THE CAMBRIDGE HISTORY
OF THE NATIVE PEOPLES OF
THE AMERICAS

VOLUME I:

North America

THE CAMBRIDGE HISTORY
OF THE NATIVE PEOPLES OF
THE AMERICAS

VOLUME I: NORTH AMERICA
Edited by Bruce G. Trigger and Wilcomb E. Washburn

VOLUME II: MESOAMERICA
Edited by R. E. W. Adams and Murdo MacLeod

VOLUME III: SOUTH AMERICA
Edited by Stuart Schwartz and Frank Salomon

THE CAMBRIDGE HISTORY OF THE NATIVE PEOPLES OF THE AMERICAS

VOLUME I

NORTH AMERICA

PART 2

Edited by

Bruce G. Trigger
McGill University

Wilcomb E. Washburn
Smithsonian Institution

CAMBRIDGE
UNIVERSITY PRESS

Published by the Press Syndicate of the University of Cambridge
The Pitt Building, Trumpington Street, Cambridge CB2 1RP
40 West 20th Street, New York, NY 10011-4211, USA
10 Stamford Road, Oakleigh, Melbourne 3166, Australia

© Cambridge University Press 1996

First published 1996

Printed in the United States of America

Library of Congress Cataloging-in-Publication Data
North America / edited by Bruce G. Trigger, Wilcomb E. Washburn.

p.   cm. – (Cambridge history of the Native peoples of
the Americas)

Includes bibliographical references and index.

ISBN 0–521–34440–9

1. Indians of North America–History.   2. Eskimos–History.
I. Trigger, Bruce G.   II. Washburn, Wilcomb E.   III. Series.

E77.N62   1996

970.004'97–dc20   95-46096
                                                                  CIP

A catalog record for this book is available from the British Library.

Volume I: North America   ISBN   0-521-34440-9 hardback   complete set

Volume I: North America, Part 1   ISBN   0-521-57392-0

Volume I: North America, Part 2   ISBN   0-521-57393-9

Volume II: Mesoamerica   ISBN   0-521-35165-0

Volume III: South America   ISBN 0-521-33393-8

CONTENTS

Part 1

CONTENTS

Part 2

ILLUSTRATIONS

PART 1

PART 2

EDITORIAL PREFACE

The North America volume of the *Cambridge History of the Native Peoples of the Americas* traces the history of the indigenous peoples living north of the Rio Grande from their earliest appearance in the New World into the 1990s. In the tradition of Cambridge histories, it seeks primarily to synthesize existing knowledge rather than to present the results of original research or to pioneer innovative approaches to the study of Native American history. Yet realizing this seemingly modest goal has been a formidable undertaking, lending credence to critics of the project who suggested that it might be premature and impossible to bring to completion. This volume draws upon the results of research by many generations of historians, anthropologists, archaeologists, physical anthropologists, linguists, and Native cultural specialists. Nevertheless, partly as a result of biases that only now are beginning to be understood, much about Native history remains poorly known among professional scholars. The co-editors were selected to represent some of the diversity within the multidisciplinary field of Native American history. One editor is an American historian, the other a Canadian anthropologist. Their political views are also quite different. By helping to ensure that a wide range of viewpoints receive serious attention, these divergences have been sources of strength rather than weakness in editing this work.

The present volume does not attempt to compete with the multivolume *Handbook of North American Indians,* or with many excellent monographs, in presenting a series of "tribal histories." Ethnic identities have shifted significantly over time in North America, as they have done in other parts of the world. Thus they do not provide a particularly useful framework for considering other important aspects of Native North American history, such as changing ecological adaptations, responses to European diseases and settlement, or the gradual development of a pan-Indian identity. In order to provide more flexible coverage, an approach has been adopted in which thematic concerns define some chapters, while regional coverage defines others.

Today no historical study can (or should) avoid self-reflection. Chapters 1 and 2 examine changing Native views of their history and the views of non-Native historians. These chapters put existing literature relating to Native American history into perspective and establish the nature, limitations, and biases of our current state of knowledge. This is followed by Chapters 3 to 5, which use mainly archaeological data to trace the history prior to European contact of hunter-gatherers (including the earliest inhabitants of North America), the development of agricultural societies in the East and the Southwest, and the emergence of stratified societies in the Mississippi Valley after A.D. 800. As the content of these chapters makes clear, this ordering does not constitute the imposition of a unilinear evolutionary scheme on this material; it merely reflects the historical order in which such societies initially appeared.

Chapter 6 surveys the nature of contact between Europeans and Native Americans in the sixteenth century, including the extent and impact of European diseases introduced at this period. This was a time when enduring European settlement was not yet established outside of Florida. Chapters 7 to 11 examine what happened to Native peoples from about 1600 to the 1880s in those parts of North America that were extensively settled by newcomers of European and African origin prior to the end of the nineteenth century. Two chapters are devoted to the Eastern Woodlands and one each to the Great Plains, the Southwest and California, and the Northwest Coast. Each chapter examines the role played by Native peoples in facilitating European settlement and the various strategies, ranging from alliance to prolonged conflict or avoidance, by which these groups sought to cope with and benefit from a European presence. These chapters also document how European demographic expansion and growing economic competitiveness made it ever more difficult for Native peoples to determine their own destinies. Chapter 12 explores the experience of the Native peoples living in all these regions from 1880 to 1960, a period when their common experience of Euro-American domination and reservation life, combined with improved communication, led Native leaders to forge a new collective identity as Indians that complemented and empowered their older ethnic identities.

Chapters 13 and 14 trace the history from earliest European contact until modern times of the Native peoples of the Northern Interior and Arctic regions of North America, including Greenland. These were areas where, until after 1945, Euro-American and Euro-Canadian settlement was minimal and where Native peoples preserved a considerable degree of political autonomy. A final chapter, by one of the co-editors, offers a personal evaluation of trends in Native North American life since 1960, a period that has seen Native people increasing in numbers and retaking ever more control of their political, economic, and cultural life. Despite continuing problems of poverty, unemployment, and dependency, especially in northern regions, these developments belie the once firmly held belief of Euro-Americans that Native people would either become physically extinct or disappear into the North American melting pot. Despite its optimism, this chapter clearly indicates the changing but persistent external pressures with which Native people still must contend.

While the topics to be covered in each chapter were decided by the co-editors, authors enjoyed complete freedom to interpret their material as they thought best. It was not easy to recruit authors for these chapters. Native American studies is a field characterized by intense specialization, with many scholars, both professional and amateur, focusing not merely on single peoples but on specific aspects of their cultures. It is not difficult to find specialists to write about Cherokee warfare, Hopi ritual, or seventeenth-century Huron history. But to find individuals able and willing to generalize on a regional or continental scale is far more difficult. The co-editors were fortunate to be able to assemble a team of young, middle-aged, and senior scholars, who could complete the demanding chores that were assigned them. Some undertook this work on short notice when prior authors were unable to write or finish their papers. Each chapter stretched the synthesizing abilities of its authors to a considerable degree. Despite generous page allowances, great concision, selection, and generalization were required in order to provide balanced coverage. While some thematic overlap between chapters was necessary, every effort has been made to eliminate simple duplication. The production schedule of collective works, as is too well known, is determined by the speed of the slowest contributor. The co-editors thank those authors who met their deadlines for patiently enduring the unconscionable delays caused by a few authors who were less prompt.

This book is written at a time when postmodern views encourage relativism and alternative histories. It is frequently maintained that every group, and indeed every individual, perceives the past differently and that there is no way to judge one version of the past to be more authentic than another. The co-editors recognize the value of alternative histories. Histories written from a feminist or minority viewpoint complement mainline studies and ultimately make possible more rounded syntheses. In North America, ethnohistory played an important pioneering role in the development of the study of minority histories.

Nevertheless, the co-editors do not accept the extreme relativist argument that alternative views of history are incommensurate and that each must be accepted on its own terms. Historical interpretations can be judged not only according to their degree of internal logical coherence (this even most extreme relativists accept), but also according to their correspondence with factual evidence. Not all histories are equally consistent, nor do they stand up equally well when tested against the growing body of documentation that historians and anthropologists have at their disposal. Anyone or any group has the right to author histories, and many do so, consciously or unconsciously, in ways that promote their own interests. Yet professional historians have a responsibility to subject all interpretations to scholarly analysis. As more historical data become available, the possibility of subjective factors wholly determining interpretations diminishes.

This publication probably marks the end of an era in Native North American historical studies. Native American history and culture were studied first by amateur and then by professional anthropologists and historians, all but a few of whom were of European descent. Their work was grounded in evolutionary and romantic stereotypes. Native peoples were viewed as illustrating what earlier stages in the development of European culture had been like and as being on their way to cultural and probably biological extinction as a result of the spread of European civilization. Whether denigrated as cruel and uncivilized or portrayed as noble savages, Native peoples were treated as essentially belonging to the past.

Over the past forty years, researches by ethnohistorians mainly of European descent have revealed the mythical status of such views by documenting the important role that Native peoples have played, and continue to play, in North American society. The accumulation of a vast body of data relating to Native Americans both before and after the arrival of Europeans has provided a sound basis for a new understanding of Indian history. In particular, ethnohistorians have realized that indigenous societies are enduring and sometimes flourishing, and rarely disappear, even under the most adverse conditions. In this way, they have discovered for themselves what has long been obvious to Native peoples. These studies not only have revealed many more details about aboriginal history but also have transformed the understanding that nonaboriginal specialists and an increasing segment of nonaboriginal North Americans have of their own history.

This new attitude became especially evident during the commemoration of the quincentenary of Columbus's arrival in the New World. In 1992, the main emphasis was not on celebrating the achievements of Europeans, as it had been in 1892, but on coming to terms with the lasting suffering that European diseases and colonization had inflicted on the Native peoples of the western hemisphere. Encouraged by a new historical understanding, fewer Euro-Americans are associating living Native peoples with the past or viewing them as existing outside the social fabric and power structures of North America's national societies. In democratic societies, knowledge that helps to dispel unfounded prejudices held by majorities about minorities is of no small importance.

The co-editors are acutely aware that this history of Native Americans has been written by Euro-Americans and Euro-Canadians. This was not for the lack of a desire or effort to recruit Native American authors. Yet, despite a growing number of Native Americans who are writing about their past, the professional study of Native American history remains largely the domain of historians and anthropologists of European descent. While Native people have played the major political role in challenging the image that other North Americans have of them, nonaboriginal historians and anthropologists have been working to dispel myths that their predecessors helped to create.

It is essential that more Native people who are interested in studying their past should become professional historians and anthropologists, so that their special insights and perspectives can contribute to the study of Native history. Just as the barrier between Native and non-Native history was replaced by a symbiotic relation once Euro-American scholars realized that Native people had played a significant role in shaping North American society since 1492, so the distinction between professional anthropologists and historians on the one hand and Native people on the other should give way to disciplines in which Native people play an increasingly important role. Such collegiality will mark the beginning of a new phase in the study of Native history.

Especially in Canada there is a growing tendency to designate Native groups by the names they apply to themselves. Sometimes this amounts to little more than a spelling change, as when Micmacs are called Mi'kmaq. But it also involves calling Montagnais Innu, Hurons Wendat, Nootkas Nuu-chah-nulth, and the people Euro-Canadians call Ojibwas and Euro-

Americans call Chippewas Anishinabe. Despite the merits of this practice and the respect that it implies for Native people, consistent use of such terminology at this time would prove confusing to an international readership that is familiar with the conventional names that Europeans have applied to these groups. Hence the co-editors have decided to retain the ethnic names and spellings utilized in the *Handbook of North American Indians,* while noting in brackets self-designations where groups who are now using these names first receive substantial mention. The usage we have adopted is little different from referring to España as Spain or Deutschland as Germany. Following Native preference and common usage, however, the modern Eskimos of Canada are regularly referred to as Inuit; those of Alaska as Eskimos. An analogous policy is applied to personal names: King Philip is preferred to Metacom and Sitting Bull to Ta-Tanka-I-Yotank.

In conformity with general usage, the term Iroquoian refers to any Indian group speaking an Iroquoian language, while Iroquois is restricted to members of the Five (later Six) Nations: Senecas, Cayugas, Onondagas, Oneidas, Mohawks, and Tuscaroras. Likewise, Algonquian refers to any group speaking an Algonquian language, while Algonquin applies specifically to a series of Algonquian-speaking bands living in and near the Ottawa Valley.

In response to complaints from historians, most notably James Axtell, that referring to collective members of indigenous groups in the singular is an ethnocentric and "nonsensical convention left over from the nineteenth century" (*The Invasion Within* [New York, 1985], xi), in this volume such groups are called Hopis, Hurons, and Utes, just as people normally speak of Germans, Italians, and Russians. Inuit is already a plural. The term prehistory is also eshewed on the grounds that it unduly segments the continuum of Native history and may falsely imply that Native peoples did not have true history prior to the arrival of Europeans. This does not mean, however, that authors do not recognize a significant difference between history based almost exclusively on archaeological evidence and that based on a mixture of texts and archaeological data or on textual evidence alone. The term tribe is also avoided except as it is used as an administrative term by the U.S. government. Finally, the co-editors have followed Francis Jennings in avoiding inherently racial expressions such as Whites, Red people, and Blacks, except as they appear in specific historical usage or as statistical categories. While it is impossible and probably counterproductive to try to keep abreast of all the latest fashions in politically correct terminology, these conventions seemed particularly important.

The co-editors wish especially to thank Frank Smith for his help in editing this volume. His contributions have gone well beyond commissioning and overseeing the production of this volume and warrant his being considered a third co-editor. They also thank Camilla Palmer, Production Editor, and David Anderson, copyeditor, for the care they have taken in guiding this manuscript through press. Trigger wishes to thank Professor Toby Morantz, McGill University, for her helpful advice at many stages in the editing of these papers.

Even a history of this size cannot cover every aspect of Native American history and in this respect it is bound to disappoint readers searching for particular facts. Nevertheless, it provides the first comprehensive history of the Native peoples of North America from earliest times to the present. It offers readers an opportunity to observe how Native peoples have dealt with the environmental diversity of North America and have responded to the different European colonial regimes and national governments that have established themselves in recent centuries. It also provides a chance to begin to compare how Native peoples have fared in Canada, the United States, and Greenland. It is hoped that it will long be a useful guide for readers around the world who are interested in the history of these peoples and will constitute a permanent record of the state of knowledge in this field in the mid-1990s, as well as a benchmark against which future progress can be measured.

9

THE GREAT PLAINS FROM THE
ARRIVAL OF THE HORSE TO 1885

LORETTA FOWLER

The mid–seventeenth through the late nineteenth centuries were times of tremendous change for the Native peoples of the Plains. They seized new opportunities presented by the arrival of Europeans and by the subsequent expansion of settlers from the United States and Canada into the trans-Mississippi West. Native peoples adapted new technologies to their own needs, elaborated and transformed their basic social and cultural institutions, and helped to create a multiethnic society in the West. For some Native groups the new opportunities enabled expansion and domination of neighboring peoples. The histories of others were shaped by a sometimes unsuccessful struggle to resist domination and dispossession. Through time, alliances shifted, as did the balance of power. Eventually, the Native peoples were overwhelmed by American and Canadian expansion and forced onto small reserves where they continued to struggle to hold on to the things they valued and to determine for themselves how they would change in adapting to new circumstances. Throughout the centuries, the decisions they made helped shape North American history.

Some of the Native peoples who occupied the Plains when Europeans first arrived in the mid–sixteenth century had been there for several hundred years or longer. Others were more recent immigrants. Over the next two centuries, more groups moved into the region, peoples who were fleeing wars among Native groups east of the Mississippi that had been brought on by European rivalries. The Great Plains region extended west from the lowland river bottom systems of the Missouri and Lower Mississippi, and gradually ascended in elevation through the grasslands, to the foothills of the Rocky Mountains. There were two adaptations to the Plains region: riverine horticultural villages, situated along the Missouri and its tributaries and along the other rivers that flowed east into the Lower Mississippi, and nomadic hunting bands that ranged in the uplands west, southwest, and northwest of the Missouri as far as the Rocky Mountains.

The riverine horticulturalists included both speakers of Caddoan languages, who had come into the Plains from the southeast about A.D. 900, and groups whose languages belonged to the Siouan family, who had moved to the Missouri from the Upper Mississippi region subsequent to the Caddoan arrival. The Caddoan peoples, the Caddos, Wichitas, Pawnees, and Arikaras, were settled on the central and southern Plains along the tributaries of the Lower Mississippi and the Lower Missouri. The Caddo groups were in what is now southeastern Oklahoma and northeast Texas, the Wichitas in Kansas, the Pawnees in Nebraska, and the Arikaras in South Dakota. Each of these peoples comprised an alliance of groups living in autonomous villages and speaking different dialects. Settled along the upper Missouri in what is now North and South Dakota were Siouan-speaking peoples known today as the Mandans and Hidatsas. They had arrived there about A.D. 1100. To the southeast in Missouri, Kansas, and Nebraska just east of the Caddoans were other Siouan-speaking groups who had come from the Ohio Valley subsequent to the Mandan and Hidatsa migration – the Missouris, Otos, Iowas, Omahas, Poncas, Kansas, and Osages.

The horticulturalists occupied permanent, often fortified villages situated on the bluffs above the river valleys. The villages also had hunting territories, where their people collectively stalked bison in the summer. The remainder of the year they tended their crops of corn, beans, squash, melons, and sunflowers. Village society among the Caddoans was stratified, with religious and secular offices held by high-status families whose members inherited important positions. Siouan societies were less stratified, but leadership also was hereditary. A great deal of emphasis was placed on religious ceremonies to ensure the success of the village crop and the hunt. Individuals with ritual authority conducted these ceremonies on behalf of the entire village.

In the mid– and late sixteenth century, Spanish explorers encountered pedestrian hunters (probably Apaches) following bison herds across the Plains, using dogs to help transport their belongings. By the late seventeenth century Native peoples of the Plains were using horses obtained from Spanish and Pueblo settlements for hunting and transporting belongings. Over the next hundred years other Native groups, some with a horticultural background, moved into the Plains from various directions, adopting a way of life based on equestrian, big game hunting in the grass-covered uplands. These peoples were organized into small family groups or bands during the winter, when they camped in sheltered areas and men hunted individually or in small groups. In the late spring the bands came together for communal hunts and ceremonial activity which continued until late fall. Hunting territories were sometimes shared with neighboring peoples; sometimes incursions were resisted. The hunting peoples' social organization was more egalitarian than the villagers'. There was ample room for individual innovation in religion and unbounded social mobility.

The nomadic groups diverged widely in language and background. Some – the Kiowas, for example – were probably there at the time the Spanish arrived, although their identity and the route they took into the Plains is largely a matter of speculation. Some, including the Cheyennes and Teton Sioux, moved into the Plains in the latter half of the eighteenth century from east of the Missouri and their routes are well documented. The nomadic hunters who occupied the Plains in the late eighteenth century spoke languages belonging to several language families. Algonquian speakers included the Blackfeet groups (Siksika, Blood, Piegan) in what is now western Saskatchewan and eastern Alberta, the Plains Crees in western Manitoba and northeastern Saskatchewan, the Gros Ventres in southern Saskatchewan, the Arapahos in northern Colorado and Wyoming, and the Cheyennes in western South Dakota. Siouan speakers included the Assiniboines (and Stoneys) in southern Manitoba and eastern Saskatchewan, the Teton Sioux in South Dakota, the Yanktons and Yanktonais in eastern South Dakota, some of the Santee Sioux in western Minnesota, and the Crows (who split off from the Hidatsas) in Montana. The Sarsis, northwest of the Blackfeet, and the Kiowa-Apaches in southwestern Kansas and northwestern Oklahoma spoke Athapaskan languages. The Kiowa affiliates of the Kiowa-Apaches spoke a Kiowa-Tanoan language and ranged from southern Wyoming south into Oklahoma. And the Comanches, who ranged in the southern Plains in southeast Colorado, southwest Oklahoma, and western Texas as well as in the Southwest, were speakers of a Uto-Aztecan language. Many of these nomadic hunters were well situated to obtain large herds of horses, but it was the horticultural villagers who initially were better able to take advantage of European trade in metal, cloth, and firearms.

The Spanish, French, and English trade with Native peoples was built upon long-established Indian trade networks. Peoples of the Plains were linked through trade systems to Pacific Coast peoples, to peoples of the

Southwest, and to societies east of the Mississippi. Native trade systems were based on trade centers and on trade fairs or rendezvous. The trade centers were located among sedentary peoples who exchanged food and other commodities to nonhorticultural and other horticultural peoples. In the Southwest, Plains peoples traded at Pecos, Piro, and Taos Pueblos, where they brought buffalo hides and dried meat and obtained corn, cloth, and turquoise. At the trade centers, ceremonial objects, including songs and other ritual knowledge, were exchanged along with material commodities.

Trade relations – both before and after European involvement – encouraged the exchange of ceremonies in whole or in part, including dances and songs. The Calumet Dance Ceremony, which had prehistoric origins, was diffused from Caddoans to the Southern Siouans and eventually, in modified form, to some of the nomadic hunting peoples. The ceremony, used for peace negotiations and for establishing or maintaining trade relations, included rituals for greeting strangers and forming alliances between peoples through the creation of a kinship bond between individuals. The visiting group's representative was ritually transformed into the "father" and the host's into the "son." The calumet, a feathered pipe stem, sanctified the proceedings.

As the Calumet Dance was diffused, through trading excursions and the Plains societies' absorption of captives, there were modifications and eventually new ceremonies that incorporated some of its aspects. Among the latter was the Grass Dance. The Omahas transferred this ceremony to the Yanktons in the nineteenth century, and the Yanktons transferred it to the Tetons, who passed it on to the other nomadic groups in the upland Plains. The ceremony combined features of the Calumet Dance and the Pawnee Irusha Dance. Once a group acquired the ceremony, it transformed it to conform to its own understandings and ethos.[1]

Similarly, the Sun Dance spread throughout the upland area to all the nomadic groups. The plan and orientation of the Sun Dance arbor and altar likely came from the Pawnee Four-Pole Ceremony and the Arikara Grandmother Cedar ritual. The rites of self-torture – in which participants pierced and tore their flesh in order to elicit attention and aid from supernatural powers – was probably suggested by the Mandan Okipa Ceremony.[2]

---

[1] William N. Fenton, "The Iroquois Eagle Dance: An Offshoot of the Calumet Dance," *Bureau of American Ethnology Bulletin* 156 (1953).
[2] Preston Holder, *The Hoe and the Horse on the Plains: A Study of Cultural Development among North American Indians* (Lincoln, Nebr., 1970), 129–30.

On the northern Plains, the villages of the Arikaras, above the Niobrara River in what is now southern South Dakota, and the villages of the Mandans and Hidatsas farther up the Missouri served as another trade center, attracting nomadic peoples from what is now Canada and from the Plains to the southwest. In the late eighteenth century, European travelers observed that Crows, Assiniboines, Plains Crees, Cheyennes, Arapahos, Kiowas, and Comanches still traded dried meat, prairie turnip flour, deer hides, bison robes, and leather goods for garden produce and Knife River flint. Teton Sioux frequented the Arikara center, along with Arapahos, Cheyennes, and Kiowas. After leaders conducted the initial ceremonial phase of the trade, individuals engaged in a private phase with men trading their products and women trading theirs.

There were at least three important trade fairs where trading partners met and exchanged goods. The Dakota Rendezvous on the Minnesota River in Minnesota was a pan-Siouan event, attracting Santees, Yanktons, Yanktonais, and Tetons. In Wyoming, the Shoshone Rendezvous linked Plateau and Great Basin peoples with the villages on the Upper Missouri through Crow middlemen. The Caddo fair in southeast Texas drew peoples from the Southwest.

TRADE RELATIONS: THE HORSE AND THE GUN

Native societies were all affected by trade with Europeans, and Indian–Euro-American relations during the seventeenth, eighteenth, and early nineteenth centuries were shaped by the trade. Neither side dominated the other, even though the exchange disproportionately benefited the Europeans and, in the nineteenth century, the Americans. The material culture of Plains peoples changed to incorporate new technology, and Native peoples influenced the patterns of trade and the trade goods themselves. The introduction of the horse and the gun, as well as the slave trade, had far-reaching effects on the economic, political, and religious organization of Native Plains societies. Diseases contracted from Europeans had a major impact on the way societies changed and on their relations with each other. Several peoples seized on the new opportunities provided by the trade to expand their territory and dominate neighboring groups, among them the Comanches and Osages on the southern Plains, the Assiniboines and Plains Crees on the northwestern Plains, and the Teton Sioux on the central and northern Plains. Political alliances among Plains peoples were

formed, dissolved, and formed again as each group struggled to accommodate to new forces in the region.

Europeans adopted Native trading practices, including gift giving,
ritual adoption, and a variety of other ceremonies. Gifts, especially guns
and special symbols of authority (medals, flags, uniforms, and staffs), were
given to men of chiefly status. The French, and later the English, incorporated the calumet ceremony, which involved ritual smoking and ritual
adoption, into their dealings with the Native peoples of the Plains. Probably European trade accelerated the diffusion of this and other ceremonies,
for the European activity encouraged the dislocation and relocation of
peoples. Europeans also introduced new elements, such as consumption of
alcohol into the ritual. Intergroup marriage occurred in the context of
trade relations. In fact, a European trader's marriage by Indian custom to a
woman of an important family was a common means of establishing trade
relations.

Trade goods such as metal pots and metal tools, including knives, hoes,
and needles, were sought by Native peoples to replace similar items made
of clay, stone, bone, and hide. Native consumers were very particular
about weight and color of textiles, and the European manufacturers accommodated their tastes. Glass beads were used in addition to quills to
decorate clothing; certain sizes and colors of beads were preferred. There
was a florescence of artistic creativity expressed in experimentation with
new materials, colors, and design and in an increasing elaboration of
design on clothing and other items of Native manufacture. The flintlock
musket, lead balls, gunpowder, and flints became necessities, for groups
without them were terribly vulnerable to well-armed peoples. The musket
was not used in the hunt, for the bow and arrow were superior; a gun
could not be fired rapidly, it was expensive, and firing it could stampede a
herd. But in battle the gun was an asset. Part of the barrel was cut off to
make the gun easier to deploy from the back of a horse, and, used as
shotguns, the muskets were very effective. Just as the horse was adapted to
Native uses, Native peoples made riding gear to accommodate their particular needs and tastes.

The horse was introduced to Plains peoples by the Spanish, then diffused northward. The Spanish built their trade network by gaining entry
into the Indian intergroup trading system. In the seventeenth and eighteenth centuries, Pueblo trade centers and fairs attracted Apaches and
some Plains traders who brought captives, hides, and skins to exchange for
Spanish trade beads, mirrors, bells, blades, wool and cotton blankets

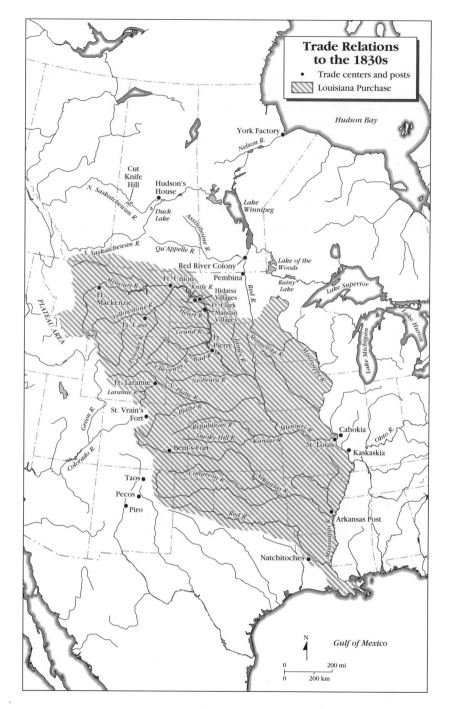

Figure 9.1 Trade relations in the 1830s: Trade centers and posts.

made by Pueblo Indians, and stock, especially horses and mules. Spanish settlements, especially those near Santa Fe, were trading horses to the Eastern Pueblos (Taos, Picos, Pecos) in the early seventeenth century. Slowly horses were diffused north and east into the Plateau and Plains areas through middlemen. In the 1660s and 1670s the Apaches traded war captives to the Pueblos in return for horses and also made stock-raiding expeditions there, and Plains groups were able to obtain some horses from the Apaches. By the 1680s and 1690s Kiowas and Kiowa-Apaches were trading some horses to Caddoan villages south of the Platte, and the Wichitas and Pawnees traded horses to Osages and other Southern Siouans, although horses still were by no means plentiful in these villages.

By the early eighteenth century the Comanches began raiding for horses in the Spanish and Apache settlements and trading them directly to the Northern Shoshones and to nomadic hunting peoples and Upper Missouri villagers at trade fairs in the Black Hills. The Shoshones traded horses to Plateau area peoples, such as the Flatheads and Nez Percés, traveling by way of the headwaters of the Colorado and Green Rivers. The Blackfeet groups and Gros Ventres in Saskatchewan country were equestrian at least by the 1740s, obtaining horses from either Plateau peoples to the southwest or Arapahos to the south, or both. Shortly thereafter, Blackfeet and Gros Ventre groups traded some horses to western bands of Assiniboines. The Crows obtained horses via the Shoshones and the Flatheads probably in the 1740s as well, which may have been a factor in their permanently migrating to the Upper Yellowstone area. The Crows brought horses to the Mandan and Hidatsa villages and so did other nomadic groups, such as the Kiowas, Kiowa-Apaches, Arapahos, and Cheyennes, who traded in Arikara villages as well. In the Mandan and Hidatsa villages, Assiniboines and Plains Crees from north of the Missouri River obtained horses in return for the guns and other manufactured goods they received from English and French traders in their country. Teton Sioux obtained horses in the Arikara villages and took them to the James River fair in South Dakota to trade to Yanktons, Yanktonais, and Santee Sioux in the 1750s. By the early nineteenth century, all the Plains groups had incorporated the horse into their way of life.[3]

In addition to being broken for riding, horses were trained for particu-

[3] John C. Ewers, "The Indian Trade of the Upper Missouri before Lewis and Clark," in John C. Ewers, *Indian Life on the Upper Missouri* (Norman, Okla., 1968).

lar kinds of specialized services: buffalo hunting by charge, winter buffalo hunting, warfare, travois pulling, carrying packs, dragging poles. Adoption of the horse for use in hunting, war, and transport had wide-reaching effects among Plains peoples.

The need to find adequate pasturage for the horses influenced settlement and work patterns among the nomadic groups. In the uplands, winter campsites had to be found where there was cottonwood bark to feed to the horses when grass was insufficient. Camps had to be moved when the horses grazed out an area. In the villages, care of the horses took time away from horticultural activity and added to women's responsibilities. Among nomadic peoples, however, horses could carry probably four times the load formerly transported by women with their domesticated dogs. The need to provide good grass led to the use of fire to encourage early growth of spring grasses and this modified the Plains environment.

The horse was used to hunt buffalo by the old methods of the surround and the drive or chase. Mounted hunters could provide a much more reliable supply of meat than could pedestrian ones. The yield was large and horses could transport the meat from the kill site to the camps, where it was cooked or dried and stored. This efficiency freed young men to undertake frequent horse-raiding expeditions. It also helped older, more established men hold a following, for men who obtained large amounts of meat were expected to share with others, and ownership of many horses enabled a man to loan some to men with few horses. Recipients of a wealthy man's generosity repaid him with loyalty in political contexts.

During the eighteenth century, warfare in the form of horse raids and revenge expeditions escalated, and war exploits were an increasingly important avenue to prestige and leadership positions. The use of horses in combat encouraged the abandonment of large, clustered groups of warriors in battle; rather, mobile, small parties became more common. There was a shift from massed, pitched battles to surprise attack by a small group. Body armor made of rawhide and large three-foot-long war shields were too cumbersome on horseback, and these were replaced by small rawhide shields, that could be easily carried by the rider and that covered only vital organs, and by leather armor for horses. Bows and lances were reduced in length to accommodate fighting from horseback. War exploits were graded to take account of the new circumstances. For nomadic upland groups, taking a gun or horse from an enemy generally was ranked high. For the horticultural villagers, bravery in the defense of the village and fields might rank higher. Warfare usually took the form of revenge expeditions before the acquisition of the horse. When horse raids led to casualties, revenge raids followed; nonetheless, horse raids assumed much greater importance in Plains warfare, particularly among the nomadic hunting groups, than did revenge raids, for the horse had become an economic necessity. When groups began to rely on trading horses and mules to Europeans, warfare escalated further. The horse-raiding parties were small groups that left camp frequently during the year. Less frequent were the larger revenge parties that went after enemy groups for the purpose of taking lives (and war trophies, such as scalps) or captives. Before the sale of captives to Europeans became profitable, children taken from enemy groups usually were adopted; women often became wives or concubines and, whether or not they did so, worked for the households of their captors. The rituals for successful horse raiding and successful revenge parties differed.

Prior to the acquisition of horses, families hunted cooperatively and the kill was equally divided. With horse ownership, status differences based on wealth emerged among individuals in the nomadic, hunting societies. Horses enabled individuals to hunt successfully. The families that owned the most and best buffalo-hunting horses and warhorses, animals that were specially trained and very valuable, formed a high-status group. Among the nomadic hunters, horse ownership was a prerequisite for leadership and was correlated with polygynous marriage. Wealthy families, with many pack horses and mules, could transport more property. They had larger tipis, more elaborate lodge furnishings, and more clothing, and could make more elaborate ritual offerings and own the most important ritual objects. The Blackfeet groups and the Kiowas had named, social categories for horse-wealthy elites and nonelites in their societies.

Successful horse raiding could help individuals of low rank gain status in the society. If the raid produced socially recognized war exploits or coups and a few horses that could be given away or used to begin building a larger herd, an individual was able to improve his position significantly in the nomadic, hunting societies. In the more stratified horticultural villages, most of the horses were given to the hereditary leaders to pay for ritual and other services. But horses and other booty could be traded to Europeans who then could give special recognition to individuals that might lead to advantages in future trading activity.

Large medicine bundles – sacred objects wrapped in hides and furs – became common among the nomadic groups after the introduction of the horse. In fact, ceremonial life probably underwent great changes, as the horse permitted more frequent visits between fairly distant tribes, during which time ceremonies and associated objects, songs, and dances were exchanged amid much gift giving. More elaborate regalia and other sacred objects could be transported easily. Among the Kiowas, the high-ranking people most often possessed the expensive medicine bundles; the lower-ranking men continued to rely on the vision quest for supernatural aid. The horse came to occupy a prominent position in religious belief and ritual among many groups. Supernatural powers could be transferred from horses to owners, and horse medicine cults assumed great importance.

There were not only wealth inequalities within societies, but peoples closest to the source of horses, such as the Comanches on the frontier of Spanish settlement or the Crows, near the Plateau horse traders, were better supplied than the more northerly groups such as the Plains Crees and Assiniboines. While a Plains Cree owner of five horses would be considered wealthy by other Crees, a Crow or Comanche owner of twenty-five animals would merit no such distinction among his people. Gradually there was a movement of some groups, such as the Cheyennes and Arapahos, southward toward the supply of horses. On the northern Plains, horse-poor peoples were more egalitarian than the groups with large herds. The latter developed new institutions to link the generous gift of horses to status and authority. For example, the Gros Ventres channeled wealth into competitive displays of generosity between individuals and mens' organizations, and into obligatory gift giving to honor certain children or fulfill religious obligations.[4]

The Comanches became preeminent among the groups that raided Southwest settlements for horses, displacing the Apaches early in the eighteenth century. They were able to dominate the upland Plains below the Platte River until the 1830s. They traded horses and mules to the Caddoans and, after the 1740s, directly to the French for manufactured goods, including firearms, although they were not as well armed as other groups allied to the French. By 1750 horse trading was probably more important to the Comanche economy than bison hunting.[5]

The Comanches were able to take advantage of Spanish-French rivalry, playing each off against the other. They traded hides and war captives for

[4] John C. Ewers, *The Horse in Blackfoot Indian Culture* (Norman, Okla., 1955); Loretta Fowler, *Shared Symbols, Contested Meanings: Gros Ventre Culture and History, 1778–1984* (Ithaca, N.Y., 1987), 30, 37–8, 65.

[5] Morris Foster, *Being Comanche: A Social History of an American Indian Community* (Lincoln, Nebr., 1991), 39.

livestock in Spanish and Pueblo settlements and, when trade was not convenient, stole stock. Comanches also traded captives and livestock to their Caddoan allies and the French in order to obtain firearms denied them by Spanish authorities, who were forbidden by the Crown to trade arms to Native peoples. Comanches were able to displace the Kiowas from the upper Platte region during 1730–1770, driving them farther east. In 1790 they made peace with the Kiowas and formed an alliance to try to prevent incursions from nomadic hunting peoples to the north and northeast. Together, the Comanches and Kiowas controlled the southern Plains uplands area between the Arkansas and Cimarron Rivers. After Americans began to settle and trade in Texas, the market for livestock increased. Mexican authorities could not pursue Comanche raiders across the border so the Comanches were able to raid deep into Mexico for stock that they traded in Texas. This livestock industry was crucial to the development of local economies throughout the region and ensured Comanche prosperity until the Americans no longer needed the trade.

Firearms were introduced into the Plains area from the northeast and southeast by the French and English. The French entered the Plains in the late seventeenth century via the Lower Mississippi watershed and later by way of the Assiniboine and Saskatchewan Rivers in Canada. In the Mississippi region, they established themselves in Illinois country and on the coast of the Gulf of Mexico where they competed with the English to the east. With Southern Siouans and Caddoans in the southern and central Plains, they attempted to form military and trading partnerships in order to obtain furs, slaves for their plantations in the West Indies and Louisiana, and other products from Native peoples. In 1699–1700 the French built Cahokia and Kaskaskia on the Lower Mississippi, from whence traders journeyed to the Native villages, especially those of the Osages. The Arkansas Post was built at the mouth of the Arkansas River in 1686, and in 1713 Natchitoches was built on the Red River where it drew the trade of Caddo and Wichita villages. French guns gave the Pawnees, Wichitas, Missouris, Otos, Osages, and Kansas an edge against Spain's Apache allies. Their Indian allies offered the French protection, access to the trade of more distant peoples such as the Comanches, and a buffer against Spanish interests. The Wichita and Pawnee villages could compete successfully with Taos for the Indian trade, for they had access to guns and French goods such as sugar and brandy.

In a particularly good position to take advantage of European trading interests, the Osages came to dominate the southern Plains east of the

Comanche sphere during the eighteenth century. The Osages played the Spanish and French off against each other, as did the Comanches. They were strategically located between the Missouri and Arkansas Rivers and thus could control the thoroughfares traders used to reach western groups. Like the Comanches, they also had a sizable population relative to other groups in the region. They were generally successful in preventing large numbers of guns from reaching their Caddoan enemies to the west, for the French could not afford to alienate them. With muskets obtained from the French, in the late seventeenth century the Osages in southwest Missouri attacked the Wichitas and Caddos to the southwest and the Pawnees to the northwest, while they stayed on good terms with the Indian groups allied with the French to the north and east in Illinois country. They successfully raided the poorly armed Caddoans for horses, mules, and slaves. The market for slaves, as well as the market for stock, dramatically increased the frequency and intensity of warfare between the Native peoples in the area. The increase in warfare had repercussions for Osage social organization: war parties were composed of brothers and other male kinsmen; thus, after marriage, couples tended to live with the bride's family rather than the groom's. In this way villages would not suffer the loss of most of their young men in the event of high casualties during a particular expedition.[6]

Because of Osage attacks, the Caddos were forced to move down the Red River, the Pawnees retreated toward the Platte River, and the Wichitas were forced south of the Arkansas Valley. By about 1750 the Osages controlled the area between the Missouri and Red Rivers.

The Kansas, located northwest between the Osages and Pawnees, had a small population of about 1,500 and were regularly exposed to disease from the travelers along the Missouri and Kansas Rivers. They had little choice but to become allied with the numerous and powerful Osages in their war with the Pawnees. Thus, the Kansas retained their territory adjacent to the Osages.

Spain took over the administration of the trade after 1763 when the French withdrew after being defeated by the British. Spain operated the trade in a similar manner to the French, even occupying the French trading posts, such as Arkansas and Natchitoches. They curtailed the slave trade and made pelts and skins the focus of trade. St. Louis was built in

[6] Willard H. Rollings, *The Osage: An Ethnohistorical Study of Hegemony on the Prairie-Plains* (Columbia, Mo., 1992); Garrick Alan Bailey, *Changes in Osage Social Organization, 1673–1906,* University of Oregon Anthropological Papers 5 (Eugene, Ore., 1973), 43–44.

1764 as a center for the Upper Louisiana trade, replacing the French centers at Cahokia and Kaskaskia.

Having driven the Caddoans out of the Arkansas Valley, the Osages began to extend their hunts into that region. In fact, some bands moved there. In the 1770s the Osages still controlled the area between the Arkansas and Red Rivers and dominated the fur trade out of St. Louis. They were able to exert their independence from the Spanish, for they also were trading with French Canadians and English.

The French and their English rivals of the Hudson's Bay Company had posts located respectively around the Upper Great Lakes and along the shores of Hudson Bay. From 1670 to 1763, first the French and then the Hudson's Bay Company, which had been granted a monopoly by the English Crown, expanded their operations west to the Saskatchewan River, with the French trade moving via Rainy Lake, Lake of the Woods, and Lake Winnipeg. The French established contacts with Plains Crees and Assiniboines largely through lower-class employees who took up residence in Native communities, often marrying Native women.

The Hudson's Bay Company catered to Native preferences in trade goods in order to compete more successfully with the French. They traded light, easy-to-carry firearms and tools and high-quality textiles. Powder, shot, tobacco, brandy, and beads also were supplied. For much of the time beaver pelts were the standard of exchange; beaver values were assigned to all goods, furs, and provisions that Indians exchanged until 1810. Most of the tobacco traded was Brazilian, twisted into a rope, treated with molasses, and sold in one-foot (30 centimeter) lengths. The Native Plains peoples preferred this imported variety to the tobacco that they grew or to that grown by the English in Virginia.

Gift giving was central to the trade. Traders tried to ensure the loyalty of leaders so that they would be reliable in bringing furs, horses, and provisions and so that they would not take their trade to rival posts. The leader of a trading party was taken into a special reception room and given, or "rigged" in, an "outfit" that was patterned after European military uniforms, with the style of the uniform indicating the regard in which the leader was held by his hosts.[7]

The Hudson Bay trade set in motion forces that helped the Blackfeet groups and the Gros Ventres to drive the Shoshones out of southern

[7] Arthur J. Ray, *Indians in the Fur Trade: Their Role as Hunters, Trappers and Middlemen in the Lands Southwest of Hudson Bay, 1660–1870* (Toronto, 1974), 139.

Saskatchewan and Alberta. It also enabled the Assiniboines and their Plains Cree allies to expand into Saskatchewan, displacing the Gros Ventres and some Blackfeet groups and dominating the fur trade during the eighteenth century. The western flank of the Assiniboines was in south-central Manitoba in the mid–seventeenth century and their Cree allies were to the north and east. By the mid–eighteenth century they controlled the major canoe routes from the west to the Bay and could dictate the terms of trade to European traders. They exchanged furs for manufactured goods, which they used for a few years; then, after marking up the prices, took west to the Blackfeet and Gros Ventre peoples in the Saskatchewan valley. Guns traded at York Factory on Hudson Bay to Crees for twelve Made Beaver (the Hudson's Bay Company's unit of exchange) were exchanged to the Crees' Blackfeet customers for thirty-six Made Beaver. With guns obtained from the Assiniboines and Crees, the confederated Blackfeet, Gros Ventre, and Sarsi warriors began to drive the Shoshones south in the 1740s. A smallpox epidemic in 1781 so weakened the Shoshones that by the 1790s they and their allies, the Flatheads and Kutenais, were pushed out of Montana west of the Rocky Mountains.[8]

In the late 1760s, after the defeat of the French, the Montreal-based North West Company took over the French sphere of the trade and pushed beyond the mid-Saskatchewan, eventually building posts up the North Saskatchewan. The Hudson's Bay Company was compelled to try to compete. The new posts, such as Hudson House, built in 1778, and others built subsequently on the South and North branches of the Saskatchewan River, eliminated the need for the Cree and Assiniboine middlemen in this area. The allied Blackfeet groups (Siksika, Blood, and Piegan), Gros Ventres, and Sarsis could sell provisions to the posts and obtain goods that way instead of relying exclusively on procuring furs. The Assiniboines and Crees, whose lands to the north and east were being depleted of fur-bearing animals and who wanted to share in the trade in provisions, began to move south and southwest into Blackfeet and Gros Ventre territory. The competition resulted in intense warfare, and by the early nineteenth century the better armed Assiniboines and Crees had driven the Gros Ventres and some Blackfeet groups into Montana where they displaced the Shoshones.

The Sioux, that is, the Tetons – a group of allied peoples who numbered in the thousands – and Yanktons and Yanktonais, also allied to the

---

[8] Ibid., 69.

Tetons and speakers of the same language, were living in east-central Minnesota in the mid–seventeenth century. They were at war with the Crees and Assiniboines to the north. The latter, being better armed, began to force the Teton, Yanktonai, and Yankton Sioux southward into the prairies east of the Missouri River. The Teton and Yanktonai Sioux subsequently pressed the Iowas, Otos, Missouris, and Omaha-Poncas, who fled west, eventually to the Missouri River in the 1680s. The Sioux also pushed the Cheyenne people west out of the valley of the Minnesota River. Continuing their expansion, by the 1740s the Tetons and Yanktons themselves had reached the Missouri River. They had begun attacking the Mandan villages at the mouth of the Heart River and the Hidatsas at the Knife River even before this. The Tetons' attacks on these villages drove the Mandans to relocate near the Hidatsas after 1750. The Arikaras, located below the Mandan directly in the path of Sioux immigration, bore the brunt.

By the 1760s the Sioux were fully equestrian and began to intensify their attacks on all the Arikara, Mandan, and Hidatsa villages on the Upper Missouri. Referred to by some contemporary observers as "the pirates of the Missouri," the Sioux were in a very good position to dominate the Upper Missouri area, for they did not need to rely on the trade on the Missouri for guns. They still traded beaver with the British on the Upper Mississippi and with the Santee Sioux who still lived in Minnesota near the British and French Canadian traders and who met the Tetons, Yanktons, and Yanktonais at trade fairs in Minnesota and eastern South Dakota. Thus, the Tetons and Yanktons harassed European traders coming up the Missouri from St. Louis and those coming from Canada down the river. With less ready access to guns the villagers had difficulty defending themselves. The Arikaras often had to rely on the Sioux for guns, at whatever prices they decided to ask. The Sioux also drove the buffalo away from the Arikara villages, so that the Arikaras had to rely on them for a supply of meat. When the Arikaras refused to trade corn and horses for an unfair rate of exchange, the Sioux raided their villages and stole what they wanted, killing villagers in the process. Until 1780 villagers vigorously opposed Sioux incursions. The Mandan, Hidatsa, and Arikara villages were very large and well fortified. The Omahas were well armed and blocked the Sioux advance south of the middle Missouri River. But smallpox devastated the villages in 1778–82 and again in 1801–2.

After the Arikaras lost four-fifths of their population in the first round of smallpox epidemics, which made it impossible for them to defend themselves against the Sioux, they combined the remnants of their thirty-two villages into two and retreated north to the Cheyenne River. They moved even farther north to the mouth of the Grand River in 1799. The Mandans and Hidatsas, whose villages had been prosperous centers of trade between Indians and Europeans, where the flow of horses from the west met the flow of guns from the north, also were devastated by small-pox in 1782 and, at the same time, harassed by the Sioux. The Omahas were weakened, as well; before the epidemics their warriors numbered 700, subsequently, 300. When Lewis and Clark arrived in 1804, they recognized the Sioux as the dominant power on the Missouri.[9]

In 1800 Spain ceded Louisiana back to France, and the United States purchased it in 1803. Soon after, Meriwether Lewis and William Clark's expedition up the Missouri helped attract Americans to the fur trade. The best country for beaver then was the Upper Missouri in Montana, in Blackfeet and Crow territory. Trappers said of Crow country that the beaver were so plentiful that they could be killed in the streams with clubs, and "Crow Beaver" was considered superior to "Missouri Beaver" because Crow women were particularly expert in processing the pelt.[10]

Euro-American traders and trappers began to penetrate the Upper Missouri. Before this, traders out of St. Louis concentrated on working the Lower Missouri, getting pelts from Osage, Oto, Kansa, Omaha, and Ponca hunters. Mandans, Hidatsas, and Arikaras had served as middlemen between the western nomadic groups and the Europeans. The Americans, representing competing trading companies, pushed up the Missouri past these villages. The villagers had little to sell but their corn. Trappers and traders also penetrated the Plains north of the Platte and the adjacent Rocky Mountains. The Arikaras attempted to prevent the traders from bypassing their villages, but they were punitively attacked by the U.S. Army in 1823 and weakened. In addition, after the War of 1812, the British had withdrawn, making it essential for the villagers to stay on good terms with the Americans, from whom they could obtain guns.

When Americans began trapping for fur in the Upper Missouri, Upper Platte, and Upper Arkansas country, they were attacked by Blackfeet and Gros Ventre groups in the north and the Crows, Arapahos, and Cheyennes

[9] Joseph Jablow, *The Cheyenne in Plains Indian Trade Relations, 1795–1840*, Monographs of the American Ethnological Society 19 (Seattle, Wash., 1950), 39, 42, 52–5. See also Richard White, "The Winning of the West: The Expansion of the Western Sioux in the Eighteenth and Nineteenth Centuries," *Journal of American History* 65 (1978), 319–43.

[10] David J. Wishart, *The Fur Trade of the American West, 1807–1840: A Geographical Synthesis* (Lincoln, Nebr., 1979), 29.

farther south. The American traders had hired their own countrymen as trappers and hunters, rather than relying on local, Native peoples to bring in furs and meat. Eventually the Crows accepted the Americans, largely because they helped them defend themselves against Teton incursions, and Crow country was trapped extensively. But the Blackfeet groups and Gros Ventres, angry at being bypassed by the trappers and hunters, repelled Americans wherever they found them and continued to trade with the Hudson's Bay Company. Conflict between Native peoples and the trappers threatened to undermine profits.

In the 1820s the American Fur Company began to squeeze out its competitors. By 1827, the company had secured a monopoly on the Upper Missouri trade. Company policy was changed in 1831, so that Native hunters could bring furs, skins, and hides to exchange at the forts. For the nomadic groups, who took advantage of the fact that the buffalo herds had moved west and northwest away from the Missouri River and who were particularly successful at procuring buffalo robes, the 1830s and 1840s were a time of prosperity, for the buffalo robe trade supplanted the fur trade on the world market. The beaver hat was out of fashion but there was a market in the eastern United States for dressed buffalo robes.

Among the groups wishing to take advantage of the opportunity to trade large quantities of buffalo robes were the Tetons, some of whom had moved west of the Missouri River into prime buffalo country. Unlike most of the Yanktons, they no longer spent the winter trapping but preferred to hunt year-round and raid for horses to trade. West of the Missouri River they came into conflict with nomadic, hunting groups, as well as with the Omahas, Poncas, and Pawnees. Teton groups contested the Plains between the Missouri River and the Black Hills, an area occupied or frequented by Kiowas, Crows, Arapahos, and Cheyennes. By 1825 Teton groups had driven the Kiowas south of the Black Hills. The Crows were pushed west to the Powder and Yellowstone Rivers. The Cheyennes had long been at odds with the Sioux, for they had defied them by continuing to bring horses to the villages on the Upper Missouri. Nonetheless, they and the Arapahos formed an alliance with the Teton groups and together dominated the central uplands area until the 1870s. Teton warfare in the nineteenth century was not merely raiding for horses or revenge, but a war to exterminate rival groups.

When the Tetons and their allies reached the Platte River country in the 1830s they fought the Pawnees, who controlled the country from the forks of the Platte south to the Republican, Kansas, and Arkansas Rivers. In

1838 the Pawnees were devastated by smallpox and, weakened, lost the Platte hunting grounds to the Tetons; they thereupon began a desperate struggle to survive against continued attacks. The Crows also suffered from smallpox and cholera in the 1840s, and they were pushed north from the Laramie River. They formed an alliance with Shoshones, Flatheads, and the Americans, in order to try to hold on to their hunting grounds in west-central Montana. To the south, in the 1820s, the Cheyennes and Arapahos drove the Kiowas, Kiowa-Apaches, and Comanches south of the Arkansas River.

Situated among the peoples still living near the Missouri River, whose lands had been seriously depleted of game, the trading posts had declining profits, and famine was increasingly a problem for all the horticultural villagers, still beset by attacks from Sioux that made work in the fields risky. The collapse of the fur trade was also instrumental in the emergence of an important bicultural group on the northern Plains.

Bicultural populations became quite influential in several places after the arrival of Europeans. St. Louis was founded in 1764 and became a major trading enclave. A creole society emerged, produced by intermarriage between Indian middlemen, French, and Spanish families. On the Texas Plains groups of descendants of Spanish and Plains Indian captives operated as traders in the nineteenth century. French-Canadian men married Indian women in all the villages of the Missouri, and their descendants have played important political roles in Native societies. Villages of these descendants often competed with other villages for political influence in dealings with Americans. Other descendants of Europeans and Native peoples formed independent mixed-blood or Métis populations that developed unique lifestyles and identities, particularly on the northern Plains and at the Red River Colony.

In 1821 the Hudson's Bay Company and the Northwest Company combined. Business was scaled down, and the labor force was cut by two-thirds. The first employees to lose their positions were the peoples of French-Indian and British-Indian descent. Many of these (of Cree and Assiniboine ancestry) established a settlement on the Red River in what is now Manitoba, at the junction of the Assiniboine River, and another at Pembina, North Dakota, and frequented the prairie to the southwest. In response to the opportunities presented by the robe trade, they followed the example of the Plains Crees and Assiniboines and began hunting buffalo in western Saskatchewan, North Dakota, and as far west as Montana. They transported meat and robes on horsedrawn carts rather than by travois. In addition, they worked as freighters in boat brigades and cart trains, as well as dog trains in the winter. At the Red River settlement, there was a population of 500 in 1821; in 1870, 12,000.[11]

After the American Fur Company resolved its difficulties with the Blackfeet and other nomadic groups in 1831, the use of steamboats made the transport of robes particularly cost-effective. The company built major depots on the Missouri in Assiniboine and Plains Cree territory (Fort Union) and in Teton and Yankton territory (Fort Tecumseh, later Fort Pierre). They also built a fort in Cheyenne, Arapaho, and Oglala (a Teton group) territory in Wyoming (Fort Laramie). Regional posts were built as well: Fort Mackenzie for the Blackfeet groups, Fort Cass for the Crows, and Fort Clark for the Mandans and Hidatsas. Only the traders William Bent, married to a Cheyenne woman from an important Cheyenne group, and Ceran St. Vrain with posts on the Upper Arkansas and South Platte Rivers, respectively, could compete. They dealt with the Cheyennes and Arapahos there, purchasing robes in the winter and horses and mules in the summer for shipment back to Missouri where emigrants were being outfitted for the journey west.

For the Plains nomads, the robe trade brought prosperity and further social change. Polygyny in some groups apparently became more common, for hunters needed more women to tan the hides that were in demand by the traders. The volume of robe trade was greater on the northern Plains, for the American Fur Company used steamships to transport robes down the Missouri. According to the trader Edwin Denig, the trader advanced hunters credit and was fortunate to receive half his due; still, the profit margin was 200–2,000 percent.[12] With access to the Upper Missouri forts and an abundance of buffalo, the Gros Ventres, Crows, and Blackfeet groups channeled the increased wealth into new ritual and political activities or elaborated on old ones.

While the nomadic groups suffered from the effects of warfare and epidemics, the villagers bore the brunt. Their denser settlement and more extensive, direct contact with European and Euro-American traders made the effects of epidemics more disastrous. Measles, whooping cough, influenza, cholera, and especially smallpox killed tens of thousands in the seventeenth through the nineteenth centuries. There were two smallpox epidemics in the late seventeenth century and seven in the eighteenth. In the 1780s

[11] Ray, *Indians in the Fur Trade*, 205.
[12] Wishart, *The Fur Trade*, 94, 99.

smallpox swept the Plains, killing one-third of the Native peoples there. Despite the traders' efforts to vaccinate Indians, in the nineteenth century there were five smallpox epidemics; the one in 1837 killed half the Native population. The Mandans were especially hard hit. In 1750 they numbered 9,000; after the smallpox epidemic of 1837, just under 150 remained. The Wichita groups also lost almost 90 percent of their population between the late seventeenth and late nineteenth centuries.

In addition to the dramatic decline in population, there were other effects of the epidemics. Captives were increasingly taken in raids and these were adopted into families to replenish population losses. Marital restrictions were altered; for example, after the 1849 cholera epidemic, the Cheyennes relaxed rules of band exogamy. Health-related rituals were introduced or elaborated. And villages that were once autonomous combined their remnants into new polities. Most were related groups who spoke the same or similar languages; others, like the Mandans, Hidatsas, and Arikaras maintained separate sections within the same village.[13]

The villagers' struggle to defend themselves against the Sioux and against Native groups from the East who were being displaced there by the westward movement of American settlers affected political organization. As warfare increasingly became an avenue to prestige and influence, clan authority and hereditary leadership in general was undermined, and villages that had a dual leadership in the form of civil and war chiefs found that the war chief, or one of the chiefs favored by the Americans, gained in power and influence.[14] In short, all these changes made the horticultural villagers particularly vulnerable to the pressures that accompanied the movement of American settlers west of the Missouri River in the 1840s.

WESTWARD EXPANSION: TREATIES AND RESERVATIONS

Trade relations had enabled some Native peoples to prosper and expand even into the early nineteenth century. But the westward expansion of the United States and Canada and their citizens initiated a process of political subordination and economic dependency that eventually overtook all the Native peoples of the Plains. The horticultural villagers were affected before the nomadic groups. Sioux attacks, competition from emigrant Native groups from the east, and the American settlers all made the

[13] John C. Ewers, "The Influence of Epidemics on the Indian Populations and Cultures of Texas," *Plains Anthropologist* 18 (1973), 104–15.
[14] See Rollings, *The Osage*, and Holder, *The Hoe and the Horse*.

villagers' positions in Kansas and Nebraska untenable. Settlers in east Texas relentlessly attacked Native peoples, friendly or not. No longer able to play one European power against another, the villagers had no choice but to try to negotiate an accommodation with the United States. At first there was some hope that Native peoples could continue to live in the same area on small reservations and adopt American agricultural technology. But in response to public pressure, the American government neglected its Native allies once their support was no longer advantageous, and, one by one, villagers were pressed to give up their homelands for small, vulnerable reservations in the midst of settlers or to leave altogether and migrate into the Indian Territory in present-day Oklahoma. In Canada also, the nomadic groups eventually were confined to small reserves.

For the nomadic peoples, the initial problem was the destruction of game that accompanied the movement of settlers westward. They also attempted an accommodation with the United States through a series of treaties, but eventually the trespass of settlers into the reserved lands of some groups led to military clashes. For other groups, off the emigrant routes or threatened by the Sioux, a military alliance with the United States offered an option. For those whose livelihood was threatened, war consumed much of the 1850s through the 1870s, as the Sioux and their Cheyenne and Arapaho allies, with some help from Comanches and Kiowas, tried to hold back the flood of immigrants. But by 1878, all the Native peoples of the American Plains had been forced onto reservations.

The villagers

In the 1790s frontiersmen began moving into the Mississippi Valley. The federal government sought to convince the Indians living there to cede their lands between the Ohio and Mississippi Rivers. Competition and conflict between Americans and Native peoples of the region led to a series of land cessions in which Native peoples gave up land in Ohio, Indiana, Illinois, Michigan, and Wisconsin during the early nineteenth century and moved west of the Mississippi where the federal government had promised them land. These Native peoples of the upper Midwest then moved into Osage and Kansa territory. Native peoples of the southeastern United States, including Cherokees, also were making forays into the Osage territory, and their numbers increased after the Indian Removal Act of 1830. As thousands of eastern Indians moved into the Lower Missouri region, the United States began to negotiate a succession of treaties with peoples already there. To facilitate emigration through and settlement of the American West, agencies were established where a federal representative tried to placate the groups adversely affected by westward expansion.

In 1808 the government obtained from the Osages the cession of southern Missouri and northern Arkansas, whereupon the Cherokees began settling these lands. In the second and third decades of the century, more cessions were obtained from Osages, Kansas, and others. In 1825 Congress created an "Indian Territory" bounded on the north by the Platte River, on the east by Arkansas and Missouri Territories, on the south by the Red River, and on the west by Spanish territory, for a permanent home for Native peoples. This land already was occupied by Osages, Kansas, Otos, Missouris, Pawnees, Poncas, and others. They were pressured to cede land to make room for eastern groups. In 1854 Congress passed the Kansas-Nebraska Act, which excised land from this Indian Territory to create the Kansas and Nebraska Territories, already settled by trespassing Americans.[15]

During the first half of the nineteenth century, the village peoples ceded most of their land and accepted small reservations where they tried to maintain their way of life molested neither by Sioux nor by settlers. The United States had promised protection to Native peoples in the "Indian Territory," which was supposed to insulate its occupants from settler incursions, but political expediency led the United States to disregard guarantees and pledges to Native peoples. In 1825 the Osages ceded lands in western Missouri and Arkansas, southern Kansas, and northern Oklahoma and reserved to themselves a tract of 125 by 50 miles (200 by 80 kilometers) in southern Kansas. They, and all the village groups, hoped to continue to farm and embark on hunting trips. In 1833 the Pawnees agreed to restrict their movements to north of the Platte River, and in 1857 they ceded their lands and settled on a small reservation in 1859. Ceded lands were sold cheaply by the federal government to settlers.

American settlers pushed into Kansas and Nebraska and waves of emigrants continued on westward, following the Platte River road through some of the best buffalo country of both villagers and nomadic Native peoples. The Osages and Pawnees, whose lands were in the path of the emigrants, tried to discourage travel and the pilfering of game by requesting tolls of sugar and coffee, and occasionally by harassment. During

---

[15] Arrell M. Gibson, "Indian Land Transfers," in *History of Indian-White Relations,* Wilcomb E. Washburn, vol. ed., vol. 4 in *Handbook of North American Indians,* ed. William C. Sturtevant (Washington, D.C., 1988), 211–29.

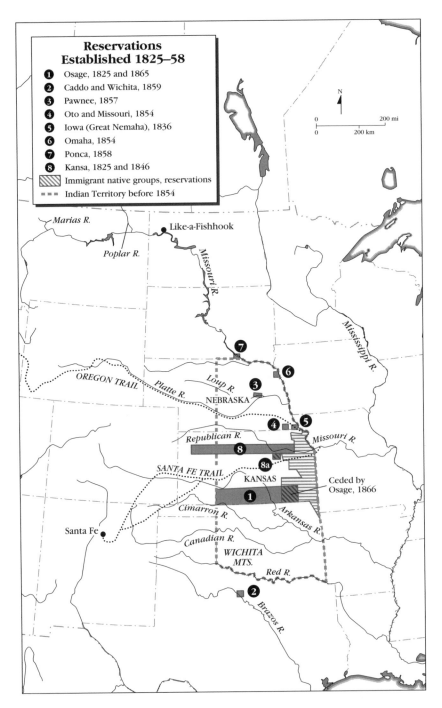

Figure 9.2 Reservations established in the United States, 1825–58.

times when food was scarce, they might steal some cattle. Americans living in Kansas and Nebraska pressured the government to remove all the Native peoples, the smaller, weaker groups as well as the Osages and Pawnees, from their reservations. These Native peoples struggled to maintain political independence and to survive in spite of drought, Sioux raids, and American incursions on the lands legally guaranteed them.

Finally, between 1859 and 1883, most of the Native peoples in Kansas and Nebraska decided that their best chance for survival as a people was to emigrate south to what remained of the "Indian Territory." Their journeys were difficult and dangerous and after they arrived in the Territory their hardships continued. But emigration to lands not coveted by settlers offered the hope of maintaining their village way of life.

The Pawnees had been in desperate circumstances since the 1820s. The buffalo range was constricting, due to the demands of the robe trade and to incursions of Native immigrants, whose presence brought about a 35 percent increase in the number of Native hunters and led to overhunting. Intergroup warfare escalated. The Pawnee villages had formed a confederacy and also were allied with Omahas and Poncas but the Tetons still outnumbered them about eight to one. The Tetons, whose alliance brought together up to 25,000 people, relentlessly attacked the Pawnees on their buffalo hunts in the South Platte and Republican River Valleys and at their villages, where raiders burned their lodges, looted their cache pits, and killed the women working in the fields. Famine was an everpresent danger. In the mid–eighteenth century, the Pawnees had numbered 20,000; by 1850, about 6,200; by 1869, only 2,400. The 1833 treaty had brought with it guarantees from the federal government that the Pawnees would be provided with guns and other assistance against the Sioux, as well as with annual payments. In spite of the failure of the government to honor these guarantees, the Pawnees were trying to make the transition from hoe to plough farming. But plough farming required more widespread fields, which made them more vulnerable to the Teton attacks.

The reservation upon which the Pawnees settled was a thirty by fifteen mile (forty-eight by twenty-four kilometer) tract on the Loup River in Nebraska, farther removed from the Platte road. Quaker missionaries acting as federal agents, who were directed both to placate Native people and to pressure them to give up their customs, arrived in the 1860s to supervise Pawnee activities. The United States failed to furnish the guns or repel the Sioux, making the Pawnees' circumstances increasingly desperate, for their Quaker agents refused to assist them in military resistance, arguing instead that the Pawnees should stop hunting so that they would be less of a target for the Sioux raids. One leader remarked that he had to sleep with his head on his revolver. Pawnees were hired as scouts to assist the army against the Tetons and Cheyennes in the 1860s. Scouting offered a means of making a living and a way to fight their enemies that did not bring federal reprisals. Two hundred men fought on the side of the Army and helped guard the route of the Union Pacific Railroad as it advanced through Nebraska.

Pawnee circumstances were extremely grave, for in addition to all these problems, grasshopper infestations and drought in the 1860s made farming unproductive, and American settlers regularly trespassed and stole the few resources that the Pawnees could protect from the Sioux. In 1866 the United States forced the Cherokees and others who had helped the Confederacy to cede some of their land in the Indian Territory for the purpose of relocating Native peoples living elsewhere. The possibility of removal to the Indian Territory was not lost on the Pawnees. Groups of Pawnees began defying their Quaker agents and moving south to Indian Territory, where they hoped to reestablish their villages in safer circumstances where they could plant and harvest cooperatively and perform their sacred ceremonies. Eventually, all the Pawnees pressed for the move and, when the religious leaders concurred, it appeared to the Pawnees to have supernatural sanction. They agreed to sell their reservation in Nebraska to the United States and, with the funds, reimburse the government for their removal expenses to the land assigned them in Indian Territory. By 1876, they had all relocated, taking with them the seeds for their crops and medicinal plants.[16]

The Osages, some of whom had been on their reservation in southern Kansas since 1825 and others since 1839, were pressured into ceding half of this reservation in 1865, but still settlers trespassed on their remaining land, burning their villages, stealing horses and crops from their fields, even moving into their homes while they were away on hunts. They were also challenged by the Cheyennes and Arapahos, who were competing over the buffalo range. Osage men enlisted with the Army to scout against the Cheyennes, but scouting activity brought further reprisals on their villages by the Cheyenne warriors. Finally, in

[16] Clyde A. Milner, *With Good Intentions: Quaker Work among the Pawnees, Otos, and Omahas in the 1870s* (Lincoln, Nebr., 1982); Alexander Lesser, *The Pawnee Ghost Dance Hand Game: Ghost Dance Revival and Ethnic Identity* (Madison, Wis., 1978), 1–52.

1870, threatened with extermination by the trespassing settlers, they decided to cede all these lands and move to Indian Territory. Even the village of about 300 Osages with French and Osage ancestry, who had a lifestyle similar to that of the American settlers, had to move, for the Americans identified them as "Indians," and as such they were fair game. Subsequently, now numbering less than 3,000, half the population settled on reservations, they all relocated on a reservation in Indian Territory between 1871 and 1874.[17]

The less populous groups – Kansas, Otos, Missouris, Omahas, Poncas, Iowas – had similar experiences. The Kansas, viewed by settlers as an obstacle to the settlement of Missouri (admitted to the Union in 1821), were forced in 1825 to cede their lands there in return for a reservation in Kansas, where they were attacked by Pawnees and again threatened by settlers. They had little choice but to sell most of this reservation in 1846 for far less than the land was worth, and confine themselves to a smaller reservation in eastern Kansas. Even this tract, which was but twenty square miles (fifty-two square kilometers), was coveted by settlers, who flooded into the area and squatted on the reservation. Attempting to appease the Americans, they sold half of the reservation in 1859. During the Civil War, Kansa men were impressed into the Union army. Military service did not guarantee their lands, however, for they were forced to sell the remainder of the reservation in 1872. Thereupon, they were assigned land in Indian Territory and started moving there in 1873.[18]

The Iowas and Otos soon followed. The Iowas ceded land in Missouri and got a reservation in southeastern Nebraska in 1836; by 1876 most had started moving to Indian Territory, where they obtained a reservation in 1883. The Otos, numbering less than 1,000, and Missouris, numbering less than 100, combined, though retaining separate political organizations, and allied with the Pawnees in fighting the Tetons. They were forced to cede land in 1854 in eastern Nebraska in return for a reservation twenty-five by ten miles (forty by sixteen kilometers) along the Kansas-Nebraska line. Leaders began trying to arrange a move to Indian Territory in 1869, and finally the reservation was sold in 1881. They obtained land in Indian Territory and moved there between 1874 and 1883, numbering about 400. There the hereditary chiefs hoped to revitalize the Oto political organization, which had been bypassed by federal officials on the reservation.

---

[17] Rollings, *The Osage;* Bailey, *Changes in Osage Social Organization.*
[18] William E. Unrau, *The Kansa Indians: A History of the Wind People, 1673–1873* (Norman, Okla., 1971).

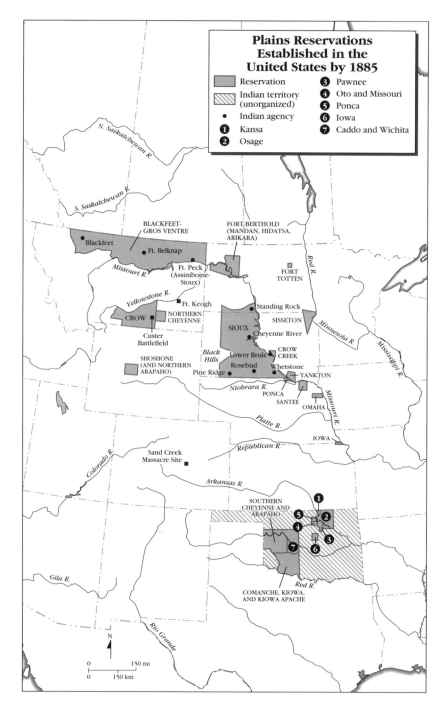

Figure 9.3 Plains reservations established in the United States by 1885.

The Poncas ceded their lands in 1858 in return for a reservation on the Nebraska–South Dakota border. They were forced to cede part of the reservation in 1865 in return for federal guarantees of inalienable title to the remainder, but shortly thereafter the government transferred title to the land to the Tetons. Congress ordered the Poncas to remove to the Indian Territory in 1876 and they started south under forced march, arriving in 1877. By 1879 a small group began a trek back to Nebraska, and upon arrival were arrested. Eventually freed due to a public outcry in the eastern United States, they received homestead allotments in Nebraska. The remainder, in Indian Territory, obtained a small reservation in 1884. Their Omaha relatives managed to hold on to a small portion of their reservation in Nebraska, which they had received in 1854 in return for land cessions.[19]

As bad as conditions were for Native peoples in Kansas and Nebraska, they were probably worse in Texas, where most of the Caddos and Wichitas lived. Wichita and Caddo groups struggled to maintain their village way of life in southwest Oklahoma (before the creation of Indian Territory) and northwest Texas. They were at peace with both Comanches and Texan settlers from the 1830s to the 1850s, despite continual trespass of settlers into their territory in Texas. When the federal government annexed Texas in 1845, Texas retained control of public lands, so the United States was unable to place the Indians on reservations until 1855, when Texas established a reservation on the Brazos River in western Texas. There, Wichitas, Caddos, and remnants of some other groups settled. Settlers in Texas were hostile, blaming them for any raids conducted by Comanches. To save them from annihilation, the United States moved them to a reservation in what by then had become Indian Territory. The threat from settlers was so great that they had to depart Texas hurriedly, leaving behind most of their property. In the vicinity of the Wichita Mountains, where the Oklahoma Wichitas and Caddos were residing, all these villages were placed on a reservation in 1859 on lands formerly assigned to the Chickasaws. During the Civil War, village life was disrupted, because some fought for the Confederacy and some for the Union, but after the war, they all returned to the reservation.

Far to the north, on the Upper Missouri, the Mandans, Hidatsas, and Arikaras did not face the problem of American emigration until the latter part of the century. In a weakened condition after the smallpox epidemic

---

[19] Milner, *With Good Intentions*, 153–85.

of 1837, the Mandans and Hidatsas decided in 1845 to move up the Missouri and found a new village, Like-a-Fishhook, in North Dakota. In 1862 the Arikaras, whose position farther south was made untenable by the Tetons, joined them there. In the new village they reconstructed their society based on old principles and, with the establishment of a company trading post, became important again in trade. Each of the three peoples occupied its own section of the village, was politically autonomous, and regulated social relations according to clan membership. Women practiced hoe cultivation and owned the corn, beans, and squash they produced; men began to learn to farm more intensively with a plow and grew wheat for sale, although they still went out on buffalo hunts. Men, primarily Arikaras, also were employed as scouts.

Due to the decline in population that resulted from epidemics, membership in the clans was reduced, which put in jeopardy the ceremonial organization. Surviving members joined another clan of the same moiety, and sacred bundles were transferred from extinct clans to surviving ones. Marriage rules of exogamy were relaxed, as well. Mandan and Hidatsa clans of the same name were equated in an effort to develop a common social system, and the ceremonial societies were merged. Intermarriage with other groups became necessary, and the villagers coped with this potential problem by insisting that the spouse be adopted and the children from the marriage raised in the traditions of the village.[20]

In 1851 the federal government called the Mandans, Hidatsas, and Arikaras to a treaty council at Fort Laramie, where their territory was defined in relation to the other Plains peoples. They were assigned the lands between the Yellowstone and Missouri Rivers. Thereafter, the federal government paid them little attention directly, for the American Fur Company's interests paralleled the government's, and its agents were relied on to transact much of the government's business. Throughout the 1850s, the Sioux terrorized the villagers, who had to beg the government for protection and assistance in the form of supplies, for they could not risk working in their fields on the outskirts of the village. The United States did not provide protection but, instead, pressured them to cede part of the 1851 territory, through which the Sioux were ranging. The remainder of these lands was made their reservation by executive order of Presi-

[20] Edward M. Bruner, "Mandan," in Edward H. Spicer, ed., *Perspectives in American Indian Culture Change* (Chicago, 1961), 187–277.

dent Grant in 1870. A federal agent arrived at the village in 1868 and began to try to pressure the Mandans, Hidatsas, and Arikaras into accepting the government's assimilation program. In 1880, the federal government reduced the size of the reservation by one-half and gave the ceded lands to the Northern Pacific Railroad.

The horticultural villagers experienced reservation life before the nomadic Plains groups. These reservations were the focus of the assimilationist policies of the United States. The rationale for them was to facilitate the "civilization" of Native peoples. Native people's experiences on these early reservations were the precursor of what was to come for the nomadic groups. Rather than facilitating their participation in American society, the reservation policy undermined their ability to compete economically with settlers. Reservations offered an opportunity for settlers to improve on a marginal existence by stealing timber, stock, and other property. It was useless to attempt to obtain legal redress, for federal courts refused jurisdiction and state courts refused to take action. Railroad companies took advantage of federal land policies to acquire and speculate in land. And the federal officials and employees who had responsibility for protecting the rights and interests of Native peoples often used their positions to profit personally, siphoning off supplies intended for the villagers. Business men cooperated with each other to make fortunes in the "Indian business" through fraudulent activity. Individuals who protested could find their lives in jeopardy.[21]

Individuals who embraced assimilationist goals found it as difficult to make a place for themselves in American society as did village communities. A noted example was the case of Susette La Flesche, an Omaha woman who excelled in boarding school and trained for the teaching profession. When she applied for a job at the school on the Omaha reservation, she was rejected as unqualified. Miss La Flesche wrote to the highest ranking federal official in Indian Affairs: "It all seems like a farce, when the Whites, who came here with the avowed object of civilizing and teaching us to do for ourselves, what they are doing for us, should, after we are prepared to occupy positions, appropriate those positions to themselves." This local agent's decision was overturned at the federal level; still, she was paid only half the salary received by her non-Indian predecessor.[22]

---

[21] See H. Craig Miner and William E. Unrau, *The End of Indian Kansas: A Study of Cultural Revolution, 1854–1871* (Lawrence, Kans., 1978).
[22] Quoted in Milner, *With Good Intentions*, 174.

The Nomadic hunting peoples in the United States

Westward expansion of American settlers and business interests threatened some Native groups in the upland Plains more than others. Some, characterized as "friendlies," had no clashes with the United States Army and even fought side by side with troops. Others, the "hostiles," resisted. The annexation of Texas in 1845, the acquisition of Oregon in 1846, and the seizure of lands in California and New Mexico by the defeat of Mexico in 1848 opened the door to western expansion. The discovery of gold in California in 1849 was a further inducement. The road west went along the Platte then up the Sweetwater to Utah, Oregon, and beyond, and down the Santa Fe Trail southwest from Kansas City along the Arkansas River and beyond. These overland routes crossed through the hunting grounds of the Arapahos, Cheyennes, and some Teton groups, in the case of the Oregon Trail, and through Comanche and Kiowa territory on the way to Santa Fe.

Trouble between American travelers and these Native peoples gradually escalated. In response, the United States arranged treaty councils with all the nomadic groups in the 1850s. At Fort Laramie in 1851, a treaty was signed with Arapahos, Cheyennes, Tetons, Crows, Assiniboines, and others. At Fort Atkinson in 1853, a treaty was signed with Kiowas, Comanches, and Kiowa-Apaches. In 1855, a treaty was signed on the Judith River with some of the Siksikas, some of the Bloods, most Piegans, and the Gros Ventres. The treaties established peaceful relations, defined "tribal" territories (albeit unrealistically), and initiated the regular issue of supplies to Native peoples to compensate for the destruction of game by the immigrants. The Blackfeet groups, removed from the immigrant routes, were unfamiliar with flour and sugar, included in the presents from the government: they threw the flour in the air to watch it fall on the grass and emptied the sugar into a stream. [23]

These treaty councils were conducted in a manner similar to the ritual surrounding trade between two Native groups. Arriving parties were saluted, there was the ceremonial smoking of pipes, and gifts were given. Native leaders expressed their group's consensus, not their individual opinions. The federal government expected that a few leaders could speak for all. In the case of the Arapahos, such an expectation was not far from the truth. Arapaho leaders had been serving as intermediaries between

---

[23] John C. Ewers, *The Blackfeet: Raiders on the Northwestern Plains* (Norman, Okla., 1958), 221.

their people and the Americans for a generation. They routinely solicited or levied "tolls" in the form of sugar and coffee from American travelers. American immigrants were a source of supplies and luxury items that groups on the central Plains had learned to crave. Leaders who were skilled at reassuring travelers and officials built reputations as friendly chiefs and were able to accumulate goods that attracted and held followers. At the 1851 treaty council the Arapahos put forth three well-known "friendly chiefs." These intermediaries and their successors in the years to come had to convince federal officials that they could influence their people. By convincing officials of their reliability, they got access to supplies which they could use to retain the support of the people. Selection of intermediary chiefs was not so easy for the Tetons, who were subdivided into many politically autonomous groups, and could not readily agree on a few representatives. In cases like these it became government policy to try to influence or dictate the selection of intermediaries.[24]

For Native peoples, participating in the council was tantamount to a promise; to the federal agents, the agreement was only legal after each leader "touched the pen," that is, a scribe made an x-mark beside his name while he touched the end of the pen. Although these treaties in the 1850s appear to have been understood by the parties, in subsequent years the practice of touching the pen allowed for provisions that had not been discussed to be inserted or provisions that had been agreed on to be omitted. Thus, treaties could be subject to accusations of fraud. After the councils, some leaders were invited to Washington, D.C., where they toured the sights, met high officials, and received special gifts symbolic of the government's trust. Such delegations were a regular feature of the diplomatic process in the late nineteenth century.

In Montana, where the Crows, Blackfeet groups, Gros Ventres, and some Assiniboines ranged, Teton groups were contesting the buffalo ground. The numerous Tetons were a serious threat to the Native peoples already there. Removed from the overland routes, the Montana groups viewed the Tetons to be more of a problem than the Americans and maintained friendly relations with the United States, the Crows eventually scouting for the Army against the Sioux in order to defend their remaining hunting territory. The Crows signed another treaty in 1868, ceding most of their land and accepting a reservation on the remainder.

[24] Loretta Fowler, *Arapahoe Politics, 1851–1978: Symbols in Crises of Authority* (Lincoln, Nebr., 1982), 25–6, 32–4.

Another serious threat was the disappearance of the buffalo. In Canada, the buffalo robe trade was in decline by the 1870s and, in the United States, not long afterwards. Instead, hides were in demand. The market for buffalo hides was in the eastern United States, where they were made into leather and used for machinery belts in factories. Hides did not need to be dressed, so Native peoples did not have an advantage in this trade. Native peoples had difficulty competing with non-Indian, professional buffalo hunters who had repeating rifles and killed the buffalo in such numbers in the United States and Canada that they were all but extinct by the 1880s.

In Montana the Southern Piegans were not disturbed by trespassing Americans until the Gold Rush of 1862, when the southern part of their territory was invaded. In 1864 Montana Territory was created, and miners and other immigrants began demanding the removal of Native peoples to northern Montana. There were depredations on both sides, and gradually the Siksikas, Bloods, and Northern Piegans began to withdraw into Canada. In the United States, troops were sent to the Piegan area in 1869 in response to pressure from the squatters. A friendly group of Piegans, sick with smallpox, was attacked without warning and massacred on the Marias River, far from the miners' settlements. There was little the Piegans could do, for they could not risk war with both the United States and the Tetons. In 1873 President Grant issued an executive order reducing the size of their reservation, without consulting or compensating the Blackfeet groups. In 1874 Congress moved the southern boundary of the reservation farther north to the Marias River. The Piegans withdrew north of the river where they could hunt undisturbed for a few more years.

The Gros Ventres, ranging to the east of the Piegans, had one-third the population of the Blackfeet confederacy and absorbed much of the Sioux attacks. Their hunting territory was far to the north of the settlements, so Americans were viewed as an asset, an ally against the Tetons, Yanktons, Yanktonais, and some Santees who flooded into Montana in the 1860s and 1870s to hunt the buffalo there. Gros Ventres allied with Crows and Upper Assiniboines in their wars with the Sioux. The Gros Ventres did not settle in the vicinity of their Fort Belknap agency until 1878.

Farther south, the 1851 and 1853 treaties did not promote peaceful relations between Americans and the Native peoples on the central and southern Plains. The emigrants along the Platte and the more southerly alternative route along the Canadian River disturbed the buffalo and otherwise adversely affected the ecology of the region. The Comanches and

Kiowas were south of the Arkansas River. Hunting was more difficult because of the emigrant traffic along the Canadian River and the Euro-American settlement of Texas. Provisions from the government, which were promised in the treaty, often did not arrive. Thus, from the Comanche and Kiowa point of view, raiding for cattle and supplies was necessary. Both Texas Rangers and federal troops tried to retaliate in the late 1850s.

The Arapahos, already feeling the effects of the decline of game, did not want hostile relations with Americans. The government supplies that once had been luxuries were becoming necessities. Blankets and cloth with which to make clothing were increasingly relied on to supplement hide clothing. Percussion and flintlock rifles were good for hunting small game. Their problems worsened as Americans settled the Smoky Hill Valley in western Kansas.

On the Platte route, some Tetons were provoked into a fight with troops in 1855 and, similarly, Cheyennes were in conflict with troops in 1857. The Cheyennes, like their Arapaho allies to the west, were finding it difficult to obtain enough game. They had suffered an unprovoked attack by troops and retaliated against two wagon trains in 1856, which brought on pursuit by troops. But these were skirmishes that did not seriously weaken the military capabilities of the Native groups.

The circumstances of the groups south of the Platte worsened in the 1860s, for Euro-American immigration increased due to the post–Civil War exodus from the East and the establishment of Dakota and Colorado Territories in 1861. Gold had been discovered near Denver in 1858, and the Gold Rush brought a flood of miners and others into the heart of Arapaho territory in violation of the 1851 treaty. Between 1859 and 1860 about 40,000 trespassers intruded on the lands of the 5,000 Arapahos and Cheyennes. The squatters and the Arapahos initially reached an accommodation, but as the game in the area disappeared and the number of settlers increased, violence began to occur. Americans, Arapahos, and Cheyennes all were involved.

In response to the deteriorating circumstances, the bands of Arapahos that ranged north into Wyoming withdrew northward and, in company with bands of Cheyennes and Tetons, stayed north of the Platte and tried to hold the buffalo ground there. The southern bands of Arapahos and Cheyennes struggled to find a way to survive. Conditions worsened when a group of volunteer militia, comprised mostly of miners determined to exterminate local Indians, attacked a camp of peaceful Cheyennes and

Arapahos who had been ordered by the Army to camp on Sand Creek in Colorado in November 1864. In the aftermath of the Sand Creek massacre, the Cheyennes, Arapahos, Comanches, and Kiowas launched a major offensive against the settlements and roads in the region that lasted into 1865. Even the northern bands participated. The ranks of their Teton allies, most of whom usually stayed on the northern Plains, were swelled by refugees fleeing west of the Missouri in the aftermath of an uprising by the Santee Sioux in Minnesota in 1862. The Upper Santees – Sissetons and Wahpetons who primarily hunted buffalo in western Minnesota and North Dakota – numbered 7,000 and were often in alliance with Tetons and Yanktonais. The Lower Santees, Mdewakantons and Wahpekutes of the Woodlands area in central Minnesota, numbered about 2,500. The uprising probably had far-reaching effects on Native peoples' decisions about how to deal with the problems of American expansion. Their awareness of the harsh reprisals taken against the Santees may have helped suppress rebellion on other reservations, even though conditions on many were deplorable during the 1860s and 1870s. But the uprising also helps explain the desperate resistance of some groups to threats to their way of life.

The Santee group of the Upper Mississippi had a long history of friendly, close interpersonal relations with traders in their country. Intermarriage was widespread and involved a set of reciprocal obligations. As kinsmen, these men adhered to Santee values of sharing, mutual aid, and respect. Yet, by the 1850s, many of the traders and mixed-blood descendants were deviating from these standards and, instead, manipulating Santee kin for personal gain. Trade had become more dependent on political connections in Washington and access to information on distribution of treaty payments rather than on creation and reinforcement of kinship ties. Such manipulations were important factors in the Santee land cessions of 1851 and 1859, in which they ceded away most of their land in Minnesota and accepted two reservations on the Minnesota River, only to see the monetary compensation go to traders and other non-Santee officials. Even more troubling was the influx of settlers who, even before the lands east of the Minnesota River were opened to settlement, trespassed, refused to enter into bonds of reciprocity, and treated the Santees with contempt. As game became increasingly scarce, Santees became more dependent on credit from traders and supplies from the government. The Santees regarded as highly immoral the fact that these supplies were not forthcoming. The threat of famine and the selective distribution of supplies that were intended for all were blamed on the traders and settlers. This led a sizable number of Santees, largely men in the warrior societies of the Mdewakantons and Wahpekutes, to the conclusion that, if not kinsmen, these non-Santees were enemies to be attacked and that, by driving them away, they might revitalize Santee traditions.

In the fighting that followed, over 500 settlers were killed in the valley of the Minnesota River, despite the heroic actions of many Santees who saved and protected settlers with whom they had ties of friendship and kinship. After large numbers of Santees were convinced that there would not be general retaliation, peace was restored. Federal officials instead allowed mobs of settlers to condemn 303 Santees, some of whom had rescued, not attacked, settlers. President Lincoln commuted the sentences of all but thirty-nine, who were executed. All the Santees, whether involved in the uprising or not, were then expelled from Minnesota. Some took up reservation life in Nebraska and the Dakotas and tried to cooperate with the government's civilization program. Others joined "hostile" groups of Tetons and Yanktonais in the upland Plains. The Santees' sense of betrayal was shared by and communicated to other Sioux groups on the Plains and contributed to the determination to resist.[25]

For the Cheyennes, the war of 1864–65 resulted in a reorganization of their society. The war chiefs attained greater influence than the intermediary chiefs who had tried to maintain peaceful relations with Americans. The military societies took their families and lived apart from the families still loyal to the peace chiefs. A new band, the Dog Soldiers, came into being and lived as semi-exiles from the rest of the Cheyennes, determined to retain control of the remaining buffalo ground on the southern Plains. Often people from other bands and sometimes other, non-Cheyenne groups would join them and participate in the raids and the fights against troops in the 1860s and 1870s, then subsequently move back to the vicinity of the forts to get supplies. The Dog Soldiers modified Cheyenne institutions to facilitate their military goals.[26]

The conflict between Americans and nomadic, Native peoples escalated during the 1860s and 1870s, and the Army responded by expanding and reorganizing. The Army increasingly relied on Indian scouts and auxiliaries after the mid-1860s. Native men served in virtually every

---

[25] Gary Clayton Anderson, *Kinsmen of Another Kind: Dakota-White Relations in the Upper Mississippi Valley, 1650–1862* (Lincoln, Nebr., 1984).

[26] John H. Moore, *The Cheyenne Nation: A Social and Demographic History* (Lincoln, Nebr., 1987), 196–8.

theater and conflict in the West. They made it possible for the Army to make contact with "hostile" Native groups on the Army's terms. In 1866 Congress provided for the enlistment of Indians as soldiers; these auxiliaries, with indeterminate enlistments unlike Euro- and African-American soldiers, could be terminated if conditions so warranted. These flexible enlistments also worked to the advantage of Native warriors, who could leave the Army when it was convenient for them to do so. Scouts were issued a uniform and a repeating carbine rifle but retained their moccasins and furnished their own horses. They took responsibility for reconnaissance, locating and following the enemy's trail, and determining their strength and identity. In practice, scouts (often with a white cloth wrapped around their heads so their comrades could distinguish them from the enemy), as well as auxiliary soldiers, engaged in combat. In fact, as Thomas Dunlay observed, "Sometimes the cliche of the cavalry's arrival just in time to save beleaguered comrades or civilians was reversed, and the cavalry was rescued at the last minute by Indians." Native warriors forced the Army to accommodate to their terrain and tactics. Thus, commanders relied on their Native allies in matters of mobility, concealment, and surprise. The small Indian ponies had more endurance than cavalry horses on the long pursuit, for they could live off grass, whereas without grain army horses weakened. The Native soldier developed more expertise than the American soldier in reloading cartridges for the breech-loading carbine, as well.

Native men assisted the Army for various reasons, assessing enlistment as an effective strategy for improving the circumstances of their people, as well as themselves as individuals. Assisting the Army against one's enemies was an advantage, for American allies improved the chance of success. Thus, Pawnees, Arikaras, and Hidatsas allied themselves with the Army against the Sioux in the 1860s in defense of their territory and, in the 1870s, assisted the Army in the Powder River war. Similarly, Crows helped the Army in Montana against the Sioux and their allies. Osage scouts also helped the Army against the Cheyennes who were competing for buffalo in the Arkansas River country. In the Indian Territory, Pawnees, Caddos, and Wichitas, who had to contend with horse raids from Comanches and others, aided the Army against nomadic groups in the 1870s. Some young men in these village societies had been to government boarding schools in the East by the 1870s. Their best chance for prestige in battle after returning to their communities lay with enlistment. Their ability to speak English was very useful to the Army, as well.

Scouting provided a man not only rations and ammunition for himself, but extra food for the family he left behind at the agency. He was allowed to keep horses and other property seized from the enemy, which brought him prestige, as did any acts of bravery during his service. At the Yankton agency on the Missouri, families were often destitute, and the pay received for service with the Army was desperately needed. Scouting also offered a means for influencing federal policy. Groups who wanted to stay on the northern Plains, rather than removing to Indian Territory, saw alliances with military leaders as a promising strategy.[27]

The federal government made a futile effort to restore peace in the upland Plains in the late 1860s. The intent was to assign the Native groups hunting in the uplands area to reservations removed from the overland routes and areas of settlement and then gradually to reduce the size of the reservations as the hunting way of life gave way to agricultural labor. Treaties were negotiated with groups on both the southern and the northern Plains.

The Southern Arapahos and some groups of Cheyennes and the Comanches and Kiowas agreed in 1865, and again in 1867 when the government realized it could not adhere to the agreement made in 1865, to accept reservations. In return, they were to receive protection from unprovoked attacks by settlers and troops and regular issues of supplies to compensate them for the loss of game.

The Comanches and Kiowas embarked on a pattern of camping near their agency where the supplies were issued, then when the supplies were depleted, leaving to raid the trails. The government was unable to make good on its promise of a reservation with sufficient provisions to make raiding unnecessary. When the Native hunters came into contact with Americans there was often trouble. There were sporadic military engagements between the Army and the Comanche and Kiowa allies between 1868 and 1875. In the 1870s commercial buffalo hunting in this region seriously cut into the buffalo herds. Professional, non-Indian hunters were armed with repeating rifles and killed animals for their hides, leaving the meat to rot. Such hunters were targets for attacks from the Native peoples. But by the 1870s the federal government was determined to crush the Comanches and Kiowas, and launched winter campaigns in which troops attacked the winter camps, destroying the families' provisions. By 1875

[27] Thomas W. Dunlay, *Wolves for the Blue Soldiers: Indian Scouts and Auxiliaries with the United States Army, 1860–90* (Lincoln, Nebr., 1982), 200.

hunger had driven the 2,500 Comanches and Kiowas back to their reservation between the Canadian and Red Rivers, this time to stay.

The Southern Arapahos tried to remain on good terms with the Americans after the treaty of 1867. The reservation they were assigned between the Arkansas and Cimarron Rivers was not feasible, being too near the settlements, and so they began a diplomatic campaign to acquire a reservation on the North Canadian River in Indian Territory. Their association with the Cheyennes endangered this effort, as well as their lives. Cheyennes were engaged in hostilities subsequent to the signing of the 1867 treaty, and the federal troops were unconcerned with distinguishing friend from foe. In 1869 the Arapahos succeeded; President Grant by executive order created a reservation for Arapahos and Cheyennes in the Indian Territory. Almost all the Arapahos and a few Cheyennes settled on the reservation and during the 1870s gave military support to the federal employees there when some of the Cheyennes threatened the agency.

Most of the Cheyennes were ready by 1867 to try to avoid war with the Americans. But Dog Soldier raids on settlers in Kansas and brutal retaliation in 1868 and 1869 from the Army, which attacked friendly Cheyennes as well as the Dog Soldiers, kept the southern Plains in turmoil. Some Southern Cheyennes moved onto the reservation where the Southern Arapahos were living; the Dog Soldiers drifted north to join the Sioux and continue the fight.

On the northern Plains, the Arapahos, Cheyennes, and Sioux groups were trying to hunt and avoid trouble with the Army. The Powder River country was still good buffalo ground, and they were determined to prevent settlement there. But when gold was discovered in Montana in 1862, miners and settlers illegally invaded these lands. The federal government sent troops to build forts along the route and protect the trespassing settlers. In response, the Sioux led a successful effort to repel them. The federal government signed a peace treaty in 1868 which established the Great Sioux Reservation and guaranteed hunting rights in the Powder River country to the Sioux and their allies.

But the Arapahos were badly weakened in the fighting. Less than 1,000, the losses they suffered led them to decide to try to obtain a reservation in the north. The Eastern Shoshones, traditional enemies of the Arapahos, had negotiated a large reservation in Wyoming in 1868, and unsuccessful overtures were made to enable the Arapahos to settle there. By 1875 the Arapahos were frequenting the agencies of the Sioux Reservation and the Army posts near the reservation; they had become dependent on the supplies they could obtain there. When another war erupted on the northern Plains, this time over trespass into the Black Hills on the Sioux Reservation, the Northern Arapahos eventually withdrew from their Cheyenne and Sioux allies and the men enlisted as scouts in the American Army during 1876 and 1877. Connections with Army officers helped them get permission to settle permanently on the Shoshone Reservation in 1878.[28]

The Northern Cheyennes also helped the Sioux in the Powder River War of 1866 and 1867, and frequented the Sioux Reservation for supplies between hunting expeditions after 1868. In 1875 they fought to keep settlers out of the Black Hills, and were with the Sioux when they defeated General George Custer on the Little Bighorn in 1876. That winter they were weakened by the Army's attacks on their winter camps. By this time the Army had enlisted upwards of 400 Indian scouts from six different Indian nations, which made the Cheyennes' efforts to evade capture more difficult. Some began surrendering at Fort Keogh in Montana at the confluence of the Yellowstone and Tongue Rivers in 1877, where Cheyenne men enlisted as scouts. The main body of Northern Cheyennes surrendered on the Sioux Reservation. The government had obtained an agreement with the Northern Arapahos, Northern Cheyennes, and Sioux in 1876 whereby they would settle permanently on the Sioux Reservation or the Cheyenne-Arapaho Reservation in Indian Territory, and the Black Hills area would be opened to Americans. Because the agreement was obtained fraudulently and included only a portion of the Sioux, the fighting did not stop.

When the main body of 1,000 Cheyennes surrendered, the government moved them to Indian Territory in 1877, as specified in the agreement of 1876. But problems immediately arose in Indian Territory. Having lived apart for several years, the southern and northern people were somewhat estranged. When they separated, each had taken one of the two Cheyenne sacred bundles, and ceremonial life had evolved somewhat differently among the two groups. One Cheyenne noted, "These northern kinsmen of ours were dressed very differently from us and looked strange to our eyes . . . They were growing more like the Sioux in habits and appearance every year. . . . Their language was changing; they used many words that were strange to us."[29]

After a year in Indian Territory, several hundred Northern Cheyennes escaped to the north. Dividing into two groups they made their way past

[28] Fowler, *Arapahoe Politics*, 42–63.
[29] Quoted in Tom Weist, *A History of the Cheyenne People* (Billings, Mont., 1977), 54.

soldiers and settlers until one group reached Fort Robinson in northwest Nebraska and asked to settle on the Sioux Reservation. Instead, many were massacred by the Army before they finally reached a settlement and were moved to the Fort Keogh area late in 1879. The other group also reached the northern border of Nebraska and was able to negotiate an agreement with the Army whereby they were moved to the Fort Keogh area in 1879 and the men enlisted as scouts. Finally in 1884 President Chester Arthur signed an executive order creating a reservation for the Northern Cheyennes on Tongue River in Montana.

The Sioux in the 1860s numbered in the thousands and were subdivided into many divisions, each of which had several subdivisions or bands. These divisions and subdivisions did not always agree on what kind of relations with Americans would best serve their interests. Some groups included descendants of European and American traders, who had developed their own subculture and their own agendas. The federal government attempted to draw the Sioux groups far away from the overland routes, distributing provisions and encouraging missionary activity at agencies that were some distance from the buffalo ground. The Yankton were effectively contained at an agency in 1859. Santee groups, exiled from Minnesota after the uprising, were settled at the Crow Creek, Santee, Sisseton, and Devils Lake (Fort Totten) agencies during 1866–7. The 1868 treaty with Tetons, Yanktonais, and some Santees who opted to join the Tetons established the Great Sioux Reservation. Four agencies on the Missouri were established on the reservation and two at the southern boundary on the North Platte and White Rivers (for Red Cloud's and Spotted Tail's Teton groups). These agencies attracted some groups, and the Army began to enlist scouts among them. Other groups roamed to the west beyond the Black Hills, periodically coming into the agencies to receive supplies. Others stayed to the north in Montana, generally shunning the Sioux agencies. Some Santees gave up on the Americans, making peace with the Métis in southern Manitoba and southern Saskatchewan and relocating there. Without signing treaties the Canadian government gave sanctuary to the Santees on condition that they remain peaceful. Between 1873 and 1877, seven reservations were created for Santee refugees in Canada.

In Montana in 1868 there were Tetons, Yanktons, Yanktonais, Santees, and some Assiniboines ("Lower Missouri" groups allied with Sioux), all challenging Crows, Gros Ventres, and Red River Métis for the buffalo ground in the Upper Missouri area as far as the Milk River.

Unwilling to frequent the Missouri agencies, they began pressing the government for an agency in Montana. A peace commission met with them in 1872 in response to Sioux attacks on Northern Pacific Railroad workers trespassing in the buffalo country. These Sioux and Assiniboines got their agency in 1873 near the mouth of Poplar River. An executive order granted reservation status to these lands in 1874. But some of the Tetons were still determined to keep Americans out of the buffalo country, and the Army began preparing for war in the Yellowstone country.[30]

The campaign in the Yellowstone area was cut short when gold was discovered in the Black Hills in 1874. This resulted in trespass by miners and others, and the government tried to treat with the Sioux in 1875 to buy or lease the Black Hills area for the miners. This effort was unsuccessful so the government ordered all Sioux to remain on the Sioux Reservation at their agencies or face attack from the Army. Hunting off the reservation was necessary to supplement the meager supplies of food at the agencies. Nonetheless, the Army began its campaign in the winter of 1876, hoping to catch as many Sioux off the reservation as possible. The Sioux suffered little harm, this the year of Custer's defeat, but subsequently they dispersed, making it easier for the Army to succeed the following winter when they received reinforcements and established forts on the Yellowstone. Congress threatened to cut off supplies to the agency Sioux, in effect pressing them along with their Arapaho and some Cheyenne allies to sign a cession agreement for the Black Hills in 1876. Large numbers of Sioux continued to resist, however. At the agencies, the Army seized the horses and guns of anyone suspected of aiding the "hostiles" and enlisted Sioux men as scouts for the winter campaign. Sioux men joined the Army to avoid the agency directives, obtain provisions for their families, and earn prestige for military exploits. The Sioux alliance was overshadowed by loyalty to band. Army commanders encouraged enlistment by promising that Sioux women and children would be taken prisoner, not killed. The winter campaign of 1877 forced most of the Tetons and their Yanktonais and Santee allies to surrender, and the Red Cloud and Spotted Tail agencies were moved north within the reservation boundary, now reduced by the cession of the Black Hills. A group of Tetons (mostly Hunkpapas under the leadership of Sitting Bull) fled to Canada and eventu-

---

[30] Raymond J. DeMallie, "The Sioux in Dakota and Montana Territories: Cultural and Historical Background of the Ogden B. Read Collection," in *Vestiges of a Proud Nation,* ed. Glenn E. Markoe (Burlington, Vt., 1986), 19–69.

ally in 1913 several hundred of them obtained a reserve at Wood Mountain; others, including Sitting Bull, had returned to the United States in 1881 and settled on reservations there. Following the defeats in the Black Hills and Montana, the Sioux resigned themselves to reservation life if not to assimilation.

Sioux groups, as widely diverse in strategies for accommodation as they were in strategies of resistance, were forced to share reservations. This diversity was an important factor in the way culture developed on Sioux reservations in the remainder of the nineteenth and the twentieth centuries, as it was on the Cheyenne and Arapaho reservation where relations between the Cheyennes and Arapahos were strained.

Nomadic plains peoples in Canada

Euro-Canadians also had difficulty accepting diversity as they began to settle the West. In the late 1850s and 1860s some settlers came to the valleys of the Red and Assiniboine Rivers, where about 12,000 Métis of French-Indian and British-Indian descent were settled. The new settlers came with assumptions of racial superiority, and these attitudes aggravated Métis resentments already present because of the Hudson's Bay Company's discriminatory policies and missionary activity that denigrated Native ways. In addition, company men who had been married to Métis women began abandoning them in order to marry Euro-Canadian women, as local prejudices adversely affected the careers of men with Métis wives. All these factors contributed to Métis anxiety. The Dominion of Canada was established in 1867 and purchased the company's lands in 1870, including the Great Plains north of the forty-ninth parallel. In these negotiations, the Métis settlement was not consulted and they feared that the government's highhandedness presaged worse to come. Métis were not assured representation in the territorial government and their land-holding system was not based on formal titles or deeds but, rather, on customary title. Thus, the Métis felt that without formal representation, their right to their lands and way of life was threatened.

These concerns motivated the Red River resistance movement in 1869, which was led by the Métis leader Louis Riel. Declaring a provisional government prior to the establishment of a Canadian administration, he tried to pressure Canada to negotiate. The Canadian government did not favor such independence and forcibly suppressed the movement. An agreement was reached in 1870, however, in which the Métis were promised land and amnesty was guaranteed for the leaders of the resistance movement. Canada reneged on the promise of amnesty and Riel and others were forced to flee to the United States. Land grants for future generations of Métis also remained a promise unfulfilled, although security of title was guaranteed those who had land. Many Métis, their rights ignored, migrated west to the Saskatchewan country, already occupied by groups of Métis hunters in the Qu'Appelle Valley, where they intended to reestablish their community on the South Saskatchewan. Others moved to Montana. When the North-West Mounted Police were created in 1873, the original intent was to employ Métis to help keep order west of the newly created province of Manitoba and prevent illegal liquor sales by Americans; but the resistance of the Métis had generated a backlash and only Canadian and British men were hired.

By 1870 the Canadian government was ready to assist Euro-Canadian settlement of the Saskatchewan country and in the building of a railroad from eastern Canada to British Columbia. The need to placate the Native peoples of the Saskatchewan region was apparent, especially in view of the fact that the Indian wars in the United States had proved to be a heavy financial burden, and the Canadian government had limited financial resources. Native peoples of the Plains also wanted to negotiate agreements about how they would be treated by the Canadians and to secure government assistance so that they would survive in the wake of the disappearance of the buffalo. Increased hunting by Métis, Sioux from the United States, and non-Indians, as well as by Crees and Assiniboines, had resulted in a drastic reduction in the size of the herds as the hunters obtained hides for the eastern market.

The Canadian government negotiated seven numbered treaties between 1871 and 1877, in which the goal was to compensate Native peoples for land cessions and to assign them to reserves. Six of these involved Plains Indians. The Red River Ojibwas and Plains Crees of Manitoba, who were signatory to Treaties One and Two, instigated the treaty councils and insisted on additional provisions that provided for supplies and assistance in agricultural development. The Ojibwas signed Treaty One in 1871 but obtained the modifications by 1873; the Plains Crees completed the negotiations for modifications by 1875. Treaty Three was signed in 1873 by Plains Ojibwas, who also insisted that assistance be guaranteed. Treaty Four was negotiated between 1872 and 1875 by Plains Crees from the Qu'Appelle area in Saskatchewan, and Treaty Six was negotiated by Plains

Crees from the Saskatchewan Valley in 1876. They insisted on help in making a transition to farming and on recognition of their rights in the area. Finally, in 1877 Treaty Seven was negotiated with Siksika (Northern Blackfeet), Blood, Northern Piegan, Sarsi, and some Assiniboine groups in southern Alberta.

About half of the Plains peoples in the area of the Qu'Appelle and Saskatchewan Rivers refused to agree to the provisions of these treaties. These were Cree and Assiniboine groups led by Piapot, and Crees led by Big Bear and Little Pine. These groups wanted guarantees that they would retain their political autonomy and that non-Indians would be prevented from hunting buffalo. They continued to hunt, fighting with Blackfeet groups over access to buffalo grounds in Alberta and Montana. After Piapot was assured that his people would receive adequate agricultural assistance, he signed Treaty Four in 1875. Big Bear and Little Pine tried to organize a confederation of Plains peoples in order to lobby the Canadian government for better treatment. Their object was to avoid violence. But the government embarked on a policy of domination, using the promised supplies as a lever. Those who complained and tried to negotiate modifications to the treaties were denied food and threatened with legal prosecution. By 1879 Little Pine had capitulated, and many of Big Bear's followers had deserted him.

Big Bear worked to get a consolidation of reserve lands in order to create a stronger political base for Cree and Assiniboine peoples, but the government opposed his efforts and insisted on scattering Native peoples on small reserves. In 1880 the government agreed to consolidation, but reneged soon after. In 1881 there began to be disturbances on reserves when food supplies ran short. The government decided to crush the holdout "non-treaty" Indians and determined not to consolidate reserves, where Native peoples in large numbers would be harder to control. More Mounted Police were sent to the area and treaty provisions were ignored. Malnutrition and starvation were all too common by 1882, when Big Bear signed the treaty. In 1884 he selected a location for a reserve. Between 1883 and 1884 he and other Cree leaders worked both to convince the government to abide by the treaty provisions and to persuade impatient followers to refrain from violence.

In 1884 the government cut funds for supplies, and lack of food drove some individuals to rob government storehouses on the reserves. Leaders began to hold councils at the Sun Dance camps, where they hoped to attract and hold followers to strengthen their influence with the government. The

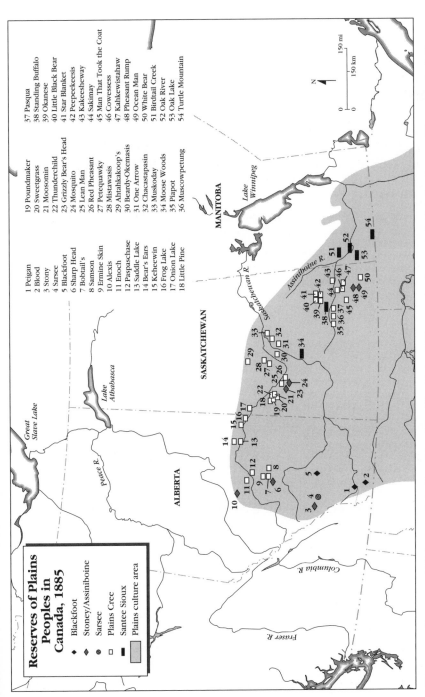

Reserves of Plains Peoples in Canada, 1885

- ◆ Blackfoot
- ◆ Stoney/Assiniboine
- ◉ Sarsee
- □ Plains Cree
- ■ Santee Sioux
- ▨ Plains culture area

1 Peigan
2 Blood
3 Stony
4 Sarsee
5 Blackfoot
6 Sharp Head
7 Bobtail's
8 Samson
9 Ermine Skin
10 Alexis
11 Enoch
12 Paspaschase
13 Saddle Lake
14 Bear's Ears
15 Keheewin
16 Frog Lake
17 Onion Lake
18 Little Pine

19 Poundmaker
20 Sweetgrass
21 Moosomin
22 Thunderchild
23 Grizzly Bear's Head
24 Mosquito
25 Lean Man
26 Red Pheasant
27 Petequawky
28 Mistawasis
29 Ahtahkakoop's
30 Beardy-Okemasis
31 One Arrow
32 Chacastapasin
33 Muskoday
34 Moose Woods
35 Piapot
36 Muscowpetung

37 Pasqua
38 Standing Buffalo
39 Okanese
40 Little Black Bear
41 Star Blanket
42 Peepeekeesis
43 Kakeesheway
44 Sakimay
45 Man That Took the Coat
46 Cowessess
47 Kahkewistahaw
48 Pheasant Rump
49 Ocean Man
50 White Bear
51 Birdtail Creek
52 Oak River
53 Oak Lake
54 Turtle Mountain

Figure 9.4 Reserves of Plains people in Canada, 1885. The Plains Ojiba people also settled with the Cree on Moosamin (21), Pasqua (37), and Muscowpetung (36). The author thanks Dr. Hugh Dempsey for his help in preparing this map.

government agents in the area used the robberies as an excuse for discrediting and ultimately arresting the leaders. Robberies and confrontations continued and a few government employees were killed by angry individuals, despite the counsel of the Native leaders. The leaders tried to appease the government but the incidents of violence were used, along with the coterminous revolt of Métis at Duck Lake, as an excuse to send troops. The troops attacked a camp of Crees, Assiniboines, and Métis on Cut Knife Hill, where the Crees drove them off and were restrained by their leaders from annihilating them. Despite this, the government arrested Cree leaders, holding them responsible for the isolated acts of violence. The strategy was to imprison them in order to weaken the Native movement to pressure the government to fulfill its treaty obligations.

The Métis in the Saskatchewan area also organized a rebellion to protest their treatment by the federal government. They had tried unsuccessfully to recruit Crees and other Native groups to their effort, but the Métis' goals and cultural background differed significantly from those of the Crees and others. The Métis feared that the government would not recognize their title to their lands in the South Saskatchewan Valley, for the government refused to negotiate treaties with them. They sent for Louis Riel, living in exile in Montana, and proclaimed a provisional government in 1885. In March of that year they clashed with Mounted Police at Duck Lake, and the government sent 8,000 troops to crush them and the other Native peoples at odds with the government. After losing two battles to the troops, Riel surrendered.

After the movement, known as the Northwest Rebellion, was suppressed, several Cree, Assiniboine, and Métis individuals were convicted of treason and were imprisoned or executed. Most of the Métis were dispersed into the fringe areas of settlement. The Plains Cree and Assiniboine groups were isolated on small reserves. As in the United States, the West could now be settled without considering the circumstances and potential contributions of Native peoples.

The opening of the Great Plains to American and Canadian settlement had profound repercussions for the Native peoples there. Resources were expropriated to benefit the federal governments and corporate interests while, at the same time, Native Plains peoples were excluded from participating in the development of the region. On reservations, these peoples struggled with remarkable success to retain a distinct sense of group identity and to pursue political independence and economic self-sufficiency against all odds.

BIBLIOGRAPHIC ESSAY

There is no adequate regional synthesis of developments during the eighteenth and nineteenth centuries that reflects recent scholarship. Francis Haines's work is useful but much of it is outdated and speculative (*The Plains Indians*, New York, 1976). Also useful is Richard White's brief sketch in *"It's Your Misfortune and None of My Own": A History of the American West* (Norman, Okla., 1991).

The best summary of Indian-Indian and Indian-European trade relations is William R. Swagerty, "Indian Trade in the Trans-Mississippi West to 1870," in *History of Indian-White Relations*, vol. 4, *Handbook of North American Indians*, ed. Wilcomb E. Washburn (Washington, D.C., 1988), 351–74. Other useful sources on Indian-Indian trade are John C. Ewers, "The Indian Trade of the Upper Missouri before Lewis and Clark," in John C. Ewers, *Indian Life on the Upper Missouri* (Norman, Okla., 1968), 14–33; Carroll L. Riley, "Pecos and Trade," in *Across the Chichimec Sea: Papers in Honor of J. Charles Kelley*, ed. Carroll L. Riley and Basil C. Hedrick (Carbondale, Ill., 1978); Carroll L. Riley, "An Overview of the Greater Southwest in the Protohistoric Period," in *Ripples in the Chichimec Sea: New Considerations of Southwestern-Mesoamerican Interactions*, ed. Frances Joan Mathien and Randall H. McGuire (Carbondale, Ill., 1986). The best summary of Plains culture history before European contact is Waldo R. Wedel, *Prehistoric Man on the Great Plains* (Norman, Okla., 1961).

On the introduction, diffusion and social effects of the horse, see John C. Ewers, *The Horse in Blackfoot Indian Culture with Comparative Material from Other Western Tribes* [1955] (Washington, D.C., 1980) and Bernard Mishkin, *Rank and Warfare among the Plains Indians*, American Ethnological Society Monograph 3 (1940). A more general work on the subject is Frank Gilbert Roe, *The Indian and the Horse* (Norman, Okla., 1955). In *Changing Military Patterns on the Great Plains*, American Ethnological Society Monograph 21 (1953), Frank Raymond Secoy discusses the effects of the horse and the gun on warfare on the southern, northwestern, and northeastern Plains. For research on the effects of the horse and trade on gender relations, as well as the status and role of women in nineteenth-century Plains societies, see Patricia Albers and Beatrice Medicine, eds., *The Hidden Half: Studies of Plains Indian Women* (Lanham, Md., 1983).

An excellent overview of the research on the fur trade era is Jacqueline Peterson and John Anfinson, "The Indian and the Fur Trade: A Review of

Recent Literature," in *Scholars and the Indian Experience: Critical Reviews of Recent Writing in the Social Sciences,* ed. W. R. Swagerty (Bloomington, Ind., 1984), 223–57. See also John C. Ewers, "The Influence of the Fur Trade upon the Indians of the Northern Plains," in *People and Pelts: Selected Papers of the Second North American Fur Trade Conference,* ed. Malvina Bolus (Winnipeg, 1972), 1–26, and Preston Holder, "The Fur Trade as Seen from the Indian Point of View" in *The Frontier Re-Examined,* ed. John Francis McDermott (Urbana, Ill., 1967), 129–39. An overview of trade in the southern and central Plains region is found in Elizabeth A. H. John, *Storms Brewed in Other Men's Worlds: The Confrontation of Indians, Spanish, and French in the Southwest, 1540–1795* (College Station, Tex., 1975). The best overview of trade in the Mandan and Hidatsa villages is W. Raymond Wood and Thomas D. Thiessen, eds., *Early Fur Trade on the Northern Plains: Canadian Traders among the Mandan and Hidatsa Indians, 1738–1818* (Norman, Okla., 1985). For Canada, see Arthur J. Ray, *Indians in the Fur Trade: Their Role as Hunters, Trappers and Middlemen in the Lands Southwest of Hudson Bay, 1660–1870* (Toronto, 1974) and "The Hudson's Bay Company and Native People," in *History of Indian-White Relations,* ed. Wilcomb E. Washburn, 335–50.

On the American fur and robe trade and nineteenth-century trade relations, see David J. Wishart, *The Fur Trade of the American West, 1807–1840: A Geographical Synthesis* (Lincoln, Nebr., 1979). Also useful are David Lavender, *Bent's Fort* (Garden City, N.Y., 1954); Richard Edward Oglesby, *Manuel Lisa and the Opening of the Missouri Fur Trade* (Norman, Okla., 1963); John E. Sunder, *The Fur Trade on the Upper Missouri, 1840–65* (Norman, Okla., 1965). A good overview of the lives of the traders is William R. Swagerty, "Marriage and Settlement Patterns of Rocky Mountain Trappers and Traders," *Western Historical Quarterly* 11 (1980), 159–80. An excellent source on the lives of Native peoples during this period is the firsthand account of the trader Edwin Thompson Denig, *Five Indian Tribes of the Upper Missouri: Sioux, Arickaras, Assiniboines, Crees, Crows,* ed. John C. Ewers (Norman, Okla., 1961).

General studies of trade goods and their use by Native peoples are Ronald P. Koch, *Dress Clothing of the Plains Indians* (Norman, Okla., 1977) and E. S. Lohse, "Trade Goods," in *History of Indian-White Relations,* ed. Wilcomb E. Washburn, 396–403. More specialized works are James A. Hansen, *Metal Weapons, Tools, and Ornaments of the Teton Dakota Indians* (Lincoln, Nebr., 1975); William Wildschut and John C. Ewers, *Crow Indian Beadwork: A Descriptive and Historical Study,* Contributions from the

Museum of the American Indian, Heye Foundation 16 (1959); John C. Ewers, "Hair Pipes in Plains Indian Adornment: A Study in Indian and White Ingenuity," *Bureau of American Ethnology Bulletin* 164 (1957); John C. Ewers, "The North West Trade Gun" in *Indian Life on the Upper Missouri*, 34–44.

On the impact of epidemics, see John C. Ewers, "The Influence of Epidemics on the Indian Populations and Cultures of Texas," *Plains Anthropologist* 18 (1973), 104–15; John F. Taylor, "Sociocultural Effects of Epidemics on the Northern Plains, 1734–1850," *Western Canadian Journal of Anthropology* 7 (1977), 55–81; William E. Unrau, "The Depopulation of the Dheghia-Siouan Kansa prior to Removal," *New Mexico Historical Review* 48 (1973), 313–28. Russell Thornton provides demographic information on Plains societies in *American Indian Holocaust and Survival: A Population History since 1492* (Norman, Okla., 1987).

Studies of bicultural populations include Tanis Chapman Thorne, "The Chouteau Family and the Osage Trade: A Generational Study," in *Rendezvous: Selected Papers of the Fourth North American Fur Trade Conference, 1981*, ed. Thomas C. Buckley (St. Paul, Minn., 1983) and Harry H. Anderson, "Fur Traders as Fathers: The Origins of the Mixed-Blooded Community among the Rosebud Sioux," *South Dakota History* 3 (1973), 233–70. See also Susan R. Sharrock, "Crees, Cree-Assiniboines, and Assiniboines: Interethnic Social Organization on the Far Northern Plains," *Ethnohistory* 21 (1974), 95–122. Sylvia Van Kirk discusses women in bicultural societies in Canada in *Many Tender Ties: Women in Fur-Trade Society in Western Canada, 1670–1870* (Winnipeg, 1980). See also John C. Ewers, "Mothers of the Mixed Bloods," in *Indian Life on the Upper Missouri* for a sketch of marriages between American traders and Native women.

There are several studies that highlight the role and effect of trade on specific peoples: Preston Holder, *The Hoe and the Horse on the Plains: A Study of Cultural Development among North American Indians* (focusing on Caddoans and the Missouri River region) (Lincoln, Nebr., 1970); Elizabeth Ann Harper, "The Taovayas Indians in Frontier Trade and Diplomacy, 1719–1768," *Chronicles of Oklahoma* 31 (1953), 268–89 (focusing on Wichitas); Elizabeth Ann Harper, "The Taovayas Indians in Frontier Trade and Diplomacy, 1769–1779," *Southwestern Historical Quarterly* 57:2 (1953), 181–201; Elizabeth Ann Harper, "The Taovayas Indians in Frontier Trade and Diplomacy, 1779–1835," *Panhandle-Plains Historical Review* 26 (1953), 41–72; Gilbert C. Din and A. P. Nasatir, *The Imperial Osages: Spanish-Indian Diplomacy in the Mississippi Valley* (Norman, Okla.,

1983); Willard H. Rollings, *The Osage: An Ethnohistorical Study of Hegemony on the Prairie-Plains* (Columbia, Mo., 1992); Garrick Alan Bailey, *Changes in Osage Social Organization, 1673–1906,* University of Oregon Anthropological Papers 5 (Eugene, Ore., 1973); Edward M. Bruner, "Mandan," in *Perspectives in American Indian Culture Change,* ed. Edward H. Spicer (Chicago, 1961). Additional works on the villagers during the eighteenth and early nineteenth centuries include W. W. Newcomb, *The Indians of Texas, From Prehistoric to Modern Times* (Austin, Tex., 1961); Mildred Mott Wedel, "The Ethnohistorical Approach to Plains Caddoan Origins," *Nebraska History* 60:2 (1979), 183–96, and "The Wichita Indians in the Arkansas River Basin" in *Plains Indian Studies: A Collection of Essays in Honor of John C. Ewers and Waldo R. Wedel,* ed. Douglas H. Ubelaker and Herman J. Viola, Smithsonian Contributions to Anthropology 30 (1982), 118–34; Roy W. Meyer, *The Village Indians of the Upper Missouri: The Mandans, Hidatsas, and Arikaras* (Lincoln, Nebr., 1977); Mildred Mott Wedel, "Peering at the Ioway Indians through the Mist of Time: 1650–Circa 1700," *Journal of the Iowa Archeological Society* 33 (1986), 1–74; Martha Royce Blaine, *The Ioway Indians* (Norman, Okla., 1979); William E. Unrau, *The Kansa Indians: A History of the Wind People, 1673–1873* (Norman, Okla., 1971). For some of these groups, no comprehensive history or ethnohistory exists.

Studies that explore trade relations among the nomadic groups through the early nineteenth century are Joseph Jablow, *The Cheyenne in Plains Indian Trade Relations, 1795–1840,* American Ethnological Society Monograph 19 (1950); Richard White, "The Winning of the West: The Expansion of the Western Sioux in the Eighteenth and Nineteenth Centuries," *Journal of American History* 65 (1978), 319–43; Gary Clayton Anderson, *Kinsmen of Another Kind: Dakota-White Relations in the Upper Mississippi Valley, 1650–1862* (Lincoln, Nebr., 1984); Oscar Lewis, *The Effects of White Contact upon Blackfoot Culture, with Special Reference to the Role of the Fur Trade,* American Ethnological Society Monograph 6 (1942); John S. Milloy, *The Plains Cree: Trade, Diplomacy and War, 1790 to 1870* (Winnipeg, 1988); Charles L. Kenner, *A History of New Mexican-Plains Indian Relations* (Norman, Okla., 1969) (Comanche). Other more general works on nomadic groups during this period include Donald J. Berthrong, *The Southern Cheyenne* (Norman, Okla., 1963); Loretta Fowler, *Shared Symbols, Contested Meanings: Gros Ventre Culture and History, 1778–1984* (Ithaca, N.Y., 1987); John C. Ewers, *The Blackfeet: Raiders on the Northwestern Plains* (Norman, Okla., 1958); Roy W. Meyer, *History of the Santee Sioux:*

United States Indian Policy on Trial (Lincoln, Nebr., 1967); John S. Wozniak, *Contact, Negotiation and Conflict: An Ethnohistory of the Eastern Dakota, 1819–1839* (Washington, D.C., 1978); John C. Ewers, *Teton Dakota: History and Ethnology* (Berkeley, Calif., 1937); Ernest L. Schusky, *The Forgotten Sioux: An Ethnohistory of the Lower Brule Reservation* (Chicago, 1975); Clair Jacobson, "A History of the Yanktonai and Hunkpatina Sioux," *North Dakota History* 47 (1980), 4–24; Mildred Mayhall, *The Kiowas* (Norman, Okla., 1962); Morris Foster, *Being Comanche: A Social History of an American Indian Community* (Lincoln, Nebr., 1991).

For an overview of the period of western expansion, see the following articles in *History of Indian-White Relations*, ed. Wilcomb E. Washburn: Arrell M. Gibson, "Indian Land Transfers"; William T. Hagan, "United States Indian Policies, 1860–1900"; Robert M. Utley, "Indian-United States Military Situation, 1848–1891"; Donald J. Berthrong, "Nineteenth-Century United States Government Agencies." Works that discuss the circumstances facing the villagers in the nineteenth century include Clyde A. Milner, *With Good Intentions: Quaker Work among the Pawnees, Otos, and Omahas in the 1870s* (Lincoln, Nebr., 1982); H. Craig Miner and William E. Unrau, *The End of Indian Kansas: A Study of Cultural Revolution, 1854–1871* (Lawrence, Kans., 1978); Richard White, *The Roots of Dependency: Subsistence, Environment, and Social Change among the Choctaws, Pawnees, and Navajos* (Lincoln, Nebr., 1983); Martha Royce Blaine, *Pawnee Passage, 1870–1875* (Norman, Okla., 1990); Grant Foreman, *The Last Trek of the Indians* (Chicago, 1946); Berlin Basil Chapman, *The Otos and Missourias: A Study of Indian Removal and the Legal Aftermath* (Stillwater, Okla., 1965); Thomas Henry Tibbles, *The Ponca Chiefs: An Account of the Trial of Standing Bear*, ed. Kay Graber (Lincoln, Nebr., 1972). Other more comprehensive studies discuss this period as well as the fur trade era: Edward M. Bruner, "Mandan"; William E. Unrau, *The Kansa Indians*; Martha Royce Blaine, *The Ioway Indians*; Garrick Alan Bailey, *Changes in Osage Social Organization, 1673–1906*. See also Francis La Flesche, *The Middle Five: Indian Schoolboys of the Omaha Tribe* (Madison, Wis., 1963).

The treaty process is discussed in Raymond J. DeMallie, "Touching the Pen: Plains Indian Treaty Councils in Ethnohistorical Perspective," in *Ethnicity on the Great Plains*, ed. Frederick C. Luebke (Lincoln, Nebr., 1980), 38–53. For a more detailed account of one such treaty council, see Douglas C. Jones, *The Treaty of Medicine Lodge: The Story of the Great Treaty Council as Told by Eyewitnesses* (Norman, Okla., 1966). And, for

Canada, see J. L. Taylor, "Two Views on the Meaning of Treaties Six and Seven," in *The Spirit of the Alberta Indian Treaties,* ed. R. Price (Edmonton, 1987), 9–45.

A good overview of the military conflict on the Plains is Robert Utley, *The Indian Frontier of the American West* (Albuquerque, N.M., 1984). On the distinction between and implications of "friendly" and "hostile" groups, see Loretta Fowler, "The Civilization Strategy: Gros Ventres, Northern and Southern Arapahos Compared," in *North American Indian Anthropology: Essays on Society and Culture,* ed. Raymond J. DeMallie and Alfonso Ortiz (Norman, Okla., 1994). On scouting, see Thomas W. Dunlay, *Wolves for the Blue Soldiers: Indian Scouts and Auxiliaries with the United States Army, 1860–90* (Lincoln, Nebr., 1982).

On westward expansion in Canada, see the following papers in J. R. Miller, ed., *Sweet Promises: A Reader on Indian-White Relations in Canada* (Toronto, 1991): John L. Tobias, "Canada's Subjugation of the Plains Cree, 1879–1885"; John Leonard Taylor, "Canada's North-West Indian Policy in the 1870s: Traditional Premises and Necessary Innovations"; J. R. Miller, "The Northwest Rebellion of 1885"; A. Blair Stonechild, "The Indian View of the 1885 Uprising." See also Gontran Laviolette, *The Sioux Indians in Canada* (Regina, 1944); Roy W. Meyer, "The Canadian Sioux: Refugees from Minnesota," *Minnesota History* 41 (1968), 13–28; Olive Patricia Dickason, "From 'One Nation' in the Northeast to 'New Nation' in the Northwest: A Look at the Emergence of the Metis," *American Indian Culture and Research Journal* 6 (1982), 1–21. For an overview, see Noel Dyck, *What Is the Indian 'Problem': Tutelage and Resistance in Canadian Indian Administration* (St. John, 1991); J. R. Miller, *Skyscrapers Hide the Heavens: A History of Indian-White Relations in Canada* (Toronto, 1989); and O. P. Dickason, *Canada's First Nations* (Toronto, 1992), 192–201, 265–89.

There are few studies of nomadic peoples' circumstances in the late nineteenth century: John C. Ewers, *The Blackfeet*; Loretta Fowler, *Shared Symbols, Contested Meanings*; Loretta Fowler, *Arapahoe Politics, 1851–1978: Symbols in Crises of Authority* (Lincoln, Nebr., 1982); Donald J. Berthrong, *The Southern Cheyenne*; William Thomas Hagan, *United States–Comanche Relations: The Reservation Years* (New Haven, Conn., 1976); Morris Foster, *Being Comanche*; Mildred Mayhall, *The Kiowas*; James C. Olson, *Red Cloud and the Sioux Problem* (Lincoln, Nebr., 1965); Ernest L. Schusky, *The Forgotten Sioux*; Raymond J. DeMallie, "The Sioux in Dakota and Montana Territories: Cultural and Historical Background of the Ogden B. Read

Collection," in *Vestiges of a Proud Nation*, ed. Glenn E. Markoe (Burlington, Vt., 1986), 19–69; Clair Jacobson, "A History of the Yanktonai and Hunkpatina Sioux"; Roy W. Meyer, *History of the Santee Sioux*. The ethnohistorical reports for the Indian Claims Commission are a good source of information on occupancy of particular areas and relations with the government over time. These have been published for most of the Plains groups in the Garland American Indian Ethnohistory Series, ed. David Agee Horr (New York, 1973–6).

In addition to studies of specific peoples, autobiography and biography offer insight on the lives of Native peoples of the Plains. Such works include Margaret Crary, *Susette La Flesche: Voice of the Omaha Indians* (New York, 1973); Dorothy Clark Wilson, *Bright Eyes, The Story of Susette La Flesche, an Omaha Indian* (New York, 1974); Gilbert Wilson, *Waheenee: An Indian Girl's Story Told by Herself to Gilbert L. Wilson* (Lincoln, Nebr., 1981) (Hidatsa); Gilbert W. Wilson, *Goodbird, the Indian* (St. Paul, 1984) (Hidatsa); Frank B. Linderman, *Pretty-Shield: Medicine Woman of the Crows* (Lincoln, Nebr., 1972); Frank B. Linderman, *Plenty-Coups: Chief of the Crows* (Lincoln, Nebr., 1962); Peter Nabokov, *Two Leggings: The Making of a Crow Warrior* (New York, 1967); Stanley Vestal (Walter S. Campbell), *Sitting Bull: Champion of the Sioux* (Norman, Okla., 1957); Raymond J. DeMallie, ed., *The Sixth Grandfather: Black Elk's Teachings Given to John G. Neihardt* (Lincoln, Nebr., 1984); Hugh A. Dempsey, *Crowfoot: Chief of the Blackfeet* (Norman, Okla., 1972); Hugh A. Dempsey, *Big Bear: The End of Freedom* (Vancouver, 1984) (Cree).

10

THE GREATER SOUTHWEST AND CALIFORNIA FROM THE BEGINNING OF EUROPEAN SETTLEMENT TO THE 1880s

HOWARD R. LAMAR AND SAM TRUETT

Coronado's despairing report in the 1540s that no gold and no fabulous cities of wealth existed to the north of New Spain led to the first realistic image the Spanish had of the Greater Southwest. Coronado and subsequent Spanish travelers to what would later become New Mexico described a land of village-dwelling agricultural Indians. These villages were surrounded by nomadic hunting and raiding Indians whose domain covered a vast area from present-day Texas to Arizona. By all Spanish accounts, it was a harsh, arid land which provided only limited means of subsistence for those living there.[1]

Such reports discouraged the Spanish authorities from formally occupying any lands north of the present-day United States–Mexico border until 1598, when Juan de Oñate received a royal patent to settle New Mexico. Nevertheless, scores of Spanish prospectors periodically penetrated the region, hoping to find the Eldorado that Cortez had chanced upon in central Mexico and Pizarro had discovered in Peru. This dream was kept alive by the very real discovery of rich silver deposits in Zacatecas far to the north of Mexico City in 1546.

Accompanying and often preceding this mining frontier were Catholic missionaries who engaged in the ambitious task of converting and "civilizing" Native Americans. Missionaries not only sought to change native beliefs, but also gathered Indians into villages around the missions where they were urged to live, to some degree, as Spaniards. Other settlers saw New Spain's northern frontier as the site of future farms and ranches on which local Indians would serve as laborers. Likewise, the dream of mineral wealth which first brought Spanish to the north was based on the

[1] George P. Hammond and Agapito Rey, eds. and trans., *Narratives of the Coronado Expedition of 1540–52* (Albuquerque, N.M., 1940).

assumption that Indians would work, as they had farther south, to extract that wealth. Even though most Spanish saw Indians as inferior, often treating them as actual or near slaves, these Europeans generally sought to include Indians, if possible, in the wider scheme of things.

Early Spanish-Indian relations in America were in some ways fundamentally different from later Anglo-Indian relations. In most instances Spanish Indian policy was not genocidal, nor did it require complete cultural assimilation. As a result, many Indian groups of the Greater Southwest survived centuries of European encroachment before the United States gained control over the Southwest in the 1850s. To the Spanish explorers, missionaries, and settlers, the Native Southwest presented an astonishing variety of lifestyles, cultures, and languages. Some groups, such as the Pueblo Indians of New Mexico, were primarily agricultural and village-dwelling. Others, like the Coahuiltecans of Texas, led a more seasonally varied hunting and gathering existence. Yet others, like the Chumashes of California, lived in a world carefully balanced between sea and land. Indeed, the diversity among the Native peoples of this region was, and remains today, greater than that found in any other part of the continental United States.

Yet despite the survival of cultural diversity, the narrative of Indian and Euro-American relations in the Greater Southwest is centrally one of change. Beginning with the first European contacts to the region in the sixteenth century – which brought alien animals and diseases as well as alien peoples – and continuing through the waves of colonial settlement, phases of imperial rivalry and racial warfare, and the passage of the region under the consecutive authorities of New Spain, Mexico, and the United States, the Greater Southwest underwent profound transformations. It was a legacy of change within which both Europeans and Indians alike would come to play significant roles. What follows here, then, is not a detailed historical reconstruction of the aboriginal Southwest – for indeed, such a project would easily fill many volumes. It is rather an attempt to map out the broader interactions between Native and European-American cultures in the region from the moment these peoples first discovered one another at the boundaries of their respective worlds.

INDIGENOUS PEOPLES

Before one can understand the broader social changes that have marked the past few centuries of Native American history in the Greater Southwest, one must first gain a sense of Native America at the time of the first European contact. Shipwrecked in 1528 on the coast of what would later become Texas, Alvar Nuñez Cabeza de Vaca was the first Spaniard to report on the Native peoples of the region. On a beach of Galveston Bay, Cabeza de Vaca and his companions first encountered a people who called themselves the Karankawas. Cabeza de Vaca was immediately struck by the contrasts between Karankawa and Spanish customs. The men of this Native Texan group went about naked, and the women wore only skirts of Spanish moss and deerskin. Both sexes were tattooed and lavishly painted. Their lower lips, nose, and other parts of the body were pierced with pieces of cane.[2]

Observed through the eyes of most Europeans, these Indians appeared both "savage" and "primitive." This judgment was strengthened by the seminomadic nature of Karankawa society. The Karankawas traveled seasonally through an area extending from the present-day Galveston Bay to Corpus Christi, Texas – a varied landscape of shallow lagoons, coastal prairies, and forested valleys. During some parts of the year, they took small canoes out along the shore and shallow bays to gather seafood, turtles, and alligators for food. At other seasons, they moved inland to hunt antelope, javelina (collared peccary), deer, bison, and bear with long bows and arrows or clubs and lances. While these subsistence strategies reveal intricate relationships between Karankawa culture and the natural world, the Spanish saw Karankawa mobility and the lack of material culture it demanded as evidence of a "primitive" economy, one which contrasted with the more sedentary, urban, and technologically elaborate economy of Europe.

Cabeza de Vaca noted the same seasonal mobility and seemingly "simple" material culture among the Native peoples to the west and southwest of the coastal Karankawas. From Corpus Christi into what is today northeastern Mexico, and inland along the lower Rio Grande, lived various seminomadic Indian groups known collectively as the Coahuiltecans. Like the Karankawas, the Coahuiltecans maintained a flexible and complex relationship to the land. At some times of year they hunted big game, such as buffalo, deer, and the javelina; at other times they lived largely on fish and on plants such as the nutritious mesquite bean. Theirs was a feast or famine economy. Survival often meant eating larvae, worms, snakes,

[2] Cabeza de Vaca, *Adventures in the Unknown Interior of America* (New York, 1961), 61 ff.; William W. Newcomb, *The Indians of Texas from Prehistoric to Modern Times* (Austin, Tex., 1961), 63–65.

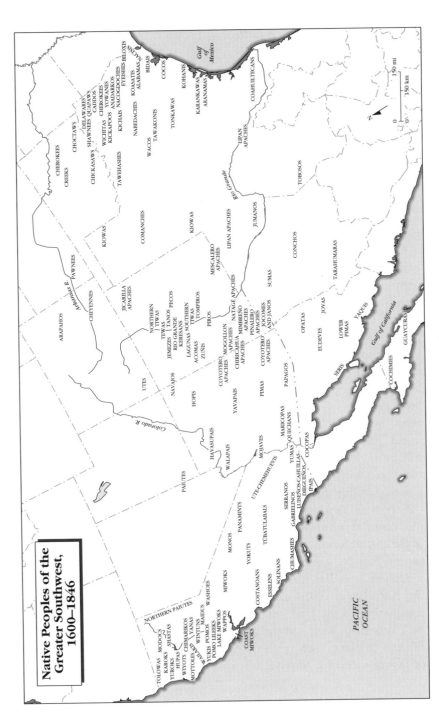

Figure 10.1 Native peoples of the Greater Southwest, 1600–1846.

earth, and even deer dung. On the other hand, the ripening of the fruit, or *tuna,* of the prickly pears typically meant days of feasting until the fruit ran out.

Even though many Europeans came to think of the Greater Southwest as a region marked almost exclusively by aridity, such was not the case in east Texas. Here, in the woodlands to the north and east of the coastal Karankawas, Spaniards encountered the Caddo Indians of east Texas and western Louisiana. The Caddos occupied a patchwork of upland pine forests and hardwood bottomlands, a landscape which yielded both game and good farming land. As a group which practiced agriculture, the Caddos were viewed by their European observers as a more "advanced" people than the Karankawas. Traveling through the region in 1541, Spanish explorer Hernando de Soto noted that their chief crops included corn, beans, squash, sunflowers, and tobacco. He also observed a system of government that appeared structurally more complex than that of the Karankawas, and a religion that echoed the elaborate ceremonial practices of the southeastern or Mississippian groups.

Other than what we can read from the accounts of such writers as Cabeza de Vaca and de Soto, little is known of the other Native populations living during the sixteenth century in what is now Texas. It is possible that Cabeza de Vaca encountered one or two groups of the Atakapans – a Native people who lived along the rivers and coast between the Karankawas and Caddos. The Atakapans appear to have been culturally related, as were the Caddos, to the Native groups of the Southeast. Their economies spanned a broad range of ecosystems; some were largely hunters and gatherers, others were agriculturalists like the Caddos, and yet others relied on fishing. The first accounts of these groups come from the eighteenth century, when the French traded among them for deer and bison skins.

Farther to the west, the Edwards Plateau of central Texas was home to the Tonkawas. These various groups lived along the river bottoms of the region, much like their Coahuiltecan neighbors to the south by hunting, gathering, and often fishing. A group which lived in a fashion somewhat similar to the Tonkawas were the Lipan Apaches of the west Texas plains. Many of the early accounts of the Lipans do not distinguish between these and related Apachean peoples to the west. Many of the Eastern Apaches, who also included the Jicarillas and Kiowa Apaches, spent spring and summer in small agricultural villages, and then left in the fall to hunt buffalo.

This diversity of Native peoples reflected the multitude of environments in what would later become Texas. At times, these regional differences were underscored by territorial or ethnic boundaries. Even though little is known about the political organization of the Karankawas, for instance, we do know that some of these Indians asked Cabeza de Vaca to become a trader to help avoid war with neighboring groups. Among the Coahuiltecans, Cabeza de Vaca witnessed even greater evidence of territorial conflict. Many of these Indians were apparently so nervous about surprise attacks that when they retired for the night, they reportedly dug trenches in which to hide and sleep, and then covered themselves with brush.

At the same time, however, the interfaces between Native Texas populations provided pathways for social and economic exchange. Many of these groups were connected to one another through trade networks which occasionally stretched the entire length of the present-day United States. Cabeza de Vaca noted that the Karankawas traded extensively with inland groups, thereby exchanging the resources of the coastal ecosystem for those of the drier regions to the west. The Coahuiltecans, too, traded with other Indians for a variety of goods which they could not or did not produce themselves. Cabeza de Vaca also reported seeing cornmeal among the Coahuiltecans of the Pecos River, a commodity undoubtedly obtained from the Rio Grande Pueblos. During his visit among the Caddos, de Soto witnessed cotton blankets and turquoise which had been traded from the Pueblo region of the Southwest. Especially after the arrival of the horse, these trade networks came to play an important role in connecting peoples and resources across the southern borderlands.

To the west of Texas, the first recorded European encounter with Native peoples was that of Francisco Vásquez de Coronado in what would eventually become New Mexico. Coronado and his party encountered in the Rio Grande Valley an Indian population unlike any they had seen north of Mexico City. The Pueblo Indians not only practiced irrigation agriculture, but also lived in permanent villages, generally appeared to be peaceful, and were intensely religious. The Pueblos were praised by the Spanish for their excellent pottery, their weaving, and their basketry. They also grew cotton to be woven into cloth, often as blankets or mantas (wraps). While being true agriculturists they also hunted deer and bison, collected all kinds of plants, and traded with various Plains Indian groups for meat and hides to supplement their agricultural economy.

The seventy or more Pueblo villages that existed when Coronado came through the Rio Grande Valley in the 1540s were all independent of one another. Not only did they speak five different languages, but they also had little or no tradition of intervillage cooperation. The population was split into two main groups of settlements: those located east of the Rio Grande, and the Western Pueblos made up of the Zuni and Hopi peoples. Perhaps more distinctive was the linguistic variation within the Pueblo cultural region. The Hopis to the east spoke a language derived from the widely distributed Uto-Aztecan family, whereas their culturally similar neighbors, the Zunis, spoke a language that was perhaps related to Californian Penutian. The Keresans, including the Acoma and Laguna Pueblos, constituted a third linguistic group which has no known affinity to any other languages. The fourth such group, the Kiowa-Tanoan family, which included the Tiwa, Tewa, and Towa subgroups, also embraced Kiowa spoken on the Great Plains.

Like the Caddos of Texas, these enclaved societies struck the Spanish newcomers as well-off, even superior to the more nomadic groups of the region, but the truth was that the margin between plenty and starvation was always a narrow one. When Spaniards following Coronado came through the region, demanding foodstuffs, supplies, clothing, grain for their horses and cattle – and later, labor – they soon found that the Pueblo villages were simply not prepared for such a drain on their resources.

Scattered to the south and east of the Pueblo villages at the time of Coronado were various nomadic and seminomadic groups which the Spanish generally grouped together under the name Apache. These Athapaskan-speaking peoples were, like the Spanish, relative newcomers to the region. They appear to have migrated south from central and western Canada between A.D. 800 and 1500 by a route over which there is still much debate. The survivors of these sixteenth-century groups are known today as the Western Apaches, the Mescalero Apaches, and the Navajos. The first of these groups consisted of five bands, known to the Spanish as the Mimbreños, Chiricahuas, Pinaleños, Coyoteros, and Tontos.

The Western Apaches originally practised a hunting and gathering economy. This may have been modified by their first contacts with the Pueblos, because by the 1600s they had developed a seasonal cycle of food gathering that included planting crops in the summer. During the spring, the Apache parties traveled, sometimes a great distance, to harvest mescal; in May they planted crops and reactivated irrigation ditches; in July they often went to harvest saguaro fruit in the Gila Valley of what is today Arizona; and in late July they moved north for a month-long harvest of acorns. Crops were harvested in September, while fall and winter were the seasons for hunting.

After the introduction of livestock herds into the Southwest, these Apaches soon came to supplement their subsistence cycle with raiding of Spanish and other Indian settlements for cattle. As they learned to ride Spanish horses, they became almost legendary for their swift daring raids. When necessary they ate horses, as well as sheep and goats. By 1700, other Apache people had moved into northern New Mexico and as far east as the arid plains of west Texas. In time these groups, consisting of the Jicarillas, Kiowa-Apaches, and Lipans, came to be called the Eastern Apaches.

The Mescalero Apaches of southeastern New Mexico bore some resemblance to their linguistic kinsmen to the west in that they were also hunters and gatherers, but they apparently did not supplement this economy with farming. Like other Apache bands the major social units were extended families which sometimes formed bands headed by an able male leader. Despite their relatively small numbers, the Mescaleros occupied – or rather seasonally traveled over – a large area ranging from the modern-day Mexican states of Chihuahua and Coahuila north to the thirty-fourth parallel, and from the Rio Grande eastward beyond the Pecos River. Because of the great variation in the geography of this region, it meant that some were more like Plains Indians in their lifestyle, living off buffalo, while others hunted deer and gathered agave and other wild plants of the hill and mountain country. The former lived in conical skin tipis, the latter in brush wickiups.

Of the Apachean peoples, undoubtedly the best known by the Spaniards were the Apache de Navihu – or the Navajos, who soon came to be considered a separate group. Yet during the early Spanish period, the Navajos were quite distinct from the sheep herding, blanket-weaving Navajo peoples that Americans came to deal with in the nineteenth century. These Indians, who raided and traded with the Spanish and Pueblo Indians, lived in the San Juan River country and called themselves the Diné, or "the people." After the de Vargas reconquest of New Mexico in 1692–96, Pueblo refugees joined their communities. By 1754 Utes and Comanches from the north attacked them and the Spaniards with such fury that they moved to the canyonlands of northwest New Mexico and northeastern Arizona. They appear to have taken with them various Pueblo Indians, who further acquainted the Navajos with herding domestic animals, weaving, pottery-making, and even constructing stone masonry hogans.[3] The Jemez Pueblos, in particular, introduced new skills and technology, concepts of religion, and ceremonial practices that together served to modify the Navajo view of the world.

Sustained relations between Spanish and Native peoples to the west of New Mexico did not begin until a century following the Spanish colonization of the Rio Grande Valley. Except for early attempts to bring missions westward to the Hopis of the northern plateau region, the colonization of Arizona began with the *entrada* of Father Eusebio Kino among the Pima (O'Odham) Indians of northern Sonora in 1687. These Natives of the Sonoran Desert occupied the "Pimeria Alta" – a region which extended westward from the Apache frontier to the Gulf of California, and northward from the Yaqui and Mayo Rivers of Sonora to the Salt River of modern-day Arizona.

Living in a region marked by unpredictable and slight annual rainfall, as well as a broad diversity of local ecosystems, the Pimas had developed three different ways of living on the land around them. The Sand Papagos, or "No Villagers," lived a nomadic hunting, gathering, and fishing existence in the driest, western part of the Sonoran Desert which bordered on the Colorado River to the west. In the somewhat less arid central portion of the Pimeria Alta lived the Papagos, or "Two Villagers" – so called because they migrated annually between winter dwellings in the mountain foothills next to permanent springs, where they subsisted on a wide range of native plants and animals, and summer dwellings in the desert plains, where they farmed at the mouths of washes following the summer rains. To the north of these two groups, along the Gila River, lived settled agriculturalists known as the Pimas, or "One Villagers."

While these larger groups each consisted of various small "rancherias" with little or no intergroup political connections, trade networks between the desert-living Pagagos and river-dwelling Pimas ensured that the diversity of the Sonoran desert ecosystems could be used to wider advantage. Under this system, the Pagagos traded plant and animal resources of the desert for corn, beans, and other agricultural goods from the Gila River Pimas. In dry years, when the Pagagos had little to trade, they sometimes exchanged their own labor for Pima crops.

Native groups to the north of the Pimeria Alta responded similarly to the ecological constraints of aridity. Yuman-speaking groups such as the Yavapais, Walapais, and Havasupais of central and west-central Arizona,

---

[3] Jesse B. Bailey, *Diego de Vargas and the Reconquest of New Mexico* (Albuquerque, N.M., 1940), 14–15.

for instance, traded both with the Hopi Indians in the east and the Colorado River peoples of Arizona and California to the west for agricultural goods. Patterns of social interaction within these groups often shifted with the seasons. At times of resource abundance, bands temporarily organized under the leadership of a chief, and families banded together to form larger units. Yet at other times, the largest sustainable social unit was often the nuclear family.

Along the Colorado River to the west, the permanence of agriculture made for a social pattern more like that of the Pimas along the Gila River. Groups such as the Mohaves, the Maricopas, and the Quechans often considered themselves as part of a larger ethnic group, and despite loose divisions into bands and local groups, cohesion was such that these peoples could often quickly muster solidarity against enemies. At the same time, trade networks linked some of these riverine peoples to groups far to the south in Mexico. These early trade connections persisted well after the Spanish *entrada,* and may help explain the later successful role of the Maricopas as mail carriers between Mexico City and California during Mexico's War for Independence from Spain.

California, the other latecomer to Spanish exploration in the Greater Southwest, represented a diversity of Native populations which arguably surpassed that of the rest of the Greater Southwest. At the time of first contact it is believed that between 275,000 and 300,000 Native peoples lived in what is now California. Although there were no Indian towns of any size, this was an exceptionally large population compared to those found in the regions of Texas, New Mexico, or Arizona. Such a population was possible because the California coast was teeming with fish, seals, sea otter, and other marine life. Its major rivers were full of salmon in season, salmon that could swim upstream all the way into the Sierra foothills and thus furnish inland groups with food. In the San Joaquin Valley and in the Sacramento River delta, tall marshes and rich grasses supported all kinds of wildlife. Vast herds of elk and deer roamed the plains and foothill regions of the San Joaquin Valley, and bear, both the smaller brown bear and the terrifying grizzly, were plentiful.

The California Indians were not agriculturalists, in part, because nature itself was so bountiful. The Indians of the Central Valley, who probably constituted a majority of the Native California population, were sustained both by hunting and by harvests of acorns from the ever-present oak trees. They also lived on the seeds of nutritious grasses which Indian women collected, pounded, and boiled into a healthy mush. Naturally those groups living near the coast depended more heavily on fish and marine life. For example, the Chumashes around Santa Barbara constructed sturdy sea-going plank boats, caulked with asphaltum, to fish or to harpoon sea otters for subsistence. More northern groups, such as the Tolowas, the Hupas, and the Yuroks, used dugouts, while those living on bays or on fresh water streams often used only simple tule or balsa rafts as a way of getting about.

Nature was not bounteous everywhere. In extreme northern and north-eastern California where the Shastas, Yanas, Modocs and northern Paiute groups lived, food was scarce and survival more perilous. The Paiutes of Mono Lake, the Owens Valley, and elsewhere east of the Sierras lived in a desert economy where food resources were so minimal that their digging for insect larvae and grub led disdainful Americans to call them "Diggers," a name they tended to apply to all California Indian peoples. Finally, in the desert areas of the southeast, the Mohaves – and along the lower Colorado River, Yumas and related groups – practiced a floodplains desert agriculture that somewhat resembled the farming practices of the Pima Indians of Arizona.

In all, the California Indians consisted of representatives of no less than six of the major linguistic families in North America: Athapaskan, Algonquian, Yukian, Hokan, Penutian, and Uto-Aztecan. Anthropologist Alfred Kroeber estimated that in 1670 as many as 118 distinctive subgroups were to be found among these major groupings.[4] Most of these California Natives had a powerful sense of territoriality, and they negotiated constantly if one group had to cross another's homeland. Their general avoidance of violence misled Europeans to assume that they were passive or even stupid.

CONQUEST AND RESISTANCE

In 1598, Zacatecan mine owner Juan de Oñate dreamed of traveling to New Spain's far northern frontier and opening up a vast landed estate worked by Indian labor. He took advantage of the recently rediscovered route to New Mexico via El Paso del Norte on the Rio Grande to bring settlers, horses, mules, sheep, and cattle to the Pueblo Indian settlements. Oñate got permission to do this, in part, because the Spanish were worried by Sir Francis Drake's forays along their Pacific coast in the late 1570s.

---

[4] See end maps in Robert F. Heizer and M. A. Whipple, *California Indians: A Source Book* (Berkeley, Calif., 1951).

Spain wanted a northern stronghold to keep the English from occupying what they believed was a waterway between the Pacific and Atlantic Oceans just to the north of Mexico.[5]

While Oñate's colony was a part and parcel of imperial diplomacy in the New World, it also rode the edge of New Spain's mining and mission frontiers. By the 1560s, silver mining towns had begun to spring up just south of the Rio Grande, and rumors of wealth set most sights farther north. At the same time, Franciscan missionaries sought royal approval to seek out new converts in the region. In 1581, Fray Agustin Rodriguez journeyed north along the Rio Grande, and was perhaps the first Spaniard to visit the Pueblos since Coronado. In 1573, Philip II of Spain had issued the Comprehensive Orders for New Discoveries, which gave missionaries the primary role in pacifying new peoples. When Oñate came to the region in 1598, his party included priests. The fortification of the north against foreign intrusion was thus initially carried out with an eye toward the pacification and conversion of the Pueblo Indians.

From the outset, however, the relations between Oñate's settlement and the Pueblos were fraught with tension and hostility. In New Mexico, as all across the far reaches of the Spanish Empire, the gap between the royal theory of conquest and its practice was a large one. The Orders for New Discoveries had sought a peaceful incorporation of Native peoples into Spanish society. It particularly sought to suppress the same sort of conquest that followed Cortés. Yet during the first year among the Pueblos, Oñate's settlers echoed past European intrusions of the New World as they took food from, raped, and sometimes murdered their Pueblo neighbors.

The process of "peaceful" religious conversion had its own set of problems. On one hand, the Pueblos were already living in permanent villages, unlike the seminomadic rancheria peoples of Sonora and Chihuahua. This meant the missionaries did not have to work as hard to create a mission community. Yet at the same time, missionizing the Pueblos was more difficult because they spoke a number of mutually unintelligible languages, each with several dialects. Unlike the Jesuits in Sonora and elsewhere in Northern Mexico, the Franciscan missionaries who came to convert the Pueblos usually did not attempt to master these Native languages and so never gained an intimate understanding of their parishioners. The stage was thus set for an unending, no-holds barred cultural confrontation.

---

[5] David J. Weber details Oñate's occupation in his *The Spanish Frontier in North America* (New Haven, Conn., 1992), 32–34, as does George Hammond, *Don Juan de Oñate and the Founding of New Mexico* (Santa Fe, N.M., 1927), vol. 1, 1–14 and 42–68.

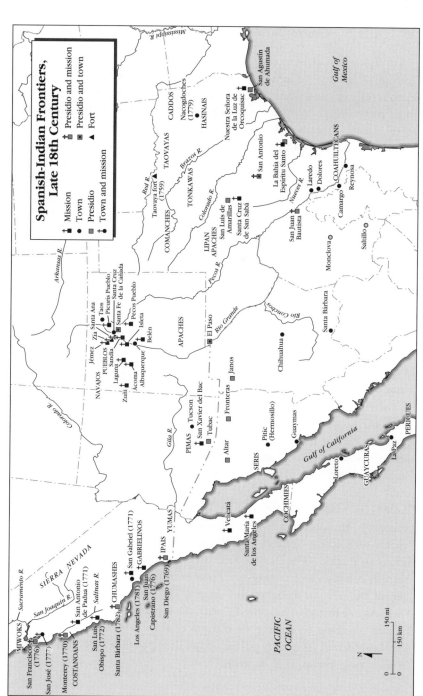

Figure 10.2 Spanish-Indian frontiers in the late eighteenth century.

Governor Oñate initially convinced the major Pueblo villages to "pledge allegiance" to him and the Spanish crown, but a year later Acoma Pueblo resisted, and Oñate engaged in a fearful siege and reduction of that mesa community. His soldiers killed many inhabitants and maimed captured resisters (see also Chapter 6). From then until the Pueblo Revolt of 1680, Indian-European relations and Indian-Indian relations went from bad to worse. Before Oñate could assert power over the region, Spanish competitors denounced him and he was recalled. A series of governors, many avaricious and corrupt, succeeded him. These governors demanded tributes of woven cloth, cattle, labor, and other items as a form of tax which the Pueblos had never paid before. The missions also demanded tribute and labor to farm mission lands. At the same time, ex-soldiers who had been granted *encomienda* lands expected Indians to labor for them.

As if these impositions were not enough, the Spanish authorities began sending captured Apache, Navajo, and Ute Indians south for sale as laborers to mining companies. That practice naturally increased an already existing Athapaskan hostility in the region. Apaches and Navajos stepped up their raids on the Spanish and Pueblo settlements, carrying away prizes of grain, cattle, horses, and children. Increased raiding forced the abandonment of three southern Tiwa villages in the 1670s.

There were other sources of discontent as well. Following the lead of other missionaries around Mexico, the Franciscans began campaigns to eradicate Native religious ceremonies. Some of the priests believed that destruction of katcina masks and other sacred objects in the kivas would break the Pueblos' will. Aided by Spanish soldiers, they raided the kivas and publicly burned masks and sacred objects. They also hanged some Indians as witches. These attacks led many Puebloans to organize for resistance. In August 1680, the Pueblos rose in a general revolt under leaders such as Popé of San Juan Pueblo and Francisco El Ollita from San Ildefonso Pueblo. The Pueblo Revolt resulted in the killing of over 400 Spanish colonists and twenty-one Franciscan missionaries, and the expulsion of the rest. In disbelief and disarray the Spanish refugees fled to El Paso. As one historian has noted, "with the expulsion of the Spaniards, the Indians set about to remove all vestiges of alien rule. European livestock was slaughtered, fruit trees pulled up, and the people waded into the river to wash away the taint of baptism."[6]

---

[6] John Kessell, "Pueblo Indians," in Howard R. Lamar, ed., *The Reader's Encyclopedia of the American West* (New York, 1977), 985.

With the hated Spanish gone, the unity achieved by the various Pueblos soon disappeared. When de Vargas led an army to reoccupy the region between 1692 and 1694, he was able to reconquer the separate villages one by one. This reconquest, as brutal as it was, did not return New Mexico to an antebellum status quo. Although trials for witchcraft continued to be held, Catholic priests gave up trying to eradicate Pueblo religious ceremonies. The *encomienda* system was abolished, and the use of Indians for tribute labor declined.

Indeed, the Spanish and the Pueblos found themselves forced into greater cooperation in order to protect their settlements against increased raids by the Apaches, Comanches, and Navajos. Such cooperation was especially necessary for the Pueblos because their numbers had undergone a dramatic decline. Their population, estimated at 60,000 in 1600, fell to about 15,000 in the 1700s, largely due to Old World diseases carried by the Spanish. So many Pueblo villages were abandoned that by 1700 only nineteen of the original sixty still existed. If the population figure of 20,000 Spanish living in New Mexico in 1700 is accurate, that meant that a total of only 35,000 Spanish and Pueblo Indians were holding out against attacks from the east, the west, and the north.

The story of New Mexico was unique in several respects. Not only had missionary and civil authority arrived simultaneously, but it was probably more coercive in its impact than at any other time in the conquest of New Spain except when Cortés took Mexico City. Moreover, the Eastern Pueblos were in a peculiarly isolated situation because Apache raiding parties between Albuquerque and El Paso denied them contact with the peoples of Chihuahua and Nuevo León. Hence New Mexico by the early eighteenth century was a complex island of severely defined ethnic enclaves. In this respect, it stood in contrast to the condition of other regions of northern New Spain at this time.

On the other hand, what the Spanish were to experience with the Upper Pimas, in present-day southern Arizona, was an extension of their experiences with the Opatas and Lower Pimas in Sonora: that is, they were a scattered people living in small rancherias who, while having notable cultural differences, shared both a similar language and like economic and social patterns. Although the Pimas and Papagos had some contact with the Spanish from the time of Cabeza de Vaca, they were not really affected until Father Eusebio Kino, an Italian Jesuit with immense energy and infinite good will, established Mission Dolores in Northern Sonora in 1687 and proceeded to work northward and westward, seeking to convert the Pimas and other groups. Kino's methods were both patently obvious and profound. He came to Pima villages with cattle and food. He never interfered in their warfare with their traditional enemies, the Apaches. Whenever possible, he placated, accommodated, and pleased the Papagos and Pimas. He was, in brief, a nonthreatening economic benefit to a group of Indians who initially seemed, in fact, to desire Spanish missions established among them.

In the end, however, Kino's efforts – like those of his countrymen to the east – were partially undone by Apache raids and a Pima revolt in 1751 against the Spanish. As with the Pueblos, even with the reassertion of Spanish authority by Juan Bautista de Anza after 1767, the Pimas and the Papagos were not really submissive. And when a Yuman uprising destroyed the mission at the Colorado River in the 1780s and broke the overland trail to California, Arizona became a no-man's land where Pimas and Papagos fought Apaches and continued their old lifestyle.

CONTESTING THE FRONTIER

While Spanish relations with more sedentary groups such as the Pueblos and Pimas were distinguished on the one hand by attempts both to pacify and convert the Native populations and on the other by resistance to these attempts, relations with the more nomadic groups of the Southwest followed a different pattern. The Spanish, as well as the Pueblos and the Pimas, saw Navajos and the various groups of Western Apaches as implacable enemies, as the Apaches in particular made these more sedentary groups the victims of their raiding economy. As a result, the Apaches and Navajos themselves often became the victims of raids rather than conversions, and Navajo and Apache captives were regularly sold as laborers for the mines of northern New Spain. In short, the Spanish did not seek to incorporate these Athapaskan-speaking peoples into their New World empire to the same extent that they had with their more settled neighbors.

And yet, the Apaches and Navajos were in ways more radically changed than their neighbors had been by contact with European culture. Both groups developed a horse culture, and eventually the Navajos adopted a sheep-raising economy and began to produce woolen blankets. This Native incorporation of Spanish animals and economic practices did not in any way, however, signify improved relations with the Spanish themselves. Between 1800 and 1850, raiding became so massive and so frequent that war became a dominant feature of Navajo society, although they raided not to kill people but to get goods or captives to sell to Mexicans. As for the Apaches, even though contact with Spaniards had profoundly altered the way they lived on the land, they nevertheless remained freer from the control of both Spaniards and other Indian populations than anyone else. Indeed, in the century after first contact the Spanish were not even sure who these hostile peoples were or what name to give them other than the Pueblo Indian word "Apache" meaning enemy.

By 1685, however, the Western Apaches had wreaked such havoc on Spanish and Opata Indian settlements in Sonora and Nueva Vizcaya that the Spanish responded by establishing forts called presidios along the northern border – one at Janos, Chihuahua in 1685, and a second to the west at Altar, Sonora in 1690. To the northeast Mescaleros and certain Eastern Apache bands were raiding into Coahuila and south into Chihuahua. What eventually emerged was a 250-mile-long "Apache corridor" stretching from southeastern Arizona to the New Mexico–Texas border. It was this dangerous war zone that prevented the Spanish from going north of the Gila River Basin in Arizona, from living in the middle Rio Grande area between Albuquerque and El Paso, and from controlling the area around Laguna and along the Conchos.

Rather than slowly gaining on these Western Apaches between 1765 and 1785, the situation became even worse. Pioneer settlements in the San Pedro Valley of modern-day Arizona were abandoned, and even presumably safe areas of Sonora, Nueva Vizcaya, and Coahuila came under attack. In short, by 1760, a century of Spanish efforts to control the Apaches had failed. Relations between the Spanish and Western Apaches only began to change in the late eighteenth century, when Charles III appointed an impressive number of able, high-ranking Spanish officials with orders to initiate a new anti-Apache policy.

If the Rio Grande settlements and the northern bordering areas of Sonora, Nueva Vizcaya, and Coahuila felt the brunt of Western Apache raids, another threat came from the Mescaleros farther east. Almost from the time of Juan de Oñate's occupation of New Mexico in 1598, the Mescaleros were subject to attacks and slave raids by the Spanish, and Spanish-Mescalero relations remained hostile well into the Mexican era. Initially aiding the United States in its takeover of the Southwest from Mexico, the Mescaleros soon came under equally hostile treatment from land-hungry American settlers. Overlapping with the Mescaleros in some areas, but extending eastward all the way to central Texas were the three major groups of Eastern Apaches. Combining farming in their mountain retreats with buffalo hunting, they were secure enough to trade with, rather than raid, the Spanish, although there were occasional confrontations. They continued to trade with the Spanish until the coming of the Americans. The Kiowa-Apaches represented yet another variation of a frequent southwestern process. Although they belonged to an Apachean linguistic group, they had in fact affiliated with the Kiowas and by the mid–nineteenth century had adopted much of the Kiowa culture. In contrast to the Jicarillas, they raided and fought the Spanish – and later the Americans – until they were forced onto reservations in the 1870s.

The Eastern Apaches expanded their territory in the sixteenth and seventeenth centuries because they incorporated horses into their economy at an early date. That acquisition, combined with the fact that huge concentrations of buffalo, antelope, and deer foraged on the grasses of the Staked Plains of modern-day Texas and New Mexico, meant that they had immediate access to fabulous game resources. However, in time the Comanches, now also mounted on Spanish horses, moved in on the buffalo hunting ground armed with superior French guns, sold to them by Indian traders stretching all the way from Louisiana across Texas and into western Kansas. By the early eighteenth century the Eastern Apaches were being punished by the Spanish for raiding their settlements, hit by the Comanches from the north, and harassed by the Wichitas to their east.

In contrast to these local Spanish visions of the Apaches as implacable enemies, the Hapsburgs and later the Bourbon kings of Spain never gave up their hope of converting, permanently settling, and trading with these Eastern Apache groups. For example, when the San Antonio missions were founded beginning in 1718, and the Apaches began to raid the town, high Spanish authorities still tried to make peace with them. On the other hand, the Canary Island settlers of San Antonio wanted them killed. By the 1730s the Apaches north of San Antonio were so desperate from being crowded by the Comanches and the Wichitas that they had to raid in order to survive, and they began to feed on horsemeat rather than buffalo.

By 1749 things had quieted down enough for the Spanish and the Apaches to hold a conference at San Antonio and initiate "at least a nominal friendship between the two groups in Texas." Somewhat like the Jumanos around El Paso and on the Rio Grande had done earlier, the Apaches were constantly moving about seeking safer locations and new allies who could protect them. Meanwhile various Franciscan fathers were pressing for missions both in central Texas and in the Nueces and Rio Grande watersheds.

Then in 1757, encouraged by rumors of a rich silver strike in the Llano River region of Texas, the Spanish agreed to establish a mission and presidio at San Saba, near present-day Menard, Texas, but a combination of internecine fighting between the padres and the soldiers, plus an understandable Apache reluctance to support the mission, suggested that the scheme would not work. Impending failure became a manifest reality when 2,000 Comanche warriors descended on San Saba, destroyed both mission and presidio, seized a herd of 700 livestock, and killed many Apaches. This defeat initiated an infamous era of Comanche-European warfare in Texas that would not end until the Red River War of 1874–5, when the last Comanche Indians were forced onto reservations.

Even the large Spanish and Apache military expedition sent out to avenge the humiliating defeat at San Saba was badly beaten by a combined force of hostile Comanches, Wichitas, and other Indian groups. The final abandonment of San Saba in 1768 and the withdrawal from the Lipan Apache missions on the Neuces did indeed mark the turning point in the history of the Texas missions and in Spain's relations with the Plains Indians.

SPANISH CALIFORNIA

Although we think of Spanish-Indian contact in the American Southwest as dating back to Coronado's expedition in 1540–1, this was not the case for Alta (Upper) California. Captain Juan Rodríguez Cabrillo had sailed north at least to San Diego Bay in 1542 just as Coronado and his lieutenants were ending their explorations and de Soto's unsuccessful southeastern expedition was sailing down the Mississippi. In 1602 Sebastian Vizcaino explored the California coast and urged colonization, but nothing came of that suggestion.

In the interim the only other Europeans to land on Upper California's shores were Sir Francis Drake and his crew, who on their trip around the world put in around the San Francisco Bay area in 1579. At the time cartographers still believed that California might be an island, and fanciful stories were told that its inhabitants were giant Amazon-like women who ruled the region and killed off the males. In the late seventeenth century, however, when Father Eusebio Kino recognized a seashell that an Arizona Indian possessed as one that could only have been traded overland from the

Pacific coast, this notion was laid to rest. "California," Kino is said to have exclaimed, "is not an island!"

Spanish interest in Alta California continued to lag although the Jesuits had established missions in Baja California by the end of the seventeenth century. What initiated the sudden rise of interest was a fear that Russians in Alaska might claim and even occupy Alta California. Charles III mounted a series of scientific expeditions along the coasts of California, Oregon, and Alaska. One of the architects of the New Spanish policy for the northern frontier was José de Gálvez, a visitador general whom Charles III had appointed to inspect and reorganize New Spain's northern borders. Gálvez insisted that any northern policy must include securing Alta California for Spain. For the first time California came to be seen as a part of the Provincias Internas.

In 1769, Franciscan father Junípero Serra and a number of missionaries and followers joined Captain Gaspar de Portolá, who commanded a military force. The journey proved to be an incredibly difficult one characterized by much suffering in the arid and mountainous terrain, but they made it to San Diego Bay. There Serra founded the first of an eventual chain of twenty-one missions that stretched along the California coast northward to Sonoma. Serra was followed to California by a second-generation frontier soldier named Juan Bautista de Anza. Anza was the son of a frontier captain stationed at Fronteras, Sonora, who had been slain by the Apaches in 1739. Having grown up in the region, Anza knew the region and its Pima-Papago and Apache populations well.

Anza liked Charles III's new Enlightenment policies and seems to have believed his own career would be furthered by supporting them. He saw the chance to open an overland route to California via Sonora and Arizona, along the Gila River to a Colorado River crossing where the Yumas lived, as a major step toward his own advancement and recognition. In 1772 Anza led a successful expedition along this route to Mission San Gabriel in California. Impressed by Anza's achievement, the viceroy in Mexico City then authorized him to lead a group of more than 200 colonists to the San Francisco Bay region. In less than a decade Spain had at last occupied at least the coast of California.

From the beginning, however, California, more than any other border region, was a mission frontier, and more specifically a fief for a set of devoted Franciscan missionaries led by Father Junípero Serra. Serra's aim was not only to convert the Indians to Christianity but to get them to become agriculturalists. That in turn meant concentrating the Native population in villages around the missions. For all their good intentions, the Franciscans went a long way toward destroying Native culture and the Indians themselves. Indians brought to the mission through persuasion or force, or enticed there by gifts, were subjected to a European work routine which included farming, ranching, building adobe churches, and accepting monogamous marriage and at least outwardly the Catholic religion.

At the superficial level there was success. All in all Serra and his successors baptized some 54,000 Indians, but at a fearful price. The impact of European diseases to which the Indians were not immune, combined with filthy sanitary conditions in the mission villages and an overwhelming sense of psychological despair, resulted in so many deaths that by the end of the mission period (1832), the population had declined to 98,000 from an estimated 300,000. With epidemics and disease disrupting established networks of political authority, the opportunities for massive rebellion were few. Nevertheless, the mission Indians did flee to the hills in great numbers and were able to stage a few minor rebellions. The lot of those at the missions was made the more miserable by mission fathers using force to make them work, abuse that was often facilitated by the presence of Spanish soldiers who could be – and often were – used to control local Indian populations.

Indian labor thus became one of the primary means by which Spanish California initially became connected to broader colonial markets. In its heyday the fathers and their Indian workers developed grain farming, gardens, and orchards and amassed extensive herds of cattle. By 1800 British and later American vessels had developed a healthy trade in hides, to be used to make shoes in New England, and tallow, to be sold to Chileans and Peruvians to make candles for their miners.

THE LATER SPANISH PERIOD

Throughout the eighteenth century older patterns of sending captured nomadic Indians south continued to be a source of income for Spanish officials, while captured Indian children became servants in Spanish or Pueblo households. A mestizo population of sorts arose, though the Spanish class system based on race remained in force and, in fact, the Pueblos resisted intermarriage with the Spanish. In between the raids of Spanish and Pueblos on nomadic Indians and those of nomadic Indians on Rio Grande settlements, an uneasy but flourishing trade continued, indeed increased, as Comanches replaced the Apaches as the dominant force in the

Galisteo Basin by the eighteenth century. The Spanish and Pueblos bargained for cash, blankets, horses, and captives at Pecos in return for buffalo hides and meat. To the north, Utes and Comanches attended annual fairs at Taos where they got horses and other items in return for hides and captives. In the 1780s after Spain had achieved a peace with the Comanches, an older Pueblo system of sending traders to these groups blossomed to the point that Spanish traders to the Comanches – the so-called Comancheros – could be found in Colorado, western Kansas, and on the arid plains of west Texas.

The late eighteenth century represented a turning point in Spanish attitudes toward its New World colonies and their Native populations. Faced with decreasing revenues from abroad, and greatly affected by Enlightenment ideas from France, the Spanish Crown initiated a series of reforms to increase the power of the secular state in New Spain. In addition to displacing frontier mission influence with a growing network of military presidios, the Crown set out to connect its vast northern holdings by networks of roads and trade – a task made particularly urgent by the Spanish purchase of Louisiana in 1763. Paths from Mexico to California were marked and traveled by the intrepid frontier captain Juan Bautista de Anza who, as already mentioned, in 1776 led colonists overland to California and as far north as San Francisco Bay. Meanwhile the determined Franciscan padre Francisco Garcés, a friend of Anza, found a way from the Tucson area to the Hopi villages. Before Garcés's impressive career was over, he had laid out trails to reach California and the northern area of present-day Arizona. In a similar fashion, Pedro Vial, a French-born gunsmith who became a Spanish citizen, was commanded to find routes from San Antonio, Texas, to Sante Fe and from Santa Fe to St. Louis.

As the Spanish Crown worked to gain greater economic control over New Spain's far northern frontier, it also faced the challenge of controlling the increased Indian depredations in the region. With decreased funding and the appalling record of Spanish military efforts against the Indians, the Spanish Crown took another lesson from France and replaced its policy of military force with one of trade and treaties. All across the Greater Southwest, the Spanish began negotiating an era of peace with the nomadic frontier groups, whether it was with the Wichitas and Apaches in central Texas or the Comanches in west Texas. At the same time, Spain tried to coordinate a general administrative policy for Louisiana, Texas, New Mexico, future Arizona, and California. In this way, it moved for the first time toward a unified vision of a "Spanish Southwest," although the name then was the northern "Provincias Internas," as these areas were seen from the perspective of Mexico City.

As officials began to write about provincial needs, small groups of Spaniards on the frontier began to spread northward and outward from the initial outposts of settlement. For the first time, something like a frontier movement similar to that in the Anglo-American trans–Appalachian West occurred as the pressure of more people led to new communities. By the 1800s New Mexico, almost without knowing it, was poised for demographic expansion and began to demand goods from abroad. There was also an increased awareness of the commercial value of trade and a new appreciation of the value of land, an appreciation one might call proto-speculative. All these developments would have significant impacts on Indian-Spanish relations, as competition for local land and resources grew, and as new commercial linkages to the outside world began to complicate local relations of economic and cultural exchange.

The expansion of Spanish cultural and economic networks had considerably less impact on the Western Pueblos, the Native Americans who lived in the Pueblos of Zuni and Acoma. In marked contrast to the experience of the Rio Grande Pueblos, the Zunis, although they had been savagely treated by Coronado in 1540 and accepted Oñate's authority in 1598, had no missionaries until 1629, and even then these officials kept leaving right up to 1821 when the Zuni mission was abandoned due to Navajo raids. To an even greater degree, the remote Hopis, living in what is now northern Arizona, never really submitted to the Spanish although one of Coronado's lieutenants successfully had attacked them and forced them to surrender in 1540. They resisted missionaries to the point that they may well have killed off the few pro-missionary Hopis among them so that there would never be a call for a missionary. When the Hopis were dying because of severe drought in the 1780s, Anza's offer of food in return for allegiance and conversion was rejected. In what is a remarkable story of resistance to acculturation despite deep internal divisions within the Hopi community, the Hopis held off the Spanish, the Mexicans, and the Americans until the 1880s.

Farther to the east, the Spanish Crown began to administer its new policies of trade and peace treaties to the Apaches from the line of presidios which marked that frontier's northern periphery. Referring to the Apaches, José de Gálvez, as visitador general, argued that we must "make peace treaties with each separate band of Indians," and persuade them to settle near the presidios, furnish them with food, introduce them to alcohol and even give them firearms (albeit inferior ones). The Spanish also sought to change another basic trait of the Apaches: their traditional hostility toward, and therefore absence of trading relations among, themselves or with other Indians and the Spanish. While these policies were formulated by José de Gálvez, it was his equally able nephew, Viceroy Bernardo de Gálvez, who put them into effect.

All the same, there were renewed attempts to engage and defeat the Apaches militarily. It was in these years that Juan Bautista de Anza, as commander at Tubac, made headway against the Apaches in southern Arizona, while General Hugo O'Conner, appointed as supreme commander of the frontier, tried mightily to reduce them elsewhere. Even though the results were slow and uneven, by 1800, many Western Apaches were living near presidios and had stopped raiding. Some had even become hangers-on and drunkards. This system, such as it was, worked until the outbreak of the Mexican War of Independence from Spain in 1811. After that date, deprived of funds for presents, food, and guns, the presidios could no longer bribe the Apaches into quiescence. A new period of devastation began during which some 5,000 Mexicans lost their lives and nearly an equivalent number had to flee the northwest settlements.

The only bright spot for the Spanish resulted from Governor Anza's defeat of a Comanche force in the 1780s, after which the Comanches traded with the Spanish and Pueblos in New Mexico until 1821. Even so, the Comanches were in the ascendancy by the end of the Spanish regime, raiding from Texas deep into northern Mexico. In eastern New Mexico, Plains Indian raids forced the abandonment of the long-established trading pueblo of Pecos in the early 1800s. By the nineteenth century the Eastern Apaches had evolved into three cultural groups. The Jicarillas had been so influenced by Pueblo contacts that they have been described as "semi-Pueblos." The Kiowa-Apaches, on the other hand, had become true Plains people, while the third group, the Lipans, could be called "semi-plains" in their lifestyle.

If one takes an overview of Spanish-Indian relations in the Southwest (including Texas but excluding California), it is clear that the Spanish Crown wanted to conquer, convert, and dominate. Granted, it tried to do so with what it considered just and fair treatment of Native Americans, based on elaborate codes of law, education, and cultural assimilation programs (largely religious ones). And, where possible, the Spanish Crown argued for a true alliance of Natives and Spanish in matters of production, defense, and even intermarriage. Yet such intentions were not always translated so clearly into actions. One can almost be certain that among the Indians of Spain's far northern frontier, the radical demographic, economic, and cultural changes that attended Spanish-Indian relations were not always considered "just and fair."

THE MEXICAN PERIOD

Changes during the early eighteenth century had less to do with local conditions on the Spanish frontier and more with political struggles which arose at the centers of Spanish power. These struggles culminated, after 1810, with the War for Independence from Spain. After Mexican independence was achieved, Indian-European relations in New Mexico and Arizona (which was still a part of New Mexico and Sonora and not a separate province) were frustrated by a shortage of funds, a much-weakened military presence, and growing conflict either among Indian groups or between Indians and Mexican nationals. To complicate matters further, there was now an American presence because of the rise of the Santa Fe trade after 1821 and the coming of Anglo-American settlers to Texas in the 1820s. The Texas Revolution in 1836 created political, cultural, and racial conflicts that greatly affected Indian relations in Texas, New Mexico, and along the Mexican-Texas border.

Yet changes were brought about by pressures from Native forces as well. By the end of the Spanish era, the Jumanos and Coahuiltecans of western Texas had been either exterminated or absorbed into other cultural groups, the remaining Karankawas were on the verge of being eliminated by Anglo-Texans, and the Lipans were at the "beck and call of settlers." Yet at the same time, the Comanches had begun to gain power on the frontier. Comanche strength was even more formidable because they were now allied with the Kiowas and Kiowa-Apaches. The ineffective Mexican response meant that the frontier in Texas would remain unstable and the Indians would hold their own until after the Texas Revolution in 1836.

Another important factor in shaping Indian and Euro-American relations during the Mexican period in Texas was increased secularization of the Texas missions. Secularization had been going on since 1794 when the mission lands at San Antonio began to be turned over to the Indians. With Mexican independence all government support ended and the missions deteriorated rapidly. Because of secularization and the anticlerical attitudes of the Mexi-

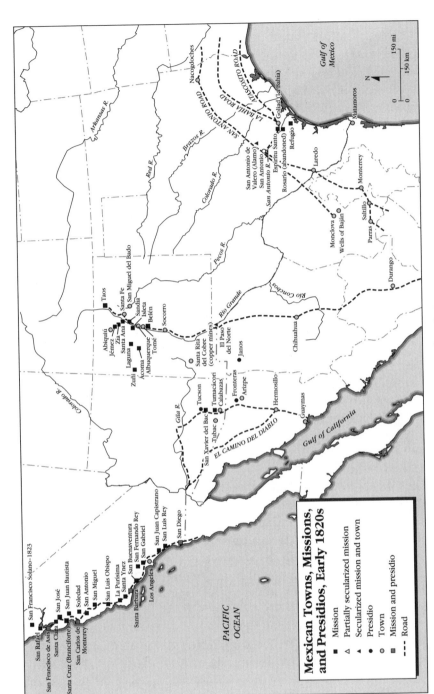

Figure 10.3 Mexican towns, missions, and presidios in the early 1820s.

can government even the important mission, San José y San Miguel de Aguayo – the "Queen of the Texas Mission" – at San Antonio, had declined precipitately. By the 1830s it had been abandoned, thereafter serving periodically as an army barracks, first for Mexican forces and later for the Republic of Texas. By 1850 the San José mission was in ruins.

Certainly the most important development in Texas during the Mexican period was the entrance of Anglo-American settlers after 1821 initially under the aegis of Stephen E. Austin. By 1830 there were more Anglo than Hispanic Texans, not counting the approximately 1,000 slaves of African origin brought by the Americans to Texas by this time. Anglo-Texan and Mexican authorities were soon at loggerheads about the coming of more American colonists, about the institution of slavery (which the Mexicans had already outlawed), and about self-government, taxes, and the requirement that one must be a Catholic to have one's marriage legitimized and the laws of inheritance applied. The result was that in 1835–6 the Anglo-Americans rose against the Mexicans, and after General Santa Anna and his Mexican troops were defeated at the Battle of San Jacinto in 1836, Texas became an independent republic headed by its first president, Samuel Houston.

Unlike the Spanish or the Mexican governments, the leaders of the new Republic of Texas did not seek accommodation with the Native peoples of Texas. They expected full solutions to military and economic conflicts between Anglo-Americans and Indians, whether by conquest or treaty, removal or extermination. Anglo-American settlers seemed to agree that the Comanches must be stopped from raiding the Texas frontiers or from using Texas as a north-south corridor by which to raid Mexican settlements. Another crisis centered around the expansion of Anglo settlers onto the lands occupied by Indians who had been forced to move into the Republic of Texas from the United States. In particular, exiled groups of Cherokees wanted to keep their Texas lands, but despite President Sam Houston's urging, the Texas Congress refused to guarantee protection to them or to any of the other peaceful Indian groups in east Texas.

Indian and Anglo-American relations declined under Houston's presidential successor Mirabeau B. Lamar. Long an opponent of Indians, Lamar joined forces with Albert Sidney Johnston, his secretary of war, and George William Bonnell, the Republic's Indian commissioner, in implementing a series of campaigns against the Indians of Texas. The Cherokees were forced to leave Texas and take refuge in what would later become the Oklahoma and Arkansas territories. Texas forces also mounted campaigns against the Comanches, pushing them back from the more settled areas. When Houston returned to office in 1841, he kept a relative peace by signing treaties with Indian groups closest to the Anglo-American settlements. Under this modus vivendi, the Wacos, Tawakonis, and southern Comanches served as a buffer between Anglo-American settlers and the more warlike Great Plains Indians to the north. As a result, Indian warfare in Texas ceased for several years.

While Texas formed frontier outposts, it came to depend more heavily on a mounted paramilitary force, the Texas Rangers, created in 1836. The Rangers were often youths from the frontier itself and in the early years were virtually their own bosses. They hated both Indians and Mexicans, yet many of their successes came from the fact that they used Indian ambush, raid-and-run fighting techniques, effectively employing the new Colt six-shooter. Despite a lack of funds, the Republic of Texas, by adopting the policies of forced removal and search and destroy campaigns by the Texas Rangers, and by the pressure of an ever-increasing number of settlers, began to achieve more control over the Texas Indian populations than the Spanish had ever done. Indian-European warfare itself, however, would continue into the 1870s and only ended then because the Plains buffalo herds had been slaughtered and the Comanches had no other food supply.

In New Mexico, a fairly long peace between the Mexican settlers and the Navajos ended in 1818, when both sides began raiding one another and continued to do so up to the time of American conquest in 1846. Similarly, New Mexico's peace with the Comanches and the Utes ended in 1820. Within the settled portions of New Mexico itself there was a notable decline both in the influence of the missions and in the number of Franciscan padres they employed. Where there had once been as many as sixty priests or missionaries in the province, this number dropped to five by 1832, echoing a similar drop of the Pueblo population from 12,000 in 1750 to under 10,000 by 1800. Since the New Mexico missions had never acquired extensive lands, and the missions themselves were largely abandoned, the 1834 secularization act could be ignored there.

In Arizona a different kind of decline had occurred. The missions were plagued both by corrupt overseers, who had been placed there to secularize them, and by Apache raiders who damaged the properties and ran off the herds. Unobstructed by presidios or soldiers, the more remote northern groups – most notably the Western and Eastern Coyotero Apaches – swept down through Arizona to raid deep into Sonora. At the same time

Mogollon, Mimbreño, Warm Springs, Natagé, and Mescalero Apaches did parallel north-south runs across southwestern New Mexico to raid Chihuahua. These terrifying raids were still occurring in 1845. So far-reaching were some of these raids that it is said Arizona Indian groups, including even the Navajos, crossed the southern Sierras to raid in California.

There were many reasons for this dramatic unraveling of the Spanish-nomadic Indian frontier. First, the Hispanic settlers still believed in the old Gálvez policy of presidial forts, present-giving, and trading. But there were no funds for any of these efforts. Second, the Indians were aggressively mistreated by the Mexicans to a greater extent than they had been under Spanish rule. Third, the central government in Mexico City was unrealistic about what it would take to maintain peace and was busy fighting its own civil wars. Presidial soldiers were not only too few in number, and seldom paid, but many did not even have adequate mounts.

Perhaps most heartening to the Indians and most unnerving to the Mexicans was the increased presence in the Greater Southwest of American fur and buffalo hide traders, and Americans now living in Santa Fe as merchants. These men did not hesitate to sell the Indians better weapons than they had ever had – indeed, better than the presidial soldiers probably had. Aided by this trade many Indian peoples, by the eve of war between Mexico and the United States, had retained autonomy and control over much of the far northern frontier of Mexico.

After Mexican independence, the new Mexican government made large land grants to Spanish colonists to develop ranchos. With the secularization of the missions in 1834, the granting of land turned into a flood. Whereas only twenty ranchos existed in 1820, by 1840 the number had increased to more than 600. Under the Secularization Act, neophyte Indians associated with the missions were also promised that they would be awarded half the mission lands for their own use.

Such was not to be the case in California. At an almost dizzying pace the rancheros acquired virtually all the mission lands with the result that for the Indian obligations to the Catholic Church were replaced by the peonage of the ranchos. Indians who did not flee inland became ranch workers, even though they did begin to live in villages or rancherias of their own again. At the same time the scarcity of labor was so great that Mexican ranchers began to raid Indian villages in California's Central Valley in order to obtain more laborers. These raids not only provoked the interior Indians to open warfare, but also gave them the excuse to launch raids themselves to procure horses and sometimes cattle.

The short period of Mexican hegemony in California from 1821 to 1846 was characterized more by exploitation than reform. The extent of this new exploitation was illustrated by John Augustus Sutter, a Swiss adventurer who founded Fort Sutter at what is present-day Sacramento in 1839. After being granted some 50,000 acres of land in the Sacramento River Valley by California's Mexican Governor Juan Alvarado, Sutter used Indians to trap fur, raise wheat, and work in weaving mills. All the while he maintained an Indian military force to keep order, punish runaways, and capture Indians in the hills for his workforce. Sutter held the power of life and death over his Indian workers. He performed marriage ceremonies, chose young women to be his concubines, and executed those Indians whom he deemed disloyal. At Fort Sutter, one can clearly see the transition in California from the Spanish theory of Indian assimilation to the Mexican policy of ruthless economic exploitation. And yet, Sutter's approach was merely a prelude to the exploitation and hostile treatment gold-rush Americans would give the California Indians.

THE AMERICAN PERIOD

Whereas three-fourths of the Indian populations in the Greater Southwest still were not under Mexican control in 1845, all of these Native groups were under some kind of control, even restraint, by 1887–88. The traumatic saga of this transformation, from both the Indian and the Anglo-American point of view, is the subject of the final section of this essay.

One might begin with the impact of trade – that great breaker of the cake of custom – on the southwestern Indians. In 1821, the newly independent Mexican government revised a long-standing Spanish policy of keeping New World colonies closed to commerce with foreigners and opened the country's northern borders to American trade. Soon a brisk business developed between Missouri merchants and the peoples of New Mexico and Chihuahua. Cloth, strouds, cutlery, and other wares came down the Santa Fe–Chihuahua trail each year in heavily loaded wagons. In exchange the Missouri merchants got furs, buffalo hides and robes, woolen blankets, silver bullion, and Spanish mules.

The Santa Fe Trail itself went through the heart of Comanche country. Every caravan had to be on guard or move in sizable numbers of wagons, as Comanche raiders would sometimes attack the trains. Indeed, the famous overland technique of a camp inside a circle of wagons at night was first used by the Santa Fe wagon trains. Confrontations between Indians and

Europeans led the Americans, like the Texans before them, to consider Comanches as enemies. Their fears were only increased by the fact that the Comanches were beginning to hunt buffalo commercially in order to trade robes and hides for guns.

Meanwhile two Missouri merchants, William and Charles Bent, worked in partnership with Ceran St. Vrain in 1834 to found a trading post on the Arkansas River in present-day southern Colorado. Fort William, or Bent's Fort as it came to be known, was soon a meeting place and point of departure for fur trappers exploiting the southern Rockies. The Bents themselves traded with Plains groups as far away as Texas. Soon American fur trappers were living in Taos and Santa Fe, New Mexico, where they were often supplied by local resident American merchants. These trappers traveled not only into the southern Rockies, but also deep into Arizona to trap along the Gila River. By the 1830s American trappers had reached California via Anza's old trail that crossed the Colorado at the future site of Yuma, Arizona. Other trapper-traders, both Hispanic and Anglo, reached California over the Old Spanish Trail and developed a small and erratic but strategically important trade in New Mexican blankets for California horses and furs.

These forays brought Americans into contact with the Apaches, Pimas, Papagos, Maricopas, and Yumas on the lower trail, and with Utes, Navajos, and California Mohave desert bands on the upper trail. With the exception of the agricultural groups in southern Arizona, these encounters between Indians and Anglo-Americans were often hostile. That these were truly *indios barbaros,* as the New Mexicans and Tucsonans called them, seemed only confirmed by constant Apache raids in Arizona and Navajo conflicts with the New Mexicans. These fights were at times so bitter that in 1845 New Mexican Governor Manuel Armijo would report that the war "is slowly consuming us."

When the United States declared war against Mexico in 1846, General Stephen Watts Kearny was placed in charge of the Army command ordered to take the province of New Mexico and then to march on to California to assist in the conquest of that province. Kearny took New Mexico peacefully and established an interim American government composed partly of former Santa Fe traders. In 1850, New Mexico was given territorial status in the Union. It quickly became clear to the first territorial governor, James S. Calhoun, that his most pressing task was to negotiate some kind of peace between Hispanic Americans and local Indians as well as between the local population and warring Indians such as the

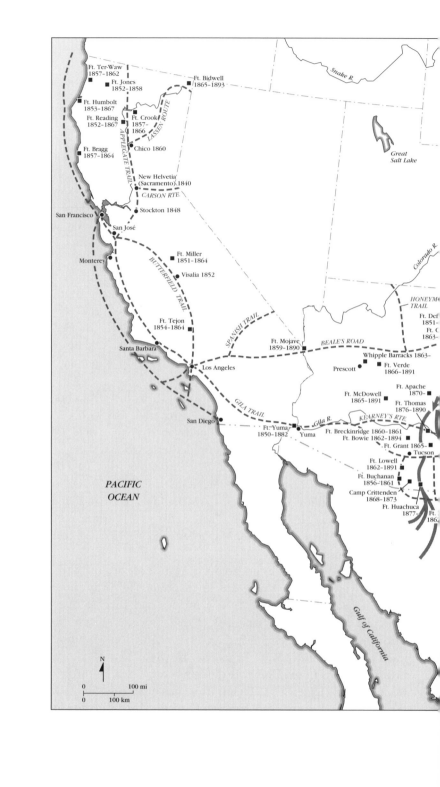

Ft. Ter-Waw
1857–1862

Ft. Jones
1852–1858

Ft. Bidwell
1865–1893

Snake R.

Ft. Humbolt
1853–1867

Ft. Reading
1852–1867

Ft. Crook
1857–
1866

APPLEGATE TRAIL

LASSEN ROUTE

Great
Salt Lake

Ft. Bragg
1857–1864

Chico 1860

New Helvetia
(Sacramento) 1840

CARSON RTE.

Stockton 1848

San Francisco

San José

Ft. Miller
1851–1864

Colorado R.

Monterey

BUTTERFIELD TRAIL

Visalia 1852

*HONEYM[
TRAIL*

Ft. Def
1851–

Ft. C
1863–

Ft. Tejon
1854–1864

SPANISH TRAIL

Ft. Mojave
1859–1890

BEALE'S ROAD

Santa Barbara

Whipple Barracks 1863–

Prescott

Ft. Verde
1866–1891

Los Angeles

Ft. Apache
1870–

Ft. McDowell
1865–1891

Ft. Thomas
1876–1890

GILA TRAIL

KEARNEY'S RTE.

San Diego

Gila R.

Ft. Yuma
1850–1882

Yuma

Ft. Breckinridge 1860–1861
Ft. Bowie 1862–1894

Ft. Grant 1865–

Tucson

Ft. Lowell
1862–1891

*PACIFIC
OCEAN*

Ft. Buchanan
1856–1861

Camp Crittenden
1868–1873

Ft. Huachuca
1877–

Ft.
186

N

0   100 mi

0   100 km

Gulf of California

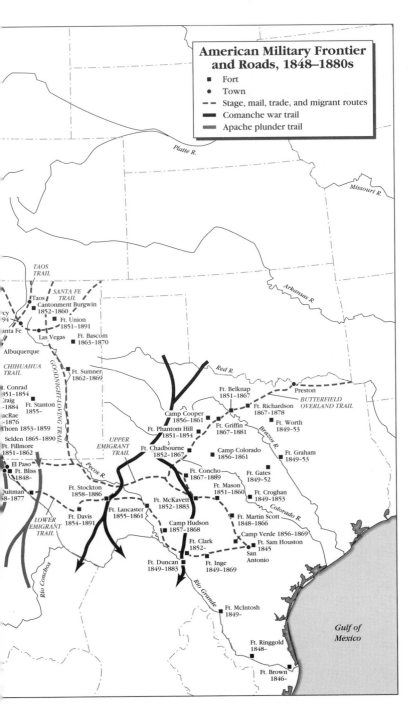

Figure 10.4 American military frontier and roads from 1848 to the 1880s.

Apaches, the Utes, and the Navajos. The need for such a peace had been underscored by a rebellion of Hispanic New Mexicans and Taos Indians at Taos in 1847, in which Charles Bent, newly appointed American governor of New Mexico, was killed.

Governor Calhoun soon discovered that like his Spanish and Mexican predecessors, he was seen as a final court of appeal for all kinds of disputes. Indians came to the Palace of the Governors in Santa Fe to complain about lost sheep or a stolen horse. In September 1851, John Greiner, Calhoun's secretary, noted wearily that "Jicarilla came in today to see Tata (Calhoun) with a long story about a horse and a mule which they say a Mexican has taken from them – all as I believe got up for an excuse to get something to eat." Pueblo Indians also asked Calhoun to settle land disputes and to end a feud between the Acomas and the Lagunas. Calhoun's successor, William Carr Lane, described his own years in office as "one eternal round of appeals, written and verbal, from Mexican and Indian, and sometimes from Americans for reparations, of every description of wrongs."

Calhoun's first goal was to get the federal government to treat the Pueblos differently from the "wild" Indians. Indeed, he recommended that the Pueblos be given property rights as well as the right to vote. Later in the decade the federal government confirmed the Pueblos' property rights but not their right to vote. As for the "wild" Indians Calhoun said they must be subdued first, then provided with an agent who should work to secure "compulsory enlightenment . . . enforced at the point of a bayonet." Toward this end, Calhoun formed territorial militia units and appointed such respected leaders as Ceran St. Vrain and Kit Carson to head them. The governor also began to sign treaties with Apache bands on the Rio Grande and with small groups of other Apaches at Jemez west of the river.

Calhoun's policies, as well-meaning as they were, were frustrated by a shortage of capable agents and supplies. His greatest problem was that the new military commander in charge of the Department of New Mexico for much of the 1850s, Colonel Edwin Vose Sumner, was a stubborn Indian and Mexican hater. Sumner refused to cooperate with Calhoun, and instead had his own plans for Indian control. Sumner first established a central command and supply center on the Santa Fe Trail near Las Vegas, which he named Fort Union. From Fort Union he proceeded to create a perimeter of small forts. To the west he located Fort Defiance in the mouth of Canyon Bonito for the purpose of containing the Navajos. To the northwest near Taos he located Cantonment Burgwin, and to the south he built Fort Craig. This defense perimeter was strengthened by subsequent commanders, and came to include other posts along the Rio Grande and farther west where the Santa Rita copper mines were located.

Supplying all these distant posts with goods that first had to be freighted down the Santa Fe Trail before they could be carried to the edge of the perimeter created a big business for New Mexico. These defense costs averaged more than $3,000,000 a year and necessitated the employ-ment of more than a thousand workers at Fort Union. With something like 8 percent of all the money in New Mexico emanating from army sources, it was no wonder that Sumner and his successors could ignore the governor in Santa Fe, for it was the military that sustained the economy. Expenditures of money, however, did not keep the peace. By the mid-1850s, the Jicarilla Apaches had attacked Cantonment Burgwin and had run off government herds near Fort Union itself.

To control the Jicarillas in what is now southern Colorado, Sumner's successor, General John Garland, built Fort Massachusetts and con-structed Fort Stanton in the south to control the Mescaleros. Despite attempts at treaty-making, Garland had a thousand troops chasing hostile Indians by 1855, and six companies of militia were campaigning against the Utes and the Apaches. The treaties that were made promised a reserva-tion system for Apaches, Utes, and Navajos, but in 1856 the Senate refused to ratify the treaties.

Just how far Americans were from controlling the "wild" Indians in the 1850s was dramatically demonstrated when 500 Mogollon Apaches in Arizona went on devastating raids. Comanches increased their attacks on the caravans on the Cimarron Cutoff, and Mangas Coloradas and his Chiricahua followers raided from Tucson east all the way to the Rio Grande. The increased pace of raiding and warfare unfortunately increased dissent among the U.S. officials in charge of New Mexico. Generals at Fort Union feuded with the governors and Indian superintendents at Santa Fe. Meanwhile the territorial delegate attacked the governor. To make matters worse the New Mexico Assembly authorized the formation of new militia companies to act on their own. Meanwhile a private vigilante militia made up of Mexican-Americans seeking spoils of war attacked the Navajos.

Despite many reversals, the American defense-offense system in New Mexico was finally beginning to have an impact on the nomadic groups when the Civil War intervened and federal troops were called back East to fight for the Union; or pro-Southern officers and men resigned to join Confederate forces. However, as soon as General Canby and Union forces rid New Mexico of Confederates, and General James H. Carleton with his California Column recaptured Arizona, the latter, assuming command at Fort Union, turned his attention to solving what contemporaries called "the wild Indian question." Carleton came at a crucial time, for Indian raids had increased to the point that in one year over sixty persons had lost their lives, thirty-four had been wounded, and an estimated $340,000 of livestock had been lost.

Carleton's Indian policy was direct and brutal. The Army would kill or capture hostile Indians until they agreed to live on a reservation, accept Christianity, and become farmers. Carleton enlisted such veteran Indian fighters as Kit Carson whom he ordered to round up the Mescalero Apaches in an unprecedented winter campaign. Defeated Indians began to fill the stockades at a fort on the Pecos River which Carleton had named Sumner in honor of the former New Mexican commander, Edwin Vose Sumner.

In over 200 years of dealing with nomadic Indians, New Mexico had never seen so much action. As leading citizens began to turn Carleton into an almost legendary hero, Carleton focused his attention on the Navajo raiders in the west. He located Fort Wingate in the heart of Navajo country and gave Kit Carson orders to effect "entire subjugation or destruction of all the men." Carson's strategy was equally ruthless. He not only conducted a series of winter campaigns, but destroyed every Navajo cornfield or food cache that could be found. The Army also agreed to pay $20 for every Navajo horse captured and $1 for every sheep taken. Soon Navajo captives at Fort Wingate began to number in the thousands. At that point Carleton unveiled the next step of his program. He ordered some 8,000 Navajos to march eastward and settle near Fort Sumner in an area called the Bosque Redondo, far from the mountains and canyons of western New Mexico. Carleton had, in fact, established not just a reservation but a prison which he himself called a "reformatory."

However, just as Carleton was being hailed as the deliverer of New Mexico, both the federal government and the climate terminated his program. The Army simply did not have and could not obtain the necessary food and supplies to feed the Navajo captives. Carleton got the Navajos to plant crops but these were ruined by drought in 1864 and by a freeze in 1865. Carleton's absolute domination of New Mexico's Indian affairs soon led politicians to oppose him and seek his removal. A contingent of anti-Carleton politicians, including Dr. Michael Steck, whose role as Indian Superintendent had been almost completely displaced by Carleton, began to urge that the Navajos be allowed to return to their home-land, saying that there they could feed themselves.

Although Congressional investigations of Carleton's Indian policy at the Bosque Redondo gave him a clean bill of health, Carleton was so unpopular he was removed in September 1866. A year later the government and the Navajos signed a treaty at Fort Sumner stipulating that the Navajos could return to their homeland. By then the Navajos had been reduced by perhaps half their 1863 population by disease and starvation. Nevertheless in the summer of 1868 the remnants of those who had made the "long walk" in 1862 struck out for the west. The emotions they experienced at seeing a familiar landscape again were overwhelming. One Navajo is recorded as saying, "When we saw the top of the mountain from Albuquerque we wondered if it was our mountain, and we felt like talking to the ground, we loved it so."

While General Carleton had failed at turning the Navajos into Christian farmers, he had broken their power. Never again would warfare be seen as the natural state of affairs in New Mexico. Raids and killings would continue up to 1885, but their impacts waned as the Anglo and Hispanic population came to outnumber that of the Indians.

In 1863 the western half of New Mexico was organized as Arizona Territory. Long dominated by Apache bands who fought the Spanish, the Mexicans, and the Pimas and Papagos, Arizona also began to undergo rapid change under American rule. The first change came when the federal government urged the construction of a railroad along the thirty-second parallel from Texas to California. The hope for this southern rail route was strengthened when gold was discovered in California in 1848 and some 10,000 argonauts took either the Santa Fe Trail or the so-called Southern Trail across Texas, southern New Mexico, and Arizona to California. In order to furnish protection to these migrants, the government built a series of forts along the route, stretching from New Mexico to Fort Yuma on the Colorado. Whereas the proposed railroad along the thirty-second parallel would not be built until the 1880s when the Southern Pacific finally joined the Texas and Pacific line east of El Paso, the Butterfield Overland Stage line began to take passengers and mail across this part of Arizona by 1858.

Just before the Civil War, American capitalists also began to develop copper and silver mines in Arizona and neighboring Sonora, and following the outbreak of war, silver was discovered in north-central Arizona at Prescott. At each of these locations, the stage was being set for nearly three decades of increased confrontation between Anglo-American settlers, miners, and federal troops on one hand, and Apachean peoples on the other. When Arizona Territory was organized in 1863, approximately 5,000 Anglo- and Mexican-Americans lived there, in contrast to the estimated 30,000 Indians who called the place home. At first it looked as if the United States might come to an understanding with the Apaches, who thought that anyone who had fought Mexicans must be potential friends. In 1852 government agents signed a treaty with the Coyotero Apaches and a year later created a reservation for the Mimbreños. Indian agent Michael Steck, a key mediator in the creation of these treaties, also persuaded the Chiricahua chief Cochise to let the Overland Mail stages go through and to permit miners to enter selected areas.

As in New Mexico, however, the Civil War had the effect of unraveling all previous understandings. The Army unwisely tried to arrest Cochise, who had helped keep the peace in the area north of the Mexican boundary (Mexican soil remained fair game for his bands). Then in 1862 several Apache chiefs including Chiricahua Apache chief Managas Coloradas were murdered by Anglo-Americans. On the other hand the Pima, Papago, and Maricopa Indians began to see the Americans as valuable allies in their own ongoing war with the Apaches. In turn, John N. Goodwin, first territorial governor of Arizona, called these groups "our well tried and faithful allies," but referred to the Apache as a "murderer by hereditary descent – a thief by prescription." In stark contrast to the Spanish-Mexican belief that Indians could be made a part of their society, Goodwin expressed the American view "that the Indian and the antelope must disappear together before the Anglo-Saxon race." He furthermore believed that the use of local militia was a more effective means to this end than the previous employment of federal troops had been.

Yet Goodwin's boasts of future Anglo-Saxon triumph hardly fit the situation at the time, and the military superiority of Arizona's newest immigrants had yet to be proved. As General John S. Mason, military commander of the district of Arizona, noted in 1865, the territory's chief mining town of Tubac was "entirely deserted, and the town of Tucson had about two hundred souls." "North of the Gila," Mason continued, "the roads were completely blockaded; the rancherias, with one or two exceptions, abandoned, and most of the settlements were threatened with either abandonment or annihilation." Even though new forts were being built, making travel through the Arizona territory safer, the Apache raids against Anglo-Americans and other Indians persisted.

The situation was made only worse as Anglo-Americans began to fight among themselves for a solution to the "Apache problem." Many Arizonans, as we have seen, held that local militia should take responsibility for subduing the "hostile" Indians. A second opinion, represented by the Bureau of Indian Affairs, felt that reservations, food rations, and clear-cut treaty relations would be the best way to bring peace to Arizona. A third group strongly advocated the transfer of the Indian Bureau to the Army. Finally in 1869 the incoming President Ulysses S. Grant announced that he would try a new "peace policy." In Arizona, this policy called for the reduction of military posts, the continued concentration of Indians onto reservations where they would presumably be "civilized," and the reform of the previous corruption of the reservation system through a new Board of Indian Commissioners which would evaluate the performance of Indian agents. Arizona Governor A. P.-K. Safford was so outraged at the military cuts that he made a special trip to Washington to get permission to form three volunteer militia companies. Meanwhile some Arizonans were sufficiently frustrated by events that they decided to take matters in their own hands. In 1871, 104 Tucson citizens and Papago Indians clandestinely invaded Camp Grant, where Arivaipa Apaches were settled, and killed 115 men, women, and children.

During Arizona's flirtation with the peace policy, General O. O. Howard did manage to attract a number of peaceful Apaches to the San Carlos and White Mountain reservations. In 1872 Howard and Thomas J. Jeffords persuaded Chief Cochise to cease warfare against American troops. Even with these efforts the peace policy failed in Arizona, and once again the Army took over and General George Crook was placed in charge of Indian affairs. Crook announced that if all Indians were not on their reservation by 1872 "they would be pursued and killed." To achieve his ends, Crook used the old divide and conquer technique of employing friendly Indians as scouts to track down hostile Indians. The technique seemed to work as more and more Apaches streamed into the reservation centers to surrender. By 1874 what had once been sustained warfare had almost ended. A new era was symbolized by Indian agent John P. Clum, who at the San Carlos reservation managed to control the Apaches there without the use of military force. Part of Clum's strategy was to give the Indians responsible duties on the reservation, an approach reminiscent of

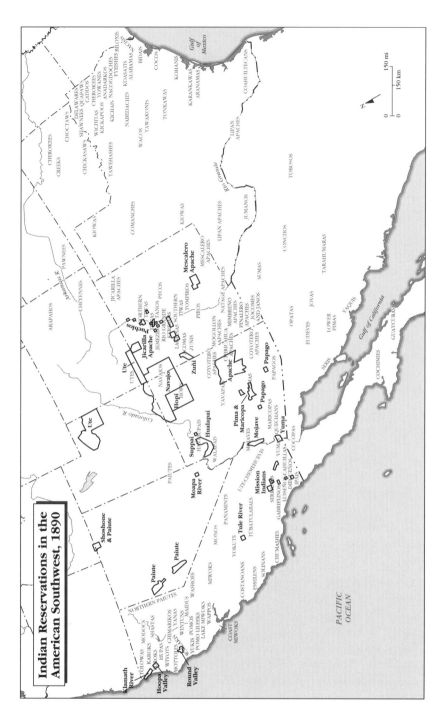

Figure 10.5 Indian reservations in the American Southwest in 1890.

that employed years earlier by the Spanish missionaries in the mission-centered Native communities.

The final crises surrounding Indian relations in Arizona came in 1885–8, when bands of discontented Chiricahua Apaches at the San Carlos Reservation, led by Geronimo, fled the reservation and began to harass the citizens of southeastern Arizona. Although Geronimo has gained the distinction in popular thought of a ruthless renegade, there were legitimate reasons for Apache discontent. With a blindness to cultural distinctions that was typical of the time, the government had brought many different Indian groups to the San Carlos agency, many of whom did not get along with the Apaches there. At the same time, corrupt agents and inadequate rations fomented yet more discontent on the reservation. Finally, the discovery of coal and copper deposits within reservation boundaries led to an invasion of the lands by Anglo-American miners and squatters, while Mormon settlers exacerbated these tensions by occupying lands at Fort Apache.

Crook's failure to bring in the Apache dissidents in 1885–6 led to local demands for a new Indian war and to Crook's replacement. In 1886 Crook's successor, General Nelson A. Miles, using Crook's skilled subordinates and his system of Indian scouts, found and captured Geronimo and his band. The older idea of Carleton's of Indian removal from their traditional "haunts" was then applied with a vengeance when the Chiricahua captives were shipped east, first to Fort Marion in Florida and later to Fort Sill in Oklahoma.

Indian and Anglo-American relations in Arizona seem in many ways a unique saga: a handful of Anglo-Americans declaring war on Indian groups who had been there from time immemorial. However, the independent spirit of many Apache groups, coupled with a professional raiding-warfare tradition that had been facilitated by the coming of the Spanish horse, had created an intolerable situation in American eyes. The eventual result was that the federal Army, urged on by local leaders and settlers, demanded subjugation and the institution of the reservation system. The Anglo-Americans had acted there, as they had elsewhere, with the assumption that Indians were destined for extinction – or at least assimilation – and that Anglo-American (and to a lesser extent Mexican-American) settlers had a manifest destiny to occupy and develop the lands of the region. Finally, the local government correctly assumed that the federal government would bring vast amounts of money to the local economy in their effort to win the day. The whole saga demonstrates that American Indian policy, like that of the Spanish, had both ruthless and benign features:

ruthless if the Indians would not be peaceful and accommodate, benign if they would live on reservations and assimilate. What no one understood on the Anglo-American side was that military defeat, confinement to a reservation, and education of the youth still did not destroy Apache culture, much less Apache spirit. Like the Spanish before them the Americans had achieved an incomplete conquest.

If the Anglo-American conquest of Native peoples in Arizona was achieved largely by military campaigns, reservations, and rations – a vast, government-run "outdoor commissary" according to one observer – the subjugation of Indians in California was of a very different kind. As suggested earlier the California Indians, while adversely affected by the Spanish mission and Mexican ranch systems, still numbered 150,000 in 1845. The coming of over 100,000 gold-seeking Americans between 1849 and 1851 created a major crisis. How were these Native peoples to be protected? Noting the monumental migrations caused by the gold rush, U.S. Indian Commissioner William Medill quickly realized that the vision that Americans had long held of a "Permanent Indian Frontier" was no longer tenable. He instead began to promote the concept of distinct reservations for Indian groups around which Anglo-Americans could settle. From 1850 onward the small reservation idea received not only the support of Medill's successors, but of Congress and the President as well.

In 1851, three federal commissioners appointed to treat with the California Indian populations concluded some eighteen treaties with a total of "139 little tribes and bands." The treaties set aside 12,000 square miles (19,200 square kilometers) of reservation lands on which the Indians were to settle and be taught farming. The government also promised to feed them during the transitional period. The opposition of California's senators, however, resulted in the defeat of the treaties in 1852. For the rest of the decade, the federal government attempted to create a better reservation system in order to overcome this opposition. But these efforts were drowned in a veritable sea of corruption and fraud. "As far as anyone can see," complained one Army officer, "the whole system is turned into a speculation for the benefit of the Agents." One result of these fraudulent actions in California was that through the combined effects of disease, starvation, malnutrition, and simple homicide, the Indian population plummeted from 150,000 in 1845 to 35,000 in 1860.

Shortly after the onset of the gold rush, a number of California Native groups found themselves embroiled in a series of skirmishes conducted by local militia or gangs of miners. In 1850, California Governor Peter

Burnett authorized the sheriff of El Dorado County to call up 200 men as a volunteer militia to punish Miwoks who had harassed emigrants on the Salt Lake to California trail, and had stolen and butchered their cattle. Over 300 men enlisted and engaged Indians in a series of skirmishes that cost the new state an exorbitant amount of money. A year later in the southern district, a local group organized to fight the Mariposa War, a military expedition that eventually gained the approval of the California legislature. Subsequent militia campaigns launched against California Indians were numerous, some twenty occurring during the Civil War period alone. Instead of solving the problem of Indian livestock theft, however, these expeditions often pushed Native peoples far from their traditional subsistence bases, increasing their dependence on raiding for survival. Anglo-American Californians responded with new invasions, leading to a deadly cycle of violence between Indians and their new neighbors.

Meanwhile beef contractors were charging unbelievably high prices to the government for cattle presumably being used as rations for peaceful Indians. Among the big profit-takers was John C. Fremont, hero of the California conquest and subsequent U.S. senator. And yet during the 1850s those reservations that did exist were so badly supplied that the Indians had to supplement their reservation fare with more traditional hunting and gathering in order to survive. At the same time, Indians in the mining areas learned to pan for gold, with which they bought coffee, sugar, and other supplies from storekeepers at exorbitant prices. They also went to work for American farmers and ranchers – the men in the fields and the women in the kitchens of Anglo-American homes. Although the demand for Indian labor declined in northern California as new immigrant workers streamed in, Indians continued to be used both as household and ranch labor in the Los Angeles area and in southern California. In Fresno County yet another variation occurred. Here Indians continued to live in communities, with their members occasionally working for Anglo-American ranchers. In yet other areas Indians were segregated by sex both in the workplace and at home, making it difficult for them to have and maintain a family. Even as their lives were profoundly altered by Anglo-American labor regimes, however, California Indians rarely, if ever, became a part of Anglo-American society.

The Indian population of California continued to decline until the twentieth century, dropping in total to about 10 percent of their original number at the time of European contact. So great was the general Anglo-American disdain for them that only since the 1960s have scholars been able to tell us much about how they survived or who their leaders were. From these studies we discover a history not only of persistence but also of ways in which shrewd leaders – especially among the southern groups of the Cahuillas, Luiseños, and Cupeños – negotiated for the survival of their peoples and whatever vestiges of "traditional" life they could preserve.

Much of the violence that occurred in California and Oregon as well as on the Great Plains after the Civil War came as part of resistance to the Peace Policy program that sought to put Indians on reservations. A dramatic challenge to reservation life occurred in northern California when Kintpuash or Captain Jack, a Modoc leader, along with sixty or seventy families, left an Oregon reservation to which they had been assigned to return to their previous home on the Lost River in northern California. When these Modocs refused to leave, the U.S. Army was ordered to use force, and in November 1872 soldiers attacked Kintpuash's village. Taking refuge in some almost impenetrable lava beds, Kintpuash held off 1,000 U.S. Army troops for four months before agreeing to negotiate. But while the peace talks were going on, the Modoc leaders decided to kill the Anglo-American members of the peace commission. Among those who died was General Edward R. S. Canby, a Civil War hero who had helped "save" New Mexico for the Union in 1862. An outraged government and nation demanded that the Modoc leaders be captured and hanged – which they were – and that their followers "be scattered among other tribes." In what had become a standard act of Indian removal, some 155 of them were sent east to Indian Territory in future Oklahoma.

As one reviews the course of Indian and Anglo-American relations in California during the first forty years (1848–88) of U.S. sovereignty over the region, the record is one of attacks, mistreatment, and misunderstanding of an extraordinarily numerous and diverse set of peoples. Most of them had been relatively peaceable but been forced to resort to raids and theft in order to survive after the influx of a huge gold-rush population. In essence, when California Indians encountered Anglo-Americans, the latter had already undergone a 250-year history of frontier warfare and Indian-European hostility. They believed that all Indians were threats and that they must be assimilated, removed, or exterminated. By 1850 removal was impossible, adequate reservations were not provided, and extermination – while practiced by local militia or miners – was not acceptable in a nation where a peace policy was presumably the official policy. Where a single-minded authority helped solve the nomadic Indian situation in American New Mexico, the California story, even more than that of Arizona, was one of divided counsels between the local and state officials and Washington, with no one consistent policy emerging. It might even be argued that a California Indian policy was the victim of too much Anglo-American democracy!

Following the admittance of Texas to the United States in 1845, the story of Indian and Anglo-American relations on the eastern edge of the Greater Southwest remained more than ever one of conflict. Before the Civil War the extreme hostility of the Texans resulted in the removal of virtually all the remaining peaceful groups north of the Red River area. Meanwhile some of the worst depredations in Texas history were taking place along the Mexican border where Lipans, Mescaleros, and Kickapoos still raided with relative impunity, while southern Plains groups – most notably the Apaches, Kiowas, and Comanches – still roamed more or less freely in certain parts of the state, as well as in Kansas and Indian Territory. Even those Kiowas who had agreed to live on the Fort Sill Reservation after the Civil War continued to move out in small parties "intent on plunder, coups, scalps, and sometimes revenge."

These raids continued during the years of the Peace Policy and greatly weakened the case for the reformers who argued that kindness, Christianization, and agricultural pursuits would turn Native Americans from their old ways. Ongoing raids on Texas settlements led to demands that the Army take Indian affairs from the hands of the reformers and civilians. Yet when the Army initiated a campaign against hostile Indians, they usually employed methods of conventional warfare. This included heavy columns of infantry and cavalry and slow-moving supply trains which were simply no match for the smaller-scale hit-and-run tactics of the Indian war parties. What the Army may have lacked in innovative techniques, however, was compensated by the dogged determination of General William T. Sherman, who headed the Army after the Civil War, and by General Philip Sheridan, commander of the Division of the Missouri. Yet in the end, the Plains Indians were not defeated so much by military action as by the killing of the buffalo herds, their main source of food, and by the relentless pressure of settlers.

One of the major aims of the federal government after the Civil War was to bring hostile Indians to the council table and write new treaties. After seven years of warfare (1861–8) in many regions, Peace Commissions – often headed by an Army general or a congressman – toured the West to make new treaties. One of these big meetings occurred at Medicine Lodge Creek, Kansas, in 1867. Present were Kiowas, Comanches, and Cheyennes, most likely representing some 26,000 fellow Indians from Texas and the southern Plains. Although the government insisted that the Plains Indians agree to live on reservations, they also promised them they could still hunt buffalo south of the Arkansas. Huge stacks of goods and guns had been brought to the Medicine Lodge Creek with the promise that if they would cede lands outside the future reservations, begin to farm, and send their children to school, such goods would be delivered annually for the next thirty years.

Yet so many raids by both Cheyenne and Comanche bands continued in southern Kansas and west Texas that Sherman decided military action was necessary. In the fall of 1868 he ordered George Armstrong Custer to conduct a winter campaign against Black Kettle and the Cheyennes. In the Battle of the Washita, November 27, 1868, Custer carried the day. But the national reaction to what many thought was an attack on a peaceful village actually strengthened the cause of the Peace Policy advocates.

Meanwhile, during one of their Texas raids in May 1871 the Kiowas barely missed attacking General Sherman himself who was on a tour of inspection, but they routed a wagon train killing seven of twelve teamsters. Sherman demanded that the leaders, Chiefs Satanta, Satank, and Big Tree, be arrested and tried for murder. In a dramatic sequence of events Satank was shot by a guard and the others were tried but later pardoned by the governor of Texas. Hostilities with the Comanches along the U.S.-Mexico border, on the other hand, continued until 1873, when Mexico agreed to let U.S. forces under Colonel R. S. Mackenzie cross the boundary line, capture the Kickapoos, and move them to Oklahoma Territory.

By the 1870s the government had built a line of forts along the Texas Indian frontier: Fort Richardson at Jacksboro, Fort Griffin near Albany, Fort Concho at San Angelo, Fort McKavett on the San Saba, and Fort Clark near Brackettville. It was around these forts that professional buffalo hunters gathered as they began to wipe out the vast southern Plains herds. By this time the Peace Policy was in such disarray that the Army was able to obtain permission to compile lists of friendly and hostile Cheyenne, Comanche, and Kiowa Indians and to move against the "hostiles." The resulting Red River War of 1874–5 was one of attrition in which U.S. soldiers were unremitting in their chase throughout the fall and into a freezing winter and spring. Finally the bands did begin to come in to the reservation, one of the last being Quanah Parker's Quahadi band of Comanches. Some leaders were imprisoned; others were put in railroad cars and transported east to St. Augustine, Florida, and confined in Fort Marion.

Robert Utley, the foremost authority on nineteenth-century Indian and Anglo-American military history, finds that by following a policy of "convergence" – that is close cooperation between commanding general Philip Sheridan and the generals and the officers in the field – the U.S. Army had not only won battles but had bodily removed the Indian leadership from the region. The result was as revolutionary for the southern Plains Indians as General Carleton's reduction and removal of the Navajos and later Crook's and Miles's campaigns against the Arizona Apaches had been. By the late 1870s, the United States had finally gained military control over Texas and the southern Plains. The eastern fringes of the Greater Southwest would no longer run red with the blood of settlers and Indians.

By 1888 the southwestern Indian "frontier" was no more. Still Indian peoples and cultures persisted whether on reserves in Indian Territory, or in the villages of the Pueblos, Pimas, and Papagos. They also survived in the vast canyonlands of the Navajos, on the Apache reservations in Arizona and New Mexico, and in almost invisible pockets in California. That persistence has continued down to the present and is part and parcel of the multiracial and multiethnic society that now lives in the American Southwest.

Earlier generations of historians have stressed the constant confrontation between Europeans and Native Americans in the Southwest. More recent scholars have been impressed by their mutual survival over more than three centuries, and, what is more, the persistence of distinctive if evolving cultures. Yet what we are dealing with in the Southwest, ultimately, is a history not simply of Indian and Euro-American interactions in the remote past, but rather of ones that are ongoing. For this reason, we must learn to address the continuities that link the historical mosaic of conquest, social change, and cultural persistence that we have encountered there to the present-day reality of Native America. For as Native peoples in the Southwest have endured, so too has their larger social context – a context of human interaction that continues to make the American Southwest one of the most diverse cultural regions on the continent. The story of the Southwest's Native past, therefore, is not only about the region's original settlers, and what happened to them in some past age. It is also a story that speaks to the many peoples who are still learning to share the same southwestern home.

The reader seeking a general introduction to Indian peoples of the Southwest and their respective cultures, languages, and histories should begin with the multivolume *Handbook of North American Indians,* edited by William C. Sturtevant and published by the Smithsonian Institution. For the history of Pueblo peoples both before and after European contact, the reader should consult the ninth volume, edited by Alfonso Ortiz, entitled *Southwest* (Washington, D.C., 1979). For all other major Native groups of modern-day Arizona, New Mexico, and west Texas – as well as of Mexico's far north – see volume 10, *Southwest* (Washington, D.C., 1983), also edited by Ortiz. Volume 8, *California* (Washington, D.C., 1978), edited by Robert F. Heizer, contains a variety of valuable essays on the far western reaches of the Greater Southwest. Hundreds of entries and essays by current scholars make these three volumes both a starting point and a constant reference tool for any student of southwestern Indian history and culture.

There are several book-length introductions to the broader history of Native peoples in the Greater Southwest. The most valuable of these is Edward H. Spicer's classic study *Cycles of Conquest: The Impact of Spain, Mexico, and the United States on the Indians of the Southwest, 1533–1960* (Tucson, Ariz., 1962), which remains the seminal text on Indian-European relations in Arizona, New Mexico, and northern Mexico's border region. Also useful is Bertha P. Dutton's *American Indians of the Southwest,* rev. ed. (Albuquerque, N.M., 1983). For the precontact period, refer to Linda S. Cordell, *Prehistory of the Southwest* (New York, 1984), and the more recent collection of Linda S. Cordell and George J. Gumerman, eds., *Dynamics of Southwest Prehistory* (Washington, D.C., 1989). An older, classic text is John C. McGregor, *Southwestern Archaeology* (Urbana, Ill., 1965).

For an introduction to historical Indian-European relations in the Greater Southwest and the U.S.-Mexico borderlands, one should begin with David J. Weber, *The Spanish Frontier in North America* (New Haven, Conn., 1992), which covers the almost three centuries of Spanish rule in the region. The Mexican period is treated in David J. Weber, *The Mexican Frontier, 1821–1846: The American Southwest under Mexico* (Albuquerque, N.M., 1982), while Howard Roberts Lamar's *The Far Southwest, 1846–1912: A Territorial History* (New Haven, Conn., 1966) provides a valuable introduction to the early American period. A recent work that considers all three eras in the context of the region's incorporation into the European "world-system" is Thomas D. Hall's *Social Change in the Southwest, 1350–1880* (Lawrence, Kans., 1989).

Finally, there are several useful bibliographic reference works on the Greater Southwest. One might begin with Ellwyn R. Stoddard, Richard L. Nostrand, and Jonathan P. West, eds., *Borderlands Sourcebook: A Guide to the Literature on Northern Mexico and the American Southwest* (Norman, Okla., 1983), but also see Barbara Valk, *Borderline: A Bibliography of the United States-Mexican Borderlands* (Los Angeles, 1988), and César Caballero, comp., *The Border Finder: A Border Series Bibliography* (El Paso, Tex., 1987). For more general reference works relevant to this chapter, see Stephan Thernstrom, Ann Orlov, and Oscar Handlin, eds., *Harvard Encyclopedia of American Ethnic Groups* (Cambridge, Mass., 1980), and Howard R. Lamar, ed., *Reader's Encyclopedia of the American West* (New York, 1987, c. 1977). Both have entries on specific southwestern Native peoples. The most useful reference for Indian-European relations during the American period is Francis Paul Prucha, *A Bibliographic Guide to the History of Indian-White Relations in the United States* (Chicago, 1977).

Earlier historical writing about the American Southwest was largely shaped by Herbert E. Bolton and his many University of California graduate students between 1900 and 1950. Bolton and his followers created a coherent history of the Spanish borderlands from scores of narrative accounts, and by editing hundreds of diaries, journals, and reports. Bolton's *Coronado on the Turquoise Trail: Knight of Pueblos and Plains* (Albuquerque, N.M., 1949), and *Rim of Christendom: A Biography of Eusebio Francisco Kino* (New York, 1936) are but two of his many major works. Despite its dated perspective, Bolton's seminal essay, "The Mission as a Frontier Institution in the Spanish-American Colonies," *American Historical Review* 33 (October 1919), 42–62, provides important information on the role of missions and missionaries in Christianizing southwestern and California Indians, and is placed in critical context in David J. Weber, ed., *New Spain's Far Northern Frontier: Essays on Spain in the American West, 1540–1821* (Albuquerque, N.M., 1979), 49–65. For a recent and more critical view of the role of the mission, see David J. Weber, "Blood of Martyrs, Blood of Indians: Toward a More Balanced View of Spanish Missions in Seventeenth Century North America," in David Hurst Thomas, ed., *Columbian Consequences*, vol. 2 (Washington, D.C., 1990), 429–48.

Bolton should be supplemented with George Hammond's and Agapito Rey's accounts of explorers and colonizers in the Greater Southwest. See, for example, Hammond's *Don Juan de Oñate and the Founding of New Mexico* (Santa Fe, N.M., 1927), George P. Hammond and Agapito Rey, eds. and trans., *Narratives of the Coronado Expedition, 1540–42* (Albuquerque, N.M., 1940). Another invaluable edited collection from this era is Charles W. Hackett's *Historical Documents Relating to New Mexico, Nueva Vizcaya and Approaches Thereto, to 1773,* 3 vols. (Washington, D.C., 1923–37). The efforts of Bolton and his students were also paralleled by such publications as Ralph Emerson Twitchell's *The Leading Facts of New Mexican History,* 2 vols. (Cedar Rapids, Iowa, 1911–12). Studies by a later generation of New Mexico scholars, such as France V. Scholes, Albert Schroeder, Frank Reeve, and others, have supplemented Twitchell. John Francis Bannon synthesized the findings of the Bolton generation of scholars in a convenient narrative text, *The Spanish Borderlands Frontier, 1513–1821* (New York, 1970). The rise of new research methods and conceptual frameworks in social history and ethnohistory have made Bolton's and Bannon's accounts seem both dated and incomplete. These early works nevertheless contain much of value to the ongoing study of the region and its Native peoples, and should not be overlooked.

Other post-Bolton scholars interested in Spain's role in the Southwest have tended to be much more critical and to focus on the Indian's side of the story. Jack D. Forbes's *Apache, Navajo and Spaniard* (Norman, Okla., 1960) finds that the Spanish brutally disrupted a working trade relationship between the Pueblos and Plains Indians. On the other hand, Oakah L. Jones, Jr., *Pueblo Warriors and Spanish Conquest* (Norman, Okla., 1966), notes how some Native Americans joined Spaniards in their conquest of other Indians. Elizabeth A. H. John was particularly distressed by the Bolton school's lack of understanding of Native American motives and actions, and responded in her *Storms Brewed in Other Men's Worlds: The Confrontation of Indians, Spanish, and French in the Southwest, 1540–1795* (College Station, Tex., 1975; republished, Lincoln, Nebr., 1981). Meanwhile, David J. Weber has recently revised and updated the synthetic borderlands perspective forged by Bolton and Bannon in his previously mentioned *Spanish Frontier in North America,* a work which reflects newer historical approaches and research in its objective treatment of both Indian and European narratives.

An issue which has recently come to the scholarly forefront as an important factor in early Indian-European relations is that of the diseases and epidemics which were perhaps the most deadly element of the European conquest. Some of the most accessible and interesting work in this area has been done by Alfred W. Crosby. Crosby's *The Columbian Exchange: Biological and Cultural Consequences of 1492* (Westport, Conn., 1972) and *Ecological Imperialism: The Biological Expansion of Europe, 900–1900* (Cambridge, 1986) provide a good introduction to this literature, while Daniel T. Reff's *Disease, Depopulation, and Culture Change in Northwestern New Spain, 1518–1764* (Salt Lake City, Utah, 1991) explores these issues within the regional context of the Greater Southwest. For the eastern fringes of the region, see Marvin T. Smith, *Archaeology of Aboriginal Culture Change in the Interior Southeast: Depopulation during the Early Historic Period* (Gainesville, Fla., 1987).

The manuscripts, published sources, and secondary works pertaining to the history of the various southwestern Native groups themselves are vast in number, and range from first-hand traveler's accounts to more complex ethnographies to more formal anthropological and historical studies. Unfortunately the majority of these works were done from a non-Native perspective, and thus reflect in many ways the particular values of the invading European cultures. The historical coverage of Indian groups in Texas, for instance, is less complete than for those farther west, a fact due just as much to a lack of European interest in these peoples as to the success of European – particularly Anglo-American – policies of removal. A convenient starting point for these more eastern populations is John R. Swanton, *The Indians of the Southeastern United States,* Bureau of American Ethnology Bulletin, no. 137 (Washington, D.C., 1946). The most reliable and convenient – if somewhat dated – anthropological overview is William W. Newcomb, *The Indians of Texas from Prehistoric to Modern Times* (Austin, Tex., 1961). Newcomb should be supplemented with Thomas R. Hester, ed., *Ethnology of the Texas Indians* (New York, 1991), which contains valuable primary materials on eastern and central Texas, and Ortiz, ed., *Southwest,* vol. 10 of *Handbook,* which looks at the more nomadic groups of west Texas. An example of newer approaches to Native Texas is Timothy K. Perttula's *"The Caddo Nation": Archaeological and Ethnohistoric Perspectives* (Austin, Tex., 1992).

The classic firsthand account of the peoples of coastal Texas is Alvar Nuñez Cabeza de Vaca's narrative (*La Relación*) first published in Spain in 1542. A recent scholarly edition is Cleve Hallenback, *Alvar Nuñez Cabeza de Vaca: The Journey and Route of the First European to Cross the Continent of America* (Glendale, Calif., 1940). A more accessible edition is Cabeza de Vaca, *Adventures in the Unknown Interior of America* (New York, 1961), trans. with annotation by Cyclone Covey. The accounts of

Hernando de Soto's encounters with the Caddoan peoples of Texas and lands to the east can be found in Edward Gaylord Bourne, ed., *Narratives of the Career of Hernando de Soto,* trans. Buckingham Smith, 2 vols. (New York, 1904). Other important firsthand accounts that discuss Texas Indians come two centuries later. See Fray Juan Morfi, *History of Texas, 1673–1779,* 2 vols. (Albuquerque, N.M., 1935), and *Lt. Colonel Athanese de Mézières and the Texas-Louisiana Frontier, 1769–1780* (Cleveland, 1914), ed. and trans. Carlos E. Casteneda, as well as Jean Louis Berlandier, *The Indians of Texas in 1830,* ed. and intro. John C. Ewers (Washington, D.C., 1969).

More recent scholarly works treating historical Indian-European relations in Texas include Elizabeth John's *Storms Brewed in Other Men's Worlds,* which provides a balanced account of Indian-Spanish relations from eastern New Mexico eastward to Louisiana in which the activities of the Mescaleros, Jicarillas, Lipan and Kiowa-Apaches, Comanches, Tonkawas, and other Indian groups are treated. Ortiz, ed., vol. 10 of *Handbook, Southwest,* also covers these groups. For more detailed information on the various Eastern Apache peoples who lived in western Texas and eastern New Mexico, see Keith Basso and Morris Opler, eds., *Apachean Culture and Ethnology* (Tucson, Ariz., 1971); C. L. Sonnichsen, *The Mescalero Apaches* (Norman, Okla., 1958); Donald E. Worcester, *The Apaches* (Norman, Okla., 1979); and Morris E. Opler, *Lipan and Mescalero Apache in Texas* (New York, 1974).

A fine anthropological study of the Comanches is Ernest Wallace and E. Adamson Hoebel, *The Comanche, Lords of the South Plains* (Norman, Okla., 1952). See also Robert S. Weddle, *The San Sabá Mission: Spanish Pivot in Texas* (Austin, Tex., 1968). The way in which the Spanish finally came to terms with the Comanches is documented in Alfred B. Thomas, ed., *Forgotten Frontiers: A Study of the Spanish Indian Policy of Don Juan Bautista de Anza, Governor of New Mexico, 1777–1787* (Norman, Okla., 1932, repr. 1969); see also his *The Plains Indians and New Mexico, 1751–1778* (Albuquerque, N.M., 1940). Connections between Comanches, Mexicans, and the Pueblo peoples of the Rio Grande are covered in Charles L. Kenner, *A History of New Mexican–Plains Indian Relations* (Norman, Okla., 1969), and more recently in Katherine Spielmann, ed., *Farmers, Hunters and Colonists: Interaction between the Southwest and the Southern Plains* (Tucson, Ariz., 1991).

American relations with the various Eastern Apache groups are covered in Newcomb, *Indians of Texas;* Dolores A. Gunnerson, *The Jicarilla*

Apaches: A Study in Survival (DeKalb, Ill., 1974); and Sonnichsen, *Mescalero Apache*, Worcester, *The Apaches*, and Opler, *Lipan and Mescalero Apache*, cited earlier. Hostilities between Americans and Comanches stimulated a number of studies, of which Wallace and Hoebel, *The Comanche, Lords of the South Plains*, is one of the most enduring. Another is Rupert N. Richardson, *The Comanche Barrier to South Plains Settlement* (Glendale, Calif., 1933). More recent valuable accounts include William T. Hagan, *Indian Police and Judges: Experiments in Acculturation and Control* (New Haven, Conn., 1966) and *United States–Comanche Relations: The Reservation Years* (New Haven, Conn., 1976), and Morris W. Foster, *Becoming Comanche: A Social History of an American Indian Community* (Tucson, Ariz., 1991).

The unsuccessful efforts to pursue a "Peace Policy" with the Comanches and their allies are treated in T. C. Battey, *The Life and Adventures of a Quaker among the Indians* (Norman, Okla., 1965, c. 1875), a volume which T. R. Fehrenbach describes as presenting "a non-Texan view from the Indian side." Utley's excellent account of the Red River War in his *The Indian Frontier* may be supplemented by James L. Haley, *The Buffalo War: The History of the Red River Uprising of 1876* (New York, 1976). The "military" solution to Plains warfare is treated extensively in Utley, *Indian Frontier* and in Paul Hutton, *General Phil Sheridan and his Army* (Lincoln, Nebr., 1985). The story of destroying the Indians' food supply by killing the buffalo is eloquently told in Mari Sandoz, *The Buffalo Hunters* (New York, 1954). In addition to Utley, *Indian Frontier*, coverage of Indian-European relations to 1888 can be found in T. R. Fehrenbach, *Lone Star: A History of Texas and the Texans* (New York, 1985, c. 1968).

For an introduction to Western Apache groups, begin with Ortiz, ed., *Southwest*, vol. 10 of *Handbook*, and Spicer, *Cycles of Conquest*. From there, one should consult articles and volumes by Albert H. Schroeder, but especially *A Study of the Apache Indians: Part 1, Apaches and their Neighbors; Part 2, The Jicarilla Apaches; Part 3, The Mescalero Apaches* (New York, 1974); and his *A Study of the Apache Indians: "Tonto" and Western Apache* (New York, 1974). Excellent recent studies of Apachean culture are to be found in Grenville Goodwin, *Social Organization of the Western Apache* (Tucson, Ariz., 1969), and Keith Basso, *Western Apache Raiding and Warfare* (Tucson, Ariz., 1971). Keith Basso, ed., *The Cibecue Apache* (New York, 1970) is a revealing study of a specific group. A convenient, brief synthesis of recent studies of the Western

Apaches is to be found in Harriet J. Kupferer, *Ancient Drums, Other Moccasins: Native North American Cultural Adaptation* (Englewood Cliffs, N.J., 1988). See especially chapter 6, "The Western Apache of the Southwest Desert," 94–122.

Evolving Spanish policy toward the Western Apaches is detailed in Spicer, *Cycles of Conquest*, 239–40, 332–3; in Max L. Moorhead, *The Presidio: Bastion of the Spanish Borderlands* (Norman, Okla., 1975); and William B. Griffin, *Apaches at War and Peace: The Janos Presidio, 1750–1858* (Albuquerque, N.M., 1988). An excellent brief account of policy is Luís Navarro García, "The North of Spain as a Political Problem in the Eighteenth Century" in David J. Weber, ed., *New Spain's Far Northern Frontier: Essays on Spain in the American West, 1540–1821* (Albuquerque, N.M., 1979), 210–16, trans. Elizabeth Gard and David J. Weber. José Cortes's *Views from the Apache Frontier: Report on the Northern Provinces of New Spain* (Norman, Okla., 1989), ed. Elizabeth A. H. John and trans. John Wheat, is an exceptionally perceptive report on the state of Apachean groups in 1799.

Western Apache-European relations after 1848 are, of course, covered in Ortiz, ed., *Southwest*, vol. 10 of *Handbook*, and in previously cited works by Goodwin and Basso. Emerging federal policies are treated in Alban W. Hoopes, *Indian Affairs and Their Special Reference to the Far West, 1849–1860* (Philadelphia, 1975). Utley, *The Indian Frontier*, covers hostilities from 1848 to the capture of Geronimo, as well as the years of the Peace Policy. There has been an enormous literature on the so-called Apache wars and such leaders as Cochise and Geronimo. In addition to works cited earlier by Sonnichsen and Schroeder, see Dan Thrapp, *The Conquest of Apachería* (Norman, Okla., 1967), John G. Cremony, *Life among the Apaches* (Glorieta, N.M., 1970, c. 1868), Odie B. Faulk, *The Geronimo Campaign* (New York, 1969), and Edwin R. Sweeney, *Cochise: Chiricahua Apache Chief* (Norman, Okla., 1991).

Navajo culture and Spanish-Navajo relations are well covered in Spicer, *Cycles of Conquest*, pp. 232–9, and in Ortiz, ed., *Southwest*, vol. 10 of *Handbook*. Henry F. Dobyns and Robert C. Euler, *The Navajo People* (Phoenix, Ariz., 1972) is a useful introduction by two outstanding anthropologists. Jack D. Forbes, *Apache, Navaho, and Spaniard* covers early relations. Garrick and Roberta Glenn Bailey, *A History of the Navajo* (Santa Fe, N.M., 1986) is a balanced recent history of the nation. A classic anthropological study is Clyde Kluckhohn and Dorothea Leighton, *The Navaho,* revised by Lucy H. Wales and Richard Kluckhohn (New York, 1962); see also Ruth M. Underhill, *Here Come the Navaho!*, U.S. Indian Service: Indian Life and Customs, no. 8 (Lawrence, Kans., 1953).

Navajo relations with the United States, which were almost totally hostile from 1848 to 1868, have been treated in Frank McNitt, *Navajo Wars: Military Campaigns, Slave Raids, and Reprisals* (Albuquerque, N.M., 1972), and more recently in William Haas Moore's *Chiefs, Agents, and Soldiers: Conflict on the Navajo Frontier, 1868–1882* (Albuquerque, N.M., 1994). The enforced removal to a reservation on the Pecos River is the subject of Gerald Thompson, *The Army and the Navajo: The Bosque Redondo Reservation Experiment, 1863–1868* (Tucson, Ariz., 1982, c. 1976), whereas the Peace Policy era is covered in Norman J. Bender, *"New Hope for the Indians": The Grant Peace Policy and the Navajos in the 1870s* (Albuquerque, N.M., 1989). Useful studies of the American period include Bailey and Bailey, *A History of the Navajos* and Peter Iverson, *The Navajo Nation* (Westport, Conn., 1981). A work that is valuable for its discussion of economic and environmental change in the American period is Richard White's *Roots of Dependency: Subsistence, Environment, and Social Change among the Choctaws, Pawnees, and Navajos* (Lincoln, Nebr., 1983).

The Pueblos have been the object of study by archaeologists, anthropologists, and historians for a long time. Beginning with studies of the Pecos ruins in New Mexico in 1882 by Adolph F. A. Bandelier, a Swiss anthropologist and historian, the story of an unbroken sequence between an ancient and a modern Pueblo past slowly emerged. See Bandelier's *A Final Report of Investigations among the Indians of the Southwestern United States, 1880 to 1885*, Archaeological Institute of America Papers, "America Series," nos. 3 and 4 (Cambridge, 1890–2). Meanwhile anthropologists such as Frank Hamilton Cushing moved to the Southwest to live among the Zunis, an example to be followed by scores of others who chose to investigate Indian life firsthand. See Jesse Green, ed., *Zuñi: Selected Writings of Frank Hamilton Cushing* (Lincoln, Nebr., 1979). A more traditional study of a Western Pueblo group is Robert C. Euler and Henry F. Dobyns, *The Hopi People* (Phoenix, Ariz., 1971), while Scott Rushforth and Steadman Upham's *A Hopi Social History: Anthropological Perspectives on Sociocultural Persistence and Change* (Austin, Tex., 1992) brings new social history approaches to the complex and often factious history of this Western Pueblo group.

Certainly the most distinguished account of Pueblo-European relations in the historic period is Edward H. Spicer, *Cycles of Conquest*. His magisterial volume should be read in conjunction with the works of two ethnologists: Edward P. Dozier, *The Pueblo Indians of North America* (New

York, 1970), and Alfonso Ortiz, *The Tewa World (Chicago, 1969), New Perspectives on the Pueblos* (Albuquerque, N.M. 1972), and his entries in Ortiz, ed., *Southwest*, vol. 9 of *Handbook*. A classic history of the Spanish period is John L. Kessell's *Kiva, Cross and Crown: The Pecos Indians and New Mexico, 1540–1840* (Washington, D.C., 1979), whereas a rich new approach to the period can be found in Ramón Guttiérez's *When Jesus Came, The Corn Mothers Went Away: Marriage, Sexuality, and Power in New Mexico, 1500–1846* (Stanford, Calif., 1991). See also Jones, *Pueblo Warriors*, and Myra Ellen Jenkins, "Spanish Colonial Policy and the Pueblo Indians," in *Southwestern Cultural History: Collected Papers in Honor of Albert H. Schroeder* (Papers of the Archaeological Society of New Mexico, 1985), 197–206. Continuing European settlement is covered in Oakah L. Jones, Jr., *Los Paisanos: Spanish Settlers on the Northern Frontier of New Spain* (Norman, Okla., 1979), and in G. Emlen Hall and David J. Weber, "Mexican Liberals and the Pueblo Indians, 1821–1829," *New Mexico Historical Review* 59 (spring 1984), 5–32. Also useful is Steadman Upham's *Politics and Power: An Economic and Political History of the Western Pueblo* (New York, 1982). Pueblo relations with the United States are covered in Dosier, *Pueblo*, Spicer, *Cycles of Conquest*, and Ortiz, ed., *Southwest*, vol. 9 of *Handbook*.

The best-known earlier anthropological studies of the Pima-Papago groups are by Ruth Underhill. See her *Social Organization of the Papago Indians* in *Contributions to Anthropology*, vol. 30 (New York, 1939). Also see Alice Joseph, Rosamond B. Spicer, and Jane Chesky, *The Desert People: A Study of the Papago Indians of Southern Arizona* (Chicago, 1949) and Frank Russell's classic study *The Pima Indians*, reprint of 1908 work, intro. by Bernard Fontana (Tucson, Ariz., 1975). Useful for economic and ecological change are Robert A. Hackenberg, *Aboriginal Land Use and Occupancy of the Papago Indians* (New York, 1974), and Robert A. Hackenberg and Bernard L. Fontana, *Aboriginal Land Use and Occupancy of the Pima-Maricopa Indians*, 2 vols. (New York, 1974). William H. Kelly, *Indians of the Southwest: A Survey of Indian Tribes and Indian Administration in Arizona* (Tucson, Ariz., 1963), Bernard L. Fontana, *The Papago Tribe of Arizona* (New York, 1974), and Henry Dobyns, *The Pima-Maricopa* (New York, 1989) are excellent recent accounts. Other studies by these authors and by writers in Ortiz, ed., *Southwest*, vol. 10 of *Handbook*, should also be consulted.

Spanish relations with the Pimas and Papagos are covered in Bolton's *Rim of Christendom*, John Francis Bannon, *The Mission Frontier in Sonora, 1620–1687* (New York, 1955), and John L. Kessell, *Friars, Soldiers, and*

Reformers: Hispanic Arizona and the Sonora Mission Frontier, 1767–1856 (Tucson, Ariz., 1976), in addition to studies of later missionaries by Peter Masten Dunne, Russell C. Ewing, and Theodore Treutlein. For the Mexican and American periods, see Paul H. Ezell, *The Hispanic Acculturation of the Gila River Pima*, Memoirs of the American Anthropological Association 90 (Menasha, Wisc., 1961), Bernard Fontana, *Of Earth and Little Rain: The Papago Indians* (Flagstaff, Ariz., 1981), as well as David Rich Lewis's recent environmental history of the Papago in *Neither Wolf nor Dog: American Indians, Environment, and Agrarian Change* (Oxford, 1994), which provides a useful introduction to the American period.

The literature on California Indians is vast, reflecting the variety and sheer number of Native peoples who lived in the region before European contact. Accounts of the many hundreds of smaller Native groups can be found in Alfred L. Kroeber, *Handbook of the Indians of California*, Bureau of American Ethnology Publication, no. 78 (Washington, D.C., 1925, repr. 1967). Kroeber was succeeded by a distinguished new generation of anthropologists, among them, Sherburne F. Cook, who published *The Conflict between the California Indians and White Civilization* (Berkeley, Calif., 1943), and *The Population of the California Indians, 1769–1970* (Berkeley, Calif., 1976); and Robert F. Heizer, who with M. A. Whipple edited *California Indians: A Source Book* (Berkeley, Calif., 1951). Heizer's *A Bibliography of California Indians: Archaeology, Ethnography and Indian History* (New York, 1977) is essential. A year later he edited *California*, vol. 8 of the *Handbook of North American Indians* (Washington, D.C., 1978).

A third generation of scholars interested in California Indians is well represented in studies by George Harwood Phillips, *Chiefs and Challengers: Indian Resistance and Cooperation in Southern California* (Berkeley, Calif., 1975), and *Indians and Intruders in Central California, 1769–1849* (Norman, Okla., 1993). See also his *The Enduring Struggle: Indians in California History* (San Francisco, 1981). For an account of Yuman peoples, see Spicer, *Cycles of Conquest*, pp. 262–78, and Henry F. Dobyns, *The Havasupai People* (Phoenix, Ariz., 1971), as well as older studies: C. Daryll Forde, *Ethnology of the Yuma Indians*, University of California Publications in American Archaeology and Ethnology, *vol. 28, no. 4, 1931; and Leslie Spier, Yuman Tribes of the Gila River* (Chicago, 1933). Cook and Phillips cover the Mexican period of California history, but an outstanding recent study is Albert L. Hurtado, *Indian Survival on the California Frontier* (New Haven, Conn., 1988) in which the Indian cultural persistence noted by Phillips is impressively documented for the American period.

Spanish occupation of California is recorded in scores of texts, chief among them Hubert H. Bancroft's magisterial *History of California, Mexico, Northern Mexican States and Texas, New Mexico and Arizona,* 7 vols. (San Francisco, 1884–90). Charles E. Chapman, *A History of California: The Spanish Period* (New York, 1921, repr. Saint Clair Shores, Mich., 1971) is still useful. An excellent recent general history is Walton Bean and James J. Rawls, *California, An Interpretive History* (New York, 1983). The "promoter" of upper California's occupation and settlement is treated in Herbert I. Priestley, *José de Gálvez, Visitor-General of New Spain* (Berkeley, Calif., 1916).

Anyone reading about the mission systems in California should read Bolton's essay, "The Mission as a Frontier Institution," along with two more critical views in Clarence H. Haring, *The Spanish Empire in America* (New York, 1952), and Bailey W. Diffie, *Latin American Civilization: Colonial Period* (Harrisburg, Penn., 1945). Maynard J. Geiger's *The Life and Times of Fray Junipero Serra . . . A Biography* (Washington, D.C., 1959) details the career of California's most prominent and powerful missionary. The settlement of the San Francisco area is well covered in Herbert E. Bolton, *Anza's California Expeditions,* 6 vols. (New York, 1930, repr. 1966), but one should also consult Theodore E. Treutlein, *San Francisco Bay: Discovery and Colonization, 1769–1776* (San Francisco, 1968). Bancroft, *History of California,* vols. 1 and 2 (1884–1885), actually written by Henry L. Oak, gives the greatest detail for the period after 1776. The role of Indian labor in Spanish settlement is covered in Robert Archibald, *The Economic Aspects of the California Mission* (Washington, D.C., 1978).

For the last years of Mexican California, vols. 3 and 4 of Bancroft's *History of California* provide great detail. They, too, were actually authored by a Bancroft ghost writer, Henry L. Oak. The ranch system, which arose after the demise of the missions and into the American period, is the subject of Robert G. Cleland, *The Cattle on a Thousand Hills* (San Marino, Calif., 1941), but must be supplemented by Hurtado's *Indian Survival,* which analyzes how Americans like John Augustus Sutter, along with other California ranchers, exploited the Indians.

For California, Hurtado, *Indian Survival,* is the most insightful recent study tracing the impact of the gold rush and agricultural settlements on Indian society, but James J. Rawls, *California Indians: The Changing Image* (Norman, Okla., 1984), traces U.S. Indian policy and local attitudes. The tragic failure to give California Indians adequate lands on reservations is traced in Rawls, Phillips, and Cook, cited earlier, and in Robert F. Heizer, *The Destruction of California Indians: A Collection of*

Documents from the Period 1847 to 1865 (Santa Barbara, Calif., 1974). See also Joseph Ellison, *California and the Nation, 1850–1869: A Study of the Relations of a Frontier Community with the Federal Government* (Berkeley, Calif., 1927); and William H. Ellison's *A Self-Governing Dominion* (Berkeley, Calif., 1950). A moving biography is Theodora Kroeber's *Ishi in Two Worlds* (Berkeley, Calif., 1965). Anglo-American policy and hostilities toward California Indians is well covered in Robert M. Utley, *The Indian Frontier of the American West, 1848–1890* (Albuquerque, N.M., 1984).

In the constant search to achieve a fuller, more balanced history of Indian people and their cultures and European interaction with them, scholars have turned to ethnohistorical approaches and studies of mutual impact as evidenced in James Axtell's *The Invasion Within: The Contest of Cultures in Colonial North America* (New York, 1985). Anthropologists have used linguistic analysis; for example, see Keith H. Basso, *Western Apache Language and Culture: Essays in Linguistic Anthropology* (Tucson, Ariz., 1990), which vividly demonstrates the crucial value of linguistic study in understanding Native American thoughts and culture.

Similarly, N. Scott Momaday's "Native American Attitudes toward the Environment," in W. Capps, ed., *Seeing with a Native Eye: Essays on Native American Religions* (New York, 1974), 75–95, uses views of nature and religion to provide a glimpse into Native American culture. Leslie Silko has analyzed "Language and Literatures from a Pueblo Indian Perspective," in *Opening up the Cañon,* L. Fiedler and H. Baker, trans. and eds. (Baltimore, 1981), 54–72.

Environmentally oriented historians have explored yet other directions. Richard White, in *The Roots of Dependency: Subsistence, Environment, and Social Change among the Choctaws, Pawnees, and Navajos,* stresses the way European takeover and exploitation of the environment turned Indians into dependents, whereas David Rich Lewis carries White's approach into the reservation era in *Neither Wolf nor Dog: American Indians, Environment, and Agrarian Change.* William Cronon and Richard White joined forces in "Ecological Change and Indian-White Relations," in Wilcomb E. Washburn, ed., *History of Indian-White Relations,* vol. 4 of *Handbook of North American Indians* (Washington, D.C., 1988), 417–29, to produce a brilliant interpretive essay. One should also see entries in the same volume: William T. Hagan's "United States Indian Policies," 51–65; Charles Gibson's "Spanish Indian Policies," 96–102; and Edward H. Spicer's "Mexican Indian Policies," 103–9.

11

THE NORTHWEST FROM THE BEGINNING OF TRADE WITH EUROPEANS TO THE 1880s

ROBIN FISHER

The experiences of the Native peoples of the Northwest were both similar to and different from those of other indigenous peoples of North America. The general patterns of adaptation and dispossession were not unlike the rest of the continent; yet there were variations on these themes that were distinctive and even unique. There was also great internal diversity within the Northwest. Geographically, the common denominators of this long, narrow region were the Pacific Ocean in the west and the mountains in the east. Otherwise the natural setting ranged from the arid, broken topography of central Oregon, through the wet, relatively rich environment of the Northwest Coast, to the cold, hard climate of the Alaskan coast and islands. Given this geographical range, it is not surprising that there was also a wide variety of indigenous cultures. Indeed there was greater cultural diversity in this region than in any other in North America. Adding to this complexity of original cultures, during the eighteenth and nineteenth centuries the Northwest was touched by most of the major imperial systems of the world. Russia, Spain, Britain, and the United States of America each had a profound influence on the region's Native people.

THE INDIGENOUS PEOPLES

By the eighteenth century, when Europeans came to the Northwest, the Native people were no longer newcomers. Over 12,000 years of accommodating to the seasonal round, they had learned to exploit the region's abundance and to survive its scarcity. From the Aleutian Islands in the north to Cape Mendocino in the south, and from the damp west coast to the semi-arid plateaus of the interior, their traditions were strong and their cultures were rich and diverse. While they were not always constant, the boundaries between groups were well defined. The rights to harvest valued resource-gathering locations were also clearly understood. In summer the people scattered over their land to hunt and gather food, in winter they congregated in larger villages and celebrated the spiritual side of life through ritual and ceremonial. Social patterns based on kinship and lineage were deeply ingrained. The extended family was the basic unit of social organization. Particularly on the coast, the societies were hierarchical and individuals knew their place in the order. Birth, wealth, and ability were the attributes of leadership; yet leaders had a mutual relationship with their people and also led by consent. Geography tended to isolate Indian groups, but trading connections extended over considerable distances, and cultures developed partly through contact with one another.

Beyond those that are obvious, generalizations about the Native cultures of the Northwest are difficult and dubious. Anthropologists draw the demarcations between the various groups along linguistic lines. There were dozens of distinct, mutually exclusive, indigenous languages in the region, representing most of the major Native language families of North America. The resulting delineations on maps suggest clarity and sharp divisions, whereas on the ground there was often a merging of dialects at the borderlines. That is not to say, however, that Native groups did not recognize clear territorial boundaries.

From north to south, the Native population was concentrated on the coast. In the far north lived the Pacific Eskimos and the Aleuts who had some cultural affinities with the Tlingits to the south, but were also distinctive. Occupying the Aleutian Islands, the Aleuts were linguistically separate from the Sugpiaq Eskimos. Between the Eskimos and the Tlingits were the Athapaskan-speaking Tanainas of Cook Inlet, who were influenced by Eskimo culture. Like all coastal groups, these people gathered most of their food from sea and shore. They developed sophisticated, open-sea hunting techniques that enabled them to survive in a harsh marine environment.

Yakutat Bay is usually seen as the northern boundary of the Northwest Coast culture area, which stretched south to what is now northern California. The northernmost groups were Tlingits. Living along the Alaska panhandle, they spoke a Na-Dene language that was related to the Athapaskan of the interior, perhaps indicating that they were comparatively recent arrivals on the coast. The Haidas occupied the Queen Charlotte Islands, except for one group, the Kaiganis, who had villages on the southern tip of Prince of Wales Island. On the adjacent mainland, Tsimshian groups spoke one of three different dialects. There were also

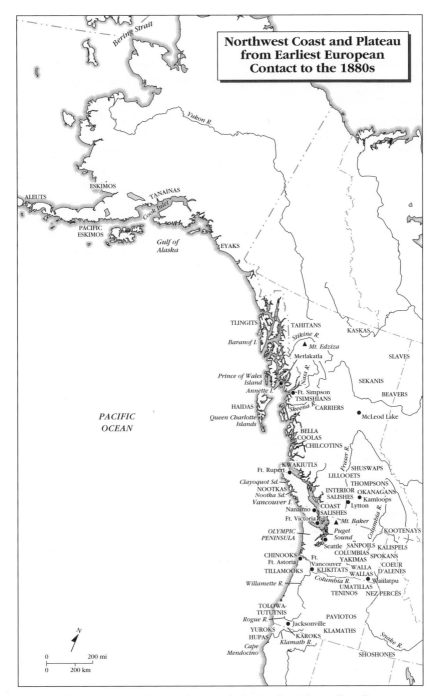

Figure 11.1 The Northwest Coast and plateau from the earliest European contact to the 1880s.

three linguistic subdivisions among the Wakashan-speaking Kwakiutls (Kwakw*a*ka'wakw), who lived on the islands and inlets of the middle coast of British Columbia. On the upper reaches of Dean and Burke channels were the villages of the Bella Coolas (Nuxalk). They formed an isolated enclave amid the Kwakiutls and were culturally similar to their near neighbors, but linguistically they were related to the Coast Salishes from whom they were separated by some distance. The west coast of Vancouver Island and the northern tip of the Olympic Peninsula were the territory of the Nootkas (Nuu-chah-nulth) whose language was distantly related to Kwakiutl. Like all the coastal groups, the Nootkas had developed a culture that was finely adapted to gathering the resources of their maritime environment, but they were the only Native people who hunted the largest of all sea animals – the whale. The rest of the lower coast of British Columbia – the east side of Vancouver Island and the adjacent mainland – and the Washington coast down to the Columbia River was occupied by groups who spoke a variety of Coast Salish dialects. After the arrival of the Europeans the Kwakiutls pushed the Salishes as far south as Cape Mudge on Quadra Island. One Salishan group, the Tillamooks, lived south of the Columbia River on the Oregon coast. Spread along this extensive stretch of coastline there was great linguistic diversity among these groups, with nearly every inlet or valley having its own subdialect. The Coast Salishes were closely related, linguistically and culturally, to the Salishes of the interior from whence they had come. Along the lower Columbia River, from the Dalles to the coast, lived the Chinooks, whose language was quite distinct from the Coast Salishes who surrounded them. The Chinooks were famous, both before and after contact, as middlemen in trade up and down the coast and into the interior. The Oregon coast south of Tillamook territory was occupied by several small but distinct linguistic groups: the Tolowa-Tututnis, who occupied the river valleys from the Umpqua to Smith River, and the Yuroks, Hupas, and Karoks, who spoke different languages but developed similar cultures along the lower reaches of the Klamath River.

Even within the Northwest Coast culture area, the similarities should not obscure the important distinctions among the groups. Some anthropologists have argued that the indigenous cultures were less elaborate and complex from north to south, but such generalizations should not be pushed too hard. There were also significant cultural distinctions between groups that were near neighbors. The cultures of the Haidas and the Tsimshians, for example, were similar but not the same; and there were considerable differences between the Haidas and the Coast Salishes farther south. Both the Haidas and the Tsimshians had matrilineal kinship structures, and in both societies the local group was divided into exogamous clans. At the same time, Haida villages were split into two clans – Eagle and Raven – while Tsimshian groups had three or even four clans – Eagle, Raven, Wolf, and Killer Whale. Or, to take another example, Haida and Tsimshian art shared many common characteristics, but the bold austerity of the figures on Haida poles contrasted sharply with the crowded, fussy groupings on many Tsimshian ones. Among the Coast Salishes, social divisions were not so clearly defined as they were in the northern groups. Kinship tended to be determined patrilineally, and clans did not exist. Coast Salish art was quite different from that of the northern coast. In the eyes of many European beholders, it was also less impressive than Haida art.

If there were cultural variations up and down the coast, there was a quite fundamental division between the coast and the interior peoples. That is not to say that there was not some cultural blending between the coast and the interior. Some villages along the Fraser River were difficult to classify as either Coast or Interior Salish, and the Dalles on the Columbia was an important point of contact between the coast and plateau groups. Archaeological evidence suggests that most coastal groups originally came from the interior and that some, like the Tlingits and Coast Salishes, were comparatively recent arrivals. Once on the coast the Indians lived off a seasonally abundant maritime environment and evolved a complex social structure, elaborate and opulent ceremonies, and a highly stylized art form. East of the coast mountains, the natural environment was less prolific and the population was much smaller. In order to gather the resources of the land, the people had to be more mobile. Partly as a consequence of their mobility, the social organization of the interior peoples was looser and, in comparison with the coastal groups, their ritual and material culture appeared less elaborate.

A number of Athapaskan-speaking groups inhabited the northern interior of the region. The Tahltans, Kaskas, Slaves, Sekanis, Beavers, Carriers, and Chilcotins were the most important of these. The Plateau country of southern British Columbia and northern Washington was the territory of Interior Salish–speaking groups: the Shuswaps (Secwepemcs), Lillooets, Thompsons, Okanagans, Columbias, Sanpoils, Kalispels, Spokans, and Coeur d'Alenes. In the far east of the region, the Kootenays spoke a distinct language that was not closely related to any of the major linguistic stocks. To the south of the Interior Salish groups, in the Columbia basin country, the Klikitats, Teninos, Yakimas, Umatillas, Walla Wallas, and Nez Percés all spoke Sahaptian tongues. The arid lands of central Oregon were most sparsely populated by the Paviotsos, who were linguistically related to the Shoshones farther east and, in the south, by the Klamaths, who spoke a separate language.

All of these interior groups subsisted on fishing and hunting. The annual salmon runs up the river systems provided a major source of food which was supplemented by hunting land mammals, such as elk, deer, and antelope. Southern Plateau groups also dug the roots of wild turnip and the onion-like camas plant. Subsistence required considerable seasonal movement. Plateau people spent the winters in protected valleys, living in earthen-roofed pit houses. During summer they moved about the higher elevations or camped at fishing places and lived in more temporary lodges.

The basic distinction between coast and interior should not obscure the great cultural variety among the inland groups. Those interior Indians who were in contact with the coast had absorbed some features of the coastal cultures. The Chilcotins, for example, had a version of the potlatch ceremony that was typical of the coastal groups. Farther east, by contrast, many aspects of Kootenay or Nez Percé culture were similar to features of the cultures of the Plains Indians, with whom they made contact during their journeys across the Rockies to hunt buffalo. The acquisition of horses from the Plains in the early eighteenth century had brought major changes to these groups. The profound impact of the horse on the Plateau cultures has been likened to the effect of the automobile on North America in the twentieth century.[1] The Indians became more mobile, adopted hide tipis and buckskin clothing, and their diet changed from being largely fish to mostly the flesh of land animals.

Prior to contact, all of these Native peoples were traders. As groups exchanged goods with near neighbors, chains of trade were formed up and down the coast and most coastal people, especially those who lived at the mouths of the major rivers, bartered with clients in the interior. Scarce and specialized items were particularly valued in trade. Dentalium, a shiny, tusk-shaped shell that was found on the northern coast, was greatly prized by the Yuroks in the far south of the region. The Nootkas gathered the shells, and they were traded south to the Yuroks who used them as a standard measurement of value. Less well known is the precontact trade in

---

[1] Carlos A. Schwantes, *The Pacific Northwest: An Interpretative History* (Lincoln, Nebr., 1989), 34.

obsidian. A volcanic glass valued for its cutting qualities, obsidian could be found in only a limited number of locations in the region. Yet it was widely distributed through trade. Obsidian from eastern Oregon, for example, has been found as far north as Namu on the central British Columbia coast, while that from Mt. Edziza on the Stikine River was scattered north to the headwaters of the Yukon and south to Burke Channel.[2] A host of other trade goods, from eulachon oil to elk hides, and from horses to human beings, were exchanged. Along with the trade in material goods and wealth items, cultural traits were also transferred from one group to another.

No culture is static and all these indigenous cultures were evolving at the time of European contact. This change was a source of strength. Far from being vulnerable and brittle, most of these Native cultures were flexible and adaptive during the early years of contact. The people of the Northwest met the newcomers on their own terms and molded the European presence to suit their own needs and priorities. As elsewhere in North America, the Native cultures remained dominant during the early period of contact and trade in the Northwest. The first Europeans who came among these people were looking for new worlds to explore and exploit. What they found was an old world where the cultures were vigorous and the people were confident in their own traditions.

THE COMING OF EUROPEANS

When Europeans first came to the Northwest they were stretched to the limit, as they grasped at the outer reaches of imperial expansion. Whether they came by sea or land, their approach to the coastline was tentative and uncertain. Stories on the coast tell of drift voyages from China and Japan, but the first documented approach from the Old World was by the Russians in the north. In 1741 Vitus Bering, having earlier found the strait that separates Asia from America, was the first European to enter the Gulf of Alaska. By the time his men returned to Kamchatka in 1742, they had acquired hundreds of sea otter pelts that fetched high prices in northern China. Before the end of the century, as many as a hundred Russian trading expeditions came to the coast. Most of these were small, private operations. The voyages became longer as the *promyshlenniki* (fur traders)

---

[2] Roy L. Carlson, "Prehistory of the Northwest Coast," in *Indian Art Traditions of the Northwest Coast,* ed., Carlson (Burnaby, 1983), 22–3.

penetrated farther eastward along the Aleutian Islands, the Alaska Peninsula, and the islands and coast of the Gulf of Alaska. Seasonal settlements were established at river mouths or in sheltered bays. Permanent settlements were not founded until the 1780s. Thus the Native people of Alaska and the Aleutian Islands were the first to be drawn into the fur trade, and the Russians had a lead of three decades over other European nations in exploiting the area.

Although it was slower to get underway, the fur trade was most intense farther south, between the Columbia River and the Queen Charlotte Islands. Responding to Russian activity in the north, the Spanish sent a series of expeditions up the coast from San Blas, Mexico, beginning in 1774. The first contact with the Native people in this area occurred when Juan Pérez met a group of Haidas off the northwest point of Langara Island in July of that year. Although this initial encounter was fleeting, it was a harbinger of things to come. The Indians paddled around the Spanish vessel throwing feathers on the water. They could not be convinced to go aboard, but when their desire to trade overcame their fear of the strangers, the exchange of goods began. The Spanish offered clothes, beads, and knives, and in return the Haidas traded some sea otter furs and a variety of handmade articles, including mats, hats, plates, spoons, ornately carved wooden boxes, and what appear to have been chilcat blankets.[3] Pérez and the crew of the *Santiago* spent two days in the area, and they left without setting foot on land. The Spanish expedition later made contact with another group of Indians in the vicinity of Nootka Sound, but again no one landed and Pérez was vague about the exact location of the meeting.

European contact with the coast south of latitude 54°40″ was not renewed until the spring of 1778, when the greatest navigator of them all, Captain James Cook, arrived at Nootka Sound, on the west coast of Vancouver Island, and spent a month refitting his vessels. Cook was the first European to set foot on the middle coast and, more importantly, his was the first extended encounter with the Native people of the area. Cook and his men established contact with the inhabitants of the summer village of Yuquot, or Friendly Cove as it would later be known by Europeans. Relations between the British sailors and the Nootka Indians were amicable and based on a good deal of mutual respect. Trade was a daily occurrence, and the crew members were impressed with the astuteness of

---

3 Tomásde la Peña and Juan Crespi, diaries, July 20 and 21, 1774, in *The California Coast: A Bilingual Edition of Documents from the Sutro Collection*, ed. Donald C. Cutter (Norman, Okla., 1969), 159–61 and 229.

the trading Indians. It was immediately clear to Cook that his Yuquot hosts had assumed the role of middlemen and were controlling the trade at the vessels, particularly when other groups of Indians attempted to gain direct access to the new source of wealth. A variety of items changed hands and, although they did not know it at the time, the most valuable articles that the seamen traded from the Indians were the pelts of the sea otter. Cook and the members of his crew recorded a great deal of accurate and valuable information about the Nootka Indians and their way of life, but the revelation that was to have the greatest impact on the history of the coast was of the prices that the sea otter furs fetched when the expedition stopped at Canton (Guangzhou) on the return voyage.

THE FUR TRADE

The appearance, in 1784, of the published account of Cook's third voyage triggered the second round of commercial development in the Northwest. Lieutenant James King drew attention to the profits to be made on furs in China, and he gave some specific advice on how to organize a trading expedition to the Northwest Coast.[4] When the British fur-trading vessel named the *Sea Otter,* under the command of James Hanna, arrived at Nootka Sound the following year, the rush for pelts was on. By the early 1790s, as many as twenty-one vessels would be on the coast during the summer trading season.

The development of the fur trade in the early years was facilitated by the continued exploration of the coastline. Cook's visit had been a reconnaissance, and other vessels followed to continue the work. Captain George Vancouver, who as a midshipman on the *Resolution* had learned his navigation from the master mariner, returned to the coast in 1792 to complete the work that Cook had begun. Over three successive summers, Vancouver surveyed the intricate coastline from Baja California in the south to Cook Inlet in the north. He charted an accurate delineation of the foreshore "through all the various turnings and windings"[5] and in the process revealed what did exist as well as what did not. He established major points of geography, such as the insularity of Vancouver Island, and, although his

---

[4] James Cook and James King, *A Voyage to the Pacific Ocean . . . Performed under the Direction of Captains Cook, Clerke, and Gore, in His Majesty's Ships the Resolution and Discovery. In the Years 1776, 1777, 1778, 1779 and 1780* (London, 1784), 3:438–40.

[5] George Vancouver, *A Voyage of Discovery to the North Pacific Ocean and Round the World 1791–1795,* ed. W. Kaye Lamb (London, 1984), 1:182.

critics would still quibble, he virtually eliminated the possibility of a navigable northwest passage connecting Europe with the Orient.

What Vancouver was unable to find from the sea, others would discover by land. In the summer of 1793, in a tiny notch in Dean Channel called Elcho Harbour, there was what one scholar has called a historic "near miss."[6] On the night of June 4 Vancouver's boat crew rested near the mouth of Elcho Harbour. The next day they examined the small inlet before proceeding down Dean Channel, leaving the spot that another European traveler, coming from the opposite direction, would reach a few weeks later. The North West Company explorer, Alexander Mackenzie, had left Fort Chipewyan in the Athabasca Country in October 1792, wintered over at the junction of the Peace and Smoky Rivers, and set out in May 1793 on a journey toward the Pacific Ocean. Mackenzie drove his men hard and traveled fast. He reached tidewater at Bentinck Arm on July 20 and two days later, on July 22, 1793, he wrote the terse inscription "from Canada, by land," on a rock on the eastern side of the entrance to Elcho Harbour. He was standing where Vancouver had been just six weeks earlier. The Indians described to Mackenzie how Vancouver had left his ship off to the southwest and come to their village in a small boat. The two Europeans had missed each other, but for the Native people, although they did not yet know the significance of these events, the connection had been made.

Vancouver and Mackenzie represented the two lines of development in the fur trade west of the Rockies. The maritime fur traders were engaged in a triangular trade that brought them from the home port to the Northwest Coast with goods to trade to the Indians for sea otter pelts that were then taken to China to exchange for tea, spices, and silk. This commerce was initially dominated by British vessels, but, by the early 1790s, most of the trading captains were Americans out of Boston. By the turn of the nineteenth century, the peak years of the maritime fur trade had passed, and it was to be superseded by the land-based trade, mostly operated by large companies.

In 1799 the Russian government, in an effort to impose order on the trade, established the joint-stock Russian American Company which was granted a monopoly to exploit the fur resources of the far north. There followed a period of southward expansion. New Archangel (Sitka) was

---

[6] Ibid., 3:931; see also Alexander Mackenzie, *The Journals and Letters of Sir Alexander Mackenzie*, ed. W. Kaye Lamb (Cambridge, 1970), 375–6.

founded in Tlingit territory in 1799, and it quickly became the center of the company's trade. By 1800 three-quarters of the company's sea otter pelts came from Sitka, and in 1808 Sitka was made the colonial capital.[7] The company extended its operations even farther south when it established Fort Ross near San Francisco Bay in 1812 to trade and grow food for the Alaska settlements, but Alaska was always the focus of its attention. The trade was better organized during this phase, though the Russians had not overcome the serious problems of supply and communications. After the company was granted a second charter in 1821, it concentrated on its northern enterprise and made some effort to tap the fur resources of the interior of Alaska. This consolidation in the north was partly in response to new competition in the south.

Within a few years of Mackenzie's transcontinental exploration, the Montreal-based North West Company was following up on his discoveries. Simon Fraser established the first permanent fur-trading post west of the Rockies and south of Russian America at McLeod Lake in 1805. After founding other forts in the north, Fraser followed the river that now bears his name to the sea. It proved to be neither the Columbia as he had expected, nor a satisfactory route to the sea as he had hoped. Another Nor'Wester, David Thompson, taking a more southerly route reached the mouth of the Columbia River in 1811 and found an American fort under construction. The attention of the United States had been drawn to the Northwest when the overland expedition of Meriwether Lewis and William Clark, which had reached the Pacific in November 1805, returned to the east and publicized their adventure. John Jacob Astor established Fort Astoria at the mouth of the Columbia as the western headquarters of his Pacific Fur Company. The fort was quickly acquired by the North West Company during the war of 1812, and it was renamed Fort George. The Montreal company now had control of the Pacific slope and a viable outlet to the sea.

It was not until after the amalgamation of the North West Company and the Hudson's Bay Company in 1821 that the fur resources of the area were systematically exploited. Under the general direction of Governor George Simpson, the Hudson's Bay Company's enterprise west of the Rockies was managed by John McLoughlin from his headquarters at Fort Vancouver. A chain of forts was established both on the coast and in the

---

[7] James R. Gibson, *Imperial Russia in Frontier America: The Changing Geography of Supply of Russian America, 1784–1867* (New York, 1976), 10.

interior, and later in the 1830s the company ran vessels up and down the coast as it continued its efforts to eliminate competitors.

There were important differences between the early maritime fur trade and the later land-based trade. The trading captains who came from the Pacific were transitory visitors. They came to the coast to do business and, when the transactions were complete, they left as soon as they could. Individually, their influence was as fleeting as their presence. The Russian traders, and later, the Hudson's Bay Company men stayed for longer periods, built permanent forts, and established more sustained relations with the Indians. Yet they were few in number, and, isolated in their little enclaves, their influence was much more limited than they were willing to admit. While the logistics at the European end of the maritime and land-based fur trade may have differed, the role of the Native people in each form of trade was much the same.

Some of the first maritime fur traders, although their objectives were primarily commercial, still cloaked themselves in Cook's mantle by expressing an interest in discovery. But it was the search for profit that sent the traders to the farthest reaches of the Pacific. At first the prospects looked good. When James Hanna took 560 sea otter furs to Canton in 1785 and sold them for 20,000 Spanish dollars, other merchants quickly calculated the wide differential between outlay and income.[8] This initial enthusiasm was shortlived, however, as the margins in the supercargos' account books became tighter and tighter. The backers of maritime fur-trading expeditions soon found that the Canton market, where sea otter pelts were a luxury item, was easily saturated, and prices fell accordingly. Even more disconcerting was the rapid increase in the price that had to be paid for furs on the Northwest Coast.

Contrary to the expectations of some early traders who had not read Cook carefully enough, the Indians were not simple-minded savages who would part with dozens of furs for a few trinkets. Rather, they were experienced, astute traders who knew all about margins of profit and how to drive a hard bargain. Some scholars have argued that Native people in other parts of North America were not motivated by profit when they engaged in trade. Instead the exchange of goods served a ritual function in establishing and maintaining political alliances and therefore price was not influenced by market factors.[9] The evidence from the Northwest Coast, however, over-

---

[8] David Mackay, *In the Wake of Cook: Exploration, Science and Empire, 1780–1801* (London, 1985), 65.
[9] A. Rotstein, "Trade and Politics: An Institutional Approach," *Western Canadian Journal of Anthropology* 3 (1972), 1–28.

whelmingly suggests that the price of furs was determined by supply and demand as well as by competition. Giving away wealth to establish prestige was an important feature of the Northwest Coast cultures, and the potlatch gave these groups a particular incentive to acquire a surplus. Thus the profit motive was not confined to Europeans. As one maritime fur trader put it, "we found to our cost" that the Northwest Coast Indians "possessed all the cunning necessary to gains of mercantile life."[10]

The first traders to arrive on some parts of the coast found that the Native people were exuberant and unrestrained sellers. On July 2, 1787, Captain George Dixon arrived at a bay on the northern Queen Charlotte Islands that would later be known as Cloak Bay. Once the Haidas had overcome their initial reticence there followed a scene "which absolutely beggars all description." The crew was "so overjoyed, that we could scarcely believe the evidence of our senses," because the Indians were falling over themselves to trade their cloaks and furs: "they fairly quarrelled with each other about which should sell his cloak first; and some actually threw their furs on board if nobody was at hand to receive them." In half an hour, Dixon obtained 300 furs.[11] But, alas for those who followed, such scenes were seldom repeated. The fur trade quickly settled down into a regular pattern, and it was a pattern of trade over which the Native people exercised a great deal of control. Whatever the preconceptions and intentions of European traders, once they got to the coast, it was indigenous demands that had to be met before furs changed hands.

Europeans had to modify their trading methods to suit the people of the coast. Captains quickly realized that the initial practice of coasting along the shoreline and expecting the Native people to paddle out to a moving vessel to trade would have to be abandoned. They had to anchor at Native villages and, subject to Native notions of time, spend longer and longer negotiating deals. Native ceremonial – singing, dancing, and the display of wealth – was usually a part of trading encounters and often irritated captains anxious to be on their way. But it was necessary to spend more time on the coast to get enough furs to make the trip to China profitable. Despite their preference for the Hawaiian climate and society, fur traders eventually found it necessary to winter over on the Northwest Coast. Even

---

[10] John Meares, *Voyages Made in the Years 1788 and 1789, from China to the North West Coast of America* (London, 1790), 141–2.
[11] George Dixon, *A Voyage Round the World; but more Particularly to the North West Coast of America: Performed in 1785, 1786, 1787 and 1788 in the "King George" and "Queen Charlotte,"* . . . (London, 1789), 199–201.

the land-based fur traders, for whom the pressure of time was less immediate, had quotas to meet. They too expressed frustration when Native
people devoted more time to winter dancing than to hunting for furs. At
the same time, they recognized that their ability to change such customs
was very limited.[12]

Nor did Native people merely control the formalities of the trade.
While ritual was important to Native people and integral to trading
relations, they were also concerned with profits. Maritime fur traders who
came back to the coast for a second or third time found that the prices
demanded by the Native people had doubled or tripled since their first
visit. Particularly in the early 1790s, as more and more traders came to the
coast, the Native people pressed for higher and higher prices, and European traders realized that the quick profits of the early years were no
longer attainable. When the Hudson's Bay Company began its trading on
the coast after 1821, its officers intended to impose their prices as quickly
as possible. But Northwest Coast people knew as much about "oeconomy"
as the governor of the company, George Simpson. Company traders
thought that the Indians demanded extravagant prices, and Simpson described them as "tiresome in their bargaining."[13] It did not take company
men long to realize that the high prices on the coast also affected the cost
of furs along the chains of intergroup trade into the interior. Instead of
trading at the forts in their own territory, the inland peoples would sell
their furs to coastal middlemen if they could obtain a higher price. As
long as the trade routes remained open and the coastal market was stimulated by competition, the interior peoples also retained a degree of independence. The "Columbia enterprise," as the company referred to its operations west of the Rockies, was one that involved astute traders on both
sides. It was not until toward the end of the fur-trade period, in the
1840s, that the Hudson's Bay Company was able to establish even the
semblance of control over the fur market.

Indigenous traders were exacting not only about price, but also about
the nature and quality of goods that they took in return for furs. As they
proved to be in other parts of North America, Native people were discrimi-

[12] See, for example, James Douglas, to Governor, Deputy Governor and Committee, October 18,
   1838, in *The Letters of John McLoughlin from Fort Vancouver to the Governor and Committee, First Series,
   1825–1838*, ed. E. E. Rich (London, 1941), 238. The general point is developed more fully in
   Robin Fisher, *Contact and Conflict: Indian-European Relations in British Columbia, 1774–1890* (Vancouver, 1977), 42–44.
[13] Sir George Simpson, *Narrative of a Journey around the World during the Years 1841 and 1842* (London,
   1847), 2:192; see also Fisher, *Contact and Conflict,* 26–33.

nating consumers. Although their demands changed over time, they were not whimsical or inconsistent, as some have argued. The hottest item in the early years of the maritime fur trade was "toes," or rough iron chisels. These were goods that had an equivalent in the recipient society and were relatively scarce. Northwest Coast people could immediately see both the use and the value of metal cutting tools. Yet they were not indiscriminate consumers even of these goods. Iron that was brittle, flawed, or could not sustain a cutting edge was usually rejected as unsatisfactory by Native traders. Nor did the demand for iron chisels last forever. As hundreds poured in, the market quickly became saturated, they lost their value, and Native traders began to demand other items in return for furs. When the demand for metal declined, cloth, clothing, and blankets became important trade items. In particular the demand for blankets remained fairly constant, and they became a staple in the trade. Native people also acquired other tastes. A taste for rum, smoking tobacco, and molasses developed, and firearms began to change hands. But the acceptance of all goods remained subject to quality. Even the famous Hudson's Bay Company blanket was rejected when it was not heavy enough. European captains, and later Hudson's Bay Company officers, had to keep up with changing demands or they would leave emptyhanded.

The old stereotype of European traders getting a stack of furs for a few beads and trinkets was never true of the fur trade on the West Coast. There were fads, but, as in all economies, they were usually shortlived. Native traders would also accept items as presents that were not a part of the actual trading deal. These baubles were offered to sweeten relations as part of the negotiations that preceded trade. When it came to a trading transaction, however, Native people were tough-minded dealers: they knew what they wanted and were determined to get it.

Native people were able to assert and maintain control over the fur-trade economy largely because of their ability to manipulate competition. From the early 1790s through to the 1840s, no European had a monopoly over the fur trade; when Indians did not get a satisfactory offer from one fur trader they could usually turn to another. Competition was always a factor on the coast, and when the fur trade moved into the interior, Indians there could trade with coastal groups when the price offered locally was not high enough. During the peak years of the maritime fur trade, when activity was concentrated at a few villages on Vancouver Island and the Queen Charlotte Islands, and there were several vessels on the coast at once, Indians could move from one trader to another comparing prices and bargaining to force them upwards. As one captain put it, "the Indians are sufficiently cunning to derive all possible advantage from competition, and will go from one vessel to another, and back again, with assertions of offers made to them, which have no foundation in truth, and showing themselves to be well versed in the tricks of the trade as the greatest adepts."[14] Richard Cleveland's barely concealed annoyance was shared by many European traders who paid the price of dealing in a competitive market.

Hudson's Bay Company managers, following their policy in other areas after 1821, intended to establish a monopoly west of the Rockies. They faced competition from two directions: in the southeast from American trappers and in the west from other coastal traders. The company quickly eliminated the first, but had much more trouble with the second. American mountain men came to the Rockies to gather furs and were particularly active in the Snake River area. They were trappers rather than traders and therefore competed directly for the fur resources with both the Indians and the Hudson's Bay Company. The mountain men worked either individually or in small groups trapping through the winter and then met at a prearranged rendezvous in the summer to exchange their furs for goods sent west by pack train. The company adopted a method that it had used in other frontier zones by sending a series of expeditions into the Snake country through the 1820s with the objective of laying the area waste of furs and thereby excluding the rival trappers. By the end of the decade, that source of competition was virtually eliminated from this southeastern boundary.

It would not be so easy on the Northwest Coast. There the company was thwarted by the competition that persisted through the 1820s and 1830s. Prices at all the company's coastal forts were affected by the visits of American fur-trading vessels, and the Russian American Fur Trading Company to the north also provided some Indians with an alternative market. The Hudson's Bay Company's most important coastal operation north of Fort Vancouver was Fort Simpson, which was established on the Nass River in 1831 and moved to a site on the Tsimshian Peninsula a few years later. Throughout the 1830s, company traders constantly complained in the fort journal about Indians holding out for higher prices because they expected the American vessels would soon be in the area or

---

[14] Richard J. Cleveland, *Voyages and Commercial Enterprises of the Sons of New England* (New York, 1865), 94.

because they knew that they could do better at the Russian forts.[15] Rather than lowering prices west of the Rockies as he had hoped, John McLoughlin had to maintain three different price levels: one in the interior, another on the coast, and a third on the coast when competitors were in the area.[16] By the early 1840s, the company was able to reduce this competition somewhat. An 1839 agreement with the Russians removed them as a source of opposition, and, by contracting to provide the Russian forts with supplies, the Hudson's Bay Company also took an important source of revenue away from American captains. Fewer vessels came to the coast, but they did not disappear entirely. As long as there was any alternative market, the coast Indians would bargain for higher prices, and the effects of their trading acumen were felt as far west as the Rocky Mountains.

Some groups of Native people and their leaders were particularly well placed to manage the fur trade. Often, because of the location of their villages, these Indians became experienced middlemen. They discouraged Europeans from trading with other groups and made sure that outlying Indians brought furs to them rather than trading directly with the vessels or forts. In this way they ensured that as many furs as possible went through their hands, so that they could control the price and, of course, add their own markup.

This is not to say that for the Native people the fur trade was simply a matter of making higher profits. At least as much as in European society, making a good deal was a source of prestige as well as profit. Indeed, among the Indians of the Northwest Coast there was a very close association between wealth on the one hand and prestige and power on the other. So Indian groups and leaders who were dealers in furs did not just increase their wealth, they also became much more powerful.

Perhaps the most famous of these trading Indians were the Chinooks, who lived along the lower reaches of the Columbia River. Indeed, their name was to become almost synonymous with trade. Given their strategic position at the mouth of one of the region's largest rivers, the Chinooks were important middlemen prior to the arrival of Europeans. They controlled the Dalles, a series of rapids upstream where the Columbia had cut

[15] John Work, Journal, February 23, 1835, Journals, 1823–51, British Columbia Archives and Records Service (hereafter BCARS); Fort Simpson, Journal, August 5, 1839, Hudson's Bay Company Archives, Provincial Archives of Manitoba (hereafter HBCA), B-201/a.

[16] J. S. Galbraith, *The Hudson's Bay Company as an Imperial Factor 1821–1869* (Berkeley, Calif., 1957), 138–9.

a deep channel. It was an ideal place for salmon fishing. Interior groups, who had less productive fishing grounds, came in large numbers to trade for salmon. The Dalles became an entrepôt where an increasing variety of trade goods changed hands. The Chinooks also traded up and down the coast. They maintained this traditional middleman role after European traders came to their territory. The Chinook leader, Concomly, became well known to the new traders. When a new language developed to facilitate trade between Indians and Europeans, it was called the Chinook jargon. The origins of this lingua franca are obscure, and it may even have begun to develop prior to contact. The jargon finally included words from many languages, including Chinook, Nootka, French, and English, and it was widely used throughout the region during the fur-trade period.

Other groups and leaders were also prominent traders. Maquinna of Nootka Sound was particularly well known during the early maritime fur-trading period. Maquinna was the name of the ranking leader among the Moachat people, who had one of their summer villages at Yuquot, or Friendly Cove. As the village became a major port of call for European traders, it was clear that Maquinna and his people controlled access by other groups on the west coast of Vancouver Island and also managed a trading network with the Indians who lived near the mouth of the Nimpkish River on the east coast of the island. Maquinna even played a role in international politics. When, in 1792 and 1794, the emissaries of Britain and Spain came to Nootka Sound to negotiate their respective claims to the area, they were guests of Maquinna at elaborate ceremonies in his winter village of Tahsis. Though he was particularly well known to European visitors, Maquinna's position as a trader was by no means unique. Wickaninish, at Clayoquot Sound, exercised similar control over the trade in that area, as did the Haida leaders Cunneah and Kow on the northern Queen Charlotte Islands, and Kotlean of the Sitka Tlingits.

Though the principles were the same, the pattern was slightly different for the land-based fur trade. Once a fort was built, a group of local Indians would set up their village close by and assert themselves as middlemen. These Indians were known as "home guards" by company men, who looked upon them with mixed feelings because of the impact that they had on prices at the fort. At Fort Simpson, for example, several Tsimshian groups moved their village to the fort and under successive leaders, each named Legaic, established control over the trade. Legaic maintained a tight monopoly over the Tsimshian-speaking Gitksan people of the upper Skeena River, which he backed up with armed force when necessary.

Controlling the powerful Haidas was less easy, but often they too had to trade through the Tsimshians rather than directly with the fort. Legaic's trading rights were a rich privilege that enabled him to enhance his prestige within his own group and his power over others. Native traditions record at least one occasion when he was able to defeat a threat to his life by humiliating his rivals with his great wealth.[17]

Indian assertiveness was also evident at a more personal level, in the marriages between Native women and company traders. The first European visitors to the coast, particularly in the north, commented on the power and authority of Native women. When fur traders became more permanent residents, as happened elsewhere in western Canada, Indian women sought marriage alliances with them for their own good reasons.[18] It made economic sense for an Indian woman to establish a kinship relation with a company trader, and they often assumed important roles as mediators between the two ethnic groups. The marriage of John Kennedy, a senior trader at Fort Simpson, to a daughter of Legaic was one of these mutually beneficial alliances. It was part of a pattern whereby Legaic married his daughters to the leaders of Indian groups with whom he traded. Now he was bringing the leader of a new, and particularly wealthy, "tribe" into his family. From the company's point of view it was only logical, as Legaic rose to preeminence, to forge a close personal connection with him. Such marriages were clearly good business, but often they were also based on strong affection, and many were lasting relationships rather than temporary liaisons. The children of such marriages formed a mixed-blood society that was smaller, but no less significant, than the Métis one at Red River. Thus fur-trade marriages and the families that resulted were another measure of the reciprocity of interethnic relations.

THE IMPACT OF TRADE

Partly because they were a controlling influence over the fur trade, most Native groups also remained in control of their cultures through this early contact period. Within their own world, they continued to be confident of themselves and their ways of life. If there was dependence during the fur-

[17] Fisher, *Contact and Conflict*, 46.

[18] This argument has been developed in detail in books that focus on the Prairies but also cite some examples from west of the Rockies. See Sylvia Van Kirk, *"Many Tender Ties": Women in Fur Trade Society in Western Canada, 1670–1870* (Winnipeg, 1980); and Jennifer S. H. Brown, *Strangers in Blood: Fur Trade Company Families in Indian Country* (Vancouver, 1980).

trade phase, it was mutual dependence. Indians began to rely on some European goods, but Europeans relied on the Indians to provide the furs that were essential to their economic success. Even the Russians in the north, for all that they exploited the Aleuts, had to rely first on them and later on the Tlingits to acquire furs. Often European traders depended on the Indians for their very survival. Some maritime expeditions and, on occasions, the inhabitants of company forts would have starved without the Indians to supply food. "Reciprocity" would therefore seem to be a better word than "dependence" to describe the nature of Native-European relations prior to the late 1840s.

Certainly the Native people cannot be said to have been conquered; although later, in the context of litigation on the land question, some Europeans would make the case that, by setting up forts, the fur traders had conquered the Indians. This argument would have more to do with politics than history.[19] Maritime fur traders were transient visitors who came to the coast in small numbers and in little vessels, while land-based traders were isolated and vulnerable in forts that could easily be destroyed. Both sides in the fur-trading relationship realized that killing potential customers was not a good way to do business. As John McLoughlin so clearly put it in 1843, "Is it not self-evident we will manage our business with more economy by being on good terms with the Indians than if at variance."[20] Although the possibility of interethnic misunderstanding was great, both sides were interested in keeping hostility to a minimum. There were individual acts of violence and a few attacks on fur-trading vessels, but they were the exception rather than the rule. F. W. Howay argued that attacks on trading vessels were common, but in the end he could only provide a few concrete examples, several of which are based on dubious evidence.[21] After the establishment of the land-based fur trade, there were few major Indian attacks on forts west of the Rockies. The Indians accepted the existence of trading posts out of self-interest, rather than because they were overawed with the power of the Europeans.

All of this is not to say that the indigenous cultures were unaltered by

[19] Canada, Parliament, Senate, *Journals,* 16th Parl., 1st sess., 1926–7, Appendix to the Journals of the Senate . . . Special Joint Committee of the Senate and House of Commons Appointed to Inquire into the Claims of the Allied Indian Tribes of British Columbia . . . , *Report and Evidence* (Ottawa, 1929), vii.

[20] John McLoughlin to the Governor, Deputy Governor and Committee, November 15, 1843, in *The Letters of John McLoughlin from Fort Vancouver to the Governor and Committee, Second Series, 1839–1844,* ed. E. E. Rich (London, 1943), 118.

[21] F. W. Howay, "Indian Attacks upon Maritime Traders of the North-West Coast, 1785–1805," *Canadian Historical Review* 6 (1925), 287–309.

the end of the fur-trade period. There was cultural change after the coming of Europeans, just as there had been before. But much of the postcontact change followed preexisting lines. While there was obviously some innovation, the overwhelming impression during this period is of cultural continuity. Traditions that had existed for thousands of years were not suddenly wiped out because some small groups of newcomers who made limited economic demands had arrived on the scene.

Some anthropologists have argued that, on the contrary, Indian cultures were stimulated by the fur trade and that the "golden age" of Northwest Coast Indian culture came after European contact. They point to the fact that the new wealth injected into the Native cultures of the middle coast by the fur trade led to increased artistic and ceremonial life.[22] More efficient metal tools made wood carving easier, and Indian leaders who controlled more wealth could "commission" more artists to work for them. The ethnographer Marius Barbeau once claimed that the totem pole actually originated as a result of the fur trade. Barbeau was wrong on that point. The accounts of early visitors to the coast make it clear that totem poles stood in front of Indian houses at the time of European contact.[23] But poles were carved more frequently and became more elaborate during the fur-trade period. The forests of tall, free-standing totem poles in front of Haida houses in the photographs taken in the late nineteenth century are indicative of many changes brought about by the fur trade. The florescence of carving was a change that involved the elaboration of preexisting forms rather than disruptive innovation.

The potlatch provides a similar and related example, both of the nature of change and of disagreement among scholars. In Northwest Coast cultures the potlatch was a ceremony in which wealth was distributed to guests in order to celebrate the power of the hosts or to signify a rite of passage.[24] Although some writers have raised doubts, the potlatch, like

[22] The point seems to have been first made by Phillip Drucker, "Archaeological Survey on the Northern Northwest Coast," Bulletin 133, Archaeological Paper no. 20, 1943, Bureau of American Ethnology, Smithsonian Institution, 27; but also by J. A. Wike, "The Effect of the Maritime Fur Trade on Northwest Coast Indian Society," Ph.D. dissertation, Columbia University (1951), p. 92; and Wilson Duff, *The Indian History of British Columbia*, vol. 1, *The Impact of the White Man*, Anthropology in British Columbia Memoir no. 5 (Victoria, 1964), 57–8.

[23] Marius Barbeau, "Totem Poles: A By-Product of the Fur Trade," *Scientific Monthly* (December 1942), 507–14; Wilson Duff, "Contributions of Marius Barbeau to West Coast Ethnography," *Anthropologica* 6 (1964), 63–96; and Phillip Drucker, "The Antiquity of the Northwest Coast Totem Pole," *Journal of the Washington Academy of Sciences* 38 (1948), 389–97.

[24] One sentence cannot begin to explain the complexities of the potlatch, about which there is a vast literature. The best general introduction to the subject is H. G. Barnett, "The Nature of the Potlatch," in *Indians of the North Pacific Coast*, ed. Tom McFeat (Toronto, 1966), 81–91.

the totem pole, existed at the time of contact, at least among some groups.[25] It became more frequent, more elaborate, and probably more widespread, when the fur trade brought new wealth to Indian societies. Beyond making the point that increased wealth led to more potlatches, however, anthropologists differ widely on the question of why they became more frequent. Few would now agree with Ruth Benedict's notion that this development reflected the megalomaniacal tendencies in Kwakiutl culture.[26] Helen Codere suggests that the potlatch became a substitute for warfare as a means of expressing the competitive drive within some Northwest Coast cultures.[27] Here again, an existing cultural element took on new significance, rather than being replaced with a completely new form.

Obviously the profits of the fur trade were not evenly distributed among Native groups. Patterns of wealth and power ebbed and flowed through the period, as some groups and some individuals benefited more than others. The Moachats of Nootka Sound were important traders in the last two decades of the eighteenth century, but gradually their supply of furs dried up. The trade passed them by, as captains preferred to go to Newitty on the northeast coast of Vancouver Island, where pelts were more plentiful. While the Indians of Nootka Sound fell into relative obscurity as traders, the Haidas offset their declining wealth with other sources of income. During the height of the sea otter trade, they had been among the wealthiest peoples on the coast. With the depletion of the fur-bearing animals, traders moved on to other places, but the Haidas began to cultivate potatoes, which they sold in large quantities. Haida artists produced "curiosities" made of wood and argilite to sell to visiting seamen: a precursor of the tourist trade in Indian artifacts. They likewise began to make canoes for export. The Tlingits also cultivated and sold potatoes. By the 1840s, they were selling them in such large quantities at New Archangel that they were a staple food for the Russians at the fort, and still there were enough left over for export. In these ways, some groups were able to regain some of their lost income as the fur trade declined.

[25] Lewis O. Saum, *The Fur Trader and the Indian* (Seattle and London, 1965), 11; for an early and detailed account of a potlatch see [Bernard Magee], Log of the *Jefferson*, July 9, 1794, University of British Columbia Library; and also Jose Mariño Moziño, *Noticias de Nutka: An Account of Nootka Sound in 1792* (Toronto and Montreal, 1970), 33; and John R. Jewitt, *A Journal Kept at Nootka Sound . . .* (Boston, 1807), 12.

[26] Ruth Benedict, *Patterns of Culture* (Boston, 1934), 222.

[27] Helen Codere, *Fighting with Property: A Study of Kwakiutl Potlatching and Warfare 1792–1930*, Monographs of the American Ethnological Society, no. 18 (Seattle, 1966), 89–97.

While some groups rose and fell, others expanded by pushing weaker peoples aside. The extension of the Kwakiutls as far south as Cape Mudge was in part made possible by the acquisition of new wealth from the fur trade.[28] The trade also led to jockeying for position within some Indian groups. When the nine Tsimshian local groups relocated at Fort Simpson, they were all living at the same place for the first time, so an acceptable order of rank, both of clans and of individuals, had to be established. By virtue of his control over the fur trade, Legaic and his group became preeminent among the Fort Simpson Tsimshians. Disparities in wealth were not new, nor were shifts in the intergroup balance of power. Yet it is equally clear that the fur trade did not simply inject new wealth into Indian societies, it also produced greater inequities. Maquinna and Legaic both became more powerful than they would have been prior to European contact because of their role as fur traders, but at the same time they both had traditional claims to positions of leadership. Lines of continuity with the indigenous past persisted, even through this time of social change.

Not all the changes that occurred within Native cultures through contact and trade were merely a matter of degree. There were also changes of kind. The European newcomers, even if they did so inadvertently, brought factors into play that the Indians could not control quite so easily. Firearms, disease, and the consequent depopulation were all indicative of the down side of European contact. Yet their impact should not be over emphasized. The precise effect of each innovation has to be looked at carefully, and their combined influence must be seen in the context of the overall process of change. Some earlier writers, who subscribed to the "fatal impact" view of Pacific history, tended to exaggerate the negative consequences of European contact.[29] Even F. W. Howay, who was probably the most meticulous student of the maritime fur trade, argued in 1942 that the trade was disastrous because it "seriously dislocated the finely balanced economic and social fabric of the Indians."[30] Nowadays it is necessary to take a somewhat more balanced view.

On the West Coast, as in other parts of the Pacific, European weapons were a good deal less powerful than voyagers assumed at the time and

[28] Herbert C. Taylor, Jr., and Wilson Duff, "A Post Contact Southward Movement of the Kwakiutl," *Research Studies of the State College of Washington* 24 (1956).
[29] The classic statement of the fatal impact idea for the wider Pacific is Allan Morehead, *The Fatal Impact: An Account of the Invasion of the South Pacific 1767–1840* (Harmondsworth, 1968).
[30] F. W. Howay, W. N. Sage, and H. F. Angus, *British Columbia and the United States: The North Pacific Slope from Fur Trade to Aviation* (Toronto, 1942), 13.

some historians have thought since.[31] In and of themselves, firearms did not necessarily confer a great advantage on European fur traders or on those Indian groups who acquired them. The smoothbore, flintlock musket, the weapon that Europeans most relied upon and also traded to the Indians, was not a very efficient, reliable, or accurate gun. Even a good quality musket under ideal conditions was slow to load, awkward to control, and revealed one's presence with the first shot. Trade muskets, however, were poor quality guns, and the damp climate of the Northwest Coast was hardly ideally suited to their use. The Native people already possessed projectile weapons of their own, but most of their fighting was done hand to hand. When it came to fighting at close quarters, the Indians were more experienced and better armed. On the rare occasions when there was concerted hostility between Indians and fur traders, Native people also had the advantages of greater numbers and knowledge of the territory. Firearms were not a major counterweight that tipped the balance of power away from the Indians. Nor was there necessarily a major increase in the level of warfare, either between Indians and Europeans or between different Native groups, in most of the Northwest during the fur-trade period.

The level of violence was greatest in the far north. Through both phases of their operations, the Russian fur traders engendered hostility and resistance among the Native people. During the eighteenth century, along the Aleutian Island chain to the east coast of Alaska, they relied on obtaining furs directly from the Native hunters rather than through middlemen. The Aleuts in particular, who were highly skilled in the tricky business of hunting sea otters on the open water from flimsy kayaks with short harpoons, were forced to gather furs by the Russians. At first pelts were demanded as tribute and hostages taken to enforce payment. These people became virtual serfs and were ruthlessly exploited. Later these practices were replaced by compulsory labor. Prior to contact, the Aleuts had lived in relative isolation. The population was sparse and the small scattered groups were not used to acting in concert, so they were particularly vulnerable to Russian pressure. The Russian fur trade was also unique in the Northwest in that Christianity went hand in hand with commerce. Missionaries of the

---

[31] The argument in this paragraph is developed in more detail in Robin Fisher, "Arms and Men on the Northwest Coast," *BC Studies,* no. 29 (spring 1976), 3–18; for other parts of the Pacific, see Dorothy Shineberg, "Guns and Men in Melanesia," *Journal of Pacific History* 6 (1971), 61–82; and K. R. Howe, "Firearms and Indigenous Warfare: A Case Study," *Journal of Pacific History* 9 (1974), 21–38.

Russian Orthodox Church baptized large numbers of Aleuts, and conversion to Christianity brought them even more under Russian supervision. The coercive Russian system naturally resulted in friction, but during this early period they were able to dominate the Aleuts.

After 1800, however, when the focus of the Russians' trade moved eastward to the Alaska panhandle, they were not able to control the powerful and unruly Tlingits. Living in a richer environment, the Tlingits were more numerous and more warlike than the people of the Aleutian Islands. They could not be exploited as cheap labor. When they did engage in trade, they came to the Russian forts as trading middlemen. The Russians had to pay the Tlingits three to five times as much for furs as they did the Aleuts. The Tlingits quickly gave notice of their fierce independence in other ways. Russian Orthodox missionaries had a much more difficult time among the Tlingits, few of whom were baptized quickly. Part of the Tlingits' objection to the Russian church was their conviction that the Aleuts had become slaves by following missionary teaching. The Tlingits detested the Russian invasion of their territory, and they could put a large and well-organized fighting force into the field. Because of their wealth from trading with Americans, they were well armed with offensive weapons and also wore a form of armor made of hide and wooden slats that provided some protection against Russian firearms. In 1802, three years after it was founded, New Archangel was attacked by a force of 600 Tlingits under their leader Kotlean. The fort was destroyed, 20 Russians and 130 Aleuts were killed, and 3,000 furs were lost. Although the Russians rebuilt their colonial capital in 1804, the antagonism between the Natives and the Russians remained. The following year the Indians struck again; this time a settlement at Yakutat was destroyed and more Russians were killed. The Russian headquarters was threatened in 1809 and again in 1813. Though the level of antagonism declined somewhat after 1820; even as late as 1855 there was a Tlingit attack on New Archangel, which by then had a population of about 1,000.[32] While the hostility between Natives and Russians in the north cannot be denied, it serves to highlight the relative absence of violence on the rest of the coast.

South of Russian territory, Indian attacks on Europeans were the exception rather than the rule. There were few attacks on trading vessels and virtually none on Hudson's Bay Company forts after 1821. For most

---

[32] James R. Gibson, "Russian Dependence upon the Natives of Alaska," in *Russia's American Colony*, ed. S. Frederick Starr (Durham, N.C., 1987), 82–5.

traders, the reciprocal benefits of the trade outweighed the potential for interethnic misunderstanding that is inherent in any contact situation. There was little to be gained by Europeans in turning their big guns on Indian villages, and Native people knew the risks they ran if they destroyed a vessel or fort. When Maquinna and his men attacked the *Boston* and killed almost the entire crew in 1803, the lesson was clear enough. There were many reasons for the attack: accumulated grievances over twenty-five years of dealing with Europeans and an angry exchange between Maquinna and the captain of the *Boston* a few days before the attack. Then there was the dissatisfaction that had developed because the fur trade was already passing Nootka by. After the attack, things only got worse. Nootka Sound was seen as too dangerous, and it was to be two summers before another vessel appeared. As trading captains avoided the area, the Yuquot people faced a declining economy and Maquinna found it less easy to sustain his leadership. Although disparities in wealth increased, the fur trade did not bring new incentives for intergroup conflict, as economic motives had already been powerful in indigenous warfare. Rivalries developed over rights to exploit the trade with Europeans, but at the same time energy expended in warfare could not be devoted to hunting and trading. In short there is no evidence to suggest that, south of Russian territory, there was a massive increase in warfare after contact, or that larger numbers of Indians died violent deaths.

While the level of warfare was something that the Indians could govern, they had little control over the introduction of infectious diseases by Europeans. At different times and in different places smallpox, venereal disease, malaria, respiratory illnesses, tuberculosis, influenza, dysentery, whooping cough, and measles all took their toll among the Native population. Most of these were introduced by Europeans into a population that had little or no immunity when the maladies first struck. Some, like smallpox, arrived about the time of first contact, while others, like measles, were so-called immigrant diseases that came later with settlers.

Smallpox was perhaps the most widespread and certainly one of the most deadly of these diseases. It was introduced by Europeans, though the timing is difficult to establish precisely. It has been suggested that it reached the Northwest as early as 1520, but there is no archaeological or historical evidence to support the contention.[33] It may have spread across

[33] Henry F. Dobyns, *"Their Number Become Thinned": Native American Population Dynamics in Eastern North America* (Knoxville, Tenn., 1983), 13–15.

the continent prior to Europeans arriving in the West and the disease was certainly observed very soon after contact. Smallpox was an extremely contagious epidemic disease, yet it came in a variety of forms of differing potency, and not all Indians who contracted smallpox died from it. Rather than being pervasive, smallpox outbreaks in the region seem to have been widely dispersed in time and place. Smallpox probably arrived on the Northwest Coast in the 1770s. There were other outbreaks on the central coast in 1801, in the north in the mid-1830s, on the Washington coast in 1853, and on the British Columbia coast in 1862.

Other diseases that were less contagious than smallpox may nevertheless have had a greater impact. Venereal disease, for example, was more prevalent, even though the means of transmission was more specific. It may well have been present in some form prior to the arrival of Europeans in the Northwest. There is possible archaeological evidence from California and British Columbia of syphilis going as far back as 500 B.C., and syphilitic skeletal material abounds in eighteenth-century material from Alaska.[34] The problem with skeletal remains, however, is that it is difficult to distinguish venereal syphilis from other treponemal bone infections, such as yaws or endemic syphilis, a nonvenereal disease of childhood. The existence of herbal remedies for venereal disease among some Native groups in the early contact period is also suggestive of precontact origins of the disease. Whether or not it already existed in the area, there can be no doubt that many of the first crewmen to come to the Northwest Coast were already infected with venereal disease and that they passed it on to large numbers of Native people. Although we still do not know whether they brought mostly mild or severe forms of the infection, venereal disease hit the childbearing segment of the population and therefore affected fertility rates.

Other maladies were particularly devastating because, once they were introduced, they persisted year after year. A form of intermittent fever that seems to have been malaria appeared on the southern coast in 1830 and over the next few years exacted a heavy toll. The Chinooks and other groups living on the lower Columbia were devastated during the early nineteenth century. One student of the subject has suggested that the Native population of the lower Columbia had dropped by 80 to 90 percent by 1840.[35] With this, as with other diseases, some of the Native peoples'

---

[34] Brenda J. Baker and George J. Armelagos, "The Origin and Antiquity of Syphilis: Paleopathological Diagnosis and Interpretation," *Current Anthropology* 29 (1988), 715.

[35] Robert T. Boyd, "The Introduction of Infectious Diseases among the Indians of the Pacific Northwest, 1774–1874," Ph.D. dissertation, University of Washington (1985), 304.

own medical practices may have done more harm than good. Taking to a sweat lodge followed by immersion in cold water only hastened the progress of the illness. But the most important point about malaria is that, unlike the epidemic diseases, it became endemic and so had a permanently debilitating effect on the population.

It is beyond dispute that disease caused significant fluctuations in the Native populations and that at least some groups suffered considerable depopulation. Nevertheless, microbes were not the only factor in the increased mortality. The nature of the European presence and the Native response also influenced the death rate. Once again, because the Russian trading system was more disruptive, the impact of disease was greatest in the north. By the end of the eighteenth century, the Aleut population had drastically declined, perhaps by as much as two-thirds. Chinook numbers were heavily depleted, as their territory became a focal point of European trading. That is not to say that there was a precisely one-to-one relationship between the number of Europeans in a particular area and the number of Indian deaths from new diseases. The effects of easily transmitted maladies may even have run well ahead of firsthand European contact. Yet it is fair to assume that more isolated groups suffered less severely from the diseases brought by newcomers.

Given such local variation, estimating the overall demographic impact of disease in the early contact period is very difficult. It has become a kind of numbers game based on very pliable evidence. In large part, the issue turns on the size of the point-of-contact Indian population, which scholars are prone to revise up or down according to their notion of the impact of disease and when the earliest epidemics occurred. The first visitors to the coast provide wildly differing estimates of the population of even a single village. When Cook was at Nootka Sound, estimates by crew members of the population of Yuquot ranged from 500 to 2,000.[36] Subsequent scholars, who reckon the precontact population of the Northwest Coast culture area to have been, say, 200,000, are making what are, at best, well-informed guesses.[37] The evidence on the impact of disease is also spotty and impressionistic. Both syphilis and smallpox result in nasty symptoms and often agonizing deaths, so reactions to even the possibility of their presence among a population were, not unnaturally, more hysterical than scientific. The pock-marked faces seen among the

[36] James Burney, Journal, April 22, 1778, Adm. 51/4528, Public Record Office, London.
[37] See, for example, Robert T. Boyd, "Demographic History, 1774–1874," in *Handbook of North American Indians,* vol. 7, *Northwest Coast,* ed. Wayne Suttles (Washington, D.C., 1990), 135.

Native people in the early contact period are not, in themselves, evidence of pandemics, but rather that some survived even the worst of the introduced diseases. Eighteenth-century observers often took deserted villages to be evidence of population decline rather than seasonal mobility. Accounts in the journals of explorers and fur traders are usually of outbreaks in particular localities, which some scholars have extrapolated to the whole of the Northwest.

Scholarly writing on the subject is therefore littered with words like "probably" and "very likely," as authors build up worst-case scenarios. The geographer James Gibson, for example, tells us, on the one hand, that disease was "rampant" on the Northwest Coast at the beginning of the nineteenth century, but, on the other hand, that the Tlingits were particularly hard hit by smallpox in the late 1830s because the last epidemic had been in either 1779 or 1795 and the new generation had little inbuilt immunity.[38] Thus, smallpox was not rampant in this area, and the time between epidemics may have been enough for the population to rebuild. The literature continues to be overwhelmingly concerned with death rates; there is little discussion of birth rates and the extent to which populations regenerated after an epidemic. The author of the most recent work on the demographic impact of disease in the Northwest explicitly refuses to consider the possibility that a population might rebound after an epidemic.[39] The question of how quickly immunity is built up after people are hit with a disease for the first time also needs to be looked at, as does the nature and impact of medical practice among both Indians and fur traders. What effect did the Hudson's Bay Company program of inoculating Indians against smallpox, beginning in the 1830s, have on the death rate? No doubt, the Indian population declined during the fur trade period, but there is room for a good deal more caution in assessing the precise extent of that decline.

The impact of so-called "virgin soil" diseases was not, of course, confined to demographics.[40] There was both a social and a psychological impact that was not necessarily commensurate with the level of mortality. It has been suggested that one consequence of introduced disease was that individuals were elevated to social positions that they would not otherwise

[38] James R. Gibson, "Smallpox on the Northwest Coast, 1835–1838," *BC Studies,* no. 56 (winter 1982–3), 61 and 66.

[39] Boyd, "Demographic history," 135.

[40] The idea of virgin soil diseases, meaning those against which there is no built up immunity, is developed by Alfred Crosby, "Virgin Soil Epidemics as a Factor in the Aboriginal Depopulation in America," *William and Mary Quarterly,* 3rd series, 33 (1976), 289–99.

have attained. As epidemics left vacancies in the higher social ranks, they were filled by people from the lower orders. For example, there was a fixed number of potlatch positions among the southern Kwakiutls. With the decline in the population, there would have been more positions than men to fill them and a flurry of potlatching as individuals of lower rank scrambled to raise their status.[41] Of course, if the death rate from disease was lower than commonly thought, the rate of social mobility would have been slower. It is also tempting to conclude that, when Native groups faced devastating new diseases that did not appear to be amenable to old beliefs and practices, they were likely to reject those traditional ideas. They "apostatized," as one ethnohistorian has forcefully argued happened among some Indian groups in eastern Canada.[42] The critics of this view have pointed out that other groups reacted in exactly the opposite way. They responded to the threat of disease by blaming it on witchcraft or by reaffirming the power of traditional spirits who, it seemed, had sent these visitations upon the people because they were offended.[43] Blanket explanations of the effect of new diseases on indigenous people will always be unsatisfactory because they obscure the variations and nuances, both between and within groups.

The impact of disease is typical of the culture contact situation generally. The Indian response to contact and trade was complex rather than straightforward. At the end of the season, trading captains or company officers could do some simple addition to see whether they had come out ahead. The effect of their presence among the Native people is less easy to calculate. Certainly the fur trade brought cultural profits and losses along with the economic ones. By the end of the period, the Indians were in some ways better off and in some ways worse off. But then change is always that way. So the question is not whether the Indian cultures had changed, rather it is were the Indians able to cope with the change, and even benefit from it, or were they devastated and demoralized?

While the fur trade may have been a mixed blessing, it certainly was not an unmitigated disaster for most of the Native people. There were exceptions, but, prior to the 1840s, most Indians had a controlling interest in the

---

[41] Codere, *Fighting with Property*, 97; see also Wayne Suttles, "Post-contact Culture Change among the Lummi Indians," *British Columbia Historical Quarterly* 18 (1954), 45.

[42] Calvin Martin, *Keepers of the Game: Indian-Animal Relationships and the Fur Trade* (Berkeley, Calif., 1978), 53.

[43] Bruce Trigger, "Ontario Native People and the Epidemics of 1634–1640," in *Indians, Animals, and the Fur Trade: A Critique of Keepers of the Game*, ed. Shepard Krech (Athens, Ga., 1981), 29–32.

fur-trade economy. Their demands had to be met by European fur traders and, in many ways, the trade was carried on according to indigenous usages that were well established before the newcomers came to the area. Even the Russian fur traders had to admit that they could not dominate the Native people as they hoped. Certainly, they were never able to manage the obstreperous Tlingits upon whom they often depended for their very existence.[44] Throughout the Northwest, the fur trade was not "an unequal trade with a primitive people," rather it was a reciprocal economic relation that Native peoples were able to exploit for their own ends.[45]

Just as the Indians exercised a good deal of control over the economics of the trade, they also kept a grip on their own cultures. To start with, fur traders were merely transitory visitors and, even when they established permanent posts, they were a tiny minority living among overwhelming numbers of Native people. Representatives of a different culture, if they are determined and aggressive enough, can have an influence out of all proportion to their numbers, but fur traders made very limited demands on the Indians. Hudson's Bay Company men clearly understood that, even if they had wanted to, they were not in a position to eradicate, or even modify, deeply ingrained Native customs. They simply lacked the power to force change. Traders came to do business and not to acquire territory, so land was not an issue. It is also significant that, with the exception of the Russians in the north, missionaries met with little success in converting Indians, either spiritually or culturally, during the fur-trade period. Indians were still free to pick and choose from among the cultural elements brought by Europeans and they chose not to accept Christianity.

The first century of European contact, from the 1740s to the 1840s, was a period of nondirected cultural change for most of the indigenous people of the Northwest. The various cultures were strong and vibrant when the Europeans arrived, and the Native people remained confident during this early contact and fur-trading period. The trade enriched the traditional cultures and change tended to run along preexisting lines. The greatest impact that the Europeans had on the Indians was the diseases that they brought with them. There can be little doubt that the Indian population declined, but the effect of disease should not be exaggerated. In the short run, European contact was not a disaster for the Native

[44] James R. Gibson, "The Russian Fur Trade," in *Old Trails and New Directions: Papers of the Third North American Fur Trade Conference*, ed. Carol M. Judd and Arthur Ray (Toronto, 1980), 223.
[45] The quote is from Howay, Sage, and Angus, *British Columbia and the United States*, 12.

people. On the contrary, Native people played a crucial and decisive role in the early postcontact history of the Northwest.

THE COMING OF SETTLERS

That was all to change, however. Throughout most of the Northwest, there were two distinct phases of relations between Natives and Europeans. While there was certainly some inevitability about the way in which the fur trade was replaced by settlement, we should not be seduced into making ahistorical judgements by attributing the consequences of settlement to the earlier era. At the same time, it is likely that, having become used to dealing with Europeans who made limited demands within the reciprocal relations of the fur trade, the Indians were ill-prepared to cope with the upheavals brought by the settlement frontier. But, ready or not, nearly all the Native people of the Northwest would face the effects of this onslaught by the end of the 1880s.

By the beginning of the 1840s, profound developments that would have a drastic effect on the lives of the indigenous people were already underway. The coming of settlers to the Northwest would end the old, interdependent economic and cultural relationship between Indian and European fur traders. Economically, cooperation would be replaced by competition. When settlers replaced fur traders, Indians would have less autonomy. As the Europeans grew in numbers and power, the pace of cultural change quickly outstripped the Native people's capacity to control it. A major transition was about to occur, as contact led to conflict.

The process of settlement began in the south. The vanguard of the settlement frontier was the American pioneers who, beginning in the late 1830s, followed the Oregon Trail to the fertile land of the Willamette Valley. Initially, their presence affected the operations of the Hudson's Bay Company more than it did the Native cultures. The settlers received some assistance from the company when they first arrived, but they soon raised noisy objections to the existence of a British monopoly company in what they saw as American territory. Seeing the writing on the wall, the company established Fort Victoria on Vancouver Island as a potential new site for its western headquarters in 1843. Then, in 1846, its worst fears were realized when the old fur-trading preserve was divided in half by the Oregon Treaty, which established the international boundary at the forty-ninth parallel. The more perceptive of the company's managers on the West Coast had realized the implications of these developments even before they had happened. James Douglas, who was then a rising star at Fort Vancouver, observed as early as 1838 that the interests of settlement and the fur trade "will never harmonize." A settlement colony, he wrote, could only flourish "by establishing a new order of things, while the fur trade must suffer by each innovation."[46] Because he foresaw the extent of the upheavals that would follow, Douglas referred to the agreement between Britain and the United States on the boundary west of the Rockies as a "monstrous treaty."[47]

South of the new border, the new order was becoming well entrenched. As settlers established farms, towns, and businesses, they soon turned their minds to the need for government. One of the distinctions that is often drawn between the United States and British North America is that, in the American West, settlement ran ahead of government, whereas, north of the border, administration was established before settlers arrived. In the Willamette Valley, the settlers joined together in 1843 to form their own, grassroots, local government which lasted until Congress approved a territorial government in 1848. The separate Washington Territory was established five years later, but, whereas Oregon became a state in 1859, Washington did not achieve that distinction until thirty years later.

The Native people, the fur trade, and the Hudson's Bay Company all had a respite in the area north of latitude forty-nine, but it could only be brief. With the establishment of the British colony of Vancouver Island in 1849, farming settlers began to arrive there too. For the first few years, their numbers were small and their influence limited. Yet, as in the Willamette Valley a decade earlier, their coming heralded a set of changes for the Native people unlike anything that they had known during the fur-trade era. The discovery of gold in the Fraser River brought a flood of miners to the area in the summer of 1858 and led to the establishment of the mainland colony of British Columbia in the same year. The two colonies of Vancouver Island and British Columbia were amalgamated in 1866 and, in 1871, British Columbia became a province of Canada.

The territory north of British Columbia remained what it had been: in many ways an exception to the generalizations that can be made about the rest of the Northwest. The Russian fur trade was in decline from the 1840s, as both the supply of, and the demand for, furs dwindled. Al-

---

[46] Douglas to Governor, Deputy Governor and Committee, October 18, 1838, in Rich, *McLoughlin's Letters, First Series*, 242.
[47] Douglas and John Work to Governor and Committee, December 7, 1846, London, Inward Correspondence from HBC Posts, Victoria, 1845–69, A-11/72, HBCA.

though the United States purchased Alaska from the Russians in 1867, the Native people did not have to deal with substantial numbers of European settlers until the Klondike gold rush at the end of the nineteenth century. The process that was underway to the south would eventually come to Alaska, and, when it did, it would not be much different because it was delayed.

South of 54°40″, whether British or American forms were followed, the establishment of government and the evolution of democratic institutions did not mean majority rule. The Native people were simply not consulted. The reciprocity that had characterized the fur-trade frontier was giving way to European domination. Both in government and on the land, growing settler power meant a declining role for the Indians. By the 1850s, European settlers were well established both north and south of the border, and their numbers would continue to grow. The Native people were outnumbered earliest in Oregon and Washington, where there were about 250,000 settlers in 1880. In that year the Indians remained a majority of the British Columbia population, but they were swamped by new immigration in the following decade, when the settler population increased from roughly 25,000 to over 70,000.[48] More important than the cold statistics, however, was the fact that throughout the Northwest the European population was growing quickly, while the Native numbers were dropping.

Settlers not only came in greater numbers, they also had quite different attitudes toward the Native people. Fur traders had tended to view the Indians as primitive partners. They often emphasized the cultural distinctions between Indians and Europeans, but their descriptions were based on considerable familiarity with, and some understanding of, the indigenous way of life. Native rituals, such as the potlatch, or pastimes, like gambling, that would outrage later arrivals to the region were described relatively dispassionately by fur traders. The custom among some Salish groups of flattening the heads of babies, a custom that shocked many European settlers, was compared by one fur trader to the habit among European women of compressing their waist.[49] Even if only out of self-interest, fur traders had at least to be informed about those aspects of Indian culture that had a bearing on trade. For example, since much of the

---

[48] The figures for Oregon and Washington are in Schwantes, *The Pacific Northwest*, 185, and for British Columbia in Fisher, *Contact and Conflict*, 202.

[49] Alexander Ross, *Adventures of the First Settlers on the Oregon or Columbia River . . .* (London, 1849), 99–100.

trading was done with Indian leaders, it was necessary to understand the nature of leadership and to know who were the ranking individuals. The boundaries and the state of relations between different Native groups were also crucial considerations for European traders. Thus, fur traders were more likely to appreciate the distinctions between the various Native cultures of the Northwest, whereas settlers were inclined to lump all Indians together with cultural generalizations. Settlers were more prejudiced than fur traders in the sense that they prejudged Native people and did not modify their views on the basis of frontier experience. Moreover, the settlers were developing an economy that did not depend on the cooperation of the aboriginal inhabitants, so the Indians were seen as a hindrance rather than a help to these new arrivals. The indigenous cultures became merely obstacles to be removed from the path of settlement, and the indigenous people were transformed in the European mind from primitive partners to hostile savages. As attitudes toward the Native people grew more negative, treatment of them became more abusive.

THE CONFLICT OVER LAND

In the face of the settler influx, the Indians would lose their land, their wealth, and their power. The first of these was land. Whether they were miners or farmers, European settlers came to new areas, like the Northwest, because they wanted to acquire land and exploit its resources. They had scant regard and no tolerance for the existing owners, particularly when these owners were seen as an inferior people who, because they appeared to make ineffective use of the land, had little claim to it. The settlers and their governments revealed their attitude to frontier land by the words that they used to describe it. In the United States, the western territory owned by the Indians was called "free land," while in British colonies areas occupied by indigenous peoples were often called "waste land." The words were different, but they spoke of similar views.

In the Northwest, the conflict over land was intensified by geography. Although the area is a vast one, the amount of fertile land is comparatively small and farm land becomes scarcer from south to north. Of British Columbia's total area of approximately 95 million hectares, for example, only about 3 percent is capable of growing crops and perhaps another 14 percent can sustain livestock.[50] Not only was good land limited, but the

50 A. L. Farley, *Atlas of British Columbia: People, Environment, and Resource Use* (Vancouver, 1979), 80.

locations that were most attractive to settlers were often exactly where the indigenous population was concentrated: the river deltas on the coast and the valleys of the lakes and rivers in the interior. In these places, the Indians possessed, and the settlers coveted, the same land for similar reasons. And, partly because the conflict was concentrated, there could be little doubt about its outcome.

By 1880 the Indians were dispossessed throughout most of the Northwest by a process that was slightly different on either side of the international boundary. The encounter began in the south, where Euro-American settlers came first because the climate was more temperate and the land was more fertile. Government officials in Oregon and Washington often had to deal with the clash over land after the fact, when settlers had already moved onto Indian property, and they were inclined to adopt wholesale measures. The first governors of the two territories, Joseph Lane and Isaac Stevens, both had a military background, having served in the Mexican War. They saw the clash over land in the Northwest more in terms of removing a threat than solving a problem. Once Oregon Territory was established in 1849, local officials were instructed to remove all the coast Indians to locations in the interior. The policy was unworkable, because the coastal groups resisted the move and the interior Indians did not want to relinquish their land to accommodate the displaced. In 1851, nineteen treaties were made with various groups along the Oregon coast and in the Willamette Valley. The Indians would not agree to removal, so the treaties provided for small reservations in local territory. Because these treaties contravened government policy, they were not ratified by Congress. The whole process only succeeded in creating much dissatisfaction among the beleaguered coastal groups.

When Washington Territory was established in 1853, Stevens continued making treaties to extinguish Indian title to the land and to define reservations. Stevens has been described as "the wrong man, in the wrong place, at the wrong time."[51] In addition to being governor of the new territory, he led a Pacific Railroad survey party into the area and was clearly identified with the forces encouraging settlement. He was an ambitious man, anxious to make his mark. He intended to move quickly and had little interest in real negotiations with the Native people. As a result he only succeeded in making a bad situation worse. He began on the coast

[51] Kent Richards, "Isaac I. Stevens and Federal Military Power in Washington Territory," *Pacific Northwest Quarterly* 63 (1972), 86.

with a series of councils in December 1854 and January and February 1855. These meetings never lasted more than a day or two, and in most cases the treaty was drawn up before the discussion began. Chinook jargon was used to convey complicated provisions, and reluctant Indian leaders were not given the time to consider what they were signing. In return for ceding their lands, they were to be given goods and instruction in useful arts, such as agriculture, and were to be placed on reservations. These reservations were as yet unsurveyed, but there were to be as few as possible so that different, and often diverse, groups would have to be lumped together on the same plot of land. Many Indian leaders left their meeting with Stevens feeling very disgruntled, and their frustration over his treatment of them soon boiled over.

In the interior some of the details may have been different, but both the process and the result were much the same. One of the largest cessions of Indian land in the Northwest occurred at the Walla Walla council, beginning in late May 1855. Stevens called on the Yakimas, Cayuses, Walla Wallas, and Nez Percés to meet with him to discuss a treaty, knowing that many of their leaders were determined not to give up their land. Here, too, he simply overrode Indian objections to confinement on limited reservations. He was particularly successful in playing pliant Indian leaders off against those who wanted to resist making a treaty. When they hesitated, Stevens, with his customary tact, warned the holdouts that, if they did not sign the treaty, "they will walk in blood knee deep." It has been argued that some groups only signed the treaty because they had already decided to drive the settlers out by force.[52] After the council was over, Stevens went on to other meetings to "negotiate" other treaties, while the Indians were left to reflect upon the fact that they had signed away over four million hectares of land in return for a few reservations. Because of the speed with which Stevens had proceeded, many Indian groups were not included in any of his treaties and they, not unreasonably, felt that they had not relinquished anything. In other instances he assumed the right of individual leaders to speak for groups over which they had no authority. Although many Indian leaders had yielded to pressure to sign, the treaties often went unratified by Washington. In the meantime, Stevens had encouraged settlers to move into the interior valleys. Rather than settling the issue,

[52] Robert H. Ruby and John A. Brown, *The Cayuse Indians: Imperial Tribesmen of Old Oregon* (Norman, Okla., 1972), 202–3.

treaty making only produced more dissatisfaction as angry Indians turned to violence in an effort to stem the settler tide.

There were constant clashes between Indians and Euro-Americans south of the forty-ninth parallel, as Indian protest led to greater coercion. Significantly, the first major outbreak of warfare occurred the year after the signing of the Oregon Treaty, when the Cayuse Indians attacked the Marcus Whitman mission at Waiilatpu, near Walla Walla. The mission had become a stopping place for pioneers on their way to the coast, and, in 1845, Whitman acted as a guide to one company of settlers traveling west. As tension built between Indians and settlers, the missionary was clearly identified with the new forces that were disrupting the Indian way of life. The immigrants brought measles with them and the disease hit the Indians hard. When Whitman's medicine failed to revive those who were dying, he was blamed both for introducing the disease and for his inability to cure it. Finally the Indians' frustration boiled over. On November 29, 1847, the Cayuses killed Whitman, his wife, and other workers at the mission, setting off the first major round of interethnic violence. There were two responses on the part of the Euro-Americans. The Hudson's Bay Company sent a party from Fort Vancouver to ransom the survivors and to persuade other Indian groups not to join the conflict. Once the hostages were released, however, a force of volunteers from the Willamette Valley took to the field against the Cayuses. After a protracted pursuit, the Cayuses finally surrendered five of their number, who were summarily hanged in Oregon City. The old fur-trade frontier of mediation was over.

Warfare continued throughout the settlement phase. The violence was perhaps most devastating for the Indians of southern Oregon. Treaties with these groups were not ratified, and there was no regulation of Euro-American encroachment on Indian land as both settlers and gold miners moved into the area. After a decade of conflict, matters came to a head in 1855–56. Individual murders and small skirmishes led to large groups of volunteers taking the field against the Indians, intending to wipe them out. One such band from the gold-mining town of Jacksonville made an indiscriminate and brutal attack on Rogue River Indians. By the time the fighting was over, all the lower Oregon Indians had either been killed or moved to reservations to the north.

There was constant warfare in Washington Territory in the latter half of the 1850s. As the implications of the treaties they had signed sunk in, Indians became very angry and, both on the coast and in the interior, they turned their anger on the settlers. Within a month of the Walla Walla council, the Yakima leader, Kamiakin, who had emerged as a leader of the dissidents in the interior, was urging his followers to drive the Euro-Americans from their territory. There were individual killings that soon escalated into running, guerilla-style attacks, and then open battles. The violence was to continue for three years. On the coast, the insurgents were led by Leschi, who launched a campaign of resistance that included an assault on Seattle. Neither side was united through the conflict. There were shifting divisions and alliances among the Indians on the advisability of taking up arms against the settlers. On the settler side, the officers of the regular Army objected to the excesses of the volunteer forces. In 1856, for example, a group of volunteers under Colonel B. F. Shaw made an indiscriminate and savage attack on a virtually defenceless group of Indians in the Grande Ronde Valley. General John E. Wool, the senior Army officer in the Pacific Northwest, felt that actions such as these only served to prolong the war. Even Philip Sheridan, who was later to make the infamous remark about "the only good Indian . . . ," was shocked by the excesses that he saw during the Washington wars. But, whatever the divisions on either side, there could be little doubt about the final outcome. One by one, the hostile Indian groups were defeated and humiliated and their leaders either killed in the field or captured and hanged after perfunctory "trials." An exception was Kamiakin, who avoided retribution by escaping to British territory north of the forty-ninth parallel.

Although most Indian groups had been defeated, the violence did not end with the 1850s. Sporadic armed resistance continued until the famous fighting retreat of Chief Joseph and the Nez Percés in 1877. The Nez Percés had done their best to live in peace with the newcomers, but even the land assigned to these Indians under treaties was not secure. Many treaties contained a clause giving the government the right to move groups to other reservations should "the interests of the territory require it."[53] As settler pressure continued to grow, government officials displaced the Nez Percés from their land in the cherished Wallowa Valley. The Indians were finally driven to violence. Some young Indians, seeking revenge for the death of family members, killed some settlers, and once again individual murders led to warfare. The Nez Percés fought a heroic campaign that lasted for several months. They were harried all the way

[53] Quoted in Alvin M. Josephy, Jr., *The Nez Perce Indians and the Opening of the Northwest* (New Haven, Conn., 1965), 311.

from their homeland to the Bear Paw Mountains, where they surrendered just fifty kilometers short of their objective: the Canadian border.

The Nez Percés, like Kamiakin, believed that things would be different in Canada, and so, to some extent, they were. But the distinctions were more apparent than real. The techniques of dispossession were different, but the end result was the same: the Indians were left without enough land to maintain a livelihood. By the 1880s, when the land that was life was gone, the means by which it had been taken would seem of little consequence.

The break between fur trade and settlement was not so sharp north of the border as it was to the south. There was also a time lag of ten or fifteen years between the settlement of the two areas. But more important was the fact that on Vancouver Island, in the 1850s, the early development of settlement was managed by former fur traders. The group administering the company colony was led by James Douglas, who was already chief factor at Fort Victoria when he was appointed governor of the colony by the British government in 1851. As the governing factor, Douglas was responsible for making Indian policy during this transitional phase. Unlike his counterparts to the south, the metropolitan authority gave him a good deal of autonomy in dealing with the Native people. The colonial office in London sent general instructions about the need to make provision for, and deal fairly with, the Indians, but the imperial government also left a good deal up to his discretion and local knowledge. As governor of the new settlement colony, Douglas put his long years of experience as a fur trader to good use. And, with escalating violence south of the border, he drew attention to American policy as a negative example.

In contrast to the wholesale, after-the-fact, approach in the United States, Douglas's Indian land policy on Vancouver Island, and later in the mainland colony of British Columbia, was piecemeal and, where possible, applied ahead of settlement. In 1850 he negotiated a series of treaties with Songhee groups in the Fort Victoria area. Under these treaties, the Indians surrendered their title to the land, were allocated reserves, and were guaranteed the right to hunt on unoccupied land and to fish as before. Rather than removal and amalgamation, Douglas's policy was to lay out several small reserves in locations that the Indians traditionally used. The Songhees' village sites and cultivated fields were reserved under the treaties: pieces of land of which Indian possession could be recognized in European terms. This policy of dealing with small groups of Indians and assigning them scattered reserves was, in part at least, to avoid the security risk that would come from bringing large groups of Indians together and locating them on combined reserves. It was an application of the old imperial technique of divide and rule. Douglas made three more treaties in the areas around the Hudson's Bay Company posts at Nanaimo and Fort Rupert. These treaties covered only a fraction of Vancouver Island, and, when the Indians of the Cowichan Valley wanted to sell their lands in the same way as the Songhees had done, Douglas refused their request. He did not make treaties in areas where he thought that there was little likelihood of settlement in the near future. Indeed, the first Douglas treaties turned out to be an exception to the general practice in British Columbia. On the rest of Vancouver Island, and on the mainland after 1858, he discontinued the practice of making treaties for want of funds to compensate the Indians for their land.

Henceforth reserves were laid out without written agreements between the parties. In the Fraser Valley, the Okanagan, and the Kamloops area, reserves were allocated without extinguishing aboriginal title by treaty. Douglas told his officials to follow the wishes of the Indians when laying out reserves and insisted that they return to extend the boundaries when he felt that his instructions were not followed. But these policies were not formalized, and they depended too much on Douglas's personal good will to survive after he left office. Later, around the turn of the century, Treaty Eight would be extended from the Prairies to cover the Peace River country in northeast British Columbia, but throughout most of the province aboriginal title was never surrendered by treaty. It was simply assumed by the British Columbia government that the allocation of reserves constituted extinguishment of title. That assumption has left the province with a legacy of litigation that continues to the present day.

Although he did not compensate the Indians for the loss of their land, Douglas did try to protect their interests in other ways. He instructed his officials to lay out reserves according to the wishes of the Native people. Once reserves were established, Douglas did all he could to see that settlers did not encroach upon Indian land. With the comment that Indians were to be, as much as possible, equal with settlers before the law, Douglas also allowed them to purchase town lots and to preempt land under the same provisions that applied to Europeans: that is, providing they resided on the claim, built a dwelling, and cultivated a certain amount of land. Very few Indians took up the option of preempting land, but Douglas's measures did succeed in taking the sharp edge off their dissatisfaction over being dispossessed.

While they did not settle the question of title in the long run, Douglas's Indian land policies did reduce the amount of interethnic friction during the early years of settlement. Although there were no Indian wars in British Columbia, there was interethnic violence. Isolated attacks by small groups and individual murders were not uncommon. But when they occurred, Douglas tried to contain the conflict by following the fur-trade tactics of selective punishment rather than mounting indiscriminate attacks on large groups of Native people. When settlers were killed by Indians, he responded by isolating the individuals responsible and meting out swift execution on the spot. During the first years of his governorship, Douglas was also reluctant to become involved in disputes among Indians. He explained this principle in 1853, when unrest developed among the Indians of northern Vancouver Island following an attack on the Koskimos by the Newittys.[54] Douglas went so far as to suggest that such quarrels between Indians were an outlet for violence that might otherwise be directed against the settlers. These methods of selective law and order were easier to apply on Vancouver Island in the early 1850s, when there were only a few hundred settlers, than they were after thousands of impatient miners poured into the gold colony after 1858.

Yet Indian-European relations were kept under control even during the gold rush. After he was appointed governor of the new colony, Douglas himself made trips to the Fraser River gold fields to impress upon the miners that both Indians and Europeans would be subject to British law. There was a good deal of interethnic tension along the Fraser Canyon in the summer of 1858. Individual killings of both miners and Indians twice threatened to boil over into serious conflict. Rumors were flying, and when dead miners were found it was automatically assumed that they had been killed by Indians. Douglas personally intervened in these situations, and peace was made between the miners and the Native people. The governor took one of the Indians involved into the government service with the comment that he would be able to help settle other disputes. He more frequently appointed Europeans as officials, of course, and the gold commissioners, who were all-purpose local government officers, played an important role in establishing law and order. Although its role ought not to be exaggerated, Douglas was able to call on the ships and men of the Royal Navy to help control this potentially turbulent frontier. Naval vessels patrolled the coast, particularly around Vancouver Island, in an effort to control the liquor trade and the trade in Indian slaves. When

---

[54] Fisher, *Contact and Conflict*, 56–7.

Indians were accused of attacking Europeans, "gunboat diplomacy" was the order of the day. Attacks on Indian villages were sometimes indiscriminate. In 1864, just as Douglas left office, the Indians of Clayoquot Sound on the west coast of Vancouver Island were alleged to have attacked and destroyed a trading sloop. Several naval vessels, including the appropriately named *Devastation,* were sent to the area, and a number of Ahousat villages were destroyed with guns and rockets.

British Columbia was a frontier that was controlled from the top down. There was less room for grassroots initiative and settler responsibility in law and government than in the American West. Because the governor was also head of the armed forces, he controlled the use of force. In Washington and Oregon, the ill-considered actions of volunteer forces often escalated the level of violence, and there was sometimes conflict between the governor and the Army over how to deal with Indians. Vigilantism, the ultimate expression of popular law and order, was not completely absent from British Columbia, but it was kept under control. The myth of British Columbia as a law-abiding and peaceful frontier should not be pushed too far, but the superficial tenor of Indian-European relations was different from what prevailed south of the border.

Control from the top was, of course, less advantageous when those at the top had little sympathy for Native people. When Douglas retired in 1864, he was replaced by officials who took a much more hard-line approach to Native issues in general, and the land question in particular. Douglas had left his more benign policies vulnerable to revision by not codifying many of them into law. They depended too much on his personal presence. When Douglas left office many Native people in British Columbia felt that they had lost a protector. It was significant that one of the few major outbreaks of violence during the colonial period in British Columbia occurred just as James Douglas left the scene.

Early one morning at the end of April 1864, a group of Chilcotin Indians killed thirteen members of the road party that was working on the Homathko River near Bute Inlet. The Indians then moved inland, where they attacked a pack train and murdered a settler. The motivation for these assaults was complex. There were undoubtedly personal grievances that arose out of the treatment of the Indians employed by the road party. There were accusations from Indians that male settlers had molested Indian women and were deliberately spreading disease. At a more fundamental level, the Indians realized that the road would provide access to more Europeans and lead to a further alienation of their land.

By attacking settlers and the lines of communication that maintained their existence, the Chilcotins were protesting against this invasion of their lands. Nor were they alone among British Columbia Indians in thinking that, with the departure of James Douglas, they had lost a proponent in their disputes with the settlers. This view seemed to be confirmed when there were loud and angry calls for vengeance against the Chilcotins at vigilante-style public meetings in Victoria. In the event, two officially sanctioned parties went into the Chilcotin country and, after those alleged to have committed the murders surrendered, they were tried and hanged.

Douglas was replaced as governor by men who were less able and less concerned about Native policy. The individual who assumed responsibility for Indian land policy after 1864 was Joseph Trutch, the Chief Commissioner of Lands and Works. Trutch had none of the fur traders' empathy for the Indians, and in his mind the development of the colonies by European settlers was the paramount concern. He referred to the Native people as violent savages and thought that they had little capacity for "improvement." In the conflict of interest between Indians and Europeans over land, there was no doubt about whom Trutch would represent. His primary concern was to take land from the Indians and give it to settlers. As in the United States, even Indian reserves that had already been laid out were not protected. He misrepresented Douglas's policies to justify drastic reductions of many reserves. When he laid out new reserves, the standard of ten acres (four hectares) per family, which had been a minimum under Douglas, became a maximum size after 1864.[55]

These policies of not extinguishing aboriginal title and of giving the Indians as little land as possible were not changed in any fundamental way when British Columbia became a province of Canada in 1871. Throughout much, though not all, of the rest of Canada, treaties were negotiated with the Native people and on the Prairies, for example, the reserves laid out in the 1870s were much larger than those on the West Coast. The federal government was at first not interested, and then not willing, to press British Columbia to conform to this standard. So, in spite of the fact that Ottawa became responsible for Indians and Indian land, the British Columbia approach of minimal recognition of Native rights has prevailed to the present day. Being deprived of their land meant that Indians of the

[55] For an account of Trutch's views and policies see Robin Fisher, "Joseph Trutch and Indian Land Policy," *BC Studies* 12 (winter 1971–72), 3–33.

Northwest were scarcely able to subsist, let alone benefit in any significant way from the developing resource economy. Whether they continued their traditional way of life or attempted to adapt to the new economy, the indigenous people were in direct conflict with an aggressive and acquisitive group of newcomers.

Those Indian groups who wished to maintain the old hunting, fishing, and gathering patterns of the past were displaced when European miners and farmers exploited the land. Even transitory gold miners, from the Rogue River in the south to the Skeena in the north, had an impact on the environment that lasted much longer than their presence. Placer mining on the Fraser River and its feeder streams after 1858 had such a drastic effect on the salmon runs that there was hardship and starvation among the Indians for several years. When settlers fenced and then ploughed or grazed the land it was no longer possible to hunt game or pick berries. In the most arid parts of the interior, disputes were, if anything, even more intense over water than they were over land. Indians faced starvation when ranchers denied them access to streams and lakes. On the coast, the resources of the sea and shore were more abundant, and the Indians had a saying that "when the tide was out the table was laid." Competition over the fishery was slower to begin, but, by the late 1860s, commercial canning operations were underway and Native people were acutely aware that they no longer dined alone.

For the indigenous people of the Northwest, the land was more than a resource, it was also the source of their cultural identity. Concepts of ownership varied throughout the region. Most commonly living sites and resource-gathering locations were the possessions of kinship groups, and most Indians had definite concepts of territoriality and trespass. Certainly all Native people closely identified with a particular locale, and it was not just a matter of physical survival but also of spiritual well-being. The Thompsons and Shuswaps believed that just as all growing things had a soul, so also did the rocks and the water, since they had all been people during the mythological age. Spirits, or land and water mysteries, inhabited particular places within their territory: the land mysteries usually caves on mountain peaks and the water mysteries lakes and ponds. When he was allocating reserves in the southern interior of British Columbia, the Indian reserve commissioner, Gilbert Malcolm Sproat, wrote to his superiors in Ottawa that "I do not exaggerate in saying that some of these Indians die if they lose their land: they take it so much to heart."[56] To relieve Native people of their land was to deprive them of the place of their ancestors and thus to take away part of their identity. To move them and give them land in another place was just as devastating.

Colonists, by contrast, came to this new place because they sought change. They saw land as an opportunity for a new life and new wealth. The newcomers were not rooted in the autochthonous soil of the Northwest. The land was there to be exploited rather than respected, let alone venerated. To the settlers the landscape seemed endless and empty, so they had little concern for the future. Even farmers were miners rather than husbandmen, who took the life from the ground. In the interior, for example, ranchers overgrazed the fragile natural grasslands and quickly turned large areas into desert. Thus, the conflict over land was as much a clash of beliefs and values as it was a struggle for resources. The battle was short, and the defeat of the Native people decisive.

THE NEW ECONOMY

While some groups held to traditional ways, others made a determined effort to develop new means of livelihood. But for these people the clash of economies, and cultures, was even more direct. Gold mining by newcomers not only disrupted food fishing, it also displaced those Indians who were already taking gold from the rivers to trade with the Hudson's Bay Company.[57] They were simply pushed aside in the stampede. Some Native groups, particularly in the southern interior of British Columbia, were raising stock on a fairly large scale. The Indians around Fort Kamloops had been raising horses to supply the Hudson's Bay Company brigades since the 1820s, and by the 1860s several Indian groups were running both horses and cattle for sale to Europeans. On the coast other groups, following the example of the Haida potato growers, were growing crops. Often the plots of land were small, but the Native people were not unsophisticated farmers. On southern Vancouver Island and in the Fraser Valley, Indian farms flourished; some had developed complicated irrigation systems, and two bands had won prizes at the

---

[56] Sproat to Superintendent General of Indian Affairs, April 18, 1879, Canada, Department of Indian Affairs, Black Series, Western Canada, Record Group 10, vol. 3, 668, file 10, 345, National Archives of Canada.

[57] Fisher, *Contact and Conflict*, 70–1.

United States Centennial Exposition in 1876 for their wheat.[58] These Indians wanted the same land for the same reasons as did the settlers. As in other parts of North America, many Indians of the Northwest were perfectly capable of making the transition from being hunters and gatherers to being successful agriculturalists.[59] But, as elsewhere, settlers would not tolerate Indian competition in what they saw as their field, so their governments made sure that Native people did not have enough land to become commercial farmers.

Some writers have asserted that, while the Indians lost their land to settlers, they nevertheless played an important role in the developing resource economy of the Northwest; that, rather than being marginalized by the settler frontier, Native people provided an important source of wage labor. The argument is most stridently made for British Columbia where, Rolf Knight tells us, the Indians "helped lay the basis of many regional economies."[60] There is no doubt that, in some areas and in some economic sectors, Indians became a part of the labor force. In the interior, during the gold rushes and after, Indians sometimes got work as packers and bearers, some simply using human effort while others worked for horse packers. As forms of transport changed, some got casual work on railway projects. A more recent and more careful study of Interior Salish bands in southern British Columbia shows that, while there was great local variation, wage labor was an important source of income for many of these Indians by the end of the nineteenth century.[61] On the coast, Indians had even more opportunities. Some entered the cash economy through the commercial fishing and canning, which began to develop at the mouths of the major rivers, beginning on the Columbia in the 1860s. Fishing for the canning companies was an extension of their traditional way of life, and by the 1880s several enterprising individuals were running gas boats. During this period prior to mechanization, the canneries were labor-intensive operations that employed large numbers of Indian workers. The inside work was hard, unpleasant, and risky and much of it was done by Native women. The dogfish oil industry also employed some coastal Indians, while others signed on as crew on pelagic sealing vessels. Many of these

---

[58] Rolf Knight, *Indians at Work: An Informal History of Native Indian Labour in British Columbia, 1858–1930* (Vancouver, 1978), 68.

[59] Sarah Carter, "Agriculture and Agitation on the Oak River Reserve, 1875–1895," *Manitoba History*, no. 6 (fall 1983), 2–9.

[60] Knight, *Indians at Work*, 23.

[61] James K. Burrows, " 'A Much Needed Class of Labour': The Economy and Income of the Southern Interior Plateau Indians, 1897–1910," *BC Studies*, no. 71 (autumn 1986), 27–46.

operations could not have survived without Indian labor. Smaller numbers of Indians worked in coal mining, logging, sawmilling, or longshoring along the coast. Hop picking for European farmers was another source of seasonal income.

While there is no doubt that Indians got jobs, it is equally clear their employment was often shortlived. Native people were usually the first workers to be laid off. Employers also hired Indians when they had no alternative, so as the settler population increased, Native people were displaced in the workforce just as they were on the land. Indian workers were thus an exploited pool of cheap and expendable labor. It is hard to imagine that the fact that some, or even most, European workers were also exploited provided much consolation.[62] Occasional employment at the whim of Europeans was hardly an alternative to owning and controlling your own land and resources. There was also no comparison between the position of Indian workers on the settler frontier and the determining role that they had played in fur-trade economics. Their tenuous and vulnerable position in the workforce confirms rather than denies the marginality of Native people after European settlement came to the Northwest.

Change is, of course, never absolute. Some Native groups, particularly in the north, remained largely unaffected by the settler economy before 1880. There were also specific economic activities in which the Indians retained a measure of independence. The trade in Indian artifacts by collectors for the world's museums reached its high point during the last few decades of the nineteenth century. Ethnographic collectors recognized that, when they had the opportunity, Indians were just as capable of driving a hard bargain over artifacts as they had been in fur-trade exchanges. The difference was that these opportunities were now few and far between. The exceptions to the rule should not obscure the fact that most Indians experienced extremely restricted opportunities and rapidly declining wealth. Artifact collectors found that poverty made Indians more willing sellers. After a poor fishing season, they were much more likely to part with valued items at lower prices. The possibility of making money during depressed times also encouraged Indians to sell ceremonial objects that they were not entitled to.[63] All these dealings tended to undermine and debase the traditional belief systems in which many of these objects had played a vital role.

---

[62] Knight, *Indians at Work*, 21.
[63] Douglas Cole, *Captured Heritage: The Scramble for Northwest Coast Artifacts* (Vancouver, 1985), 16, 295–307.

THE DECLINE OF CULTURES

Declining wealth meant declining power. Within most Indian cultures, particularly those on the coast, wealth was power. The wealthiest individuals and groups were, by virtue of their wealth and property, able to give away more and hence were the most influential. During the fur-trade period, increased wealth had been injected into many Native communities. Now there was a reverse trend as the resource wealth of the Northwest fell into new hands. Native people felt their power and prestige slipping away. While it was still possible, some Indians withdrew from contact with Europeans and apparently succumbed to a malaise that came from the loss of cultural self-confidence. The Ethnological Society of London was told in 1867 that many Indians on the west coast of Vancouver Island no longer came to Victoria "in their former free independent way, but lived listlessly in their villages, brooding seemingly over heavy thoughts."[64]

As power declined within Indian cultures, they also lost their autonomy in relation to the Europeans. Indian protest took various forms, but it was always ineffective. When they complained to individual Europeans about losing land, their views were quickly dismissed as either misguided or of no consequence. When Robert Brown of the Vancouver Island Exploring Expedition found in 1864 that many Indians complained about the lack of compensation for their land, he spoke to them of the benefits the colonists brought them. The Indian, he wrote, "harps on his wrongs without ever thinking of any alleviating circumstances."[65] South of the international boundary, after negotiations proved completely one-sided, frustrated Indians turned to violence, even though that was equally futile in the long run. Protest was less violent, but no more effective, in British Columbia. Indians addressed the government through letters and petitions in the 1860s, and they soon formed organizations to express their grievances. A number of interior groups met at Lytton in 1879 to form a self-help committee that would work to improve social and economic conditions among the Indians as well as to press for a resolution of the land question. The measures advocated by the Lytton meeting were no different from those proposed by European philanthropists, but the settlers were horrified by the potential threat to their security posed by any combination of

[64] Gilbert Malcolm Sproat, "The West Coast Indians of Vancouver Island," *Transactions of the Ethnological Society of London*, n.s. 6 (1868), 254.
[65] John Hayman, ed., *Robert Brown and the Vancouver Island Exploring Expedition* (Vancouver, 1989), 124–6.

Native groups. So even this harmless organization was squashed. It would be well into the next century before the Native people of the Northwest had any influence on politics and policy.

Powerlessness was especially debilitating for the indigenous people, given the major cultural disruptions that they faced by the middle of the nineteenth century. As well as appropriating land and resources, the European settlers introduced some undesirable aspects of their civilization to the Northwest. Liquor was made available to the Indians in increasing amounts during the settlement phase. In 1854 and again in 1860, the colonial government of Vancouver Island passed legislation that prohibited the sale or gift of liquor to Indians, but laws passed in Victoria or New Westminster had little effect on the distant reaches of the coast or far-flung valleys in the interior. Throughout the region, many Indians turned to drinking as a form of escape. With the European population composed disproportionately of single males, the prostitution of Indian women became common. The changing relations between European men and Indian women were a measure of the shift from cooperation to exploitation with the coming of settlement. Indian women came to the growing centers of population, like Victoria and Seattle, as well as to the small towns and mining camps to earn money from prostitution. Women could earn twice as much as prostitutes in Victoria, for example, than they could up the coast. By the early 1860s, large numbers came every summer to earn money in this way. Some were able to enhance their family's social position with the wealth they acquired, but the exchange was scarcely a healthy one.

Drunkenness and prostitution brought the attendant evils of degradation and disease. The impact of European diseases was exacerbated by poverty and malnutrition, and the increased mobility of many Indians accelerated the spread of epidemics. After the gold rush to the Fraser River, Victoria developed as a supply town and Indians from up and down the coast were attracted to it by the economic opportunities. There was a large concentration of Native people living in and visiting Victoria in March 1862, when there was an outbreak of smallpox. As more and more Indians became infected, they were driven away from the town by frightened citizens. Rather than being contained at the source, the highly contagious disease was carried up the coast as northern Indians returned home, infecting others wherever they made a landfall. The disease was carried at least as far north as the Queen Charlotte Islands. The 1862 smallpox epidemic was only one of many diseases that hit the indigenous peoples of the Northwest.

Yet we should still be careful about estimating population decline in the nineteenth century. Contemporary remarks about smallpox converting Indian "camps into graveyards" should be treated with some caution, as should statements by more recent commentators that the 1862 epidemic reduced the Indian population by one-third.[66] As during the fur-trade period, disease hit some groups more severely than others. After more than 100 years of contact, there must have been some generational immunity to European diseases. Particularly in British Columbia, thousands of Indians had been vaccinated against smallpox by the 1860s.[67] Accurate counts by census-takers of the Native population of the Northwest were only beginning by the 1880s. It is interesting to note that in British Columbia between 1881, when the first reasonably accurate census was taken, and 1901 the Indian population dropped only from 25,661 to 25,488.[68] Although the death rate was still high, it seems that the birth rate was compensating for the losses. To the south, the rate of decline appears to have been greater. The estimated Indian population of Washington and Oregon in 1860 was 31,000 and 7,000 respectively, but by 1890 it had dwindled to 11,181 and 4,971, or a total of 16,152.[69]

There can be no doubt that many Native people died from disease after the coming of settlers to the Northwest. The debilitating effects of losing close kin cannot be measured by population figures and were made worse by the accompanying social upheaval. Numbers aside, the impact of disease was like that of the settlement frontier: the pace of change often outstripped the Native peoples' ability to cope with it. Old cures for illness had proved ineffective against smallpox, just as the traditional social forms could not deal with the crisis that settlement brought to Indian cultures. Many settlers assumed that the Native people would soon die out, and in the late nineteenth century there seemed to be some evidence to support that view. The corollary of such thinking was that, since the Native people were likely to disappear, there was no need to worry about providing for them.

[66] R. C. L. Brown to James Douglas, February 18, 1863, British Columbia, Colonial Correspondence, file 214 (BCARS); Duff, *Indian History of British Columbia*, 43.
[67] Fisher, *Contact and Conflict*, 116.
[68] Canada, *Census of Canada, 1880–1* (Ottawa, 1882), 4:11 and Canada, *Fourth Census of Canada 1901* (Ottawa, 1902), 1:285, 2.
[69] The 1860 estimates are from Robert H. Ruby and John A. Brown, *Indians of the Pacific Northwest: A History* (Norman, Okla., 1981), 175; and the figures for 1890 are from United States, Department of the Interior, *Abstract of the Eleventh Census: 1890* (Washington, D.C., 1894), 55.

NEW RELIGIONS

Amid all this cultural disruption, the one group of Europeans that seemed to offer Native people a clear vision of the future was the missionaries. They came to the Northwest sometimes conscious of their personal limitations, but with a prodigious confidence in the power of their God, in the efficacy of their religion, and in the superiority of their culture. They were not simply the representatives of nineteenth-century evangelical Christianity, they were also advocates of European "civilization." They came with the firm intention of effecting social as well as religious change among the Indians. Those few missionaries who came to the area during the fur-trade period had, even by their own admission, only a superficial impact. The Russian Orthodox missionaries to the Aleuts in the far north provide a partial exception to this generalization. The fur trade was particularly disruptive to these people, and so large numbers of them had turned to Christianity. But as long as Native people retained their cultural confidence and had the freedom to be selective about what they accepted from the Europeans, they showed little interest in missionary teaching. With the upheavals of the settlement frontier, however, Christianity became more attractive to many. Indeed, some historians of Christian missions to indigenous peoples have argued that a degree of cultural disruption is a prerequisite for missionary success: that only when old ways and values are proving ineffective, or are being called into question, will new ones be considered.[70]

There can be no doubt that the missionaries of the various denominations were aggressive agents of change, both spiritual and secular, among the Native people of the Northwest. The most important denominations were the Russian Orthodox in the north, and, farther south, the Roman Catholic, Anglican, Methodist, and Presbyterian. Roman Catholic missionaries may have been slightly less dogmatic about changing Native customs that did not conflict directly with Christian teaching, but all of them required more than spiritual change of their converts. Along with an inner conversion to the new religion, thorough-going changes in outward behavior were called for, so that the Christian Indian would become a completely new being in every way. With their vivid understanding of sin and its consequences in hell, missionaries saw spiritual conversion as an urgent matter. But the temporal side of their work was no less pressing than their spiritual

---

[70] Fisher, *Contact and Conflict*, 124.

responsibilities. As one of the most prominent missionaries to the Northwest coast, William Duncan, put it, "Christianity meant nothing less than the subversion of every evil work and no compromise."[71]

Such missionary rhetoric has led many historians to the conclusion that they were totally at odds with Native cultures. While the missionaries would never have admitted it, there were points of correspondence between the missionary role and traditional culture. Although the missionaries objected strenuously to the potlatch and winter dances of the coast Indians, these ceremonies and rituals were those of a people accustomed to exploring the spiritual dimension of life. Ultimately, Indian spirituality was not entirely incompatible with Christianity. Native people of the Northwest, as elsewhere, paid homage to spiritual and mythical beings who in return were expected to work for humans: to protect them and help provide for their needs. If they were to accept the Christian God, and he proved effective, his name could simply be added to those of the existing deities. Within many Indian cultures, the connection between the spiritual and the material world was made by the shaman who, like the missionary, fulfilled the functions of both doctor and priest and called on the assistance of spirits to cure physical maladies. Because their roles were similar, the missionary and the shaman often came into sharp conflict; but because the Native people knew the role of the shaman, they could appreciate some of the missionaries' intentions. Indian societies also produced strong leaders. Although chiefs led through prestige and influence rather than power and authority, Indian societies, particularly on the coast, were definitely hierarchical, and leadership was clearly defined and understood. Sometimes the conversion of an Indian leader could influence the decisions of followers. Many missionaries had strong and forceful personalities, and they usurped traditional leadership roles at the same time as they built upon them.

The syncretic mixing of traditional spirituality and Christianity began with the earliest missionaries to arrive in the Northwest. When the Russian Orthodox church sent its first representative to the Alaskan Islands in 1793, many Aleuts had already been baptized by fur traders. The Aleuts were susceptible to missionary influence partly because there was much overlap between Native and Orthodox beliefs and symbolism. The Aleuts therefore integrated their traditional beliefs with the teaching brought by

[71] Duncan to David Laird, May 1875, Church Missionary Society Archives, North Pacific Mission, British Columbia, Original Letters, Journals, and Papers, Incoming, 1857–80, C-2/0, University of British Columbia Library.

the newcomers. When Orthodox missionaries began work among the Tlingits in the mid-1830s, they continued their tradition of considerable toleration for Native customs. Russian Orthodox missionaries, unlike many to the south, were encouraged to learn the Indian languages. Another objective was to train Native people to be clergymen. Like the Russian American Company, the Russian Orthodox church relied heavily on Native and mixed-blood people to do its work. Not all Orthodox missionaries lived up to these ideals, and some resented their reliance on the local people, but in principle the Russian missions were based on give and take. Russian Orthodox influence among the Tlingits was always weak, and those who did accept baptism may have done so more for commercial and political than for spiritual reasons. Russian missionaries remained most successful among the Aleuts, although with the sale of Alaska to the United States in 1867, the status of the church suddenly changed. Its missionaries continued to work among the Native people of Alaska even after it became a foreign land, but their influence declined in the late nineteenth century, as other denominations began proselytizing. By the end of the century, the Russian Orthodox church operated only sixteen of a total of eighty-two missions in Alaska.[72]

Though it is easy to be critical of the missionaries, it is also important to remember that in a situation of rapid change they were the one group of Europeans who planned a future for the Indians. In contrast to many settlers who believed that the Native people would simply disappear, the missionaries took the more optimistic, humanitarian view that colonization need not be a complete disaster for the indigenous people, provided the right steps were taken quickly to save them from the worst effects of settlement. Ironically, to the extent that they pacified the Native people, the missionaries assisted the advance of settlement. At the same time, they often had an uneasy relationship with the settlers as they worked to protect the Indians from the worst effects of the new frontier. They frequently, for example, acted as advocates for the Indians in negotiations with government officials over the land question. They did have an ulterior interest in the land issue, since they believed that, if the Indians became settled farmers, missionary work would be made easier. But the Indians could only settle if sufficient good land were reserved for them. So, ulterior motives aside, the missionaries were correct in their view that the Native

[72] Sergei Kan, "The Russian Orthodox Church in Alaska," in *Handbook of North American Indians*, vol. 4, *History of Indian-White Relations*, ed. Wilcomb E. Washburn (Washington, D.C., 1988), 514.

people had to have some viable economic base if they were to play a significant role in Northwest society.

Yet, even in the chaotic circumstances of the settlement frontier, the missionaries did not merely impose their will upon the Native people. Few missionaries ever achieve all they set out to do, and those in the Northwest were no exception. There is always a discrepancy between missionary objectives and indigenous responses, and, while the missionaries were dogmatic in their approach, the Native people were flexible in their reaction. Some Indians totally rejected missionary teaching, while others found it completely convincing, and there was a range of opinion in between.

As the Cayuses showed at Waiilatpu in 1847, the missionary presence and example could become quite unacceptable to the Indians. The Whitmans had been particularly strident in their denunciation of Native ways and their demands for change. They also became too closely associated with the buildup of settlers west of the Rockies. The violence of the Cayuse attack was exceptional, and the Whitmans and their associates were the only missionary martyrs in the Northwest. But other Indians firmly rejected the missionary message. Resistance more usually took the form of efforts to reassert traditional Native culture in the face of the missionary inroads, and was particularly strong among those who had an investment in a continuation of the old lifestyle. But, just because older people and Indian leaders frequently rejected Christianity, it does not follow that only slaves or people of low rank were converted. The largest groups of Indians still holding traditional beliefs were on the coast, particularly among the Nootkas of the west coast of Vancouver Island and to a lesser extent the Indians of the northern coast. The tensions between those of different views often divided Native communities in these areas into pro- and antimissionary factions.

Many Native people in the Northwest enthusiastically embraced Christianity. Perhaps the best-known example was the missionary community that William Duncan established in the 1860s among the Tsimshians at Metlakatla on the northern British Columbia coast. In his day, Duncan was as famous for his success as the Whitmans were for their failure. Duncan established a community of converts, isolated from other Tsimshians and from what he saw as the debilitating influence of the colonists. The original small group of fifty was swelled by new arrivals until Metlakatla was a thriving village of several hundred. Duncan enforced a set of rules in an effort to manage every aspect of the daily lives, both

spiritual and temporal, of his followers. Some regulations prohibited traditional Tsimshian customs such as the potlatch or consulting the shaman
when ill, while others enjoined the villagers to attend church and school
regularly and to be neat, clean, and industrious in their daily lives. And
these were only the minimal expectations that Duncan had of those who
joined him. Duncan knew that he was demanding radical change, discipline was strict and rigorously administered, and he intended to have
absolute control over the community.[73]

Nor was Metlakatla an isolated example of missionary authority. By the
end of the nineteenth century, when missionary influence was probably at
its peak, most Indians in British Columbia identified themselves as Christian. A census taken by the Department of Indian Affairs indicated that,
of a total population of 24,696 Indians, 19,504 called themselves Christian. Only 2,692 were enumerated as "pagan," while the religion of
another 2,900 was unknown.[74]

Those who accepted missionary teaching did so for a variety of often
mixed motives. Some converts no doubt observed only the form of the new
religion. Contemporary skeptics often claimed that Native Christians
merely recited the church liturgy without making any real change in their
daily lives. Many were attracted by the novelty of the ritual and the
teaching. Scholars have sometimes argued that indigenous people accepted Christianity only out of a desire for the material benefits that the
missionaries brought. In many cases economic gain may have been the
dominant motivation, yet some Indians clearly approached Christianity on
the level of ideas and embraced it for theological reasons. There were those
who made a complete change in their beliefs and way of life, and for them
conversion was the total experience that the word implies.

Perhaps the most common pattern of missionary influence was an
initial period of rapid progress followed by gradual disenchantment.
Such was certainly the reaction to the Methodist missionary Thomas
Crosby, who began work at Fort Simpson in 1874. The Tsimshians had
invited Crosby to their community and initially responded to his teaching with enthusiasm. But they welcomed him for their own reasons and
accepted his guidance only as long as it brought the results they wanted.
When Crosby failed to deliver, particularly in negotiations with governments on the land issue, his authority withered away. Even the religious

[73] For a detailed account of the "Metlakatla system," see Jean Usher, *William Duncan of Metlakatla: A
Victorian Missionary in British Columbia* (Ottawa, 1974), 63–90.
[74] Canada, *Sessional Papers*, 8th Parl., 5th sess., 1900, no. 14, 499.

life of the village developed outside his control.[75] At Metlakatla, William Duncan sometimes faced similar insurgency. In 1877, during Duncan's temporary absence, there was a revivalist movement in the village. In part at least, it involved a reassertion of traditional Tsimshian spirituality, but it was also an indication that some were dissatisfied with Duncan's authoritarian leadership. The missionary returned and reasserted the appearance of control, but over the next decade the dissension became worse. When Duncan had a falling-out with the Church Missionary Society over liturgy and ecclesiastical authority, Metlakatla divided into pro- and anti-Duncan forces. The two groups also squabbled over the ownership of land in the village. By 1887, factionalism had so divided his community that Duncan took a group of followers to form New Metlakatla on Annette Island in Alaska. But continuing tensions, and particularly Duncan's inability to accede to Indian leadership, left him isolated and lonely. The missionary's credibility gone, the community went its own way.[76]

An encounter with Christianity followed by disillusionment could lead to new forms of religion that were a mixture of old and new elements. Prophet cults sprang up in many parts of the region, particularly among the Plateau groups in the interior, but also on the coast.[77] These syncretistic religions combined aspects of Christianity with traditional spirituality. In many cases, they evolved from the guardian-spirit quest. The Anglican missionary John Good recalled one such movement along the Fraser River in the 1870s. The Indian prophet and his followers looked forward to the day when the Europeans would be ejected from the land and all that they had taken would be restored to the Indians.[78] The Dreamer religion attracted followers among a number of groups in Washington and Oregon. The Wanapum (Sahaptin) prophet Smohalla was particularly influential, and Indians flocked to his village at Priest Rapids on the Columbia River. They gathered to perform the ritual dances and to listen to the prophecy that Indians would someday reinherit the earth. Typically such cults arose from cultural dislocation at a time when Euro-Americans had become dominant and more rational means of resistance were thought to

[75] See Clarence R. Bolt, "The Conversion of the Port Simpson Tsimshian: Indian Control or Missionary Manipulation?" *BC Studies*, no. 57 (spring 1983), 38–56.
[76] Peter Murray, *The Devil and Mr. Duncan* (Victoria, 1985), passim.
[77] Christopher L. Miller, *Prophetic Worlds: Indians and Whites on the Columbia Plateau* (New Brunswick, N.J., 1985), 42–62; Wayne Suttles, "The Plateau Prophet Dance among the Coast Salish," in *Coast Salish Essays* (Vancouver, 1987), 152–98.
[78] Fisher, *Contact and Conflict*, 140–1.

be ineffectual. In the Mount Baker area of northern Washington one prophet leader, known as the Mormon prophet, advocated complete isolation from Euro-Americans.

Less anti-European and more permanent in its influence was the Shaker Church. Like most of these indigenous religious movements, it arose at a time of turmoil, when Native people were faced with the pressures of change. Its founder, John Slocum, was a Squaxin Indian from Puget Sound who lived a quite unremarkable life until 1881, when it is said that he rose up from the dead. He returned with a message for his people that they live moral, upright lives and reject evils such as alcohol. Slocum had also been given healing powers. He attracted a large following among his own and neighboring peoples, and the sect later expanded to other parts of the region: south into Oregon and north into British Columbia. Indian Shakerism combined traditional spirituality with both Protestant and Roman Catholic influences. In the shaking trances that conferred the power to heal and exorcise evil, there were similarities with the traditional guardian-spirit religion of the Coast Salishes. It has also been suggested that elements of the Shaker religion came from the earlier Prophet Dance movement in the Plateau area. This ritual, which dated from the late eighteenth century, was based on the belief that by dancing like the dead in the other world, Indians could renew their world and bring about the return of the dead. Over time, it combined more Christian elements, while reacting against the growing disruption of traditional culture. Like most of these Native spiritual movements, the Indian Shakers initially attracted a good deal of opposition from missionaries and Indian agents. Later, when it was clear that the church had a beneficial social influence on the reserves, the objections of government officials were more muted. The Shaker Church became more secure from external threat after it was legally constituted in 1892 and incorporated under Washington State law in 1910, with a structure similar to most Protestant denominations. Since then, dissension within has been a more serious threat to its survival. The Shaker Church, in spite of its structure, emphasized respect for individual thought, and differences of opinion were difficult to keep under control. The major line of division has been between those who want to move the church closer to Protestant Christianity and those who want to preserve traditional elements. Yet, even this debate indicates that the Shaker Church, along with all the other "adjustment cults," was representative of the increasing tendency for missionary Christianity to become integrated into Native culture.

THE END RESULT

In the long run then, missionary dogma was more malleable than the wider effects of the settlement frontier. With the exception of the far north, where settlement still lay in the future, by the 1880s Native people throughout the region were dispossessed by the newly dominant culture. They had lost their land and with it the means of maintaining an independent livelihood. Their numbers continued to decline and their traditional cultures were eroded away. Indian protest against the treatment they received was ignored, and even their efforts to help themselves were discouraged. Native people were seen as either doomed or largely irrelevant by many newcomers, who had few regrets about the dislocation of Indian cultures. The races became more separate as Native people were confined to isolated reserves and made unwelcome in the society of settlers. Governments mounted a sustained attack on traditional society, but did little to replace it with a new way of life.

The dominant people's notion that cultures could be simply legislated out of existence found its clearest expression in two pieces of federal legislation passed in the 1880s. At one level the Canadian Potlatch Law and the American Dawes Act were simply two more assaults on the Native way of life. Yet, at another level, they were the work of reformers who believed that they could legislate an improvement in Indian conditions. If Native people could be weaned away from "heathen" customs and cajoled into becoming small farmers on individual plots of land, so the argument went, they would become more like Europeans and the "Indian problem" would be solved. But these laws were designed to assimilate Indians into a society that offered them no place.

In both cases, pressure for the legislation came from missionaries and Indian agents. Government officials in British Columbia felt that the potlatch was, in the words of one of them, "a foolish, wasteful and demoralizing custom," and their opinions were shared by most churchmen.[79] The ritual was fundamental to Northwest Coast Indian culture, and it was partly for that reason that its opponents saw it as the most formidable obstacle in the way of "civilizing" Native people. Vocal demands finally convinced the Canadian federal government to pass a law prohibiting potlatching and winter dancing. Thus, a clause in the 1884

[79] W. H. Lomas to I. W. Powell, February 27, 1884, RG10, vol. 3, 628, file 6, 244 (1), National Archives of Canada.

amendment to the Indian Act stated that "Every Indian or other person who engages in or assists in celebrating the Indian festival known as the "Potlatch" or in the Indian dance known as the "Tamanawas" is guilty of a misdemeanor and shall be liable to imprisonment."[80] South of the forty-ninth parallel, Indian agents argued that, if Indians were given individual allotments of land, they would be less inclined to roam about in search of food. Some Indians were assigned allotments under the provisions of treaties, but without individual title they were reluctant to make improvements. So the General Allotment, or Dawes Act, was passed by the United States government in 1887, in an effort to turn Indians into individual property owners and settled agriculturalists. The act established a procedure for dividing reservations into individual homesteads. Indians who received these allotments then became citizens of the United States.[81] Many of the reserves in the interior of Washington and Oregon were brought under the provisions of the Allotment Act.

If the reformist intent of these laws was clear, their application and effect were ambiguous. The potlatch law was impossible to enforce consistently. The Canadian federal government did not have enough Indian agents to apprehend all those who took part in the ceremony, and the first charges under the new law were dismissed with the judgment that the offences were not clearly defined. British Columbia Indians responded in a variety of ways to this legal attack on their culture. Some gave up potlatching altogether, while others continued as before. Still others potlatched in secret or modified their ceremonies to circumvent the law. Nor did the Dawes Act turn the Indians south of the border into American-style small farmers. The intent of the legislation, in the words of the Commissioner of Indian Affairs, was to turn "the American Indian" into "the Indian American."[82] But the good intentions of reformers in Washington only triggered another assault on reserve land in the Northwest. Thirty years after the Dawes Act was passed, approximately three million acres (1,200,000 hectares) of land had been taken from Indian reserves in the Northwest and passed into the hands of Europeans.[83] The further loss of land led to more poverty and greater economic dependence.

Although the assault on the indigenous way of life by settler society was

---

[80] "An Act to Further Amend 'The Indian Act, 1880,' " Canada, *Statutes of Canada*, 1884, 47 Vict. c. 27.

[81] "An Act to Provide for the Allotment of Lands in Severalty to Indians . . . ," *The Statutes at Large of the United States of America*, 1887, vol. 24, 388–91.

[82] Quoted in Wilcomb E. Washburn, *The Indian in America* (New York, 1975), 242.

[83] Ruby and Brown, *Indians of the Pacific Northwest*, 268.

unrelenting, neither the Indians nor their cultures completely disappeared. For the Native peoples of the Northwest the late nineteenth century was a period of survival under pressure. There can be no doubt that the pressure was great. As the settlers became more aggressive toward Native cultures, many Indians could not cope with the pace of change. They faced upheaval and disruption, but their cultures did not entirely crumble away. Even in the 1880s, many Native groups, particularly in the far north, were relatively isolated from European contact. Other Indians became defensive in the face of the settler onslaught, and determined to conserve what they could of their culture. Some made major changes in their way of life and yet were not assimilated into the dominant culture. Through all the turmoil that was brought to their world, the Native people of the Northwest endured and adapted as they waited for that time in the future when they could assert themselves once more.

BIBLIOGRAPHIC ESSAY

The literature on the Northwest, both anthropological and historical, is characterized by an overwhelming fascination with the coast and by the fact that virtually none of it is written by Native people. Ever since Franz Boas and his students and collaborators began their work in the late nineteenth century, the scholarly study of Native cultures has been dominated by anthropologists. Historians, by contrast, were comparative latecomers to the field.

Academic archaeology is also a relatively recent development, and, so far, archaeologists in the Northwest have been more concerned with examining detailed evidence than with drawing out larger generalizations. An introduction to precontact times is provided by Roy L. Carlson, "Prehistory of the Northwest Coast," in Carlson, ed., *Indian Art Traditions of the Northwest Coast* (Burnaby, 1983) and Knut R. Fladmark, *British Columbia Prehistory* (Ottawa, 1986). Carlson also has a statement on the "History of Research in Archaeology" in Wayne Suttles, ed., *Handbook of North American Indians*, vol. 7, *Northwest Coast* (Washington, D.C., 1990).

Indeed, many of the general points that can be made about the scholarship on the region are reflected in this volume of *The Handbook of North American Indians*. It confirms the concentration on the coast and it is "tribal" in its approach: in the sense both that it deals with individual groups and that it is dominated by the anthropological tribe, presided over by a council of elders. Apart from the essays on particular Native groups, there are useful sections that discuss the development of research in the area and outline the history of culture contact, and the extensive bibliography is a good place for any researcher to start. Yet this volume is a statement of current wisdom rather than an exploration of new ideas, and interdisciplinary possibilities are limited by the editors' decision that, while anthropologists may be historians, historians cannot be anthropologists. More synthetic accounts of the ethnographic cultures of the coast appeared in earlier introductions, the best of which is still Philip Drucker, *Cultures of the North Pacific Coast* (San Francisco, 1965). There are no equivalent general studies of the cultures of the interior. June Helm, ed., *Handbook of North American Indians,* vol. 6, *Subarctic* (Washington, D.C., 1981) deals with some of the Native groups of the interior of British Columbia, Alaska, and Yukon, but the volume on the plateau has yet to appear.

When it comes to Native history since the coming of the Europeans, British Columbia is better served for general accounts than either the states to the south or Alaska. Wilson Duff, *The Indian History of British Columbia,* vol. 1, *The Impact of the White Man,* Anthropology in British Columbia Memoir no. 5 (Victoria, 1964) is a very brief overview. Robin Fisher's *Contact and Conflict: Indian-European Relations in British Columbia, 1774–1890* (Vancouver, 1977) is a more detailed examination of the impact of the fur trade and then the settlement frontier on the Indians of British Columbia. The closest equivalent on the American Northwest is Robert H. Ruby and John A. Brown, *Indians of the Pacific Northwest: A History* (Norman, Okla., 1981), which is a good survey written for a popular audience.

The generalisations made in the survey histories need to be tested by closer studies of particular groups, and here Oregon and Washington are better served than British Columbia. Joanne Drake-Terry, *The Same as Yesterday: The Lillooet Chronicle the Theft of Their Lands and Resources* (Lillooet, 1989), published by the Lillooet tribal council, is an exception to this rule as well as a sign that Native groups are beginning to write their own history. Another example, written by a non-Native scholar, is Peter Carstens, *The Queen's People: A Study of Hegemony, Coercion and Accommodation among the Okanagan of Canada* (Toronto, 1991). There are several histories of particular groups south of the border. A classic is Alvin M. Josephy, Jr., *The Nez Perce Indians and the Opening of the Northwest* (New Haven, Conn., 1965). The prolific authors Robert H. Ruby and John A. Brown have written several such volumes, including *The Cayuse Indians:*

Imperial Tribesmen of Old Oregon (Norman, Okla., 1972) and *The Chinook Indians: Traders of the Lower Columbia* (Norman, Okla., 1976). Stephen Dow Beckham has described the particularly depressing history of the Indians of southern Oregon in *Requiem for a People: The Rogue River Indians and the Frontiersmen* (Norman, Okla., 1971).

Just as some Native groups have been more favored by historians, some aspects of the history of the Northwest are more fully discussed in the literature than others. The fact that the fur trade was more important in the north than the south is reflected in the fact that Canadian historians have given it more attention than American scholars. One of the earliest students of the maritime fur trade was F. W. Howay, and his work can be sampled in "An Outline Sketch of the Maritime Fur Trade," Canadian Historical Association, *Report* (1932), 5–14, and "Indian Attacks upon Maritime Traders of the North-West Coast, 1785–1805," *Canadian Historical Review* 6 (1925), 287–309. A more recent survey of the early fur trade is James R. Gibson, *Otter Skins, Boston Ships, and China Goods: The Maritime Fur Trade of the Northwest Coast, 1785–1841* (Montreal, 1992). Not all of Gibson's views are shared by other historians. Robin Fisher argues that Native people had more control over the trade in "Indian Control of the Maritime Fur Trade and the Northwest Coast," in Del Muise, ed., *Approaches to Native History in Canada*, National Museum of Man, Historical Division Paper, no. 24 (Ottawa, 1977), and over the Indian-European power relationship in "Arms and Men on the Northwest Coast, 1774–1825," *BC Studies* 29 (spring 1976), 3–18. The letters and journal of fur traders published by the Hudson's Bay Record Society shed much light on the land-based fur trade, particularly E. E. Rich, ed., *The Letters of John McLoughlin from Fort Vancouver to the Governor and Committee, First Series, 1825–1838; Second Series, 1839–1844; and Third Series, 1844–46* (London, 1941, 1943, and 1944). E. E. Rich also began the scholarly examination of the economic role of Indians in the fur trade in "Trade Habits and Economic Motivation among the Indians of North America," *Canadian Journal of Economics and Political Science* 26 (1960), 35–53. There is room for much more work on fur trade economics in the far West along the lines of Arthur Ray's *"Give Us Good Measure": An Economic Analysis of Relations between the Indians and the Hudson's Bay Company before 1763* (Toronto, 1978), which deals with the Prairies. Other writers have analyzed fur trade marriages and the mixed-blood families that resulted in works that focus east of the Rockies but also include West Coast examples. See on this subject Sylvia Van Kirk, *Many Tender Ties: Women in Fur-Trade*

Society in Western Canada, 1670–1870 (Winnipeg, 1980), and Jennifer
S. H. Brown, *Strangers in Blood: Fur Trade Company Families in Indian
Country* (Vancouver, 1980). Partly because few North American historians
read Russian, the fur trade in the far north has received limited attention.
Useful introductions are found in James R. Gibson, "The Russian Fur
Trade," in Carol M. Judd and Arthur Ray, eds., *Old Trails and New
Directions: Papers of the Third North American Fur Trade Conference* (Toronto,
1980), and, by the same author, "Russian Dependence upon the Natives
of Alaska," in S. Frederick Starr, ed., *Russia's American Colony* (Durham,
N.C., 1987). Trade on the Northwest Coast was not confined to furs, as
Douglas Cole reminds us in *Captured Heritage: The Scramble for Northwest
Coast Artifacts* (Vancouver, 1985).

   Government policy on Native people, particularly regarding land, is
discussed in the general and group histories already referred to and also in
a number of more specialized studies. Robin Fisher looks at the making of
Indian land policy in British Columbia in Robin Fisher, "Joseph Trutch
and Indian Land Policy," *BC Studies* 12 (winter 1971–2), 3–33. His
views, particularly on James Douglas, have been challenged by Paul
Tennant in *Aboriginal Peoples and Politics: The Indian Land Question in British
Columbia, 1849–1989* (Vancouver, 1990). Robert E. Cail, *Land, Man,
and the Law: The Disposal of Crown Lands in British Columbia, 1871–1913*
(Vancouver, 1974) includes a couple of solid chapters on Indian land
policy. In *Isaac I. Stephens: Young Man in a Hurry* (Provo, Utah, 1979),
Kent Richards examines the Washington governor's role in treaty making.
Government policy was not confined to depriving Native people of their
land. Barry M. Gough describes the role of the Royal Navy and also
exaggerates its importance in the suppression of Native people on the
British Columbia coast, in *Gunboat Frontier: British Maritime Authority and
Northwest Coast Indians, 1846–90* (Vancouver, 1984). For an account of
the Canadian government's largely unsuccessful effort to ban the potlatch,
see Douglas Cole and Ira Chaikin, *An Iron Hand upon the People: The Law
against the Potlatch on the Northwest Coast* (Vancouver, 1990).

   One of the pressure groups that pushed to eliminate the potlatch was
the missionaries, and their work, in this and other areas, has received a
good deal of attention though much of the writing still concentrates on
missionary objectives rather than Native responses. Sergei Kan provides a
good introduction to the "The Russian Orthodox Church in Alaska," in
Wilcomb E. Washburn, ed., *Handbook of North American Indians*, vol. 4,
History of Indian-White Relations (Washington, D.C., 1988). Missionary

personalities are examined in Jean Usher, *William Duncan of Metlakatla: A Victorian Missionary in British Columbia* (Ottawa, 1974), Peter Murray, *The Devil and Mr. Duncan* (Victoria, 1985), and David Mulhall, *Will to Power: The Missionary Career of Father Morice* (Vancouver, 1986). Clarence R. Bolt's "The Conversion of the Port Simpson Tsimshian: Indian Control or Missionary Manipulation?" *BC Studies,* no. 57 (spring 1983), 38–56 is a welcome sign that more attention should be given to the Native reaction to missionary Christianity. Indian prophet movements are examined in Wayne Suttles, "The Plateau Prophet Dance among the Coast Salish," in *Coast Salish Essays* (Vancouver, 1987) and more recently in Christopher L. Miller, *Prophetic Worlds: Indians and Whites on the Columbia Plateau* (New Brunswick, N.J., 1985). On the Shaker Church, see H. G. Barnett, *Indian Shakers: A Messianic Cult of the Pacific Northwest* (Carbondale and Edwardsville, Ill., 1957) and Pamela T. Amoss, "The Indian Shaker Church," in Wayne Suttles, ed., *Handbook of North American Indians,* vol. 7, *Northwest Coast* (Washington, D.C., 1990).

One aspect of Native history that needs to be examined more closely is the extent to which, in spite of the dispossession of the settlement phase, Indians played a role in the postsettlement economy. Rolf Knight, *Indians at Work: An Informal History of Native Indian Labour in British Columbia, 1858–1930* (Vancouver, 1978) is a foray into this area, but it is, as the author admits in his title, an informal history: long on generalization and short on detailed evidence. Others have looked more closely at specific case studies. Examples are James K. Burrows, " 'A Much Needed Class of Labor': The Economy and Income of the Southern Interior Plateau Indians, 1897–1910," *BC Studies,* no. 71 (autumn 1986), 27–46, and Daniel L. Boxberger, "In and Out of the Labour Force: The Lummi Indians and the Development of the Commercial Salmon Fishery of North Puget Sound, 1880–1900," *Ethnohistory* 35 (1988), 161–90. With more detailed studies like these, we will be able to make better generalizations about the region as a whole.

Another question that requires more work is the effect of disease on the Native people of the Northwest. In spite of studies such as Robert T. Boyd, "Demographic History, 1774–1874," in Wayne Suttles, ed., *Handbook of North American Indians,* vol. 7, *Northwest Coast* (Washington, D.C., 1990) and James R. Gibson, "Smallpox on the Northwest Coast, 1835–1838," *BC Studies,* no. 56 (winter 1982–3), 61–81, many questions about diagnosis, epidemiology, and death and birth rates remain unanswered.

Perhaps surprisingly there have been few attempts to make comparisons between the Canadian and American parts of the Northwest. One exception is Robin Fisher, "Indian Warfare and Two Frontiers: A Comparison of British Columbia and Washington Territory during the Early Years of Settlement," *Pacific Historical Review* 50 (1981), 31–51, but there is certainly scope for more fruitful investigation of the similarities and differences between the two countries within the region.

12

THE RESERVATION PERIOD, 1880–1960

FREDERICK E. HOXIE

Few objects might appear more alien to traditional Native American cultures or more remote from Indian history than the steam locomotive. In nineteenth-century America, railroads symbolized the power of modern technology and the growth of non-Indian society. Railroads also traced the context in which Native life would be lived in the reservation period.

In 1880, if one were to superimpose a map of railroad lines over a map of North American Indian populations, the separation of most Native people from the bulk of the continent's population would be clear. Native communities in present-day Oklahoma, New Mexico, and Arizona lived beyond the reach of steel rails, while the Indians on both sides of the international border running west from Lake Superior to Puget Sound knew of the locomotive as only a distant rumor. In 1869, great celebration had accompanied the completion of a narrow line from Omaha, Nebraska, to Sacramento, California, but little had been done in the depression-ridden years immediately following to expand the total system. Even in the aftermath of the American Civil War (1861–65) and Canadian Confederation (1867), most Indian people, whether they were Creeks in Oklahoma, Assiniboines in Montana and Saskatchewan, or Ojibwas around the Great Lakes, had little contact with American and Canadian citizens.

In 1960, if one were to repeat the exercise of superimposing transportation lines on a map of Indian population, it would be clear how drastically Native life had been altered in the intervening eight decades. While many Indian people still lived in relative isolation in 1960, the non-Native majority in the populated regions of both the United States and Canada could reach most Indian communities and resources in a matter of hours. Rail lines, all-weather highways, and air transportation routes multiplied the available avenues of access. In the mid–twentieth century, most Native people outside the Far North could not avoid regular contact with non-Indians.

As telegraph and telephone communication supplemented face-to-face contact, the number and intensity of the cross-cultural meetings between Indians and outsiders increased. For government officials, missionaries, and business organizations, ready access to Indian people meant they could devise uniform approaches – or policies – to Native communities. Their ideas, their educational programs, and their economic interests crowded in on Native people and became an inescapable part of the Native environment.

Indians of the mid–twentieth century experienced an odd reversal of the immigration process which so enriched the United States and Canada. In contrast to the movement of peoples from distant lands who traveled across broad oceans to a new continent, Native people witnessed the sudden arrival of foreigners on their very doorsteps. For Asian and European immigrants (and the French Canadian and African-American migrants who moved from one part of the continent to another) the "golden door" – or the open road – symbolized an eagerly sought launching pad into modernity; for Indians it signified an unwanted end to cherished traditions and the spoliation of their country.

It is useful to explore the meaning of the reservation era by examining maps from 1880 and 1960, but it would be misleading to assume that traffic on the nations' new roads and rail lines moved only in one direction. The rise of modern, industrial nations in North America did not simply complete a 400-year conquest; it also made possible unprecedented levels of communication and cooperation among members of the continent's aboriginal population. Such contacts in turn spawned a wide array of social and political organizations, which conditioned modern Native life and structured relations between Native people and the non-Indian majority.

The existence of highways and airports meant that Indians were vulnerable to "intrusions" from non-Indian missionaries and businessmen, but the reverse was also true: non-Indian law courts, business centers, and book publishers were increasingly accessible to Native Americans. The product of this mutual involvement was the formation in each country of new versions both of indigenous cultures, and, ultimately, of the larger nations that surrounded them.

Between 1880 and 1960, Canada and the United States defined Native homelands as "reserves" (Canada) or "reservations" (United States). Whether these areas were reserved by Native peoples for their own use in formal negotiations, or assigned to them by national authorities, they normally represented what remained of the original Native domain. These areas contained more than real estate. They encompassed religious and historic sites, community resources, and Native institutions. For their inhabitants and others who traced their origins there, reservations were cultural homelands. As a consequence, the borders between reserves and the nations which surrounded them, like the borders which previously had separated "Indian country" from "civilization," were cultural and political frontiers. Despite the permeability of modern social relations — the fact that over time Indians and non-Indians could travel and interact with growing freedom — reservations in the period from 1880 to 1960 continued to be arenas of exchange, negotiation, and conflict, places where Native traditions encountered non-Native demands.

This chapter will describe the major struggles that occurred between 1880 and 1960 as Indian people in the continental United States and southern Canada worked to sustain and defend their reserves and the cultures they embodied. (The experience of the Native peoples of the Arctic and Subarctic regions will be described in subsequent chapters.) It will also identify how the contentious relationship between the two nation states and Native peoples affected the evolving cultures of Indian America.

THE ASSAULT, 1880–1900

During the last two decades of the nineteenth century, the combined efforts of government officials and private citizens were uniformly bent in the interest of reducing the size of the Indian land base and gaining access to Indian resources. While these efforts were certainly not new (reservations had first been established in Virginia and Quebec in the seventeenth century), the wealth contained in Native landholdings, together with the skyrocketing population of both continental nations, made the future of North American Indians a subject of public debate. For the first time in each country's history, it was impossible to remove Native people to areas beyond the line of settlement. The assault on Indian lands and resources was therefore combined with an unprecedented array of efforts to "civilize" the Indian nations.

By 1900, most Indians in both countries were surrounded by outsiders. In Canada, 100,000 Natives (1.3 percent of the national population) lived on five million acres (2.023 million hectares) of land divided into 1,500 reserves. In the United States, approximately 250,000 Natives lived among nearly 76,000,000 other people on 200 reservations occupying nearly seventy-two million acres (29.14 million hectares). Except in the most remote areas, the indigenous peoples of both countries were vastly outnumbered by rapidly growing populations of ambitious outsiders.

In 1880 rail lines had only begun to penetrate the northern regions of Michigan, Wisconsin, and Minnesota, home to more than 20,000 Native people. In that same year there were fewer than 200,000 Euro-Americans in the Dakotas, Montana, and Wyoming combined; they shared that vast territory with perhaps 100,000 Indians. Similarly, Manitoba, Alberta, and Saskatchewan had few Euro-Canadian settlements, and the eastern portions of Washington State contained huge stretches without any concentrations of European population. In the American Southwest, towns like Albuquerque and Phoenix maintained non-Indian majorities, while rural areas in both Arizona and New Mexico Territories were overwhelmingly Indian in population and character. Standing between the Southwest and the older settlements of Louisiana and Arkansas was Indian Territory, with more than 100,000 Native people and still considered an Indian homeland. As the only part of North America which was not governed directly as a state, province, or territory, Indian Territory was unique.

In 1880 it would have been reasonable to suppose that the immigrant populations of the United States and Canada had reached the natural limits of their respective territories. Cities and factories clustered around eastern transportation points and harbors; mechanized agriculture had spread to the most accessible areas of each country. There was little need to expand into the arid, frigid, or heavily forested regions that now supported the bulk of the continent's Native people. One could have supposed in 1880 that the future expansion that might be required for the extraction of coal, timber, or precious metals from "unoccupied" areas could be accomplished without massive non-Indian settlement.

But each country viewed its "unsettled" regions as more than warehouses of resources, for both nations faced the continuing problem of forging a unified national identity and strengthening national institutions on a continent which fostered regional differences and cultural separatism. In the United States and Canada, "unsettled" areas were objects of fantasy, places where dreamers hoped the tendency toward fragmentation might be reversed by exciting national projects (such as railroad building) and the promise of a fresh start. Politicians, businessmen, and reformers alike could all paint their destinies on the seemingly "blank" regions that lay just beyond their control. Some sought the spread of railroads and commerce, others the extension of churches and schools, still others saw in the West or North the solution to urban crime and lawlessness. On both sides of the forty-ninth parallel, these non-Indian dreamers believed that the extension of "civilized" settlement was intimately connected to the creation of a national identity that excluded Indian cultures. This common allegiance – together with the booming population figures in both countries – explains the intensity of the settler assault on Native communities at the close of the nineteenth century.

The 1880s were years when Native people faced rapid reductions in the amount of land under their control. They either lost title to land through government seizures, or they were faced with an existence constrained by narrow boundaries which had previously been established but never before been enforced.

In the Great Lakes region, timber and rail interests sought access to minerals and timber. The Wisconsin Central Railroad reached Ashland, Wisconsin, on the southern shore of Lake Superior in 1877, touching off a riot of mining speculation, timber cutting, and industrial growth. In the wake of this change, local Ojibwa people at the Bad River, Lac Court Oreilles, and Lac Du Flambeau reserves were besieged with demands from businessmen who wanted access to their lands. These bands had ceded large areas to the United States in 1837, 1842, and 1854, and had resettled on reservations, but pressures on their remaining land base continued. During the 1880s and 1890s, these reservations were surveyed into eighty acre (32.4 hectare) parcels and assigned (or "allotted") to individual tribal members. "Surplus land" (the area left over after each member received an allotment) was sold and opened for Euro-American settlement. Through this method up to half the land within the Ojibwa reservations passed to Euro-American ownership.

Under the allotment system in Wisconsin, "Indian" lands remained under nominal Ojibwa ownership, but an order from the Secretary of the Interior in 1882 permitted tribal members to sell off the valuable timber that stood on their property. As a result, battalions of small timber-cutting outfits invaded the north woods and contracted with Ojibwa landowners to take their pine forests off their hands. In 1888, 731 of these contracts were approved, funneling over 190 million board feet (58 million meters) of timber into the American industrial machine and thousands of dollars into Ojibwa pockets. While the timber boom brought temporary prosperity to the region, it encouraged further encroachments on Indian communities and destroyed the forest environment which had supported Ojibwa communities for centuries.

On the Canadian Plains, seven treaties had been negotiated in the first decade following Canada's purchase of Rupert's Land from the Hudson's Bay Company in 1870 (see Chapter 13). These agreements had secured national title to all of the territory between Lake Superior and the Rockies in advance of Euro-Canadian settlement. In 1880, that settlement was eagerly anticipated as more than twenty-five million acres (10.1 million hectares) of former Indian land had been ceded to the Canadian Pacific Railway as a stimulus to construction. In the ensuing decade the company turned to the business of settling farmers along its lonely track and the economy of the region shifted rapidly from the fur trade to agriculture. Quickly, the Cree, Assiniboine, and Blackfeet residents of the region learned that the boundaries which had been nothing but marks on paper in the 1870s had became practical points of separation. As in the Great Lakes region, the spread of non-Indian enterprise meant both pressure on their borders and the transformation of traditional means of livelihood. On the Plains during the 1880s, the buffalo disappeared, the Hudson's Bay traders moved north to more isolated lands, and starvation became a familiar part of Native life.

South of the forty-ninth parallel, Plains communities under United States jurisdiction experienced a similar process. The American government expanded its ownership of Plains territory during the 1880s. Earlier treaties, such as those negotiated by the Indian Peace Commission at Medicine Lodge, Kansas, and Fort Laramie, Wyoming, in 1867 and 1868, had set aside huge areas as Indian homelands and hunting preserves. These agreements were drawn up at a time when the United States Congress was trying to ensure the construction of the Union Pacific Railroad and avoid the expense and controversy of a major Indian war. In the 1880s, with additional railroads snaking their way west along northern and southern routes and the military power of the Plains peoples broken, federal agents emulated the Canadians, exchanging promises of annual subsidies for large parcels of Indian land.

During the 1880s, the Colorado Utes, the Minnesota Ojibwas, the Lakota Sioux, the Crows, Blackfeet, and Assiniboines of Montana, the interior Salishes of eastern Washington, the Bannocks and Shoshones of Idaho, and several Oklahoma peoples lost over seventy million acres (28.3 million hectares) of their territory to the United States through a series of imposed land-sale agreements. As in the Canadian West, the impact of this land loss came upon the groups somewhat gradually. The completion of three additional transcontinental lines – the Southern Pacific (1881), Northern Pacific (1883), and Great Northern (1892) – spelled, first, the end of the buffalo, and, then, the arrival of non-Indian cattlemen and farmers.

A similar process involving vast unsettled areas took place in Oklahoma and represented the opening effort by the United States to breach agreements made with eastern emigrant peoples a half century before. When they were forcibly removed from Georgia, Alabama, Florida, and Mississippi in the 1830s, the so-called "civilized tribes" had been promised a permanent home west of the Mississippi. Because these groups had sided with the Confederacy in the Civil War, new treaties were imposed on them in 1866. These agreements reaffirmed the American government's recognition of the Oklahoma homeland, but they allowed for a vastly increased federal presence in the territory. They permitted the construction of rail lines across Indian land and provided for the cession of the entire western half of the territory to the United States for use as a home for relocated Western Indians.

During the 1880s, the reconstruction treaties in Indian Territory facilitated the erosion of the area's distinctive status. Federal actions curbed the reach of Native law and custom, producing predictable results. The new railroads authorized in the agreements brought large numbers of non-Indians into Native areas and disrupted the operations of local governments. Federal officials began relocating Midwestern and Plains peoples to the newly "opened" lands in the western portion of Indian Territory. While some Indian groups resisted this process (most notably the Cheyennes and Poncas), by 1890 there were twenty-one reservations in Indian Territory containing nearly seventy different peoples. Finally, the rising value of their lands prompted many groups to lease millions of acres of pastureland to Texas and Kansas cattle companies; these transactions brought yet another influx of non-Indians into the territory.

Railroad construction, the forced migration of Indian peoples into Oklahoma, and large-scale cattle leasing encouraged the notion that Indian Territory would soon be open for Euro-American settlement. This expectation grew during the 1880s when it became clear that the relocated groups would not fill all the "unclaimed" areas in western Oklahoma and that the supply of homestead land in other parts of the West was beginning to run out. Groups of "boomers" began to agitate for a federal purchase of unassigned Indian lands and to organize parties of

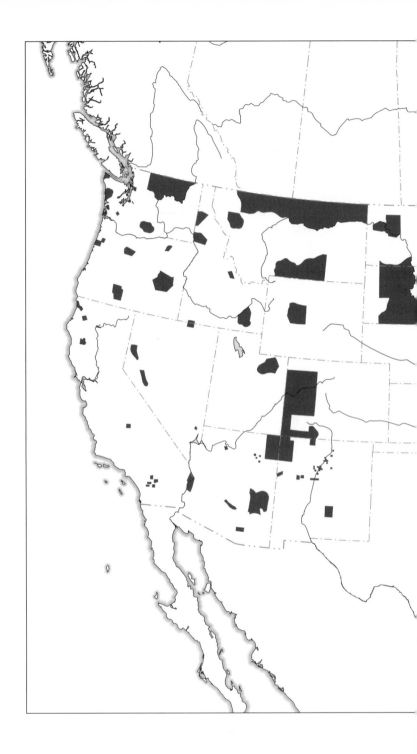

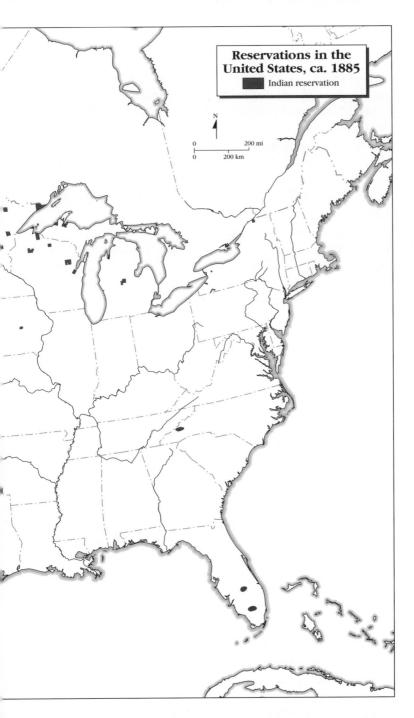

Figure 12.1 Reservations in the United States, ca. 1885.

squatters (or "sooners") who settled in the territory without authorization. Indian political leaders and lawyers battled these outlaws in Congress and the courts, but the arithmetic of politics and the force of racial prejudice undercut their efforts. In 1890 Congress organized Oklahoma Territory on property purchased from the Creeks and Seminoles. The land rush was on. Pressure for other Indian groups to sell "unused" lands intensified, and each new cession set off a fresh cycle of demands. In 1907, when Congress (over the objections of Indian leaders) admitted Oklahoma to the Union, the new state contained no reservations and non-Indians outnumbered Native Americans seven to one.

The 1880s were years of dramatic development in the plateau and coastal areas of Washington, Oregon, and Idaho. Inland peoples found farmers and ranchers pressing them for further land cessions, and fishing peoples faced competition for access to their most productive bay and river sites. In Whatcom County, Washington, for example, along the shores of Puget Sound, the Euro-American population increased more than fivefold during the 1880s, while the Indian population remained constant. The decade saw the first fish wheels installed along the banks of the Columbia River and the first corporate-sponsored fish traps in Puget Sound. Each of these innovations allowed newcomers to harvest many times the numbers of fish that had traditionally been obtained by netting and spearing. In 1883 the Northern Pacific Railroad reached the West Coast, providing shipping points for commercial farmers who were filling the inland valleys of the region and transportation lines for miners who pushed into Yakima, Colville, and Coeur d'Alene lands in their search for precious metals. In retrospect it is not surprising, then, that the 1880s also produced land-sale agreements (most notably at Colville, Coeur d'Alene, and Fort Hall) and an energetic government campaign to persuade fishing peoples such as the Lummi to turn to farming.

During the 1890s, with Washington and Idaho now admitted to the Union as states, the region's shift to commercial agriculture and the mechanized harvesting of aquatic resources accelerated. Indian leaders protested when they discovered commercial traps at their traditional Puget Sound fishing locations or were excluded from ancient netting sites along the Columbia, and they attempted to resist the seemingly constant expansion of spur lines and branch roads across their lands, but the assault on their territory continued. The Klamaths, for example, opposed the transfer of 87,000 acres (35,200 hectares) of ponderosa pine land to the California and Oregon Land Company, only to be told by the Indian Office that if they did not agree to to the sale, the property would be transferred without compensation. In southern Idaho, the railroad town of Pocatello grew up in the center of the Fort Hall reservation, setting off an irresistible demand for land cessions to be made by the resident Bannock and Shoshone peoples.

Farther north, along the Pacific Coast of Canada, Native communities widened their contacts with government officials, traders, and missionaries, but continued to feel less direct pressure on their landholdings and lifeways. At the same time, provincial authorities in British Columbia asserted that they held title to the entire area; they refused to recognize any aboriginal rights held by the local indigenous population. The result was a cycle of confrontations that has continued into our own time.

For the first two decades following British Columbia's entry into the Canadian confederation in 1871, the disinterest of local authorities in Indian affairs and the weakness of federal power caused the national government to rent a lighthouse tender, the *Sir James Douglas,* for $70 per day whenever it needed to send its agents up the coast from Victoria. European settlement increased during these years, however, and miners began to move through the interior regions of the province, so questions of land title and legal jurisdiction grew in importance and complexity. Nevertheless, Native people continued as the majority population, and some were powerful enough to resist Canadian expansion. At a meeting with a royal commission in 1884, for example, angry Tsimshian leaders asked, "How can the Queen own the land? She has never paid for it! She has not got it by conquest! Therefore she must have stolen it."[1] Following that encounter, disgusted Tsimshian people at Metlakatla, spurred on for his own reasons (see Chapter 11) by Methodist missionary William Duncan, actually left British Columbia and took up residence on U.S. soil at nearby Annette Island, Alaska. These and other disputes caused government forces to grow (the Canadian Indian Service finally purchased a gun boat in 1890), and they inspired Native organizations in the Northwest to become among the most sophisticated and tenacious lobbyists and legal strategists on the continent. One group representing British Columbia's Capilano Band took its appeal directly to King Edward VII in 1906.

The struggle over the potlatch ceremony dramatically illustrates both

[1] Quoted in Barry M. Gough, *Gunboat Frontier: British Maritime Authority and Northwest Coast Indians, 1846–1890* (Vancouver, 1984), 183.

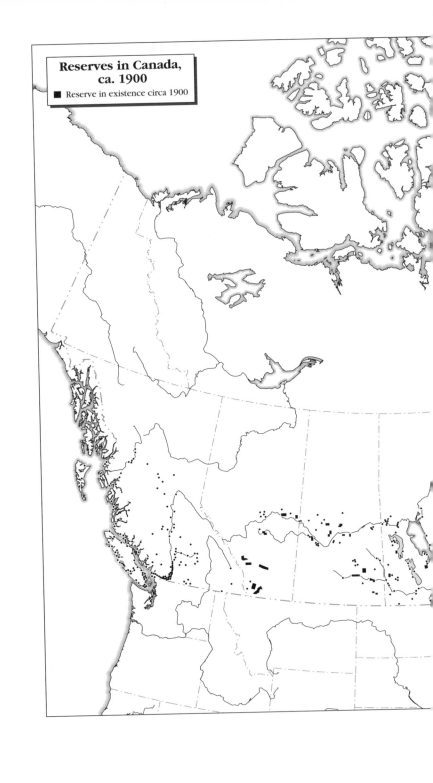

Reserves in Canada, ca. 1900

■ Reserve in existence circa 1900

Figure 12.2 Reserves in Canada, ca. 1900.

British Columbia's effort to extend its authority into remote areas of the Northwest and the active resistance of the province's Native people. Potlatches were grand celebrations held by coastal peoples which featured feasting and massive give-aways of handicrafts and trade goods. A potlatch was an opportunity for hosts to display their generosity and reinforce social relationships within a community. To the agents of Victorian civilization, however, they appeared wasteful and barbarous. In 1884 the Canadian parliament outlawed the potlatch and began to suppress it, but the ceremony flourished. This cultural battle continued through the 1890s, and few Indians were persuaded that their traditions were evil. Historian Robin Fisher has noted, for example, that when anthropologist Franz Boas first visited one coastal group in 1886 "he had to assure them that he was not a government agent before they would accept him. . . . they made it clear that they would not follow the orders to give up potlatching and that they despised the Indian administration."[2] By the turn of the century the ceremony had been driven underground, but its revival following the repeal of the 1884 law in 1951 demonstrated that potlatching had been kept alive in some form during the years of suppression.

Even Indians living east of the Mississippi felt a surge of Euro-American expansion during the 1880s. The United States Census for 1880 reported slightly over 11,000 Native Americans in the Northeast and Southeast, approximately 5 percent of the national Indian total. These people lived in isolated, rural communities and were generally not recognized by the federal government as tribes. Nevertheless, groups like the Mashpees of Massachusetts and the Lumbees of North Carolina maintained town and group traditions and tried to prevent the extension of non-Indian settlement. During the 1880s and 1890s their communities faced unprecedented pressures.

The town of Mashpee on Cape Cod had been established as a Christian Indian settlement in the seventeenth century, and its communal lands had been protected since then by both colonial and state governments. In 1869 the state of Massachusetts removed these restrictions and non-Mashpees began buying up most of the town's cranberry bogs and ocean-front lots. As the century drew to a close, therefore, the town's residents had moved silently from independent lives as landowners who farmed and fished for a living, to the dependent status of wage earners and tenants.

In North Carolina, Indian people feared the legal and cultural institu-

---

[2] Robin Fisher, *Contact and Conflict: Indian-European Relations in British Columbia, 1774–1890* (Vancouver, 1977), 207.

tions of the New South as much as they feared the expanding railroads and textile mills. In that state as in others in the region, the rise of Jim Crow laws (which mandated separate schools and public accommodations for the races) threatened to lump Native Americans with local African-Americans. In 1885 the Lumbee community, which had previously been defined as consisting of "free people of color," successfully petitioned the state legislature to recognize them as "Croatan Indians," named after a coastal island which had figured in the story of the "lost" sixteenth-century English colony at Roanoke. This state recognition exempted the group from attending the newly established African-American schools and offered them the possibility of escaping other forms of segregation. In the aftermath of this victory, Lumbees opened their own Indian schools and launched a teacher-training institution that became Pembroke State University. The Lumbees hoped that these steps would hold off the expansion of segregationist institutions and protect their distinctive sense of community.

The great exception to this decade of unrestrained non-Indian expansion occurred in the most isolated region of the continent outside the Arctic and Subarctic: the American Southwest. There railroad expansion and mineral exploration dislocated Native communities, but relatively little property changed hands. The Navajos were the most prominent exceptions to the experiences of other groups in other places. Rebounding from the horror of their collective imprisonment at Bosque Redondo in the 1860s, the Navajos doubled their population between 1870 and 1900 and moved peacefully from hunting and gathering to a predominant reliance on herding and farming. While the village peoples of the region (the pueblos of the Rio Grande, Hopi, and Zuni) suffered continual pressure on their outlying lands during the 1880s and 1890s (indeed, it was at this time that Hopis and Navajos began their century-long struggle to control the same grazing and hunting territory), there were no major land cessions in the territories of Arizona and New Mexico.

For most Native Americans, however, the disruptive arrival of non-Indians in their neighborhoods forced them to function in a cash economy. Native Americans had begun to slip into the orbit of the market almost at the point of first contact in the sixteenth and seventeenth centuries, but it was not until the late nineteenth century that cash threatened to eradicate self-sufficiency as the principal means of subsistence for most Indians. Indians in Massachusetts, New York, and North Carolina labored as sailors, domestic servants, and agricultural laborers. In the Great Lakes region, an Indian population of approximately 50,000 spread itself across both sides of the international border amid a Euro-American population in excess of fifteen million. These Native people made a living through farming, fishing, and trading in northern areas that remained isolated from Euro-American settlement, and worked for wages elsewhere.

On the Plains, agriculture and cattle production became an option, particularly after 1883 when the buffalo became extinct and the establishment of new reservation boundaries made it difficult for Indian people to pursue other animals. In both the United States and Canada, the land cession treaties of the 1860s and the 1870s contained provisions for agricultural training and development to replace hunting as the basis for subsistence. Government agents in both countries found many groups, such as the Dakotas of Manitoba and the Yankton Sioux along the Missouri River, eager for this new technology. Despite the hardships accompanying early wheat and corn farming in the region, Native leaders quickly saw that draft animals and labor-saving devices could produce cash crops that might become a substitute for the fur trade and the buffalo hunt.

In the 1880s there was reason to believe that Natives might shift to agriculture with relatively little difficulty. Groups on the Canadian Plains pooled their resources to purchase mowers, rakes, and self-binders and tried out new seed supplied by the Central Experimental Farm in Ottawa. In the United States, agents divided their reservations into districts and assigned Euro-American farmers to them who organized model gardens to teach agricultural techniques and demonstrate the rewards of hard work. These efforts seemed to bear fruit. For example, a recent study of the number of acres cultivated per person on thirty-three reservations during this period shows that twenty-seven of them (82 percent) sustained an annual growth rate of more than 5 percent, despite the fact that most of the communities examined had no experience with commercial farming.

Unfortunately, in the 1880s progress did not necessarily bring prosperity. Indian farmers were hampered by bad weather and the uncertain supply of government tools and seed. Fixed on their reservations, individuals could not move to better soil or to a site closer to the expanding railroad lines as conditions changed. Even Indian groups with a history of prosperity, such as the "Five Civilized Tribes" of Oklahoma and the fishing peoples of the Northwest Coast, were made vulnerable by a rapidly expanding cash economy. They could not match the capital outlays of industrial corporations (such as the Alaska Packers Corporation) or the political influence of wealthy cattlemen and large landowners.

Like the Oklahoma Indians, the Indians of California, that is, those who had survived the whirlwind of the gold rush and the chaos of American settlement, were familiar with the workings of a cash economy. Nevertheless, during the 1880s and 1890s, the expansion of California's non-Indian settlements – and the rapidly rising value of Native lands – placed the state's Native communities at risk. Because most California Indians did not live on reservations, title to their lands was often unclear or nonexistent. In the last two decades of the century, despite the efforts of a congressional commission chaired by the Quaker reformer Albert Smiley, and the legal appeals of local Indians and their supporters (one case, *Barker v. Harvey* [1901], made it to the Supreme Court), thousands of California's Native people lost their homes. The most dramatic of these dispossessions occurred in 1903 at Warner's Ranch near San Diego, where villages of Cupeño, San Luiseño, and Kumeyaay Indians were evicted by a large landowner, and moved by the Army to a new reservation. Leaving their community churches and graveyards behind, the people of Warner's Ranch were marched to a new reservation home in the Pala Valley.

The extension of Euro-American property ownership and the advent of a cash economy were an outgrowth of government action. However much non-Indians might celebrate the "invisible hand" of capitalism or the "rugged individualism" of men like railroad tycoon James J. Hill or the Oklahoma oil baron J. Paul Getty, the destruction of landholding by Native groups, which enriched both men, required the frequent use of federal power. Both Hill's Great Northern Railroad and Getty's empire of wells began with the appropriation of what had recently been Indian assets.

The enthusiasm for capitalist expansion did more than open Indian resources to outsiders. It also inspired the government agents responsible for Native welfare in Canada and the United States to superimpose "civilized habits" on the Indians' shattered lifeways. If traditional cultures were going to be obliterated, government officials reasoned, a replacement would be needed quickly. Between 1880 and 1895 the U.S. Office of Indian Affairs started twenty off-reservation boarding schools and opened or expanded day schools at every agency; during this period, annual appropriations for Indian education rose from $75,000 to over $2 million. Canadian officials visited the United States and were particularly impressed by the "industrial training" schools, such as the one at Carlisle, Pennsylvania. Appropriations for such schools became a part of the Indian Department's annual budget in 1884, and by 1896 there were twenty boarding schools (largely operated by Christian missionary organizations) in Manitoba, British Columbia, and the Northwest Territories. At the turn of the century, a uniform, government-mandated curriculum was being imposed on more than 30,000 Indian children across the continent.

Other "civilized" institutions sought to forge a new pattern of life in Indian communities. In the United States, Courts of Indian Offenses and reservation police forces appeared at most agencies during the 1880s. First authorized in 1878, Indian policemen were government employees who reported to the local agent and were supported when necessary by regular Army troops. In 1883 Congress expanded this system by establishing Courts of Indian Offenses to punish those who disobeyed reservation authorities. The Indian Office hoped that Indian judges and policemen would ensure that the pressing necessities of working, attending school, and abandoning traditional ways would be recognized and followed by all the Indians who lived on reservations. On reserves in the Canadian West there was no equivalent to the Indian police. There, the North-West Mounted Police had jurisdiction over both Indians and non-Indians, and these officers were frequently called upon to enforce the provisions of the Indian Act. These included an amendment passed in 1895 which elaborated on the government's previous banning of the potlatch ceremony by declaring that anyone who engaged in ceremonies involving the giving away of "money goods or articles," or the "mutilation of the dead or living body of any human being or animal" would be subject to arrest and imprisonment. Such extensive controls were even extended to "civilized activities"; a statute approved by parliament in 1930 permitted the arrest of an individual found "misspending or wasting his time" in a poolroom!

Christian missions had long been a fixture in most North American Indian communities, but during the 1880s, the churches forged an alliance with both the Canadian and U.S. governments' "civilization" efforts. In the United States the tradition of separating church and state prevented religious societies from implementing federal policies, but mission personnel and Christian values were an integral part of every reservation community. Canadians were explicit about their reliance on the churches to spread "civilization" to Indian people. In both countries, Indian people faced a common front of government officials and Christian churches; both advocated the suppression of traditional lifeways and both taught that there was no alternative to the Indians' adopting private property, capitalism, and Victorian standards of morality.

The fullest expression of the American government's commitment to replacing communal with capitalist values came in 1887, when President Grover Cleveland signed the General Allotment Act into law. Anticipated by allotment provisions in treaties and agreements approved over the previous half-century, the new law granted the president the authority to direct the division of any reservation into individual landholdings. Following this process, the Executive was authorized to negotiate with Native leaders for the sale of all unclaimed (or "surplus") lands. Called the Dawes Act in honor of its Senate sponsor, Massachusetts Senator Henry L. Dawes, the new law became the principal vehicle for facilitating non-Indian access to Indian lands. Between the time of its passage in 1887 and its repeal in 1934, this "reform statute" was called upon to dismember most of the reservations in the United States. (Indian Territory was broken up under a different statute – the Curtis Act – and both New York State and the communities of the arid Southwest were exempted from the law.) When a final accounting was made in the 1930s, government officials estimated that the Dawes Act had brought about the loss of over 90,000,000 acres (36.4 million hectares) of Indian-owned land.

There was no general allotment law in Canada, but the 1869 Indian Act contained provisions to allow federal authorities to issue individual land titles to any resident of an Indian reserve who appeared to be "a safe and suitable person for becoming a proprietor of land." The allotment provisions of the Indian Act were initially implemented in southern Ontario, but they did not become a central feature of Native life because Indian landowners were only allowed to sell their farms to members of their band. Relatively little land passed to non-Indians because Canadian reserves were so much smaller than their American counterparts (an average size in Canada at the end of the nineteenth century was 3–4,000 acres [1,200–1,600 hectares] compared to 300,000 or more acres [121,400 hectares] in the United States). As a result, even though Canadian Indians were repeatedly subjected to sermons on the virtues of individual land ownership – and many saw their lands pass to the control of Euro-Canadians who leased their property rather than purchased it – there was less pressure placed on them by non-Indians to dispose of a band's "surplus."

Despite the breadth of the assault on Indian communities in the 1880s and 1890s, the reach of non-Indian businesses and bureaucrats varied from agency to agency. In areas with large, scattered populations (such as the Navajo reservation and the isolated villages of the Pacific Coast) the authority of non-Indians was uneven and sporadic; individuals faced the government's courts and missionaries when they "came in" to trade or enroll their children in the schools, but otherwise they were able to live their daily lives without interference. For a growing majority of communities, however, "the agency" (consisting of some combination of government office, guard house, school, blacksmith, warehouse, and Christian mission) was a constant, intrusive factor in their lives.

Not surprisingly, the pressures of the 1880s met resistance. Most Indian groups were unconvinced by the government's frequent promise that the sale of "excess" lands would satisfy European settlers, and their leaders resented the constant pressure for more concessions. It seemed that treaties and agreements were no sooner made than an Indian Office representative appeared to discuss redrawing what the Indians had believed were "permanent" reservation boundaries. Indian leaders frequently complained that the government treated them as if they had no rights. Angered by such official duplicity, many groups simply refused to negotiate.

For example, the Teton Sioux of Dakota Territory defeated two separate attempts to reduce the size of their reservation during the 1880s. Led by famous old warriors such as Sitting Bull, Gall, and Red Cloud, the various bands insisted on maintaining the relatively generous boundaries established at Fort Laramie and recorded in their treaty of 1868. The Hunkpapa leader Sitting Bull even traveled to other reservations to urge their chiefs to send the government officials packing. In Oklahoma, as the Dawes Act was being debated in Congress, both the "civilized tribes" of the east and the newly resettled Plains communities in the west met to form a united front against allotment and land sales and to dispatch a team of lobbyists to Washington, D.C.

Unity worked for a time, but it could not resist the political and economic momentum of the era. In 1889, as North and South Dakota prepared to join the Union as states, a commission headed by veteran Indian fighter General George Crook bullied the Sioux into an "agreement" which opened millions of acres west of the Missouri River to Euro-American settlement. In Indian Territory the Kiowas tried to stop a similar 1892 land sale with a federal injunction. Their efforts carried the case to the United States Supreme Court, but they were ultimately defeated when the justices announced their decision. Balancing congressional power against old promises made in treaties, the Court in *Lone Wolf v. Hitchcock* declared that "the power exists to abrogate the provisions of an Indian treaty." An exultant Commissioner of Indian Affairs immediately reported to Congress that *Lone Wolf* "will enable you to dispose of land without the consent of the Indians."[3]

Aware of these defeats, other Indian groups tried sabotage. In 1889, when Smithsonian anthropologist Alice Fletcher came to the Nez Percé reservation to supervise the allotment and sale of that group's lands, she reported that boundary markers for new Indian homesteads were regularly removed by angry Indians. Other forms of noncooperation could be found elsewhere. Parents hid their children from reservation policemen and others who came to enroll them in schools or balked at taking up unfamiliar farming and ranching techniques. While some missionaries were successful, others discovered that Native people were boycotting their services. Occasionally, resistance turned violent.

The most dramatic example of Native opposition to expanding federal authority in the 1880s came on the Canadian Plains. There the Cree leaders Poundmaker and Big Bear had grown increasingly outspoken in their opposition to the new system of numbered treaties. With perhaps 10 percent of their population dying each year, the buffalo gone, and rations frequently cut off by the government as a way of forcing bands to comply with its orders, these tribal elders began to feel that there was no alternative to resistance. Interband councils and a series of "thirst dances" in the summer of 1884 seemed to lay the foundation for a movement that would bring together representatives from across the Plains and produce a set of revised treaties. With the example of the defeated American Indian groups before them, Big Bear and the other leaders made it clear that they did not want a military confrontation.

At the same moment as these "hostile" bands were mobilizing their members, Louis Riel, a Métis leader who had played a prominent role in the mixed-blood community's stand against the Canadian authorities in Manitoba in 1869–70, returned north from exile in Montana and rallied support among his old followers in what is now Saskatchewan. Hoping that the region's 20,000 Indians might unite with its 4,800 Métis, Riel decided to act. On March 19, 1885, the Métis of the village of Batoche on the Saskatchewan River arrested the local Indian agent, seized control of the town, and declared the existence of a new provisional government. In the following weeks, hundreds of Indians, led largely by frustrated young warriors from Big Bear's and Little Pine's bands, joined in the rebellion

[3] *House Report* 443, 58 Congress, 2nd Session, 4–5. For a fuller account of the *Lone Wolf* decision and its impact, see Frederick E. Hoxie, *A Final Promise: The Campaign to Assimilate the Indians* (Lincoln, Nebr., 1984), 152–162.

against the Canadian authorities. The leaders remained aloof, however, and large-scale Cree support for the Métis never materialized.

Riel's rebellion revealed the fragility of the Canadian government's hold on the Plains. Federal officials were aware that Indian involvement in the uprising was minimal, but they were quick to take advantage of Euro-Canadian fears of a general Native revolt. Immediately upon hearing of the revolt, Edgar Dewdney, Canada's Commissioner of Indian Affairs for the North-West Territories, requested that troops be sent to Alberta by way of the new trans-Canada rail line, and he declared that any Indian found off his reserve would be considered a rebel. The army retook Batoche in mid-May and set off to capture the resistance leaders. Big Bear's family escaped into Montana, as did hundreds of Métis, but the chief and his colleague Poundmaker surrendered to Canadian officials in July. By then, the fighting was over. Trials ensued – as did continued migrations into Montana – and on November 16, Louis Riel was hanged. Significantly, however, the eight other men who received capital punishment for participating in the rebellion were all Indians. Six Crees and two Assiniboines were hanged on November 27. These executions marked the end of the government's suppression of the Riel uprising. It provides grisly proof that the revolt marked a dramatic defeat for the Plains Indians as well as for the mixed-blood Métis.

In the United States during these years, the government's response to the few instances of direct Indian resistance to Euro-American expansion was similarly swift and brutal. Chiricahua and White Mountain Apaches who fled their reservations in the 1880s found themselves pursued across the rugged southwestern landscape and into Mexico by hundreds of regular Army troops. Even after their leaders Geronimo and Naiche surrendered for good in 1886, the government insisted on shipping all suspected hostiles (including several Apaches who had served Army units as scouts) to Fort Pickens and Fort Marion prisons in Florida. The Apaches were transferred to Fort Sill, Oklahoma, in 1894 where they remained as prisoners of war until 1913. Geronimo died in 1909.

In Montana in 1887, a small group of young Crows rode noisily through their reservation's headquarters, shooting at buildings and persuading their agent that a general rebellion was in the offing. Again, retaliation was swift. By the time Sword Bearer and his "hostile" band had been subdued (and the leader killed), several hundred troops had been dispatched to the field by the Army's commanders in Washington, D.C.

The bloodiest conflict in North America during this period occurred in

1890 along Wounded Knee Creek on the Pine Ridge Sioux Reservation in the newly admitted state of South Dakota. Following a now common pattern, local Indian Office officials responded to the outbreak of an Indian religious revival – the Ghost Dance – among the Sioux by massing federal troops around the Native camps. The expectation was that the assembled units would intimidate the Sioux as they had the Crows, or that they would divide the group into a small, violent minority and a large, "reasonable" majority. Neither hope was fulfilled. The Pine Ridge and Rosebud Sioux communities were many times the size of the small Apache and Crow groups, and their leaders were not men who trusted officers of the U.S. Army: they were battle-hardened veterans of campaigns against the Americans in eastern Montana in the 1860s, as well as of Colonel George Armstrong Custer's famous defeat along the Little Bighorn River in 1876.

The new religion had begun in Nevada where, during a total eclipse of the sun on New Year's Day, 1889, a Paiute man named Wovoka or Jack Wilson received a message of peace and right living from the Creator. Son of a religious leader, and already respected as a "weather doctor," Wilson began preaching and receiving delegations from an ever-widening circle of western Indians. Assisted by speedy rail service, his message spread to groups in California, Arizona, Wyoming, Oklahoma, and the Dakotas. During the summer of 1890, growing numbers of Lakota began to perform the round dance Wilson had prescribed as an imitation of the sun's course.

Taken aback by the government's nervous reaction to the new religion, the Ghost Dancers and their sympathizers at Pine Ridge and the other Sioux reservations withdrew to isolated areas and considered their response. They feared a Euro-American attack no less than the Euro-American authorities feared a tribal uprising. As fall turned to winter, the dancers and the military moved farther and farther apart from each other. Each side waited for the other to act out its worst fears.

The tragedy began on December 15 at the Standing Rock reservation when, acting on the orders of Agent James McLaughlin (and supported by regular Army units), a detachment of Indian policemen killed Sitting Bull while placing him under arrest. The death at the hands of the government of a man who for three decades had been the apostle of Sioux resistance stretched the tension between Indians and soldiers as tight as piano wire. Within days, the Miniconjou leader Big Foot, fearing that he too would be "arrested," mobilized his band at the nearby Cheyenne River agency and began moving the group away from the reach of the local agent and his policemen. Big Foot was apprehended by elements of the Seventh Cavalry near Wounded Knee Creek on December 28. The following morning, as the band was being disarmed and other military units continued to pursue elusive and ambiguous Ghost Dancers elsewhere at Pine Ridge, shots rang out over the frozen prairie.

Disputes continue over who fired the first shot, but when the army's repeating rifles and mobile artillery fell silent, 146 Sioux men, women, and children (including the Miniconjou chief who had been too ill to leave his tent) lay dead on the battlefield. Twenty-five soldiers had perished in the fighting.

Resistance to Euro-American encroachments continued after Wounded Knee. For example, Redbird Smith of the Cherokees and Chitto Harjo of the Creeks continued to oppose the dissolution of Indian Territory and the allotment of Indian lands long after both events had occurred. Elsewhere Chippewa (Anishinabe), Cree, and Winnebago people who opposed government programs on their reserves simply left their agencies and tried to establish new communities on unclaimed lands in Wisconsin and Montana. Nevertheless, the killing in South Dakota drove home to Native people the reality of Euro-American domination. Despite the humanitarian outrage expressed by citizens who were sickened by the Wounded Knee murders, it was clear that in the United States, as in Canada, direct opposition to government policy would be treated as a challenge to national power and would be met with force.

RE-CREATIONS OF NATIVE LIFE, 1900–1920

In 1900 it would not have been unreasonable for an outside observer to conclude that the scale and brutality of the recent assault on Indian communities would soon destroy the Indian way of life. With Native lands and resources transformed into commodities that Euro-Americans could buy or lease, Native traditions outlawed or debased, and so many Native leaders destroyed, it appeared that most of the continent's indigenous people were entering a period of social and economic domination.

Miraculously, while the domination took place and its consequences grew more horrible, the experiences neither stripped away everything that made Indian people distinct, nor severed the threads of memory that bound Native Americans to their past. All the instruments of two modern nation states were bent in the service of cultural destruction; yet the inventiveness, strength, and obstinate endurance of these communities preserved them – altered but whole.

Indian people have long insisted that "religion" and daily life are closely intertwined. As a consequence, there are several points in the histories of most Native peoples when political crises have inspired new religious leaders and new rituals. For example, the Delaware Prophet called for the renewal of old lifeways in the bloody aftermath of the Seven Years War, and the Wanapam (Sahaptin) leader Smohalla advocated an end to sales of "mother earth" as Euro-Americans began surrounding his kinsmen at the western end of the Oregon Trail in the 1850s. It is not surprising, then, that the accelerating assault on Indian communities in the 1880s and 1890s contributed to yet another series of religious innovations.

In December 1881 two rail lines entered Laredo, Texas. From the east, the Texas-Mexican line connected the dusty, Rio Grande town to the gulf port of Corpus Christi. As it cut across southern Texas, the new railroad passed through part of the small area where peyote (*Lophophora williamsii*) will grow in North America. While this east-west road was being completed, Laredo became the southern terminus of a rail line running north to Austin, Texas, and on to Indian Territory. For the first time, peyote buttons, which been used in religious rituals in the Rio Grande Valley for centuries, could be transported cheaply and in bulk to Indians living outside their immediate area of cultivation.

Many stories surround the origins of peyote in modern Oklahoma, but most sources agree that during the 1880s Lipan Apache men began to conduct all-night ceremonies centered on the use of the plant among the Oklahoma Comanches and Kiowas. Their activities were supported by steady shipments of peyote over the new rail lines. ("It is kept by almost all the little stores in Greer County," one Euro-American resident reported in 1886.)[4] Two Lipan teachers, Pinero and Chiwat, are frequently identified as early apostles of the peyote ritual, but they were surely joined by others whose names have been lost and by local disciples who quickly mastered the rite.

The "peyote religion" had many elements that appealed to reservation communities at the turn of the century. It focused on the peyote button as a source of inspiration and did not depend on a specific place or Indian group's tradition for its power. It promised to restore the health of partici-

[4] Quoted in Omer C. Stewart, *Peyote Religion: A History* (Norman, Okla., 1987), 62.

pants both through the ritual itself and through group sanctions against alcohol use. Peyotists emphasized the Christian-like aspects of their faith – they often mentioned the similarity of peyote and the Christian sacrament and reported that Jesus appeared in their visions – but the ritual had an unmistakable Indianness: it included drumming and singing in the Native language, it lasted through an entire night, it was egalitarian, and its object was communion with an unseen, but immediate spiritual world.

The appeal and mobility of the peyote ritual was unprecedented. Between 1900 and 1920, the religious use of peyote moved north from Oklahoma to the Winnebagos of Nebraska and Wisconsin and the Ojibwas of Minnesota, west to Taos Pueblo, and across the Plains to the Sioux of the Dakotas, the Cheyennes and Crows of Montana, the Shoshones and Arapahos of Wyoming, and the Utes of Utah. While the official record is unclear, there is good reason to believe that peyote use had also spread to the Canadian Plains by the mid-1920s.

In each new community, the peyote ritual was led by "road men" who had learned it from other practitioners and who trained others to assist them in their work. This first generation of leaders – John Rave among the Winnebagos, Frank Bethune among the Crows, Jim Blue Bird among the Sioux, and Lorenzo Martinez at Taos Pueblo – were formidable advocates for the new religion. They posed no military threat to the government, and they accepted most of the Indian Office's regulations concerning the adoption of Euro-American lifeways. But as they pursued their calling to spread the faith, they began to form a powerful new infrastructure of Native American leadership.

Most prominent of the early Peyote leaders was the Comanche chief Quanah Parker. The son of a prominent warrior and Cynthia Ann Parker, a Euro-American captive, Quanah spent his young adulthood as a committed opponent of American expansion, raiding settlements in Texas and fighting bravely at the battle of Adobe Walls in 1874. Once he agreed to settle on the Comanche reservation in 1875, however, Quanah professed friendship for all Euro-Americans and adopted his mother's family name as his own. Despite the fact that he insisted on keeping multiple wives, he otherwise cooperated fully with the new "civilization" program. He also acquired an admiration for the American constitution. In the 1890s, for example, when the Oklahoma Territorial legislature was debating the prohibition of peyote use, Parker stated his case in terms a Euro-American could not ignore: "I do not think this Legislature should interfere with a man's religion."⁵ He repeated this argument frequently during the next two decades, and certainly inspired – although he did not live to see – the formal incorporation of the Native American Church in Oklahoma in 1918.

Oklahoma peyotists formed the Native American Church "to foster and promote the religious belief . . . in the Christian religion with the practice of the Peyote Sacrament . . . and to teach . . . morality, sobriety, industry, kindly charity and right living." The new organization represented thousands of believers in the state. It quickly became a persistent enemy of prohibition legislation in both Oklahoma and in Washington, D.C., and it spawned affiliated churches in other states with large peyote congregations. The Native American Church of the United States was organized in 1944 as an umbrella organization. Its first elected officers were from the Cheyenne, Kiowa, Crow, and Oto peoples, reflecting its pan-Indianness as well as its ties to the original road men who shipped their peyote north from Laredo in the 1880s.

The rapid rise of the peyote faith provides the most dramatic example of religious reorganization among Indian peoples in the first decades of the twentieth century, but it was by no means unique. In virtually every Indian community, Native leaders attempted to understand their new condition in religious terms. The Ghost Dance, for example, which had continued to draw followers even after the killing at Wounded Knee, provided a coherent religious solution to recent events for many groups. Jack Wilson (or Wovoka) continued to sell the red paint which was emblematic of his vision to followers across the Great Basin and Plains, and to repeat his message of peace, hard work, and sobriety until his death in 1932. Among the Indians who persisted in following him were the Kiowas, Comanches, and Pawnees of Oklahoma, Sioux groups in Saskatchewan, and Shoshones in Wyoming.

In the Pacific Northwest, two other visionary movements – the Dreamers and the Indian Shaker Church – survived into the twentieth century and offered a similar kind of hope. While their practitioners could trace these movements' origins to a tradition of visionary prophets that had begun long before the arrival of Europeans, twentieth-century Dreamers and the Shakers each began with a new, founding vision. The Dreamers were Plateau people, followers of Smohalla (1815?–95) and Skolaskin (1839–1922); the Shaker Church was founded in Puget Sound by a

⁵ Ibid., 75.

Squaxin man named Squsachtun, or John Slocum (1842–97) (see Chapter 11). Each of these leaders called on his followers to form congregations of hardworking, sober believers.

Both Smohalla and Skolaskin rejected the government's assimilation program. Instead they advocated the preservation of traditional subsistence – gathering and fishing – and the adoption of an ascetic, religious life. Skolaskin urged his followers to spend their Sundays reciting prescribed prayers. Despite their peaceful message, both dreamer prophets and their followers were actively suppressed by federal authorities. Skolaskin was imprisoned at the military prison on Alcatraz Island between 1889 and 1892 for subverting reservation discipline, but he returned to the Colville Reservation following his release and continued to criticize both private land ownership and Christianity. By the turn of the century, various forms of the Dreamer faith, often called the Longhouse or Feather religion, had spread across the interior Northwest and were forming both a formidable buttress for Native values and a remarkable vehicle for the preservation of Native leadership.

John Slocum's vision was pointedly Christian, for it taught that sinners would to to Hell and pious practitioners of the new faith would ascend to Heaven. Also like the Christian missionaries around them, Slocum's followers erected churches and dispatched teachers to surrounding Puget Sound communities. In time, the group also adopted a hierarchy of bishops and priests.

The rise of new faiths is a distinctive feature of early-twentieth-century Indian religious life, but the period was also marked both by the persistence of older spiritual traditions and by an expansion of Indian participation in organized Christianity. Despite federal bans on the potlatch, the Plains Sun Dance, vision quests, and other forms of Native ceremony, Indian communities continued to value ancient religious practice and to revere elders who had special religious power. In Canada, for example, the Blackfeet held modified Sun Dances which did not involve the "mutilations" prohibited by the Indian Act. In the United States, the ritual actually spread during this period, moving west from the Plains to the Utes and Shoshones in Utah and Idaho.

In the early twentieth century, Native Americans in both the United States and Canada also took part in Christian worship in growing numbers. Indian pastors, such as Philip Deloria among the Sioux, the Nez Percé Billy Williams, and the many Native leaders among the Oklahoma Creeks and Cherokees, reaffirmed indigenous values in a new setting.

They preached the teachings of Jesus, but accepted the existence of distinct Indian communities and encouraged group activities. For example, they encouraged the formation of lay organizations, women's clubs, and community service groups. Among the Papagos preservation of the tribe's chapel dedicated to Saint Francis Xavier honored both the sixteenth-century Jesuit father and the community's own history of survival through two centuries of outside rule.

Running parallel to the religious inventions, survivals, and accommodations in the first two decades of the twentieth century were a variety of cultural innovations. Pow-wows, community festivals, and fairs allowed groups to gather in explicitly secular settings that local Euro-Americans would find acceptable. The result was the emergence of a range of pan-Indian activities that both reinforced local affiliations and forged new ties among Native groups. The Grass Dance, for example, which in the nineteenth century had been the property of Pawnee and Omaha warriors, was appropriated by Teton Sioux and other Plains communities and became a central feature of multigroup gatherings. Practitioners of the new dance also adopted the Omahas' deer-hair head roaches and feather bustles, which quickly became the mark of a "traditional" Indian dancer across the American and Canadian Plains.

The Grass Dance was frequently performed at community gatherings called by the government. Assembled to celebrate the fourth of July in the United States or Dominion Day (July 1) in Canada, Indian people would win permission to "honor" their national government with a dance. Carrying over the tradition of the warrior societies that had inspired the original dance, the Grass Dancers also used these occasions to provide for the needy in their communities with generous distributions of food and clothing. Other activities quickly ensued: dancing and drumming competitions, visits from (and return visits to) distant tribes, women's and children's dances, and displays of traditional crafts. All this activity was amplified by rail and automobile transport and encouraged whenever the events occurred near a tourist center.

In the Southwest, tourists riding the Santa Fe Railroad or venturing along the nation's expanding highway system encountered Indian ceremonies that were clearly religious but that were either partially Christian or practiced by groups that were so small and isolated that they seemed harmless. The Hopi snake dance and the seasonal dances among the Rio Grande pueblos attracted curious visitors and were publicized by local boosters and such magazines as Charles Lummis's Los Angeles–based *Land of Sunshine.* In Tucson, colorful dances performed by refugee Yaquis from Mexico played a central role in winning local sympathy for them. The group's ultimate acceptance by U.S. officials in 1978 capped a struggle for cultural survival that had begun nearly a century earlier.

East of the Mississippi other groups took advantage of the growing American tolerance for secular expressions of Indian community life. In Mississippi, 2,000 Choctaws who had resisted all efforts to remove them to Oklahoma with the rest of their people followed the earlier pattern of the North Carolina Lumbees and sought a legal designation that would set them apart from the state's African-Americans. Aided by an odd coalition of Catholic missionaries, local segregationists, and academics, the Mississippi Choctaws succeeded in winning a federal reservation in the central section of the state. In New England and the Canadian Maritimes, where small and frequently unrecognized communities had continued to hunt and fish for a livelihood, the first two decades of the new century brought a growing involvement in tourism as guides and service workers, and the beginnings of intergroup gatherings. These pow-wows were built on old lines of association and alliance among Passamaquoddy, Penobscot, Maliseet, and Micmac (Mi'kmaq) bands in the north, and New England Algonquian groups farther south. The process of renewed affiliation was formalized among some of the groups in 1926 with the formation of the Algonkian Council of Indian Tribes.

The transfer of cultural activity to the political arena occurred in a number of settings. In 1912 in Alaska, the Alaska Native Brotherhood was founded to represent coastal communities, including the Tlingits, Haidas, and many Tsimshians. Presbyterian missionaries assisted the organizers of the first meeting and all its affairs were conducted in English. The Brotherhood (and its companion organization, the Alaska Native Sisterhood) urged the protection of Native resources and called for an end to school segregation and other forms of local discrimination. Beginning in the 1920s, the group's leader was William L. Paul, Jr., a Tlingit graduate of the federal boarding school at Carlisle, Pennsylvania.

On the Plains, the Sioux communities, which had been divided into several reservations during the nineteenth century, began to meet together to discuss their common belief that the government's acquisition of the Black Hills in 1876 had been so fraudulent that it might well be reversed in court. In 1911 representatives from nine communities (including their old battlefield comrades from the northern and southern Cheyenne agencies) united to form the Black Hills Council. The group elected James

Crow Feather, a young, bespectacled boarding school graduate, its chairman and began to plan a legal strategy for prosecuting their claim against the United States. The courts and Indian groups would spend seven decades pursuing the case, but the gathering in 1911 marked a new departure for a people who had been at war with the United States only twenty-one years before.

In New Mexico, another legal challenge to an apparent land seizure also served as a rallying point for a large group of disparate communities. The boundaries of Pueblo lands in the Rio Grande Valley had never been clearly established, and this had encouraged squatters to ignore their titles. Responding to this illegal settlement, the Pueblo communities organized a collective challenge to the intrusion based on their common cultural bond. Because the Pueblo people were nominally Christian and held their land under fee simple Spanish titles, the American courts had traditionally viewed them as citizens rather than dependent Indians. The Pueblo appeal, therefore, was for recognition of themselves as Indian communities. Their victory in 1913 further strengthened their intergroup ties and led ultimately to the formation of the All Pueblo Council in 1922.

Indian Territory's passage from Native homeland to the State of Oklahoma (admitted to the Union in 1907) afforded numerous opportunities for intergroup cooperation and political organization. Cherokee members of the Ketoowa Society, a conservative religious group, established a committee under Redbird Smith to resist allotment and additional Euro-American settlement. Smith collected like-minded leaders from the other Five Civilized Tribes and formed the Four Mothers Society to carry on the battle. At first the group hired lawyers and Washington lobbyists to represent it, but as statehood began to appear inevitable, the society altered its strategy, urging passive resistance and the revival of old town-square grounds modeled on nineteenth-century ceremonial centers. Among the Creeks Chitto Harjo led a similar movement which tried to disrupt and sabotage the allotment process. United States marshalls arrested the Creek leader and ended the "Snake Uprising." As a result of both movements, however, forceful opponents of "civilization" would continue to function throughout the old Indian Territory during the twentieth century.

Other Oklahoma leaders tried to make the best of statehood. Peyotists appeared at the first Oklahoma constitutional convention to defend their religion, some tribal politicians vied for state office, while others worked to defend Indian lands and resources under the new order. As a result,

Indians were represented both among the new state's political establishment (Robert L. Owen, a Cherokee, was one of Oklahoma's first U.S. senators) and among its critics.

A short-lived national version of these early intertribal organizations, the Society of American Indians, was founded in 1911 on the campus of Ohio State University by a group of educated Indians and their Euro-American supporters. Membership in the society was limited to Native people, but Euro-Americans were recruited as "associates," and most of the organization's activities took place away from Indian reservations. The group established a journal (*Quarterly Journal*, 1913–15; *American Indian Magazine*, 1915–20) and opened a Washington office. The society was influential when it lobbied for generally popular reforms such as the creation of a special court of claims for Indians or improved health care on the reservations, but it was quickly weakened by more divisive issues and by its failure to win a significant following among Native groups. By 1920 disputes over a society position on the use of peyote and the abolition of the Bureau of Indian Affairs (together with an empty treasury) set the Society of American Indians on the road to oblivion. Despite its failure, however, the group brought together a growing cadre of educated, middle-class Indian leaders, such as Charles A. Eastman (Sioux), Carlos Montezuma (Yavapai), Gertrude Bonnin (Sioux), Sherman Coolidge (Arapaho), Laura Cornelius (Oneida), and Arthur C. Parker (Seneca), and laid the groundwork for an unprecedented kind of national Indian organization.

In Canada, the ongoing disputes over land titles along the Pacific Coast inspired the organization of the Allied Tribes of British Columbia in 1915. Like its American counterparts, the Allied Tribes was led by Natives who were largely Christian graduates of government schools. In the East the Six Nations reserve at Brantford, Ontario, and the Mohawks of St. Regis each refused to accept councils imposed on them by federal authorities and filed protests with parliament and the general public. The government's response, which journalist Boyce Richardson has called "one of the most reprehensible acts in the history of Canadian democracy," was to adopt in 1927 a new statute making it an offense for anyone to raise money for the purpose of litigating for Indian rights.[6] Such measures only encouraged further organization and protests. The moderate Grand General Indian Council of Ontario (founded with the help of missionaries in

---

[6] Boyce Richardson, "The Indian Ordeal: A Century of Decline," *The Beaver* (February–March 1987), 36.

the 1870s) and the more radical Mohawk Workers Club at the Six Nations Reserve continued to function.

The first two decades of the new century were thus marked by religious, cultural, and political reorganization and revival. In each of these areas Indian people found ways to organize their communities, both to shore up damage done in the previous quarter-century and to devise ways of participating in the alien, non-Indian world. Thus, while marked by suffering and dislocation, the early twentieth century witnessed the beginnings of modern Indian nationalism in North America.

Unfortunately, in the realm of economics there were few steps taken toward a parallel re-creation of Native material existence. In the business world the assault of the late nineteenth century continued, as did the rising cost of participating in national economic life. The period from 1900 to 1920 marked the end of rural self-sufficiency throughout most of North America and the final shift of both the United States and Canada to an urban, industrial economy. The only role available for Native people in this new order was a peripheral and dependent one.

This transformation was the direct result of government action. In the early twentieth century, for example, the allotment act came to dominate the economic lives of most Indians in the United States. In addition to producing a direct loss of more than ninety million acres (36.4 million hectares) through the sale of "surplus" tribal lands, the severalty act pushed Native people onto small homesteads which they frequently lost once they had received title to them in fee simple. These titles, called fee patents, gave individuals full ownership of their lands, making the property vulnerable to local property taxes and exposing its owners to the entreaties of land speculators and loan sharks. The practice of issuing these patents to Native land owners grew increasingly popular with government officials during the early twentieth century, reaching its peak between 1915 and 1920 when more than 20,000 Indians were forced to accept fee patents to their land, more than twice the number that had been issued since the original adoption of the Allotment Act in 1887.

Other factors added to the hardships faced by Indians who tried to participate in the Euro-American economy. In order to produce profits, for example, Indian crops needed to be sold on the open market and delivered to distant customers. Unfortunately, many reservations remained remote from the nation's transportation system, however expansive it may have become. In addition, in an era when Euro-American farmers were expanding the average size of their farms and investing in new crops and machinery, Indian farmers were being assigned homestead-size plots and issued horses and wagons. Finally, non-Indian agricultural interests with the requisite capital and transportation resources were eager to lease Indian lands for their own profit. As a result Indians with relatively fertile and well-situated land, such as the Montana Crows, the Yakimas in central Washington state, and the Papago (Tohono O'Odham) residents of irrigated reserves in Arizona, were encouraged to lease their property to Euro-Americans. By 1920 the thousands of Indians who still farmed had little opportunity to produce above the level of subsistence; participation in the larger, market economy was a forgotten dream.

In Canada in the 1890s, Indian Commissioner Hayter Reed made the limitation of Indian farming on the Prairies an explicit part of his administration. He announced in 1889 that in order to learn proper work habits Natives should emulate the "peasants of various countries" who cultivated their crops with hand tools, grew produce for home consumption, and maintained no more than a cow or two. Reed insisted that Canadian Indians give up their agricultural machinery, abandon cooperative patterns of farming, and content themselves with a hand-to-mouth existence. His department began dividing reserve lands into forty acre (16.2 hectare) plots, and his employees policed their charges to ensure that the Indians broadcast their seed by hand, cut their crops with hand scythes, and threshed their wheat with flails. By the time he left office in 1897, Indian agriculture had been so devastated that most observers believed that Natives were incapable of becoming farmers.

On the surface, ranching would seem to have offered Indian communities the most promising opportunities for economic well-being. Cattle and sheep ranching lent themselves to communal effort, and they were ideally suited to the isolated environment of so many reservations. Indeed, many Indian groups had a tradition of ranching success. Nevertheless, the early years of the twentieth century were marked by repeated failures. Euro-American competitors aggressively captured available water and ignored reservation boundaries, so even accomplished ranching communities, such as the Papagos of southern Arizona or the Arapahos of Wyoming, found it impossible to run profitable herds on their land. On the northern plains, large non-Indian ranching interests with ready cash at hand leased large tracts of reservation land before a tribal herd could get established. Ed Lemmon, for example, leased (and fenced) an 865,000 acre (350,000 hectare) area on the Standing Rock Sioux Reservation in 1902. Other cattlemen made similar arrangements at the Rosebud Agency in South Dakota and at Montana's Fort Peck. In the Pacific Northwest, fishing and farming offered the only viable forms of economic activity, but here too federal actions limited Native communities to subsistence-level enterprises and wage labor. Unable to protect their legal right to the region's catch, or to gain access to the capital necessary for industrial fishing, Native people in the Northwest were largely confined to manual labor on farms and in Euro-American–owned canneries. The situation in Western Canada for fishing communities was, if anything, worse than in the United States because, with smaller reserves and without treaty-guaranteed fishing rights, Canadian Indian communities had fewer opportunities to harvest their traditional food source on anything approaching a commercial scale. Inland areas offered little beyond seasonal employment in the rapidly expanding hops fields and apple orchards. Indian labor gangs moved through Washington, Oregon, and British Columbia, but their wages did little to relieve their marginal status in the region's economy.

In the Southwest, Navajo sheep herds offered yet another example of a Native industry limited by policy to subsistence-level activity. While the Navajo adoption of sheep from the Spanish is a mark of cultural innovation, desperate conditions on their vast Arizona and New Mexico reservation meant that Navajos had no opportunity to consider the commercial development of their "crop." Moreover, the government's desire to individualize and "civilize" the Navajos (even though allotment was limited to only a few districts on the reserve) foreclosed any discussion of a communal herd or enterprise. As a result, the image of patient Navajo herders and their expanding herds is one of a survival strategy, not a commercial venture.

One area where Navajos did engage in a new commercial venture during the first decades of the new century was in the sale of blankets and silver jewelry. The arrival of the railroad on the reservation (in 1881) and the rising demand for Native handicrafts promised an expanding market and escalating prices. Navajo people were certainly aware of this trend, for they shifted quickly during the 1880s and 1890s from mutton to wool production and from small- to large-scale jewelry making. In 1870 there were three trading posts on Navajo land; in 1900 there were seventy-nine; in 1920 there were 144. Nevertheless, Navajos profited little from this growing market. Traders controlled marketing through their access to transportation and they eliminated competition by holding federally issued licenses. A free market in handicrafts would have run counter to the government's "civilization" program, which was based on the assumption that Indians were "dependent people." In handicrafts as in sheep, cattle, fish, and grain, then, Native communities demonstrated an ability to function within a market economy, but did not gain the power that would enable them to compete with non-Indians.

The rigid controls imposed on Canadian bands by the Indian Act, together with the smaller size of their reserves, conspired to push Natives there even further from participation in the marketplace. Indian farmers were required to request permission before selling their farm products to outsiders, and government officials had broad authority to administer band property for the group's benefit. Worried that too much of this property was "idle," Parliament in 1911 enacted a measure which allowed a local magistrate to expropriate Indian land adjoining a town if such action was judged to be in the "interest of the public." When this occurred, the local magistrate was to compensate and resettle the Indians who were displaced. In this atmosphere, there was no active role for Indian groups in the industrial or agricultural development of local economies. It is perhaps for this reason that the government felt the need in 1930 to guarantee Native people the right to hunt for food on unoccupied Crown lands.

Between 1900 and 1920, Indian communities in North America began the process of re-creating the religious, cultural, and political institutions that Euro-Americans had attacked during the assault of the previous two decades. In an age of great hardship, Native people adapted to institutions and lifeways introduced from the outside, invented new forms of their own, and resisted coercive policies when possible. In the process, they laid the foundations for a new version of Indian culture in the twentieth century.

THE AGE OF PUBLIC REORGANIZATION, 1920–1940

"Union is the outstanding impulse of men today, because it is the only way by which the individual and collective elements of society can wield a force and power to be heard and their demands recognized." This opening sentence of the first public declaration issued by the Canadian League of Indians in late November 1919 was written by Frederick Ogilvie Loft, a Mohawk veteran of World War I who was determined that the organization would "claim and protect the rights of all Indians in Canada by legitimate and just means."[7] Loft's words reflect both ongoing concerns – protecting the interests of Indians in a hostile environment – and the impact of the Mohawk veteran's residence in a liberal, democratic state. Rooted in the Native protest groups which had begun to emerge in the early twentieth century and modeled on the trade union movement, which was gaining strength across North America, the League of Indians intended to bring political pressure ("force and power") on the government. Like other reformers of his day, Loft believed that the best way to bring about change was to articulate his community's "rights" and have them "recognized" by the government.

Frederick Loft's call for political action on a national scale sounded new in 1919, but his statement reflected a strategy that would have potent appeal in the decades ahead. During the 1920s and 1930s Native leaders attempted to mobilize their communities and defend their interests in public actions which reflected deep faith in the possibilities of reform. Both the victories and the defeats of those years would foster a reorganization of Indian life and make possible the reemergence of Native cultures into the public life of the United States and Canada.

During the 1920s non-Indian attitudes toward Native Americans shifted decisively from hostility to pity. While difficult to date, it appears that this transition occurred in a number of areas simultaneously. In popular life, the Boy Scout movement (which was introduced to the United States in 1910) incorporated Indian traditions and Indian lore into its rituals and made these subjects appealing to young people across North America. In the world of literature, the decade witnessed the popular and critical success of Oliver La Farge's *Laughing Boy,* a Pulitzer Prize–winning story of a Navajo couple caught between tradition and modernity. And among academics, anthropologist Franz Boas and his protégés, such as Robert Lowie and Ruth Benedict, took control of their discipline, turning it dramatically away from older conceptions of Indians as people who lagged behind Europeans in all aspects of social development and promoting the concept of cultural pluralism. The enmity that had marked most encounters between the races at the turn of the century was being replaced by curiosity and unfocused sympathy.

Opportunities proliferated for the expression of this sympathy during the 1920s, for it was during this decade that a series of U.S. government

[7] Quoted in Peter Kulchyski, " 'A Considerable Unrest': F. O. Loft and the League of Indians," *Native Studies Review* 4 (1988), 95.

investigations began to reveal the poverty and dislocation of Native life in painful and undeniable detail. In 1923, a "Committee of One Hundred" appointed by the Secretary of the Interior reported that "the great objectives of our benevolent desires have not been attained." The committee called for increased spending in the fields of education and health. Congress created a special investigations subcommittee early in 1928 to gather more information regarding the "condition of the Indians," and later that same year a privately financed study, *The Problem of Indian Administration,* was released and received wide attention.

Directed by social scientist Lewis Meriam, and written by a team of nine experts which included Henry Roe Cloud, a Winnebago graduate of Yale, *The Problem of Indian Administration* contained data on health, education, economic development, social life, and government programs. The results were shocking. For example, Meriam and his staff reported that the infant mortality rate among Indians in the 1920s was more than 190 per 1,000 births, higher than that for both "Whites" (70.8) and "Blacks" (114.1). They noted that Native people suffered inordinately from tuberculosis, pneumonia, measles, and trachoma, but that the government spent only about fifty cents per person on health services. Looming over these grim figures were the twin demons of poverty and malnutrition. Nearly half of all Indians had an annual income of under $200, and the government's highly publicized boarding schools spent eleven cents per child per day for food. Amid the "Roaring Twenties," it was clear that thousands of Native Americans knew hunger as a daily reality.

The Meriam Report and its kin made clear that the bleakness of Indian life in the 1920s had its origins in the policy of allotment. Whether it was because they no longer owned their lands, or because they had lost control of their resources through the Indian Office's generous leasing program, Native Americans in the decade after World War I had been barred from participating in the economies of the United States and Canada.

Public sympathy for the social and economic conditions in Indian communities, together with the increasing rate at which Native people met and shared their common concerns, spurred an ever-widening circle of political activity in Indian communities in the United States and Canada. Much of this activity involved increasingly sophisticated protests against government policies. One of these which prompted opposition in both the United States and Canada was the move to extend citizenship to all the Indians in both countries. South of the forty-ninth parallel, approximately two-thirds of the Native population had become citizens by treaty stipulation or some specific act of Congress; but over 100,000 individuals still remained outside the national polity. North of the line, status Indians had technically been eligible to apply for citizenship since the passage of the 1869 Indian Act (provided that they give up their band affiliation in the process). Not surprisingly, however, only 320 individuals had exercised that option between confederation and 1920. In the aftermath of World War I, both countries' Indian bureaus expressed support for the mandatory enfranchisement of all Native people.

In the United States, many tribal elders from the Plains and Midwest regions and the leaders of several Pueblo communities in New Mexico had deep reservations about citizenship. How would it affect federal protections for their lands and resources? Would it undermine the powers of the fledgling Indian organizations? The Iroquois Council at Onondaga, New York, declared that it would not accept citizenship if it were offered. Responding to these concerns, Congress in 1924 passed the Indian Citizenship Act which declared "all noncitizen Indians" to be citizens, and at the same time provided that their new status would "not in any manner impair . . . the right of any Indian to tribal or other property." For the moment, the fact that Arizona, Utah, and other states denied Indians the franchise did not concern Indian people as much as the fact that Congress seemed to be recognizing an emergent form of dual citizenship – national and Indian – in the new act.

In Canada, the protests against national citizenship were louder and more united than they were in the United States. There, the various Indian Acts had declared repeatedly that band membership and federal citizenship were incompatible. Therefore, the compulsory extension of the national franchise would automatically sever an individual's ties to his community. As a consequence, in 1920 Indians across the country mobilized to oppose a government bill providing for the enfranchisement of individuals against their will. The result bordered on high comedy. Deputy Superintendent of Indian Affairs Duncan Campbell Scott urged the parliamentary committee with jurisdiction over the measure *not* to notify the Indians concerning the measure because opponents would "flood" Ottawa. Representatives of the Six Nations of Ontario, the Allied Tribes of British Columbia, and the League of Indians testified anyway, claiming that national citizenship would destroy their communities.

Despite the presence of government officials who wished to enfranchise people without their knowledge and potential citizens who told parliament that citizenship would do them harm, parliament approved the

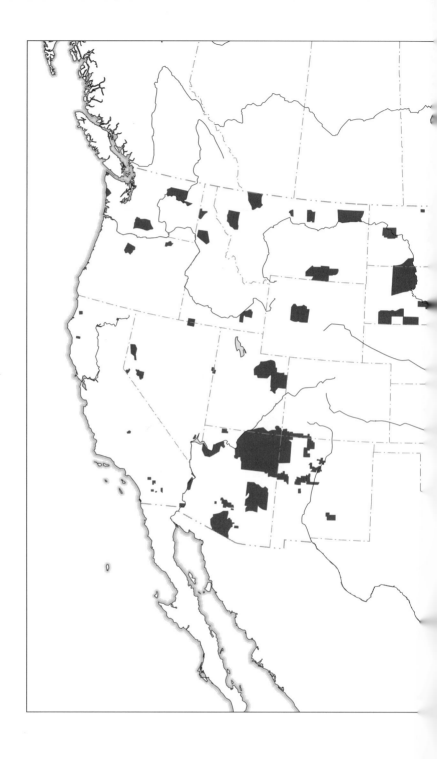

Figure 12.3 Reservations in the United States, ca. 1960.

government's bill. The majority agreed with Superintendent Scott that the "whole point" of the measure was "to continue until there is not a single Indian in Canada that has not been absorbed into the body politic, and there is no Indian question, and no Indian Department."[8] Protests continued, however, and the measure was repealed by W. L. Mackenzie King's new Liberal government which took office late in 1921.

Another government initiative common to both the United States and Canada in the 1920s was a renewed attempt to suppress Indian dances and ceremonies. In 1918 the Canadian parliament declared dances involving "mutilation" and "give-aways" to be "summary offenses," so that local agents could now order the newly reorganized (and renamed) Royal Canadian Mounted Police to arrest and incarcerate offenders without the formality of a trial. Both 1921 and 1922 proved to be record years for arrests of this kind. In the United States, Commissioner of Indian Affairs Charles H. Burke, a former congressman from South Dakota, issued an order in 1921 which was a copy of the Canadian law, except that it also prohibited ceremonial activities that fostered "immoral relations" and the "destruction of clothing or other useful articles."

Indians in both countries protested these orders and actively worked to subvert them. For example, two neighboring Canadian bands sidestepped the ban on leaving their reserves to participate in ceremonies by holding an event on their common border. Non-Indians in both countries also rose to the Indians' defense. The most outspoken of these new critics of government-imposed morality was a young social worker from New York City named John Collier. A veteran of the pre–World War I settlement house movement who sympathized with the preservation of ethnic traditions among European immigrants, Collier became interested in Indian affairs during a trip to Taos, New Mexico, in December 1920. Impressed by the beauty and antiquity of Southwestern Pueblo cultures, the reformer quickly saw the link between the suppression of Indian traditions and the subjugation of other minority peoples. In 1922 the thirty-eight-year-old Collier began to work full time toward, as he put it, "rectifying a number of wrongs and contributing to a new public opinion" concerning American Indians.

The principal vehicle for Collier's efforts was the American Indian Defense Association, which he founded with the support of a group of

---

[8] E. Brian Titley, *A Narrow Vision: Duncan Campbell Scott and the Administration of Indian Affairs in Canada* (Vancouver, 1986), 50.

wealthy New Yorkers and Californians early in 1923. Employed as the executive secretary of the organization at twice the salary of the Commissioner of Indian Affairs, Collier traveled to Washington, D.C., and reservation communities across the country to denounce attacks on Indian communities. He was concerned at first primarily with the preservation of Pueblo lands, but Burke's "dance ban" quickly drew him into cultural issues as well. Collier's attacks on the Indian Office earned him the hatred of missionaries and their supporters, thereby ensuring that his handsome salary would seldom be paid in full, but he persisted. Working in concert with Indian leaders in the Southwest, Collier insisted that what many saw as the government's duty to "Christianize" Native people was in fact an attack on religious freedom. As the peyotists had learned a decade earlier, this was a potent appeal in an increasingly multiethnic country. By 1926 attitudes had shifted sufficiently that a measure proposed by Montana Congressman Scott Leavit to give Commissioner Burke's antidance order the force of federal law (a proposal Collier had condemned as "A Bill Authorizing Tyranny") was defeated.

During the 1920s and 1930s, sympathy for the welfare and traditions of Indians frequently stimulated non-Indians to defend Native lands and resources. Sensing a shift in public attitudes, Indian leaders across the continent pressed a variety of legal challenges against the United States and Canada, demanding greater recognition for themselves from government officials and publicly questioning the long-standing notion that their constituents should advance themselves simply by emulating Euro-American behavior and developing individual plots of land.

Symbolic of this reemerging struggle between Native leaders and national officials was the conflict between the hereditary chiefs of the Six Nations reserve in Ontario and the Canadian government. The chiefs of the Six Nations had acquired their lands from the British in compensation for their assistance during the American Revolution and therefore could not be described as being leaders of a "subject people." Nevertheless, in an effort to "manage" this community more efficiently, the Department of Indian Affairs assigned Royal Canadian Mounted Police to Ohsweken in 1923 and in 1924 conducted an election for a new band council. Opposing these actions was the council of hereditary chiefs led by Levi General, a Cayuga chief called Deskahe. Deskahe petitioned King George V in London and even traveled to Geneva to present his case before the League of Nations. There he attracted support from the international press as well as from the delegates of small countries, but he did not deter the Canadian authorities. Nevertheless, the struggle between the "chiefs" and the elected council would continue, energized – and complicated – by each group's access to assistance and publicity.

Similar struggles against federal authority took place in the United States. In the nineteenth century the U.S. Court of Claims had been the forum angry Euro-Americans had used to recover damages suffered from alleged Indian "depredations." By 1892 suits claiming $25,000,000 had been filed against various Indian groups; happily for the Indians, barely $500,000 had been paid out. In the twentieth century, the Indian groups themselves took the offensive, filing suits for wrongful seizure of land, damage to property, and failure to carry out treaty promises. In addition to the highly publicized Black Hills claim brought formally by the Sioux in 1923, cases were filed by Native groups from California, the Southwest, the southern Plains, and the Midwest. By 1930 the Commissioner of Indian Affairs complained that the court's docket was so crowded that the cases could not possibly be heard before the end of the century. Other kinds of claims – for water, access to fishing sites, and the right to hunt without state restriction – were also pressed in the federal courts.

Because legal actions were generally initiated by a group of community leaders, any victory in their legal struggle served automatically to enhance their community standing and their legitimacy as Native leaders. Among the Sioux, for example, the 1923 filing before the Court of Claims bestowed upon Henry Standing Bear and other young educated men a role in tribal affairs they would otherwise not have had. Similarly, in 1926, when Duwamish leaders in Puget Sound asked the courts to set aside several treaty provisions because the articles in question had never been translated into their Native language, they became the speakers for their group.

The most outstanding example of a new Indian leadership legitimized by its battles with the United States arose in the Rio Grand Valley in 1922. In that year, a group of New Mexico politicians led by Senator Holm O. Bursum sponsored a bill in Congress that essentially would have validated the claims of non-Indian squatters to Pueblo lands. Aroused by John Collier, Stella Atwood of the General Federation of Women's Clubs, and other non-Indian reformers, most of the state's Indian groups sent representatives to a meeting at Santo Domingo on November 5, 1922. This unprecedented "All Pueblo Council" issued an appeal "to the people of the United States" that was reported in the following day's editions of the *New York Times, Tribune,* and *World.* Editorials supporting their statement quickly appeared as well in the *New Republic* and *The Nation.* Critics accused Collier of orchestrating the gathering, but the council dispatched a delegation to lobby Congress against the proposed bill and the group continued to function.

Despite the energy of those who increasingly opposed government assimilation programs and efforts to open Indian resources to outsiders, it would be a mistake to assume that Native leaders were always united or that opposition to "civilization" and federal action was uniform. Many Indians agreed with government officials and church leaders who argued that there was no alternative to the adoption of "civilized" ways. Native Christians were among the most outspoken members of this group.

In 1921 an interdenominational Protestant group reported that twenty-six churches conducted missions among tribal communities in the United States; they counted 597 Indian churches and 268 Native American ministers serving an estimated 110,000 people. The same report estimated that there were 336 Catholic churches, chapels, and schools across the country serving more than 61,000 communicants. According to the survey, nearly one-half of the 400,000 Native people in North America were nominal Christians.

During the 1920s Christian Indians developed a number of organizations to communicate with one another and to speak out on public issues. The Home Missions Council (which represented the major Protestant denominations), the YMCA, and the YWCA formed a Joint Central Committee on Indian Affairs to coordinate the work of its members. The Bureau of Catholic Indian Missions played a similar role for Catholic Indians. Both organizations supported the use of federal money for religious instruction (although each opposed funds going to the other), and both sent lobbyists to Congress to testify in support of federal legislation outlawing the religious use of peyote. Both organizations also raised private funds for religious schools. Most prominent among these were the large Catholic boarding establishments such as St. Labre and St. Francis on the Northern Cheyenne and Rosebud reservations, and two Protestant institutions: Bacone College in Muscogee, Oklahoma, and Cook Christian Training School in Phoenix, Arizona. The latter two schools were explicitly devoted to the training of Indian preachers and church workers; both expanded their programs during the 1920s and 1930s.

The Christian presence in virtually every Native community during the 1920s produced Indian leaders with strong ties to the ideals of Euro-American "civilization." Such people were often at odds with the community's elders. Jacob Morgan, for example, one of the first Navajos to embrace Christianity, organized a congregation of the Christian Reformed Church in Farmington, New Mexico, in the 1920s. His success there formed the basis for his later involvement in Indian politics. Among the Rio Grande Pueblos, the attack of the All Pueblo Council on Commissioner Burke's antidance order was itself condemned by a "Council of Progressive Christian Indians," a group of boarding school graduates who resented the traditional leadership's defense of "outgrown customs." Elsewhere Christian leaders opposed the spread of peyotism and joined local missionaries in urging their kinsmen to attend school and work for wages in the local economy.

But the growing Christian and "progressive" elements of Indian communities were not always disruptive. At Wind River, Wyoming, for example, an Arapaho "Christmas Club" annually distributed gifts and sponsored a yuletide feast for the whole group, Christian and non-Christian alike. Called "those who hang things on a tree" in the Arapaho language, club members were thereby able simultaneously to perpetuate the traditional Arapaho virtue of generosity and to celebrate a major Christian holiday – while evading the government's ban on give-aways. Similarly, while mission schools taught a curriculum mandated by outsiders, they could also serve as a focus of community life, particularly in a time of rising tensions between Indians and local Euro-Americans. In the Rocky Mountain West, the Sacred Heart and Saint Ignatius Missions among the Coeur d'Alenes and Flatheads, which had been established in the middle of the nineteenth century, played this role. They provided a place for Indian people to gather and a vehicle for community solidarity. In the 1910s, when the future anthropologist D'Arcy McNickle lived near the mission at St. Ignatius, he was impressed more by the spiritual strength of his fellow Salish and Kootenay Indians than by the teachings of the local priest.

As the decade of the 1930s began, formal organizations became a regular feature of Indian life in the United States. Political, social, and religious groups in reservation communities formed themselves into clubs and informal factions. These loosely affiliated bodies joined with like-minded people from other reservations, or used some other vehicle, such as a Christian church or a reform organization, to multiply their strength. Both locally and nationally, Native Americans demonstrated that there were now enough educated people available to carry their concerns before a national audience of non-Indians, and enough organizations to sustain their interests in a variety of public arenas. It was in the course of this revival of indigenous organizations that John Collier became the United

States Commissioner of Indian Affairs. His record twelve-year tenure in that post ratified the developments already underway within Indian communities and established the institutional underpinnings for their continuation through the hostile decades that followed his departure.

In the aftermath of his landslide victory in the 1932 presidential election, Franklin Roosevelt selected Harold Ickes to be his Secretary of the Interior. A Chicago lawyer and civic reformer who had been active in Theodore Roosevelt's "Bull Moose" campaign of 1912, Ickes was a close friend and supporter of John Collier and a charter member of the Indian Defense Association. In the 1920s Ickes had also opened his Winnetka, Illinois, home to delegations of Pueblo leaders when they were forced to change trains in Chicago on their way to lobby officials in Washington, D.C. To the horror of missionaries and many Indian Office personnel, Ickes nominated Collier for the commissionership. Yet amid the crises and frenzy of Roosevelt's first hundred days, Collier was approved without serious opposition.

During his first year in office the new commissioner declared that religious freedom would be respected at all Indian agencies, he abolished the practice of holding mandatory Christian services at boarding schools, he saw to it that nearly all the debts the government had claimed Indian groups owed from their treasuries for past appropriations were canceled, he stopped the sale of allotted lands, and he intervened to settle remaining disputes over Pueblo lands in favor of the Indians. The 1920s agenda of the Indian Defense Association was now federal policy. Ben Reifel, a Rosebud Sioux college graduate who was working as an agricultural agent on the Pine Ridge Reservation in 1933, recalled that after explaining Collier's philosophy to an elderly Sioux, the man sat there, stroked his braids, looked off in the distance, and pronounced the Lakota equivalent of "Well, I'll be damned."[9]

In 1934 Collier sought to codify his new approach to Indian policy by submitting an Indian Reorganization Act to Congress. He proposed four new ideas: First, Indian communities would be authorized to organize themselves into self-governing units which could also act as private corporations for business purposes; second, Congress would pursue a policy of promoting Indian traditions; third, the allotment system would be abolished and procedures established to consolidate Indian lands and return

[9] Kenneth R. Philp, ed., *Indian Self-Rule: First-Hand Accounts of Indian-White Relations from Roosevelt to Reagan* (Salt Lake City, Utah, 1986), 54.

individual homesteads to Indian control at the death of the allottee; and fourth, a national court of Indian affairs would be created to hear cases involving the newly organized Indian governments. Reaction to the proposal was intense. Many Indian landowners resented the idea that their property would be controlled by a new Native authority. Missionaries objected to government action that would support traditional culture. And a wide array of legislators could not accept the idea that newly authorized Indian organizations might act to reverse the century-old notion that Native people should assimilate into the non-Indian majority.

When the Indian Reorganization Act (IRA) became law in June 1934 it had been stripped of its most controversial provisions. There was no Indian court, no statement of support for Indian culture, and no requirement that previously allotted land would eventually come under the jurisdiction of Indian authorities. Nevertheless, the new law offered the stunning prospect of the U.S. government acting to restore and reorganize the indigenous governments and community organizations it had previously sought to destroy. Additional legislation was approved in 1936 to extend the IRA to Alaska and Oklahoma. In the years to come, therefore, despite a constantly disappointing level of federal appropriations, and the persisting difficulty of applying a general statute to reservations with widely differing conditions and cultural traditions, Indian groups throughout the United States would have an opportunity to write and approve community constitutions. Two hundred and fifty-eight local referenda were held under the new law. One hundred and sixty-four communities decided to organize under the IRA; ninety-four rejected it.

Collier himself was stunned by the Indian opposition to the IRA. He believed that the new law had been enacted to *defend* Indian life and Indian culture. Tempered by the bitter exchanges with missionaries and government bureaucrats in the 1920s, he paternalistically assumed that he spoke for the Indians and that his Native opponents were either misinformed or acting as puppets of sinister interests. His partisan campaigns for Indian groups to adopt the new law – conducted at Indian congresses held across the country – were viewed by many Native leaders as heavy-handed and coercive. His Native critics charged that the commissioner threatened to cut their annual appropriations and their eligibility for other federal programs if they failed to support the new plan.

By the time Collier left office in 1945, much of the Indian criticism of the reorganization act was inseparable from criticism of the commissioner himself. In 1937 the Senate Indian Affairs Committee held hearings on the administration of the Indian Bureau and was told by one witness that John Collier represented "atheism, communism and unAmericanism." Beginning in the late 1930s bills were filed to repeal the IRA; one passed the committee in 1944, but it was never considered by the full Senate.

Despite the dominant presence of John Collier, opposition to the IRA was not caused only by personal resentment. Indian allottees who had managed to hold onto their land campaigned actively against reconstituting Indian councils elected by popular vote and therefore possibly controlled by their landless fellow Indians. These same satisfied individuals often argued as well that the informal Indian councils that existed on most reservations and which managed lands and resources that remained unallotted were adequate and need not be replaced. Finally, defenders of the status quo pointed out that a "reorganized" Native group would still be dependent on the federal bureaucracy and the local non-Indian economy. Aside from allowing reservation communities to organize into federally chartered corporations, the new law contained no program for economic development. In short, the IRA appeared to institute self-administration rather than self-government. Two prominent battles over local ratification of the law illustrate these positions.

The Navajo reservation appeared to be an ideal candidate for self-government. Spread across four states, the Navajos had no tradition of central government and a pressing need to adopt community regulations regarding economic development, mineral leasing, and education. A democratically elected council organized under the IRA appeared to be an ideal way to govern their vast territory. Prior to the passage of the new law, however, a series of government investigations had established that the Navajos were grazing perhaps three times as many livestock – sheep, goats, and horses – on their reservation as the land could sustain. The Indian Office attempted to arrange a voluntary reduction in the Navajo herds during 1933 and 1934, but their arguments were poorly made, the hard-pressed Navajos resisted, and heavy-handed administrators ultimately ordered a specific quota of sheep to be taken from each subagency without regard to herd size. Stock was seized and frequently destroyed in full view of its former owners. When the IRA referendum was held in June 1935, 98 percent of the eligible voting population participated and the measure was defeated by 384 votes.

The stock reduction issue was probably crucial to the Navajos' rejection of the IRA, but their vote was also affected by an ongoing dispute between groups allied with Chee Dodge, who identified himself with traditional headmen but who supported the Collier reforms, and Jacob Morgan, a Christian leader from the northeastern section of the reservation whose attacks on the New Deal represented the view of younger, better-educated Navajos. In its aftermath, government officials insisted that the Navajos continue to consider a "tribal" charter, but the debate revolved around contests between these two men and their followers. Through four years of struggle, Morgan consistently opposed the stock reduction program, Collier, and the government's efforts to institute a Navajo government. When an election was finally held in 1938 to choose a new chairman – following a set of regulations imposed on the Navajos by the Indian Office – Morgan won in a landslide.

On the Rosebud Reservation in western South Dakota the IRA touched off a similar contest between community interest groups. Supporters of the new law included business-oriented boarding school graduates such as Sam Lapointe, who believed Indian corporations could become instruments for economic development, and young, landless individuals who saw participation in reservation affairs as a way to overcome their handicaps. Opposing them were supporters of the Black Hills claim case, whose Treaty Council was now two decades old. The claims advocates imagined a new "tribal" organization would undermine their authority and dilute their long-standing assertion that the United States should deal with the Sioux on the basis of past treaties, not as minority groups deserving social welfare legislation.

In New York State, the claim of Native sovereignty lay behind the Iroquois objection to the IRA. Like their fellow tribesmen in Canada, the New York Iroquois considered themselves a sovereign people whose relationship to the national government rested on treaties dating from the eighteenth century and earlier. As in Ontario, a minority of the New York group, led by men such as the Tuscarora anthropologist J. N. B. Hewitt, argued that the new system would end the "tyranny and corruption of the traditional chiefs," but when the vote came, the "traditionals" prevailed. The Wisconsin Oneidas, exiled to the Midwest for a century, were the only Iroquois community to accept the IRA.

Repeatedly, then, the IRA and other aspects of the New Deal policy were subsumed within the increasingly active arena of Native politics. The Klamaths and Crows, whose "unity" and "progress" had seemed promising to Collier, rejected the measure. In Oklahoma, opponents of the New Deal organized the American Indian Federation and opposed Collier because they believed his endorsement of traditional Indian ceremonialism was anti-Christian. They were also able to point out the difficulty of serving Indian needs in a state where, because there were no reservations, Indians came under the jurisdiction of local government agencies.

While the Indian Reorganization Act was the central legislative reform of the 1930s, other New Deal actions supported the development of a more vigorous Native life. In the field of education, W. Carson Ryan, a holdover from the Hoover administration, worked to implement programs that would move Native American children out of boarding schools and into community-based institutions close to home. When he resigned in 1935, Ryan was replaced by the president of the Progressive Education Association, Willard W. Beatty. Under these men the number of day schools in Indian communities rose from 132 to 226, and boarding school enrollment dropped from 22,000 to less than 15,000. At the same time, Congress passed the Johnson-O'Malley Act which authorized the Indian Office to contract with public school districts for the education of Indian children in exchange for a per capita payment. By 1938 contracts of this kind were in effect in four states: California, Washington, Minnesota, and Arizona. Many of Ryan's and Beatty's proposals were lost in the tightening budgets of the late 1930s, and attending public schools was rarely a solution to problems of poverty and discrimination; nevertheless, Indian families could see educational possibilities before them that had not been available in the bleak days of the missionary schoolmaster. The schools, like the new Indian organizations, might become something other than an alien imposition; they might serve as a focus for community involvement and growth.

Even before the IRA became law, the New Deal was an economic presence in many Indian communities. During his first weeks in office, John Collier and Harold Ickes established an Indian division within the new Civilian Conservation Corps. Like its bureaucratic "parent," the Indian Emergency Conservation Work program (IECW) provided public service employment to needy individuals. Between 1933 and 1942 more than 85,000 Indians participated in IECW projects on, or near, their reservations. They planted trees, repaired drought-ravaged range land, and took part in job-training classes. Similar programs administered by the Public Works Administration (PWA) employed thousands of Indians on road and bridge construction projects. Both the IECW and the PWA helped reduce suffering on the reservations, but neither addressed the two basic sources of poverty: the loss of Indian land and resources that had occurred during the Dawes Act period and the absence of investment capital for community economic development.

John Collier promised his Indian constituents that community organization would ultimately pay economic dividends. He had proposed that the new Indian governments would take control of all reservation land, and that their federally chartered corporations would benefit from substantial congressional largesse. When it emerged from Congress, however, the IRA provided only that reservation governments could acquire land and that they could participate in a revolving loan fund. While both provisions of the act were implemented during the 1930s – raising Indian expectations and fueling dreams of self-sufficient reservation economies – they did little to reverse the dominance of the non-Indian economy over Native life.

Only a few communal Indian enterprises received generous support. In 1937 the Northern Cheyennes received a $2 million loan to develop their cattle herd, but the fact that they remained an unallotted reservation made them an exceptional case. Most loans to Indian corporations were for less than $50,000, and of the $5.5 million in loan commitments made by 1944, more than half had gone to individuals. Most loans were used for the purchase of stock, seed, machinery, or fishing boats, and virtually all were repaid (the default rate was less than 1 percent), but their small size and relatively small total indicates that the beneficiaries of the New Deal's economic development programs were members of the Indian groups who were already successful farmers and ranchers. Commercially oriented Indians, people who were active in the new Indian councils, or individuals who had managed to succeed in the pre–New Deal era, were the most likely to pass the Indian Office's stringent loan requirements and to acquire additional stock or machinery.

The impression that the 1930s brought an alleviation of poverty, but no fundamental realignment of reservation economies can readily be confirmed by reviewing the modest shifts in Indian landholding that took place in the Collier era. Of the 2.75 million acres (1.1 million hectares) acquired by Indian groups between 1934 and 1940, over one million acres (405,000 hectares) were added to reservations from the public domain and another one million came from the purchase of submarginal lands by the Resettlement Administration and the reacquisition of Indian lands which had been opened to Euro-American homesteading but never claimed. Only 20 percent of the total was acquired by Native groups through purchase or exchange with allottees. In other words, most of the desirable lands which had been lost over the previous half-century remained beyond the Indians' grasp. The bulk of the territory they did acquire was either unsuitable for development or marginal grazing land; it could not be the basis for new businesses and new employment.

In Canada there was no specific parallel to the American New Deal, but there were indications that the political agitation and cultural concerns of Indian people were receiving increased attention. In 1938, after more than six decades of wrangling and protests organized by the Allied Tribes, the government of British Columbia formally ceded nearly 600,000 acres of Indian reserve land to the federal government, thereby ensuring that they would be exempt from seizure by local interests. Throughout the nation, the supreme authority of Indian agents and Mounties continued, but changes in the United States — particularly in the area of Indian education — attracted the attention of government officials and inspired local leaders to step forward. The Indian Associations of Alberta (1939) and Saskatchewan (1944) were formed during this period, as was the ambitious, but short-lived, North American Indian Brotherhood, a national organization founded by the Squamish Andrew Paull, a veteran of the British Columbia land struggle who had been reared under the influence of Oblate priests.

Indian people in North America had never intended or expected to disappear, and yet the headlong agricultural and industrial development of the United States and Canada in the late nineteenth century had seemed to promise them nothing but isolation and defeat. By 1940, however, there appeared to be space in both the legal and the cultural life of the United States that Indians could begin to exploit in order to sustain communities and their ethnic identities. During the 1930s, the decline of the national administration's commitment to the eradication of Indian ways, and the hobbled but genuine expansion of public Indian organizations had made it seemingly impossible to argue that Native people would or should become a "vanishing race." As Canada and the United States entered the prosperous postwar era, both nations wrestled with the emerging conflict between Native and national citizenship.

SURVIVAL IN AN URBAN WORLD, 1940–1960

In January 1944, as allied forces massed in Great Britain for the final assault on Hitler's Europe, Secretary of the Interior Harold Ickes wrote in a popular magazine that the 25,000 Indians who were at the moment serving in the American armed forces "see in a victory of the democracies a guarantee that they too shall be permitted to live their own lives." The secretary's words reflect the idealism of the war era. They illustrate the American government's belief that a victory over the Nazis and the Japanese would usher in a new age of brotherhood in which every racial group would prosper through a combination of national citizenship and public aid. Ickes's words did not anticipate the survival and growth of Indian cultures in North America; indeed, he did not foresee the extent to which the Native vision of freedom was sharply at odds with the expectations of most other citizens. In the 1940s and 1950s, while most non-Indians in the United States and Canada pursued goals of affluence and social homogeneity, most Indian people were forced to explain why their participation in national life should not require them to surrender their traditions and their Native rights.

The war brought Indians and Euro-Americans together as never before. Twenty-five thousand Indians served in the American forces, but nearly twice that many people (perhaps 50,000) left home during the war to work in defense plants or to live near loved ones. The conflict was punctuated by constant labor shortages, epitomized by the visits of large transportation trucks to distant Navajo trading posts. "The drivers offered the few English-speaking Navajos a dollar a head or two dollars a head . . . to gather up a truckload of workers," one man recalled. "Navajo men were packed in trucks to standing room only."[10] Perhaps most important, however, when Indians and Euro-Americans found themselves together during the war years, they seemed to have a great deal in common.

Separated from their people and integrated into Euro-American units, Native American soldiers were not threatening to their Euro-American colleagues. Similarly, while Indian soldiers suffered from Euro-American society's stereotypes (for example, they were frequently referred to as "natural scouts"), they experienced little direct discrimination. Civilian workers lived in integrated areas, received the same pay as Euro-Americans, and generally were accepted socially. In addition, since the Indians who left their reservations either had jobs or wore uniforms, there were no obvious social differences between themselves and non-Indians. Finally, the war produced a new pantheon of Indian heroes. These included the son of Navajo chairman Jacob Morgan who died on the Bataan

---

[10] Quoted in Garrick Bailey and Roberta Glenn Bailey, *A History of the Navajos: The Reservation Years* (Santa Fe, N.M., 1986), 199.

"death march" Osage Air Force General Clarence L. Tinker, who was killed in 1942 at the battle of Midway, Lieutenant Ernest Childers, a Creek man who won the Congressional Medal of Honor in Italy in 1943, and Ira Hamilton Hayes, who was among the small group of Marines who raised the American flag atop Mount Suribachi on the island of Iwo Jima in 1945. A Pima from Arizona, Hayes became a national celebrity who toured the United States to sell war bonds and became the subject of a Hollywood movie.

Following the war, Indians and Euro-Americans seemed to revel in their common experience. In 1945 the Marine Corps announced that a secret detachment of Navajos had served as "code talkers" in the Pacific, confusing Japanese intelligence units by communicating with each other in their Native language. Movie makers quickly adopted this fact, and Indians with walkie-talkies became a staple of the cinema battle field, while back on the reservation the Navajo code-talkers association culti-vated the image of wartime heroism and became a potent political force. Many Native groups staged elaborate welcome home ceremonies, while others celebrated their warriors' skill and courage. Kiowa veterans, for example, revived the nineteenth-century Gourd Dance society, and sev-eral Sioux communities equated their veterans with the honored warriors of the 1870s.

In Canada up to 6,000 Indians served in the armed forces. Because the changes in national Indian policy in the prewar years had been less dra-matic in Canada, the nation's pride in the Native contribution to victory was mixed with a sense that "something should be done" for its indigenous people. In 1945 federal authorities still operated on the assumption that one could not be both "Indian" and "Canadian" simultaneously. As a result, Indians did not receive the same benefits as other veterans and continued to be denied the right to vote, own property, stay at certain hotels, and sell produce on the open market. Responding to public pro-tests over this discrimination, parliament in 1946 created a special joint committee to consider a fundamental reform of the Indian Act. For three years the group heard testimony on Indian health, legal status, education, and economic development. Affluent Canadians were horrified to learn that only 113 Indians in the entire country had reached Grade 9 in 1946, that the death rate among Natives suffering from tuberculosis was fifty times that of Euro-Canadians, and that many northern Natives were actu-ally shorter and smaller than they had been at the turn of the century. By the time parliament received the report and moved toward action, the public had developed an unprecedented awareness of what the nation's tremendous progress had cost its Native people. Yet the federal franchise was not extended to include status Indians until 1960, and Indians were not allowed to vote in Quebec provincial elections before 1969.

In the United States gloomy reports from Indian country stimulated a renewed interest in policy reform. Below the forty-ninth parallel most of the attention was focused on the deterioration of economic life on rural reservations. Part of this decline was relative, for the war had brought new prosperity to urban areas and had not produced any significant development of Indian farms or businesses. The sixty-three Hupa veterans who returned from the war to their reservation homes in northern California, for example, found little had changed there except the rising presence of non-Indian lumbermen and businesses. As they settled back into their prewar routines, the returnees found social barriers between themselves and Euro-Americans lessening and the local economy shifting from farming to wage labor. Unable to support themselves through traditional pursuits, they looked for jobs "in town" or survived on seasonal employment.

During the postwar years, rural non-Indians turned to public works projects to revive their local economies. When it was completed in 1942, for example, the Grand Coulee Dam was the world's largest single source of electricity. Despite the fact that it destroyed innumerable Indian fishing sites along the Columbia River and undermined the subsistence economies of the Yakima and Colville reservations, the dam was viewed as a model of regional development. It seemed destined to bring prosperity to the inland farming areas of Washington and Oregon. Following a disastrous flood along the Missouri River in the spring of 1943, an even larger program of dams and hydroelectric plants was proposed by the Army Corps of Engineers for the nation's heartland. The Pick-Sloan project eventually constructed five major dams along the Missouri, destroying in the process over 550 square miles (1,425 square kilometers) of Indian land. The constituents for projects of this kind were rural boosters and large-scale farmers and ranchers. Indians had no role in the planning or construction of these dams, and most of them were entirely unaware of what was envisioned until ground was broken.

During the 1940s the widening gap between the economies of Indian and Euro-American communities, together with the memory of wartime prosperity, produced a new understanding of reservation poverty. To non-Indians the problem was no longer lack of education or training, but the isolation and "overpopulation" of reservations. A report in *Time* magazine in

1947, for example, noted that many Indian groups faced not just poverty, but starvation because their herds were small, their farms nonexistent, and there were no plans for development in reservation communities. A 1948 Interior Department report on the Navajo economy confirmed this impression with the declaration that the "maximum" development of all reservation resources would produce an adequate income for only half of the group's 65,000 members. It appeared obvious that the solution to this situation was the integration of Indians into the prosperous national economy.

Some Indian leaders encouraged this idea. The Alaska Native Brotherhood, for example, had successfully organized a Maritime Workers' Union during the early 1940s to represent both fishermen and cannery workers. The union quickly affiliated with the American Federation of Labor and seemed to demonstrate that Native people could blend successfully into the modern economy. The success of a parallel group in British Columbia made a similar point. Indian groups with rich resources, such as the Klamaths of Oregon, also seemed ready to participate more fully in business affairs. Members Wade and Ida Crawford argued forcefully during the 1940s for some kind of arrangement whereby the Klamaths themselves could manage their timber lands. Similar arguments were made on behalf of the Menominees of Wisconsin and the Flatheads of western Montana, both tribes with substantial timber wealth, and a long history of education and cooperation with missionaries.

Postwar discussions of Indian economic development also felt the effects of dramatic changes in two inversely related public attitudes. On the one hand, the ethnocentrism which had produced various government "civilization" programs earlier in the century declined in the postwar era. The revelation of Nazi war crimes, together with the dramatic independence movements in Africa and Asia, produced an atmosphere in which a policy of government-sponsored assimilation appeared not only cruel, but anachronistic. At the same time, these same events brought about a rise in support for the notion that Indians should have equal rights with other citizens. "Why don't a veteran of World War II have the right to vote?" an Apache man named Lester Oliver wrote to his congressman in 1946.[11] Responding to questions of this kind, politicians supported the repeal of restrictive legislation and the bolstering of citizenship rights.

In Canada, the 1951 revisions of the Indian Act repealed the ban on both

---

[11] Quoted in Donald L. Fixico, *Termination and Relocation: Federal Indian Policy, 1945–1960* (Albuquerque, N.M., 1986), 17.

the potlatch ceremony and the Sun Dance. Significantly, however, the government's new measures also tried to reduce the economic isolation of Native people and to respond to experts like the anthropologist Diamond Jenness who called for the "liquidation of Canada's Indians" as a distinct community. The tradition of federal control over Natives held firm, however, and the changes brought by the 1951 Act were limited. It was not until much later, with the publication of the infamous "White Paper" report by Prime Minister Trudeau's government in 1969, that federal officials would propose the complete abolition of the Indian Department and the replacement of Indian status with undifferentiated national citizenship.

In the United States in 1947, the President's Committee on Civil Rights expressed outrage that returning veterans in New Mexico and Arizona were being denied the right to vote. Both states permitted Indians to vote the following year, and tribal members responded by coming to the polls in large numbers. In 1952, New Mexico's 47,000 Native American voters were considered an important enough bloc to warrant a visit to Gallup's Inter-Tribal Indian Ceremonial by presidential candidate Dwight Eisenhower. Five years later, Utah became the last state to drop its opposition to Indian voting. In a similar vein, the decade of the 1950s witnessed the end of long-standing restrictions against the sale of liquor to Indians.

Sympathy for Indian rights also helped win passage of the Indian Claims Commission Act in August 1946. Conceived originally as part of John Collier's New Deal, the claims commission was intended to give all Indian groups an opportunity to win monetary compensation from the government for violations of treaties, mismanagement of resources, or violations of common standards of "fair and honorable dealing." As it moved toward congressional approval, however, the commission came to be justified as a measure to resolve all outstanding disputes between Indians and the government. Thus, when President Truman signed the Indian Claims Commission Act into law, he declared that it would allow Indians to reach a "final settlement" of all their claims so that they could "take their place without handicap or special advantage in the economic life of the nation and share fully in its progress."[12]

In the prosperous and nationalistic 1950s, Indian communities and their traditions appeared both economically disadvantaged and politically backward. The experience of World War II demonstrated that Native

[12] Quoted in ibid., 28.

people could be integrated into the country at large, and the course of postwar events seemed to indicate that returning to the traditionally oriented thinking of the 1930s would be both unfair and unproductive. Despite the high-minded rhetoric of equality in the immediate postwar years, non-Indians had yet to take seriously the traditions or the leaders of Native communities.

By the time the war hero Dwight D. Eisenhower became president in January 1953, the logic of completely incorporating Native Americans into a homogeneous national society seemed unassailable to most non-Indians. Politicians and bureaucrats had fallen under the thrall of their own arguments. During the first summer of the new administration, a bipartisan group in Congress approved two measures which would translate the powerful language of assimilation into policy. The first, House Concurrent Resolution 108 (HCR 108), stated simply that it was the "sense of Congress" that a group of Indian tribes named in the act should be "freed from federal supervision" at an early date. While it had no immediate impact, this "termination" resolution was intended to mark a clear departure from previous assumptions that the protection of Native communities should be the goal of federal policy. The second measure was a unanimously approved new statute called Public Law 280 (PL 280). PL 280 unilaterally turned civil and criminal jurisdiction on most Indian reservations in California, Minnesota, Nebraska, and Wisconsin over to the states, thereby effectively abolishing the reservation police and court systems which had operated throughout the twentieth century. President Eisenhower turned aside criticism of the act upon signing it, when he declared that PL 280 represented "still another step" in the Indians' movement toward "complete political equality."

The passage of HCR 108 and PL 280 formalized federal efforts to terminate the historic relationship between American Indian communities and the national government. During the remainder of the 1950s, termination was a theme running through a wide variety of new laws and administrative initiatives. Most prominent among these were termination laws passed in 1954 setting out the procedures for abolishing federal protection for the Klamaths of Oregon, the Menominees of Wisconsin, and a group of similar tribes in Utah, Oregon, and Texas. The first of these – the Southern Paiutes – were formally terminated in 1957; the Menominees were the last to be cut off when their termination went into effect in 1961. Throughout the process, Bureau of Indian Affairs officials "negotiated" with the Indian groups over final disposition of their assets and other details, but Indian leaders were told bluntly that termination was inevitable and protest would be futile. By the time the policy was renounced by President Richard Nixon in a special message to Congress in 1970, over 13,000 tribal members and 1.3 million acres (445,000 hectares) of Indian real estate had been "freed" of federal control. While these losses represented a tiny fraction of the Indian estate and population, they were large enough to inject a new fear of federal authorities into the life of every Native community in the country.

During the 1950s the rhetoric of equal opportunity also inspired efforts to dismantle the Bureau of Indian Affairs. Attendance at federally funded schools remained steady during the 1950s, but enrollment at public schools increased by more than 60 percent. There seemed to be no alternative to the gradual assimilation of all Indian children into locally run schools that had no special Indian identity. In the area of health care, Congress responded to continuing bleak reports on life expectancy and criticism of BIA inefficiency by beginning in 1952 to transfer Indian hospitals and other facilities to state control. In 1954 all responsibility for Indian health was shifted from the BIA to the Public Health Service.

Finally, what was becoming known as the "termination policy" came full circle by providing funds to support the migration of Indians to cities, the movement that during World War II had first suggested that Indians should be integrated into the national economy. Government relocation offices assisted probably no more than one-quarter of the 122,000 Indians who moved to cities between 1940 and 1960, but these agencies helped shape the urban migration, and they gave government officials a policy fig leaf with which to cover their obligations to the Indians who were being stripped of federal support. Migration to booming, modern cities could be held up as the answer to those who remained "outsiders" on outmoded, poverty-stricken reservations.

The first postwar "relocations" were of Navajos, forced by the deteriorating economic conditions on their reservation to migrate to cities like Denver and Los Angeles. Most of the employment provided to these first migrants was seasonal labor. As other Indian groups joined the stream, the Indian Bureau expanded its efforts, but continued to specialize in placing unskilled laborers in urban jobs. This haphazard approach changed in 1954, when the BIA created a Relocation Branch to supervise the permanent resettlement of Native Americans in urban areas. By 1961 this branch was maintaining offices in Chicago, Los Angeles, Denver, San Francisco, San Jose, Oakland, Dallas, and Cleveland, and had supervised the movement of more than 30,000 individuals to new homes in the city. Conceived in the wake of a migration that was already taking place, and defended by terminationists who claimed that urban employment was the answer to Indian poverty, the relocation policy could not succeed. The new city dwellers had been forced to move by circumstance rather than choice, they were poorly prepared for the rigors of city existence, and they were vastly outnumbered by strangers who were at best indifferent to their needs and traditions. Even though some critics charged that up to 75 percent of relocated Indians quickly returned home, the number of urban Indians increased dramatically during the 1950s. The result was an expanding group of Native American communities in the eight cities with relocation offices, as well as in urban centers close to reservations (such as Seattle and Oklahoma City). These communities contained a growing, but frequently changing population of unskilled workers who continued to view their reservations as "home." Like other neighborhoods of newly arrived, unskilled workers, these areas were frequently marked by poverty, poor housing conditions, alcoholism, and crime.

Despite the failure of relocation as a policy, however, Indian migration to the cities bore some unexpected fruit. First, city living created a small, but important, Indian middle class. Not only did some migrants who found stable occupations and decent housing later come home to lead their people (for example, Navajo Chairman Peter MacDonald, Winnebago leader Reuben Snake, and Cherokee Chief Wilma Mankiller), but they also produced children who played prominent roles in Indian life during the 1960s and 1970s. In addition, urbanization and poverty together created the need to form new Indian organizations. By the end of the 1950s Chicago, Minneapolis, Oakland, Cleveland, Los Angeles, and Oklahoma City each contained an "Indian center" which served as a gathering point for newcomers. Some of these centers evolved into social service agencies, while others became sites for pow-wows, political rallies, and religious meetings. The centers were by definition pan-Indian, and through their activities, from bowling leagues to canoe clubs to soup kitchens, they maintained the idea that Native people had more in common with each other than they did with the thousands of strangers now surrounding them.

The logic of termination began with conditions both Euro-American policymakers and Indian leaders recognized. In the 1940s there was a consensus that the war experience had contained some valuable lessons, that reservations were not economically viable, and that Indians deserved

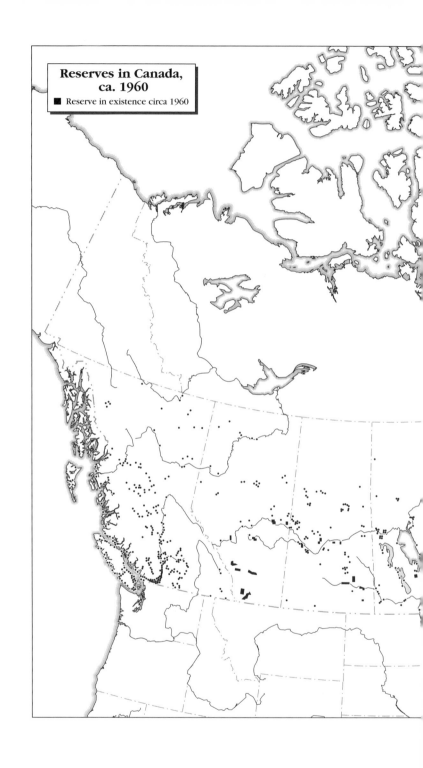

Reserves in Canada, ca. 1960

■ Reserve in existence circa 1960

Figure 12.4 Reserves in Canada, ca. 1960.

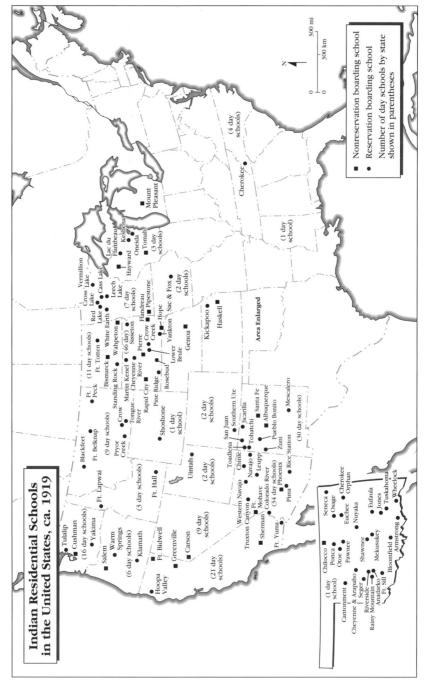

Indian Residential Schools in the United States, ca. 1919

■ Nonreservation boarding school

● Reservation boarding school

Number of day schools by state shown in parentheses

300 mi

300 km

N

Tulalip
Cushman
(16 day schools)
Yakima
Salem
Warm Springs
(6 day schools)
Klamath
Ft. Bidwell
Greenville
Carson
(21 day schools)
Hoopa Valley
Ft. Lapwai
(3 day schools)
Ft. Hall
Blackfeet
Ft. Belknap
(9 day schools)
Pryor Creek
Tongue River
Crow
Shoshone
(1 day school)
Uintah
(2 day schools)
Ft. Peck
(11 day schools)
Ft. Totten
Red Lake
Cass Lake
Leech Lake
Cross Lake
Vermillion
Lac du Flambeau
Keshena
Oneida
Tomah
Hayward
(7 day schools)
(3 day schools)
White Earth
Bismarck
Standing Rock
Martin Kenel
(46 day)
Cheyenne River
Sisseton
Wahpeton
Pierre
Flandreau
Hope
Pipestone
Crow Creek
Lower Brule
Yankton
Sac & Fox
(2 day schools)
Genoa
Rapid City
Pine Ridge
Rosebud
Kickapoo
Haskell
Cherokee
(4 day schools)
(1 day school)
Mount Pleasant
Southern Ute
San Juan
Jicarilla
Toadlena
Chinle
Navajo
Tohatchi
Santa Fe
Albuquerque
Pueblo Bonito
Zuni
Leupp
Mescalero
(30 day schools)
Western Navajo
Truxton Canyon
Ft. Mohave
Sherman
Colorado River
Phoenix
Rice Station
Pima
Ft. Yuma

Area Enlarged

(1 day school)
Cantonment
Cheyenne & Arapaho
Seger
Riverside
Rainy Mountain
Anadarko
Ft. Sill
Bloomfield
Armstrong
Chilocco
Ponca
Otoe
Pawnee
Shawnee
Mekusukey
Seneca
Osage
Euchee
Nuyaka
Eufaula
Jones
Tuskahoma
Wheelock
Cherokee Orphan

Figure 12.5 Indian residential schools in the United States, ca. 1919.

equal protection under the law. Had Indian leaders of the 1940s been without strong ties to their cultural traditions – had history begun in 1941 – the iron logic of economic development, civil rights, and bureaucratic efficiency might well have destroyed the legal underpinnings of Native communities in the United States. As it happened, however, the legacy of the past came forcefully into play during the termination era. The persisting values which Native leaders believed were basic to their identity and which – even in the cosmopolitan rush of modern cities – still set them apart from other Americans fueled a sense of allegiance and unity that was expressed in a variety of ways.

Native governments, recognized haltingly in the 1930s, functioned bravely in the hostile environment of the 1940s, providing a living argument for their own continuation. New organizations emerged during these years as well, formulating coherent counterarguments to termination and winning non-Indian support for their views. The threat of losing a set of distinctive institutions – from Bureau of Indian Affairs schools to tribal courts – stimulated the development of a multifaceted Indian identity rooted in the universal language of nationalism and self-determination. When the termination era ended, therefore, Native leaders knew that they had been the leading instruments of its defeat. That knowledge would carry them forward to the end of the century.

One measure of the Native government activity in the 1940s was the Indian response to the creation of the Indian Claims Commission. Under the legislation approved in 1946, Native groups had five years to register their claims against the United States for unlawful or unconscionable seizures of land. When the deadline came in 1951, 370 petitions had been filed; these were later separated into 615 separate dockets. The Claims Commission Act also set 1957 as the year by which all cases would be heard and settled. Because of the huge Indian response, the life of the commission was repeatedly extended. When the body formally went out of business in 1978, it turned its sizable remaining caseload over to the United States Court of Claims.

In addition to providing an incentive for Native groups to mobilize themselves, the Claims Commission brought Indian leaders, attorneys, and scholars together to prosecute their complaints against the United States government. While the legal arena militated against substantial involvement in the cases by Indians (all cases were heard in Washington, D.C., for example), the claims process made many individuals aware of the law's potential as an instrument of Native government. Where Indian groups had previously needed Bureau of Indian Affairs' approval to engage a lawyer, Indian communities were now largely free to select their counsel, commission the necessary historical research, and otherwise plan their cases. In the process, both because of the length of the proceedings and the number of cases (many groups were involved in more than one docket), Native leaders developed close relationships with their lawyers and researchers, and claims cases often generated interest in other kinds of legal action.

Lawyers representing the Sioux tribes in their ongoing claim for the seizure of the Black Hills prosecuted the case before both the Claims Commission and the Court of Claims. By the time that case was settled by the Supreme Court, the Sioux were already involved in a number of other claims proceedings in which they were represented by some of the same attorneys who had worked for them previously. In fact, in the course of litigating their claim, Sioux leaders determined that they no longer wanted cash for the hills, but preferred a return of land. As a consequence they engaged new attorneys and began designing an entirely new approach to the case. While the effort has yet to satisfy Sioux complaints against the U.S. government, it has provided a remarkable opportunity for the development of a sophisticated legal strategy to defend the Sioux's interests in court.

In addition to placing them in nominal control of their cases, the Claims Commission Act also provided successful Native governments with a major decision to make: how to spend money awarded them. The tribunal awarded a total of more than $818 million to the Native groups. Individual awards ranged from $2,500 to the Poncas to over $29,000,000 to the Indians of California. None of these funds could be distributed, however, until the Bureau of Indian Affairs approved a disbursement plan. Unfortunately, the terminationist atmosphere of the 1950s frequently poisoned negotiations between Native groups and the Indian Office. Native leaders argued for distributing the funds to members on a per capita basis both because their constituents were clamoring for money and because they feared a large group treasury would be used by federal officials as a sign that a group was "ready" to be "set free." Government officials, on the other hand, tried to relieve their own budget problems by having Native groups pay for federal services out of their award money. The Menominees were the most notorious victims of this process; they watched as hundreds of thousands of dollars received from their claims cases were spent to facilitate their own termination. Despite these difficulties, however, the Indian Claims Commission created a situation in which Native governments – even ones in danger of being terminated – were being asked to plan for the long-term economic development of their reservations. One of the largest early awards was $31.7 million which went to the Utes in 1951. Native leaders won high praise from both politicians and the popular press when they decided to use the funds for livestock, schools, and hospitals, rather than to distribute it to individuals.

Outside the claims process, Native governments were frequently presented with opportunities to flex their fledgling muscles. The Arapaho council, for example, supervised the annual distribution of profits generated by a collectively owned ranch. The Bureau of Indian Affairs viewed the ranch as a training ground for individuals who could learn to be stockmen by working there. Bureau officials urged profits be distributed in the form of block grants or low-interest loans to enterprising young Arapahos. The council, on the other hand, viewed the ranch as an ongoing communal enterprise and distributed its earnings in small monthly checks to tribal members. The group took a similar attitude towards royalty payments for mineral development and traders' fees. During the 1950s the council also took an active role in tightening tribal membership requirements so as to maximize individual payments. As a consequence, the Arapaho council played a central role in the group's economic activities during the 1950s.

Most aggressive was the Navajo Tribal Council, which had earned the support of its constituents during its battle with John Collier and the stock reduction program of the 1930s and which became increasingly assertive in response to the economic hardships of the immediate postwar years. Faced with widespread poverty, the Navajo leadership lobbied for approval of a special rehabilitation act which was approved by Congress in 1950. In addition to promising more federal aid, the new law granted the Navajo council the power to allocate revenue from mineral development to Indian needs. When the provision was written, the Navajos earned under $500,000 per year from their mineral wealth; by the 1960s, income from this source averaged more than $14 million annually. This increase amplified both the authority and the ambition of the council. During the 1950s, Navajo leaders developed their own court system, took control of their police force, developed a community power authority, and began a newspaper. In the words of historian Peter Iverson, the decade "witnessed the birth of the Navajo nation."[13]

---

[13] Peter Iverson, *The Navajo Nation* (Westport, Conn., 1981), 82.

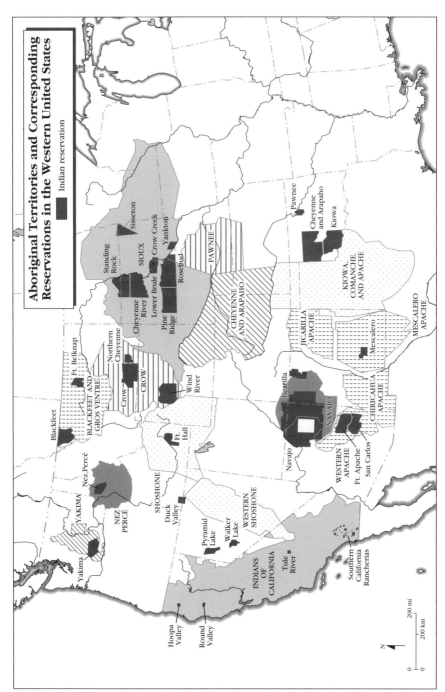

Figure 12.6 Aboriginal territories and corresponding reservations in the western United States.

In the past, active groups of leaders from different Native groups had frequently cooperated with one another, sometimes forming regional organizations to support some common concern. National Indian organizations had been short-lived; they were either dominated by Euro-Americans, or led by Native Americans with few ties to local communities. In the postwar decade, increased public discussion of Indian policy, together with the threat of termination, stimulated the development of the first Native organization in the United States that could reasonably claim to represent all Indians. Ironically, the National Congress of American Indians began with a meeting in the offices of the Commissioner of Indian Affairs.

John Collier called a group of Indian employees of the Bureau of Indian Affairs into his office in 1942 to discuss the appointment of a Native person to represent the United States in a research project in South America. The group responded that they could not make such a selection because they did not represent American Indians. Following this encounter, a group of these employees, led by D'Arcy McNickle and others who worked as liaison officers with the new tribal governments, began discussing the need for a new organization. In 1944 a Chippewa leader, Mark L. Burns, called together the first convention of the group. Representatives from twenty-seven Native groups gathered in Denver in November of that year and elected Judge Napoleon B. Johnson the first president.

While its early meetings attracted a number of older leaders who had worked closely with Euro-American reformers and churchmen, the National Congress of American Indians was from its inception an organization that assumed the persistence of Indian life. The organization's constitution declared that it was founded "to preserve Indian cultural values," as well as "to secure and to preserve Indian rights under Indian treaties with the United States."[14] Membership was open both to Indian individuals and Indian organizations, but its early leaders saw themselves as advocates for the nation's Native communities. The National Congress of American Indians worked to avoid rivalry and backbiting. In its early years it endorsed the union activities of the Alaska Native Brotherhood, lobbied for passage of the Navajo-Hopi Rehabilitation Act, and supported the political agendas of the Arizona Inter-Tribal Council and the Affiliated Tribes of Northwest Indians.

As support for termination grew, the National Congress of American

---

[14] Hazel Whitman Hertzberg, "Indian Rights Movement, 1887–1973," in Wilcomb E. Washburn, ed., *Handbook of North American Indians*, vol. 4, *History of Indian-White Relations* (Washington, D.C., 1988), 313.

Indians moved to center stage as the principal defender of Native governments. In 1953, the year Congress passed House Concurrent Resolution
108 and Public Law 280, Joseph R. Garry of the Coeur d'Alenes (who was
also an Idaho state legislator) was elected president of the organization. He
pledged to defend the status of Native tribes as "nations within a nation."
That same year the National Congress of American Indians altered its
constitution so that only recognized tribes could be organizational members (Indian individuals could still belong), and its new executive director,
a Sioux social worker named Helen Peterson, began to prepare for an
"emergency conference" on the termination crisis for 1954.

In February 1954, representatives of forty-three Native groups – which
together comprised more than one-third of the nation's Indian population –
gathered in Washington to plan a counterattack on Congress and the Indian
bureau. The conference adopted a "Declaration of Indian Rights," which
spoke directly to the popular idea that reservations were anachronistic
provinces of despair. "Reservations do not imprison us," the NCAI statement declared, "they are our ancestral homelands, retained by us for our
perpetual use and enjoyment. We feel we must assert our right to maintain
ownership in our own way, and to terminate it only by our consent."[15] The
Association on American Indian Affairs (formed in 1936 by the merger of
Collier's Indian Defense Association and the New York–based Eastern Association on Indian Affairs), *Christian Century* magazine, and other reform
interests also opposed termination, but the unity and commitment of the
all-Indian National Congress of American Indians proved most persuasive.

As the termination threat eased in the United States in the late 1950s, the
National Congress of American Indians continued to play a major role in
Indian life. Not only had it won high praise for its lobbying efforts in the
crisis, but it had injected two new elements into the public discussion of
Indian affairs. First, it had made clear that a federal program for Indians that
did not have Indian support would not succeed. The logic of termination
was so persuasive to non-Indians and it fit so snugly with the prevailing
political attitudes of the day that it seemed for a time to be irreversible. The
National Congress of American Indians' response was direct and undeniable: articulate, educated Indians simply did not accept termination as a
policy. They insisted on continued recognition for Native traditions and
reservation communities. Once this point was made, it was impossible to
justify termination as being carried out "in the best interests" of the Indians.

15 Ibid., 315.

Second, the termination struggle brought sharply into focus the common bond Indian people in the United States shared with one another. By declaring that their reservations were "ancestral homelands," the National Congress of American Indians' leaders were forging a new basis for pan-Indian identity. Rather than linking themselves together solely on the basis of race or culture, the authors of the National Congress of American Indians' declaration were asserting that they shared a separate national heritage. They opposed termination because the policy would eradicate their political and cultural "homelands" and they asserted that their claim was as legitimate as that of any third world independence movement. While maintaining their loyalty to the United States, Indian leaders in the termination struggle were claiming that their citizenship rights included a special right to a permanent reservation homeland. Native leaders argued that Indian lands were not to be submerged in the larger nation, but preserved as beacons of culture and guarantees of continued community survival. Such language would prove potent in the decades to come.

In 1983, while reflecting on both the termination era and the Menominee tribe's struggle to regain their "tribal" status, their former chair, Ada Deer, identified what she believed was the lesson contained in those events. "I want to emphasize," she declared, "especially to Indians, that they can decide what they want. You do not need the Bureau of Indian Affairs or any other group telling you what to do. You can make a decision and work for it."[16]

The counterattack on termination did not succeed completely. While the Menominees won a restoration of their "tribal" status in 1973 and the Klamaths were successful a decade later, other, smaller groups never regained federal protection for their homelands. Moreover the apparent logic of termination continued to appeal to non-Indian politicians long after the term had become unmentionable in serious discussions of Indian affairs and was to become a major issue in Canada in the 1960s. Nevertheless, the end of the 1950s marked the completion of Indian efforts in the United States to rebuild and reorganize their communities in the aftermath of the European conquest. By 1960 it was clear that Ada Deer was correct: Native people had both the skills and the resources to survive in the legal and political arenas. It was also clear that their presence – despite the persistence of intense local antagonism – was perceived by the population at large as a national asset. Indian communities

[16] Ada Deer quoted in Kenneth R. Philp, *Indian Self-Rule*, 141.

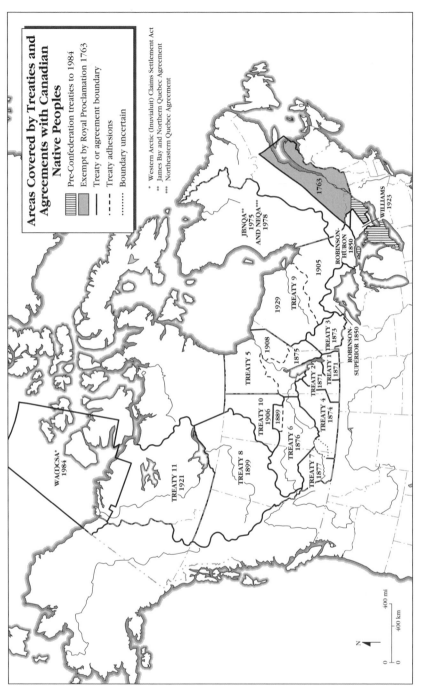

Areas Covered by Treaties and Agreements with Canadian Native Peoples

Pre-Confederation treaties to 1984

Exempt by Royal Proclamation 1763

Treaty or agreement boundary

Treaty adhesions

Boundary uncertain

* Western Arctic (Inuvialuit) Claims Settlement Act
** James Bay and Northern Quebec Agreement
*** Northeastern Quebec Agreement

WAQCSA*
1984

TREATY 11
1921

TREATY 8
1899

TREATY 10
1906

TREATY 5

JBNQA**
1975
AND NEQA***
1978

1763

1929

TREATY 9

1905

1908

1889

1875

TREATY 6
1876

TREATY 7
1877

TREATY 4
1874

TREATY 1
1871

TREATY 2
1871

TREATY 3
1873

ROBINSON-
SUPERIOR 1850

ROBINSON-
HURON
1850

WILLIAMS
1923

N

0   400 mi

0   400 km

Figure 12.7 Areas covered by treaties and agreements with Canadian Native peoples.

could imagine a permanent existence within the United States and, while the threat of termination was still to be faced in Canada, Native people there had acquired the same political skills and will to defend their identity as had Indians to the south. Such a future could not have been imagined in 1880.

BIBLIOGRAPHIC ESSAY

A number of general works contain extensive descriptions of the reservation period. These include Francis P. Prucha's definitive history of United States Indian policy, *The Great Father: The United States Government and the Indians* (Lincoln, Nebr., 1984); vol. 4 of the Smithsonian Institution's *Handbook of North American Indians,* ed. Wilcomb Washburn (Washington, D.C., 1988); *The Canadian Indian: A History since 1500,* by E. Palmer Patterson (Don Mills, Ont., 1972); Olive P. Dickason's, *Canada's First Nations: A History of Founding Peoples from Earliest Times* (Toronto, 1992); and Edward H. Spicer's *A Short History of the Indians of the United States* (New York, 1969). The latter volume, one of many general histories available, is by an anthropologist and is particularly perceptive about the cultural changes described in this essay. A similarly interpretive overview of Canadian Natives is Boyce Richardson, "The Indian Ordeal: A Century of Decline," *The Beaver* (February–March 1987), 17–41.

Several bibliographical tools can assist further reading in the history of the reservation period. Chief among these are the two volumes by Francis Paul Prucha: *A Bibliographical Guide to the History of Indian-White Relations in the United States* (Chicago, 1977) and *Indian-White Relations in the United States: A Bibliography of Works Published, 1975–1980* (Lincoln, Nebr., 1982). A parallel guide to Canadian materials is Robert J. Surtees, *Canadian Indian Policy: A Critical Bibliography* (Bloomington, Ind., 1982). For a guide to U.S. government documents relating to Indian affairs, a central source of primary material on this period, see Edward E. Hill, *Guide to the Records in the National Archives of the United States relating to American Indians* (Washington, D.C., 1981).

The general assault on Indian lands and lifeways has been the subject of a variety of works that tend to focus either on national policymaking or on local administration. Among the studies of national policy in this period are Frederick E. Hoxie, *A Final Promise: The Campaign to Assimilate the Indians, 1880–1920* (Lincoln, Nebr., 1984); Robert Wooster, *The Military and United States Indian Policy, 1865–1903* (New Haven, Conn.,

1988); and E. Brian Titley, *A Narrow Vision: Duncan Campbell Scott and the Administration of Indian Affairs in Canada* (Vancouver, 1986).

More specific studies of particular regions or tribes in Canada include Sarah Carter, *Lost Harvests: Prairie Indian Reserve Farmers and Government Policy* (Montreal, 1990); and Robin Fisher, *Contact and Conflict: Indian-European Relations in British Columbia, 1774–1890* (Vancouver, 1977). Similar, focused studies on communities in the United States include H. Craig Miner, *The Corporation and the Indian: Tribal Sovereignty and Industrial Civilization in Indian Territory, 1865–1907* (Columbia, Mo., 1976); Donald J. Berthrong, *The Cheyenne and Arapaho Ordeal: Reservation and Agency Life in the Indian Territory, 1875–1907* (Norman, Okla., 1976); and William T. Hagan, *United States–Comanche Relations: The Reservation Years* (New Haven, Conn., 1976).

The massacre at Wounded Knee, the central military event of the 1890s, is the subject of Robert M. Utley, *The Last Days of the Sioux Nation* (New Haven, Conn., 1963). The classic account of the entire Ghost Dance movement is still James Mooney, *The Ghost Dance Religion and the Sioux Outbreak of 1890* (Washington, D.C., 1893).

In a number of other works which examine a longer time frame, the assault on land and resources is a central concern. Among this group are Karen Blu, *The Lumbee Problem: The Making of an American Indian People* (Cambridge, 1980); Florence Connolly Shipek, *Pushed into the Rocks: Southern California Land Tenure, 1769–1986* (Lincoln, Nebr., 1987); Daniel L. Boxberger, *To Fish in Common: The Ethnohistory of Lummi Indian Salmon Fishing* (Lincoln, Nebr., 1989); and Edmund Jefferson Danziger, Jr., *The Chippewas of Lake Superior* (Norman, Okla., 1978). Finally, *The Blackfoot Confederacy, 1880–1920: A Comparative Study of Canadian and U.S. Indian Policy* (Albuquerque, N.M., 1987) by Hana Samek offers a unique, comparative portrait of tribal life on both sides of the Canadian-U.S. border during the height of the assault.

The early twentieth century, marked by quiet in national policymaking and peace in "Indian country," has rarely attracted the attention of scholars. Nevertheless, a number of histories focus on events in this period. Among these are Omer C. Stewart, *The Peyote Religion: A History* (Norman, Okla., 1987); Robert H. Ruby and John A. Brown, *Dreamer Prophets of the Columbia Plateau: Smohalla and Skolaskin* (Norman, Okla., 1989); Robert L. Bee, *Crosscurrents along the Colorado: The Impact of Government Policy on the Quechan Indians* (Tucson, Ariz., 1981); significant sections of *A History of the Indians of the United States* (Norman, Okla., 1970) by Angie Debo; Frederick E. Hoxie, *Parading through History: The Making of the Crow Nation in America, 1805–1935* (Cambridge, 1995); and two outstanding tribal profiles by Loretta Fowler: *Arapahoe Politics, 1851–1978: Symbols in Crises of Authority* (Lincoln, Nebr., 1982) and *Shared Symbols, Contested Meanings: Gros Ventre Culture and History, 1778–1984* (Ithaca, N.Y., 1987).

The beginnings of Indian participation in "white" political institutions is the subject of Hazel Hertzberg, *The Search for an American Indian Identity: Modern Pan-Indian Movements* (Syracuse, N.Y., 1971). Two biographies present the lives of Charles Eastman and Carlos Montezuma, two Indian leaders who attempted to speak for their people during the early twentieth century: Raymond Wilson, *Ohiyesa: Charles Eastman, Santee Sioux* (Urbana, Ill, 1983); and Peter Iverson, *Carlos Montezuma and the Changing World of American Indians* (Albuquerque, N.M., 1982).

The period of the 1920s and 1930s has received substantial attention, much of it focused on John Collier and the history of the Indian "New Deal." Collier's early career is the subject of a masterful biography by Lawrence C. Kelly: *The Assault on Assimilation: John Collier and the Origins of Indian Policy Reform* (Albuquerque, N.M., 1983). The implementation of Collier's reforms is vividly portrayed in a compilation of speeches and reminiscences entitled *Indian Self-Rule: First-Hand Accounts of Indian-White Relations from Roosevelt to Reagan,* ed. Kenneth R. Philp (Salt Lake City, Utah, 1986). For an insightful history of the era from the point of view of a prominent Native American scholar, see Vine Deloria, Jr., and Clifford Lytle, *The Nations Within: The Past and Future of American Indian Sovereignty* (New York, 1984).

There are few published studies of reservation communities in the era of the New Deal reforms. A classic portrait, commissioned by the Indian Office itself, is Gordon Macgregor, *Warriors without Weapons: A Study of the Society and Personality Development of the Pine Ridge Sioux* (Chicago, 1946). More recent scholarly profiles of this period in "Indian country" include Donald L. Parman, *The Navahos and the New Deal* (New Haven, Conn., 1976); Laurence W. Hauptman, *The Iroquois and the New Deal* (Syracuse, N.Y., 1981); Thomas Biolsi, *Organizing the Lakota: The Political Economy of the New Deal on the Pine Ridge and Rosebud Reservations* (Tucson, Ariz., 1992); and Terry P. Wilson, *The Underground Reservation: Osage Oil* (Lincoln, Nebr., 1985).

As with other periods, the years following World War II have primarily interested historians of federal policy who have tracked and explained shifts in government action. These scholars have produced a number of fascinating studies, including Michael L. Lawson, *Dammed Indians: The Pick-Sloan Project and the Missouri River Sioux, 1944–1980* (Norman, Okla., 1982); Larry W. Burt, *Tribalism in Crisis: Federal Indian Policy, 1953–1961* (Albuquerque, N.M., 1982); and Donald L. Fixico, *Termination and Relocation: Federal Indian Policy, 1945–1960* (Albuquerque, N.M., 1986). A provocative series of essays that focus primarily on this period was edited by Vine Deloria: *American Indian Policy in the Twentieth Century* (Norman, Okla., 1985). An exception to the general interest in national policy are two studies of the Navajo tribe which give special care to that tribe's remarkable political development in the 1940s and 1950s: Peter Iverson, *The Navajo Nation* (Westport, Conn., 1981); and Garrick Bailey and Roberta Glenn Bailey, *A History of the Navajos: The Reservation Years* (Santa Fe, N.M., 1986).

13

THE NORTHERN INTERIOR, 1600 TO MODERN TIMES

ARTHUR J. RAY

The postcontact experience of the Native peoples of the boreal forest zone has been fundamentally different from that of aboriginal groups living in all other areas of North America. The fur trade has remained important for Subarctic Natives ever since they first encountered Europeans. In most places Europeans have not pushed them off the land because extensive agriculture is not possible. Native languages continue to flourish. Apart from the fur traders, it is the missionaries and government agents who have had the greatest effect on the Native population. Yet, even these officials had little impact on the Natives before the early part of the twentieth century. This means the continuity with the recent past is very powerful in the Northern Interior. Today Native societies strongly reflect their aboriginal roots, two to four centuries of fur-trading traditions, the work of missionaries, and most recently, the impact of government programs.

The Northern Interior has what outsiders perceive to be a hostile climate, where extremes, not averages, govern life. Summers are fleeting; winters are severe. The boreal forest extends from near the Labrador coast west-northwest almost 5,500 kilometers into central Alaska. However, it is by no means an unbroken forest. The eastern two-thirds of the region is the land of the rocky Canadian Shield, where continental glaciers stripped vast portions of the uplands bare of soil so they do not support extensive tree growth. In this Shield country, forests primarily grow in the sheltered lowlands beside the countless lakes, rivers, and streams. Here is where Indians found most of their large game, chiefly woodland caribou and moose, small prey and fur bearers, and waterfowl. Here fish also abounded, the key staple species being white fish, sturgeon, and lake trout. Toward the northern limits of the forested Shield, barren ground caribou in small herds seek shelter during the winter from the frigid, wind-swept barren lands.

To the northwest, the landscape of the sprawling Mackenzie River drainage basin has a very different appearance from that of the Shield. Mostly this is a poorly drained lowland, covered with glacial and river deposits mantled by a heavy forest. The same animal species found in the Shield region are present here also, but moose were once particularly abundant in the southern sections toward the Athabasca and Peace Rivers. The whole basin teams with beaver and muskrat. Toward the delta Arctic fox are plentiful. This animal also ranges eastward through the northern fringes of the boreal forest, including the lands adjacent to Hudson Bay and James Bay.

NATIVE PEOPLES AT CONTACT

The Northern Interior is the traditional homeland of Native peoples who spoke many dialects of two major linguistic families. At the time of European contact, the Athapaskan speakers inhabited the boreal forest country lying to the northwest of the Churchill River; Algonquian speakers occupied the Churchill Valley and all the woodlands to the eastward except for the Labrador coast, which was occupied by the Inuit (see Chapter 14).

The Athapaskan and Algonquian groups were alike in that they were hunter-fisher-gatherers who lived beside lakes and rivers for most of the year. However, there were important regional variations in their patterns of subsistence which reflected the subtle but significant variations in the biogeography of the region.[1] Most of the Athapaskan peoples living in the lower Mackenzie Valley, and the area to the east and south toward the Churchill River, combined caribou hunting with fishing and the gathering of berries in season. In contrast, Athapaskan groups living in the headwaters of the Yukon River and along the Liard and its tributaries depended more heavily on moose, although woodland caribou were also important. The Alaska plateau peoples also had a big game hunting economy. In the Peace River and Athabasca River areas, hunters seem to have focused on bison and moose. Most Algonquian hunters favored moose if it were available. Where this animal was absent or present only in small numbers, they mostly stalked caribou. Both Algonquians and Athapaskans hunted and trapped a variety of furbearers to obtain pelts for winter

---

[1] J. H. McAndrews and G. C. Manville, "Plate 17: Ecological Regions, ca. A.D. 1500" and "Plate 17A: Descriptions of Ecological Regions," in ed., *Historical Atlas of Canada*, R. C. Harris, vol. 1 (Toronto, 1987).

clothing. Some of these animals, most notably beaver, provided important supplies of meat.

Faunal remains in archaeological sites suggest that throughout the Subarctic both hunting and fishing were important. It is difficult to tell from this evidence which activity was more important because mammalian fauna tend to be overrepresented archaeologically. It is clear, however, that fishing contributed more to the diet of Natives who lived along the north shore of the Gulf of St. Lawrence eastward from the Saguenay River. Here fishing, eel trapping, and the hunting of sea mammals were more significant than the quest for moose or caribou. Early European accounts furthermore suggest that fishing was more consequential than hunting throughout the Algonquian area, except for the caribou-hunting zone of northern Quebec. Fishing also seems to have been the dominant activity for Athapaskans living in the upper Yukon River country and in the adjacent territory of the Liard River. Throughout the Northern Interior, Indians caught most of their fish during the open-water season between late spring and early autumn, but some groups also set gill nets beneath the ice in winter, depending on the availability of other game.

These various subsistence activities strongly influenced the patterns of social and economic organization that developed in the different parts of the region. Moose and woodland caribou are most effectively hunted by small parties. This meant that the small hunting group composed of a few patrilineally or bilaterally related families was commonplace throughout the primary moose-hunting territory. During the open-water season, fishing and the hunting of water fowl became more important. Related winter hunting groups, which usually occupied adjoining territories (very often situated in the same watershed), came together to form local bands at a good fishing site or strung out along a waterway. If fishing were very productive, these summer encampments could support a substantial number of people.

Unlike the solitary moose or small troops of woodland caribou, the barren ground caribou is much less predictable in its migratory habits but its herd size is frequently in the thousands. Rather than stalking this creature in small parties, it made more sense to employ a variety of hunting techniques that required large parties of men and women. For example, the Chipewyans, who at the time of contact lived along the forest edges northwest of the Churchill, commonly employed the chute and pound during the spring and autumn migrations and in the winter when the animals foraged in the shelter of the forest. The hunting parties drove herds up chutes, made of clusters of stones and brush spaced at intervals, into a fenced pound or enclosure fashioned from brush. Inside the pound the caribou became entangled in numerous snares. The hunters easily dispatched the trapped animals with bows or spears. Alternatively, when the caribou were migrating, hunters often attacked them from land, or sometimes canoes, as they crossed rivers or lakes.

Generally the barren ground caribou-hunting groups were larger than those which sought their subsistence in the full boreal forest, but like the latter, members were related patrilineally or bilaterally and group sizes fluctuated considerably with the seasons and availability of food. In this instance, the migratory rhythm of the barren ground caribou was the determining feature. Along the northern forest fringes west of Hudson Bay the winter hunting groups, or local bands, which lived off the chute and pound, numbered from 400 to 1,000 at the time of initial European contact; they were never fewer than 200. The regional bands which co-alesced from these local groups to prey on the migrating herds were substantially larger.

Conflicting lines of archaeological, documentary, and oral evidence mean that scholars probably never will be in complete agreement about the contact locations of all the various Subarctic societies. The problem is that contact had a disruptive effect on population distributions in many areas, particularly the central and western portions of the region, before the arrival of the first recorded European observers. [2]

Most of the Algonquians of the central and eastern boreal forest region spoke various dialects of Cree, although linguists are divided as to whether to classify the distinctive eastern dialects as separate languages. There are three eastern dialects, Montagnais, Naskapi, and Eastern Cree, which are associated with regional groups identified in the early European records: the Montagnais (Innu), Naskapis, and East Main Crees. People speaking various dialects of Western Cree occupied the region extending from the Harricanaw River in southern James Bay to the upper Churchill and Saskatchewan Rivers.

[2] Examples are discussions of the locations of the northern Ojibwas, Woodland Assiniboines, and Western Woods Crees. For the Assiniboines see Arthur Ray, *Indians in the Fur Trade* (Toronto, 1974); for the Ojibwas see Charles A. Bishop, *The Northern Ojibwa and the Fur Trade* (Toronto, 1974); for the Western Woods Crees see James G. E. Smith, "Western Woods Cree," in *Handbook of North American Indians*, vol. 6, pp. 256–8; and for the Great Lakes–central Subarctic see Conrad E. Heidenreich, "Plate 37: Re-establishment of Trade, 1654–1666," and "Plate 38: Expansion of French Fur Trade, 1667–1696," and Conrad E. Heidenreich and F. Noël, "Plate 39: Trade and Empire, 1697–1739," and "Plate 40: France Secures the Interior, 1740–1755," in the *Historical Atlas of Canada*, vol. 1.

The Ojibwas (Anishinabes) were the only northern Algonquians who spoke a language that was different from those of the Crees. They lived along the north shore of Lake Huron and in the eastern portion of the upper Michigan Peninsula. The Ojibwas differed from their Cree neighbors in other important respects. Most noteworthy, the abundant fishery in their territory and substantial populations of moose and woodland caribou meant that they resided in twenty or more villages of 100 to 300 persons each.

Beyond Lake Nipigon dwelled various Cree bands who now collectively are referred to as the Western Woods Crees. While scholars generally are in agreement about the eastern location of these people on the eve of contact, they disagree about the southern and western limits of their territory. For example, early postcontact data suggest that the Siouan-speaking Assiniboines had occupied the Rainy River, Lake of the Woods, and Winnipeg River area for a considerable length of time. Some archaeologists challenge this conclusion. They have long argued that the analysis of "protohistoric" pottery from the area hints that Crees, and perhaps Ojibwas, lived in the area. Unless new data come to light, this controversy about the southern boundary likely will persist. It is certain that Western Woods Cree groups lived in the lower Churchill River and Reindeer Lake region, but the western margins of their territory may have extended as far west as Lesser Slave Lake.

The Chipewyans, who spoke a dialect of Athapaskan, lived to the north of the Churchill River along the edge of the forest and in the adjacent tundra. The Beavers were their Athapaskan neighbors to the southwest. Their dialect was different from that of the Chipewyans. However, this was not a sharp division, the Beaver dialect being the least defined of the regional variants of Athapaskan. The Dogribs and Yellowknives (who share a common Athapaskan dialect with the Slaveys and Hares) lived to the northwest of the Chipewyans. The Slaveys held the territory along the Liard and Mackenzie Rivers as far north as Great Bear Lake. The Kaskas flanked them to the southwest and the Mountain Indians to the northwest. Two groups of Hares dwelled just to the north and west of Great Bear Lake. Eastern Kutchin bands held the lower Mackenzie River between the westernmost Hares (the Rapids Hares) and the delta, while their western relatives occupied the lands to the west as far as the Chandalar River, an upper tributary of the Yukon. The Kutchins speak a dialect that is unintelligible to most of their Athapaskan neighbors. The Yukon Valley was occupied by the Athapaskan-speaking Tutchones, Hans,

Tananas, and Koyukons, while to the south were the Ahtnas, Tanainas, Kolchans, and Ingaliks.

Archaeological data suggest that Northern Interior people were involved in only a small amount of long-distance trade before contact. It mostly concerned exotic resources of great value, such as native copper from the Great Lakes and Coppermine River areas, silica from northern Quebec and the Northwest Territories, and obsidian from the Pacific slope.[3] Although they used some of this material to make essential equipment, mostly they fashioned such equipment from locally obtained raw materials – bone, hides, fur pelts, bark, roots, wood, clay, and stone. Families worked as a unit to meet their needs. Men made most of the weapons (bows, stone-tipped arrows, and lances) and built the canoes (used mostly by the Algonquians and southern Athapaskans). Women provided most of the household equipment (summer lodge coverings, canoe coverings, bone fleshers, bone needles, bark containers, baskets, pottery), fashioned the clothing, and made the snowshoes. Both men and women created stone knives, stone burins for etching bone and wood, fishing equipment (gill and dip nets made of babiche or willow cordage, weirs, bone hooks, and sinew lines), snares, and traps (pit as well as deadfall types).

The socioeconomic organization of the Subarctic bands was very adaptable. They had no hereditary leaders. Rather, for various economic tasks, Indians tended to follow the individual who was best suited to head the group, such as someone skilled in beaver hunting or another in moose hunting. The winter hunting group was usually led by the most experienced and skilled hunter, often a father to the other men, or following his death, a brother. Headmen, at all levels, were expected to be generous, to have abilities as speakers, and to be endowed with supernatural powers. This was particularly important because these were societies in which leaders had no real authority, so that their status imbued them only with a degree of influence. Bands acted only after their members had reached a consensus. Thus, a leader had to be effective at counseling and convincing others that it was in their interest to follow him. The councils of the larger summer or regional bands consisted of the leaders, or elders, of the assembled winter hunting groups. Customarily one of these men acted as spokesman for the rest when dealing with outsiders.

The social organization of the Ojibwas may have been somewhat more

---

[3] J. V. Wright and Roy Carlson, "Plate 14: Prehistoric Trade," *Historical Atlas of Canada*, vol. 1.

elaborate than that of their Cree neighbors. As noted above, the Ojibwas lived in semisedentary settlements whose bands had animal names. This has led some scholars to conclude that the Ojibwas may have had patrilineal clans on the eve of contact. Others reject this suggestion. Early European data regarding Ojibwa social organization are too scanty to reach any firm conclusions about this question.

For all Subarctic people, individual and group survival depended upon teamwork. Accordingly, all of them regarded a willingness to share as an essential social value. For this reason they expected their leaders to set good examples through their generosity. General reciprocity was the most common type of economic exchange among closely related people. According to this scheme, band members shared their possessions and food with those in need without expecting repayment in kind within a specified period of time. However, the giver understood that the receiver would return the gesture if their respective situations were reversed in the future. In this way, general reciprocity linked band members together through bonds of mutual obligation. These were particularly useful when food resources failed for some, but not all, neighboring bands.

Transactions with non-kin groups were different. Generally these exchanges served economic and socio-political goals. When establishing or renewing relations with outsiders, elders exchanged gifts of equal value. If the parties hoped to establish or perpetuate long-lasting bonds, they often intermarried, thereby extending kinship boundaries. After the leaders took care of the diplomatic gestures, barter exchange proceeded. As noted above, for most areas of the Subarctic we assume that little interregional trade occurred because there would have been little exotic material to exchange. The principal exception was the area of the upper Ottawa River, Lake Nipissing, and the country to the north of Lake Huron. There the Nipissings, Ottawas, and Ojibwas seem to have had close trading ties with the Hurons (Wendats) and Petuns. They supplied these agricultural peoples with furs, hides, garments, and native copper (from Lake Superior) in exchange for corn, tobacco, raccoon pelts, and black squirrel cloaks that originated in the country to the south.

It is not entirely certain what aboriginal land tenure systems were like on the eve of contact. Based on field work undertaken in 1913, Frank G. Speck suggested that the Algonquian groups of the eastern Subarctic operated a family hunting territory system. According to this scheme each family claimed a certain tract of land for their exclusive use, although we now know that the system was more flexible than that represented by

Speck and that most of the resources of the land continued to be shared by members of the larger winter hunting group. Families husbanded the fur and game resources on these tracts by hunting sections in rotation. Speck's informants said that families had a very strong sense of trespass. His idea that family hunting territories were aboriginal has been questioned by later scholars on the basis of lack of evidence. Today it is generally believed that the land tenure system that he observed resulted from the Indians' long participation in the fur trade, in some cases over several hundred years, and their growing reliance on sedentary, nonmigratory, furbearing animals such as beaver.[4] Before the family hunting territory system evolved, it seems likely that bands would have hunted the same tract of land every year with access to subsistence resources available to all band members. It is not clear how Indians dealt with scarce resources. The historical record suggests outsiders had to obtain permission from a band to cross its territory for purposes of trade or to hunt on its lands.

Unlike Europeans, Northern Interior Natives thought all natural phenomena had life and good or evil power. Hunters sought contact with the supernatural world through the vision quest and dreams. They were very careful to show respect for the spirits of the animal species on which they depended lest they offended these spirits, who would not give over more animals to the hunter. The hunter showed his respect, usually by ritually disposing of the bones of his fallen prey and, after European contact, by making an offering of tobacco at the subsequent feast. (Tobacco, though a herb of American origin, became available throughout the North largely as a result of the fur trade.) Sometimes religious beliefs led groups to avoid hunting certain animals. Most Athapaskans, for instance, would not touch river otter because they associated this animal with the spirits of the dead. Those who had special ability to commune with the spirit world became shamans and performed rituals to aid in this spiritual contact. These healed the sick and helped predict the location of game animals. Shamans often employed scapulimancy, which involved scorching the shoulder blades of large game animals and reading the maplike cracks that developed as evidence of where game could be found. Many Algonquian shamans also engaged in the shaking-tent (conjuring) rite, in which they entered a specially constructed lodge in order to converse with the spirits. The supernatural world permeated the Subarctic hunter's life to a greater

---

[4] For a good synopsis of this historical debate see Adrian Tanner, "The New Hunting Territory Debate: An Introduction to Some Unresolved Issues," *Anthropologica* n.s. 28 (1986): 20–1.

degree than is conveyed in early European writings, for it was a subject seemingly closed to the European visitor.

THE ERA OF THE EXPANDING FUR TRADE

The first recorded European contact with the boreal forest region is that of Jacques Cartier on the Labrador coast in the summer of 1534. The "wild and savage folk" clothed in furs whom he met there and along the north shore of the Gulf of St. Lawrence likely were the Montagnais. These Indians probably were familiar with Breton fishermen before Cartier's arrival. Forty years later Spanish Basque whaling activity had expanded considerably and twenty to thirty vessels were hunting in the region each year.

Tadoussac, at the outlet of the Saguenay River in the heart of Montagnais country, eventually became the most important port for French Basque ships. In the sheltered harbor whalers rendered their oil. Here they also developed a trade with their Indian hosts. They exchanged European manufactures for deer skins, marten (the closest North American equivalent to the highly prized sable), bear, otter, and seal. However, the demand for fur initially was not sufficient for the development of a trade that was independent of whaling or fishing.

The establishment of the fur trade as a practicable enterprise by itself came about once the felt hat became the fashion rage in Europe. First mentioned in Chaucer's time, this hat became very popular after 1550 and remained an essential item of fashionable European dress for the next 300 years. The underwool of beaver made the best felting material, so the demand for this fur expanded rapidly. However, by the middle of the sixteenth century beaver had been nearly exterminated in northwestern Europe and there were only two major preserves left – Siberia and northern North America.

The establishment of the land-based fur trade with beaver as the dominant staple was a bonanza for the Indians. Beaver cloaks were their most important article of winter dress. They wore these cloaks with the hair turned inward. After several winters of use the long guard hairs were worn off leaving behind only the underwool. Feltmakers prized these "coat beaver" pelts because they could make felt from them merely by shearing off the remaining wool. Parchment or unworn skins, on the other hand, had to be sent to Russia for processing. There manufacturers had developed a jealously guarded, cost-effective technique for removing the guard hairs. For these reasons, in the late sixteenth century and throughout the seventeenth century, traders paid a premium for coat beaver (see also Chapter 6).

Judging from early-seventeenth-century French observations, the Indians fully understood their economic advantage. Although Europeans hotly competed for the trade, the enterprise remained profitable for them throughout the late sixteenth century. By 1580 the volume of business had expanded to the point that it became worthwhile for European merchants to specialize in the enterprise. In 1581 the first French trading vessel set sail for the Gulf of St. Lawrence. Four years later merchants from St. Malo annually were sending five to ten ships to the St. Lawrence River. Besides vying with one another for the favor of the Indians, the merchant newcomers still had to contend with European fishermen and whalers, who continued to barter with these Indians as they had done for the previous fifty years. However, the role these part-time traders played in the industry declined thereafter.

While the Europeans struggled among themselves for dominance in the emerging enterprise, Indians built their own networks and sought to monopolize the inland traffic in furs and trade goods. The Montagnais became the first major group to do so. This circumstance placed them in a good position to act as middlemen and control the traffic for their own benefit. By acting in this manner, they obtained the furs the Europeans prized without having to abandon the food-rich coastal environment for the poorer interior. For this reason the Montagnais were reluctant to give neighboring groups permission to cross their territory to reach the Europeans. It was a privilege they granted only to their closest allies.

The network which the Montagnais established revolved around two trading hubs – Tadoussac and Lac St-Jean. Tadoussac, of course, served as their principal contact point with Europeans and remained the most important Indian-European trading center in the Gulf area until at least 1608. At Lac St-Jean the Montagnais conducted the bulk of their business with Algonquins (an Ottawa Valley–based Algonquian people who also became middlemen in the fur trade) and East Main Cree groups. During a visit to the St. Lawrence River in 1608, Champlain learned that the Montagnais received their furs from bands living as far north as James Bay. But, in order to protect their interest, the Montagnais refused to take Champlain to their lakeside trading base or to the headwaters of the St. Maurice River in 1610.

While the Montagnais expanded their network to the north and west, their Five Nations Iroquois neighbors to the southwest also were seeking to obtain European goods. The problem that Iroquois groups such as the Mohawks faced was that they had limited fur resources and no direct access to European traders except by way of the lower St. Lawrence River. The threat of their incursions into the St. Lawrence Valley led Algonquins and Montagnais to avoid the area and channel most of their trade northward between the upper Ottawa River and Lac St-Jean.

Greater and more sustained French involvement in the Native realm began in 1599 when the French government granted a ten-year trading monopoly to Pierre de Chauvin de Tonnetuit and François Gravé Du Pont. In a departure from previous practice, Chauvin built a permanent trading post at Tadoussac in an effort to protect this monopoly. Although this experiment failed and the permanent post had to be abandoned in favor of a summer one, it signaled a shift in the trading policies of French merchants. By then it had become clear to them that the Northern Interior was the primary fur area and, therefore, they had to make a concerted effort to tighten their links with Indians from that region, even if it were at the expense of Native groups who lived farther south. To accomplish this, the French became more involved in Native political and military alliances. The reason was simple enough. The Montagnais, the key people in the fur trade at the turn of the century, sought aid because the Mohawks were harassing them. Chauvin seized this opportunity in 1602 and promised the Montagnais that he and his associates would help them subdue their enemies. At first he limited this aid to the provision of a steady supply of metal hatchets, knives, and other weapons. Chauvin did not take part in the continuing warfare. So the Montagnais of Tadoussac sought the additional warriors they needed to combat the Mohawks by allying themselves with Algonquins living in the area between the upper St. Maurice and Ottawa Rivers. To make the alliance attractive to these people, the Montagnais gave them the right to come and trade directly with the French. They also welcomed the Etchemins (or Maliseets) from the south side of the gulf. By 1603 the alliance among these various peoples had been firmly established. Over 1,000 Algonquins, Montagnais, and Maliseets gathered that summer in Tadoussac to celebrate a recent triumph over the Iroquois.

Now the French trading company decided to move beyond Tadoussac and establish a colony and trading station at Quebec. By building a post there they would be in a better position to enforce their monopoly against rival European traders. Also, the Indians at Tadoussac had become so expert at playing rival European merchants against each other that they had turned the summer rendezvous into an auction and had driven fur prices upward to the point that they were seriously eroding profits. By moving farther west, Champlain and his backers hoped to overcome this problem.

Although the French move would undermine the economic position of the eastern Montagnais groups, they consented to it anyway. They needed their French allies and Champlain assured them that the new colony would serve their interests. During the summer of 1608 Champlain built his "habitation" at what would later become Quebec City. It immediately became a major trading center frequented by the Montagnais and their allies. In an effort to secure peace in the valley and thereby expand the trade of the new post, Champlain and Gravé Du Pont decided to take a more active part in the Indian conflicts. In 1609 Champlain and nine of his men accompanied a Montagnais war party which defeated a group of Mohawks on Lake Champlain. The following summer Champlain joined forces with another group of Algonquin, Huron, and Montagnais warriors that annihilated a second party of about 100 Mohawks. The Mohawks did not seriously threaten the St. Lawrence Valley again until 1634.

The French traders' expansion of their activities upriver to the Montreal area under Champlain's direction had major implications for the Montagnais traders from Tadoussac and Quebec. This development further undercut their economic position, but there was little these Indians could do about it because of their continuing dependence on French military aid. They limited their opposition to spreading disquieting rumors in the interior in the hope of weakening the new partnerships that Champlain was promoting. The Algonquins, on the other hand, had a mixed reaction to Champlain's advance. They welcomed the prospect of having direct contact with the French in their own territory, but feared, with good reason, that Champlain was intent on bypassing them too so that he could establish relations with their Huron and Nipissing trading partners. As early as 1611, Champlain made overtures to the Hurons, and in 1612 he expressed an interest in finding a route to James Bay – a trading area of the Nipissings. In 1613 Champlain set out for the Ottawa River intent on exploring a route to the Bay, but the Allumette or Kichesipirini Algonquins who lived on the upper Ottawa River refused to let him pass. They took this action to protect their strategic position on the Ottawa River, which enabled them to control the trade of the upper Ottawa region and to charge tolls of all who passed. They did not want Champlain to undermine their position by making direct contact with the Nipissings and exploring the country to the north. But, like other Algonquin groups, the Allumettes were keen to have the French move closer to them, so they encouraged Champlain to build a post at Montreal.

At about this time the political climate in the Ottawa Valley changed as the area came under more frequent attacks by the Oneidas and Onondagas, who, like the Mohawks, were members of the Five Nations Iroquois Confederacy. These people raided the area to plunder the Algonquins of the growing supplies of European goods they were receiving through the rapidly expanding trade. Faced with this menace, the Algonquins sought and received help from the Hurons. In return, they granted the Hurons the right to pass through their country to deal with the French. Partly for this reason Champlain did not encounter any opposition when he passed through Allumette country in 1615. Thus, like the Montagnais before them, the Ottawa Valley Algonquin bands began to yield their short-lived role as middlemen for reasons of defense. By the mid-1630s the Hurons had largely replaced the Algonquins and Montagnais as the leading middlemen in the French fur trade.

The spatial evolution of the fur trade in the period between 1581 and the 1630s is instructive, because it highlights a process that continued for another 200 years until the industry stretched right across the Northern Interior to the lower Mackenzie River and into the headwaters of the Fraser River on the Pacific slope. As soon as this commerce began, Indian trading specialists quickly emerged who carried European goods to their inland partners and returned with their furs. The European effort to bypass these Native entrepreneurs to get at cheaper supplies of fur led them to extend their lines of communication, thereby adding to their fixed overhead costs. High volumes of fur returns were needed to cover the additional expenses. European merchants attempted to achieve this goal by encouraging Indians to exploit older areas at levels that exceeded the local carrying capacities; they drew more Indians into the system from new areas; and they pressured their home governments for monopoly privileges vis-à-vis fellow nationals. The Indians confounded the Europeans' efforts, however, because, every time the latter managed to circumvent one group of Native middlemen, another one emerged to take their place. So, the trading frontier expanded rapidly and Indian entrepreneurs were always at the cutting edge. Often conflict and population migrations took place as they pushed forward. This is why we rarely obtain a pristine view of the aboriginal world from European explorers.

Scholars disagree about the extent to which the first 100 years of European contact altered the daily lives of Indians living in the eastern boreal forest. It is likely that by 1580 Indians were carrying some European goods as far west as Georgian Bay and James Bay, and probably beyond. By the 1630s these articles would have been common throughout the region east of a line drawn between these two places. Archaeological data and historical records suggest that the Indians incorporated European goods into their cultures in definable stages. Initially they prized such goods because they were exotic and probably they believed that these articles had special supernatural powers. Many groups buried their dead with their prized European goods. Very quickly, however, Indians learned to appreciate the utilitarian and military advantages which these new wares offered, and this heightened their demand for them. As we have seen, securing supplies of metal hatchets, knives, and projectile points for military purposes became a major concern of all groups living between Tadoussac and the Huron country, and the differential rates of acquisition shifted the balances of power among the various groups. These weapons also were useful in the hunt and axes and knives in domestic life.

In addition, Indians greatly appreciated a variety of other items. Undoubtedly cloth and copper and brass kettles were the most notable of these. Metal kettles had a major impact on the domestic life of migratory peoples. To cook food in easily transportable aboriginal bark containers women had to resort to the tedious task of using heated stones to boil water. Once they had metal pots they could much more easily boil food over an open fire. Thus, boiled fish and meat, stews, and soups became mainstays of the diet. When copper pots wore out Indians reworked the metal into knives, beads, and other items. Long before Europeans arrived on the scene, local Indians had worked native copper which they obtained from the vicinity of the Upper Great Lakes by a route that ran east across central Quebec to the Lac St-Jean area. So, reworking copper did not pose new challenges.

It is not clear how long traditional technologies continued to be important in this region following the adoption of European trade goods. Most likely some of the Montagnais living near Tadoussac and near Champlain's habitation at Quebec were the only groups to become dependent on European goods for their economic survival before the 1630s. Nevertheless, the trade did bring about some fundamental changes in subsistence patterns. For example, the expansion of economic intercourse between the Algonquins and the Hurons led the former to develop an appetite for corn. Like the Nipissings who were long-standing trading partners of the Hurons, the Algonquins obtained large supplies of this food in trade. Corn was attractive primarily because it was an ideal voyaging food. As groups began to travel more extensively for trading and warfare, the demand for this product increased. The Montagnais who lived close to the French began to value corn meal imported from Europe for the same reasons.

In the years between 1630 and 1670, several developments took place which seriously disrupted the lives of Native people in the eastern Subarctic. Although scholars have postulated that European diseases reached the area earlier, there is no evidence that pestilence caused widespread death during the first 100 years of contact. Most of the scattered accounts of illness and death suggest that the problems were localized. However, between 1634 and 1640 several major outbreaks took place which caused widespread suffering. In 1634 an epidemic broke out at Trois-Rivières and spread to the Saguenay River, through the Ottawa Valley, and to the Hurons. If this illness was measles, which seems likely, it would have infected a very high proportion of the regional Native population and caused a significant number of deaths. In 1636–7, influenza and probably scarlet fever swept the same region. Two years afterward smallpox broke out and spread as far north as James Bay. This was the most deadly of all the contagions to reach the region and mortality rates ran above 50 percent. Calvin Martin has suggested that epidemics like smallpox so shattered the Native world that they caused Indians to reject many of their traditional religious views and activities, particularly concerning conservation practices. He argues that Indians blamed the spirit game keepers for causing the havoc and decided to wage war on the animals. Martin suggests that this is why Indians overhunted game and furbearers. However, while no doubt the chaos that these epidemics created led the Natives to do much soul-searching, there is little evidence that supports Martin's suggestion. On the contrary, Native religions were much more adaptable to changing circumstances and Indians generally did not blame animals for their misfortunes. Initially they believed that witchcraft practiced by hostile Indian neighbors, or by the French, caused their suffering.

Increasing warfare among Indian peoples proved to be equally disruptive in the region. By the 1640s the Iroquois living south of Lake Ontario had been well-armed by the Dutch. Meanwhile, the French continued to limit the acquisition of firearms to their Indian converts. With the military advantage now decidedly resting with the Iroquois, their raids became bolder, better organized, and more deadly. In 1647 and 1648 the eastern Iroquois blockaded the lower Ottawa River and dispersed the Algonquin bands living there to the east, north, and west. Between 1647 and 1651, the Iroquois systematically assaulted and scattered the remaining Algonquins, Hurons, Petuns, and Nipissings. The Algonquin bands from the Madawaska area fled all the way to James Bay, while some of the surviving Nipissings headed northwest toward Lake Nipigon. The remainder of the Nipissings, the Christian converts, settled near the French post of Trois-Rivières, established in 1634. In 1651–2 the Iroquois struck the western Montagnais living at the headwaters of the St. Maurice River sending them fleeing eastward in fear to Lac St-Jean. The plight of these various refugees prompted other Native groups living beyond the Huron country and the Ottawa Valley to take flight. Most of the Ojibwas and Ottawas (Odawas), for example, sought refuge by moving west along the south shore of Lake Superior. A few of them moved into the Green Bay area. By the early 1650s the French inland fur trade was in tatters and the Native world had been completely disrupted.[5]

After a brief hiatus between 1649 and 1654, when Indians living in the western Great Lakes region were cut off from the French on the lower St. Lawrence, the Indians took the initiative and reestablished contact. In 1654 a party of Ottawas and refugee Hurons and Petuns from Green Bay ventured to Montreal to trade. Some of the furs which they brought had been obtained from their neighbors, suggesting that, despite the turmoil of the previous years, these bands were intent on continuing to act as middlemen in the French network. When they returned to their new homeland, missionaries and *coureurs de bois* (unlicensed traders) followed them. In 1656 over thirty Frenchmen voyaged to the area, including Pierre-Esprit Radisson and Médard Chouart des Groseilliers. Groseilliers had spent the previous two years in the region on an official mission to encourage more Indian traders to visit the colony on the St. Lawrence. During the next four years, trade expanded in the Lake Michigan and Lake Superior regions. Montreal, established in 1642, became the major center for this trade and thereafter surpassed Trois-Rivières, Quebec, and Tadoussac in terms of the volume of furs obtained. Hundreds of Indians came every year to take part in the great Montreal trading fairs.

While the groups living on the margin of the region renewed their participation in the business, more remote groups also became involved. By 1660 it appears that Cree bands from as far away as the eastern Lake of

---

[5] For a detailed presentation of these movements see Plates 37–40, *Historical Atlas of Canada*, vol. 1.

the Woods country, the upper English River area near Lac Seul, and the western James Bay region all took part. Most of these more westerly groups did not travel to Montreal. Rather, they dealt with Indian middlemen. The great western trading rendezvous apparently was located on Lake Nipigon, where western Crees and some Siouan-speaking Assiniboines from the boundary waters area of Minnesota and Ontario met with the immigrant Nipissing and Ojibwa traders. Trade from Lake Nipigon also extended northeastward to James Bay. East of this bay, the Montagnais continued to operate their system. By 1660 it encompassed all of the East Main country in northwestern Quebec and extended into central Labrador.

In 1658 the Iroquois again went to war against the French. Between 1661 and 1664 they made a concerted assault on the Montagnais, raiding as far as Lac St-Jean and Lake Nipissing, disrupting the regional trading network in the process. The French counterattack into Mohawk country in 1666 cowed the Iroquois, bringing peace to the Northern Interior once again. This led a substantial number of Ojibwas and Ottawas to return to their former homeland along the southeastern shores of Lake Superior and the northern shores of Lake Huron. Peace also meant that it was safer for the French to venture into the interior. Growing numbers of *coureurs de bois* obtained their outfits in Montreal, and headed into the Great Lakes region and the Northern Interior. Increasingly these men carried the trade to the interior, and the number of Indians who visited Montreal began to decline, particularly after 1670.

The year 1668 marked another important turning point in the history of the region. That year the English dispatched their first shipload of goods to James Bay from London. The idea of establishing direct contact with the heart of the Northern Interior by sea was a French idea. While traveling in the Upper Great Lakes region during the winter of 1659–60, Radisson and Groseilliers concluded that the cheapest way to reach the fur-rich country north of Lake Superior was by way of Hudson and James Bays. Also, it became clear to them that southern James Bay already was a major trading place for Indians. In the early 1660s they tried to persuade French colonial officials and the home government to back a seaborne trading venture into the region. After failing to get government support and their involvement in an abortive attempt to mount an expedition from Boston in 1663, they turned to the English court of Charles II. There, with the help of the king's cousin, Prince Rupert, the two Frenchmen secured the financial backing they needed. However, they were unable to set sail to the Bay until the summer of 1668. The first expedition involved two ships, but only one of them, the *Nonsuch,* with Groseilliers on board, made it to the "bottom of the bay" in late summer. The crew passed the winter near the outlet of the Rupert River, where they were favorably received by local Crees who exchanged a substantial number of prime northern furs during the spring of 1669. By the time this ship returned to London in the autumn, the financial backers of the enterprise had taken steps to organize themselves into a company for the purposes of conducting trade on a long-term basis. They secured a charter from Charles II on May 2, 1670 as the Hudson's Bay Company. Of great importance, the royal charter gave the company title, in effect, to all the lands drained by waters flowing into Hudson Strait, the area which they named Rupert's Land, and monopoly trading privileges within this vast country.

Having obtained the charter, the English traders faced the task of establishing regular trade with people they knew little about. This job became the responsibility of the governor and committee, who were a small group of men elected by the shareholders from among their ranks at the company's annual general court. In the company's formative years the governor and committee turned to Radisson and Groseilliers, particularly the former, for advice on all aspects of the Canadian operations. For this reason, the Hudson's Bay Company's early trade provides important clues about the way the French trade had operated since the late sixteenth century, given that latter trade served as the model.

To establish relations with Indians on a sound footing, the governor and committee ordered their men to follow those customs of the country that seemed most appropriate. Thus, in the Bay area, transactions between Indians and the company followed long-established Native trading traditions. Economic intercourse between the two parties always involved two components – gift exchange and barter. Gift-giving was a Native practice, a type of balanced reciprocity, that served to establish or renew trading and political alliances. Indians usually came to the posts in small parties (called "gangs" by the traders) led by one or several "trading captains." Large gangs also included "lieutenants." Of course, these terms were not appropriate, in the sense that the Indian leaders had no authority by virtue of their position. Instead, they recruited their followers by promising to look after their interests at the post. Trading captains had to know the routes to the various posts and be good negotiators with traders and Indians whose territories they had to cross on the way. Following the lead of the French, the Hudson's Bay Company traders made presents to the Indian captains to secure their favor and acknowledge their special importance. Normally an important leader received a captain's outfit, which consisted of a hat, a regimental jacket, a pair of pants, and miscellaneous adornments. In addition he and his followers received some food, usually biscuits and prunes, tobacco, and rum. While handing out these gifts, the trader in charge of the post delivered a welcoming speech and smoked the calumet. The trading captain then reciprocated by giving a present of furs to the post manager consisting of several pelts he had collected from among his followers. Once these pleasantries were concluded, barter trade commenced.

In order to engage in barter trading on an accountable basis, the London directors decided to use the staple of the trade, a prime winter beaver pelt (coat or parchment), as the unit of account, which was called the "Made Beaver" [MB]. Every year the governor and committee sent out two price schedules to each post. In the "Standard of Trade" they listed the MB prices of the company's goods and in the other, the "Comparative Standard," they gave the current MB prices for the various furs other than beaver that the Indians came to sell. One of the most remarkable facts about the MB system is that it was so well suited to the business that it remained in use in many areas of the North until after World War I. When furs other than beaver dominated local trading activity, the company sometimes used an alternative standard. For example, marten figured prominently in the James Bay area and the posts used "Made Marten" besides the MB.

One of the biggest challenges that the governor and committee faced in the first years of the company's existence involved selecting goods that would be acceptable to the Indians. Radisson played an especially important role in helping them deal with this problem. He and the committee were aware that their Indian customers already had well-defined demands for goods. Because the Crees were accustomed to French goods, the directors made a concerted effort to supply them with these articles, or reasonable copies of them. The governor and committee focused their early concern toward obtaining suitable arms, ammunition, and metalwares, suggesting that these categories of goods were of paramount interest to the James Bay Natives in the 1670s.

Even though the governor and committee initially depended heavily on Radisson's advice when choosing their inventories, they also solicited Indian feedback about the goods the company was shipping to the Bay. Seeking Native reactions in this way became a standard operating procedure of the company, and it gave the Indians a chance to exert a strong influence on the development of the company's trade good inventories.

The establishment of the Hudson's Bay Company afforded the local Crees and their allies the opportunity of having contact with European traders without having to go through Indian intermediaries or traveling through the territories of other bands. Already in 1662 and 1663 Crees from the James Bay area had dispatched envoys to Quebec to ask the French to send missionaries to them. Apparently they made this request in the hope of forging commercial and military links with the French in an effort to ward off Iroquois raiders who were reaching as far north as James Bay. The French responded to this initiative in 1663 by sending three traders, accompanied by a large party of Indians, to the Rupert River, where they conducted a lively trade. However, this expedition did not go as far as James Bay. So, when the Hudson's Bay Company men arrived on the scene, they met Native people who had been involved in the fur trade for a considerable length of time and who were eager to improve their strategic position in the enterprise. The construction of posts at the outlets of the major rivers flowing into the bay – Charles Fort on the Rupert River, 1668; Moose Factory, on the Moose River, 1673; Fort Albany on the Albany River, 1675; York Factory, on the Hayes River, 1682; and Churchill Fort on the Severn River, 1685 – gave them that opportunity.

Hudson's Bay Company records make it clear that the Swampy and Western Crees moved quickly to capitalize on their new advantage. Just twelve years after the company received its charter, Governor John Nixon reported that the Crees were using their English firearms to establish a cordon around the Bay and thereby deny to more distant Indians direct access to Fort Albany. The Siouan-speaking Assiniboines of the Winnipeg River area and bordering parklands were the only outsiders they exempted from the blockade. Apparently the Assiniboines obtained free access because they had forged an alliance with their Cree neighbors sometime in the late precontact era in order to carry on their battles against the Dakota Sioux from a position of greater strength. According to Nixon, the Assiniboines and Crees raided Siouan territory in part because they wanted to "steal their beavers."

Although Fort Albany was an important trading place for the Assiniboines and southwestern Crees in the early 1680s, it was the construction of York Factory in 1682 that had the greatest impact on them. The Hayes River–Echimamish River route leading inland from this post provided the easiest canoe route into the interior and enabled York Factory eventually to become the most important fur-trading and warehousing center in western Canada before confederation in 1867. The Assiniboines and Crees living about Lake Winnipeg were ideally situated to take control of the inland trade of this post during its first century of development. They wasted no time in doing so. Using their superior military strength, gained by having steady access to Hudson's Bay Company firearms, they intensified their wars with the Dakota Sioux to the south, and pushed westward between the Churchill and Saskatchewan rivers. From 1694 to 1720 the Crees fought the Chipewyans along the middle and lower Churchill River and clashed with the Beaver Indians in the upper Churchill River country toward Lake Athabasca. In these conflicts the Crees pushed back the Beaver and Chipewyan frontiers.

Apparently the Cree-Chipewyan conflict cost many lives. James Knight, who was in charge of York Factory in 1716, reported that Indians told him that as many as 6,000 men had died in recent battles along this frontier. Granting that this undoubtedly was an exaggeration, it does suggest the scale of the conflict. Widespread hostilities also existed along the southern margin of the forest. Here the Assiniboines seem to have suffered heavy losses.

The construction of Fort Churchill (soon renamed Fort Prince of Wales) in 1717 had a major impact on the Chipewyans. The Hudson's Bay Company built this post on the Churchill River to establish regular trade with these people, who had previously come to York Factory. However, the contact had been intermittent because the Crees frequently attacked Chipewyan trading parties. With the help of the arms they obtained from the new post, the Chipewyans began to fight back against the Crees, stopping their advance in the lower Churchill River region by the middle of the century. Before 1763 the Chipewyans primarily served as middle-men to the more distant Yellowknives and Dogribs because their own territory was not well stocked with furbearers.

The first half-century of Bay-side trading led to further disruptions, as Assiniboine and Cree groups pushed westward and northward searching for new fur supplies and trading partners. Through warfare this new group of Indian middlemen advanced the trading frontier as far west as the Athabasca River area by 1715. Meanwhile, the southeastern Woodland Assiniboines were pulling away from the war-torn portions of their traditional territory between Lake of the Woods and Lake Winnipeg. Since very few Chipewyans were able to penetrate the northern Cree perimeter by this date, Athapaskan-speakers remained peripheral to the fur trade. Likewise some of the Plains Indians who had visited York Factory in its earliest years, such as the Blackfeet and Bloods, rarely appeared after the 1720s. There were two reasons. First, the Assiniboines and Crees now carried the trade to the prairies. Second, as the Plains groups acquired horses they became unwilling to make long canoe voyages to Hudson Bay. Farther east, the Montagnais, Ottawa, and Ojibwa middlemen had lost most of the carrying trade, since their Cree suppliers no longer depended on them. Therefore, these eastern groups had to obtain an increasing share of the furs they sold to the French through their own trapping activities.

Whereas the founding of the Hudson's Bay Company represented a boon to the Crees, this development posed an immediate threat to the French. Now the French trading empire centered on the St. Lawrence faced English challengers on its northern as well as its southern flanks (the English had replaced the Dutch south of Lake Ontario in 1664). The returns carried home on the *Nonsuch* in 1669 made it abundantly clear to the French that the Hudson's Bay Company had the prospect of garnering the bulk of the highest quality beaver if it remained unopposed. At first French colonial officials and merchants responded cautiously, in order to avoid taking any actions that might disrupt the good relations which existed at the time between the English and French monarchs. In 1672 Father Charles Albanel made a brief overland visit to southeastern James Bay. Immediately thereafter the French built a post on Lake Mistassini which drew a substantial number of Rupert River Indians away from the Bay to trade. In 1679 Louis Jolliet obtained the support of some Montreal merchants, and he too led an expedition to James Bay. On his return, Jolliet recommended taking action to evict the English from the Bay or the French would lose the northern trade. Responding to these concerns, a group of merchants rallied behind Charles Aubert de La Chesnaye in 1682 to form the Compagnie du Nord, and they received a charter from the King of France three years later, permitting them to trade into Hudson Bay.

Even before the French company received its royal charter, it took steps to challenge the Hudson's Bay Company. In 1682 it sent Jolliet to build a post at Lake Nemiscau. It also sent Radisson and Groseilliers, who by then had defected from the English, to build a post on the outlet of the Nelson River not far from York Factory. They occupied this establishment for three years before withdrawing. In 1686 the Compagnie du Nord launched its boldest strike. It sent 105 men overland from Montreal under the command of Pierre de Troyes and they captured all three of the

Hudson's Bay Company's posts on James Bay. Significantly, except for a small party of Crees, most of the local Natives did not take sides in the struggle. The few Swampy Crees who did offer help to the French were angry with the postmaster at Fort Albany who they claimed had beaten them. In 1693 the Hudson's Bay Company retook Fort Albany, the most important trading establishment on James Bay, and held it thereafter. However, a year later the company suffered a major setback on Hudson Bay when the French seized control of York Factory and held it for the next twenty years (renaming it Fort Bourbon). Thus the English and French reached a stalemate in the Hudson and James Bay area which lasted until the end of the War of the Spanish Succession (1702–13). Of critical importance to the local Indians, European traders remained on the scene to supply their growing needs and desires.

In 1713 England and France signed the Treaty of Utrecht, ending the War of the Spanish Succession in Europe. This accord had important repercussions for Indians of the Northern Interior because it changed some of the fundamental spatial characteristics of the trade. The French agreed to withdraw from the Bay, but they retained the right to send traders into the interior of Rupert's Land. Previously the French had pushed their inland empire from their St. Lawrence Valley base as far as the western shores of Lake Superior, where they built posts at Kaministiquia and on Lake Nipigon, which they operated between 1678 and 1698. During this time French traders also probed farther west – Jacques de Noyon building a temporary post on Rainy Lake in 1688. Once peace between England and France was reestablished in 1713, the French made plans to renew their northwestern expansion. In 1717 they reopened Fort Kaministiquia and Fort Nipigon, placing them within a new command, the *Postes du nord,* which included the northwestern Lake Superior area and beyond. In 1726 the French built a post at Michipicoten to tap the southwestern hinterland of James Bay. In 1728 Pierre Gaultier de Varennes et de La Vérendrye took command of the Postes du Nord and launched a vigorous exploration and trading campaign with the help of his sons and the financial backing of colonial merchants. By 1748 he and his sons had extended his network of posts as far as Lake Winnipegosis (Fort Dauphin) and the lower Saskatchewan River (Forts Bourbon and Paskoya).

Of great significance to the Indians, the Hudson's Bay Company did not respond to these French initiatives by moving inland. By doing so the company would have incurred substantially greater operating costs without having any guarantee that it would obtain enough additional furs to pay for them. For these reasons the Hudson's Bay Company decided to leave the inland trade in the hands of its Indian entrepreneurial partners. This was a wise business decision, even though it left the company politically vulnerable to its critics, who railed at it for "sleeping by the frozen sea" and not living up to its imperial responsibilities by meeting the French face-to-face. The volume of the company's fur returns declined in the face of the French advance, but it turned handsome profits nonetheless, largely because rising beaver prices on the London market helped offset diminished volumes. Also, the company's fur-pricing structure was very profitable.[6]

The Indians benefited from English-French commercial rivalries in a variety of ways. Although the French had moved into the heartland of Assiniboine and Western Cree territory by the 1740s, they did not completely displace Indian middlemen because the cargo capacity of the French canoe-oriented overland transportation network was not sufficiently large to bring in enough goods to satisfy the Indian demand. In particular, bulky and heavy items like kettles, guns, powder, and cloth could not be carried inland in large quantities. So Indians still had to visit the Hudson's Bay Company's Bay-side posts to obtain additional supplies of these commodities. Soon the Hudson's Bay Company officials learned that Indians were willing to make the long and difficult trek to the Bay only if the company assured them that the posts always had all of the supplies they needed. Accordingly, after 1716 the company adopted the policy of always keeping a two-year supply of trade goods on hand to cover the possibility that a supply ship might fail to reach its destination, such as happened at York Factory in 1716. That year a large party of Indians waited in vain for the ship and departed in an ugly mood.

As other Native groups had done before them, the Assiniboines and Crees took advantage of competitive market conditions to press the English and French traders for better prices for their furs. The Hudson's Bay Company's post account books provide us with a measure of the degree to which the Indians succeeded. As the trade evolved, the annual price lists primarily served to set the minimum prices for the company's goods and provided the bookkeepers with the values they needed to tally their accounts. The company's traders tried their best to obtain as much for their

---

[6] Arthur J. Ray, "Buying and Selling Hudson's Bay Company Furs in the Eighteenth Century," in *Explorations in Canadian Economic History: Essays in Honour of Irene M. Spry*, ed. D. Cameron (Ottawa, 1985), 95–115.

trade goods as the local market conditions permitted. This meant they charged more than the minimum in nearly all instances.

The Hudson's Bay Company officers advanced their prices by using a variety of tactics. One of these involved dickering over the quality of the furs which the Indians brought to exchange. The company's "Comparative Standard" only listed prices for prime furs; hence, the traders had considerable latitude when determining what they would pay for all other grades. It also became common practice in the earliest years of operations for officers to buy furs on averages. This involved offering an Indian a price for his pack which took into account the proportion of prime, medium, and low grade furs it contained. This custom provided Hudson's Bay Company men with more flexibility in their fur pricing than would have been the case had they bought skins one at a time. Buying on averages also expedited exchange, thereby reducing the company's transaction costs.

Besides dickering over fur prices, Hudson's Bay Company traders also sought to make gains by simply charging more for goods than the "Standard of Trade" specified, or they used shortened measures when dispensing commodities such as cloth, powder, shot, and brandy.

The company traders recorded the net gains that they made each year as a result of using these various strategies. They listed this in their account books as "overplus." This was the MB value of the returns that exceeded what the official standards called for, given the quantity of goods the Indians purchased. The bookkeepers determined the "overplus" simply by subtracting the worth of the goods exchanged (valued according to the "Standard of Trade") from the total value of the returns received (rated at the "Comparative Standard"). The surviving Hudson's Bay Company account books for the period before 1763 show that the traders always made overplus. Their markups over the standards of trade ranged from 40 to 60 percent. The volume of "overplus" achieved at a given post fluctuated considerably from year to year depending on the intensity of French competition.

The Indians had some leverage in this circumstance, because the English traders depended on them for information about French operations and prices. Hudson's Bay Company traders complained that their Native customers readily told them about those French prices that were more generous than the company's, but were unresponsive when asked which Hudson's Bay Company prices were more favorable to them. In any event, when faced with very competitive circumstances, the Hudson's Bay Company men had to meet the Indians' demand to "take pity on us" and give us "good measure" or they ran the risk of losing their trade. At these times the company's postmasters had to be more liberal and settle for a smaller volume of "overplus."

However, the company's traders did not have a free hand to respond to Indian economic pressure. By the 1740s the governor and committee had become accustomed to receiving certain levels of "overplus" at the various posts, even though they did not understand how it was obtained. So, if a trader failed to satisfy the committee's expectations without having a very good explanation, he risked receiving a strong admonishment or dismissal. Also, the officers could not adjust the official standards without first obtaining the governor and committee's approval.

Generally the governor and committee opposed any moves to lower prices or pay more for the Indians' furs no matter how strongly their officers argued for such changes. For example, in the 1720s and 1730s the French rated a prime marten pelt as equal to a beaver. The Hudson's Bay Company, on the other hand, priced them at one-third of a beaver. The local Crees repeatedly pointed out this glaring discrepancy to the company's post managers who in turn petitioned the London committee to permit them to meet the French price. The London committee refused all their requests. Marten was worth even more than beaver on the London market and the company reaped a handsome profit from the price differential. The committee was not willing to abandon this economic advantage to placate the Indians as long as fur volumes remained high enough to make a good gross profit.

Because the committee believed that once they lowered prices Indians would resist subsequent increases, they rarely reduced them. However, periodically the governor and committee did raise the "Standard of Trade" in spite of Indian protests. Normally this was done only when the price of buying goods in England had risen to the point that profit margins were seriously threatened. So, one of the striking characteristics about the Hudson's Bay Company's standards of trade during the eighteenth century was that they moved upward in a stepwise fashion. Long periods of time elapsed between general increments. The relative stability of the standards meant that they served as the reference point for Indians and traders when bargaining. This is why Indians usually asked for "full measure and a little over" and the traders tried to give them less.

Besides being price-sensitive, Indian consumers proved to be very demanding about the quality of the trade goods the traders offered to them and the suitability of these items for their mobile lifestyle in the intemperate

Subarctic climate. Indians took advantage of competitive conditions to get the goods they wanted. For example, the Hudson's Bay Company initially imported long-barreled East Indian land rifles. Apart from being difficult to haul around in canoes and in the bush, the trigger guards on these guns were not large enough to allow a hunter to use a gloved hand during the winter. To address this latter problem, the company had its gunsmiths enlarge the trigger guards. In the early eighteenth century the French shortened the gun barrels to between three and three and one-half feet (92 to 107 cm), making the muskets much lighter and easier to handle. The Indians liked them immediately and carried their new French arms down to the Bay to show the Hudson's Bay Company men what they now expected. The company's officers purchased a few of these arms and sent them to England, where the company's gunsmiths copied the new design and improved it. By the middle of the century, these smaller muskets accounted for the bulk of the firearms trade at the company's James Bay posts and a significant share at York Factory and Fort Churchill.

Although the governor and committee devoted a lot of attention to meeting the Indians' demands for high quality, lightweight firearms, their Native customers continued to complain throughout the eighteenth century. Indians pressed for even lighter weapons. The problem was that, once the company produced firearms of the length Indians desired, the only other way to reduce the weight involved thinning the walls of the barrels. This made the weapons prone to explosions that usually had disastrous consequences for Indian hunters. After attempting to deal with these conflicting concerns through the 1730s and 1740s, the governor and committee finally told their postmasters to inform the Indians that they would have to decide whether they wanted lightweight firearms or reliable ones.

The Hudson's Bay Company also faced considerable Native criticisms regarding other metal goods that it supplied. For example, although copper and brass kettles were very popular, the Indians wanted lighter ones. Once again it seems that technological constraints made it difficult for the company suppliers to meet the Indians' exacting requirements. The company experimented with thinner gauges of metal, only to have the Indians complain that too often the bottoms dropped out of these kettles or the walls cracked.

One of the key reasons that the Hudson's Bay Company faced these kinds of problems with its metal goods was that English manufacturers had no experience with making tools and weapons for use in the Subarctic climate, where extremely low temperatures made the metal brittle and even the slightest defects caused articles to break. Compounding the problem, in the eighteenth century most of the Indians lived long distances from the posts. This meant that they could visit a gunsmith or tinsmith to have repairs made only once or twice a year. For these reasons, Indians had become very discerning consumers. Also, some groups came to depend on these weapons for their survival. Considering this, it is not surprising that Hudson's Bay Company traders reported that Indians became remarkably astute and readily spotted the most minute casting flaws in gun barrels and other metal goods.

The Indians showed similar discrimination concerning cloth. In the beginning they preferred French cloth to that of English manufacture. However, by the 1730s, the Hudson's Bay Company managed to obtain cloth from England, which the Indians regarded as superior. They became particularly fond of cloth from Stroud, appropriately called stroud. To satisfy the Indian demand for this type of cloth, French traders smuggled English stroud into New France from Albany. Ironically, by the 1740s Indians began to arrive at the Bay-side posts with "French strouds" and demanded that the Hudson's Bay Company furnish them with the same!

The Indians forced the French and the Hudson's Bay Company to court their favor in other ways. They complained about the quality of goods partly as a ploy to get traders to lower their prices. Gift-giving before trade became more elaborate as rival parties tried to show that they were more generous than their opponents, raising Indian expectations with each round. Also, Indians came to expect very generous credit terms. Very early in the fur trade it became a common practice to "outfit" Indians on credit. Under the outfitting system, traders advanced staple items on credit. The amount of credit given out depended on the average return of an individual. Credit provided an Indian with an incentive to trap; it gave the trader a moral claim on his future returns; and it assured the trapper that he would have the tools and equipment he needed even if his previous hunt had been a failure. Initially the Natives probably regarded trader credit as a type of balanced reciprocity; soon they came to regard it as a means by which a trader proved his concern for their welfare. Under competitive conditions traders not only felt the need to be more generous to show their good faith, but also often discouraged Indians from honoring the debt they owed to the opposition. The journals of the English and French traders contain many complaints that competition "unsettled the Indian's minds," leading many of them not to pay their debts. Granting that some Indians defaulted when the enticements to do so were strong, it is likely that Europeans exaggerated the problem. In any event, when trading rivalries were strong, Indians demanded and received liberal credit.

By the time the French withdrew from the Northern Interior in 1763, the fur trade reached from the Atlantic Coast westward to the foothills of the Rocky Mountains and northward to the boreal forest–tundra boundary as far west as Great Slave Lake and Great Bear Lake. By this time the enterprise had a differential impact on the various peoples of the region.

One very important change had taken place in terms of European fur demand. Coat beaver no longer was the prized fur. By the beginning of the eighteenth century, Western Europeans had learned the secret for processing parchment beaver and therefore no longer had to send it to Russia. English and French traders now preferred parchment skins because they were of a more uniformly high quality than coat beaver. This shift in demand had considerable implications for the Indians. To satisfy the changing European market, Indians had either to increase their total beaver production, if they wished to continue to wear beaver coats, or to adopt alternative winter clothing.

Given that this change did not serve the Indians' best interests, it is not surprising that they strongly resisted it. For example, as the market for coat beaver weakened at the end of the seventeenth century, these skins piled up in the warehouses and at the trading posts. The Hudson's Bay Company directors ordered their men to inform the Indians that the company no longer wanted these skins. When simple persuasion failed, the London committee recommended that their officers take stronger action. The directors suggested that they assemble the Indians and burn some coat beaver in front of them to show how little the company valued these skins. Some of the officers followed these instructions, but others declined to do so, saying that it would offend their Native clientele.

The governor and committee were mindful of some of the economic implications which the proposed changes would have for Native people. They sent some sheepskin coats to their posts to see if Indians would be willing to wear them in place of their traditional winter garments. The Indians flatly rejected this idea, and they continued to press the Hudson's Bay Company and the French to take their coat beaver. In spite of their persistence, however, the trade in this commodity began a gradual decline until the middle of the nineteenth century, by which time it had largely ceased. This subtle shift meant that over time the industry placed more pressure on beaver stocks. As these stocks dwindled, the Indians were increasingly motivated to stop wearing beaver coats in the winter and to substitute European clothing instead. It may be that this process already was well underway by the middle of the eighteenth century. Data from Hudson's Bay Company posts show that parchment beaver returns usually exceeded those of coat beaver between 1720 and 1780. Furthermore, the difference normally was much greater at the James Bay posts than at Fort Churchill and York Factory.

Hudson's Bay Company merchandise sales figures reveal that in the early years, firearms and ammunition accounted for almost 50 percent of the total value of Indian expenditures at the various posts. Subsequently, Indians bought a greater array of goods. In particular, cloth and blankets, both used for clothing, increased in relative importance from 1720 to 1780. In the James Bay area, these commodities were more important than arms and ammunition after 1730. The same pattern emerged later at York Factory in the 1770s and Fort Churchill in the 1780s. This confirms that European clothing materials were in greater demand over time. It also suggests that men directly benefited the most from the early trade, given that expenditures on hunting tools and weapons predominated, and women more from the later one, considering that they traditionally made most of the clothing and domestic goods. Yet, apart from bands living next to trading posts, it is unlikely that very many Indians had become dependent on European clothing.

The trade of metal tools and utensils, such as axes, hatchets, knives, and kettles, does not show any pronounced long-term trend during the middle of the eighteenth century. Between 1720 and 1780, these items accounted for 5 to 15 percent of the value of Indian purchases in the James Bay area and from 10 to 30 percent of those at York Factory and Fort Churchill. By the 1760s, kettles probably had displaced Native pottery among the Assiniboines and most of the Algonquian groups, and it is likely that stone tools and weapons yielded to European imports. Metal axes and ice chisels were particularly important during this period, because hunters used them to break open frozen beaver lodges in the winter.

Brandy and tobacco were the two leading luxury items. The traders distributed substantial quantities of these two commodities in the pre-trade gift exchanges, but these presents served to heighten rather than satisfy Indian demand. Brandy was more important in the James Bay area, comprising 10 to 30 percent of the values of sales between 1730 and 1760, whereas on western Hudson Bay it amounted to just under 10 percent. Tobacco was more popular at the latter posts, amounting to 10 to 20 percent of the turnover, than it was around James Bay, where it accounted for less than 10 percent of sales. Although Indians consumed substantial quantities of alcohol while visiting the trading posts, there is little evidence to suggest that this was having any seriously disruptive effects on their societies at this time. Most groups still lived considerable distances from trading posts, and they apparently carried only small quantities of alcohol home with them. Indians mostly drank only once or twice a year. Nearly all the tobacco that the Hudson's Bay Company sold consisted of Brazil tobacco. Imported from Brazil to London by way of Portugal, this molasses-treated tobacco was twisted into ropes which were then coiled into "carrots." Hudson's Bay Company accounts show that Indians were extremely fond of this tobacco, which the French did not have, and that they were willing to travel great distances to obtain it. For this reason, the governor and committee sought to obtain the highest quality Brazil tobacco that was available.

It is very difficult to estimate accurately the extent to which Native people living to the south and east of the Churchill River had become dependent on the fur trade by 1763. It is probable that European goods had become well integrated into the Native economies, given the volume and nature of sales at Hudson's Bay Company posts and taking account that these posts secured a smaller share of the fur returns than did French ones. Yet, even though they depended on these goods for their newly emerging lifestyle, the Indians remained in a strong position vis-à-vis the Europeans thanks to the competitive nature of the fur trade. Very few Europeans took part in the enterprise and widespread resource depletion had not yet occurred. To this date most of the rapid spatial expansion of the industry took place because of European and Native commercial rivalries.

By encouraging the expansion of commercial hunting and trapping activities, the fur trade provided a catalyst for changes in the aboriginal land tenure systems. As long as subsistence needs predominated over fur hunting for exchange purposes, the traditional practice of sharing resources continued. Yet, the fur trade began to emphasize individual and family interests and the development of more sharply defined rights of access to resources. The replacement of eastern middlemen in the fur trade by new groups to the west made bands living in northern Quebec and Ontario increasingly reliant on their own trapping efforts and local resources. Also the expanded demand for parchment beaver encouraged them to take more beaver. In contrast to woodland caribou and moose, beaver do not migrate but remain in the same general territory. As Indians began to shift the focus of their economy in this way, it offered them both the option and the incentive to develop more sharply defined territorial boundaries and a stronger notion of trespass concerning commercially prized species.

Hudson's Bay Company records provide clear evidence that this development was taking place in the James Bay area at least as early as the 1740s. Indians continued to share basic subsistence resources with their neighbors, but they reserved the fur bearers on their land for themselves. Family hunting territories served as management units, and commercially valuable fur bearers became the focus of Indian concern. As fur and game stocks dwindled later in the century, this orientation grew stronger as we shall see.

The debt system also encouraged Indians to take a more individualistic approach to resource management. The traders extended credit to individual trappers, not to groups. Hunters who were "steady," reliable, and always paid their debts received more credit than those who did not. Hence they were better able to look after their families, dispense largess to their friends, and provide evidence of their supernatural powers. In this way individual performance became linked with status for those Indians who were being drawn into the emerging fur trade society.

This society began to take shape as soon as the French *coureurs de bois* entered the region and its development accelerated with the establishment of trading posts. When European traders appeared Indians courted their alliances through marriages, and the French readily accepted these overtures. The *coureurs de bois* quickly learned that Indian women were essential companions for travel in the north because they possessed knowledge and skills that were necessary for survival and, in addition, cooked, cut wood, prepared the camps, and provided companionship. Also, Native women facilitated trade through their kinship connections. Others who followed later adopted the practice begun by the *coureurs de bois*. Although the Hudson's Bay Company directors frowned on fraternization and forbade their men to develop liaisons with Native women, their officers and servants ignored the ruling. We have no way of knowing how many Native people were offspring of these Indian-European unions by 1763. However, their numbers were substantial. By that time bands of Indians lived near most trading posts. Many, if not most, of the members of these groups, called Homeguard Indians by the Hudson's Bay Company, were of mixed descent. Traders referred to these people of French-Native ancestry as "*bois brulés*" or "Métis" and those of English- and Scottish-Native background as "mixed-bloods" or "country born."

1763 – 1821: AN ERA OF DESTRUCTIVE COMPETITION

The nearly six decades between 1763 and 1821 were a time of momentous change in the fur trade. Control of the Montreal-based fur trade passed from French and French-Canadian merchants to those of Scottish, English, and colonial American background. This new group of entrepreneurs, using a labor force of French Canadians, mixed-bloods, and Indians, pushed the fur trade well beyond the limits of the old French network and fought the Hudson's Bay Company to a standstill.

Indian hostilities around the eastern Great Lakes briefly hampered efforts to reestablish the northwestern trade after the British conquest of Quebec. The growing resentment of the Indians about their altered circumstances came to a head in May 1763 when the Ottawa chief Pontiac initiated an uprising to drive out the British (see Chapter 7). It was the fall of Fort Michilimackinac on June 2, 1763, which most directly affected the northwestern fur trade, since it was located on the main route to the west.

With the establishment of peace in 1765, Montreal-based traders no longer faced the threat of attack as they pushed westward. However, they encountered a legal barrier. In order to prevent a recurrence of the kinds of trading abuses that helped provoke the Pontiac uprising, British authorities established a series of trading regulations in 1764 which specified that all traders had to obtain a license and conduct their affairs only at posts where an official of the Indian department was present. Furthermore, traders were not supposed to infringe on the charter of the Hudson's Bay Company. Merchants from the province of Quebec (created in 1763) took exception to these restrictions, and some British officers ignored them. In 1765 Alexander Henry obtained a monopoly on the trade of Lake Superior from the commander at Fort Michilimackinac and a new era of inland expansion began. In 1768 the British government abandoned its effort to regulate the trade, having decided that it was too costly to do so. Instead, it passed the responsibility on to colonial authorities to administer it as they thought best. The Governor of Quebec immediately authorized licensed traders to go beyond Lake Superior and into the heart of Rupert's Land, thereby setting the stage for a rapid expansion of the fur trade into what was to become the Canadian Northwest.

The first phase of the advance took place between 1765 and 1774. During this time the St. Lawrence–based traders took the initiative and reestablished or constructed posts at Sault Ste. Marie, Grand Portage, on

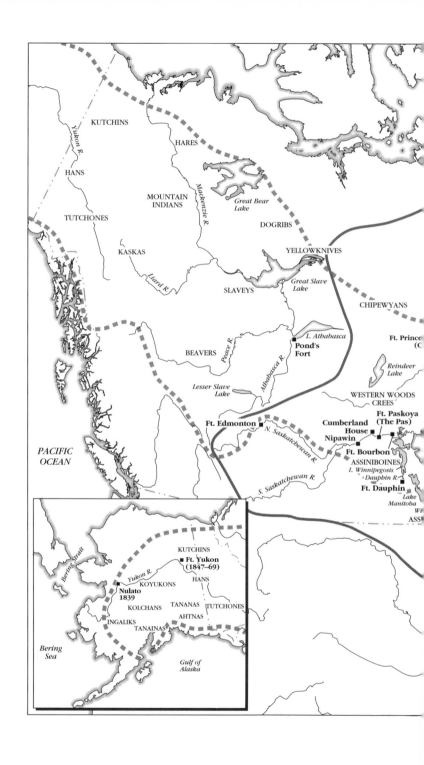

KUTCHINS

Yukon R.

HARES

HANS

MOUNTAIN
INDIANS

Mackenzie R.

Great Bear
Lake

TUTCHONES

DOGRIBS

KASKAS

YELLOWKNIVES

Liard R.

Great Slave
Lake

SLAVEYS

CHIPEWYANS

Ft. Prince
(C

Peace R.

L. Athabasca

BEAVERS

Pond's
Fort

Athabasca R.

Reindeer
Lake

Lesser Slave
Lake

WESTERN WOODS
CREES

Ft. Paskoya

PACIFIC
OCEAN

Ft. Edmonton

N. Saskatchewan R.

Cumberland
House

(The Pas)

Nipawin

Ft. Bourbon

ASSINIBOINES

L. Winnipegosis

Dauphin R.

Ft. Dauphin

S. Saskatchewan R.

Lake
Manitoba

Wi

ASS'

Bering Strait

KUTCHINS

Ft. Yukon
(1847–69)

Yukon R.

KOYUKONS

HANS

Nulato
1839

TANANAS

TUTCHONES

KOLCHANS

AHTNAS

INGALIKS

TANAINAS

Bering
Sea

Gulf of
Alaska

Figure 13.1 Contact locations of Native groups and major trading posts in the Subarctic.

the lower Assiniboine River, at the outlet of the Dauphin River, on the Saskatchewan River near Cedar Lake, at The Pas, and at Nipawin. From these establishments the Montreal-based traders (referred to hereafter as "Nor'Westers") dispatched many men to comb the country for the Indians' furs. The Hudson's Bay Company responded only slowly to this great challenge. In 1766 it reestablished its Henley House way station to encourage Indians to travel to Fort Albany to trade.

The year 1774 marked a significant turning point for the Hudson's Bay Company when it established Cumberland House as its first inland trading post. By this date it had become clear to the governor and committee that the policy of "sleeping by the frozen sea" was no longer practicable in the face of the onslaught by the Nor'Westers. They simply were carrying away too many of the Indians' furs. This sparked off a period of unprecedented competition that did not end until 1821. The Nor'Westers continued to be in the vanguard of the expansion. They carried the trade into the Athabasca-Mackenzie region, beginning in 1778 when Peter Pond built a small post on the lower Athabasca River. They extended their operations across the Rocky Mountains into central British Columbia (called New Caledonia) following Alexander Mackenzie's overland exploring expedition to the Pacific Ocean completed in 1793 (see Chapter 11). To carry out the vigorous campaign of expansion and battle against the older, financially more secure Hudson's Bay Company, the Nor'Westers had to minimize competition among themselves and pool their resources. They had entered the field as a series of small partnerships involving one or more wintering partners, who conducted the business in the interior, and one or more Montreal merchant partners, who obtained and dispatched the trade goods and disposed of the furs. To push on into the Athabasca area, several of these smaller partnerships joined forces on the Saskatchewan River in 1776 and formed the North West Company. Dominated by Scots entrepreneurs, this organization proved to be an intimidating force for the Hudson's Bay Company throughout most of the period before 1821.

The spatial expansion of the two trading networks during this forty-seven year period had a strong impact on all aspects of Native people's lives in the central and western portions of British North America. The two opposing camps of traders built over 600 posts throughout the Northwest. Most of these were temporary facilities, permanent posts being located mostly at strategic sites along the principal transportation routes. Yet their number demonstrates that a fundamental change had taken place in the spatial character of the enterprise and its impact on the environment. The proliferation of posts meant that, by 1821, most Indians located south and east of the Peace River lived in relative proximity to a trading post. Thus, there no longer was a role for Indian middlemen in this region. Easier access to trading posts also removed one of the constraints on Native consumption, since they no longer had to carry their purchases long distances to their home territories.

The construction of many posts and the development of the transportation system needed to supply them led to a substantial increase in the fur trade labor force. Beginning in 1774, the Nor'Westers and Hudson's Bay Company men probably numbered fewer than 300 men. By 1820, they totaled over 1,800.[7] This substantial increase created problems for the Europeans and expanded economic opportunities for Native people.

From the earliest days of the fur trade, Europeans had sought to control their operating expenses by minimizing the consumption of expensive imported foods and living off the land as much as possible. Also, the trading companies needed to stockpile these foodstuffs at key locations along their routes in order to minimize critical boat or canoe cargo space. For this reason, they turned to the Homeguard Indians to supply them with meat, fish, and a variety of collected foods. Each post retained at least one, and more often several, Natives to hunt game. The Europeans supplemented the food they obtained from their post hunters by purchasing additional quantities from other Indians who came in to trade. These additional purchases were particularly important at the key posts where traders stockpiled food for the passing brigades. Between 1774 and 1821, provisioning became a major activity for Subarctic Native peoples and it enabled them to supplement their earnings from trapping.

There were several areas where Native provisioning was especially important for the operation of the transportation system. One of these was the Rainy River–Winnipeg River region. Here the Ojibwas, who immigrated into the region after 1730 in the wake of the Assiniboines' withdrawal, provided large quantities of fish (whitefish and sturgeon), wild rice, and Indian corn. The Ojibwas had begun to cultivate the latter crop more extensively following the destruction of the Hurons in the 1640s. The market for this commodity, which the Nor'Westers generated, provided them with the incentive to increase their output. Between 1795 and 1821 the Ojibwas took advantage of the fierce trader rivalries to increase

---

[7] D. Moodie, B. Kaye, V. Lytwyn, and A. J. Ray, "Plate 65: Peoples of the Boreal Forest and Parkland," *Historical Atlas of Canada*, vol. 1.

the price of all the provisions they supplied. West of Rainy River country, the Prairie region was the most critical food basket for the northwestern fur trade. Pemmican, dried meat, and grease from this region enabled the brigades from Hudson Bay and the Rainy River to reach the Athabasca-Mackenzie country. Within the boreal forests, the Peace River district was the surplus food producer of utmost strategic importance. Beaver Indians living in the middle and upper parts of the valley and Crees who had pushed into the lower portions hunted wood bison, moose, and elk, providing the traders with the pemmican, dried meat, and grease that the brigades needed to tap the Mackenzie Valley and push on into New Caledonia. These supplies were so critical that the North West Company employed a variety of means, including force, to prevent the Hudson's Bay Company from establishing itself in the area between 1802 and 1815.

The traders also turned to the Indians for a variety of other country items which became essential to the conduct of the trade. The most notable of these commodities included canoes, canoe supplies, and sinews or pack cords. Both the North West Company and the Hudson's Bay Company came to depend on Ojibwa canoe builders in the English River–Rainy River country for many of the northern canoes, *canots du nord,* that were critical for expansion into the northwest from Lake Superior and Fort Albany.

During this period the trading companies also found it necessary to recruit Native laborers. The Nor'Westers did so from the outset. Between 1805 and 1820, three-quarters of the North West Company's labor force consisted of French Canadians, including a substantial number of men of French-Indian descent, as well as of Iroquois from the Montreal area. The Hudson's Bay Company was slower to follow the Nor'Westers' lead. From the earliest days the governor and committee forbade their officers to hire Indians, primarily because they did not want them being drawn away from fur-trapping activities. This policy became unworkable in the late eighteenth century, however, because of labor shortages. The company was not able to hire enough men in the Orkney Islands and mainland Scotland, its favorite recruiting areas, to push forward with a vigorous program of inland expansion. The Napoleonic Wars made the situation worse. The need for additional laborers led the Hudson's Bay Company to reverse its policies about recognizing country marriages and the employment of Native people. The company hired increasing numbers of mixed-bloods to meet its acute summer labor shortages. These Natives mostly worked on the boat and canoe brigades and served as general laborers around the posts. Significantly, the directors still disapproved of hiring Indians.

The employment practices of the two companies strongly influenced the trading post societies that were beginning to emerge. At the North West Company posts Scots and English wintering partners constituted the small upper class. Beneath them were the French Canadian and Indian voyageur and laboring class. At Hudson's Bay Company forts, English and Scots officers occupied the uppermost echelons of the community. Beneath them were the permanent laborers, mostly Orkney men, who in turn were graded into skilled and unskilled workers. The seasonal, mixed-blood employees occupied the lowest rung. In this way, the stratification of the work force along cultural and racial lines had a very strong impact on the lives of the people who were included in the social orbits of the trading posts.

The intense competition for the Indian's furs, particularly between 1795 and 1821, strongly affected most Native groups in the Northern Interior. Many of them suffered as a result. As the Chipewyans became more deeply involved in the enterprise, many of them shifted into the full boreal forest (a move fur traders encouraged), where furbearers were more abundant and barren ground caribou did not divert them. The decimation of their Cree foes by smallpox in 1781–2 made it easier for them to make this move. By 1821 Chipewyan bands had taken possession of most of the area to the north of the Churchill River and east of the Athabasca River. This expansion led to the emergence of three geographically distinctive groups of Chipewyans. These were the Caribou Eaters, who continued much as before along the forest-tundra borderlands, the Athabascas who lived near Lake Athabasca, and those who now occupied the upper Churchill River region.

Among the profoundly negative effects of the fur trade during this period, the highly competitive market encouraged Native people to overtrap furbearers, particularly beaver, throughout the forest country lying between the Churchill River and James Bay. New trapping technologies accelerated the process. In the late nineteenth century, it became commonplace for hunters to use leg-hold traps with castoreum bait. This highly effective technique was not as selective as the older method, which allowed the hunter to pick the animals he killed. Also, archival records suggest that environmental forces may have contributed to the slaughter. It seems that particularly widespread epidemics of tularemia (a periodic fever) struck beaver and muskrat populations around the turn of the century. Compounding this problem, Native and European provision hunters also seriously reduced moose and woodland caribou populations.

These two developments created a serious crisis for the Native groups, since they placed their trapping economy at risk and put some of their traditional food sources in jeopardy. The Native groups, particularly the Cree and Ojibwa bands in what is now northern Ontario, responded by attempting to husband the dwindling fur and game on their hunting lands. The problem, however, was that neither they nor the Europeans had a system of authority that could regulate access to resources. Making matters worse, the North West Company traders brought in their own Iroquois trappers when they were not satisfied with the productivity of local Natives. It is not surprising that local Natives often deeply resented these new intruders. Unfortunately, the unbridled competition, which continued until 1821, meant that the slaughter of furbearers and game proceeded unabated in spite of the growing awareness of the problem. By 1821 the English River–Rainy River area had been so adversely affected that Indian bands living there could not obtain enough caribou skins to make their moccasins.

This destruction of the resource base had several important consequences. It further eroded the Natives' economic position in the industry and made them more reliant on the European fur traders. Also, Indians began to change their attitudes about sharing the produce of their lands because they had to husband their declining stocks of furbearers and game animals. A more sharply defined sense of territory began to emerge. Indians living in the country then known as the Little North (the area between James Bay, Hudson Bay, and Lake Winnipeg) started to exhibit a strong sense of territory and trespass. They complained bitterly about any outsiders who transgressed on their lands to trap. The stronger sense of territory that was emerging also may have been a result of the stabilization of Indian populations that was beginning to take place in this region. By 1821 the widespread dislocations were over and the Northern Ojibwas had taken possession of the areas previously vacated by Assiniboine and Western Cree groups between Lake Nipigon, Red River, and eastern Lake Winnipeg.

The ruinous competition of this era also had very negative effects on Native social life. In their efforts to secure the furs of local Indians, traders attempted to win the loyalties of headmen, or trading captains. Sometimes the trading captains brought together many men from a large number of different bands, probably helping to create the later trading post bands. If European traders failed to win the loyalties of local trading captains, they often appointed another Native to act on their behalf. Such actions were disruptive and created internal tensions within Indian bands. The use of alcohol was even more disruptive. Previously the Indians' infrequent access to this commodity served to minimize its destructive potential. By 1821 this was no longer the case for most areas to the south and east of the Mackenzie Valley.

The manner in which the European and Indian economies joined together in the fur trade encouraged alcohol abuse. As we have seen, Europeans adopted the Native custom of exchanging gifts before commencing barter exchanges. Under highly competitive circumstances this custom became very costly, because traders attempted to be more generous than their rivals. Giving away large quantities of brandy or rum was one way of holding these expenses in check, since these drinks were cheaper than most other commodities. Trading alcohol was highly lucrative for the same reason. For Hudson's Bay Company men, trading brandy also afforded an excellent opportunity to gain more "overplus" because they diluted it one-third (on average) before sales. For these reasons, the fur trade encouraged Native people to increase their consumption of alcohol very rapidly. In conjunction with the increasingly disruptive nature of the trade, this consumption encouraged domestic violence and intergroup conflict. Sometimes Europeans became entangled in the cross fire, because most of the drinking took place at or near the trading places.

The traders themselves also caused serious disruptions to Native societies. For example, the Nor'Westers often used very dubious means to collect debts that Indians owed to them. One of these involved seizing the wives of Indian men who were in arrears and "selling" them to fellow traders or employees for the amount of the debt. Nor'Westers also intimidated Indians with beatings and threats of violence. In the Peace River area, abuses of this sort led many of the Beaver to withdraw from the trade temporarily.

Generally the period between 1790 and 1821 was a mixed blessing for the Native people. They were able to obtain higher prices for their furs, provisions, and country-made articles, such as canoes and snowshoes. Similarly, European trade goods became cheaper, more abundant, and more accessible. Social relations were established among groups over larger areas, and stronger leadership probably became more acceptable. But there were negative aspects to the trade which probably canceled out these advantages in the long term. Fur and game stocks were badly depleted over wide areas. Most Indians traded a high degree of economic independence for interdependence with Euro-Canadians. Their social fabric had been seriously disrupted by conflicting trading factions within some bands and by the central role which alcohol had assumed in the business.

THE SHIFTING BALANCE OF ECONOMIC POWER, 1821–1870

The amalgamation of the Hudson's Bay Company and the North West Company in 1821 represented a momentous change for the Native people, since it fundamentally altered the character of the trade. The union of the bitter rivals resulted from two pressures. The two companies had driven each other to the brink of financial ruin and could not continue their struggle much longer. Also, the British government had become alarmed about the lawlessness in the Northwest and the adverse effects that it was having on Native people. In particular, members of the British parliament wanted to bring an end to the alcohol trade. So, the government encouraged the amalgamation of the two companies and granted the combined firm a twenty-year monopoly on the fur trade of Rupert's Land and the Northwest (the Mackenzie Valley and the Pacific drainage area).

The new Hudson's Bay Company immediately set about reorganizing the fur trade. George Simpson (later Sir George) began to take control of the Canadian operations of the company beginning in 1821, when the governor and committee appointed him governor of the Northern Department, which included all of the territory between western Hudson Bay, Lake Winnipeg, New Caledonia (in British Columbia), and the Arctic coast. In 1826 Simpson also assumed the governorship of the Southern Department (present-day northern Ontario and Quebec) and in 1839 the committee made him governor-in-chief of all Canadian operations. By that date, the company had established posts in Labrador and had leased the King's Posts on the lower St. Lawrence River.

In the 1820s and 1830s, Simpson and the London Committee focused their attention on blocking the advance of American traders from the south, putting the fur trade on a sustained yield basis, and economizing operations. They developed a comprehensive strategy to achieve these objectives. To protect the heartland of the Canadian fur trade, they decided to create a "fur desert" along the American border to the east of the Rocky Mountains and in the Oregon country to the west of them. By depleting the resources of these areas, they would make it not worthwhile for Americans to reach farther north to trade furs.

Behind the fur desert frontier, the company launched a conservation program that aimed at nursing back the depleted beaver populations. The scheme had several important components. Simpson recognized that Indians were reluctant to cut back on their beaver trapping, because they needed the income to buy supplies and also to obtain meat in those areas where moose and woodland caribou had been depleted. The company's beaver conservation program had several key components: it closed posts in areas where beaver stocks were particularly low and opened new ones in places where the animal was more abundant; it encouraged Indians to hunt other furbearers, particularly muskrat, when ecological and economic conditions were favorable for doing so; it established open and closed seasons to discourage the trapping of low-value summer pelts; it banned the sale of steel-spring leg-hold traps in 1822, except in frontier regions exposed to American opponents; and in 1826 it introduced a quota system which limited each district to one-fifth to one-half of its average beaver return in the three-year period between 1823 and 1825.[8]

At first the company's scheme achieved little success. The officers in charge of the districts earned most of their incomes from their collective share of a portion of the company's fur-trading profits. So it was in their short-term interest to obtain as many furs as possible. Often this meant accepting furs from Natives living in adjacent districts where company officers enforced the rule. Many Natives attempted to circumvent the plan in this way for several reasons. Although they were painfully aware that beaver were in sharp decline, they needed to hunt beaver for food and income. Besides their pressing economic circumstances, Natives likely opposed the company's plan because they looked at the problem differently. Traditionally Indians believed that the welfare of animals rested with the game keepers of the spirit world. Successful hunting in the future depended on maintaining the goodwill of these spirits, so perhaps they did not see human conservation as crucial in protecting the beaver numbers.

In any event, the Hudson's Bay Company found it necessary to take additional steps to make their program work. In 1839 it reduced beaver quotas and threatened to dismiss any officer who exceeded his quota. This

[8] Arthur J. Ray "Some Conservation Schemes of the Hudson's Bay Company, 1821–50: An Examination of the Problems of Resource Management in the Fur Trade," *Journal of Historical Geography* 1 (1975), 49–68.

measure was more effective, and by the 1840s beaver were rebounding. In 1844 the company decided to rescind many of the restrictions.

In 1828 Governor Simpson suggested that the company consider assigning tracts of land to families as another way of dealing with the conservation problem. When putting forward this idea, he noted that it would only work in the extensive districts like the Albany where there were few Indians. The governor observed that such a scheme was not feasible in areas where Indians still depended heavily on "Rein Deer" or where there were no reliable fisheries. In other words, as long as Native people remained dependent on mobile large game, a more restrictive territorial system would not work. The governor and committee liked Simpson's proposal and suggested that he go further and give Indians a bonus for each beaver lodge they preserved on their allotted territories.

Although Simpson correctly anticipated that a fundamental shift in the orientation of the Native economies would have to occur before the new tenure system would take hold, the depletion of moose and woodland caribou created instability which prevented this shift by stimulating yet another cycle of population migration. Indians moved out of the western Hudson Bay lowlands around York Factory to the mission at Norway House on Lake Winnipeg, where they could obtain food through laboring, or to the fringes of the Red River colony. Migrations also took place from the Island Lake, Nelson River, and English River districts. Many Crees and Chipewyans abandoned the Lesser Slave Lake and upper Churchill River areas for the Saskatchewan District around Fort Edmonton in order to escape starvation. As long as these kinds of population dislocations were taking place, it was difficult to carry out Simpson's band territory scheme. Widespread warfare between Native groups was an additional hindrance. In the longer term, however, band migrations probably helped the scheme by bringing the remaining populations more in balance with the depleted resources. In any event, it is clear that the destruction of woodland caribou and moose populations, and the growing importance of fish and hare for subsistence, created an ecological setting that was more favorable to the development of a family hunting territory system. The Hudson's Bay Company used its monopoly position between 1821 and 1870 to encourage this trend.

The establishment of a monopoly fur trade throughout most of the Northern Interior had other important implications for Native people. In their efforts to increase the profitability of the fur trade, Simpson and the governor and committee introduced an austerity plan in the 1820s to eliminate the excesses that had characterized the business between the 1790s and 1821. Profligate gift-giving before trade was one of these. The large ceremonial exchanges became a thing of the past. "Steady and reliable" Natives received small presents when they came to trade, on the reigning sovereign's birthday, and at Christmas and the New Year. Similarly, the company made efforts to trim or eliminate Indian debts, but with little effect. Credit trading was an essential part of their relations with Indians.

Simpson also thought that the elimination of competition would afford the company an opportunity to lower the quality of its merchandise and thereby enhance profit levels. The Indians strongly resisted this idea, and the governor and committee did not insist on it. The most important retailing change that took place during this period involved the elimination of alcohol in most areas and the substitution of tea. Also, flour, used mostly to make bannock, became more important where country foods were limited. By the end of the nineteenth century, tea and bannock emerged as key staples for many Native people.

Many of the proposed economic reforms did not take place at least partly because of Indian resistance to them, even though the Indians' economic position within the industry had deteriorated following the renewal of the company's monopoly. The fact was that the company still absolutely depended on exploiting the Indians' cheap labor in the bush. One of Simpson's and the company's overriding concerns was to discourage Indians from leaving the woodlands, a fundamental goal of the Hudson's Bay Company into this century.[9] Economic reforms, which seriously undermined the quality of life for Native people, would work to undermine that objective.

Some of the economic reforms that the company initiated in the 1820s played an instrumental role in bringing about important social changes. Immediately after the amalgamation, the company closed many redundant inland posts and slashed its labor costs by 25 percent. Simpson achieved the latter reduction by lowering wages and laying off at least 250 men. One of the groups whom he targeted for layoffs were the servants who had large families (mostly Native). He did this because it had long been a company tradition to support these families, but this responsibility had become a substantial additional burden for the organization.

[9] Arthur J. Ray, *The Canadian Fur Trade in the Industrial Age* (Toronto, 1990), 49.

After 1825 the company attempted to hire recruits from Britain (mostly Scotland), the St. Lawrence, and Rupert's Land. The scheme did not work very well, however, because economic developments in Europe and Canada meant that the company's wage rates became increasingly uncompetitive. So, as time passed, the company had to hire more Natives from Rupert's Land with the result that Indians and mixed-bloods comprised the largest component of its work force by the 1850s.[10] Recruits from the Red River area proved to be the most difficult to manage because they had alternative economic opportunities. However, by the 1860s, even Natives recruited from the most remote districts were successfully demanding higher wages and were becoming more independent.

Even though Natives began to play a more central role in the company's operations after 1821, their position in the fur-trade hierarchy deteriorated in many respects. Before 1821 men of mixed ancestry were able to advance from the lowest ranks into the officer class. After the amalgamation, the company severely restricted such upward mobility and a rigid, racially biased class system emerged. "Indians" occupied the lowest echelons of the labor force as seasonal workers who did general maintenance jobs or helped man the canoe and boat brigades. Many mixed-blood men found seasonal employment at these same jobs, but a substantial number of them also secured permanent (contract) appointments for a range of positions involving general labor or the skilled trades. The mixed-bloods mostly learned these latter skills by apprenticing with European servants. These latter men largely comprised the elite of the laboring class. The company's commissioned officers ranked above them. After 1821, the Hudson's Bay Company recruited its officers in Europe, which meant that servants no longer could move upward into the officer class.

The company's older and well-established officers resented this development. Most of them had Native families and the company's hiring practice now meant that their sons could not follow them. These officers protested and the governor and committee responded in a half-hearted fashion by creating the position of apprentice postmaster. After serving at least five years in this position, mixed-blood men could receive a junior officer appointment as a postmaster, usually at an "outpost." From the perspective of the Native sons and their fathers, this new scheme was entirely unsatisfactory. It merely highlighted the company's racist policy, since

---

[10] Carol Judd, "Mixed Bands of Many Nations, 1821–70," in *Old Trails and New Directions: Papers of the Third North American Fur Trade Conference,* ed. Carol Judd and Arthur J. Ray (Toronto, 1980), 127–46.

European recruits did not have to serve an apprenticeship. Few Native sons ever gained officer status by this route.

The social mobility of Natives in fur-trade society was further limited by changing marriage practices. In the earliest days of the business most fur traders took Indian wives by following a blend of Indian and European marriage customs, known as *marriage à la façon du pays*. By the early nineteenth century wintering partners and company officers preferred to marry mixed-blood women, who they thought had higher status than Indian women. Generally these country unions were stable. When Euro-Canadian men retired from the country they often arranged to have their wives and children placed under the protection of another trader (a practice known as "turning off"). Alternatively, the Native women returned to their own relatives. In these ways, the welfare of the families was assured.

Governor Simpson's behavior upset these social customs. He not only refused to recognize Margaret Taylor, mother of two of his children, as his country wife, but suddenly at the age of forty-three he married his eighteen-year old English cousin, Frances Simpson, thereby establishing a new social norm for senior officers. Thereafter, company officers who took Native wives instead of European ones did so with the knowledge that such unions might have adverse effects on their long-term careers.

Partly, Simpson's actions were merely symptomatic of new trends that were beginning to take place because of the acceleration of the industrial revolution in Britain, the development of Victorian morality, the maturation of the Red River colony, and the growing influence of missionaries. It became increasingly commonplace for men from Britain to be very concerned about upward mobility, to delay marriage, and to chose their mates very carefully. Although these men often remained unmarried until late in life, they did not abstain from sexual liaisons. As a result, after 1821, the officer recruits were less inclined to follow older fur trade social practices. This meant that Native women often found themselves in very uncertain relationships with European men and their social status suffered as more of these men ultimately married European women. After 1821, it was not socially acceptable for a company officer to marry an Indian woman. Mixed-blood women were not very suitable either unless they had been educated at Red River. Moreover, Protestant missionaries, who competed with company officers for status in a growing number of fur-trading communities, frowned on mixed marriages. These ministers usually brought European wives with them.

In interior Alaska Natives began to feel the impact of European expansion toward the close of the eighteenth century after the Russians had begun expanding along the south coast in the late 1780s. Soon Russian goods made their way to the interior along Native trading routes. The establishment of the Russian post of Nulato on the lower Yukon River in 1839, and the construction by the Hudson's Bay Company of Fort Yukon eight years later at the confluence of the Yukon and Porcupine Rivers, brought the Athapaskans of interior Alaska face-to-face with the newcomers. This drew them more heavily into the fur trade and the pace of culture change accelerated. Russian Orthodox missionaries arrived with the traders, but they were few in number and had a minimal impact. The people remained only nominally Christians at best until the middle of the twentieth century.

END OF THE OLD ORDER, 1867 – 1921

The period between confederation and the end of World War I was a time of profound change in the Northern Interior. The Canadian government became directly involved in Native affairs for the first time. Meanwhile, the expanding industrial economies of Western Europe and North America began to transform the North in fundamental ways.

In 1870 the Hudson's Bay Company relinquished its trading monopoly and title to Rupert's Land for 1.5 million dollars, a one-twentieth share of the land of the fertile belt (the prairie-parkland area), and title to the developed land around its trading posts. The Canadian government gained sovereignty over the region and assumed the legal responsibility for the welfare of the Native people. Previously this responsibility had tacitly rested with the company. Even within the borders of future provinces, Indians and Indian lands were reserved for federal jurisdiction according to the terms of the British North America Act.

The government's first concern involved extinguishing Native title to the lands it needed for various economic expansion schemes. The precedent for obtaining this title through comprehensive treaties already was well established in British North America. The Robinson-Huron and Robinson-Superior treaties, signed in 1850, had alienated Indian lands in the area between the southern limit of the Hudson Bay drainage and Lakes Superior and Huron (see Chapter 8). These two treaties provided the Indians with a one-time payment when treaties were signed, annual annuities, reserves, and the right to continue to hunt and fish on undeveloped crown lands. The eleven treaties (and treaty adhesions) that the government negotiated, between 1871 and 1929, with Indians living in most of the wooded territory stretching from James Bay to the lower Mackenzie River included these key provisions.

Indians tried to achieve a variety of objectives through treaty negotiations. In the early 1870s, the Ojibwas living about Rainy River and Lake of the Woods wanted to lease rights-of-way for railways and telegraph lines as well as timber and mineral rights. These Ojibwas already had diversified their economies in response to local changes that were taking place because of the construction of the Dawson Road between the Lakehead and Red River. In contrast, their neighbors who lived near Osnaburgh Lake were still heavily committed to the fur trade. These Ojibwas hoped to improve their economic position by obtaining enough annuity money to pay for their annual outfits and thereby reduce or eliminate their need for credit from fur traders. Besides proposing a per capita annuity of five dollars ($25 for chiefs and $15 for headmen), the government negotiators offered these Ojibwas a collective annual allowance of $1,500 for ammunition and twine to help them with their hunting and fishing activities. In addition, the government promised to help them develop gardens, mostly for potatoes, to supplement their traditional supplies of game that were becoming more uncertain because of excessive hunting pressures.

These various economic concessions were sufficient to get the groups around Osnaburgh Lake to sign. Having divided the Indians in this way, the southern Ojibwas had little choice but to accept these terms, and government negotiators concluded Treaty Three in 1873. Generally speaking, the later treaties provided roughly the same level of compensation to other Indians, except for Treaty Nine in 1905, which provided only a four dollar annuity. Initially the annuity, ammunition, and twine allowances did subsidize continued Indian participation in the fur trade. However, by the late nineteenth century price inflation began seriously to erode the value of these economic benefits.

In later treaty discussions, such as those for Treaty Eight (ceding northern Alberta), Indians expressed their alarm about the killing of their hunting dogs and the wholesale destruction of game and fur-bearing animals by Euro-Canadian hunters and trappers who were using poisoned bait and practicing a policy of "cleaning out" an area of its furbearers. Government officials shared the Indians' concerns. The collapse of the bison-hunting economies on the Prairies in the 1870s and early 1880s had forced the government to shoulder a potentially very heavy financial burden in its efforts to provide the relief needed to ward off starvation. The government was anxious to avoid a similar catastrophe in the boreal forest. Accordingly, the negotiators promised the Indians that steps would be taken to deal with the problem.

While desiring protection from Euro-Canadian hunters and trappers, who were becoming commonplace in the North by the turn of the century, Indians also wanted assurances that government laws and regulations would not threaten their traditional way of life. Their concern arose in the 1890s, after the province of Ontario and the federal government passed the first game laws. During the Treaty Eight discussions, negotiators assured the Indians that their traditional vocations would not be disrupted by government schemes. The problem for the Indians, however, was that the hunting rights clauses of the treaties gave the government the right to pass such regulations when necessary. Subsequently, provincial and federal parliaments exercised this option and the courts have upheld their actions. Only in the landmark "Sparrow" decision, rendered in 1990, did the Supreme Court recognize the special relationship of aboriginal people with the land and living resources. That judgment stated that aboriginal rights had not been (and cannot be) extinguished or curtailed except through legislation that has that objective as its clear and plain intention. Furthermore, conservation legislation, and regulations flowing from it, that seek to limit these rights have to be justified. Previously many Native groups saw their rights eroded in the name of conservation even though government officials often provided no scientific evidence of a need for it.[11]

The year 1873 marked the beginning of one of the longest and most severe worldwide depressions of modern times. This calamity sent fur prices and sales plummeting, and recovery did not begin until the late 1880s. The Hudson's Bay Company reacted to the crisis by carrying out an austerity program and paying the Indians less for their furs. Meanwhile, the company made substantial investments in steamboat services in the Prairie and Athabasca-Mackenzie regions in order to increase its cargo capacity and reduce its dependence on Native laborers. The latter objective was particularly important to company officials, who feared that future economic developments would make the Native labor force more

---

[11] Peter W. Hutchins, "Commentary: Supreme Court of Canada, Ronald Edward Sparrow v. Her Majesty the Queen and the National Indian Brotherhood/Assembly of First Nations, et al., Interveners" (Montreal, 1990 [unpublished]). The "Sparrow" case addressed the issue of the federal parliament's right to limit Native salmon fishing rights under the Fisheries Act.

expensive and difficult to manage by offering alternative employment opportunities.

The construction of the Canadian Pacific Railway had an even more revolutionary impact on the fur trade. Delayed by political scandals and the crippling depression, construction of the line was not completed until 1885. The railway provided fur buyers with cheap access to the southern portions of old Rupert's Land, breaking the Hudson's Bay Company's tight grip on the fur trade. Equally important, the construction of telegraph lines to major Canadian cities broke the company's monopoly on current fur prices. Buyers now had instant access to the latest trends in all the major market centers. These developments set the stage for unprecedented competition once fur markets began to rebound in the late 1880s, and the boom times lasted until 1921 when prices crashed temporarily.

The market integration brought about by railway and telegraph construction (a second, more northerly transcontinental railway system was completed in 1915) made it possible to conduct the fur trade in new ways. Cash fur-buying became an important component of the business in frontier areas adjacent to major transportation arteries. Indians welcomed this development. It enabled them to obtain the highest prices for their furs and bargain rates for the supplies they needed. Many of them traveled to towns situated along the railway lines where they did their shopping for "fancy goods" (mostly dry goods). By the early 1920s, some Indians bought merchandise through Eaton's catalogs. Hudson's Bay Company traders complained that many Indians only bought groceries and other staples at their posts and that profit margins on these commodities were very low compared with those on dry goods.

Cash fur-buying affected the business in other ways. Previously, fur traders bought an Indian's entire fur collection, paying him an amount that took into account the range of furs included in his return. In contrast, cash dealers generally targeted their fur-buying to the highest grades of particular species, for which they offered the best prices. Indians disposed of the remainder of their furs at more traditional outlets such as Hudson's Bay Company posts. These two developments meant that the company's profit margins on fur-buying and selling shrank substantially.

By skimming off the most valuable furs at the height of the trapping season, cash buyers also made it more risky for trading companies to advance goods to Indians on credit. For this reason, the Hudson's Bay Company repeatedly attempted to restrict credit. However, Indians thought that the company had an obligation to provide advances, and they regarded any attempt to deny them as a breach of faith. Company officials learned this the hard way. In 1914 the British government temporarily closed the London fur market in response to the outbreak of World War I. Faced with this problem, and fearing a collapse of fur markets worldwide, the company's directors ordered their men not to buy furs and not to extend any credit to their Indian customers. That order proved to be disastrous. The Indians felt betrayed at the very time American buyers were combing the North in record numbers. Indians welcomed their cash. In later years, officers regarded 1914 as the black year in the fur trade, because the company apparently never regained the confidence of many of its traditional customers even though credit trading resumed in 1915.

One of the reasons that the Hudson's Bay Company had difficulties regaining Indian loyalty was that it already faced a horde of competitors, and the outbreak of hostilities aggravated the situation. The wartime disruptions of the international fur-marketing system gave merchants in New York and St. Louis a golden opportunity to challenge the traditional centers of London and Leipzig, Germany. The highly profitable businesses the American auction houses established, beginning in 1914, encouraged merchants in Montreal and Winnipeg to follow suit in 1920 and 1921 respectively. The competition that developed between rival auctions, fur brokerage firms, and raw fur dealers affected the northern fur trade in several important ways. Major fur sales took place with increasing frequency. This reduced the amount of capital northern traders needed and also their risks, because they could turn over their fur inventories much more rapidly. Furthermore, auction companies and brokerage houses extended liberal credit to independent traders and trading companies in order to obtain their consignment business. In these ways, rising demand, improved transportation and communication systems, market integration, and metropolitan rivalries made it possible for legions of competitors to flood the North during World War I. They recklessly spent cash buying furs.

Some of the firms which the Hudson's Bay Company faced were very formidable. In 1899 Revillon Frères of Paris commenced trading operations in Canada and very quickly established a network of posts that covered most of the Subarctic. This firm was particularly aggressive in James Bay, the traditional heartland of the Hudson's Bay Company. By 1913 the Northern Trading Company of Edmonton operated throughout the Athabasca-Mackenzie area, where it strongly challenged the Hudson's Bay Company and Revillon Frères. In 1918 the furriers Lamson and Hubbard of Boston purchased several trading posts in the same area and registered their Canadian enterprise as Lamson and Hubbard Canadian Company Limited. By the end of World War I Lamson and Hubbard had built their organization up from seven to thirty-five posts and they had extended their trading sphere eastward to Hudson Bay. However, the Athabasca-Mackenzie region remained the center of their operations. By the end of the war, rival traders roamed throughout most of the North; they were particularly active in northern Ontario and the Athabasca-Mackenzie district, where steamboats or railways provided cheap access.

As in the earlier era of the Nor'Westers, the unbridled competition had positive and negative effects on the Native people. On the positive side, Natives obtained more for their returns and received a portion of these payments in cash. This meant they no longer had to spend all of their income at Hudson's Bay Company stores. Thus merchandising became highly competitive. In some areas, such as in the lower Mackenzie River district, Native purchasing power exceeded their consumer demand. Many of them banked their surpluses at the trading posts. By 1920 most of the Hudson's Bay Company posts in this country were in debt to their Indian customers. Also, in the Athabasca-Mackenzie district, the quest for furs encouraged Lamson and Hubbard Company, the Northern Trading Company, and the Hudson's Bay Company to expand their steamboat operations in order to haul ever larger loads of trading goods. The completion of the second transcontinental railway line improved access to northern Ontario. These various developments meant that throughout the Northern Interior Native people had a greater array of merchandise available to them at lower costs when fur prices hit record high levels. In response they consumed more. Of particular importance, canned foods became important to them for the first time. Also, their consumption of "fancy dry goods" increased sharply.

On the other hand, the rush for Canadian furs had some very adverse long-term effects on the Native economies. For the first time, European trappers came north in growing numbers, lured there by soaring fur prices. Some were brought to the North by trading companies, particularly Lamson and Hubbard, who used these men in areas where they did not obtain the quantities of furs they wanted from local Indians. Many of the newcomers combined trapping and fur trading with prospecting, lumbering, mining, and other activities. These people moved in and out of the trapping economy with the fluctuations in the business cycles; when fur prices were high, or the economy was in recession, they trapped. Generally European trappers, particularly the part-time ones, were "high-liners" who did not care about the long-term impact that their activities had on fur and game resources; they were ruthless in pursuit of their prey, often dynamiting beaver dams, and thereby adding to the fur and game depletion problems that normally arose when fur markets were buoyant. Equally troublesome, these trappers often trespassed on the traditional hunting lands of Indian bands. In some areas the intruders forced Indians off their homelands. Hudson's Bay Company officials in the Athabasca-Mackenzie district said that European trappers had become the scourge of the industry by the end of the Great War.

MARGINALIZING THE NATIVE PEOPLE, 1921–1945

The decades of the 1920s and 1930s were times of considerable uncertainty as the world economy fluctuated between recession (1920–1), inflation (1922–8), depression (1929–39), and renewed inflation (1939–45). Fur markets strongly reflected these cycles, and the downturns took their toll on the Hudson's Bay Company's largest rivals. Lamson and Hubbard Company did not survive the recession of the early 1920s and ceased operations in 1923. The Northern Trading Company went into receivership in 1925, but managed to survive, albeit in a very shaky state, as Northern Traders until 1939. Revillon Frères lost money throughout the 1920s. In 1926 the Hudson's Bay Company bought controlling interest in the organization. In spite of this injection of cash, the firm continued to lose ground. The depression dealt a fatal blow, and in 1936 the Hudson's Bay Company bought the remaining assets.

One of the reasons that Revillon Frères continued to operate as late as it did was that the Hudson's Bay Company was not eager to wrap up the operation. Company directors feared that the Canadian government and the Native people would react adversely to any moves that seemed intent on eliminating competition. Also, the Hudson's Bay Company had regarded Revillon Frères as a "sane competitor," one that paid realistic prices for furs. Company managers believed that by dividing local markets between these two firms it was more difficult for smaller operators, who had lower overhead costs, to establish themselves. In the end, as a result of the activities of individual buyers, competition for northern furs continued to escalate between 1920 and 1945, even though the Hudson's Bay Company's largest opponents fell by the wayside. The use of bush planes widened these buyers' abilities to contact hunting camps directly. For this reason, the company's share of Canadian fur returns shrank. By the eve of World War II the Hudson's Bay Company obtained barely one-quarter of the wild fur output of Canada.

Generally, the Native economies did not fare very well during this period of boom and bust. Although the aggregate value of Canadian fur production rose markedly between 1920 and 1945, a growing share of the output consisted of ranched furs. By the close of the period, nearly all the silver fox and almost one-half of the mink production came from ranches. These were two furs of very high value. Resource depletion was the main reason for this development. Prices soared as the wild stocks of these furs dwindled under increased trapping pressures. Ranching provided one way of dealing with this problem. Fur garment manufacturers sought other solutions. One of the most important of these involved dying and treating cheaper utility furs (particularly muskrat and rabbit) to make imitations of the high-priced and increasingly scarce luxury species.

Generally these developments had adverse implications for the Native people of the Northern Interior. They did not benefit from ranching activities. Nearly all the silver fox operations were located on Prince Edward Island, and most of the mink farms were situated near Toronto. The prices of utility furs, such as hare, muskrat, and squirrel, remained comparatively low. Furthermore, the population cycles of some of these furs, particularly hare and muskrat, are very erratic. This meant that many Native people, particularly those from "muskrat country," depended increasingly on those furbearers which provided a meager and very unreliable return. In this regard the fur trade of the early twentieth century was very different from that of the seventeenth and eighteenth centuries, when beaver dominated.

The growing problem of resource depletion had other negative effects. Federal and provincial governments felt compelled to play more active roles in conservation management programs. Various game acts and regulations established open and closed seasons for most key furbearing animals in the Northern Interior. Although the first acts were passed as early as the 1890s, enforcement was patchy at best before the 1930s. Sometimes local closed seasons for certain species, most often beaver, extended over several years and caused serious hardships for Natives. Also, in the late 1930s and 1940s government agencies, often with Hudson's Bay Company participation, created preserves for beaver and muskrat. By the late 1940s nearly all the land surrounding James Bay had been set aside, as well as large tracts in Manitoba and Saskatchewan along the Saskatchewan River. Within these preserves, officials severely restricted hunting and trapping activities. Although Native people argued that many of these conservation schemes violated their treaty rights to hunt and fish, the courts ruled otherwise. On the other hand, in some areas, such as Quebec, the Indians gave up beaver hunting and managed conservation programs themselves, using a system of "tallymen," or Natives who kept count of the beavers in the conservation area.

The introduction of registered traplines marked another major innovation in conservation efforts. According to this scheme, governments issued licenses to hunters which gave them exclusive trapping rights in designated tracts of land. Officials hoped that this system would reduce conflicts between Natives and Euro-Canadians and facilitate proper game management. The province of British Columbia introduced the first trapline programs in 1925. Other jurisdictions followed over the next twenty-five years: Ontario in 1935, Alberta in 1937, Manitoba in 1940, Quebec in 1945, Saskatchewan in 1946, the Northwest Territories in 1949, and the Yukon in 1950.[12] Although government officials intended this scheme to help protect Native peoples from Euro-Canadian incursions, in many areas it had the effect of further curtailing Native hunting rights on undeveloped crown lands. But these conservation measures did bring back the beaver.

Native people faced other serious economic problems. In the late nineteenth century, many of them had a growing array of economic opportunities available to them outside the declining fur trade. The shortage of workers in the North meant that they could find alternative or supplemental employment in railway construction, mining, lumbering, tourism, and other new economic development projects. The annual reports of the Department of Indian Affairs reveal that many Natives in Northern Ontario took advantage of these opportunities. However, the large waves of European immigration to Canada at the turn of the century altered the regional labor market and Native people were displaced from the work force. Manpower shortages during World War I temporarily alleviated this problem, but thereafter employment prospects for Natives diminished.

Although the introduction of commercial aviation to the North after

---

12 Milan Novak, "The Future of Trapping," in *Wild Furbearer Management and Conservation in North America*, ed. Milan Novak et al. (Toronto, 1987), 92.

World War I was a boon to traders and trading companies, it dealt a harsh blow to the Natives. It opened even the most remote areas to Euro-Canadian trappers, who had previously concentrated their activities near major transportation corridors. Also, bush plane services eliminated work for Indian canoemen who hauled outfits to the more remote outposts. Aware that the use of the bush plane would adversely affect its Native trappers and workers, the Hudson's Bay Company responded slowly to the advantages of commercial air services. However, by the late 1930s, it had to follow the lead of its opponents in order to remain competitive. Aviation also made southern society and values more easily available and gave Indians access to more specialized medical care.

The completion of railway lines to Churchill, Manitoba, in 1929 and James Bay in 1932 had a similar impact. These lines opened new areas to Euro-Canadians and led to the displacement of Native workers, as the Hudson's Bay Company adjusted its transportation system to take advantage of cheaper railway service. The community of Moose Factory suffered the most from this development. For nearly a century it had been the Hudson's Bay Company's major port of entry for northern Ontario and Quebec. There the company employed large numbers of Native people as longshoremen, boat builders, and repairmen at its Moose Works. In addition, it hired many men to carry supplies into the interior. As early as 1900, company officials noted that Moose Factory was no longer a fur-trading community, because most of the Native men earned the bulk of their incomes by working for the company. Besides their immediate families, these Native workers supported many relatives who settled around the fringes of the community. These people had abandoned the bush because it was becoming increasingly difficult to make a living by trapping. So, when the Hudson's Bay Company closed down the Moose Works, the local Natives suffered severe economic hardships and the community never recovered. To this day many local residents lament the arrival of the railway.

Although structural changes in the economy may have had the greatest adverse impact on the community of Moose Factory, Natives elsewhere faced similar problems. Throughout the North many natives no longer could survive solely by hunting and trapping, in spite of rising fur prices. They needed summer employment to supplement their trapping incomes. The Hudson's Bay Company had been aware of this fact since the late nineteenth century and had used this knowledge to its own advantage. It rewarded with summer work trappers who regularly paid their debts. The most reliable of these men were sometimes provided with shanties at major posts such as York Factory and Moose Factory. The company sought alternative economic opportunities for its Native trappers when it began to trim its labor force in the late 1920s and 1930s. Together with the Department of Indian Affairs, it encouraged Indians to develop crafts. To support this effort the company's stores provided space to sell Native handiwork.

The problem was that this program was not sufficient to meet the worsening plight of Native people. They needed substantial additional economic support. Since 1870, it had been the Canadian government's responsibility to provide the aid that was needed, but it proved very reluctant to do so. Between the early 1870s and the early 1890s, the government faced serious financial problems: it had to cope with the lingering depression; it struggled with problems that arose because of the collapse of the Native bison-hunting economies on the Plains; and it worked to raise the money needed for major development projects. Given these concerns, government officials were very reluctant to help any Natives who lived beyond the boundaries of treaties, even if they had an obligation to do so. Furthermore, these officials feared that any form of regular economic help would only serve to make Native people permanent wards of the state.

Under these circumstances, missionaries and the Hudson's Bay Company often had to look after the economic needs of the Native people. Concerted missionary activity in the central and western Subarctic had begun after 1821, and the pace quickened in the closing decades of the nineteenth century. Missionaries became an important catalyst of change in the Subarctic beginning in the nineteenth century. In 1840 the Rev. James Evans, who was working at Norway House, devised the Cree syllabic script which revolutionized communication among Native people and continues to be used today. Syllabics were later adapted for Athapaskan and Inuktitut. In many areas the competition between Protestant and Catholic missionaries was ferocious, with Hudson's Bay Company officials frequently helping Protestant ones to gain a foothold. Protestant missionaries were accompanied by their Euro-Canadian wives, altering the dynamics of Indian–Euro-Canadian relations in trading post communities. Catholic missionaries introduced French as a second language to a large number of Indians in northern Quebec. By the early twentieth century Protestant and Catholic missionaries were actively proselytizing throughout the entire Subarctic, and both of these groups had stations in many of the larger settlements, where they provided religious instruction and schooling. When possible, the missionaries and the fur traders provided Indians with help in the form of food and clothing.

Although the Hudson's Bay Company traditionally provided such help, after confederation many company officials increasingly were unwilling to continue the tradition. They believed that, without the advantages of a trading monopoly, these relief costs were too burdensome. Accordingly, by the close of the nineteenth century company officials began to press the government for reimbursements for the aid they rendered. The government reluctantly provided them. Subsequently, the government authorized the Hudson's Bay Company, other trading companies, and missionaries to provide aid on its behalf in areas that were beyond the reach of Indian agents, so long as it did not exceed established spending guidelines. In this way, the government reluctantly began to assume some of the social overhead costs of the fur trade that had formerly been borne by the Hudson's Bay Company. At the same time, government agents were increasingly attempting to dictate to Native people how they were to constitute themselves politically, to interfere in local-level politics, and to regulate Native life in conformity with the Indian Act. These pressures intensified as more Euro-Canadians and Euro-Americans were stationed in the north during World War II.

The American takeover of Alaska in 1867 and the introduction of steamboats on the Yukon River two years later hastened similar processes in the far-Western Subarctic. Most significantly, the introduction of repeating rifles led to a depletion of caribou and an increased exploitation of moose. As a consequence, communal hunting practices began to yield to more individualistic ones. At the turn of the century Euro-American settlers introduced fish wheels, which could be used in the large, muddy rivers. The Kolchans adopted this device; soon fish became the mainstay of their diet, and families spent most of the open water season at fish camps. By the late 1930s they had abandoned many of these fish camps, choosing instead to settle into a few larger settlements located along the main rivers. From these communities they ran traplines in winter. The adoption of outboard motors in the 1930s made it easier to live this way. This and other expensive technological advances forced the Kolchans to take a more active part in the wage economy. Traditionally, the mining and transportation industries provided most of the seasonal work, which supplemented trapping incomes.

THE MODERN ERA, POST-1945

After World War II, the circumstances of Native peoples changed drastically once again. Fur prices crashed after the war and remained depressed until the end of the Korean conflict. Meanwhile, the prices of manufactured goods soared. These developments meant that fur trapping became a marginal economic activity. During this period the Canadian government became much more heavily involved in all aspects of Native peoples' lives. In 1945 the government introduced its family allowance program, which paid every Canadian family six dollars per month for every child under the age of sixteen. Shortly thereafter, Native people became eligible for benefits under the program. Although Natives welcomed this benefit, it did not greatly alleviate their economic stress.

Soon the government used the family allowance program to force Native families to send their children to school by threatening to withhold payments to parents of truants. This was intended as a further promotion of the government's assimilationist policies. Although these coercive tactics had mixed results, in some areas Native families did move to towns and settlements where their children could attend school. In these instances, the household began to replace the winter hunting group as the primary economic unit. Furthermore, the women's and children's participation in the bush economy diminished. Increasingly, they remained in the settlements while the adult males operated their traplines. Over time, an ever smaller portion of the population depended on the fur trade. The school curriculum reinforced this trend by failing to teach children any of the skills they needed to survive in the bush and by being insensitive to Native traditions.

More recently the Native people have been threatened by vast development projects. The two most celebrated of these are the James Bay hydroelectric venture and the Mackenzie Valley pipeline proposal. On April 30, 1971, the Quebec government unilaterally announced a 5.6 billion dollar hydroelectric generation scheme for the southeastern James Bay area. The original plan envisioned flooding some of the most productive fishing and trapping areas of the Crees of Rupert House, Nemiscau, Waswanipi, and Mistassini. These Crees, who had not been consulted prior to the announcement, strongly protested against the government's plan, and they, with the initial help of the Indians of Quebec Association and of environmental groups, initiated legal proceedings to block the project. Justice Albert Malouf's decision upholding the Crees' injunction against the project forced the government to negotiate with the bands who would be affected by the proposed development. These negotiations resulted in 1975 in the James Bay and Northern Quebec Agreement between the Quebec government and the Grand Council of the Crees of Quebec (formed August 1974) as well as with the Inuit. It was later modified to include the Naskapis.

Through their negotiators, the Crees obtained very important concessions from the Quebec and federal governments. These included over $90 million in compensation; a modification of the plan to reduce the negative impact on the fishery of the lower La Grande River; a precise definition of their rights in three different categories of land (one of these categories conveys exclusive hunting rights); equal representation on the joint Quebec-Cree Hunting, Trapping and Fishing Coordinating Committee, established to manage wildlife resources in the area; recognition that Crees' subsistence needs take priority over the interests of other groups when managing these resources in the tracts where the Crees did not retain exclusive hunting rights; the establishment of an income security program for hunters and trappers; and the creation of a Cree Regional Authority to represent all Crees on government bodies and to coordinate various social and economic programs.

The 1975 agreement has affected the lives of the people of the James Bay region in many important ways. Perhaps the most striking impact has been the emergence of a coherent regional society from the isolated and fragmented band villager-oriented one of the earlier era. This new society is largely the result of the actions of the Cree Regional Authority; increased Cree input into improving local educational, economic, and health systems; and the greatly improved regional transportation (Air Creebec) and communication system that knits the communities together more closely.

The advancement in the standard of living that the Crees have achieved under their own auspices and direction since 1975 has been very striking. This has been accomplished by strengthening the hunting and trapping sector of the local economy and by expanding other employment opportunities. Significantly, by the early 1980s, more Crees operated as full-time hunters than had been the case on the eve of the James Bay agreement, thanks largely to the income security program for hunters and trappers and their families, which guarantees full-time hunters a minimum cash income plus an allowance for every day they spend in the bush. Also the trappers' marketing interests were now promoted by the Cree Trappers

Association. The expansion of social services and the construction and maintenance of new houses, schools, and other government facilities provided most of the new jobs. As in earlier years, most of this employment was available in the summer and did not conflict with hunting and trapping activities.

Today opinions are divided about whether or not the benefits which the Crees obtained from the James Bay agreement adequately compensate them for the concessions which they made and whether they have adequately protected themselves from further mega-projects. However, considering that they were forced to negotiate under extremely adverse circumstances, the Crees did achieve striking gains. Most importantly, they managed to retain strong control over the direction of social and economic development in the James Bay region. To date they have exercised that power to make sure that the changes taking place are compatible with their traditional values. They have also successfully opposed a hydroelectric project at Great Whale River and a proposed one on the Nottaway, Broadback, Rupert River system that would further jeopardize their traditional way of life. As of 1995, faced with the uncertainties of Canada-Quebec politics, the James Bay Crees appeared more united than ever before and are asserting themselves internationally.

The Mackenzie Valley pipeline proposal had a very different fate. In 1971 a consortium of multinational oil companies put forward a seven billion dollar scheme to transport natural gas from Alaska and Mackenzie delta fields through the valley to southern markets. Native leaders and environmentalists promptly voiced concerns about the impact which this vast undertaking would have on the local ecology and economy. In response to their concerns the federal government established the Mackenzie Valley Pipeline Inquiry in 1974 and appointed Justice Thomas Berger as commissioner. Between 1974 and 1976, the Berger commission traveled to communities throughout the region to hear testimony from local residents.

The Dene, Métis, and Inuit spoke eloquently against the proposal; they voiced fears that the project would destroy their way of life and argued that it should not go forward until their Native claims were settled. In 1977, after carefully considering their objections and the testimony of experts who supported and opposed the project, Berger recommended to the federal government that a pipeline not be built in the Yukon and that construction of one in the Mackenzie Valley be delayed for at least ten years. He concluded that the proposed pipeline would not solve local Native economic (employment) problems and that the social costs of the project would be very high; he was also sympathetic to the Dene, Métis, and Inuit position that no development should proceed until their outstanding claims were settled. Berger reasoned that the Native residents would not be in a position to benefit fully from pipeline construction and maintenance until new governmental institutions and programs were established and land claims settled.

While the Berger hearings were underway the Dene sought, and obtained in 1973, a caveat to stop resource exploration on their homelands. The Northwest Territorial supreme court justice who listened to their appeal stated in his ruling that he did not believe that Treaties Eight and Eleven had extinguished Dene aboriginal title because he doubted that the chiefs who had signed them understood the terms. In any event, the Denes and their Métis relatives were encouraged, and two years later they issued the Dene Declaration demanding an equitable settlement of their land claims and self-government within Canada. Changing public opinion in Canada toward aboriginal rights issues, fostered in part by the Berger inquiry, and the prospect of endless court challenges led the government of Canada to agree to begin negotiations with the Denes in 1981. Successively, the entrenchment of existing aboriginal and treaty rights into the Canadian constitution (Section 35[1]) in 1982 and the introduction of a more flexible federal claims policy in 1986 facilitated the process. In 1988 the Mackenzie Valley Denes and Métis signed a comprehensive land claim agreement in principle. Two years later, however, at their annual assembly they rejected the accord. One of the reasons Dene leaders did so was because they concluded that the *Sparrow* decision, concerning the relations of aboriginal people with the land and living resources, indicated aboriginal rights might be more extensive than previously thought. In spite of their rejection, however, the leadership decided that the various regional Dene and Métis groups should have the option of seeking separate agreements based on the principles of the 1988 accord.

Farther west, their neighbors in the Yukon signed an umbrella agreement-in-principle with the federal and territorial governments. This compact set aside 16,000 square miles of settlement lands, on which aboriginal rights will continue, and it establishes guidelines for the various member nations to negotiate their final agreements.

While comprehensive claims negotiations moved forward, the residents of the Northwest Territories took steps to take greater control over their political affairs. Their goal was to create provincial-style governments that protected Native heritage and accommodated consensus decision making at the local level. In 1982 the inhabitants of this region took part in a plebiscite and voted to divide the area in two – a western region where Denes, Métis, and Euro-Canadians dominated and an eastern zone where the Inuit held the majority. Subsequently the Western Constitutional Forum, consisting of representatives of the various groups residing in the western portion of the territory, and the Nunavut Constitutional Forum representing the populace of the eastern Northwest Territories, now called Nunavut, held discussions to define the boundary and to begin to formulate constitutions for their respective areas. The two forums reached a preliminary boundary agreement in 1987, which the people of the Northwest Territories approved in a second plebiscite five years later. Work on the new constitution and land claims negotiations continue in the western area. The task has been more difficult here than in Nunavut for the people are of divergent backgrounds and have conflicting interests.

In central Alaska, after World War II, various kinds of government payments, mostly welfare, furnished a growing portion of Native incomes as fur prices slumped and wage earning opportunities declined. Outside the economic sphere, the introduction of schools in the 1940s and 1950s was one of the most important changes to take place in the region. Similar to other areas of the Northern Interior, schools furthered the nucleation of the population into fewer and fewer settlements. In turn, this encouraged those young Natives, mostly men, who wanted to participate in hunting and trapping activities to drop out of school.

In the late 1960s the Kolchans joined together with other Alaskan Native groups in the Alaska Federation of Natives to press their land claims. When the Alaska Native Claims Settlement Agreement was signed in 1971, they were entitled to a share in the substantial cash settlement and a portion of the 15.6 million acres (6.3 million hectares) earmarked for Athapaskan-speaking groups. Regional and village corporations invest the money and manage the land to promote long-term development and attempt to alleviate economic hardships in the Native communities.

BIBLIOGRAPHIC ESSAY

Glimpses of the Native people at the time of initial contact with Europeans are available in a variety of published accounts. The earliest of these to describe the Indian groups who lived north of the Gulf of St. Lawrence and the Great Lakes were written by many of the same French observers who are discussed in previous chapters. Most important are the journals and letters of Jacques Cartier, Samuel de Champlain, and the Jesuits. The accounts of Pierre Gaultier de Varennes et de La Vérendrye portray the contact world for the area between Lake Superior and the forks of the Saskatchewan River. These papers are available in *Journals and Letters of P. G. de Varennes de La Verendrye and His Sons,* ed. L. J. Burpee (Toronto, 1927).

Undoubtedly the most important records pertaining to the Northern Interior are those of the Hudson's Bay Company. E. E. Rich provides an overview of the history of this company's central role in the mercantile fur trade in *The Fur Trade in the North West to 1867* (Toronto, 1967). For a discussion of its declining position in the industrial fur trade see Arthur J. Ray, *The Canadian Fur Trade in the Industrial Age* (Toronto, 1990). Only a small fraction of these voluminous documents have been published to date, mostly by the now defunct Hudson's Bay Record Society. Of the papers this society published, *James Isham's Observations on Hudson's Bay, 1743,* ed. E. E. Rich (London, 1949) and *Andrew Graham's Observations on Hudson's Bay, 1767–91,* ed. G. Williams (London, 1969) are the most perceptive. Collectively these two men spent more than forty years on Hudson Bay dealing with Indians. Their reminiscences are very solid amateur ethnographies; also, Isham and Graham provide unparalleled insights into the conduct of the early fur trade. Glimpses into the daily life at the bayside posts in the eighteenth century are available for Fort Albany in 1705–6 in *Albany Hudson's Bay Miscellany, 1670–1780,* ed. G. Williams (Winnipeg, 1975); for Fort Churchill in *The Founding of Churchill Being the Journal of Captain James Knight . . . 1717,* ed. James F. Kenney (Toronto, 1932); and for Moose Factory in *Moose Fort Journals, 1783–85,* ed. E. E. Rich (London, 1954).

Although the Hudson's Bay Company slept by the frozen sea for most of the eighteenth century, it did dispatch men into the interior to gather information on the geography of Rupert's Land, the Native people, and the activities of its opponents. Probably the best known of these accounts, and certainly the most important source of information on the Northern Interior, is Samuel Hearne's *A Journey from Prince of Wales's Fort in Hudson's Bay to the Northern Ocean, 1769, 1770, 1771, 1772,* R. Glover, ed. (Toronto, 1958). Hearne traveled along the boundary between the boreal forest and tundra and wrote the earliest detailed descriptions of northern Athapaskans in their home territories. Once the company moved inland after 1774, the number of its inland posts proliferated rapidly, but very few of the records of these establishments have been published. One of the most important of these presents the post journals for Cumberland House during its first few years of operations, *Cumberland and Hudson's House Journals, 1775–82*, ed. E. E. Rich (London, 1948). The Hudson's Bay Company archives are located in the Provincial Archives of Manitoba in Winnipeg.

Following the collapse of the French empire in North America, American, English, and Scottish traders based in Montreal took over the interior fur trade, carrying it beyond the Saskatchewan River into the Mackenzie River drainage basin and the Pacific slope. Alexander Mackenzie played the leading role in this expansion, and his journals provide the first recorded observations of Native life in these two regions; see *The Journals and Letters of Sir Alexander Mackenzie*, ed. D. Kaye Lamb (Toronto, 1970). The most important of the published papers of the Nor'Westers who followed Mackenzie are *David Thompson's Narrative, 1784–1812*, ed. R. Glover (Toronto, 1962); *The Letters and Journals of Simon Fraser, 1806–1808*, ed. W. Kaye Lamb (Toronto, 1960); and Daniel Harmon's *Sixteen Years in Indian Country*, ed. W. Kaye Lamb (Toronto, 1957). Thompson traversed much of the country between York Factory and the lower Columbia River. He left particularly good accounts of the Woodland Crees and Ojibwas. Fraser's and Harmon's published writings, on the other hand, provide the first readily available descriptions of the Pacific slope portions of the Northern Interior after Mackenzie.

George Simpson (later Sir George) provides an excellent sketch of the Athabasca Department at the height of Hudson's Bay Company–North West Company rivalry in his *Journal of Occurrences in the Athabasca Department . . . And Report*, ed. E. E. Rich (London, 1938). Immediately after the merger of these two rivals the Hudson's Bay Company appointed Simpson governor of the Northern Department, which stretched from Hudson Bay to the Pacific Coast. In 1824–5 he made an inspection trip of a large portion of this department. His account of this voyage is available in *Fur Trade and Empire*, ed. F. Merk (Cambridge, Mass., 1968). It provides a very good depiction of the fur trade during the time when the Hudson's Bay Company's monopoly was at its height.

A number of narratives about life in the region during the era of the industrial fur trade are available. Among the most useful are J. W. Anderson, *Fur Trader's Story* (Toronto, 1961); Philip Godsell, *Arctic Trader* (London, n.d.); Hugh Mackay Ross, *The Apprentice's Tale* (Winnipeg, 1986); Sydney Augustus Keighley, *Trader-Tripper-Trapper: The Life of a Bay Man* (Winnipeg, 1989); and Peter Baker, *Memoirs of an Arctic Arab: The Story of a Free-trader in Northern Canada* (Yellowknife, 1976). For Native perspectives see John Tetso, *Trapping Is My Life* (Toronto, 1970) and Tom Boulanger, *An Indian Remembers* (Winnipeg, 1971).

The scholarly literature dealing with the Northern Interior is very extensive. A comprehensive overview of Native societies of the Northern Interior before and after contact is available in *Handbook of North American Indians, Vol. 6, Subarctic,* ed. June Helm (Washington, D.C., 1981). This volume also includes an exhaustive bibliography. Aspects of the cultural geography of the area up to the eve of European penetration are portrayed by J. V. Wright in "Plate 9: Cultural Sequences, AD 500–European Contact," *The Historical Atlas of Canada,* vol. 1, ed. R. C. Harris (Toronto, 1987).

The classic general study of the Canadian fur trade is Harold A. Innis, *The Fur Trade in Canada* (Toronto, 1977 [1930]). W. Eccles provides a concise overview of the early French fur trade in *The Canadian Frontier, 1534–1760* (Albuquerque, N.M., 1969). The standard reference on the northern English trade is E. E. Rich, *Hudson's Bay Company,* 3 vols. (Toronto, 1960). For an excellent popular overview of the company's history see Glyndwr Williams, "The Hudson's Bay Company and the Fur Trade: 1670–1870," *Beaver Magazine of the North* (autumn 1983). A summary picture of the industry from contact to the twentieth century is Arthur J. Ray, "The Fur Trade in North America: An Overview from a Historical Geographical Perspective," in *Wild Furbearer Management and Conservation in North America,* ed. Milan Novak et al. (Toronto, 1987), 21–30.

A pioneering work dealing with the impact of the fur trade on Native people in the eastern portion of the Northern Interior is A. G. Bailey, *The Conflict of European and Eastern Algonkian Cultures, 1504–1700* (Toronto, 1969 [1937]). In this study Bailey challenged the earlier work of F. G. Speck, "Family Hunting Territories and Social Life of Various Algonkian Bands of the Ottawa Valley," *Canada Department of Mines, Geological Survey, Memoir* 70 (Ottawa, 1915) and "The Family Hunting Band as the Basis of Algonkian Social Organization," *American Anthropologist* 17 (1915), 289–305, which asserted that the land-tenure systems found in the Northern Interior in the early twentieth century were of aboriginal origin. Instead Bailey argued that they were the product of the fur trade. For an excellent overview of the continuing land tenure debate see *Who Owns the Beaver? Northern Algonquian Land Tenure Reconsidered, Anthropologica (Special Issue)* 28 (1986), ed C. A. Bishop and T. Morantz.

In *Keepers of the Game* (Berkeley, Calif., 1978) Calvin Martin put forward the highly controversial thesis that early contact, particularly the epidemic diseases Europeans introduced, shattered traditional worldviews and led Indians wantonly to destroy the animals they depended upon. In a collection of essays edited by Shepard Krech III, *Indians, Animals, and the Fur Trade* (Athens, Ga., 1981), several prominent ethnohistorians challenge Martin's ideas.

Intergroup trading relations in the Gulf of St. Lawrence and eastern Great Lakes region in the sixteenth and seventeenth centuries are discussed in Bruce Trigger, *The Children of Aataentsic*, vol. 1 (Montreal, 1976) and *Natives and Newcomers* (Montreal, 1985). Native participation in the Hudson's Bay Company fur trade is explored in depth in a series of important monographs. Daniel Francis and Toby Morantz focus on the eastern James Bay region before 1870 in *Partners in Furs* (Montreal, 1983); Charles A. Bishop examines the impact the fur trade had on the Ojibwas of northern Ontario before 1945 in *The Northern Ojibwa and the Fur Trade* (Toronto, 1974); and Arthur J. Ray explores this topic with respect to the Western Crees and Woodland Assiniboines in *Indians in the Fur Trade* (Toronto, 1974). Whereas Ray stresses the role of the early fur trade as an agency of change in the lives of the Western Crees, more recently Dale Russell in *The Eighteenth Century Western Cree and Their Neighbours* (Ottawa, 1991) and Paul Thistle, *Indian-European Trade Relations in the Lower Saskatchewan River Region to 1840* (Winnipeg, 1986) downplay the industry's impact. J. C. Yerbury considers Athapaskan involvement in *The Subarctic Indians and the Fur Trade, 1680–1860* (Vancouver, 1986). Kerry Abel likewise explores this topic in *Drum Songs: Glimpses of Dene History* (Montreal, 1993), but she also considers their responses to changing social and economic circumstances from the late nineteenth century to recent times. In *"Give Us Good Measure"* (Toronto, 1978) Arthur J. Ray and Donald B. Freeman show how the Native and European economies joined together in the Hudson's Bay Company's fur trade before 1763. Various social and economic aspects of the Subarctic fur trade are addressed in a collection of essays edited by Shepard Krech III, *The Subarctic Fur Trade: Native Social and Economic Adaptations* (Vancouver, 1984).

The development of fur trade society and the changing positions of Indians and Métis within it are discussed by Sylvia Van Kirk, *Many Tender Ties: Women in Fur-Trade Society in Western Canada, 1670–1870* (Winnipeg, 1980) and Jennifer Brown, *Strangers in Blood: Fur Trade Company Families in Indian Country* (Vancouver, 1980). A good overview of missionary activity in the north is John Webster Grant, *Moon of Wintertime: Missionaries and the Indians of Canada in Encounter since 1534* (Toronto, 1984).

With the exception of Bishop's and Abel's works, most of the above studies spotlight the pre-1870 era. The only studies that focus on the fur trade after that time are Harold A. Innis, *The Fur Trade in Canada* (New Haven, Conn., 1930) and Arthur J. Ray, *The Canadian Fur Trade in the Industrial Age* (Toronto, 1990). The more important ethnographies dealing with this era are Adrian Tanner, *Bringing Home Animals: Religious Ideology and Mode of Production of the Mistassini Cree Hunters* (St. John's, 1979); R. W. Dunning, *Social and Economic Change among the Northern Ojibwas* (Toronto, 1959); Edward S. Rogers, *The Round Lake Ojibwa,* Occasional Paper 5, Art and Archaeology Division, Royal Ontario Museum (Toronto, 1962); Robert Jarvenpa, *The Trappers of Patuanak,* National Museum of Man Mercury Series: Canadian Ethnology Service Paper 67 (Ottawa, 1980); and Hugh Brody, *Maps and Dreams: Indians and the British Columbia Frontier* (Vancouver, 1981). Important regional histories are Ken S. Coates, *Best Left as Indians: Native-White Relations in the Yukon Territory, 1840–1973* (Montreal, 1991) and Julie Cruikshank, *Life Lived Like a Story: Life Stories of Three Yukon Native Elders* (Lincoln, Nebr., 1990).

An account of the negotiations of Treaties One to Seven by a government negotiator is Alexander Morris, *The Treaties of Canada with the Indians* (Toronto, 1979 [1862]). For Treaties Eight and Eleven, see Rene Fumoleau, *As Long as This Land Shall Last: A History of Treaty 8 and Treaty 11, 1870–1939* (Toronto, 1974).

The early Cree reactions to the James Bay hydroelectric proposal are brought together in Boyce Richardson, *Strangers Devour the Land: The Cree Hunters of the James Bay Area versus Premier Bourassa and the James Bay Development Corporation* (Toronto, 1975). The impact of the project on Cree life is thoroughly discussed by Richard F. Salisbury in *A Homeland for the Cree: Regional Development in James Bay, 1971–1981* (Montreal, 1986). Thomas Berger provides a good account of the Mackenzie Valley Pipeline Commission which he headed in *Northern Frontier, Northern Homeland,* rev. ed. (Vancouver, 1988). Native testimony before the commission is available in Martin O'Maley, *The Past and Future Land: An Account of the Berger Inquiry into the Mackenzie Valley Pipeline* (Toronto, 1976). Aspects of Dene life at the time of the inquiry are explored in Mel Watkins, *Dene Nation: The Colony Within* (Toronto, 1977). In *Home and Native Land: Aboriginal Rights and the Canadian Constitution* (Toronto, 1984), 89–110, Michael Asch discusses the efforts to accommodate Native concerns in future government arrangements in the Northwest Territories.

14

THE ARCTIC FROM NORSE CONTACT
TO MODERN TIMES

DAVID DAMAS

FIRST CONTACTS: NORSE AND THULE PEOPLES IN THE
EASTERN ARCTIC

The Norse colonists

When Erik the Red (Eirikr Thorvaldsson) and his followers landed in
southwest Greenland near the end of the tenth century, they discovered
traces of previous inhabitants, including the remains of dwellings, parts of
skin boats, and stone implements. Archaeologists agree that these were
remains of people of the Dorset culture (see Chapter 3). Late Dorset people
probably inhabited the west Greenland coast to the north of the Holsteinsborg region in the period A.D. 700 to 900 and thus preceded the
Norse occupation by about 100 years. While Dorset people lived in other
parts of Greenland during Norse times, there is little likelihood of meetings between the two groups.

The Norse settlers distributed themselves in two colonies, which were
designated the Eastern Settlement and the Western Settlement, although
both were located on the southwest coast of Greenland. They lived for up
to five centuries a life which combined animal husbandry with hunting sea
mammals and some terrestrial animals, fishing being a minor occupation.
Chief domesticates were sheep and goats, though cattle, pigs, and horses
were also kept. In the farms, scattered deep in the fjords, the Norse used
meadows for grazing their animals and harvesting hay to feed them over
the winter. It appears that they experimented with growing domesticated
grain but were unsuccessful. Exports to Europe included hides, fats and
oils, falcons, and walrus ivory. The Norse in Greenland clothed themselves
in garments made from the wool of their sheep and partly in animal skins.
Their houses were substantial structures with frames of driftwood and
walls and roofs covered with sod. Population estimates for these colonies

329

are 4,000 to 5,000 for the Eastern Settlement, and 1,000 to 1,600 for the Western Settlement at peak periods.

First contacts between Norse and the ancestors of modern Inuit of the Thule culture are usually assigned to about the beginning of the thirteenth century. Norse sagas and Inuit legends agree that these contacts took place around the Disko Bay region, some distance north of the Western Settlement, in the course of hunting trips. The historian Finn Gad notes that "The small *History of Norway* . . . tells mainly of bloody combats, but the archaeological finds reveal that peaceful contacts must also have existed. No doubt a certain wariness was present at the beginning, but the relations may have been quite peaceful."[1]

The main theme of the Inuit legends about the Norse is why and how the Eskimos exterminated them. In several of the tales "an Eskimo is made responsible for the origin of the enmity between the two people, but the merciless attack by the Norse is meant to justify the counterattack by the Eskimos that exterminated the Norse."[2] Such a situation is consistent with the traditions of the vendetta, which has been a widespread Inuit practice and was certainly a part of Norse tradition as well. One tale describes an attack by a "pirate ship" which sacked the Norse settlement and exterminated its inhabitants, except for five women. These women subsequently intermarried with Inuit. This tale is the only one extant which suggests amalgamation of Norse into the Thule population. The historicity of these legends is questionable because of their late recordings; moreover, the locations of several of them shift from one version to another, as for instance, from the Eastern to the Western Settlement.

While there is some evidence for extensive Norse hunting expeditions to the north, those parts of the west coast were the domain of the Thule people, who were "bound to territories where ice hunting was possible and where the whale and walrus were sufficiently numerous. Accordingly, they kept to the northern part of Greenland until changing climatic conditions forced them southward."[3] The presence of Norse materials in Thule sites has been used to define the Inuksuk (or Inugsuk) phase of that culture. Such occurrence does not mean that physical contacts, involving exchange or pillage, necessarily took place. Instead, those materials could have been collected by the Inuit from abandoned Norse farms. As early as 1936 the

[1] Finn Gad, *The History of Greenland* (London, 1970), 1:100.
[2] Inge Kleivan, "History of Norse Greenland," in vol. 5, *Arctic, Handbook of North American Indians*, ed. David Damas (Washington, D.C., 1984), 552.
[3] Gad, *The History of Greenland*, 1:102.

archaeologists Therkel Mathiassen and Erik Holtved noted that Inuksuk sites in the Julianehab (Eastern Settlement) region are found part way up the fjords, where it was judged that the ice edge would have been located during the thirteenth through the fifteenth centuries, while the Norse farms were at the heads of the fjords. They assumed that the two zones of settlement were inhabited simultaneously and that the Inuksuk people expanded up the east coast in the second half of the fourteenth century. Mathiassen found that fully 80 percent of the artifacts are the same as those discovered in pure Thule sites.

The possible contemporaneity of late Norse and Inuksuk cultures raises the fascinating question of the disappearance of the Greenland colonies and the role of the Inuit in that demise. Inge Kleivan reviewed the various theories, including epidemics, lower fertility, pirate attacks, extermination by Inuit, emigration, and intermarriage and absorption into the Native population. She concluded that "none of the many different theories that have been propounded to explain why and how the Norse disappeared from Greenland has advanced sufficient evidence for the solution to the puzzle. Most probably there were several different factors operating."[4] One theory which combines some of these factors is advanced by Thomas McGovern. He thinks that while the Western Settlement may have been overrun by the Thule/Inuksuk people, the Eastern Settlement was too populous to have suffered such a fate. He cites competition for resources in a situation which assumes co-occupation of the Eastern Settlement region. McGovern also argues that the failure of the Norse to adopt ice hunting (mainly of the ringed seal), or inadequate clothing in times of cooling climate, may have accounted for their disappearance.[5]

Climatic change and economic conditions in the eastern Arctic

Christian Vibe has evolved a model of periodic fluctuations in climate from first Norse occupancy to the present day which is based on changing conditions of sea ice in waters surrounding Greenland and in the Arctic Archipelago.[6] Historians and archaeologists have eagerly, but not always accurately, cited his formulations. In Vibe's scheme there was a "drift ice

[4] Kleivan, "History of Norse Greenland," 555.
[5] Thomas H. McGovern, "The Economics of Extinction in Norse Greenland," In *Climate and History*, ed. T. M. L. Wigley, M. J. Ingram, and G. Farmer (Cambridge, 1981), 404–34.
[6] Christian Vibe, "Arctic Animals in Relation to Climatic Fluctuations," *Meddelelser om Grønland* 170/5 (1967).

stagnation stage" prior to A.D. 1150, which was accompanied by a cool, stable climate favorable to reindeer (caribou) hunting, a practice which he links to the appearance of the Thule people in north Greenland. That period was followed by "drift ice pulsation" and "drift ice melting" stages from A.D. 1150 to 1340, when a warmer climate prevailed which would have been favorable to whaling in Baffin Bay. But the increased moisture of that period would have made hunting of land animals unproductive. Deep winter snows and occasional icing rains would have made it difficult for caribou and musk oxen to forage and consequently would have reduced their numbers. These stages were followed by another "drift ice stagnation" phase between A.D. 1340 and 1450, when the climate was again relatively cold and dry, and during which time the Inuksuk people migrated south taking advantage of colder and longer winters with their ice hunting economy. Land mammal hunting would have been profitable as well, and Vibe thought that the Inuksuk people eliminated the Western Settlement early in this period. Further "drift ice pulsating" and "drift ice melting" phases followed, from A.D. 1450 to 1560. Warmer conditions during these stages would have shifted the harp and ringed seal ranges father north, and the moisture would have created deep winter snows that depressed the caribou populations. Vibe suggests that the disappearance of the Eastern Settlement may have been due to the absence of seals in that region during the early part of this phase. Meanwhile some of the Inuksuk people headed north up the east coast "to follow the seal." Several aspects of Vibe's formulation are intriguing as well as persuasive, but the paucity of accurate dating – indeed its virtual absence for the southernmost and the east coast of Greenland – leaves much to be resolved.

Norse-Thule contacts in North America

With the discovery of Norse remains at L'Anse aux Meadows at the northern tip of Newfoundland, it is no longer doubted that they reached that region. Norse sagas, especially *The Greenlander's Saga* and *Erik the Red's Saga,* recount voyages of discovery to the west and south of Greenland during the period A.D. 986 to about A.D. 1020. Lief, Erik's eldest son, is usually given credit for the discovery and naming of Baffin Island (Markland) and Labrador (Helluland), as well as Vinland, now identified with Newfoundland, on his voyage of 1002–3. Other landings were probably made, and eventually evidence for such may be found to the south on the North American mainland.

It had been earlier assumed that the Natives encountered in Newfoundland were Dorset people. Yet, on the basis of recent archaeological findings, William Fitzhugh puts both Newfoundland and the southern half of the Labrador coast beyond their range during the entire period of probable Norse contacts. The first encounter with "skraelings" (a term used by the Norse to designate all Native people) appears to have been in Hamilton Inlet, and the people encountered probably belonged to the Point Revenge Indian culture. Yet, between A.D. 1000 and 1400 Thule, Dorset, Point Revenge, and Norse could all have come into contact within a very small geographic range in northern Labrador.[7] Only a few fragments of archaeological evidence suggest or indicate Norse contacts with peoples of Newfoundland and the North American mainland. The Natives whom the Norse encountered in Newfoundland would most likely have been the Beothuks.

Robert McGhee has marshaled all the evidence, including Inuit legends, Norse sagas, and archaeology, regarding far-flung Norse-Native contacts in the Canadian Arctic as a whole. He concludes that "contacts between North American natives and Norse probably occurred more frequently and over a greater area than recorded in historical accounts."[8] Such contacts were possibly most frequent during Norse voyages to Labrador for timber. The effects of Norse contacts on Thule people were probably very minor. Meteoric iron from Greenland, Siberian iron, and native copper were as notable additions to Thule artifact assemblages as were the few examples of Norse iron that have been found in such association. There is no evidence for epidemic disease spreading to the Thule people, and there was little motivation for the Norse to trade with them.

THULE TO INUIT: THE TRANSITION FROM
ARCHAEOLOGICAL TO HISTORICALLY RECORDED
CULTURES IN THE ARCTIC

Transition in Greenland

During the period of Norse occupation of Greenland and visits to North America, roughly A.D. 986 to 1450, there occurred a simultaneous set of

---

[7] William W. Fitzhugh, "Winter Cove and the Point Revenge Occupation of the Central Labrador Coast," *Arctic Anthropology* 25/2 (1978), 170.
[8] Robert McGhee, "Contact between Native North Americans and the Medieval Norse: A Review of the Evidence," *American Antiquity* 49/1 (1984), 21.

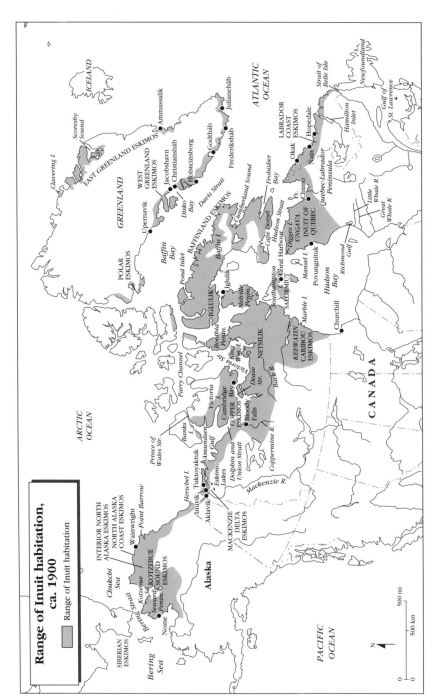

Figure 14.1 Range of Inuit habitation, ca. 1900.

changes in Arctic cultures which operated largely independently of any contacts with Europeans. In Greenland the Inuksuk culture had some Norse artifacts superimposed on a base of classical Thule culture. This probably happened shortly after the arrival of Thule peoples in Greenland, and about the time of first Norse settlement in the southwestern parts of Greenland. The culture of the Inuit who reached Greenland appears to have been little different from that of the region north of Parry Channel from which they came. They relied heavily on the ringed seal, which was probably hunted at all seasons, supplemented by whale hunting in skin boats. As the Thule people moved south during the Inuksuk phase, certain adjustments were made in response to altered ecological conditions. Richard Jordan sees polar bear hunting declining south of Disko Bay, and ringed seal hunting was also less important. Harp, hooded, and common seal hunting was increasingly important south of Holsteinsborg, where dog traction also disappeared as an adjustment to more temperate conditions. Settlement patterns and house type remained unchanged until the period of later contacts. Certain art forms showed alterations during the Inuksuk period, and the practice of intering of bodies in caves was introduced, as evidenced by a well-preserved series of female mummies.

The transition in the Central and Western Arctic

Thule people had populated most of the Canadian Arctic coast from Amundsen Gulf eastwards, including parts of the southern tier of the archipelago and Boothia and Melville Peninsula, Baffin Island, and parts of both coasts of Hudson Bay, between A.D. 1200 and 1300. Later, perhaps during the same period that Inuksuk people were moving southward in Greenland, the northern tier of islands above Parry Channel was abandoned, perhaps because of the disappearance of whales. As in the case of archaeological interpretations of the southward movement of Inuksuk, McGhee attributes this movement in the Central Arctic to climatic deterioration, with increased ice cover making the northern islands uninhabitable.[9]

The process of transformation from Thule to ethnographic Central Eskimo culture proceeded as a greater emphasis on land animals and winter sealing came to characterize adaptations throughout coastal Central Arctic

---

[9] Robert McGhee, "Thule Prehistory of Canada," in Damas, ed., *Arctic*, 374.

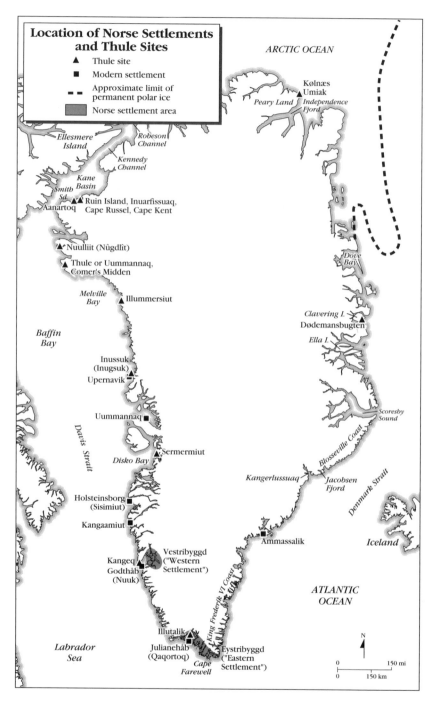

Figure 14.2 Location of Norse settlements and Thule sites in Greenland.

regions. On Baffin Island, the traditional earth-covered, whalebone-raftered Thule houses were replaced by the *qarmat,* which employed skin roofs on the remains of previous Thule dwellings, a practice still encountered in southern Baffin Island by Boas in 1883–4. Elsewhere the domed snowhouse became the chief winter dwelling. One of the major economic shifts over much of the Canadian Arctic was the decline of whaling and wholesale adoption of sealing at winter breathing holes. McGhee notes, however, that the whaling economy had never been established among the Copper and Netsilik peoples in the regions from Boothia Peninsula westward to Dolphin and Union Straits, due to shallow waters and the absence of large whales. In that region, Thule culture had been based on caribou and seals from its beginning. Little is known about the late Thule culture of the eastern shore of Hudson Bay. It arrived as late as 1400 in the Ungava region and only after that time expanded down the coast of Labrador. In the latter region, the emphasis on whale hunting and the occurrence of permanent winter dwellings indicate a continuing closer resemblance to Thule than is found elsewhere in the Canadian Arctic.

Western Thule regions began in the Mackenzie delta. In comparing Thule with modern Inuit cultures, Mathiassen found by far the greatest retention of Thule traits in the western Arctic. Permanent settlements and dwellings (though different from Thule houses to the east because of availability of wood), and the strong emphasis on whaling, point to great affinity. Beluga hunting became the dominant pursuit in the Mackenzie region and continued into the twentieth century, while hunting large whales has remained important from Point Barrow around the northwestern corner of Alaska. In the Kotzebue region, however, whales seem to have been scarce after about A.D. 1400, after which time there was a shift to fishing in the rivers and caribou hunting. Movements of people from the coast into the interior of northern Alaska appear to have increased dramatically in the seventeenth century, leading to the origin of the year-round caribou hunters of the ethnographic period.

In summarizing the relationship between Arctic archaeological and ethnographic cultures, McGhee expresses the view now endorsed by all Arctic prehistorians: "In summary then, archeology has provided fairly certain evidence that all Canadian Eskimo tribes of the historic period are descended biologically and culturally from the Thule people who first swept across the area from Alaska after the tenth century. Thule Culture is the historical factor that explains the biological, linguistic, and cultural similarities of all Eskimo between Bering Strait and Greenland."[10]

THE REDISCOVERY OF AMERICA AND EARLY WARFARE AND TRADE IN THE EASTERN ARCTIC

The fifteenth century saw the severance of ties between Greenland and Scandinavia and by its end the disappearance of the Greenland colonies themselves. The waning years of that century and beginnings of the next also brought the rediscovery of Newfoundland by John Cabot (1497) and of Greenland by the Portuguese João Fernandes sailing from the Azores (1502), but there is no record of contacts with Inuit on these voyages.

Sixteenth-century contacts in the Newfoundland-Labrador region

There is considerable controversy regarding the people encountered in these regions during the sixteenth century, particularly in the Strait of Belle Isle. Breton fishermen and Basque whalers certainly made contact with people there. Yet Thule/Inuit occupation seems to have been largely confined to the northern half of the Labrador coast and certainly to the regions north of Hamilton Inlet, although occasional trading or raiding trips may have been made as far south as the north shore of the Gulf of St. Lawrence. We learn little from the extant accounts about the culture of the Inuit in Labrador during the sixteenth century. The famous Augsburg Print of what appears to be an artist's conception of an Inuit woman and her child who were brought back to Copenhagen is dated 1566, but the provenance of the depicted Inuit is obscure.

Post-Norse contacts in Greenland and Baffin Island

It seems likely that the deteriorating climatic conditions during the fifteenth and sixteenth centuries brought on a heavy accumulation of pack ice all around Greenland, which to a large extent accounted for limited contacts from the outside. A number of abortive attempts were made to reach the Norse colonists who were thought to be still surviving, but only one of these expeditions actually landed in Greenland, and it failed to

[10] Ibid., 376.

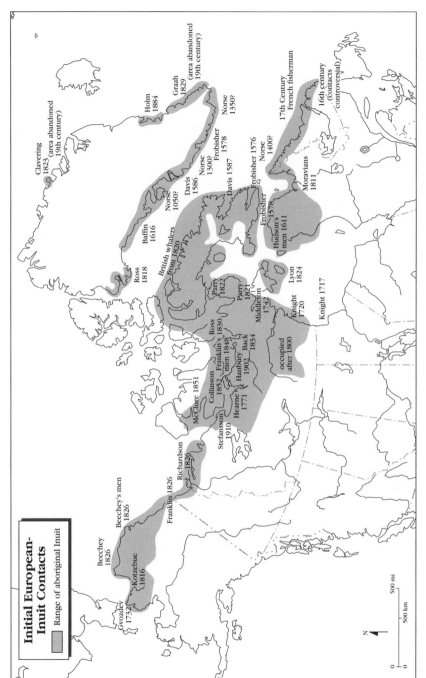

Initial European-Inuit Contacts

Range of aboriginal Inuit

Gvozdev 1732
Kotzebue 1816
Beechey 1826
Beechey's men 1826
Richardson 1826
Franklin 1826
Clavering 1823 (area abandoned 19th century)
Holm 1884
Graah 1829 (area abandoned 19th century)
Norse 1050?
Norse 1300?
Norse 1350?
Baffin 1616
Davis 1586
Frobisher 1578
Davis 1587
17th Century French fisherman
16th century (contacts controversial)
Frobisher 1576
Norse 1400?
Frobisher 1578
Moravians 1811
Hudson's men 1611
British whalers from 1820
Ross 1818
Ross 1830
Parry 1822
Parry 1821
Lyon 1824
Franklin's men 1848
Middleton 1742
Knight 1720
Knight 1717
occupied after 1800
McClure 1851
Collinson 1852
Hanbury 1902
Back 1834
Stefansson 1910
Hearne 1771

N

0 ————— 500 mi
0 ————— 500 km

Figure 14.3 Initial European-Inuit contacts in Canada.

make contact. The search for the Northwest Passage to the Orient began in earnest with the voyages of Martin Frobisher, between 1576 and 1578. The accounts of his three visits to the eastern Arctic provide the first historical descriptions of Inuit since the brief references of the Norse period. On the first voyage, of 1576, Inuit were encountered in southern Baffin Island. The nature of contact, a mixture of warfare and trade, set the stage for Inuit-European relations for some years to come. In the case of Frobisher's three voyages, the balance was heavily toward hostilities. These were brought on both by the Natives' eagerness to secure iron and other European goods by whatever means, and by the attempts of the English to capture Natives to display at the English court. During an initial period of friendly relations, Inuit men showed great familiarity with the ship by doing gymnastics in the rigging. This suggests that previous contacts are likely, the most probable candidates being the Basques, who were already operating in the waters to the south of Baffin Island. Five of Frobisher's men were captured on the first trip, and the English carried off an Inuk man who died on the voyage back to England. On the second trip, that of 1577, the English seized two women, a child, and a man, as a result of which relations deteriorated rapidly into a pitched battle. The chronicler of the second voyage, Dionyse Settle, gives a rather detailed description of the Inuit of Frobisher Bay, which he laced with his ethnocentric evaluations. We are told that their skin color was much like that of Englishmen who worked in the sun, that they ate much of their meat raw, and that they had the habit of eating grass "like beasts devouring the same." Their dogs were said to be "not unlike wolves," though usually black in color. The skin clothing worn in summer is described, and many layers of garments exaggeratedly posited as being the winter costume. Two dwelling types are mentioned, the skin tents used in summer and "ovens" used in winter, the description of which identifies them as the *qarmat,* or skin-roofed, sod-walled structures of the historical era for that region. Weapons, including sinew backed bows and stone, bone, and iron tipped arrows, are described in detail. The presence of iron implies either trade relations for meteoric metal from north Greenland, or some sort of direct or indirect European contact. Both kayaks and umiaks are depicted in detail, the latter employing gutskin sails. While Settle remarks on the barrenness of the country, he also mentions large herds of caribou. Some very disgusted comments are made about the eating habits of the Inuit, for instance, "there is no flesh or fishe, which they find dead, smell it neuer so filthy, but they will eate it as they find it, without any other dressing, a loathsome spectacle either to the beholder or hearers."[11] Cannibalism is assumed, but no proof of this practice is offered.

During the third voyage, undertaken in 1578, Frobisher's ships landed in Greenland and made contact with Inuit, probably in the Godthab region. The Natives fled their encampment when approached, leaving behind some dogs and their tents containing artifacts. Among these was a box of nails, which clearly indicates unrecorded contact. After discovering Hudson Strait, some of his men landed on the southern or mainland shore and engaged in trade with Natives, with the usual exchange of knives, looking glasses, bells, and other trinkets for fresh meat.

The next explorer to enter the eastern Arctic, John Davis, appears to have planned his meeting with Inuit more carefully. In the company of his first voyage of 1585, he included an orchestra which was greeted with enthusiastic singing and dancing by the natives of the same Godthab region earlier visited by Frobisher. Davis's initial impressions cast the Inuit in a very favorable light: "They are very tractable people, voyde of craft, or double dealing, and easie to be brought to any civilitie or good order."[12] Although Davis crossed the strait which now bears his name to Baffin Island, no encounters were reported with the Natives of that region.

On his second voyage (1586), Davis returned to the Godthab region. At first he and his men were greeted warmly, but thievery by the Inuit quickly soured relations. Relations came to a head when English sailors were pelted with stones and the Inuit stole an anchor from one of the ships. With almost saintly magnanimity, Davis continued to distribute gifts, but shortly afterwards came another attack with stones. Davis says of his subsequent actions, "I changed my courtesy and grew to hatred. Myself in my own boat, well manned with shot, and the bark's boat likewise in pursuit pursued them and gave them divers shot, but to small purpose by reason of their swift rowing."[13] Davis's observations on the people of Greenland included their eating raw meat, the apparent use of baleen ("fins of whales") for nets, and that many men bore wounds which he attributed to their warlike nature, but which were more likely the result of hunting accidents. A vocabulary of thirty-nine words was collected on this second voyage, though the rough orthography makes them difficult to identify with Greenlandic

[11] Vilhjalmur Stefansson, ed., *The Three Voyages of Martin Frobisher* (London, 1938), 1:23.
[12] Albert H. Markham, ed., *The Voyages and Works of John Davis* (London, 1880), 8.
[13] Ibid., 23.

terms. Other peaceful trading contact was made farther up the Greenland coast, but when, on returning southward, Davis's ship skirted the
Labrador coast, there was more violence. Five men who went ashore
were attacked by "the brutish people of this country who lay secretly
lurking in the wood." Only one escaped. There is, again, uncertainty
regarding the ethnic identification of the Natives of the Labrador region
located south of Hamilton Inlet.

About three weeks after Davis and his flagship left the Godthab
region, his other ship, the *Sonneshine,* called there and encounters with
the Inuit repeated the inconsistency and ambiguity that had characterized earlier contacts in that locale. While the first men who went ashore
were immediately attacked, the next day the crews joined with the Inuit
in a football game. Other people encountered farther north traded with
the English, but then a fight broke out over a kayak which had been
traded and which the Natives strove to recover. There was less contact
with Inuit during Davis's third voyage, that of 1587, but at some
location along the west coast of Greenland a boat which was being
assembled on an outlying island was dismantled by the Inuit for its
nails. Later, peaceful trade was established. After crossing Baffin Bay,
Davis had another meeting with Natives. Trade ensued, but the English
were by this time too wary to be lured ashore.

Thus, as the sixteenth century ended, contacts in west Greenland, Baffin
Island, and more briefly, with Inuit in the Ungava and Labrador regions had
occurred. The descriptions of these encounters depict a culture which exhibits definite changes from the Thule phase of Arctic history. The people met
with by Europeans were a mystery to the explorers. The apparent cordiality
which characterized trading contacts could quickly change to a variety of
hostile, and at times, it seemed to the English, spiteful and even malicious
acts. For the most part both Frobisher and Davis behaved themselves with a
great degree of caution and even magnanimity in their relations with the
Inuit. Expectations that such behavior would ingratiate them to the Arctic
inhabitants were sorely disappointed. English diaries included a number of
highly ethnocentric evaluations of the Inuit. The Inuit were prepared to use
any method, peaceful or not, to acquire European artifacts, especially metal
products. The English usually rationalized capturing Natives as taking
hostages to ensure good behavior, but it would appear that there was an
over-eagerness to take people in order to display them before the court as
curious people from a far-away land. Such readiness to kidnap was surely not
conducive to peaceful relations.

European-Inuit contacts in the seventeenth century

The patterns of hostile relations interspersed with interludes of trade continued in the eastern Arctic into the seventeenth century. In 1612 William Baffin experienced the same combination of thievery by the Greenlanders when their numbers were large, and their fleeing when smaller numbers of them encountered the English. In Hudson Strait, John Knight and his mate walked over a hill and were never heard of again. In 1611 Hudson's mutinous crew was attacked at Digge's Island at the northeastern entrance to the great bay, without apparent provocation and while ostensibly trading peacefully. Four men were killed.

While contacts along the Labrador coast doubtlessly continued, and perhaps on Baffin Island as well, the bulk of information for the next century comes from Greenland. These relations between visiting Europeans and the Inuit were for some time no better than earlier. In 1604 the Danish-Norwegian King Christian IV hired two Englishmen, John Cunningham and James Hall, and the Dane Godske Lindenov to reestablish contacts with the Norse colonists who were presumed still to be living there. Lindenov appears to have kidnapped two Inuit and an attack by natives ensued. When the ships returned the following year, a captured Inuk had been trained to convert his fellows to Christianity, but he died during the voyage. Other captives were taken and one man jumped overboard. By this time, little rationalization was offered for taking prisoners back to Europe. The Greenland Trading Company was founded in 1635, but it would be many decades before it became an important force in contact. Although sporadic trading took place throughout the seventeenth century, Gad writes of contact as follows:

Between 1605 and 1660 Danish-Norwegian as well as Dutch ships had kidnapped about thirty Eskimos and brought them away from their homes. To us this seems brutal and inhuman, but to be honest we must remember that human value and dignity were unknown concepts in Europe at that time. Just as the Eskimos considered themselves "real human beings", *inuit,* and all others strange beings, so the Europeans regarded the so-called "barbarians" as animals that were strange enough to be exhibited in the market-place for money.[14]

The capture of Inuit provided subjects for study by two famous and serious scholars of the day. The Danish royal historian and pastor Claus Lyschander published a long poem in 1608, which was an appeal to restore European

---

[14] Gad, *The History of Greenland,* 1:238.

contacts with Greenland and rediscover the descendants of the Norse set-tlers believed to be still living there. The poem contained descriptions of the inhabitants based on observations of captives whom he had seen and on the accounts of explorers. Another scholar who reported on the seventeenth-century Greenlanders was Adam Olerius. In his studies of the Orient he found physical resemblances between the Inuit captives and inhabitants of the latter area. While much of Olerius's published description concerned physical characteristics, some of his comments were based on travelers' accounts of Native behavior. In contrast to Lyschander he distinguished more clearly between what he had observed and merely heard about the Inuit. He recorded that they had brutish eating habits, and that their personalities were characterized by sullenness, timidity, shyness, and suspi-cion. He also mentioned more positive traits, based on his own observations of captives, whom he describes as being "a quiet people who quickly under-stand what they are taught," although he was puzzled by their unwilling-ness or inability to learn Danish or German. Based largely on the accounts of explorers, Olerius provided detailed descriptions of kayaks and umiaks, which had fascinated the early explorers. Most significant, perhaps, he was the first to state in print that the then inhabitants of Greenland were not descended from the Norse colonists.

Another account published in 1658 by L. de Poincy, who had visited Greenland, produced a very favorable image of its inhabitants. He stressed their friendliness, fondness for children, and civility in dealing with strangers. Together with his discussion of the trading activities of Nicolas Tunes, these favorable impressions suggest that by the second half of the seventeenth century relations with the Inuit in Greenland had become more peaceful and mutually trusting than had been the case earlier.

THE EIGHTEENTH CENTURY: PACIFICATION IN THE
EAST AND FIRST EUROPEAN PENETRATION OF THE
CENTRAL AND WESTERN ARCTIC

Greenland in the 1700s

Greenlander contacts in the opening years of the eighteenth century were largely with Dutch whalers who, while taking large numbers of mammals in the Davis Strait–Baffin Bay region, also carried on brisk trade with the Natives, at least along the eastern shores of those waters. A number of

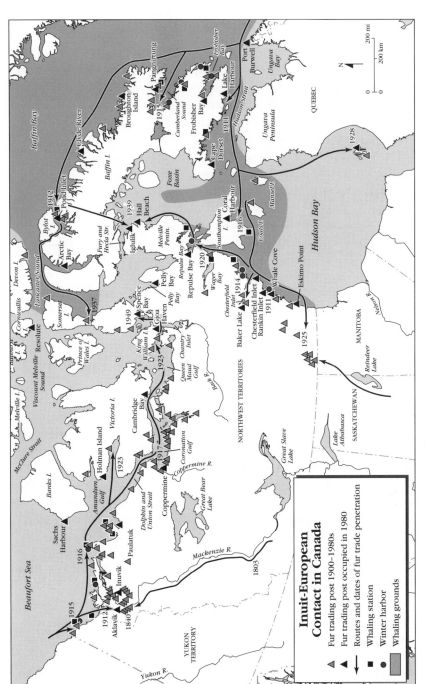

Figure 14.4 Inuit-European contact in Canada.

useful articles were brought in, but the Dutch refrained from trading firearms or powder out of fear for their own safety. The profit that the Dutch derived from hides and blubber probably far exceeded the cost of goods traded for them. The introduction of tuberculosis as well as the likelihood of alcohol use and of sexual excesses by the sailors seem to have characterized these contacts.

The year 1721 was a landmark in Greenlandic history. Hans Egede and his small band of Norwegian Lutheran missionaries and their dependents arrived, establishing the first European settlement since the Norse occupation. In the next few years a number of missions and trading stations were established along the west coast, beginning with Godthab in 1728 and continuing with Christianshab in 1734, Jakobshavn in 1741, and Frederikshab in 1742. While the missionaries were learning the Inuit language and trying to convert the Greenlanders to Christianity, the trading operations, which functioned in conjunction with the missions, had to compete with the Dutch until the Royal Greenland Trade Department began to enforce a monopoly after 1774. Gad writes that "by 1782 all the West Greenland colonies had been established as well as many intermediate trading posts and whaling stations" and by 1776 the coast of Greenland was closed to all foreign ships.[15] Personnel in each of the colonies included not only the missionaries and traders but also a number of hired craftsmen. The traders periodically visited outlying Inuit settlements to sell their wares. During the century the variety of trade goods increased, and around 1740 the Dutch began selling firearms, gunpowder, and lead for making bullets. Before the Dutch competition ceased, the Danish-Norwegian traders also began to sell these items. Trade was thus increasing and replacing the often hostile relations of earlier years. The trading companies had a deliberate policy of keeping hunting the principal occupation, and in this connection discouraged the aggregation of the Inuit population. This philosophy of protectionism and conservatism was to characterize most of the long history of contact in Greenland.

Hans Egede and his followers had begun their mission with the hope of rescuing the descendants of Norse settlers from paganism, but they quickly discovered that there were no survivors from the early colonies. Their chief program then was to translate the Bible into Greenlandic and to educate the Natives, largely in religious matters. While Egede and his

[15] Gad, "History of Colonial Greenland," in Damas, ed., *Arctic*, 558.

sons operated under difficult conditions, they succeeded in overthrowing the power of the shamans in a surprisingly short time. Meanwhile, German Moravian missionaries began, in 1733, to compete for Inuit souls. The Moravian approach was more successful for some time in that their missionaries were laymen who taught practical crafts as well as giving religious instruction. A certain concentration of population developed around the chief colonies, which necessitated the introduction of welfare aid, especially distributing provisions. Also prominent in eighteenth-century Greenland was interbreeding between European men and Inuit women, which created an intermediate group largely made up of illegitimate offspring in the first generation, but which was later to become the basis of an ethnic group that was "to form the nucleus of the population of West Greenland."[16]

Toward the end of the century, efforts were made by the Royal Greenland Trade Department to revive whaling, an occupation which had lagged just previously. While eight stations were established, no great success was possible as a result of the decline in the number of whales in Greenland waters at that time. The Instruction of April 19, 1782 established two inspectorates, the first attempt at organizing the great island politically. Provisions were made for the welfare of offspring of mixed marriages, and alcoholic beverages were forbidden. Fair trade regulations and the organization of social welfare in times of famine were also provided for by the legislation. Pricing schedules were set and medical assistance expanded. While the provisions of the Instruction implemented measures that generally sought to promote enlightened and liberal relations with the Greenlanders, a period of stagnation was to follow.

Eighteenth-century developments in Labrador

Early in the century French influence became important in southern coastal Labrador, with Quebec-based sealing and cod fishing operations maintaining year-round establishments. Some trade was carried on with Inuit as far south as the Strait of Belle Isle, where their summer excursions brought them. But these contacts were brief and uneasy, often displaying the hostility that had characterized earlier contacts in that region.

Contacts also occurred with Dutch whalers, many of whom traded in

[16] Ibid., 563.

Greenland and, while returning south, in Labrador. Trade relations became somewhat more stabilized after 1743, with the opening of a post in Hamilton Inlet by the Quebec merchant Louis Fornel. Baleen was the product traders most desired at this period. After a hiatus during the Seven Years' War, both Britons and Americans attempted to revive the baleen trade, but open hostilities with the Natives again became commonplace. The governor of Newfoundland attempted to establish a truce with the help of the Moravians in 1765. Although this attempt did not bring immediate and lasting peace, conditions seem to have improved, especially after mission-trading stations were opened along the coast by the Moravians. They established Nain in 1771, Okak in 1776, and Hopedale in 1782, thus covering a considerable length of the coast before the end of the century. In addition to their primary purpose of proselytizing, the Moravians were very active in trade, which soon brought them into competition with more southerly European traders. "By maintaining regular trade with the Inuit, the Moravians hoped to make their mission as self-sufficient as possible, while at the same time reducing one of the prime motives for Inuit journeys to European traders in southern Labrador."[17] One of the immediate effects of this contact with the Moravians was virtual abandonment of much of the northern part of the coast by the Inuit in order to be closer to the mission trade centers. However, the subsistence elements of the economy continued to dominate, and J. G. Taylor has provided a description of the seasonal economic cycle at this time which can be identified as essentially traditional, although the introduction of firearms was to alter subsistence more drastically.

Early explorations in the central and western Arctic

Hudson Bay had been penetrated as early as 1610 by Hudson and by 1615 by William Baffin, and was visited by other seventeenth-century explorers such as Thomas Button and by Jens Munk, who wintered at the site of present-day Churchill. Except for the description of the brief bloody contact by Hudson's men noted above, there is no account of the inhabitants of the area until a Hudson's Bay Company post was established at Churchill by James Knight in 1717. Both Inuit and Chipewyans began to trade there.

---

[17] J. Garth Taylor, "Historical Ethnography of the Labrador Coast," in Damas, ed., *Arctic*, 517; Taylor *Labrador Eskimo Settlements of the Early Contact Period* (Ottawa, 1974).

There is evidence that Inuit had been coming to that locale for timber for some time. The area also was noted for its large numbers of beluga. Knight sailed north in 1719 in two sloops, apparently for exploration as well as trade, but made no contact with the Natives. In wintering at Marble Island his entire crew died, leaving behind valuable wood and iron, which was a source of artifacts for the Inuit of the area for some years to come.

Hearne's trip to the mouth of the Coppermine River, which he reached in July 1771, was the first European penetration to the coast of the Central Arctic. During it his Athapaskan companions made a premeditated attack on an Inuit encampment just below Bloody Falls. The wariness of the Inuit of this region in their later encounters with explorers can be understood, at least in part, in terms of such hostile interaction with the Indians. It was not possible for Hearne to learn much about the culture of these Inuit, although he noted abundant caribou, musk oxen, fish, and seal in the region. Hearne encountered no Inuit during his outward and return trip through the Keewatin Barrens, but he noted signs of their presence, which indicated a deep seasonal penetration.

The Arctic Ocean was reached at another point before the turn of the nineteenth century, with Alexander Mackenzie's 1789 trip to the coast by way of the river that now bears his name. While he made no actual contacts with Inuit during his journey, his account vividly portrays his Indian companions' fears regarding possible contacts with their northern neighbors. Abandoned Inuit villages were visited and their permanent winter houses described. It appears that during Mackenzie's brief stay in the delta, the Inuit were hunting for caribou at Eskimo Lakes, some distance to the east, where they stored large quantities of meat for the coming winter. Whatever ironware the Indians in the area had appears to have come from the Inuit. This implies that the trade network which emanated from Siberia, later described by Vilhjalmur Stefansson, was already in force before the end of the eighteenth century. In the northern Alaskan domain of the Inuit, direct European contact had not yet taken place, although Captain Cook had explored the coasts of northwest Alaska as early as 1778.

Summary of eighteenth-century contacts

At the end of the eighteenth century Inuit culture showed wide variation from the east to west with regard to the effects of contacts. In Greenland and Labrador significant contact had taken place and settlements had been established by Europeans. While earlier trade had been sporadic and had brought supplies of European implements and other goods into the Arctic in an irregular fashion, after the establishment of trading posts in the area the flow became more regular. While earlier contacts had always been uneasy and characterized by frequent outbreaks of hostility, pacification was achieved in Greenland and Labrador before the end of the century. The road to acculturation was opening, with the chief agents of these processes being missionaries. Conversions were taking place slowly, but the cumulative effect was felt before 1800. Trade in animal products became an important adjunct to the subsistence economy of the Inuit, but was devoted largely to the acquisition and replacement of tools and weapons that would help to procure local game rather than provide other sources of food. The post at Churchill and the northward cruises of trading sloops along the west coast of Hudson Bay brought some European goods into the purview of certain groups of Inuit in the Central Arctic and doubtlessly stimulated intergroup trade long before direct contacts with Europeans had occurred. Yet, vast areas of the central regions still lay beyond the range of the explorations, and the life of the people of those regions was almost completely unaffected.

THE NINETEENTH CENTURY: PROTECTIONISM IN THE EAST — EXPLORERS, WHALERS, AND THE INUIT

Greenland: economic stagnation and preservationism

The end of the eighteenth and the early years of the nineteenth century were a time of great difficulty for the administration of Greenland and for the Greenlanders themselves. By that time, English whalers were encroaching in definite competition with the Royal Greenland Trade Department. According to Gad, all kinds of excesses accompanied contacts with whaling crews, in that "the Greenlanders neglected their jobs and hunting and often sold their animal hides, clothes, kayaks, and hunting gear for gin."[18] A financial crisis in Denmark and Norway aggravated these problems, and the influence of the missions was weakened through cutbacks in personnel which were not remedied by the training of native catechists. Isolation came with the Napoleonic wars and especially, in 1813–14, with the war between Sweden and Norway, following Norway's separation from Den-

---

[18] Gad, "History of Colonial Greenland," 565.

mark. After that conflict, Greenland fell solidly under the hegemony of Denmark. Economic conditions did not improve until after 1830.

Meanwhile European exploration of the coasts continued and resulted in the discovery of previously unknown Inuit. First among these discoveries was John Ross's encounter in 1818 with a small group of Inuit in Northwestern Greenland whom Ross named "Arctic Highlanders" and who apparently regarded themselves as the only people in the world. An outstanding feature of this contact with the Polar Eskimos was their relative unconcern for European iron objects, which as we have seen dominated encounters with other Greenland Inuit and in the Canadian Arctic. Ross attributed this to their possession of artifacts made from meteoric iron. On the other hand, they were very covetous of wooden objects, and quickly overcame their initial fears and caution by aggressively attempting to steal such objects. Ross's description of their material culture, which included narwhal-tusk harpoons and sleds made of whale bone, attests to the absence of wood in the region.

Exploration and contacts along the ice-choked east coast of Greenland lagged behind those of the west coast. In 1823 Captain D. C. Clavering met briefly with Inuit in the far northeast, but this group was never again encountered. Farther south, however, contact between East Greenlanders and their western neighbors had been taking place for some years around the south end of the island. This contact appears to have been broken off shortly before first direct European contact, which is recorded by Holm, who wrote an ethnography of the people of the Ammassalik region of the east coast based on his visit in 1884–5.

As Helge Kleivan points out, a hybrid culture "grew to fill the vacuum left by intensive missionary work that had obliterated traditional Eskimo intellectual culture, or for the time at least, had driven it underground."[19] Establishment of a teacher's college for training Greenlandic catechists in Godthab in 1845 "contributed profoundly to formation and dissemination of a homogeneous colonial intellectual culture," since the curriculum included not only religious subjects but also world history, zoology, and geography. Another important event was the establishment of the periodical *Atuagagdliutit*, which was published in Greenlandic and provided the seeds of a Greenlandic literature that was to flourish in the twentieth century. Homogenization of local cultures was brought about by training teachers from west Greenland, who worked in outlying regions and estab-

---

[19] Helge Kleivan, "Greenland Eskimo: Introduction," in Damas, ed., *Arctic*, 524–5.

lished the west Greenlandic dialect as the lingua franca of the whole island. Self-identity of Greenlanders as *Kalaallit* had already emerged by the end of the eighteenth century, and these later developments served to strengthen the idea of a single people sharing common causes, rather than the local identification with the *-miut* suffix, which generally among the Inuit refers to vaguely defined local populations.

Throughout the nineteenth century, the Danish administration continued to adhere to its policies of maintaining a hunting economy as the principal Native industry and excluding foreign elements from trade and other contacts. Although some efforts were made to develop commercial fishing, the results were indifferent. Gad concludes that "At the end of the nineteenth century, the economy of West Greenland had still not been straightened out, and at the same time, there was political stagnation in Denmark."[20]

Labrador: technological change and hybrid cultures

With the establishment of the Moravians as traders as well as proselytizers along the Labrador coast in the late eighteenth century, Inuit trading journeys to the south ceased about 1800. The missionaries were reluctant to trade firearms at the beginning of their stay in the region, because of the extent of warfare that had ravaged the coast. As pacification was achieved, and with trade in firearms already established between ships along the northern part of the coast and the unconverted Natives who lived there, this restriction was lifted.

The Moravian mission operated on a profit-making basis in its trade with the Inuit, the profits to be used in support of Moravian missions elsewhere in the world. After 1830, however, competition came with the advent of a group that was to become known as the Settlers. These largely English immigrants settled at various points among the inner fjords, and their presence was regarded with considerable anxiety by the Moravians. While the missionaries played down the question of competition in trade, they regarded the Settlers as a morally disruptive force, especially with regard to their sale of alcoholic beverages to the Inuit. In time, however, the Settlers were incorporated into the Moravian congregations. By that time their orientation had shifted from trading to hunting and fishing. The Settlers tended to identify themselves as

[20] Gad, "History of Colonial Greenland," 569.

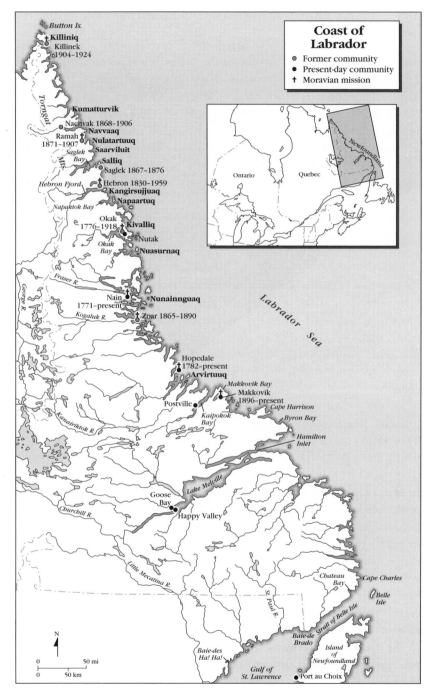

Figure 14.5 Coast of Labrador, showing dates of founding (and closing) of
settlements and present-day communities.

"Whites" and were dubbed *kablunanajok* (*qablunaayuq*) or "one who resembles a white man" by the Inuit. After initial intermarriage with Inuit women, they practiced a high degree of group endogamy. Throughout the nineteenth century Settlers strove to maintain a separate society. After being admitted into the Moravian congregation, special services were held for them in English, while the Inuit were addressed in their own language, which had been encouraged and maintained by the missionaries as part of their general philosophy of cultural preservation. This policy, of course, excluded certain pagan practices, such as polygyny, traditional dances, and shamanism. The education of Settler children actually lagged behind that of the Inuit during the nineteenth century, due largely to their scattered settlement and inaccessibility to centers of habitation.

Relations between the Inuit of coastal Labrador and the Indians of the interior had been warlike from precontact times onward, although there were some indications of rapprochement during the nineteenth century. Hostilities had been promoted by the alliance of French with Indians, which included supplying firearms to the latter. Once they had firearms, the Inuit ranged farther inland. By 1800 these journeys resulted in chance encounters with the Indians, which in time took on a peaceful character.

By the second half of the nineteenth century, the rich coastal fishing grounds began to be heavily exploited by Newfoundland fishermen. They sailed north in their schooners just before the breakup of ice each spring to compete for the best fishing grounds as the ice dispersed from the fjords. The mission at Hopedale reported that 400 schooners had been working in that vicinity in the summer of 1869. In the latter part of the century, these numbers increased, and it has been estimated that, between late June and early October, about 30,000 fishermen in 1,000 to 1,200 vessels cruised the coast annually. While the missions deplored the presence of so many outsiders, whom they regarded as morally depraved, relations between the fishermen and the Inuit appear to have been largely harmonious, despite competition for the same fish stocks, especially the cod. The Inuit were especially enthusiastic about the presence of new sources of trade and the gifts which the fishermen brought to the country. There was a certain amount of fraternization between the two groups in Inuit summer camps that were remote from mission influence. For instance, the Newfoundlanders sometimes joined in Inuit dances. Some genetic interchange doubtlessly occurred during this period as well. Population estimates of those classed as Inuit range from 1,625 for 1773 to 806 for 1829, with an apparent recovery from the epidemics of the early part of the century to 1,065 in 1840, and a relatively stable population, ranging from about 1,000 to a little over 1,300, during the remainder of the century. Fluctuations within that range reflected serious local population losses from epidemics. While the importance of contacts with Settlers, Indians, and the Newfoundland fishermen during the nineteenth century may be underrated, it is clear that in most phases of Inuit life in Labrador, the Moravian church still maintained its hegemony and would continue to do so into the next century.

The Hudson Bay region in the nineteenth century

Travel for trade eastward from Hudson Strait and the east coast of Hudson Bay may have taken place as early as 1750, and certainly did after 1830, when Fort Chimo was established in Ungava Bay. This post was closed between 1842 and 1866 due to lack of trade, although trade there resumed again later. Other trade contacts began in 1750 with the founding of a post at Richmond Gulf, about halfway down the east coast of Hudson Bay, which it was hoped could exploit the mine deposits believed to exist there. But neither this search for minerals nor fur trading was successful, and the post was moved south to the margins of Inuit country at Little Whale River in 1756. It was only after moving to the site of Great Whale River in 1837 that trading became permanently established along the coast.

The west shore of Hudson Bay saw the emergence of the Caribou Eskimo, with an inland adaptation that was unusual for Inuit. The annual trips of Hudson's Bay Company sloops northward from Churchill had ceased before the end of the eighteenth century, and about that time the coastal areas were mainly deserted as sites of year-round habitation. The reasons for the strong inland orientation, which characterized settlement after that time, are uncertain. It has been variously attributed to the wide use of guns and nets, which made survival in the interior practicable, the shallowing of seas which may have impeded seal hunting along the west coast, and the desertion of the Keewatin interior by the Chipewyans, whose numbers were decimated by smallpox. Probably a combination of some or all of these factors operated to create the predominately inland orientation that was to endure well into the twentieth century.

Inuit and explorers: the search for the Northwest Passage

While early European exploration of the North American Arctic had been stimulated by the hope of finding a commercially feasible route to the Orient, by the nineteenth century this goal had been largely abandoned. Instead, the concern shifted to charting the boreal coastline of the continent, though prizes were also offered for the navigation of the Northwest Passage. In the course of these explorations, contacts were made with Inuit which, although in many cases of a fleeting nature, supplied information about the locations and customs of those people.

The accounts of Captains William Parry and George Lyon from their expedition of 1821–3 provided the best insights into the life of the Inuit of the vast Central Arctic regions that had yet appeared. While wintering first at Winter Island, at the base of Melville Peninsula, and later at Iglulik, at its north end, Parry and Lyon had opportunities to observe the life of the group later known as the Iglulik Eskimos. Lyon gives an especially detailed account of these contacts. We learn of the seasonal hunting at breathing holes in winter, and the great emphasis on sea-mammal hunting year-round, of the capture of walrus and beluga, and the importance of caribou hides for clothing. The construction and use of the domed snowhouse was also described, as was the use of dogs for winter traction. The kayak was again described in detail as had been the case for Inuit to the east. Lyon especially fraternized with the Inuit of the region, often sharing his cabin with them. He provides us with numerous impressions of Inuit character, praising their honesty above all other traits. Incidents of theft were few and easily forgiven by the captains of the *Fury* and *Hecla*. Lyon deplored the tendency for the Inuit to beg from the ships before energetically pursuing the hunt, but it would be unrealistic to expect that the Inuit should be driven by a work ethic when sumptuously supplied ships were close at hand and the generosity of the English had already been demonstrated. Lyon and Parry were shocked at the libertine sexual mores of the Iglulik Eskimos, as well as by their apparent indifference to the suffering of the sick and aged, and by what the Europeans conceived of as their callousness regarding death and the deceased. Lyon also depicted them as being exceedingly envious of one another and was deeply disappointed at what he perceived as their extreme lack of gratitude. But he was also impressed by the affection often shown between husband and wife and, especially, that shown to children.

While Parry and Lyon were trying vainly to navigate the Northwest Passage by ship, Sir John Franklin had commenced his overland explorations far to the west. During the course of his expedition of 1819–22, when he explored from the mouth of the Coppermine River eastward, he saw Inuit near Bloody Falls, but they fled on his approach. During his second expedition, of 1825–7, Franklin's initial encounter with the Mackenzie Eskimos was decidedly unpleasant. The Inuit were aggressively thievish and treacherous in their dealings. This behavior was later rationalized by the Natives on his return trip, when better relations had been established, by their being unable to resist the presence of so many valuable articles in the boats of the expedition. Ironically, Franklin had planned to distribute gifts in order to ensure his peaceful passage through the region. The eastern detachment of this expedition, under John Richardson, also met with thievish attacks on their boats by Mackenzie people, and bloodshed was avoided only by considerable restraint and coolness exercised on the part of the English. As Franklin moved westward from the Mackenzie delta, he encountered Inuit who were more peacefully disposed. These people had been engaged in trade with the Inuit of northwestern Alaska as well as with Indians who traveled north to the coast for the purposes of trade. These contacts thus identified two routes by which articles from Siberia were reaching the Arctic coast of northeastern Alaska and the Mackenzie region. Stefansson thought that such material was actually moved as far east as Hudson Bay during the nineteenth century.

While Franklin's explorations reached westward along the uninhabited coast of northern Alaska, Frederick Beechey's expedition in the ship *Blossom* proceeded northward and eastward from the northwestern corner of the continent in an unsuccessful attempt to establish contact with him. The Beechey expedition advanced as far east as Point Barrow in 1826, before the hostile actions of Natives forced a retreat. A notable feature of this expedition was the collection of a number of Inuit artifacts. When the *Blossom* returned to the Kotzebue region, the temptation of salvage was too much for the Inuit, and their aggressive actions resulted in a sequence of attacks which led to the death of one Native.

The Russian expedition under A. F. Kashevarov[21] explored the same northwestern region of Alaska in 1838, and received a friendly reception

[21] James W. VanStone, "A. F. Kashevarov's Coastal Explorations in Northwest Alaska, 1838," David H. Kraus, trans., *Fieldiana: Anthropology*, 69 (1977).

until it reached the vicinity of Wainwright, when thievery was again experienced. Aside from describing unfortunate contacts with the Inuit of northwestern Alaska, Kashevarov's account, which is much more complete than those of earlier visitors to the region, is notable for its description of Inuit customs. It contains details of hunting practices, clothing, and housing.

The expedition of Sir John Ross of 1829–33 penetrated the area of the Central Eskimos. Three winters spent in their country produced lively contacts and the first descriptions of one of the most inaccessible groups, the Netsiliks. While the Netsiliks were not hostile or aggressive in their contacts with the English, theft was occasionally a problem. Ross's impressions of the Netsiliks were generally more favorable than Lyon's concerning the Igluliks. While Lyon's observations were balanced or at least mixed, Ross's were almost totally positive. For instance, the indifference shown the aged and the envy and lack of gratitude which Lyon had described were denied by Ross in his account of the Netsiliks.

In assessing such varying depictions of Inuit, the possible subjectivity of the observers as well as regional variations in Inuit character must be considered. On balance, the encounters of these two expeditions with the Inuit of the Central Arctic were more peaceful than those experienced by European explorers in the eastern and western sections of Inuit country. The Ross expedition was notable for the work of the captain's nephew, James Clark Ross, who adopted dog sleds, fur clothing, and camping in snowhouses on his explorations, which commenced in the month of April, well before a season earlier thought feasible. While the trade items and gifts which reached the Inuit through expeditions such as those of Parry and Ross were in the long run of little significance, the abandonment of Ross's *Victory* in Netsilik country not only was a boon in metal and wood to people who had been previously all but lacking in these commodities, but also stimulated intergroup trade. Other exploratory trips which resulted in brief contacts with the Inuit of the Central Arctic include that of George Back in 1834 to the mouth of the river which now bears his name. In trying to navigate the Northwest Passage, the two ships of Sir John Franklin, the *Erebus* and the *Terror,* were imprisoned by ice in Victoria Strait in 1846, and the great explorer died the next spring. The next year, 1848, saw the demise of the entire crews of the two ships, a tragic episode that was, in part, witnessed by Netsiliks as the men trudged south and east along the coasts of King William Island.

Inuit and explorers: the search for Franklin

The three-year absence of Franklin's expedition had by 1848 instituted the search that was to dominate the exploration of the Central Arctic for the next several decades and to result in further contacts between Inuit and Europeans. Richardson returned to the regions where he had traveled more than two decades before, this time in the company of John Rae. Remembering his earlier experiences, Richardson took special precautions when a large group of Mackenzie Eskimos approached his boats in kayaks and umiaks, but nevertheless experienced further unpleasantries. After some peaceful trading his boats were grabbed by kayakers and the English were forced to fire on them. Brief contact was made with Copper Eskimos that summer by Richardson and Rae. Over the next two summers, Rae explored the mainland and southern coast of Victoria Island for traces of Franklin, but because of the seasonal cycle, which found the Inuit inland in summer, he had few encounters with the Natives of those regions. One encounter is, however, notable. When Rae gave presents to Inuit he met along the south coast of Victoria Island, they could not believe that no return was expected. Rae also revisited caches he had established and observed that, though they likely had been discovered by Inuit, they had not been molested.

Beginning in the early 1850s, ships entered from both Atlantic and Pacific approaches in search of the missing seamen of the *Erebus* and *Terror*. From the west, the joint expedition of Robert McClure in the *Investigator* and Richard Collinson in the *Endeavour* passed Point Barrow in the summer of 1850. Collinson spent the next winter near the present Canadian-Alaskan border, where he and his men experienced a year of constant struggle with the Mackenzie Eskimos, who proved to be as aggressive and thievish as they had been in encounters with previous exploratory parties. Meanwhile McClure had entered Prince of Wales Strait before wintering on Victoria Island, where there were some meetings with Copper Eskimos. More importantly, the summer of 1852 saw his navigation of the west and north shores of Bank's Island, followed by abandonment of the *Investigator* in 1854. This led to the eventual discovery of the ship by the Copper Eskimos, who thereafter for a number of years traveled to it for metal and wood.

Collinson wintered near the place that McClure had visited the year previously and made brief observations of the Inuit. In the following summer, 1852, his ship followed the south coast of Victoria Island and in one encounter the English experienced the same disbelief on the part of the

Inuit regarding receipt of gifts without recompense that Rae had earlier. It is not surprising to one who has studied the exchange systems of the Copper Eskimos that such would have been the response, since among themselves some very definite systems of balanced reciprocity were practiced. Collinson's *Endeavour* spent the winter of 1852–3 in the vicinity of Cambridge Bay and, from accounts of contacts in this center of Inuit activity, one is able to piece together the outlines of a seasonal cycle, which included breathing-hole sealing on the ice of Dease Strait in winter and caribou hunting, especially during the autumn migration. Collinson reports that he met with "a kind-hearted and well-disposed people,"[22] whose diet was mainly fish, which were abundant in both the sea and lakes of the region.

While a number of the search expeditions ranged far to the north of Inuit country and indeed well beyond the route of Franklin's ill-fated journey, others, notably those of Rae in 1853–4, Leopold McClintock in 1857–9, Charles Francis Hall in 1864–9, and Frederick Schwatka, in 1878–9, entered the immediate region of the demise of the Franklin expedition and brought back relics long after hope of rescue had been abandoned. But very little was learned about the inhabitants beyond what Ross had produced, except for brief references to locations of groups and the game hunted at certain seasons.

Inuit and explorers: an assessment

During the "age of exploration" that occupied much of the nineteenth century, a number of contacts had been made with various groups of Inuit in the central and western Arctic. The outlines of the distribution of the various groups were recorded as well as some often lively, but usually uneven, descriptions of their customs. European goods and supplies were carried and dispersed through trade or gift-giving by the explorers, but not in great quantities, and they served mainly to establish rapport rather than to initiate or extend commercial relations. Items received from the Inuit consisted mostly of food and clothing, together with some ethnological artifacts.

A number of hostile clashes and other unpleasant incidents occurred between explorers and Inuit, especially in the western American Arctic,

---

[22] Richard Collinson, *Journal of H.M.S. Enterprise, on the Expedition in Search of Sir John Franklin's Ships by Behring Strait, 1850–1855*, ed. T. B. Collinson (London, 1889), 285.

which were reminiscent of early contacts in Greenland, Baffin Island, and Labrador. There is little evidence of actions on the part of the nineteenth-century explorers that could be said to have justified them. It is not easy to explain why contacts of a hostile nature took place with greater frequency in the eastern and western Arctic than in the Central Arctic. Perhaps relative numbers of Inuit and Europeans account in some measure for this contrast. Very often, in the more densely populated western regions small crews of boats were overwhelmed by large numbers of kayakers. The aggressive and even warlike nature of the Mackenzie Eskimos can perhaps to some extent be linked to the virtually constant state of conflict between them and neighboring Indians, especially the Kutchins.

Nineteenth-century exploration resulted in the emergence of individual Inuit from among the faceless multitude that appears in earlier accounts. Sir John Ross provided several detailed sketches of individual Netsiliks, and Lyon distinguished clearly among the personal characteristics of a number of named individuals. Most notable of these individuals were the interpreter-hunters hired by the explorers. The Hudson Bay region Natives, Augustus and Ooligbuck, who accompanied Franklin's first two expeditions, are examples, as is the Greenlander Hans Hendrick, who accompanied the expeditions of Elisha Kane, Isaac Hayes, C. F. Hall, and George Nares to the north. The Labradorean, Johann August Miertsching, a Moravian convert, served with McClure, and the Baffinlander Ebierbing (Joe) and his wife Hannah took part in no fewer than five Arctic expeditions. These Inuit served the explorers to whom they were attached with loyalty and dedication and often demonstrated considerable bravery in meetings with strange peoples. Accounts depict them as individuals who combined all the Christian virtues with the skill and knowledge vital to survival in the Arctic that one would expect of traditional northern Natives.

Inuit and whalers

While Basque and Dutch whalers had operated in Labrador, Greenland, and eastern Baffin Bay as early as the sixteenth century, by the middle of the eighteenth century this activity had fallen off. By 1820, English whalers had expanded their operations to the west side of Davis Strait and Baffin Bay with renewed success. Whales, killed or wounded but not recovered, drifted ashore on Baffin Island and were eagerly salvaged by the Inuit for their meat and blubber. W. G. Ross suggests that numbers of wrecks of whaling ships also must have provided useful materials.[23] The regions of most important whaling activity at this time were around Pond Inlet in the north and Cumberland Sound farther south. But it was only after about 1850, when Scottish whalers established shore stations in the latter locale, that direct contacts with Inuit were regularized. By the time Boas visited the region for his geographical and ethnological investigations in 1883–4, activities at these stations had already declined because of the diminishing number of whales. The use of firearms over a thirty-year period did not appear to have resulted in any drastic reduction of game, but had enhanced the number of animals that were being taken. Caribou were by then hunted year-round, and the use of traded whaleboats had apparently increased the capture of sea mammals. Trade with groups not in direct contact with the whalers also seems to have been stimulated.

The northwestern Hudson Bay region of Roes Welcome Sound became the chief locus of whaling activity after 1860, as substantial stocks were discovered there. Overwintering of American whaling vessels resulted in yearly contacts with the Inuit that extended into the twentieth century. These contacts brought about the relocation of people, including the southward movement of the Aivilingmiut, as well as a shift in the ranges of a number of Netsiliks who migrated there from their traditional hunting grounds around Boothia Peninsula and King William Island. The Aivilingmiut in particular adopted an annual pattern of camping around ships frozen in for winter. Inuit men hunted at the floe edge for sea-mammal meat and blubber and in the interior for caribou meat and for musk-oxen hides, which were sold as carriage robes in the south. Women acted as seamstresses to provide warm winter clothing for the sailors. In the spring and summer, Inuit men also helped to crew the boats engaged in whale hunting. Payment for such services usually took the form of whaleboats, firearms, and metal tools. There was, as well, the beginnings of a trade in white fox furs. While there was genetic interchange as a result of these contacts with nineteenth-century whalers in the eastern Arctic, and while various diseases were introduced, there is no clear evidence for large-scale depopulation. Those Inuit who camped around the wintering vessels or

[23] W. Gillies Ross, "Commercial Whaling and Eskimos in the Eastern Canadian Arctic 1819–1920," *National Museum of Man, Archaeological Survey of Canada, Paper* 99 (1979), 251–2.

had direct contact with whaling stations in the east-central Arctic benefited most directly from the flow of goods, but others traded with them
and goods diffused some distance from these centers. These goods probably did not make major changes in the economy or cultures of these
more remote groups. For example, firearms could pass from group to
group, but steady supplies of ammunition were necessary for them to
make a substantial impact on hunting, and these supplies could not be
provided on a regular basis, except in the immediate vicinity of the
ships. Large areas and significant numbers of Central Eskimos continued
to be unaffected by the presence of whalers on Baffin Island and in the
Hudson Bay region during this whaling period.

Whaling activity in the western Arctic commenced later than in the east,
but, by 1848, American whalers were operating with great success in the
Chukchi Sea, and, by 1854, in the Point Barrow region. After 1889,
Herschel Island was the favorite overwintering site, and between that year
and 1906, when the industry collapsed, as many as fifteen ships were frozen-
in there between whaling seasons. While highly generalized depictions of
Inuit-European contacts have stressed "domination," "destruction," "exploitation," "demoralization," and depopulation, these interpretations are in
many cases greatly distorted and overgeneralized. For western Arctic whaling, however, such depictions have strong bases in fact. Whalemen crews
were recruited from many parts of the world and, whether they were "black-
birded" from Pacific islands or "shanghaied" in the saloons of San Francisco,
many served unwillingly and their selection was not designed to produce a
seaman elite. The crews are described as having been "as hardy, brave,
lecherous, and murderous a collection of toughs as ever walked the earth or
sailed the seven seas." Alex Stevenson contrasts the nature of contact around
Herschel Island with that of the Hudson Bay region: "The week long orgies
after the arrival of the fleet are a striking contrast to the conduct of American
whalers operating in Hudson Bay, in the eastern Arctic."[24] The most dramatic testimony to the traumatic nature of the contact of the Mackenzie
Eskimos with this whaler element is the drastic decline in their numbers.
Mid-nineteenth-century population estimates range from 2,000 to 2,500;
by the end of the whaling period only 200 to 300 remained of the bold and
aggressive people who had hampered exploration and terrorized their Indian
neighbors.

---

[24] Alex Stevenson, "Lawless Land," *North* 16/1 (1969), 29; "Whaler's Wait," *North* 15/5 (1968), 28.

THE EARLY TWENTIETH CENTURY: STABILIZATION
AND RETRENCHMENT

*Greenland: expansion into the hinterland, legislative reform, and
economic experiments*

The west coast of Greenland continued to be the administrative, cultural, and economic focus of Greenland society, and the extension of its influence into the more remote regions had begun by the end of the nineteenth and beginning of the twentieth century. While a mission and store had been established in East Greenland in 1894, it was only in 1904 that a school was founded at Ammassalik; hence the region lagged behind in achievement of full literacy in Greenlandic. East Greenland was administered directly from Denmark, but provisions for medical care were less advanced for many years than was the case for the west coast; the first nurse arrived as late as 1932, and the first resident physician only in 1940. In 1925 a colonization scheme moved a number of people north to the Scoresby Sound region.[25] This proved a fortunate venture, for the region was one of superior marine resources, and in addition, local coal deposits provided an important source of fuel. Both of these East Greenland communities continued on a largely subsistence basis, with trade in skins and furs, especially sealskins, providing the only source of European goods.

The Polar Eskimos of northwestern Greenland remained relatively autonomous and isolated into the twentieth century.[26] Travel over Melville Sound to the Upernavik region, initiated by the Danish Literary Expedition in 1904, resulted in some trade, cultural interchange, and intermarriage. Establishment of a trading post at Thule by the explorer-ethnologist Knud Rasmussen provided a steadier supply of European goods to the region after 1910 and a Lutheran mission began nearby in 1909, but conversion of the Natives was not complete until 1934. The influence of Rasmussen continued until his death in 1933. While he sought to maintain the hunting economy and as much of the traditional culture as was practicable, he also instituted a system of local government, which included the few Danish residents as well as men from the Native community. The Danish administration did not assert itself in the region until 1937.

[25] Robert Petersen, "East Greenland before 1950," in Damas, ed., *Arctic*, 622.
[26] Rolf Gilberg, "Polar Eskimo," in Damas, ed., *Arctic*.

Farther south on the west coast, in the centers of population, legislative measures affected the lives of Greenlanders. The Greenland Church and School Act of 1905 ensured that schooling remained firmly in the hands of the Lutheran Church. The Moravians had withdrawn from Greenland in 1900. The Act also provided that the Royal Greenland Trade Commission continue to regulate commerce. But the Administration and Trade Act of 1908 sought to separate the functions of administration and trade by establishing separate commissions. This plan failed, and, by 1912, the two departments were merged under a single director. Other aspects of the Act of 1908 continued in force. Foremost was establishment of municipal councils, which were composed entirely of Greenlanders. These bodies were charged with settling local disputes not concerning Danish residents. The councils also administered new sources of funds, which were secured by a 20 percent tax paid by the Royal Greenland Trade Commission on its Greenland exports and a 2 percent tax on salaries of all residents who earned wages.[27]

The early years of the twentieth century also saw some important changes in the economy of the west coast. A warming trend extended the ranges of Subarctic or temperate zone fishes, such as cod and halibut, northward, with a concomitant shift of sealing regions farther to the north. These conditions brought on an increase in commercial as well as subsistence fishing along parts of the coast that were affected. Sheep raising, an occupation that had been practiced by the Norse, was revived in the eighteenth century, and considerably expanded in the early twentieth century. That industry remained a risky business, susceptible to the effects of severe winters even in southernmost regions of Greenland. Fox farming was introduced in 1913, but, as a result of the collapse of the fur market after 1930, it did not prove highly successful.

The most significant legislation in the first half of the twentieth century was the Act of the Administration of Greenland of April 18, 1925, which organized administrative districts and defined voting rights as well as eligibility for office for both Greenlanders and Danish residents. It also required compulsory education for children aged seven to fourteen, but schooling opportunities beyond that level remained few. Health facilities and administration of justice were also provided. Industries which had been or were to be developed in Greenland were to operate on a self-financing basis. Indeed, throughout the first half of the century, only modest support flowed into

[27] Gad, "History of Colonial Greenland," 570.

Greenland from Denmark, mainly in the form of Old Age Security payments. Protectionism continued, as foreign commodities which were regarded as being harmful, especially alcohol, were officially denied to Greenlanders. Education remained in the hands of the Lutheran church and Greenlandic continued to be the language of instruction.

While the economy followed an uneven course and was severely affected by the worldwide depression in the 1930s, national identity continued to develop, especially as a result of the growth of a Greenlandic written literature. This literature had begun during the nineteenth century with the publication of a newspaper in Greenlandic, but now flourished in mediums such as the theater, novels, poetry, and songs, and largely freed itself from the primary concern with Christian religious themes that had characterized the inception of the movement.

Labrador: the decline of Moravian hegemony[28]

By the beginning of the twentieth century, cod fishing had become an occupation of primary importance for Inuit as well as Settlers along the coast of Labrador. It provided a steadier source of income than did the fur trade, while subsistence fishing and sealing continued as other important economic pursuits. By 1900, the gulf between the growing material wants of the population and the means for satisfying them had reached crucial proportions. While the mission stations continued as the chief trading corporation, problems of mismanagement and the desire to continue on a profit-making basis were undermining the effectiveness of the trade and its service to the Inuit and the Settlers. The mission stations sought to control acculturation by limiting wares to what they regarded as necessities and discouraging "luxury" products. The initial desire for a wider variety of goods by the Inuit soon resulted in considerable debts and eventually in the tightening of credit. The failure to resolve these problems caused the Moravians to withdraw from trade, which they relinquished to the Hudson's Bay Company. In 1926 a special agreement was drawn up with the Newfoundland government by which the Hudson's Bay Company was given the right to import its stock of goods without paying duty. In return, the company was to be charged with the responsibility for administering public relief. By 1934 the relief provision was

---

[28] The following is based on Helge Kleivan, *The Eskimos of Northeast Labrador: A History of Eskimo-White Relations, 1771–1955* (Oslo, 1966).

withdrawn from the Hudson's Bay Company, and, beginning the next year, social assistance was issued by the Newfoundland Rangers, a policing body which entered Labrador at that time.

There was little interest in commercial fishing or the sale of sealskins during the period of Hudson's Bay Company involvement. The company encouraged subsistence hunting and fishing during the summer in order that men and their dogs would be supplied with stored food during the trapping season. This made more time available for trapping the white fox during the winter season. The Hudson's Bay Company exercised a firmer control over trade in white fox pelts than had the Moravians during their period of trading dominance, since by the 1920s competition from trading schooners plying the coast had diminished greatly. The prices for furs dropped dramatically during the Great Depression of the 1930s and there were fluctuations in the supply of furbearers; hence trapping had become an unsteady source of income by the beginning of World War II.

Traders, police, and missionaries in the central and western Arctic[29]

The trade in white fox pelts, which was to become the chief basis of connection with the outside economy in the vast regions of the Central Arctic, had its start during the whaling period, but only in that period's dying phases, after the beginning of the twentieth century. Between 1900 and 1915, 3,924 fox furs were traded to whalers in the eastern Canadian Arctic. This number was equaled or surpassed in certain years at single Hudson's Bay Company posts after the trade had been fully established. It was only when trading posts had been founded within the ranges of various Inuit groups that the industry flourished.

Between 1911 and 1923, a string of posts from southern to northern Baffin Island and on both shores of Hudson Bay were supplied from the east. In the Mackenzie delta and eastward to King William Island, posts were supplied from the west. With very few exceptions, they made trade accessible to all the Inuit groups of Arctic Canada. The fur trade peaked, along with prices, during the 1920s, and in that decade a large number of firms competed for white fox pelts. During the depression years, however, as a result of declining prices most of the companies folded, and by the end of that period the Hudson's Bay Company almost fully controlled that

[29] The following is based on David Damas, "The Contact-Traditional Horizon of the Central Arctic: Reassessment of a Concept and Re-examination of an Era," *Arctic Anthropology* 25/2 (1988), 101–38.

trade in Arctic Canada. In some locales, the Hudson's Bay managers issued government-derived relief rations and supplies as well as medical aid. The regular supply of rifles, ammunition, nets, wooden boats, and steel traps encouraged a spiral of economic and social change. Changes in extractive techniques also altered seasonal patterns of hunting. In some regions where breathing-hole sealing had been the only dependable source of winter subsistence, floe edge and waterhole-sealing with rifles was now possible. More successful sea-mammal hunting was also possible in summer from wooden boats, using rifles. Elsewhere, where large migratory herds of caribou appeared, hunting was especially enhanced by the use of rifles, and some formerly coastal people moved inland each winter. The adoption of new hunting methods and the incorporation of trapping into the economy were largely responsible for major changes in settlement. Instead of large winter aggregations on the sea ice associated with breathing-hole sealing, or similar aggregations at fishing sites or caribou drives, with dispersal into small nomadic hunting groups for much of the summer season, a new pattern emerged. This was the advent of small, usually sedentary, hunting-trapping sites, from which hunting excursions and trips to traps radiated. Large aggregations now occurred at the points of trade, usually at Christmas and the end of the trapping season, while periodic trips to the posts for trade were usually made by the men alone.

Another important agency, the North-West Mounted Police (after 1920, the Royal Canadian Mounted Police), entered the Canadian Arctic during the same period. In the nodal whaling locales of northwestern Hudson Bay and Herschel Island they actually preceded the traders. Their goal was to enforce game laws, to ensure fair trading practices between whalers and Inuit, and, especially in the case of Herschel Island, to control the riotous behavior which accompanied the presence of whalers. Beginning in 1921, the Council of the Northwest Territories met on a regular basis in Ottawa in order to establish and maintain policies and regulations in the Canadian North. A ban against musk-oxen hunting had existed since 1917 and attempts were later made with less success to enforce closed seasons for caribou. As early as 1922, the council established licensing "except for natives or half-breeds except when hunting for others." The council also regulated opening and closing of trading posts. In general, it tried to keep in communication with whatever problems arose in the North, but, in reality the Royal Canadian Mounted Police were the only effective agents of the government. In addition to enforcing game and other laws, their duties included taking censuses, ascertaining conditions of life, issuing relief, and in some cases dispensing medical aid to the Inuit. These functions were carried out mainly in the course of annual dog sled patrols, which endeavored to reach all the villages and encampments within the region of each detachment. The overall application of southern Canadian laws and regulations, as well as the nature of punishment for offenders, were liberal and not oppressive.

Missionary activity had begun in 1894 on Baffin Island, with the Anglican Rev. E. J. Peck in the Cumberland Sound region. His translation of hymns and parts of the Bible into a syllabary spread a means of communication in the Inuit language throughout much of the east-central Arctic in subsequent years. A series of missions was established throughout the Canadian Arctic during the same period as the spread of trading posts, so that, by the mid-1920s, most Inuit groups in those regions had been exposed to the gospel either through the Roman Catholic faith, as dispensed by Oblate fathers, or by Anglican missionaries and catechists. Primacy of appearance in each district usually determined which of the two faiths was adopted, and subsequent conversions across the Protestant-Catholic boundary were few. It is most difficult to judge the depth of Christianization that was achieved during this period, and shamanism continued to exercise influence. What were conceived to be the immoral sexual practices of the Inuit, especially spouse exchange, were much deplored, as was infanticide, a practice that was also a concern of the Royal Canadian Mounted Police. There is evidence that these customs still occurred in the outlying camps or villages, which for the largest part of each year operated as relatively autonomous communities.

The fur traders also replaced whalers as the chief means of contact in northern and western Alaska. These regions were the source of migrations which repopulated the Mackenzie delta and surrounding regions, though numbers never were as high as they had been before the catastrophic influx of American whalers. The delta region was an important nodal locale for the fur trade, from northeastern Alaska to King William Island in Netsilik country. Not only did the Mackenzie River provide the conduit for most goods from the south from which the vessels belonging to small free traders and to the various major fur companies drew their supplies, but the delta itself was an area rich in furbearers, especially mink, beaver, and muskrat.

In northwestern Alaska, the gold rush encouraged relocations of some peoples to the vicinity of Nome, where there were some wage labor opportunities around the turn of the century and for a few years afterwards. The introduction of domesticated reindeer into that region, and eventually to the north coast and finally to the Mackenzie delta, provided a reliable source of food for large segments of the Inuit population of the western Arctic during the 1920s and 1930s. The eventual collapse of the reindeer industry resulted from a number of factors, including competition in Alaska by at least one large commercial firm, the reluctance of the Inuit to become fully committed herders, the desertion of some animals to join caribou herds, and failure to develop an export market. While reindeer provided meat and skins for local use, they never rivaled the fur trade as a source of income to purchase the equipment and supplies which had now become necessities. For North Alaska, policing activities were largely in the hands of the U.S. Department of the Treasury, Revenue Marine and confined to their summer cruises. Missions had been established in the Seward Peninsula region by the end of the nineteenth century, and while several Protestant denominations competed for converts, it was the Moravians who emerged as the dominant faith. As they had done in Labrador, the Moravians provided the beginnings of both medical and educational facilities in northwestern Alaska.

Summary: culture contact in the 1900–40 period

Shortly after the turn of the century, Greenland entered into a period of legislative changes as well as economic experiments designed to raise life on the island above a principally subsistence level. At the same time, the Danish administration sought to make this possession self-supporting. While the experiments in subsistence-plus activities enjoyed some success, they were eventually limited by the depression of the 1930s. Meanwhile, the sense of identity of Greenlanders, as a group of mixed racial and cultural composition, continued to strengthen and finally emerged as a definite nationality differentiated from Danish residents. On the Labrador coast the Moravian mission had ceded its economic control to the Hudson's Bay Company but retained its influence over education and health as well as religion. Commercial fishing activity gave way to an increased emphasis on the fur trade, which experienced a sharp decline during the depression years.[30]

In the Central Canadian Arctic, while police applied largely judicious and mild control over the lives of the Inuit and missionary activity was only partially successful in altering their religious beliefs, these agencies were important in dispensing medical and material aid. The fur trade brought

---

[30] Peter J. Usher, *Fur Trade Posts of the Northwest Territories, 1870–1970* (Ottawa, 1971), 28.

about more profound changes. The most obvious of these were economic in character, though the location of people was affected as well. While cases of starvation were rare during this period in the Central Arctic and reduced nomadism and improved subsistence facilities were positive changes, continued high rates of infant mortality and deaths from epidemics kept populations essentially level. Moreover, while there was no overall decline in game or success in hunts, there were good years and bad during this period, and in the latter cases survival was often made possible only through issuing rations.

Using population levels as a gauge of prosperity and general well-being, the picture for the Arctic as a whole during these years was an uneven one. Clearly the Greenlanders enjoyed superior health and living conditions; between 1900 and 1940 the population increased by nearly 50 percent. In Labrador there was only a slow recovery or possibly even a further decline from the slump that had occurred in the nineteenth century, for epidemics continued and medical facilities were still meager. In the population-depleted Mackenzie region, the influx of Alaskans did not nearly compensate for the demise of the original Inuit population. A number of these immigrants established themselves as trappers along the coast to the eastward. Indians, Euro-Canadians, and Métis together outnumbered the Inuit in the trading regions of the lower Mackenzie according to a 1941 census.[31] There appears to have been a drastic depopulation of the interior of Alaska and the region around Kotzebue Sound in the late nineteenth century, due apparently to famine, disease, and, in the case of the interior peoples, some migration to the coast. The Kotzebue region, however, showed a doubling of population during the forty-year period considered here and the coastal settlements of sea hunters to the north also showed increases, though it is not clear to what degree these swelling coastal populations were due to immigration from the interior.

WORLD WAR II AND ITS AFTERMATH: ENDING OF
ISOLATION AND THE SEEDS OF A NEW LIFE

Greenland: the slow evolution of social reform

Greenland assumed geopolitical importance during World War II as a result of its proximity to the shipping lanes which fed the Allied war

---

[31] "Population of the Mackenzie District: 1941," Department of Indian Affairs, Public Archives of Canada, RG85, vol. 64, file 19.

effort in Europe and the concomitant need for the United States to control air space in the North Atlantic. Under the Kauffman Treaty the United States was given the right to establish air bases in Greenland. With the occupation of Denmark by the Germans, administrative officers acted independently of the mother country, as had been provided for in the Administrative Law of 1925. Both U.S. and Canadian consulates were established in Godthab. A Northeast Greenland Sled Patrol, made up of Greenlanders, succeeded in routing a series of German weather stations which had been set up on the east coast to aid naval, especially U-boat, activities in the North Atlantic. The cryolite deposits in southern Greenland acquired great importance at this time because of their use in the manufacture of aluminum. A flood of new commodities entered the country through the American military presence. Gad notes that "the war had shown that Greenland could not exist in a military vacuum. Nor could it continue to be an economic vacuum. This criticism was gradually acknowledged politically."[32] Active implementation of programs that effectively improved conditions was, however, to take some years. The state of postwar Greenland was such that immediate cures would not be possible, for as Helge Kleivan indicates: "The socioeconomic conditions of 1945 were those of underdevelopment: there was widespread poverty, inadequate and unhygienic housing, an alarming health situation, and deteriorating possibilities for maintaining production technology. . . . This situation had developed over a very long period, despite the undeniable fact that Danish colonial rule had been marked by an unusually benevolent attitude."[33]

Inequality of status between Greenlanders and Danes was also marked. In 1946 a five-year plan for development was devised largely by people in Denmark who had little appreciation either of conditions in Greenland or of Greenlandic attitudes and aspirations. Political changes in Denmark under the Social Democratic party, which took office in 1947, brought more substantial progress through the appointment of the so-called "Big Commission," which was formed in 1948 and composed of four Danish and five Greenlandic representatives. This commission produced a voluminous report in 1950, the most immediate result of which was the G-50 plan instituted that year. The basic idea of the plan was to create a market for wage labor by developing a commercial fishing industry. The program

[32] Gad, "History of Colonial Greenland," 574.
[33] Helge Kleivan, "Contemporary Greenlanders," in Damas, ed., *Arctic*, 700.

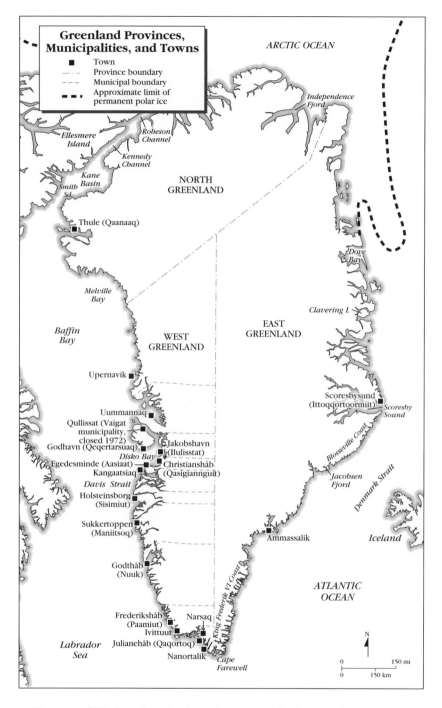

Figure 14.6 Modern Greenland provinces, municipalities, and towns.

also called for the relocation of large numbers of people from small settlements to the towns, which was to be accompanied by a massive housing program. One of the most substantial provisions of the G-50 plan was to abolish the monopoly of the Greenland Trade Commission and to open trade with countries other than Denmark. The plan had "a strange inconsistency" in that modernization, especially the massive housing program, was to be accomplished without the development of a program to train Greenlanders for skilled occupations. The result was an immediate and large-scale influx of Danes into Greenland. The inequality in occupations and pay between the two ethnic groups increased perceptions of social and economic inferiority on the part of Greenlanders.

On the political front, the Constitution of 1953 provided for abolition of colonial status for Greenland, which was incorporated into the Kingdom of Denmark with two seats in the Danish Parliament. But the equality implied by this legal act did not in fact materialize, as differences in occupational and pay levels persisted. Certain improvements in living conditions, especially in health care and housing, had been made in the 1950s. A reduction in mortality and a strong increase in fertility had occurred, but major changes in education and economic conditions were still on the horizon in 1960.

Labrador: temporary prosperity and the effects of confederation

The government of Newfoundland began to take a more active role in the affairs of coastal Labrador after the Hudson's Bay Company, "plagued by rising expenses and trade deficits," pulled out of the region in 1942. The trading operations were taken over by the Newfoundland Department of Natural Resources. World War II created a boom in the value of indigenous products, and wage labor opportunities grew for the Inuit and Settlers of the coast of Labrador. Prices for fox furs doubled, and the demand for codfish increased, although the prices of store products also rose. A number of men found employment in the construction of the American air base at Goose Bay and at expanded lumber operations in two locales.

These economic improvements were short-lived: "In the 1940s the administration and economy of Northern Labrador was in great disarray and undergoing considerable change."[34] Much of this flux was due to the

---

[34] Anne Brantenberg and Terje Brantenberg, "Coastal Northern Labrador after 1950," in Damas, ed., *Arctic*, 689.

declining influence of the Moravian missions and the withdrawal of the Hudson's Bay Company, combined with the rapid decline of wartime prosperity after fighting in Europe ceased. Major changes were to come after confederation with Canada in 1949, though a period of conflict over spheres of jurisdiction ensued between Ottawa and the Newfoundland government. The latter expanded its participation in areas of social welfare, and education was transferred from the Moravians, which led to a more secular curriculum. Both marine and air services were expanded and a telephone system installed. The economy, however, reverted to prewar conditions, with fishing and hunting for subsistence predominating. During the course of the 1950s, government-directed centralization of settlement removed most of the population from the northern sections of the coast. Part-time wage labor opportunities in the towns, centralization of schooling, availability of medical facilities, and lower prices for furs and sealskins were factors in this "urbanization." Changes of a more major character were to follow in the next decade.

Canada: wartime isolation and the advent of centralization

The vast areas of the Canadian Arctic were affected by a sharp rise in fox-fur prices about 1940. For a few years, this rise coincided with periods of ample supplies of fur. It was also a period of considerable isolation, except in Frobisher Bay and at Coral Harbor, on Southampton Island, where American air bases were established that brought the Inuit into increased contact with outsiders. Elsewhere the all-Native hunting-trapping camp focused on point-of-trade settlements continued throughout the war and for some years afterwards.[35]

The Hudson's Bay Company enjoyed an especially strong period of prosperity. The beginnings of increased Canadian government involvement came with the institution of the family allowance program, which was fully implemented in the Arctic by 1947. The influx of these funds, although small amounts by southern Canadian standards, significantly enhanced the income of the Inuit. These payments also came at a crucial juncture, in that there was another slump in fox-fur prices about the same time. During the late 1940s, income from family allowances outstripped that derived from the fur trade. The situation improved somewhat with rising fur prices after 1950, but soon other, more profound changes took place in Canada's North.

---

[35] Damas, "The Contact-Traditional Horizon."

While the period from full establishment of the fur trade throughout the central and eastern Arctic until about the middle 1950s had been one of stable relations between Inuit and the few non-Natives living in the area, as well as with the outside world, major changes occurred in these relations in the years that followed. These included the large-scale centralization of the Native population in a small number of communities. In some cases, construction opportunities, such as those associated with building of DEW line (military radar) sites, was a factor. In others, local game failures, especially a general decline in caribou, which took place during the 1950s and early 1960s, drew people to the newly forming centers. The always uncertain market of the fur trade and the expanding material wants of the Inuit were other factors. Certainly convenience of administering relief, medical, and educational programs was enhanced by this concentration. One of the chief problems that accompanied this centralization was unemployment, as it became apparent that in many locales subsistence hunting and the fur-trade work did not provide a sufficient economic base.[36]

A most important move designed to combat this problem was the growth of the Inuit art industry. Beginning at Cape Dorset at the extreme southwestern corner of Baffin Island, in 1949, and shortly thereafter at Povungnituk, on the east shore of Hudson Bay, Euro-Canadian agents introduced the industry in soapstone carvings (see also Chapter 15). Art had played little part in traditional Canadian Inuit culture, though during the latter part of the nineteenth century whalers had promoted carving in ivory. Formerly soapstone had been used only for lamps and cooking pots, but now, with this material being widely distributed and a market developing in southern Canada and elsewhere, soapstone carvings began to provide an important source of cash for a number of skilled carvers.

In the Mackenzie delta region trapping had replaced hunting as the chief economic pursuit in the 1920s and had continued as such even through periods of slumping fur prices in the 1930s and late 1940s. While drops in the value of furs were general throughout the North at these times, they were less dramatic in the case of muskrats, the most important quarry for trappers in the delta region, than with white fox. A rise in fur prices occurred briefly in the early fifties. Shortly afterwards, the new settlement of Inuvik was constructed. Thereafter, general failure

36 Frank G. Vallee, Derek G. Smith, and Joseph D. Cooper, "Contemporary Canadian Inuit," in Damas, ed., *Arctic*.

of the fur market helped to accelerate centralization in the delta, especially at Inuvik itself. While some hunting and trapping continued, radiating outward from such large population centers, a combination of wage labor earnings and the not insignificant influx of social legislation funds, principally family allowances and old age pensions, contributed more to the total economy.

Alaska: wartime prosperity and postwar readjustments

Alaska's involvement in World War II was much greater than that of Arctic Canada, especially because of the Japanese presence in the Aleutians. It also had far-reaching consequences for the lives of Native Alaskans, including the Inuit of the northern part of that territory. As Jenness remarks, "from Ketchikan to Point Barrow Alaska seethed with activity."[37] The most obvious and dramatic effect of the war on the Inuit of Alaska was the movement of men to military bases at Nome, Kotzebue, and Barrow. Construction and service occupations provided new sources of income for Native men, as did handicraft sales and fur clothing manufacture for women. Trapping, hunting, and herding receded as the most important work for many of the North Alaskan Natives. The process of centralization began with the war, but continued thereafter. Barrow's population grew from 363 in 1940, to 951 in 1950, and 1,274 in 1957. For Kotzebue, the figures for the same years were 372, 623, and 854.[38]

Responses to perceived inequalities in income and occupational levels, as well as probably racially motivated discrimination, stimulated the passage of the Anti-Discrimination Act of 1945 by the territorial legislature. While some sources perceive an improvement in interethnic relations as a result of this act, the picture is uneven. One tangible outcome of the law was the election of two Eskimo members to the territorial House of Representatives in 1948, but other benefits were not as immediately evident. Drunken behavior in the larger centers of population and excessive drinking lowered Inuit resistance to tuberculosis, which was the chief health problem at the time. Another, more persistent association was between poor Native health and inadequate housing. Housing projects included one at Point Barrow and a much more ambitious and regionally more comprehensive effort organized by the Alaska Housing Authority,

[37] Diamond Jenness, *Eskimo Administration, I: Alaska* (Montreal, 1962), 40.
[38] Ibid., 41.

which resulted in 990 houses being built in thirty villages. While these housing projects, which were designed to reduce the spread of disease and to increase general comfort, resulted in lowered death rates and rising birth rates, the battle against tuberculosis was to be won only after antibiotics became available some years later. Alaskan Natives, including the Inuit of the northern part of the territory (later to become a state), did not achieve a modern level of education during World War II or the decade and a half which followed. In 1950, 87 percent of Native children of school age were in school, but education did not usually extend beyond the sixth grade. By 1960, only a handful of Eskimos (including Inuit, Aleut, and Yuit) had received post-secondary education and only about one-fifth of these had graduated from colleges or universities.

THE 1960–1990 PERIOD: THE AWAKENING OF INUIT
POLITICAL CONSCIOUSNESS

Greenland: the emergence of the home rule "state"

The legislative actions of the 1950s, principally the G-50 plan and the Constitution of 1953, had achieved mainly symbolic improvements for the Greenlanders. The attendant frustrations resulted in the G-60 plan of 1960 which, however, perpetuated familiar contradictions. While the chief objective was to increase Greenlandic participation in the island's affairs, the improvements called for required further importation of Danish labor and management. For instance, the largest part of housing construction went to domiciles for the ever-growing transient Danish population. Both Greenlandic and Danish numbers continued to grow, but while Greenlanders increased 75 percent from 1948 to 1969, the Danish resident population rose 700 percent during that same period. While subsidization of Greenland had increased from 41 million to 567 million Danish Crowns, the rise in population largely canceled out actual improvements during that period. The population explosion also brought in its wake a number of social problems. With rising numbers of people, more housing, more medical facilities, more occupational opportunities, more training programs, and, ultimately, of course, a greater flow of monies from the mother country were needed. One possible solution to this population crisis was emigration to Denmark. In 1971 there were about 6,000 Greenlanders living in Denmark, amounting to about 15 percent of those still at home. Such relocation was usually only temporary, for schooling and other training. Birth control measures were introduced in the 1960s, and these led to a drop in births by 1964. Greenlandic women were a force in legalizing abortion which took place in Greenland in 1974, some time after it had been effected in Denmark.

The centralization of population in large centers was accelerated partly by Danish policies and partly by the attraction of "urban" living and the possibilities of wage employment. By 1981, nearly half the population lived in towns of 3,000 or over. This centralization and other acculturative factors resulted in increasing social ills of various kinds, including alcoholism, suicide, homicide, and an alarming prevalence of venereal disease, which has been estimated as 100 times higher than in Denmark. The presence of large numbers of single Danish men on the island doubtlessly accounted for an extremely high rate of illegitimate births, estimated at as high as 50 percent of all births from Greenlander mothers in some districts. The breakdown of the extended family system, which was encouraged by the program of separate family housing and emigration from village to town, resulted in both the economic and the emotional isolation of unmarried mothers, as well as the deterioration of the situation of the aged, another group who traditionally were accommodated within larger kinship units.

During the 1970s, a group of educated "young radicals" became active politically and started the first realistic moves toward achieving self-determination for Greenlanders. As in the past, when these radicals began to win seats in the Provincial Council, they acted as individuals, but soon actual Native political parties were formed, which quickly dominated Greenlandic politics. In 1971, the Siumut or "Forwards" movement began, which became a formal party in 1977. This group has been described as a moderate socialist party. Opposition came quickly with the appearance of the Atassut or "Connecting Link" party, which was regarded as "conservative-liberal" and had loose connections with the Social Democratic party in Denmark. Contemporaneous with the formation of Siumut as a party was the emergence of the Marxist Inuit Ataqatigiit or "Human Fellowship" party.

Even before it become an official party, Siumut dominated the impetus toward what was to become the Home Rule movement, and it was largely the pressures that its members applied that led to the formation of the Commission on Home Rule in 1975. This body submitted proposals which resulted in the Greenland Home Rule Act of November 29, 1978, implemented May 1, 1979. This act provided that authority over foreign relations, defense policy, and financial support would continue under Danish control, but that Greenlanders would have charge of local government, taxes, fishing, hunting, herding, vocational education, health services, rent control, and similar functions. Greenlandic was designated as the official language, but Danish would continue to be taught also. Ideally, subsidies from Denmark would be neither increased or decreased, but more importantly, transferrals of monies would be made as a lump sum, instead of being regulated according to the detailed system of allocated priorities formerly applied.

Major legislative reorganization resulted from the Home Rule Act. The Provincial Council was replaced by an assembly, the Landsting, which was made up entirely of popularly elected officials, with elections to be held every four years. In 1984 there were eleven members from the Siumut party, eleven from the Atassut, and three from Ataqatigiit. The success of the degree of self-government achieved by the Landsting was greeted with considerable surprise in many quarters, and Greenlandic politicians succeeded in controlling internal economic affairs as provided for by the Home Rule Act. However, ironically a small group of bureaucrats and politicians concentrated power in their hands and became isolated from the constituencies whose support their liberal, and partly left-wing, ideologies had been designed to win. In the mid-1980s, a local government official commented that "Greenland survives on artificial respiration from Denmark."[39]

Canada: regionalism and Inuit unity

The decade and a half that followed World War II had been a period of major adjustments brought about by a strong centralization of settlement in Labrador, northern Quebec, and the Northwest Territories, including the Mackenzie delta. After 1960, centralization intensified and was accompanied by a host of social and economic problems. In later years, diverse regional concerns, especially those relating to the emergence of politically significant divisions of Arctic Canada, stimulated the development of a number of Inuit organizations to deal with these problems. At the same time, recognition of problems which were common to the whole area encouraged increasing communication among the Inuit of the entire Canadian Arctic.

[39] Per Langgard, "Modernization and Traditional Interpersonal Relations in a Small Greenlandic Community," *Arctic Anthropology* 23/1&2 (1986), 308.

The coast of Labrador: provincial policies and Native responses

In the early years after Newfoundland had joined the Canadian confederation and until the mid-1960s, while the federal government of Canada provided the chief funding for the various programs that were implemented, Ottawa did "not formally recognize its constitutional responsibility toward the province's Natives."[40] Meanwhile, the Newfoundland provincial government expanded its administrative services for the Labrador Coast. Its policy was based on the premises that the northern part of the coast, which was inhabited by the Inuit, had little economic potential and that relocation of the population to such centers in southern Labrador as Goose Bay and Happy Valley was the only realistic solution to local problems. By the 1960s, it became clear that the emigrants could be neither culturally assimilated nor economically accommodated, so that a solution to their problems had to be sought within northern Labrador. In order to supplement the subsistence economy and the sources of income from occasional construction work and transfer payments, several fishery projects were introduced or expanded by the Northern Labrador Service Division. Pickling of Arctic char for export had begun as early as 1942; in 1968 a smoked char operation was introduced, and by the early 1970s char fishing was restricted to Labradorean fishermen. Commercial salmon fishing was also encouraged. Unfortunately, these activities resulted in declines of both species and strict quotas for their takes had to be established. The cod fishery, which had been the mainstay of commercial fishing for many decades, went into a sharp decline by the late 1960s, but by 1980 signs of recovery were apparent. While certain fluctuations in the success of the fishery projects were experienced, they were able to employ a large portion of the available work force. Problems arose in connection with environmentalist attacks on the sale of sealskins, as a result of which subsistence hunting and fishing continued to be the main and most reliable occupations on the coast. A sharp rise in previously depleted caribou herds provided an important source of food after the Newfoundland government removed its strict game laws regarding caribou in 1978.

In 1973 a Native organization, the Labrador Inuit Association (LIA), was founded as a response to several Inuit concerns. The main objectives of the organization were to strengthen Inuit culture and to organize land claims, although it later became involved in economic and environmental matters

[40] Brantenberg and Brantenberg, "Coastal Northern Labrador after 1950," 689.

as well. The Labrador Inuit Association also became an affiliate member of the Inuit Tapirisat of Canada, which was becoming the chief organization coordinating the concerns of a number of regional groups. The Labrador Inuit Association admitted Settlers into their organization and subsequently, in 1975, it received federal funding support. This inclusion was a major step, in that it served to bridge an ethnic gap that had existed for a century and a half, despite common economic practices, and to unite two groups that, by this time, shared a large body of concerns. The land use and occupancy study, when submitted in 1978, was immediately accepted by Ottawa, but it took two more years of negotiations until Newfoundland also agreed. Concessions made by the Labrador Inuit Association were that they would relinquish aboriginal rights and not seek self-government.

A number of developments occurred to strengthen Inuit culture in the late 1970s and the 1980s. Perhaps the most important of these was establishment of the Labrador Inuit Cultural Centre, Torngarsuk. There was also participation in campaigns against mineral and oil exploration and, by 1982, the Inuit had gained full control over the fishing industry in northern Labrador. Extra-local political affiliation extended beyond the Inuit Tapirisat of Canada to membership in the Inuit Circumpolar Conference which expressed Inuit concerns at an international level. By the 1980s, the Labrador Inuit Association was firmly established as the official organization representing the Inuit and Settlers of Labrador and had gone a long way toward achieving its objectives. But, as in Greenland, the economic base remained uncertain. There was still a substantial gap between rising costs and expectations. The same social problems of alcohol abuse, crime, and violence had arisen as in Greenland.

The Inuit of Quebec: shift in hegemony and internal dissent

In the early sixties, the Inuit of northern Quebec were experiencing the same challenges as those in the rest of Arctic Canada: compulsory education, mechanization of individual transport, some depletion of local resources, the social ills brought on by centralization, and, above all, adjusting to the welfare state era which by then had emerged. What made the situation special and even unique for the Inuit of Quebec was, first, the struggles for political dominance between the Canadian and Quebec governments and, second, the repercussions following in the wake of the James Bay and Northern Quebec Agreement.[41] The contest

---

[41] Bernard Saladin d'Anglure, "Contemporary Inuit of Quebec," in Damas, ed., *Arctic*.

between the federal and provincial governments coincided with the advent of Liberal party control in Quebec in 1960, and the next decade saw a tug of war between the two governmental levels. One of the first steps toward provincializing the Quebec North was replacement of the Royal Canadian Mounted Police by the Sûreté du Québec, and shortly after there was a duplication of agents of the two governments in each of the communities. By 1970, the federal government decided to divest many of its responsibilities to Quebec. There were, however, generally negative reactions from the Inuit population with regard to the establishment of such a degree of Quebec control as was planned, particularly as the Inuit themselves had not been consulted. One response was the formation of the Northern Quebec Inuit Association in 1971.

The Quebec government under Premier Robert Bourassa treated this association as representing the Inuit of the entire province when negotiations over impending hydroelectric development began about that time. After the James Bay and Northern Quebec Agreement was ratified in 1975, profound changes were to take place in the lives of the Quebec Inuit. The conditions of the agreement provided that three classes of land rights were to be recognized. The first category gave exclusive rights to each village. This category comprised only 1 percent of the entire area. A second class of land allowed Inuit exclusive hunting, fishing, and trapping rights, and accommodations had to be made by those carrying out mineral or other exploitation. But in the third category, which comprised by far the largest part of the total area, Inuit enjoyed no special rights. Compensation for losses included giving greater authority to local communities in matters such as education, reforms in the justice system, and regional jurisdiction over transportation, communication, health, social services, and economic development. In addition, there were monetary compensations totaling $90 million. The Makivik Corporation was formed to administer these funds.

The majority of the Inuit agreed to ratify the agreement, but an important dissident group formed which considerably dulled its impact. The communities of Povungnituk, Ivujivik, and some people from Sugluk, refused to recognize the agreement and set up their own organization, the Inuit Tungavingat Nunami. Local support for the organization proved to be inadequate and eventually outside subsidization had to be secured. Objection was directed against keeping only 1 percent of land for exclusive use by Inuit, and the members of this organization regarded themselves as defenders of Inuit rights.

Meanwhile other local organizations sprang up which raised difficulties in negotiations with the Quebec government. Eventually all parties recognized the problems resulting from these divisions within the Inuit community. The upshot of this was the formation of the Nunavik Constitutional Committee on April 10, 1989. On December 15, 1989, a constitution was drawn together and later presented to the Quebec government for consideration. The new organization was to supplant earlier bodies.

The central Arctic: from the "hamlet ideal" to Nunavut

For the vast regions of the Northwest Territories, the process of centralization which had begun by 1960 accelerated rapidly in the next decade. An Eskimo Camp Study Committee reported that only about one-fifth of the Inuit of these regions still lived in year-round, hunting-trapping camps in 1967. As the in-gathering process gained force, a definite philosophy of administration evolved. The image of northern communities modeled after villages and hamlets in southern Canada emerged, implying that every Canadian should have access to proper housing, compulsory education, adequate medical aid, and sanitation, as well as to recreational, communication, and transportation facilities. But, while in the case of southern communities local resources and taxation provided much of the support for such facilities, in the Arctic they were possible only through a wholesale implementation of the welfare state, with support coming largely from southern Canada.

Several housing programs swept the Northwest Territories, each providing successively greater comfort and requiring less individual financing of construction and heating costs. While hunting and trapping could still be carried out from the new centers, especially with the aid of mechanized transport, the costs of purchasing and maintaining the equipment, fuel, and other supplies needed to continue this way of life rose rapidly as inflation gripped the whole nation. Commercial art, service occupations, and construction employment were all helpful, but in the end heavy subsidization continued to be required in order to uphold the standard of living accepted as desirable by the government, and now expected by the Inuit.

While substantial advances were made in health care, which led to rising populations, psychological and social disorders were notable. Much of the marital strife, crime, and violence was traced to overuse of alcohol, and some communities became "dry" in order to avoid such difficulties. Progress in education moved slowly, with few students continuing beyond grade 6 and almost all delayed in terms of age-grade levels. Yet, beginning in the 1970s, a relatively well-educated youth began to assume prominence in the Inuit communities, and provided the impetus for the political movements of the 1970s and 1980s.

In 1975 important political changes took place. The Territories were divided into two ridings (electoral divisions), the Western Arctic and Nunatsiak, each now represented by a member in the federal House of Commons. Election of Inuit members to the newly reorganized Northwest Territory Assembly (formerly the Northwest Territory Council) increased, so that seven of ten Arctic constituencies were represented by Inuit members in the 1979 election. In 1971 the Inuit Tapirisat of Canada was formed and soon became the overarching organization of a number of regional organizations that were formed in the 1970s. These included the aforementioned Labrador Inuit Association, as well as several others from the eastern and central Arctic, and the Committee for Original People's Entitlement (COPE), which represented the western Canadian Arctic. One of the important moves initiated by the Inuit Tapirisat corporation was the Nunavut proposal, which sought division of the Northwest Territories into two sections with one, Nunavut, being largely Inuit country. Certain problems were encountered in dealing with the Dene Nation and the Métis Association regarding boundaries. But, on January 15, 1987, agreement was reached with Inuit representatives, and a timetable was established for steps leading toward ratification by the federal government, which was scheduled for October 1, 1991. Meanwhile, before this finalization of Nunavut as a separate territory was complete, a comprehensive land claim settlement was made between the Tungavik Federation and federal and provincial governments in the spring of 1990. The agreement, which is described as the "last major northern land claim," included providing the Inuit of Nunavut with $580 million to be allotted over a fourteen-year period and confirmed title to 350,000 square kilometers of land. The land allotment included about 10 percent of the region and subsurface mineral rights among a number of provisions which put a large measure of control of the area in Inuit hands. The establishment of Nunavut strove toward recognition of the Inuit as a distinct people of Canada, along with "the protection of traditional cultures and lifestyles, and aboriginal rights, as well as certain rights of self-government, rights to lands, and protection of existing economic resources."[42]

---

[42] "Last Major Land Claim Settled," *Arctic Petroleum Review* 13/1 (1990), 3; Vallee, Smith, and Cooper, 671.

Inuit of the Mackenzie Delta: "Bystanders in the economic scene" and the pipeline crisis

Establishment of Inuvik in the mid-1950s accelerated the centripetal forces in the delta region and, by the mid-1960s the trapping industry, based in a large number of outlying camps, which had long flourished was reduced to a decidedly secondary activity operating out of the centers of Tuktoyaktuk, Inuvik, Aklavik, and a few points to the east of the delta. While this in-gathering process and its effects have been noted for other Arctic regions, especially for the period after 1960, the delta had special problems, for it was a region of multi-ethnic populations, with both Indians (Dene) and Métis as well as a number of Euro-Canadians living there. With the locating of the Western Arctic administration, which was dominated by southern Canadians, in Inuvik, the Inuit now comprised only a minority group and one which had a low level of full-time employment as well as low incomes. By 1968, there was a promise of new employment possibilities with discoveries of oil in the region. But plans for building a pipeline for natural gas from the Prudhoe Bay discoveries through the delta and southward alarmed the inhabitants of the region. They feared that the pipeline would cause spillage that might result in environmental destruction and adversely affect the movements of caribou. These threats, together with land claims, resulted in the formation of COPE in 1970. By 1978, COPE had reached an "agreement in principle" with the federal government on their land claims, and on June 5, 1984, the Western Arctic Claim was finalized by a ratification vote of the Inuit of the region (Inuvialuit) after agreement was reached between the federal government and representatives of COPE. The claim allocated the Inuit 91,000 square kilometers of the 435,000 "they traditionally used and occupied," including 11,000 square kilometers located around actual settlements, involving both surface and subsurface rights. The claim also provided for the Inuvialuit to receive $45 million between 1984 and 1997 as well as specific provisions for Native management of game in the regions concerned.[43]

The Berger Inquiry into the pipeline development released a report in 1977 which gave strong support to Native resistance and was instrumental in postponing pipeline construction, but the picture appeared to be changing by 1990 with Ottawa becoming increasingly interested in building the line.

[43] *The Western Arctic Claim* (Ottawa, 1984).

Alaska: the road to settlement and the threat of termination

By the 1960s, the American government's policy of termination had largely been abandoned. A new policy of "equal opportunity" was proposed, but it proved difficult to implement and many Alaskan Natives regarded it as "a subtle form of White paternalism" rather than any realistic improvement in conditions. The Alaska Statehood Act of 1958 did not immediately resolve any of the problems confronted by Native peoples, including the Eskimos of Alaska. The act stated that Alaskan Natives should not be dispossessed of any lands currently used or claimed by them, but allowed the new state government to claim more than 104 million acres (42 million hectares). In addition, during the 1960s mineral and oil companies also laid claim to large parts of the state that Eskimos and other Native peoples considered to be their own land. Other issues arose during the 1960s which could have had profound effects on the Native peoples. A plan (Project Chariot) was entertained by the Atomic Energy Commission to blast a harbor with nuclear explosions in northwest Alaska. The Rampart Dam Project would have flooded large areas of the interior of Alaska. Enforcement of a long neglected international Migratory Wildfowl Treaty seriously affected hunting practices. These plans were all discussed without consultation with the Natives and thus caused Native people to begin to organize resistance. Their chief response came in 1966 with the formation of the Alaska Federation of Natives, an alliance of eight regional organizations. This body carried out most of the negotiations which led to the Alaska Native Claims Settlement of 1971. The settlement did not grant Native people all they sought due to fierce opposition from some members of Congress. The White House staff played an important role in achieving the eventual agreement and Native leaders praised President Nixon for his role.[44]

One provision of the settlement was that regional corporations and 200 villages would receive monies to be used on both regional and village levels for operating business and other ventures. Of the regions, the Arctic Slope Regional Corporation, the NANA Regional Corporation, and about

---

[44] Ernest S. Burch, Jr., "The Land Claims Era in Alaska," in Damas, ed., *Arctic;* Wilcomb E. Washburn, *Red Man's Land/White Man's Law* (New York, 1971), 130–3; Bradley H. Patterson, *The Ring of Power: The White House Staff and Its Expanding Role in Government* (New York, 1988), 36–7.

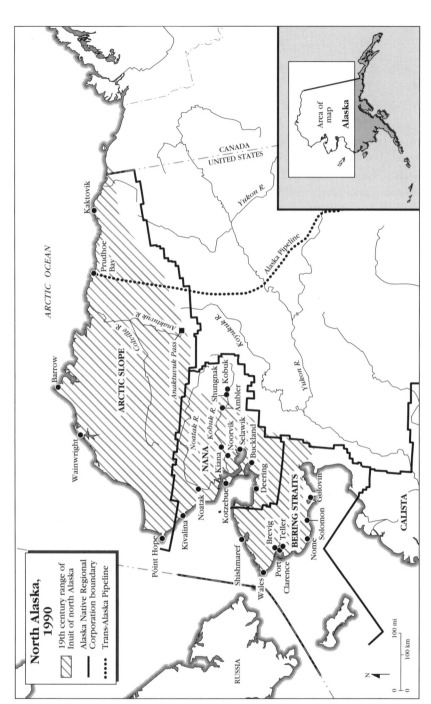

**North Alaska,
1990**

- 19th century range of
  Inuit of north Alaska
- Alaska Native Regional
  Corporation boundary
- Trans-Alaska Pipeline

Figure 14.7 North Alaska in 1990.

half the Bering Straits Native Corporation were Inuit speakers, the latter sharing land grants and monies with Yuit speakers. These three regional organizations received $185.9 million in cash entitlement as well as large land areas. Both land selection and cash aspects of the settlement have proved difficult to resolve. Land settlement negotiations extended well into the 1980s and many claims remained in an "interim conveyance" stage. Most of the money was issued to the regional and village corporations and 10 percent was to be paid by them directly to individuals. A balance was to be struck between amount of land and cash paid, with those receiving less land getting more cash.

The most difficult part of the settlement was that only a twenty-year period was to apply to its conditions, a provision which in fact was an extension of the termination policies that had been tried earlier with Indians in the "lower forty eight" states. This meant that only those who had been living on December 18, 1971, would benefit directly from the act. It meant also that, after December 18, 1991, shares in the Native corporations could be transferred to non-Natives and that Native land would become liable to taxation. There was, in addition, anxiety regarding the financial failure of several of the corporations by the 1980s, and fear that others would go under as well. In response, the Alaska Federation of Natives lobbied for changes in Washington, and, in February 1988, President Reagan signed a bill which amended the original act. This included lifting the restrictions on rights for those born after the settlement date in 1971, and altering restrictions on stock alienation and land taxation.

After statehood, certain improvements had been effected. Between 1960 and 1980, housing projects were sponsored by both state and federal governments, and schools came under greater local control. Supermarkets, television aerials, and mechanical vehicles transformed the outward appearances of villages, but "The extent to which Eskimo and Aleut villages changed culturally and socially during the same period is less clear. . . . The one really significant and pervasive change has been the extent to which Natives have taken over control of their own affairs at the regional and village levels."[45] As the 1990s began, the most crucial concern of the Eskimos of north Alaska was the presence of oil operations on the North Slope and the degree to which they threatened wildlife, especially the migrations of whales, which remained an important quarry for the hunters of the region.

[45] Burch, "The Land Claims Era in Alaska," 661.

THE PAN-ESKIMO MOVEMENT AND THE FUTURE OF
THE INUIT

Throughout the long history of contacts with Westerners, the image of the Inuit has undergone significant changes. The impressions of bellicose and thieving xenophobes, as Europeans perceived them in early contacts in the eastern and western parts of the North American Arctic, can be contrasted with those of more benign, but inscrutable, Natives encountered in central regions. Then, there were the apparently passive and largely withdrawn people of much of the area in later times, especially the Inuk hunter-trapper of the fur-trade era. Today a new image has emerged. This is one of an assertive, intelligent, articulate, and politically aware people, who have gained considerable unity and influence through a number of organizations. The influence which Inuit have gained through the actions of such organizations is especially remarkable in view of the continuing economic dependency that exists throughout the entire North American Arctic. While some local developments, such as the fishing industries of Greenland and Labrador, tourism, craft production, and wage opportunities, show some promise, there are few prospects for comprehensive economic development that will eliminate the need for government support in the near future. One view of this dependency has been expressed by an official of the Northwest Territory government, who pointed out that only about one billion dollars a year has been required for subsidization of Native peoples in the Territories while the national budget is on the order of $110 billion.[46] Similar situations prevail in Greenland and Alaska as well in relation to the Danish and American budgets.

Meanwhile, Inuit political influence expanded to an international level with the founding of the Inuit Circumpolar Conference (ICC) in 1977. Assemblies of Inuit from Greenland, Canada, and Alaska have met every third year and the fifth meeting of the ICC included observers from the Soviet Arctic as well. Early sessions were concerned with organizational matters and, by 1983, the ICC had achieved Non-Governmental Organization status in the United Nations. Among the concerns which have dominated ICC discussions and resolutions have been those of the environment. The thrust of Inuit environmental interests does not conform to that of most Western environmental movements. For instance, there is obvious opposition to moves by Greenpeace toward banning seal hunting. In the

[46] Marc Malone, "Irwin Report: The View from Yellowknife," *Northern Perspective* 17/1 (1989), 14.

case of the Inuit, most environmental concern has to do with preservation of wildlife as resources to be exploited. In many places, in traditional times, the precariousness of existence did not allow the luxury of limiting kills. Yet, while regional and temporal shortages of game did occur and produce conditions of hardship, no overall decline in game in the Arctic was associated with Inuit hunting practices. With rising populations, however, uncontrolled game harvesting cannot be sustained. The fact that Inuit communities have accepted and observed quotas of certain animals, such as polar bear and large whales, shows that they appraise realistically the limits to which hunting can be pursued.

Another area of concern – regulation of research – was discussed at some length at the fourth ICC assembly, held in Kotzebue in 1986. While both applied and pure research were acknowledged as important, Inuit controls definitely constricted anthropological research. For some time, clearance of village or hamlet councils has been required for research to commence. In the renaissance period of ethnological field work in the 1960s "gifts" of small monetary value were sufficient to establish rapport and to compensate for various services. By the 1980s, information became regarded by Inuit as a highly marketable commodity and field budgets had to swell to accommodate rising costs of research with human subjects. Archaeologists and physical anthropologists also were subject to restrictions against disturbing sites, especially those containing human remains.

A brief summary of some of the discussion topics of the fifth ICC assembly, held in July-August 1989, suggests the range of concerns that Inuit were addressing at the end of the eighties. No fewer than forty-two resolutions were passed including ones on AIDS, the Porcupine Caribou Herd, militarization, fetal alcohol syndrome, conservation strategy, marine mammal protection, and shipping. It should be clear from this list that the Inuit find themselves involved in environmental, health, and security concerns that are global in nature, as well as with concerns of a more local character.

In the 1990s Inuit concern with gaining political influence and self-determination continued to grow. For Greenland implementation of transferral of governmental functions from Denmark according to the provisions of the Home Rule Act had brought about profound changes. One of the most prominent of these was the reduction of provision of public funds by Denmark from 80 percent in 1979 to 50 percent in the final decade of the century.

For Inuit living in Arctic Canada north and west of Hudson Bay the most important recent event has been the final ratification of the Nunavut Agreement on May 25, 1993, with the provisions outlined earlier. While the agreement specifies quotas for most game, there had been a recent movement opposing the existing prohibition against hunting migratory waterfowl during the spring months.

For the Inuit of Quebec resolution of the objections of dissidents against the James Bay Agreement is still pending, nineteen years after the agreement was ratified. Another question has been raised by the lawyers of the Makivik Corporation representing those Quebec Inuit who were relocated to the High Arctic in the 1950s. Whereas some contradictory reports regarding the conditions experienced by these people were aired in 1990–1,[47] it now appears that favorable government response will be forthcoming regarding claims for compensation for hardships endured.

In the Labrador region problems of land claims and self-government by the Inuit continue to lag behind the rest of Canada due to conflicts between the federal government and that of Newfoundland.

A number of problems are yet to be resolved concerning the aftermath of the Alaska Native Claims Settlement Act. In the words of one observer, writing in 1992, "chronic obstacles hinder its completion." He lists several chief problems, including those of land conveyance, lack of financial stability of Native corporations, and continuing holding of large sums of money in escrow by the Internal Revenue Service, and adds "the final resolution of these issues is probably years or decades in the future."[48]

On the international level the growing influence of the ICC is being expressed most strongly in its representation at a series of conferences. In addition to their own Sixth General Assembly held at Inuvik in July 1992, representatives attended several others which spread the influence of the ICC well beyond the Eskimo area. Concern with environmental issues has continued to be a central theme of the organization, involving both controlling pollution and safeguarding hunting rights. In this connection support was gained for ICC espousal of such rights at an international meeting of conservationists in Perth, Australia, in 1990 and was hailed by the president of the ICC as a major defeat for the anti-hunting lobby present. Other participation included the 1992 meeting of the International Whaling Commission, the so-called Earth Summit held in

---

[47] Frank James Tester and Peter Kulchyski, *Tammarniit (Mistakes)* (Vancouver, 1994), 102–4.
[48] Steven McNabb, "Native Claims in Alaska: A Twenty-year Review," *Etudes/Inuit/Studies* 16 (1992), 85.

Rio de Janeiro in June of the same year, and the United Nations Working Group of Indigenous Peoples held in Geneva in July 1991. In reporting on her attendance at the latter conference, the ICC representative, an Alaskan Inuk, may well echo the sentiments of Inuit throughout the Arctic today:

The legacy of outside control is what indigenous people are fighting against. Since the time of first contact there has always been strong resistance to assimilation. Today, there continues to be an unwavering determination to identify both self and community as indigenous, despite rapid social, environmental, and economic change. Indigenous peoples are responding to 500 years or more of oppression.[49]

In the case of the Inuit, among such indigenous peoples, deference to perceived omnipotence of bearers of dominant cultures has given way to more active responses. These are taking the form of organized pressures being exerted toward representative bodies of major states to rectify perceived abuses and omissions. Further, the above references indicate that such a reaction has now begun to gather force on a global scale as the Inuit see themselves as sharing many of the problems of other indigenous peoples.

BIBLIOGRAPHIC ESSAY

This chapter deals with inhabitants of Arctic North America, who are properly designated Inuit as based on their own word for "people." Others grouped together with the Inuit into the Eska-Aleut or Eskimo-Aleut linguistic family include the Yuit speakers of the Bering Sea and Alaskan Pacific coast regions, as well as Aleut speakers of the Aleutian Islands and part of the Alaskan Peninsula (see Chapter 3). There has been the tendency, beginning in the 1970s, to replace the term Eskimo by Inuit in referring to all these peoples and to prehistoric Arctic populations. Such usage has two main shortcomings. On the one hand, the uncertainty of linguistic and genetic affiliations of most carriers of archaeological cultures (with the exception of Thule) limits its usefulness, and, on the other, the populations of Yuit and Aleut speakers do not have the term Inuit in their vocabularies.

Beginning with Boas, there have been several attempts to apply the

49 Dalee Sambo, "Indigenous Human Rights: The Role of Inuit at the United Nations Working Group on Indigenous Peoples," *Etudes/Inuit/Studies* 16 (1992), 28.

concept of "tribe" to Arctic peoples on the basis of the Native usage of the suffix *-miut* or "inhabitants of." Yet this element refers often to small and evanescent entities that inhabit specific locales for varying periods of time. Large groupings are designated by the *-miut* suffix only by outsiders, who apply names of constituent groupings to a much larger population. Helm's definition of "tribe" as based on her studies of Northern Athapaskans is more appropriate here: "the greatest extension of population throughout which there is sufficient intermarriage to maintain many sided communications." This association is applicable to such major groupings as the Netsilik, Copper Eskimos, and Iglulik Eskimos. For a more complete discussion of usages of Inuit and Eskimo and for "tribes," see "Introduction," by David Damas and Ives Goddard to *Handbook of North American Indians,* vol. 5, *Arctic,* ed. D. Damas (Washington, D.C., 1984).

The transition from archaeological to historically documented cultures is dealt with for Greenland in volume 1 of Finn Gad, *The History of Greenland* (London, 1970). Inga Kleivan, "History of Norse Greenland" in the *Handbook of North American Indians,* vol. 5, ed. David Damas (Washington, D.C., 1984), addresses the question of Norse-Thule Inuit contacts in Greenland. Robert McGhee, in several publications, including *Canadian Arctic Prehistory* (Toronto, 1978), attributed a southward movement of Thule to climatic changes, and he explored the possibility of Thule-Norse contacts in the Canadian Arctic in "Contact between Native North Americans and the Medieval Norse: A Review of the Evidence" in *American Antiquity* 49 (1984), 4–26. Vilhjalmur Stefansson's *The Three Voyages of Martin Frobisher* (London, 1938) documents the first post-Norse contacts with Inuit. Other explorers' accounts of encounters with Inuit in this early period are *The Voyages and Works of John Davis,* ed. Albert H. Markham (London, 1880) and *The Voyages of William Baffin,* ed. Clements R. Markham (London, 1881).

Eighteenth-century explorers' accounts dealing with European-Inuit contacts are few, exceptions being Samuel Hearne, *A Journey from Prince of Wales's Fort in Hudson's Bay to the Northern Ocean,* ed. Richard Glover (Toronto, 1958); and Andrew Graham, *Andrew Graham's Observations on Hudson's Bay 1767–1791,* ed. Glyndwr Williams (London, 1969). Mission reports, especially those of the Moravians, formed the basis for much of volume 2 of Finn Gad, *The History of Greenland* (London, 1973) and for J. Garth Taylor, "Labrador Eskimo Settlements of the Early Contact Period," *National Museum of Man, Publications in Ethnology* 9 (Ottawa, 1974), major sources for the eighteenth century.

For most of the North American Arctic, the nineteenth century represented a period of European exploration and discovery of a number of Inuit groups, while in Greenland and Labrador it was a period of advancing acculturation. Volume 3 of Finn Gad, *The History of Greenland* (Copenhagen, 1982) and Helge Klievan "The Eskimos of Northeast Labrador: A History of Eskimo-White Relations, 1771–1955," *Norsk Polarinstitutt Skrifter* 139 (Oslo, 1966) are the definitive works for the eastern Arctic for the century. Accounts of explorers that provide descriptions of Inuit for the period include: John Ross's meeting with the Polar Eskimos in *A Voyage of Discovery . . . in His Majesty's Ships Isabella and Alexander* (London, 1819) and for the encounters farther to the west, Sir William Parry, *Journal of a Second Voyage for the Discovery of a Northwest Passage* (London, 1824) and Ross, *Narrative of a Second Voyage in Search of a Northwest Passage* (Philadelphia, 1835). Contact between Inuit and American whalers in the eastern Arctic, as chronicled in Inuit oral tradition, is documented in Dorothy Harley Eber, *When the Whalers Were up North* (Montreal, 1989).

Sir John Franklin's *Narrative of a Second Expedition to the Shores of the Polar Sea* (London, 1828) describes contacts with the Inuit of the Mackenzie delta and the northeastern Alaska region. Further information from those regions as well as about the theretofore little-known Natives of Victoria Island came in Captain Richard Collinson's report, *Journal of H.M.S. Enterprise, on the Expedition in Search of Sir John Franklin's Ships*, ed. T. B. Collinson (London, 1889).

At the western extremity of Inuit country, Frederick Beechey, *Narrative of a Voyage to the Pacific and Beering's Strait* (2 vols., London, 1831, 1832) and "A. F. Kashevarov's Coastal Explorations in Northwest Alaska, 1838" *Fieldiana: Anthropology* 69 (Chicago, 1977), ed. James W. VanStone provide the basis of our information on first contacts with the Natives of northwestern Alaska. Wendell H. Oswalt, *Eskimos and Explorers* (San Francisco, 1979) furnishes a useful summary for all time periods and all Eskimo regions.

The period of direct ethnological observations began during the 1880s resulting in such publications as Gustav F. Holm, "Ethnological Sketch of the Angmagsalik Eskimo," *Meddelelser om Grønland* 39 (Copenhagen, 1914 [Danish version 1888, MOG 10 (2), 43–182]); Franz Boas, "The Central Eskimo," *6th Annual Report of the Bureau of American Ethnology* (Washington, D.C., 1888), which presented not only a detailed description of Baffinlanders based on Boas's field work in 1883–4, but also a compilation of materials on other Inuit groups; and for Alaska, John Murdoch, "Ethnological Results of the Point Barrow Expedition," *9th Annual Report of the Bureau of American Ethnology* (Washington, D.C., 1892).

There followed a hiatus in ethnological field work in the Arctic, but during the ensuing years, records of whalers provided the basis for such information on the Inuit as appears in W. Gillies Ross, "Whaling and Eskimos: Hudson Bay 1860–1915," *National Museum of Man, Publications in Ethnology* 10 (Ottawa, 1975). John Bockstoce, *Whales, Ice, & Men* (Seattle, Wash., 1986) depicts relations between whalers and Inuit for the western Arctic, as do articles by Alex Stevenson, including "Whaler's Wait," *North* 15(5) (1968), 24–31.

The true flowering of Arctic ethnology began with publication of Knud Rasmussen, *The People of the Polar North* (London, 1908) and Stefansson's account of first European encounter with elements of Copper Eskimos in *My Life with the Eskimo* (Macmillan, 1913). Later, the addition of Jenness's fourteen volumes, especially *The Life of the Copper Eskimos* (Ottawa, 1922), made that people the most intensively documented of any Inuit group. Ernest W. Hawkes, "The Labrador Eskimo," *Department of Mines, Geological Survey Memoir* 91 (Ottawa, 1916), and, for Alaska, "The Dance Festivals of the Alaskan Eskimo," *University of Pennsylvania Museum, Anthropological Publication* 6(2) (1914), 5–41 were based on field work during this period, as was Kaj Birket-Smith, "Ethnography of the Egedesminde District," *Meddelelser om Grønland* 66 (Copenhagen, 1924).

The culmination of the great ethnographic era of Inuit studies came in the Fifth Thule Expedition, which visited nearly every grouping from Baffin Island in the east to the Inuit-Yuit boundary in Norton Sound in the west. The ten volumes of the *Report of the Fifth Thule Expedition 1921–24* (Copenhagen, 1925–52) deal with material culture, linguistics, oral tradition, religion, and physical anthropology, as well as providing censuses for each locale visited. Representative of the volumes in the series of "The Netsilik Eskimos" by Knud Rasmussen (Copenhagen, 1931), "Material Culture of the Iglulik Eskimos" by Therkel Mathiassen (Copenhagen, 1928), and "The Caribou Eskimos" (2 vols., Copenhagen, 1929) by Kaj Birket-Smith.

Little subsequent ethnological field research was carried out until after World War II, exceptions being that reported in Erik Holtved, "The Polar Eskimos, Language and Folklore, Parts I and II," *Meddelelser om Grønland* 152(1–2) (Copenhagen, 1951); and two studies from the Keewatin barrens, *Vie et coutumes des Esquimaux caribous* (Paris, 1944) by Jean Gabus and *Terre stérile* (Paris, 1949) by Jean Michea. The period also saw publication of two general works, *The Eskimos: Their Environment and Folkways* (New Haven, 1932) by Edward M. Weyer, Jr., and *The Eskimos* (London, 1936) by Kaj Birket-Smith, which have remained as principal texts on Inuit and related peoples. The present author has drawn on Hudson's Bay Company, Royal Canadian Mounted Police, and other government records in "The Contact-Traditional Horizon of the Central Arctic" *Arctic Anthropology* 25 (1988), 101–38 by David Damas, which explores relations between Inuit, fur traders, and police.

Post-war ethnological field research began in the Alaskan region with the work of Robert F. Spencer, published in "The North Alaskan Eskimo: A Study in Ecology and Society," *Bureau of American Ethnology Bulletin 171* (Washington, D.C., 1959). Dealing with more contemporary matters for northwestern Alaska is James W. VanStone, *Point Hope: An Eskimo Village in Transition* (Seattle, 1962).

The rebirth of Inuit studies in the Canadian Arctic came with a series of community studies beginning in the late 1950s. Representative of this research are James W. VanStone and Wendell H. Oswalt, *The Caribou Eskimos of Eskimo Point* (Ottawa, 1959) and Frank G. Vallee, *Kabloona and Eskimo in the Central Keewatin* (Ottawa, 1962). Meanwhile, the French scholar Jean Malaurie's research in northwestern Greenland had resulted in *The Last Kings of Thule* (New York, 1956).

Post–World War II studies have dealt with a number of topical and theoretical interests. Social structure and social relations were the special focus of A. Balikci, "Development of Basic Socioeconomic Units in Two Eskimo Communities," *National Museum of Canada, Bulletin 202* (Ottawa, 1964), with David Damas, "Igluligmiut Kinship and Local Groupings," *National Museum of Canada, Bulletin 196* (Ottawa, 1963) and Lee Guemple, "Inuit Adoption," *National Museum of Man, Ethnology Service, Paper 47* (Ottawa, 1979) being examples of such concerns from the Canadian Arctic, and Ernest S. Burch, Jr., *Eskimo Kinsmen* (St. Paul, Minn., 1975) for northwestern Alaska. Concern with conditions of change grew as a principal interest in the dynamic postwar period. For Greenland, Helge Kleivan, "Culture and Ethnic Identity," *Folk,* 11–12 (1969–70), 209–34 dealt with postwar problems, while *The White Arctic,* ed. Robert Paine (Toronto, 1977) concerned conditions of Inuit-European relations in the Canadian Arctic and Charles C. Hughes "Under Four Flags," *Current Anthropology* 6 (1965), 3–69 surveyed the entire Eskimo area in this regard.

Interests of the Fifth Thule expedition have been brought forward and developed in the work of Eugene Arima in his treatment of material culture in "A Contextual Study of the Caribou Eskimo Kayak," *National Museum of Man, Ethnology Service, Paper 25* (Ottawa, 1975), and in oral tradition (with Zebedee Nungak) in "Eskimo Stories from Povungnituk, Quebec," *Na-*

tional Museum of Canada, Bulletin 238. Insight into Inuit psychology comes from Jean L. Briggs, *Never in Anger* (Cambridge, Mass., 1970).

Linguistic studies have been carried out for many years including early works by Samuel P. Kleinschmidt and William Thalbitzer, and analyses by Swadesh, including "Eskimo-Aleut Languages," *Encyclopedia Britannica* 8 (1962), 706–7. More recent contributions include "The East Greenlandic Dialect in Comparison with West Greenlandic," *Objets et Mondes* 15(2) (1975) by Robert Petersen, whose ethnological contributions are well known to scholars of Greenland. A summary of linguistic studies by Anthony C. Woodbury can be found in "Eskimo and Aleut Languages," in *Handbook of North American Indians,* vol. 5 (Washington, D.C., 1984).

Important physical anthropological studies for the area include Lawrence Oschinsky, *The Most Ancient Eskimos* (Ottawa, 1964); Emöke Szathmary and Nancy Ossenberg, "Are the Biological Differences between North American Indians and Eskimos Truly Profound," *Current Anthropology* 19 (1978), 673–701 and Szathmary, "Human Biology of the Arctic," in *Handbook of North American Indians,* vol. 5 (Washington, D.C., 1984).

Concern with governmental relations between the nation states of the Arctic and the Inuit include: Diamond Jenness, *Eskimo Administration,* 5 vols. (Montreal, 1962–8), which compares policies of the Danish, Canadian, and American governments; Ernest S. Burch, "The Land Claims Era in Alaska," in *Handbook of North American Indians,* vol. 5 (Washington, D.C., 1984); and several recent articles by Scandinavian authors, for instance, "The Impact of Public Planning on Ethnic Culture: Aspects of Danish Resettlement Policies in Greenland after World War II," by Marie-Louise Deth Petersen, *Arctic Anthropology* 23 (1988), 271–80; and for Canada *The Road to Nunavut* (Montreal, 1988) by Quinn Duffy.

Charles A. Martijn has traced the development of Inuit carving in "Canadian Eskimo Carving in Historical Perspective," *Anthropos* 59 (1964), 545–96, a theme carried forward in much more extensive work by Nelson H. H. Graburn, including "Commercial Inuit Art: A Vehicle for the Economic Development of the Eskimos of Canada," *Inter-Nord* 15 (1978), 131–42. Current concern with the role of environmentalists is the topic of several articles and the book *Animal Rights, Human Rights* (London, 1991) by George W. Wenzel.

Several periodicals have featured articles on the Inuit, including the Danish publications *Meddelelser om Grønland* and *Folk; Arctic* (Montreal and Calgary), *Arctic Anthropology* (Madison and Fayetteville), and *Etudes/Inuit/Studies* (Quebec).

The literature on the Inuit is extensive and will continue to grow; hence a survey like this can hope only to be representative rather than comprehensive. An attempt has been made to draw together our knowledge of the Inuit and other Eskimo peoples in *Handbook of North American Indians*, vol. 5, *Arctic*, where archaeological, historical, linguistic, physical anthropological, and ethnological materials are represented. Most germane to this survey are the chapters "History of Research before 1945" by Henry Collins and "History of Ethnology after 1945" by Charles C. Hughes. Accounts of recent political activities and developments in all regions of Inuit habitation can be found in "Collective Rights and Powers," in *Etudes/Inuit/Studies* 16 (Quebec, 1992).

15

THE NATIVE AMERICAN
RENAISSANCE, 1960–1995

WILCOMB E. WASHBURN

The recent history of Native Americans is both complex and controversial. Complex because of the rapid cultural change that has occurred in the twentieth century, particularly in the last half of the century; controversial because both Indians and non-Indians perceive that change differently. The perception of the status of Native Americans as the twentieth century comes to a close is like the classic perception of a glass half full of water. Some see it half full; some see it half empty. Some Native Americans, and some non-Native Americans, focus on the negative side (the empty half of the glass) and see what is missing rather than what has been gained. Indeed, as Native Americans achieve more, there are many who emphasize, with increasing vehemence, what they have not achieved. An example is the question of tribal self-government. In 1991 Native American leaders, in a meeting with President Bush, urged that the right of tribal governments in the United States to have jurisdiction over non-Indians and over Indians not members of the tribe claiming jurisdiction be "restored," ignoring the fact that the Supreme Court decisions that mandated those restrictions did not claim to take such powers away, but ruled that they did not in fact exist. Indian leaders sought to overturn these Supreme Court decisions by urging the introduction of bills in Congress to "restore" those powers. The fact that they assumed that such bills would pass an overwhelmingly non-Indian Congress is a measure of the growing confidence that Native Americans possessed in the second half of the twentieth century. Their confidence was partially justified. While unwilling to recognize tribal power to prosecute non-Indians, Congress did recognize tribal authority to criminally prosecute non-member Indians. Even more indicative of the changing character of relations between Indians and non-Indians in the late twentieth century is the fact that, responding to the negative reaction of Indian peoples, the U.S. government moved decisively away from a "termination policy" in the 1950s, a policy that threatened the very existence of tribal governments, to what Presidents Reagan, Bush, and Clinton have all termed a "government-to-government" relationship among tribal, state, and federal governments.

The following chapter will deal with various aspects of the Native American presence in the United States, Canada, and to a lesser extent Greenland, and try to demonstrate that, from a comparative and historical point of view, the status of Native people is improving in significant ways in all three countries and that the term "Native Renaissance" can legitimately be applied to the recent progress of the descendants of the first Americans.

THE ABORIGINAL POPULATIONS OF THE UNITED STATES AND CANADA

American Indians and Alaskan Natives (Inuit and Aleuts) in the United States in 1990 numbered 2,015,143, up from 1,423,043 counted in the 1980 census, constituting about one-half of 1 percent of the total U. S. population. By way of comparison, Canada's aboriginal population – Indians, Inuit, Métis, and people of mixed Native origin – is less than half that of the United States but constitutes about 3 percent of Canada's total population. Included in the U.S. total are not only those who identify themselves exclusively as American Indians but a second category of individuals who report their race as Indian but include non-Indian ancestry in their ethnic background. Formerly designated "mixed bloods" or "half-breeds," they are now categorized as "American Indians of Multiple Ancestry." A third category – over five and one half million in 1980 and nearly nine million in 1990 – who identify themselves as non-Indian but claim Indian ancestry are known as "Americans of Indian Descent" and are not included in the official Indian count.[1]

---

[1] The statistics for this and following paragraphs are drawn from the U. S. Censuses of 1980 and 1990, as reported in C. Matthew Snipp, *American Indians: The First of This Land,* A Census Monograph Series prepared for the National Committee for Research on the 1980 Census (New York, 1989); *Statistical Record of Native North Americans,* ed. Marlita A. Reddy (Detroit, 1993); Paul Stuart, *Nations Within a Nation: Historical Statistics of American Indians* (New York, 1987); and *Statistical Abstract of the United States, 1994,* 114th edition (Washington, D.C., 1994). For Canadian statistics, see *Canada Year Book 1994* (Ottawa, 1993). Statistics Canada conducts a census every five years. The census of June 4, 1991, has been reported in various publications, including *Profile of Canada's Aboriginal Population* (Ottawa, 1995), *Ethnic Origin* (Ottawa, 1993), *Language, Tradition, Health, Lifestyle and Social Issues* (Ottawa, 1993), and *Canada's Aboriginal Population by Census Subdivisions and Census Metropolitan Areas* (Ottawa, 1994). See also Viviane Renaud and Jane Badets, "Ethnic Diversity in the 1990s," *Canadian Social Trends,* winter 1992 issue (Ottawa: Statistics Canada), 17–22.

The lowest point in North American Indian population was reached in 1890 when the Indian population of the United States was approximately 228,000. The probable range of pre–European-contact North American Indian population was between two and five million. While the Indian population of the United States increased only slightly between 1890 and 1950, it began a precipitous rise between 1950 and 1990 – 47 percent between 1950 and 1960, 51 percent between 1960 and 1970, 72 percent between 1970 and 1980, and 38 percent between 1980 and 1990. Even though the birthrate of the United States Indian population is nearly twice that of the United States as a whole, the largest portion of the Indian population growth in recent years has come from increased self-identification on the part of those who previously had not identified themselves as Indian or who, prior to the policy of racial self-identification established in 1960, had been identified by census takers as other than Indian. Self-identification in the 1960s, 1970s, 1980s, and 1990s was affected by ethnic pride and by the benefits increasingly accruing to identified American Indians through programs administered by government, foundations, and educational institutions.[2]

In the United States the largest Indian populations are located in the south and west, the smallest in the east. Oklahoma has the largest Indian population (252,000 in 1990), followed by California (242,000), Arizona (204,000), and New Mexico (134,000). Cherokees constitute the largest single tribe (308,132), followed by Navajos (219,198), Chippewas (103,826), and Sioux (103,255). Over one-half of all American Indians reside in rural or nonmetropolitan areas, compared to one-quarter of the United States population generally. Although the urban Indian population increased rapidly in the 1960s and 1970s, the rate of migration to such areas slowed significantly in the 1980s and the number is still under 50 percent. One-quarter of all Indians reside on reservations, most of them in rural areas.[3]

Statistical comparisons between the Indian and African-American populations of the United States are important because both groups are recognized to be disadvantaged and their status is often seen as a test of the sincerity and concern of the majority Euro-American population. By 1980 Indians had reached economic parity with African-Americans, as measured by both employment and income, and had achieved a slight

[2] Snipp, *American Indians*, 10, 71, 145.
[3] *Statistical Record of Native North Americans*, Tables 51, 52, 132, 138, 139; Snipp, 77, 85, 235.

edge in 1990. Between 1970 and 1980 Indian life expectancies overtook those of African-Americans.[4]

The long-range demographic trends are liable to make serious inroads upon the exclusively Indian character of the United States Indian population, since 48 percent of American Indian men are married to non-Indian women and the same percentage of American Indian women are married to non-Indian men. Will American Indians intermarry themselves out of existence? Earlier expectations that Indians would disappear through disease, warfare, or assimilation have all proved to be mistaken. Disappearance through intermarriage may prove equally illusory, especially since American Indian history has shown repeatedly that blood quantum bears only a very tangential relation to self-identity and lifestyle. Nevertheless one must take seriously the projections of the United States Office of Technology Assessment that the number of persons with one-half or more Indian blood quantums will decline in the next 100 years from 87 to 8 percent. While these projections foresee the number of American Indians increasing in 100 years from 1,295,450 (in the thirty-two states that its forecast covers) to 15,767,206 in 2080, over 90 percent of these persons will have less than one-half Indian blood quantum. Nevertheless those with greater than one-half Indian blood quantum in 2080 are projected to amount to 1,292,911, about the same number as the total Indian population of these thirty-two states in 1980.[5]

The proportion of descendants of aboriginal people in Canada is larger than in the United States. Of Canada's twenty-seven million people slightly over one million, according to the 1991 census, reported having Aboriginal origins, either as their only ancestry or in combination with other origins, an increase of 41 percent from the 1986 census. When single and multiple responses are combined, 783,980 people reported North American Indian ancestry, 212,650 reported Métis, and 49,255 reported Inuit. As in the United States demographic factors cannot entirely explain this increase, which must be attributed in part to a heightened awareness of Aboriginal issues and a diminished reluctance to identify oneself as having Native ancestry. The 1991 census figure is larger than the Native population thought to have existed at the time of the arrival of Europeans, though the extent of that population is still a matter of widely varying estimates. Whatever the pre-European contact Indian

---

[4] *Statistical Record,* Table 536; Snipp, 69, 125, 135, 209, 249, 317.
[5] Snipp, *American Indians,* 158, 166, 167.

population of Canada, the number declined drastically. By 1867, as a result of disease, starvation, and warfare, there were between 100,000 and 125,000 Indians, 10,000 Métis and half-breeds, and 2,000 Inuit, numbers that had declined even further by 1920.[6]

Native people are concentrated unequally in the Canadian provinces. In the Northwest Territories, the majority of the population (51 percent) reported single Aboriginal origins, with sharply declining portions in the Yukon, Manitoba, Saskatchewan, Alberta, British Columbia, Ontario, Quebec, and the Atlantic provinces. Cree and Ojibwa are the two Aboriginal languages most spoken by adults living on Indian reserves and settlements, Cree by 30,210 (45 percent) North American Indian adults who report speaking an Aboriginal language, and Ojibwa by 11,875 (18 percent). Among North American Indians living off reserves who report speaking an Aboriginal language, 19,000 (10 percent) report speaking Cree and 9,530 (5 percent) report speaking Ojibwa.

Approximately 65 percent of the total Indian population of Canada (both status – those registered as Indians under the Indian Act – and nonstatus Indians, as well as Métis) live in rural areas, while 35 percent live in urban or semiurban areas. Since the 1960s an increasing number of Native people have moved away from their reserves or home communities, usually to seek greater economic opportunities in non-Native urban centers.

Canada's Indian population is divided into 592 bands. Like the tribal organizations in the United States, the Canadian bands have many powers of self-administration. Native people do not pay income tax, provincial tax, or certain excise taxes when they live and work on their reserves. There were 2,284 Indian reserves and settlements comprising 12.6 million hectares (30.5 million acres) in 1985, which amounts to approximately 7.6 hectares (nineteen acres) per status Indian compared with sixty-two hectares per status Indian in the United States. This means that 0.2 percent of land is reserved for 3 percent of the population, compared to 4 percent of the land for 0.5 percent of the Indian population in the United States. The average band membership is fewer than 700 individuals. Several bands have fewer than fifty members, the largest about 13,000.[7] The fact that so many Native people live in small, isolated communities scattered across northern Canada (and Alaska) has made the

[6] *Canadian Encyclopedia,* 2nd ed. (Edmonton, 1988), p. 1448; *Statistical Record,* Table 766; Statistics Canada, *Profile of Canada's Aboriginal Population* (Ottawa, 1995), Table 1; and Statistics Canada, *Ethnic Origin* (Ottawa, 1993), 1.
[7] *Canadian Encyclopedia,* 1449.

provision of medical services, education, and job opportunities for these groups more difficult than elsewhere in North America.

POLITICAL RENAISSANCE

Despite the mandate provided by the Indian Reorganization Act of 1934, Indian tribal governments in the United States were not "reborn" overnight. Indeed, the process was long and hard. Most skeptical of all about the true nature of the authorizing legislation were the Native Americans themselves. Many tribes – most notably the Navajo Nation – refused to accept the authority granted by the act. One of its most liberal and astonishing features was the provision that Indian tribes had to accept the act before it applied to them. Because of the long history of government actions that were in opposition to Indian interests, many Indians drew the logical inference that anything the government wanted them to do must *not* be in the Indian interest. A sense of powerlessness had been accepted by tribal leaders long used to manipulation and coercion by Bureau of Indian Affairs bureaucrats.

Because of the pervasiveness of this dependency and sense of powerlessness, the federal government had difficulty inducing the tribes to avail themselves of the new authority granted to Indian tribes under the Indian Reorganization Act and subsequent acts in the 1960s, 1970s, and 1980s. Despite these grants of power and the increasing number of Indian employees of the Bureau of Indian Affairs, hired under the "Indian Preference Laws" (provisions of various laws incorporated in Section 472 of 25 U. S. Code), the BIA, as the Bureau was traditionally called, was unable to convince tribal leaders that they – the Native Americans – had regained control of their destiny. Following the Supreme Court's decision in *Morton v. Mancari* (1974), which upheld Indian preference against Mancari, a disgruntled non-Indian employee, not only in terms of a "narrow" or "original" preference in hiring, but also in terms of an "expanded" preference involving any personnel action (such as promotion and transfer), the number of Indian employees in the Bureau rose steadily to its present level of 87 percent. Despite the almost total dominance of Indian employees within the Bureau, tribal chairmen continued to insist that their hands were tied and initiative denied by Washington. At the same time the Bureau of Indian Affairs bureaucrats insisted that they could not act for the tribes because authority lay with tribal officials! In fact the stalemate was attributable both to the unwillingness of tribal officials to believe that their shackles had indeed been removed and to the residue of restrictive regulations. The old way of doing things allowed tribal representatives to blame all problems on the BIA and to use the agency as an excuse for anything that went wrong on the reservation. One can understand the frustration experienced by Senator Robert Kennedy in the 1960s when he sought to correct some of the problems he was told were caused by an insensitive BIA. When he floated the idea of abolishing the BIA and distributing its functions to other agencies, the Native Americans reacted with outrage. "The BIA may be a son-of-a-bitch," the feeling was, "but it is *our* son-of-a-bitch." A similar reaction emerged in Canada in 1969 when government officials proposed a similar shifting of responsibilities.[8] Fear of losing existing rights and economic support underlay opposition to change in both countries.

Even with the advent of the Reagan administration in 1981, in which the relationship between the federal government and the Indian tribes was specifically declared to be a "government-to-government" relationship, skepticism continued to impede the full flowering of that relationship. When President Reagan himself, addressing students at Moscow State University in May 1988, showed in his answer to a question about the Indians that he was unaware of the nature of the relationship, it is not surprising that most American citizens and many American Indians remained ignorant or skeptical. Nevertheless, the government-to-government relationship does exist, built upon the solid base of the tribal governments created, or re-created, by the Indian Reorganization Act of 1934. Among the many examples of the government-to-government relationship are the cross-deputizing of law officers by neighboring states and tribes. Often the governmental functions of tribal authorities are questioned, as in the issuance of tribal automobile license plates in place of state license plates, first initiated by the Red Lake Chippewas in 1974. Often such disputes must be resolved by the Supreme Court of the United States, as in the case of *Oklahoma Tax Commission v. Sac and Fox Nation,* decided May 17, 1993 (No. 92–259), in which the Court held that Oklahoma could not impose income taxes or motor vehicle taxes on tribal members who lived in "Indian Country," which it defined as formal and informal reservations, dependent Indian communities, and Indian allotments, whether restricted or held in trust by the federal government. The court

---

[8] Kenneth R. Philp, ed., *Indian Self-Rule: First-Hand Accounts of Indian-White Relations from Roosevelt to Reagan* (Salt Lake City, Utah, 1986).

noted that the United States recognizes and encourages the tribe's sovereign right to self-governance within "the family of governments in the federal constitutional system." States have been surprised to discover that, in the absence of appropriate extradition agreements, some tribal governments have refused to turn over fugitives to states demanding their return.

The fact that much of the financial support for tribal governments and enterprises comes from appropriated funds authorized by act of Congress — which in the 1980s amounted to almost three billion dollars annually for programs dealing with Indians — makes it difficult for many Americans to take tribal governments seriously. While their authority to tax individuals and businesses living or operating on tribal land has been upheld by the Supreme Court, most of their financial base is still provided by the federal government. Despite its derived and limited character, the sovereign power of Indian tribes has been repeatedly upheld by the Supreme Court of the United States.

One of the areas in which tribal governments have been successfully involved is that of Indian health. The Indian Health Service, which was placed under the Public Health Service of the Department of Health and Human Services by the Transfer Act of August 4, 1954 (P.L. 83-568), has had a significant impact on the state of Indian health. The Indian Self-Determination Act of January 4, 1975 (P.L. 93-638) gave the tribes the option of managing Indian Health Service programs in their communities. Many did. At the end of the decade of the 1980s more than one-third of the service units, which administer health services delivery, were operated by tribes. While the Indian Health Service operated forty-five hospitals and tribes only six, the tribes operated many more of the smaller health centers and health stations than did the Indian Health Service. The Indian Health Care Improvement Act (P.L. 94-437) of 1976, as amended by P.L. 96-537 in 1980, had as its seven-year goal the elevation of the health status of American Indians and Alaska Natives to a level equal to that of the general United States population. Its service population in 1987 comprised over a million Indians and Alaska Natives in thirty-two states on or near reservations. Under the leadership of Everett R. Rhoades, M.D., a Kiowa Indian, from 1982 until 1991, the Indian Health Service quietly but effectively moved to achieve its goal.[9]

One of the most active ongoing debates over the character of tribal

9 Indian Health Service, *Trends in Indian Health – 1993*, more cautiously defines the IHS's goal as "to raise the health status of American Indians and Alaska Natives to the highest possible levels" (Preface i, and 1).

governments concerns their representative character. The structure of representative government among contemporary Indian tribes was largely established as part of the revolution in Indian affairs associated with the Indian Reorganization Act of 1934. Constitutions were prepared by the Bureau of Indian Affairs for those Indian tribes desiring to avail themselves of the opportunity to govern themselves. Critics accused the BIA of providing "boiler plate" constitutions, all of a single rigid character, but in fact the Bureau, with the advice of a corps of anthropological advisors, was careful to make allowances for preexisting political structures, such as the political authority of Hopi village religious leaders when that authority was recognized by a majority of the residents of particular Hopi villages.

But because John Collier had built the Indian Reorganization Act upon the idea of *tribal* identity and unity, the earlier autonomous village, band, and clan units among the Hopis, as well as among other "tribes," were subsumed under the tribal identity recognized by the federal government. Where subtribal units remained viable and important, as among the Hopis and the Sioux, the unity or legality of the tribe as a political entity was sometimes challenged by dissident elements. Such divisions are still at the root of most challenges to the authority of tribal governments by factions within the tribe and by Euro-American supporters outside the tribe. Critics have argued that tribal governments are unrepresentative because they fail to reflect the preexisting and traditional patterns of authority. They also have maintained that some tribal governments are controlled by energy companies intent upon exploiting the mineral resources of the reservations at the cheapest cost. Charges that tribal governments are corrupt and mere "puppets" of an insensitive federal government bureaucracy are also frequently made.[10]

The dispute within the Navajo Nation over tribal governance in the 1980s illustrates many of the conflicts and misunderstandings that becloud United States Indian policy. Tribal leadership among the Navajos in the 1970s and 1980s was divided between two leaders: Peter MacDonald and Peterson Zah. Their contrasting styles of dress illustrated the different approaches each took toward governing the Navajo Nation. MacDonald (called by his political enemies "MacDollar") usually appeared in pinstriped suits, flew around the country in a private jet, and dealt with

---

[10] Wilcomb E. Washburn, "On the Trail of the Activist Anthropologist: Response to Jorgensen and Clemmer, JES 6:2, 6:3," *Journal of Ethnic Studies* 7 (1979), 89–99; Wilcomb E. Washburn, "Anthropological Advocacy in the Hopi-Navajo Land Dispute," *American Anthropologist* 91 (1989), 738–43.

corporations and governments in a regal manner. Zah, a populist and one-time legal activist in the Navajo Reservation branch of the Office of Economic Opportunity, dressed the part of a 1960s activist and rhetorically attacked corporations and those seeking to do business with them on the reservation. Leadership of the Navajo Nation alternated between the two in periodic elections, belying the charge that the Navajo electoral process was "rigged" by outside forces. What does seem clear is that corruption and favoritism did exist and that MacDonald used tribal funds to reward friends and business partners. Evidence of this corruption, along with other cases of tribal misappropriation of funds, was brought out in 1989 in the special report of an investigating committee headed by Senator Dennis De Concini of New Mexico. The committee derived its investigative and oversight responsibilities from the authority given Congress in the Constitution "to regulate Commerce with foreign Nations, and among the several States, and with the Indian Tribes."[11]

Because the powers of the tribal chairman, particularly in relation to the tribal council and tribal courts, are unclear and evolving, a number of efforts to force MacDonald out of office were initially unsuccessful. The tribal council ultimately voted to suspend him from office – even though he continued to receive his $55,000 salary – until potential criminal charges against him were resolved. The council took possession of the chairman's suite of offices, while MacDonald campaigned through the reservation arguing his case. On July 20, 1989, two Navajos were killed by tribal police and eleven injured during a pro-MacDonald march on the tribe's administration and finance building. MacDonald, buffeted by charges involving tribal, state, and federal courts, as well as being assailed by his political rivals on the reservation and harassed by outside American Indian Movement activists, finally lost control of the situation. On October 17, 1990, he was found guilty in Navajo tribal court on forty-two counts of accepting bribes, violating the tribe's ethics laws, and conspiracy. His son was found guilty of twenty-three similar charges. He was also convicted of separate charges in federal court and sentenced to fourteen years in prison. His supporters believe he was victimized by his political opponents.[12]

Tribal government has been influenced not only by local, state, and

[11] 101st Congress, 1st Session, Senate Report 101–216, *Final Report and Legislative Recommendations: A Report of the Special Committee on Investigations of the Select Committee on Indian Affairs, United States Senate* (Washington, D.C., 1989), 181–211.

[12] Peter MacDonald, *The Last Warrior: Peter MacDonald and the Navajo Nation* (New York, 1993), 313–65.

federal governments, but by nontribal Indian organizations and by non-Indian specialists in Indian affairs. The twentieth century has seen the rise of national or pan-Indian organizations, such as the National Congress of American Indians (NCAI) and the American Indian Movement (AIM), which have phrased their recommendations and demands in terms of all Indians rather than of single tribes. The NCAI is a loose organization of tribes and individuals, which comes as close as any organization to being the official spokesman of tribal governments. AIM, on the other hand, is a radical organization of individual Indians who more often than not challenge existing tribal governments, as AIM did in the siege of the Oglala Sioux village of Wounded Knee, South Dakota, in 1973. Similarly, in Canada, the twentieth century has seen the rise of national, pan-Indian, organizations such as the Assembly of First Nations, the Métis National Council, and the Inuit Committee on National Issues. Because the Native political process requires the non-Native majority to be persuaded to support Native aspirations, pan-Indian organizations, with their larger resources, are more capable than individual tribes of presenting "the Native" case to non-Natives bewildered by the multiplicity of small tribes and conditioned to think of Natives as a single entity.

Non-Indian specialists – largely anthropologists – have become increasingly involved in the politics of Native Americans in recent decades. American anthropology "grew up" on studies of Native Americans. There was, therefore, a long tradition of working with particular tribes. Increasingly, individual anthropologists became advocates for one tribe against the federal government (or against another tribe), or for one faction of a tribe against another. In the 1970s anthropologists were drawn into issues such as the establishment by Indian activists of the Yellow Thunder Camp in a national park near the Sioux reservation; the siege of Wounded Knee, taken over by a group of AIM radicals in 1973; the "Trail of Broken Treaties" (1972) and "The Longest Walk" (1978), when many Indians marched on Washington to protest government violations of Indian treaty rights; and the relocation and boundary dispute between the Hopi and Navajo tribes that has been a continuing bone of contention between those neighboring peoples. Many anthropologists saw their efforts as helping to redress the imbalance in relations between Indians and Euro-American governments that had persisted over the previous century, but their efforts were not always seen as helpful by established tribal governments challenged by other tribes or by dissident elements in the Indian community.

The political turmoil of the 1960s and 1970s, which challenged the very legitimacy of tribal governments on Indian reservations, was gradually replaced by more conventional political debate over the validity of the policies particular tribal governments were following. Many of the radicals of the 1960s and 1970s, such as AIM leaders Dennis Banks and Russell Means, ceased their attacks on tribal governments as political entities and sought rather to influence the course of those governments. John Collier was, in effect, vindicated. Tribal governments were rescued and restored to power, in the context of English law and American government, yet without losing their Indian character. Indian politics was directed inward rather than outward, as Indian confidence in the reality of the government-to-government relationship with the states and the federal government overcame their initial skepticism.[13]

In Alaska the most significant political changes were incorporated in the Alaska Native Claims Settlement Act of 1971. A unique feature of the legislation was its establishment of Native economic corporations that were expected to supplant and replace tribal or village political organizations. These economic corporations, into which non-Natives could not "buy in" until after the expiration of twenty years, sought to insert Native Alaskans into the economic world of the twentieth century "without," as the act put it, "establishing any permanently racially defined institutions, rights, privileges, or obligations," as the federal government had done in the case of Indian tribes in the "lower forty-eight" states in the Indian Reorganization Act of 1934. The unusual form of the Alaskan Native settlement derived in part from the fact that Native Alaskans were few in number and organized in small, isolated clans and villages rather than in large tribes as some Indians were in the "lower forty-eight" states, and in part from the fact that both Euro-Americans and Natives wanted to avoid replicating the legally complex and economically inefficient reservation and trusteeship system characteristic of those states.

Despite the fact that the Alaska Federation of Natives had supported the provision for an economic rather than a political approach to the problem, the rapid approach of the period when non-Natives could buy into the Native corporations generated a movement in the 1980s to provide for a continuation of the special status of Alaskan Natives; perpetuation of the exclusively Native character of the corporations even after the period of guaranteed exclusive Native ownership specified in the act of

[13] Wilcomb E. Washburn, *Red Man's Land/White Man's Law*, 2nd ed. (Norman, Okla., 1995).

1971; protection of undeveloped land held by Native corporations from taxation, loss through court action, and bankruptcy proceedings; and provision for those Natives who did not benefit from the original settlement. Native efforts to enhance Native sovereignty by transferring corporate lands to tribal authority, such as remained in the absence of legally acknowledged tribal territories, were rebuffed. Instead Congress allowed corporations to set up state-regulated trusts that could own the land on behalf of Native shareholders. Congress also added a "disclaimer" that the amendments were intended neither to help nor to hinder claims of tribal governments. What powers tribal governments might have under these so-called "1991 amendments" to the act (signed into law, P. L. 100–241, by President Reagan in February 1988) were, to a great degree, left to the courts to decide. The uncertainty persisted throughout the administration of George Bush; in the administration of Bill Clinton, Interior Department Assistant Secretary for Indian Affairs Ada Deer, on October 15, 1993, in Anchorage, announced the publication of a list of federally recognized tribes in Alaska. Deer hoped that this executive action, which asserted that recognized Alaska tribes possessed the same tribal status as tribes in the "lower forty-eight," would be accepted by the courts. The ultimate political status of Alaska Natives remains to be determined.

The evolution of Canadian Indian policy has roughly followed that of the United States but at a different pace and in a very different constitutional and legal setting. The government of Canada was never comfortable with the notion of "aboriginal title." The phrase does not appear in any of the land claims settlements proposed by the government in the 1960s. Aboriginal title and sovereignty were recognized in practice by British colonial administrators and acknowledged in the Royal Proclamation of 1763, which allowed lands of "Indians with whom We are connected" to be surrendered only to the Crown. Yet Canadian courts, particularly those of British Columbia, until the 1970s, generally rejected the idea that the Proclamation either created, or recognized, a preexisting right of aboriginal title. Still earlier, French colonial policy had never acknowledged Indian title to the land, and no land surrender treaties had been made with the Indians of Quebec and the Maritime provinces under French jurisdiction. Only half of Canada's legal-status Indians have treaties with the Crown. Métis and nonstatus Indians (those of Indian ancestry who had lost their legal Indian status through intermarriage with Euro-Canadians or by signing away their land rights) seemed further evidence of the government's diminished legal obligation to many of its citizens of Indian origin.

The rights of Canadian Indians were first comprehensively defined in the Indian Act of 1876 (39 Vic. cap. 18), which formed the basis of all future Indian acts. The act provided for the right of status Indians to reside on the reserve assigned by the government to their band, freed them from most taxes, and gave adult males the right to vote in band council elections (women received the right to vote only in the 1951 amendment). The subject of a preexisting aboriginal title to Indians lands, however, was generally ignored or rejected until continuing Native agitation and increasingly favorable court decisions brought it once again to the fore in the 1970s and 1980s.[14]

Indian policy in Canada in the immediate post–World War II period, like that in the United States, was based on the assumption that the Indians would eventually be assimilated into the larger Canadian body politic. The first Indian was elected to the federal parliament in 1968 and since then Native people have served as Members of Parliament, Cabinet Ministers, Senators, provincial legislators, and the lieutenant-governor of Alberta. Although studies such as the Hawthorn-Tremblay report, based on research by an interdisciplinary team of researchers sponsored by the Canadian government, recommended that Indians keep privileges but be given greater self-determination and be encouraged to participate in Canadian society, in general it was assumed that "Indians," as "Indians," would disappear as they became Canadians.[15] From a government perspective, even the treaties signed with Indian bands in the nineteenth and twentieth centuries were merely "a means of providing transitional protection of an indigenous people who were faced with eventual assimilation or extinction."[16] By 1969 the last Indian agents were gone and band councils began administering housing, education, and other functions under Indian Affairs supervision. By 1984, 187 bands were fully operating their own schools, mainly in British Columbia and on the Prairies, and the last of the federal residential schools closed in 1988. The Canadian government wanted to revise the Indian Act, but Indians wanted special rights honored and land and treaty rights settled first. Consultations in 1968–9 led

---

[14] Sally M. Weaver, *Making Canadian Indian Policy: The Hidden Agenda 1968–1970* (Toronto, 1981), 18, 19, 32, 69; Robert Surtees, "Canadian Indian Policies," in *Handbook of North American Indians,* vol. 4, *History of Indian-White Relations,* ed. Wilcomb E. Washburn, (Washington, D.C., 1988), 90; Bruce Clark, *Native Liberty, Crown Sovereignty: The Existing Aboriginal Right of Self-Government in Canada* (Montreal, 1990).

[15] H. B. Hawthorn, ed., *A Survey of the Contemporary Indians of Canada: A Report on Economic, Political, Educational Needs and Policies* (Ottawa, 1966–7).

[16] J. Rick Ponting, ed., *Arduous Journey: Canadian Indians and Decolonization* (Toronto, 1986), 31.

Indians to believe that they would be involved in the process of revising the Indian Act. But when Canada's Indian policy was reformulated in a 1969 White Paper, during the prime ministership of Pierre Trudeau, a strong proponent of individual as opposed to collective rights, none of these hopes was realized. The White Paper called for a termination of all special treatment of Indians, including the abolition of rights and privileges incorporated in the Indian Act of 1876 and in treaties made both before and after Confederation in 1867. This policy, which had analogies with the "termination legislation" that attracted United States legislators in the 1950s and 1960s, was forcefully defended by Prime Minister Trudeau and his Minister of Indian Affairs, Jean Chrétien. In an address in Vancouver in August 1969 Trudeau asserted flatly that "we say we won't recognize aboriginal rights."[17]

The government's White Paper was what one scholar has called "the embodiment of the liberal ideology" that dominated the Canadian government at the time. It reflected an honest view that equality of treatment of all Canadians, the rejection of paternalism on the one hand and special rights on the other, was the appropriate direction in which Indian policy should move. It was a forward-looking rather than backward-looking approach in the opinion of its supporters. Both the content of the White Paper and the way in which it was presented, however, caused an unexpected Indian reaction and the ultimate withdrawal of the document. The document, compiled in great secrecy, was presented to the House of Commons on June 25, 1969 by Jean Chrétien, who asserted that the paper was a response to Indians' demands for a change in the historical relationship between them and the government. Indian leaders, who had been flown to Ottawa the night before the announcement, had been sketchily but inadequately briefed by Chrétien shortly before the announcement of the policy in the House of Commons and invited to sit in the gallery during the announcement. Their presence gave the appearance of full consultation (if not agreement) with the government.[18]

After the initial shock of the announcement had worn off, spokesmen for the various Canadian Indian organizations began to speak out against the assumptions underlying the new policy and the claim that they had participated in its formulation. Canada's Native organizations had devel-

---

[17] Peter A. Cumming and K. Aalto, "Inuit Hunting Rights in the Northwest Territories," *Saskatchewan Law Review* 38:1 (1973–4), 222–323, quoted in Michael Asch, *Home and Native Land: Aboriginal Rights and the Canadian Constitution* (Toronto, 1984), 8.

[18] Weaver, *Making Canadian Indian Policy*, 168, 169, 204.

oped a powerful national voice and had an ability to make their influence felt in Ottawa, as had similar Indian organizations in the United States. They responded to the government's White Paper of 1969 with the publication in 1970 of a "Red Paper" entitled *Citizens Plus*. The government's "White Paper" looked toward the termination of the special legal status of Indians as it derived from treaties, and their integration into the larger Canadian society. The Indian "Red Paper" demanded the preservation of treaty rights and the retention of the special status they possessed under their treaties. In addition, the "Red Paper" demanded compensation for the taking of the Natives' aboriginal rights. Neither Canadian courts nor the government had at that time accepted the obligation to compensate for aboriginal title. Moreover, the Canadian courts, unlike their judicial brethren south of the border, did not at that time presume to declare an act of the Canadian parliament unconstitutional. Opposition to the government's White Paper increased, with Canadian Indians staging a series of occupations of government offices and demonstrations in Ottawa. These led to the White Paper being withdrawn in March 1971. By highlighting and cementing extreme positions the issuance of the White Paper may have been, as one Canadian scholar has put it, "a costly and unwise *strategy* . . . for which both Indians and government will pay for many years to come."[19]

The debate was acrimonious. Canadian Native leaders, such as Clem Chartier, vice president of the Métis National Council, informed Prime Minister Trudeau that God gave the Natives the land that became Canada and that it would always remain theirs. In a meeting with Chartier and other Indian leaders on March 16, 1973, Trudeau countered by noting that "God also sent Columbus across" and demanded of the Native leaders: "When do you stop reading history? Only when the white man came?" In the verbal play that marked the conference Chartier retorted that "We have thousands of years of history on this land; you have 200 years of history. . . . It all belonged to us, and we shared it." Such public dialogue provided a background to the soul-searching and political calculations that were to lead to an attempted resolution of the issue of Native rights. The issue was doubly complicated because of the powerful role of provinces, such as Quebec and British Columbia. The provinces resisted Trudeau's attempt to have them assume the social and economic responsibility for Indians (the political responsibility remaining with the federal

[19] Ibid., 204.

government), and sometimes rejected federal claims in political matters. Thus British Columbia refused to admit that the Royal Proclamation of 1763 applied to it, and denied the Indian claim to aboriginal land title. The provincial position was upheld by the Supreme Court of Canada in 1973, on appeal from the Supreme Court of British Columbia, in the case of *Calder v. Attorney General of British Columbia*. Though the court was evenly divided on the merits of the case, Calder lost on a technicality. By 1989, however, when the Gitksan-Wet'suwet'en land claim came to the Supreme Court of British Columbia, the concept of a preexisting aboriginal title had been accepted, and the court was faced with determining whether that title had been explicitly or implicitly extinguished.[20]

The James Bay and Northern Quebec Agreement of 1975 has been described as the first modern Native claims settlement in Canada. It left the Inuit and Cree communities in Quebec with substantial control of their political, economic, and social affairs, a cash settlement of $232.5 million over twenty-one years, exclusive ownership of 5,543 square kilometers, and limited hunting rights over areas surrendered to Quebec. Since that time the Crees have established a regional government for their holdings in Quebec, which has provided a model for the development of regional Native governments in Manitoba and other parts of northern Canada.

On March 21, 1974, Prime Minister Pierre Trudeau asked Justice Thomas Berger of the British Columbia Supreme Court to head the Mackenzie Valley Pipeline Inquiry to look into the "social, economic and environmental" impacts of the Mackenzie Valley pipeline, designed to tap the rich energy resources of Alaska and the Canadian North. Justice Berger's commission, in the years that followed, provided a sympathetic hearing to the aspirations of Inuit and Indians that was not limited to social, economic, and environmental issues but which opened up the most fundamental legal and political questions concerning the status of Canada's Native population (see also Chapter 13). The commission's report set in motion a national debate that would reach its climax in the decade following.[21]

Prime Minister Trudeau's comparison of French and Indian aspirations in Canada, and his emphasis on the danger of making concessions to the claims

[20] *New York Times*, March 17, 1973; Paul Tennant, *Aboriginal Peoples and Politics: The Indian Land Question in British Columbia, 1849–1989* (Vancouver, 1990), 213–26.
[21] Thomas R. Berger, *Northern Frontier, Northern Homeland: The Report of the Mackenzie Valley Pipeline Inquiry*, rev. ed. (Vancouver, 1988).

of one group for fear of stimulating those of the other, was to seem prophetic during the 1990 constitutional crisis over the Meech Lake Accord designed to harmonize French-speaking Quebec's aspirations with those of Canada's mainly English-speaking provinces. The delicate agreement, which recognized Quebec as a "distinct" society, collapsed in part as a result of the actions of Elijah Harper, an Indian legislator from Manitoba, who held the agreement hostage to an equivalent recognition of Canada's Indian Nations. The old problem of how to achieve an "equal partnership between the two founding races" of Canada, which has bedeviled Canada since at least the 1860s, in the 1990s threatened to unravel because Canada's Indians now presented more forcefully than ever before their claim that *they* were in fact the original founding "race" and therefore worthy of equal recognition alongside the French and the English intruders.[22]

Many Canadians, including highly placed politicians, seemed reluctant in the early 1990s to concede to Indian governments any claims to sovereignty or even to come to grips with formally defining the nature of self-government. Yet clearly the Native population of Canada had moved to a position of enhanced power and autonomy. The most important legal issues in the 1990s focused on the fight over recognition of past land losses and compensation for them, but subsidiary issues included subsistence hunting rights, recognition of non-status Natives (a Métis issue), and band authority. In all of these areas the trend was toward providing more encompassing authority for Native peoples. In the words of Justice Thomas Berger, Chairman of the Alaska Native Review Commission (established by the Inuit Circumpolar Conference and by the World Council of Indigenous Peoples) as well as of the earlier Canadian Mackenzie Valley Pipeline Inquiry dealing with the Subarctic, there was a "world-wide movement of indigenous people for self-rule or self-determination." While Canada was far from fully recognizing this Native claim to self-rule and self-determination, and while it did not recognize band authorities as existing on a government-to-government basis on the order of U.S. policy, it was engaged, as were many other nations around the world, in redefining its relationship to the ethnic minorities – whether aboriginal or immigrant in character – within its national borders.

The early stages of the debate had resulted in the 1951 revision of the Indian Act of 1876, and the renewed debate unleashed by the Trudeau White Paper of 1969 led ultimately to the Constitution Act of 1982,

---

[22] Pauline Comeau, *Elijah: No Ordinary Hero* (Vancouver, 1993).

which affirmed existing aboriginal and treaty rights and included within the definition of "Aboriginal peoples of Canada" the Indians, Inuit, and Métis. However, the precise meaning of the recognition of existing aboriginal and treaty rights was left undefined in the constitution and the subject of continued debate and negotiation between the government and Native organizations. A House of Commons Special Committee on Indian Self-Government (the Penner Committee) issued a report in 1983 recommending the establishment of Indian governments as another order of government separate from the federal and provincial. Whether these goals will be realized depends upon future negotiation and debate between descendants of Canada's Aboriginal peoples and of its later immigrants.[23]

The reluctance of the Canadian government to recognize an inherent Native right to self-government retained from their history as a free people, preferring rather to encourage individual bands to seek municipal-type powers subordinate to provinces, led to heightened tensions with Native people. The appropriation by the municipal government of Oka, Quebec, of land claimed for over 200 years by the Kahnesetake Mohawks in order to expand a golf course precipitated a crisis on July 11, 1990. This involved the highly publicized seventy-eight-day armed defence of the land claimed by the Mohawks at Oka and the blockage of bridges and railroad lines passing through the nearby Mohawk reserve of Kahnawake by armed Mohawk "warriors" from nearby reserves (and from across the U.S. border). Although ultimately dispersed by the Canadian army, this resistance led to a ground swell of sympathy for the Indians among Anglo-Canadians, who were already disillusioned with the government of Brian Mulroney, while it embittered relations between Native people and franco-phone non-Natives inside Quebec.

The 1970s also saw demands by Inuit and Indians in northern Canada for self-government and recognition of aboriginal title to their lands. These demands, in the 1980s, were met with a new flexibility and understanding on the part of the Canadian government, which agreed, after many years of negotiation under a land claims process established by the federal government, to turn over extensive areas of the Canadian Arctic to a greater measure of Native control. Because of the large numbers of non-

---

[23] Leroy Little Bear, ed., *Pathways to Self-Determination: Canadian Indians and the Canadian State* (Toronto, 1984), 133; Thomas R. Berger, Speech on "Land Claims: 14 Years Later" to Maryland Colloquium on Public Philosophy, Washington, D.C., May 10, 1985, mimeographed, 7; Thomas R. Berger, *Village Journey: The Report of the Alaska Native Review Commission* (New York, 1985); *Canadian Encyclopedia*, 1451; Douglas Sanders, "Government Indian Agencies in Canada," in Washburn, ed., *Handbook of North American Indians*, vol. 4, 283.

Native Canadians in the Northwest Territories, the decision to grant a greater degree of political and economic control over the northern areas to the descendants of the aboriginal inhabitants was a difficult one for the Canadian government. The policy moved forward step by step, culminating in the Nunavut Final Land Claim Agreement, signed on May 25, 1993, by Prime Minister Mulroney, Northwest Territories Government Leader Nellie Cournoyea, Tungavik Federation of Nunavut President James Eetoolook, and other Inuit leaders. The agreement, which covered the Eastern Arctic, confirmed the commitment to proceed to parliament with legislation that would create the Nunavut Territory by 1999 giving 17,500 Inuit (80 percent of the population of the designated area) ownership of 350,000 square kilometers of land, of which approximately 36,000 square kilometers will include mineral rights. In addition, the rest of the Northwest Territories, with its headquarters in Yellowknife, would become increasingly self-governing and move toward provincial status. The Inuit of the Western Arctic also entered into a separate agreement, the Inuvialuit Land claim, on June 5, 1984, which provided them with ownership of 11,000 square kilometers of land with surface and subsurface rights and another 78,000 square kilometers without gas and oil rights.[24]

The increasing participation of Native Canadians in the governance of the northern territories of Canada has resulted in numerous name changes everywhere in this region. Thus the name of the Inuit village of Frobisher Bay, at the head of the bay in which the English explorer Martin Frobisher in 1576 hoped to find the Northwest Passage to China, has been officially changed to Iqaluit, although the long inlet itself retains his name. Similarly, Hudson Bay continues to commemorate the European explorer for whom it is named, while the smaller geographical locations within it that are of most concern to the Native population revert to their Native designations. Whether names venerated in Canadian history, such as Resolute Bay and the Mackenzie River (named for the explorer Sir Alexander Mackenzie who traced its route in 1789), will be changed will be thrashed out in the context of the new partnership between the descendants of Canada's northern Aboriginal population and the descendants of her more recent immigrants.

The same liberalizing tendencies that have changed the character of relations between Native and non-Native populations in the United States

---

[24] *Canadian Encyclopedia*, 1521–4; Little Bear, *Pathways*, 79; Indian and Northern Affairs Canada, Communique 1-9324, May 25, 1993. Ken Coates, ed., *Aboriginal Land Claims in Canada* (Toronto, 1992), 167–94.

and Canada have also been operative in Greenland. Because of the situation during World War II, when Greenland was effectively cut off from any Danish administration, Greenlanders achieved a working experience with self-government. That experience was maintained following the reintroduction of Danish administration after the war.

In 1975 a committee composed entirely of Greenlanders proposed the development of a home rule system for Greenland. A commission on the subject was created which, in 1978, presented formal proposals for a Home Rule Act, which became law on November 29, 1978, and effective on May 1, 1979, after overwhelming approval by Greenland's residents, of whom about 40,000 were Native Greenlanders and 10,000 Danes. The act gave Greenland the same political autonomy as the Faeroes, another Danish possession. While remaining a constituent part of Denmark, which retained absolute jurisdiction in constitutional, foreign, and defense affairs, together with national finances, Greenland began to exercise authority over domestic affairs, taxation and duties, and control of the fishing industry, as well as moving to take over various Danish-subsidized activities such as social welfare, church affairs, and education. Political power under the act was shifted to a new Greenland assembly elected by popular vote and an executive administration elected by the assembly. Greenlanders were also recognized to have certain "fundamental rights" to Greenland's natural resources: that is, the possibility of controlling the exploitation of any mineral wealth that might be found under Greenland's vast icecap.

By an "accident of history" Greenland was brought into the European Community along with its mother country in 1973, before Home Rule, even though in the Danish referendum on the subject in the previous year Greenlanders voted 2 to 1 against entering. In 1983 the Greenlanders were again asked their views on the subject. Denmark promised that it would abide by their decision. Greenlanders voted 52 to 46 percent for withdrawal. Although withdrawal from the European Community, which took place on January 1, 1985, meant the loss of approximately $30,000,000 a year in direct grants from the Community, and might eventually call into question the continuing financial support – covering over half the cost of running the country – provided by Denmark, the sense of identification with fellow Inuit of Canada and Alaska provided a greater attraction than Europe.

This "Nativist" trend in Greenland was further stimulated by the formation in 1977 of the Inuit Circumpolar Conference, which sought to link

Inuit people from all the circumpolar nations, including the Soviet Union. The almost total dominance of fishing over other economic activities in the rich waters surrounding Greenland, and the fear that Native exploitation of this resource might be threatened by decisions taken in Brussels, headquarters of the European Community, was another factor in Greenland's relaxation of its former ties with Denmark.

LEGAL RENAISSANCE

The period since 1960 has seen a rapid development of Indian law in the United States. The system of tribal courts and tribal police, organized in the nineteenth century as an expedient way of utilizing Native Americans to police and judge themselves (critics would say to impose Euro-American law and order upon Indians), has helped to establish the permanence and validity of tribal governments. Many of the approximately 150 tribal courts and Courts of Indian Offenses were established according to the provisions of tribal constitutions adopted under the Indian Reorganization Act of 1934. At the same time, as the power and reach of the judicial branches of tribal governments have been extended, Indian judges have often found themselves in conflict with tribal chairmen and councils. The lack of professional training of tribal judges, and the acceptance of informal procedures in tribal courts, have stimulated protests from some Indian litigants and from some outside observers.

Indian courts, which one federal court in 1888 described as "mere educational and disciplinary instrumentalities by which the government of the United States is endeavoring to improve and elevate the condition of these dependent tribes to whom it sustains the relation of guardian" (*United States v. Clapox,* 35 F. 575, 577), were thrust into a more fundamental and central role by the 1959 decision of the Supreme Court in *Williams v. Lee* (358 U.S. 217). In that case the Supreme Court ruled that a non-Indian storekeeper on the Navajo Reservation could not use the Arizona state courts to collect a debt owed by a Navajo Indian residing on the reservation. "There can be no doubt," the court ruled, "that to allow the exercise of state jurisdiction here would undermine the authority of the tribal courts over Reservation affairs and hence would infringe on the right of Indians to govern themselves." Although the court complimented the tribe for "strengthening the Navajo tribal government and its courts," its decision may have rested more on hope in the continued development of the Navajo legal system than on a full understanding of its existing character. In particular the court seems to have been unaware of the potential opposition between the tribal government and the tribal courts that was eventually to develop. In subsequent years the import of the ruling was not fully grasped either by the tribe itself or by the Bureau of Indian Affairs. Tribal courts remained underfunded and underdeveloped.

The 1960s and 1970s saw the slow development of the Indian court system, stimulated by the heightened attention to Indian law provided by the increasing number of judicial decisions at all levels affecting Indians, and by the work of organizations such as the Native American Rights Fund, established in 1970 in California (moving to Boulder, Colorado, in 1971) to provide expert legal advice and representation for hundreds of tribes and individuals. This organization initially was supported financially by the Ford Foundation and later by other foundations, business, and government. The growth of the Indian court system was marked by the establishment in 1968 of the National American Indian Court Judges Association, which sought to improve and upgrade the Indian court system through research, professional advancement, and continuing education, while furthering tribal and public knowledge and understanding of the Indian court system.[25]

The status of tribal courts was given its strongest push by the Supreme Court's decision in *Santa Clara Pueblo v. Martinez* (436 U.S. 49) in 1978. The case involved an Indian woman, Julia Martinez, who claimed that her individual rights under the U.S. Constitution were violated by a tribal ordinance that prohibited her children by a non-member of the tribe (though an Indian) from becoming enrolled members of her tribe. On appeal to the Supreme Court, the highest court held that her rights as a U.S. citizen must give way to tribal regulations, discriminatory as they might be toward women. The rights of individual Indians against their tribal governments, rights created by the Indian Civil Rights Act of 1968 (82 U.S. Stat. 73), the high court ruled, could only be vindicated in tribal courts. For federal courts to intervene would violate the sovereign immunity of the tribal government.

Yet were tribal courts prepared to assume the role thrust upon them by the Supreme Court? There was no tradition of judicial review of tribal legislation by tribal courts. There was no historical process similar to that by which U.S. courts were able to assume this prerogative, so rare in the

---

[25] National American Indian Court Judges Association, *Indian Courts and the Future: Report of the NAICJA Long Range Planning Project* ([Washington, D.C.], 1978); Washburn, *Red Man's Land/ White Man's Law.*

world. The tribal courts had established their ability to deal with both civil and criminal cases (other than major crimes, which were reserved to the federal courts). Yet the Indian court system, which had been consciously freed from the technicalities of procedure and form characteristic of non-Native courts, was now being asked to deal with responsibilities for decisions of a more fundamental character. Would the informal, subjective, traditional, common sense approach of Indian judges untrained in either U.S. or Native law be equal to the heavy responsibilities thrust upon them? Clashes soon occurred between judges and tribal chairmen. Many of the latter, who had often appointed the judges to their positions, were in no mood to be told that their decisions could be reversed by their appointees. Tribal councils also sometimes assumed an authority to legislate that transcended the right of the tribal courts to question or repudiate.

Perhaps the most hopeful development in the field of Indian law in this period was the effort to develop a corpus of Indian common law that can apply the "traditions," "customs," and "usages" of individual tribes to the determination of tribal disputes. Indian customs and usages are fully a part of the powers that the tribes have reserved, and that right has been recognized by the United States. If Indian common law is to come into being, in the opinion of one commentator, it "must be written down so it will be the same for all" within the tribe. Tribal judges should therefore be leaders in developing tribal law not only through written decisions but by participating in the development of tribal codes.[26]

The creation of the Navajo Peacemaker Court in 1982 expressed the hope of the leaders of one tribe to blend traditional Indian values with formal Euro-American court procedures. The Peacemaker Court incorporated a tradition of informal mediation into the formal legal structure of the tribe. It attempted to deemphasize the adversarial format of Euro-American–derived courts and provide justice that was private, inexpensive, and accessible, and at the same time met the ends of compensation and reconciliation. By making the court a new division of the trial court and providing for enforcement through the regularly constituted Navajo court structure, the Navajo experiment was able to link past and present in a legal structure suitable for the Navajo future.[27]

The legal record in the United States on the subject of land claims, fishing rights, hunting rights, water rights, recognition of non-federally

[26] James W. Zion, "Harmony among the People: Torts and Indian Courts," *Montana Law Review* 45 (1984), 274, 279.
[27] James W. Zion, "Navajo Peacemaker Court . . . ," *American Indian Law Review* 11 (1985), 89–109.

recognized tribes, and other aspects of the Indian–Euro-American relationship is massive and need not be recounted in detail. Suffice it to say that in all these areas there has been continual growth and widening of Indian rights since 1960. The principle that rights established by nineteenth-century treaties must be respected by twentieth-century courts despite intervening changes of circumstances has been established. Often the definition of those rights has turned on the interpretation of obscure phrases. The "original intent" of those who formulated the treaties has been the subject of bitter debate. In the fishing rights cases in the State of Washington, much hinged on the meaning of the phrase found in the treaties negotiated in 1854 and 1855 that in exchange for relinquishing their interests in certain lands the Indians would be given small parcels of land for their exclusive use and protected in their "right of taking fish at usual and accustomed grounds and stations . . . in common with all citizens of the Territory." The Supreme Court, in *Washington et al. v. Washington State Commercial Passenger Fishing Vessel Assn. et al.* (443 U.S. 658, 1979), upheld the ruling of a lower court that the phrase meant that present-day Indians and non-Indians should share the take of fish on an equal basis. The court noted that the United States had previously used the phrase "in common with" in two treaties with Great Britain that dealt with fishing rights in waters adjoining the United States and Canada and that those treaties were interpreted by the Department of State during the nineteenth century to give each signatory country an "equal" and apportionable "share" of the take of fish in the treaty areas. The court concluded that "Nontreaty fishermen may not rely on property law concepts, devices such as the fish wheel, license fees, or general regulations to deprive the Indians of a fair share of the relevant runs of anadromous fish in the case area. Nor may treaty fishermen rely on their exclusive right of access to the reservations to destroy the rights of other 'citizens of the territory.' "

Equivalent judicial interpretations in other areas have upheld the rights of Native Americans in asserting their unique authority, derived for the most part from treaties, to hunt without the restrictions placed on non-Indians and to preserve their priority in the utilization of water rights when those are challenged by non-Indians. Judicial determinations have not always pleased the tribes or their attorneys, but recent courts have in general rendered judgments that recognize the sovereignty generally acknowledged in the seventeenth and eighteenth centuries and gradually eroded in the nineteenth and early twentieth centuries.

The one area of law in which the Supreme Court has caused Native Americans some anguish is in its rulings denying tribal authorities the right to punish nontribal members for offenses committed on tribal territory. In *Oliphant v. Suquamish Indian Tribe* (435 U.S. 191), the Supreme Court, in 1978, sharply limited the right of Indian tribes to assume such authority in the face of the historical record (which the court read as denying such intent on the part of Congress) and in the absence of any basic rights that those accused, as nonmembers of the tribe, would otherwise possess against their tribal accusers. The decision in *Oliphant* does not mean that Indian tribes have no power over non-members residing in tribal territories. They have the power to tax and regulate businesses of outsiders on the reservation. But the court wanted to assure non-Indians that they would not be subject to criminal prosecution under procedures at variance with those to which they were accustomed and in the formulation of which they had no say.

Perhaps the best evidence that tribal existence is enjoying a renaissance is the fact that many non-federally recognized "tribes" are still attempting to become recognized. Many of these are remnants of historical Native peoples, particularly in the eastern portion of the United States, whose political unity was shattered by war, disease, or migration, and whose descendants intermarried with non-Indians as well as other Indian groups and gradually lost much of their earlier tribal identity and culture. An office in the Bureau of Indian Affairs considers applications from individuals professing to constitute such tribes, a number of whom have successfully achieved federal recognition and are now able to enjoy the support provided by the federal government to recognized tribes. Among the tribes recognized in recent years are the Mohegan Tribe of Connecticut, the Catawba Tribe of South Carolina, and the Ione Band of Miwok Indians of California. The impressive panoply of legal rights surrounding Indian tribes, their courts and councils, is built on the recognition by the United States, virtually uniquely among the nations of the world, of the independent, self-governing, permanent, and persisting character of the aboriginal tribes, whose source of authority is treated as inherent and not derived from the American state.

ECONOMIC RENAISSANCE

Can one speak of an Indian economic renaissance in the face of the powerful and prevailing external view, and in many cases the terrible reality, of

Indian poverty, unemployment, disease and despair? A good case can, in fact, be made for this view. Indians are economically less well-off than most other North Americans, especially in northern and other more remote regions, but the gap between the Indian and the non-Indian population is closing. Most surprising is the fact that Indians, once perennially at the bottom of any statistical study of economic well-being in the United States, are now no longer so in several significant categories, including income and education, as noted in the first section of this chapter. According to 1980 census statistics, the median family income for United States Indians ($13,724) surpassed that for African-Americans ($12,598), while remaining well below that of Euro-Americans ($20,835). The equivalent 1990 census statistics were $20,025, $19,758, and $22,429. In the field of education, increasingly a vital element in a nation's economic well-being, the number of Indians twenty-five years or older who have had twelve years of education is now 55.5 percent in comparison with an African-American figure of 51.2 percent and a Euro-American one of 68.8 percent. The number of high school graduates or higher for the ten largest American Indian tribes (as a percentage of persons twenty-five years or over) rose from 55.8 percent in 1980 to 65.6 percent in 1990. The overall United States percentage during the same period rose from 66.5 percent to 75.2 percent. Problems of an enormous character remain, but the trends suggest the validity of the term renaissance, and the remainder of this section will attempt to describe and define the upturn in Indian economic well-being.[28]

Poverty and disease were the most prominent characteristics of United States Indians in the early twentieth century, at which time the Native American population was at its lowest ebb, less than a quarter of a million people. Since that time the movement of population, health, and economic statistics has been up, particularly in the wake of the "New Deal" innovations of Commissioner of Indian Affairs John Collier. Under the Indian Reorganization Act pushed through Congress under his guidance, Indian tribes were reconstituted, economic corporations established, and credit facilities made available so that the power of Indians in the economic field could be established. Although this recovery was slow and partial rather than rapid and revolutionary (see Chapter 12), it neverthe-

---

[28] Snipp, *American Indians*, 249, 317, and Table 8.10; Bureau of the Census, *1990 Census of Population: Social and Economic Characteristics, U.S.* (Washington, D.C., 1993), Table 8; Edna L. Paisano, Population Division, U.S. Bureau of the Census, "Selected Characteristics of American Indian Tribes for the United States," mimeographed, November 1994.

less marked a distinct turning away from the philosophy of despair that had formerly dominated Indian economic life. Along with this economic recovery has come a dramatic population recovery, noted in the first section of this chapter.

Nevertheless there were many failures and disappointments in the course of this economic renaissance, particularly when the government sought to encourage tribes to shift from one economic activity to another. In the case of the Navajo Nation, where the U.S. government, concerned that the growth of sheep herding was destroying the ability of the Navajo land to sustain itself, sought to curb the herds, the Navajo opposition was so strong that it directly affected the tribe's willingness to accept the Indian Reorganization Act (IRA). Other tribes experienced successful conversions to new economic activities. Among them were the Jicarilla Apaches, who initially resisted acceptance of Collier's suggestion that they adopt a formal tribal government under the Indian Reorganization Act, but who eventually, in 1937, voted to accept a constitution that reflected both the spirit of the IRA and the traditions of the tribe. The tribe, at this point, in the words of its Native Jicarilla historian, "entered into an unmatched era of economic development" and "changed from a dying, poverty-stricken race to a prosperous people with a thriving livestock economy."[29]

Some observers have assumed that Indian economic problems stem from the continued existence of tribalism. The movement to "terminate" the federal trust responsibilities for Indian tribes, identified with the administration of Dwight D. Eisenhower in the period 1953–61, was a reflection of that feeling. The idea pervaded leaders of both political parties that the reservation and the trust relationship were holding Indians back economically. The belief that Indians should be integrated into the larger society had been an underlying assumption of non-Indians despite John Collier's extraordinary achievement in overturning the assumption long enough to effect the passage of the Indian Reorganization Act in 1934.

Termination acts affecting the Menominee Indians of Wisconsin, the Klamath Indians of Oregon, and four small bands of Indians elsewhere, passed the Congress in 1954. Other tribes were targeted for termination, under House Concurrent Resolution 108, which judged them to be ready for "freedom from federal supervision and control." It was argued that the tribes selected for termination were those expected to do well economically

[29] Veronica Tiller, *The Jicarilla Apache Tribe: A History, 1846–1970* (Lincoln, Nebr., 1983), 159, 172–3.

when removed from federal supervision. It was hoped that with the successful termination of federal supervision over these selected tribes, termination could be applied to others, and eventually the federal government might be able to "get out of the Indian business."

The leading figure behind the termination legislation was Senator Arthur V. Watkins of Utah. A devout Mormon, conservative in his views, he sincerely believed that the Indians needed to be "freed" from government control. As chairman of the Senate Subcommittee on Indian Affairs he was able to steer legislation to "free the Indian" from "wardship status" through the Congress, most of whose members knew little or nothing of Indian matters. Few members of his committee regularly attended the hearings on the subject.

The results of the termination legislation of this period proved disastrous to the tribes involved. Thrown headlong into the competitive world of American economic life without the supervision to which they had for so long been accustomed, the tribes proved unable to sustain themselves or their members. Whether they were coerced or willingly moved toward termination is a much debated point. Scholars have concluded that the Menominees were coerced into accepting termination in the belief that they had no option in the matter. The Klamath case seems more ambiguous. There, the desire of many individual Klamath members to obtain per capita payments from the sale of their rich timberlands resulted in apparent Klamath acquiescence in the process. The wasteful dissipation of the timber payments in the purchase of consumer goods such as automobiles by individual Klamaths did not, in the opinion of those justifying the process, invalidate the correctness of the policy.

Because of the work of a charismatic Menominee woman, Ada Deer, who headed a tribal organization called Determination of Rights and Unity for Menominee Shareholders (DRUMS), the Menominees were eventually able to reverse the termination legislation of 1954 and regain, though with diminished resources, the trust status given up at that time. They were aided by the support of pan-Indian organizations such as the National Congress of American Indians, and by friendly non-Indian anthropologists. The Menominee Restoration Act of 1973 achieved this purpose and, in the words of one scholar, "signaled the official end of the policy of termination."[30] The entire story of Menominee termination and

[30] Nicholas C. Peroff, *Menominee Drums: Tribal Termination and Restoration, 1954–1974* (Norman, Okla., 1982), 227.

restoration is a complex one, with characteristic internal factional disputes, outside involvement by well-wishers and ill-wishers, and gender conflicts within the tribe. As is usual in Indian affairs, the critical work had to be done in the larger context of American society and Washington politics. Yet it is an inspiring example of the ability of an Indian people to shape their own destiny, even to the point of forcing the U.S. government to reverse its course. A measure of the impact of Ada Deer's work is that she was made Assistant Secretary for Indian Affairs in the Department of the Interior in the administration of Bill Clinton.

Despite the reversal and repudiation of the termination legislation of the 1950s, the assumption of eventual assimilation of American Indians into the larger society and economy prevailed even during the "Great Society" period of President Lyndon B. Johnson. In the hearings on the Indian Resources Development Act of 1967, July 13 and 14, 1967, Secretary of the Interior Stewart Udall introduced the legislation by comparing it in importance to the Indian Reorganization Act of 1934. With support from Robert L. Bennett, Commissioner of Indian Affairs, and an Indian himself, the Johnson administration proposed to allow Indian tribes, when incorporated by charter in accordance with the provisions of the proposed act, to "acquire, hold, and dispose of property, including trust or restricted property," and "to sell, mortgage, invest, or otherwise use, pledge, or dispose of trust or restricted property including tribal funds deposited in the U.S. Treasury." Secretary Udall noted that the trust status of Indian land "has been a barrier to certain kinds of development in the past." Udall believed the trust relationship could be altered "to enable Indians to participate in normal economic activity, but still not eliminate the trust precipitously." Udall foresaw the Indians moving down the road "toward the right kind of ultimate independence." When queried by Chairman Wayne N. Aspinall as to whether by "ultimate independence" Udall meant doing away with reservations as such, Udall responded that "I think this is undoubtedly the ultimate end result; yes." Elaborating further, Udall noted that "I am a gradualist – gradual termination."[31]

Far from succeeding in "freeing the Indian" from the guiding hand of the federal government, the 1960s saw increased dependence upon Washington, as a part of the overall thrust of the Johnson administration's "war on poverty" and push to create the "Great Society" the president envis-

---

[31] House Committee on Interior and Insular Affairs, *Hearings on the Indian Resources Development Act of 1967, 13 and 14 July 1967* (Washington, D.C., 1967), 33, 39, 40, 45, 48.

aged. Every agency of government, not just the Bureau of Indian Affairs, seemed to "discover" the Indian and money appeared embarrassingly easy to come by. Other agencies of government – by legislative, judicial, or administrative determination – were allowed to include Indians among the recipients of federal funds, and "Indian desks" were created in virtually all the large government agencies. One such office, originally the Indian Division of the Office of Economic Opportunity, was transferred to the Department of Health, Education and Welfare (HEW, later to become the Department of Health and Human Services) and its name changed to the Office of Native American Programs. In 1974, the name was again changed to the Administration for Native Americans.[32]

As a private organization – Americans for Indian Opportunity, headed by the Comanche LaDonna Harris – put it in a paper entitled "Colonization of Indian Economy," submitted to the House Interior and Insular Affairs Committee for its hearings on Indian Economic Development Programs, June 26, July 10 and 24, 1979, "Tribes have learned through experience that dollars are most likely to come through the art of learning what projects are [that] granting agencies want to fund." The result, as Chairman Morris K. Udall of the Committee on Interior and Insular Affairs noted in a hearing held March 12, 1979, was that "This tends to be to the advantage of the tribe with the best program of grantsmanship and the best hustlers who know their way through this bureaucracy, and not necessarily the tribes with the greatest need."

The Economic Development Administration, for example, between 1966, when Indian reservations were designated as eligible for assistance, and 1979, spent half a billion dollars for economic development in Indian country. Among the favorite projects, which tribes soon learned to demand, were industrial parks. Of forty-eight industrial parks built, the EDA reported in 1979 that only twenty-three had any business or industrial activities on them.

Tourism projects were also favored by the EDA. In the early 1970s the EDA committed $75 million to tourism development. "The majority of the projects," the EDA conceded, "have experienced a multitude of operating problems, most of which are related to management."[33]

---

[32] House Committee on Interior and Insular Affairs, *Hearings on Indian Economic Development Programs, March 11, 12, 17 and April 3, 1979* (Washington, D.C., 1979), 68.

[33] Testimony of Harold Williams, Deputy Assistant Secretary, Economic Development Administration, U.S. Department of Agriculture, in House Interior and Insular Affairs Committee, *Hearings on Indian Economic Development Programs, March 12, 22, 27, and April 3, 1979*, part 1 (Washington, D.C., 1979), 273; ibid., 7, 42–43, 136.

Another attempt to aid Indian reservation economies was by the Comprehensive Employment and Training Act (CETA), first enacted in 1973 and reauthorized in 1978. CETA, in the view of the Department of Labor, which administered the grants under the act, "mesh[ed] perfectly" with the Indian Self-Determination and Education Assistance Act of 1973 (P.L. 93-638).[34]

The numerous programs designed to improve the Indian economic condition resulted in what Chairman Morris K. Udall of the Committee on Interior and Insular Affairs called a "nightmare" when recorded on a chart showing the interrelations between government agencies and the Native American community. As the Sioux Franklin Ducheneaux, Special Counsel on Indian Affairs to the committee, noted, "This chart, somewhat incompletely, shows the duplicating and overlapping of Federal efforts in the area of economic development and Indian reservations." Ducheneaux noted that across the top of the chart "you will see Interior, Commerce, Agriculture, and HEW as major Departments involved in this effort, and below it the departmental agencies, the Bureau of Indian Affairs, the Economic Development Administration, the Office of Minority Business Enterprise, the Rural Development System, the Farmers Home Administration, the independent agencies – the Small Business Administration – and under HEW the Community Services Administration, and the Administration for Native Affairs, also under HEW."[35] The list could go on and on.

It is little wonder, then, that it took six pages just to list the titles of federal programs of assistance to American Indians in the table of contents of the 295-page publication *Federal Programs of Assistance to American Indians: A Report Prepared for the Senate Select Committee on Indian Affairs of the United States Senate* by Richard S. Jones, Specialist in American National Government of the Congressional Research Service, printed for the use of the Select Committee on Indian Affairs (Washington, D.C., August 1985). The programs available covered the gamut from the Department of Agriculture's Food Distribution Program on Indian reservations to the Veterans Loan Program of the Small Business Administration.[36]

The rush by agencies of government to do something for the Indians in

[34] Statement of Lamond Godwin, Administrator, Office of National Programs, U.S. Department of Labor, in ibid., 88, 309–10.

[35] Ibid., 5–6, 69.

[36] 99th Congress, 1st Session, Senate Report 99-81, *Federal Programs of Assistance to American Indians* (Washington, D.C., 1985), 5, 287.

the 1960s and 1970s reflected not only the optimism of the period but a compassionate concern for Native Americans brought on by Indian militancy and Euro-American guilt feelings. Yet there was no clear assumption of purpose in these programs other than to ameliorate the economic lot of Indians and to enhance their political power. Conflicts of interest within or between tribes and with their non-Indian neighbors were often ignored. Even influential Indian organizations, such as LaDonna Harris's Americans for Indian Opportunity, conceded that "There was a tendency in 'Great Society' programs in general and Indian programs in particular to ignore fiscal accountability requirements in the early days because of a lack of experience on the part of the grantees." The Americans for Indian Opportunity report also noted that "One rule of thumb that should be kept in mind is that any business that is run like a governmental agency is doomed to failure whether it be tribal or federal."[37]

The early history of the American Indian National Bank, formed in 1973 as a "financial vehicle to combine the resources of Indian tribes and people as a source of lending funds to help their economic development," provides an unhappy example of how the best intentions could be frustrated by poor administration. The bank was capitalized at about $1.5 million. When a new director was asked to take over the direction of the bank in 1978, capital had declined to a low point of $52,000. The bank had lost its initial capitalization through charge-offs of uncollectible loans. Conley Ricker, the new director, established new lending policies and found ways to secure loans with collateral that previously had not been used. Tribes were required to come up with a secondary source of repayment other than the primary source. The bank found a way that tribes could pledge the interest on their certificates of deposit, which are managed for them by the Bureau of Indian Affairs, as a way to secure loans. The history of the American Indian National Bank illustrates both the dangers and the opportunities inherent in Indian involvement in the private sector of the American economy under conditions established by the federal government.[38]

Even the most ardent advocates of the Indian cause became persuaded

---

[37] Chapter 3, "Barriers to Development," in Americans for Indian Opportunity, Report on "Colonization of Indian Economy," presented by LaDonna Harris, June 26, 1979, in House Interior and Insular Affairs Committee, *Hearings on Indian Economic Development Programs, June 26, July 10 and 24*, part 2 (Washington, D.C., 1980), 145, 148.

[38] Testimony of Conley Ricker, Chief Executive Officer of Indian National Bank, in U.S. Senate, Select Committee on Indian Affairs, *Hearings on Oversight of Economic Development on Indian Reservations, April 29, 1982* (Washington, D.C., 1982), 87, 88, 92.

that the system of the 1970s was not working, despite the extraordinary sums disbursed. Joseph B. DeLaCruz, the fiery president of the National Congress of American Indians, while bemoaning the policies instituted by Ronald Reagan when he became president in 1981, conceded that "Our dependency upon outside assistance is our Achilles heel." DeLaCruz urged tribes to "recognize and utilize the economic power of their resources to influence public opinion." Particularly important was the need to "eliminate" the "misconception that seems to pervade the general public . . . that Indian people drain the treasury while contributing little to the general economy."39

Members of Congress were also, by the 1980s, convinced that a new approach had to be found. Senator Mark Andrews, of North Dakota, noted that "We have searched, during the two decades I have been privileged to be in Congress, for new ways that we can stimulate job opportunities on the reservation, and every time we come up with a new one it seems like a will-o-the-wisp to disappear again because it does not interface with what the tribal people need or it is simply impractical at the beginning." Chairman of the Select Committee on Indian Affairs William S. Cohen of Maine, in introducing a hearing on the economic condition of Indian reservations, noted that "the single and perhaps most striking feature of this condition is the great dependency of Indian tribes on the professional and financial assistance of the Federal Government."40

The American example could be matched by equivalent problems in programs designed to help the Canadian Native population. Canada's debate over Indian policy in the 1970s took place in the context of a tremendous increase in federal support for Indian communities that had, however, a paradoxical result. As one resident of an Ojibwa village put it "the kids see their parents getting everything for nothing; the government provides welfare money; the government provides jobs; the government gives free houses." Violent and senseless rage and destruction of property is the way youth in this particular Ojibwa village worked out their sense of powerlessness and worthlessness.41

The particular village at which this social pathology was observed was also one that had been relocated in the 1960s by the Canadian government

---

39 Joseph B. DeLaCruz, Statement delivered at 6th National Indian Timber Symposium, Spokane, 1982, printed in ibid. 14–15.
40 William S. Cohen, quoted in ibid., 1–2.
41 Anastasia M. Shkilnyk, *A Poison Stronger than Love: The Destruction of an Ojibwa Community* (New Haven, Conn., 1985), 33.

to handle more efficiently the social services being provided in increasing amounts to the Natives of the village. The relocation was ostensibly done at the request of the band, but in fact was engineered by non-Indian administrators who had little understanding of, or respect for, Indian culture. The tribal members went reluctantly because of their increasing dependence on the government for support. The move deprived them of some of their traditional ties to the land of their forefathers. They gave up growing their own food and resorted to purchasing it in stores, for example.

The federal operating budget in Canada for Indian Affairs for 1990 has been estimated at $2.5 billion, just over half of what Ottawa spends annually on all programs directed towards Native peoples. This is a large burden for a country with a total population only one-tenth that of the United States. Yet one student of Canadian Indian affairs has noted that "it is one of the most compelling paradoxes of our public policy that ever increasing government expenditures on Indians finds an exact parallel in ever increasing indices of social disintegration on their reserves." What was the "implacable logic" that produced an outcome so "contradictory to the intent" of those who promoted the policy that it was interpreted in some quarters as "an implicit acceptance of Indian genocide"![42]

To answer this question it is not adequate to consider merely the facts of cultural relativism, and the resulting misunderstanding by the representatives of each culture of the imperatives of the other; nor is it enough to attribute the impasse merely to Eurocentric arrogance or Native intransigence. Rather it is necessary to consider the use and abuse of concepts like development, modernization, socialism, colonialism, and imperialism by the intellectuals and politicians who determined the direction of Indian policy in Canada as well as in the United States. Most of the intellectuals who provided the theoretical explanations upon which Indian policy was based in this period were committed to the concept of the welfare state.[43] From the best of motives and most sophisticated intellectual assumptions, governments in Canada applied in the 1970s and 1980s policies that sought to supply Native American communities with the same generous benefits and supports being provided to non-Native communities, although these benefits often did not take account of the fact that economically and educationally many Native communities started at a far less favorable level. The results were often to destroy the modest compromises

---

[42] Ibid., 170, 234–5; Olive P. Dickason, *Canada's First Nations: A History of Founding Peoples from Earliest Times* (Toronto, 1992), 418.

[43] J. R. Ponting and Roger Gibbins, *Out of Irrelevance* (Toronto, 1980), Introduction, xii.

and gradual adjustments that Native American societies were making to the changing economic, political, and social circumstances of their lives, and to induce in their place a culture of dependency characterized by easy welfare payments (which discouraged preexisting subsistence activities even in situations where they remained viable); bureaucratic expansion of tribal and band governments (which promoted factionalism by enhancing the economic and social distinctions between Native people related to those in control of tribal governments and those without such a connection); and the disintegration of traditional networks of social control in the face of catastrophic increases in alcoholism and child neglect.

How did good intentions result in such disastrous consequences? In part, those determining Indian policy did not listen to Indian views on the subject of the changes induced in Indian societies by the federal and provincial governments, even though "a sham-like series of consultative meetings" was sometimes organized to give the appearance of serious consultation. Yardsticks for measuring the character and the effectiveness of changes in Indian society were drawn from the dominant society and were mechanically focused on delivering "services" to Indians at the lowest cost and with the greatest efficiency. Too often much of the cost of these services was eaten up in salaries and administrative expenses in the Department of Indian Affairs, which in Canada remained largely non-Indian. That the "benefits" of modernization, heaped unthinkingly upon Indian communities, might result in social regression, disfunction, and dependency rather than in beneficial development seems never to have been imagined by those implementing the changes. As Anastasia M. Shkilnyk noted in her study of the Ojibwa community at Grassy Narrows in Ontario, not only were subsistence activities based on hunting, trapping, and fishing lost in this community but traditional rites of passage, such as the puberty vision quest and courtship and marriage rituals, as well as traditions of sharing and mutual help, were eroded, abandoned, or destroyed as a result of the growing dependence upon the welfare state introduced into the Indian community in the 1950s, 1960s, and 1970s. Only the traditional rituals of death seemed to retain their relevance.[44]

Canada in the 1990s was engaged in a renewal of the debate over its Indian policy. A professor of economics at McGill University asserted that "the solution for Indians' problems . . . is . . . : End reservation collectivism, privatize the land (perhaps distributing it by lottery), distribute

[44] Ibid., xvii; Shkilnyk, *Poison Stronger than Love*, 92, 235.

all remaining cash settlement money to individuals, cash out to individual Indians the present value of all special welfare programs, institute democratic elections with the same rules for representative government by which the rest of us live and grant Indians full and equal citizenship, with the same rights and responsibilities as all other Canadians or Americans." He supported his assertion claiming that "as soon as Indians leave the reservation their problems dissipate." Specifically he noted that the poverty and unemployment rates of off-reservation Indians in the United States were only half of what they are for reservation Indians. Income and education were similarly higher.[45]

Advocacy of what appears to be a renewed effort at termination as a solution for Native economic problems remains speculative and debatable, even though both Indians and Euro-Americans concede the inadequacy of the present economic model. Ross O. Swimmer, former Principal Chief of the Cherokee Nation and former assistant secretary for Indian Affairs, conceded that "the welfare state in most of Indian country is not healthy" and that the "U.S. welfare system, as ordered by Congress, requires failure in order for people to receive benefits." But, he noted, "there is nothing wrong with a group of people holding land or other assets in common." Competent tribal leadership, according to Swimmer, "can solve the problems if allowed to succeed instead of encouraged to fail."[46]

Whether a communal and tribal (collectivist if you will) approach to Indian life is better than an individualistic and nontribal approach will continue to be debated in the future as it has been in the past in both the United States and Canada. Yet the deficiencies of a collectivist approach need not necessarily be an inevitable concomitant of tribal government. If Poland, Hungary, the Czech Republic, and Tanzania (cited by George Manuel, president of the Canadian National Indian Brotherhood from 1970 to 1976, as a model for Canada's Natives) can lift the dead hand of centralized control from their economies, it is not impossible for Indian nations to do the same, while retaining and even enhancing their communal identity and political autonomy within the larger national units of which they are a part. But whereas in the 1960s and 1970s Indian and non-Indian leaders alike looked to the federal governments for solutions to their problems, in the 1990s they are increasingly looking to the market and to individual and tribal initiatives.[47] In the United States, tribal

---

[45] Tom Velk, *Wall Street Journal,* September 7, 1990.
[46] Response of Ross Swimmer to Velk in letter to editor, *Wall Street Journal,* October 9, 1990.
[47] Ponting, *Arduous Journey,* 38.

governments are eagerly seizing on gambling casinos as enterprises that can bring economic prosperity quickly to their people. The Mashantucket Pequots in Ledyard, Connecticut, a tribe with fewer than 300 members whose casino earns an estimated $600,000,000 a year, is the most spectacular example. Such casinos are permitted under the U.S. Indian Gaming Regulatory Act of 1988 if operated on Indian lands pursuant to a tribal ordinance and in conformance with a tribal-state compact. Whether high-stakes gambling is the appropriate vehicle for the recovery of economically depressed reservations became, in the 1990s, a hotly debated issue among both Indians and non-Indians.

Too often the bureaucracies in whose hands Indian programs were entrusted, in both Canada and the United States, seemed to be principally concerned with protecting and expanding their departments rather than with providing Indians with the same level of services already offered to the larger society. "Doing good to Indians" became a rationalization for self-serving consumption of public funds. It is not surprising, then, that Indian affairs bureaucrats would view the trend to promote Indian economic development outside the smothering embrace of the bureaucracy with some alarm. In the United States A. David Lester, commissioner of the Administration for Native Americans of the Office of Human Development Services, for example, worried about a too rapid Indian economic growth, particularly on the part of the energy-rich tribes forming the Council of Energy Resource Tribes. In testimony before the House Committee on Interior and Insular Affairs, March 27, 1979, Lester warned that "uncontrolled growth in the body is essentially cancer" and went on to state that "uncontrolled economic growth has similar repercussions in the social, political institutions, and systems of the tribe."[48]

The extent of the dependency that had grown to unite Indian tribes in the United States and the bureaucrats who serviced them with government funds was highlighted in the testimony presented by Sandra L. Cadwalader, executive director of the Indian Rights Association, on July 10, 1979, before the Committee on Interior and Insular Affairs of the House of Representatives. The association had undertaken two economic survey studies to measure the impact of selected Indian economies on the surrounding non-Indian communities. In its study of the Uintah-Ouray Ute Tribe of northeastern Utah, comprising 1,680 Utes living on the reservation, the association noted tribal income in fiscal year 1978 of $16,496,062, of which

---

[48] A. David Lester, in *Hearings* (see note 33), 67.

nearly $7 million came from royalties on oil and gas leases on tribally owned lands, $2 million from seven tribally run enterprises, including a resort, $2 million from interest on Treasury and other investments, and $5 million in federal grants for 34 separate programs in health, education, job training, alcoholism counseling, environmental projects, and law enforcement, including the construction of new tribal offices. Nearly half the sources of Ute personal income ($7 million in all) came from dividends paid out by the tribe to its members on earnings from the oil and gas leases. Most of the remainder of the personal income was from the tribal payroll. The tribe and its enterprises employed 320 tribal members or 89 percent of all employed Utes. "Almost all of the other 40 employed tribal members worked at the BIA agency office at Fort Duchesne, or for another branch of the federal government." The report went on to note that "Incredibly, there were no Utes in private employment." Twenty-five Utes were self-employed, however, mostly as ranchers.[49]

The attitude of self-employed Indian cattlemen among the Utes and elsewhere in Indian country can be divined from the testimony of John Frederick, president of the American Indian Cattlemen's Association, during the same hearings. Frederick, who described himself as "half Indian and half cowboy" and "born and raised on the Fort Berthold Indian Reservation in North Dakota," complained that tribal governments were inevitably swayed by the majority of tribal voters "from the lower income less productive segment; therefore, each and every candidate must be vitally concerned about the social welfare programs that provide resources to those voters, mostly in the form of government subsidies in one form or another." The tribal government, in its concern with this less productive element of the tribe, "discriminated against or at least discouraged from more aggressive business development" what Frederick described as "the more progressive business men." "I think the time has come," Frederick concluded, "to put more emphasis on the business segment of our reservation population and less on the social welfare program aspect if we expect to have Indian people ever determine their own destiny." The attitude expressed by Frederick has found theoretical support in the work of the Political Economy Research Center (PERC), a research and educational foundation in Bozeman, Montana, that focuses primarily on environmental and natural resource issues. Terry L. Anderson and his colleagues at PERC, in a series of books and articles building on the "new institutional

[49] Sandra L. Cadwalader, in *Hearings* (see note 37), 166–8.

economics" and "public choice" theory, have proposed a radical change in reservation economies in which more reliance is placed on the free market and less on the supposedly protective "trust" relationship with the federal government.[50]

With the electoral victory of Ronald Reagan, cutbacks in the social welfare component of Indian, as well as non-Indian, programs began to be made. Though Indian leaders expressed concern and outrage at the cutbacks, the Reagan administration attempted to fulfill what it regarded as its mandate to reduce the role of government in the economic life of the American people and to allow private enterprise to function where government control had previously impeded such enterprise. Not that the Reagan administration attempted to subvert Indian tribal governments. Far from it. In President Reagan's statement of January 24, 1983, on Indian policy, the president reaffirmed President Richard M. Nixon's 1970 policy statement proclaiming self-determination for Indian tribes without termination. President Reagan was even more explicit in promising to deal with the tribes on a "government-to-government basis" and committing the United States government "to foster and encourage tribal self-government." To signal his commitment to the new policy the president moved the White House liaison for federally recognized tribes from the Office of Public Liaison to the Office of Intergovernmental Affairs, which maintained liaison among federal, state, and local governments. The policy statement noted that federal policies since 1975, "instead of fostering and encouraging self-government . . . have by and large inhibited the political and economic development of the tribes." The statement asserted that "Excessive regulation and self-perpetuating bureaucracy have stifled local decision making, thwarted Indian control of Indian resources, and promoted dependency rather than self-sufficiency."[51]

In order to facilitate execution of the new policy for economic development, the president, when issuing his new policy statement, appointed a Presidential Commission on Indian Reservation Economies. That commission submitted its *Report and Recommendations to the President of the United States* in November 1984. The commission found numerous obstacles to Indian reservation economic development, among them incompetence at both the tribal government and Bureau of Indian Affairs level. It noted

---

[50] John Frederick, in ibid., 228–33. For the work of the Political Economy Research Center, see, Terry L. Anderson, ed., *Property Rights and Indian Economies* (Lanham, Md., 1992), and Anderson's *Sovereign Nations or Reservations: An Economic History of American Indians* (San Francisco, 1995).
[51] Press Release, The White House, Office of the Press Secretary, January 24, 1983.

that "the training and counseling bureaucracy consumes more funds on itself than it contracts directly to tribes." It observed "a Byzantine system of overregulation" that "actually deters investment by raising costs, creating uncertainty, and undermining local initiative." It noted that the BIA "consumes more than two-thirds of its budget on itself,. . . leaving little for investment purposes."

The commission also noted that because of the trust status of Indian land and the doctrine of sovereign immunity from legal suit, businesses were discouraged from attempting to function on the reservations. From a structural point of view the problem was, the commission noted, that "the goals of tribal government are different from businesses." With the reservation economic activities regulated and managed, in one form or another, by federal, state, local, and tribal governments, "an environment hostile to private sector development" existed.[52]

The commission's report has helped begin a revolution in Indian reservation economic development, but one that is still far from complete or even fully underway. Many of the same problems noted by the commission were cited in the reports published in 1986 in *An American Indian Development Finance Institution: A Compendium of Papers Submitted to the Select Committee on Indian Affairs of the United States Senate,* April 1986 (99th Congress, 2d Session, S. Prt. 99-142, Washington, D.C., 1986).

Slowly and reluctantly Indian tribes have made an adjustment to the policy initiated under Reagan, which was carried over into the administration of George Bush. Though loud objections have been expressed by Indian leaders, there was, in the late 1980s and early 1990s, a growing belief, particularly in the context of the worldwide collapse of regimes based on centralized state planning, that local initiative and intelligent adaptation to the surrounding free market can stimulate reservation economies. Enterprising tribal leaders, such as Philip Martin of the Mississippi Choctaws, have put new life into some reservation economies. The Choctaw tribe, under Martin, became one of the top twenty employers in the state, with five auto-related electronics factories and a greeting-card operation. The Choctaw success owes much to Martin's skill as a political leader and as a businessman, as well as to tribal tax advantages, excellent location, and a nonunionized labor force. The tribe has shown that, in its corporate capacity, and without losing its political identity, it can succeed

---

[52] Presidential Commission on Indian Reservation Economies, *Report and Recommendations to the President of the United States* (Washington, D.C., 1984), part 1, 21, 39.

in the economic market place. It does not need to base its economic life on a relationship of dependency with the federal government. Yet most other tribes have not been as successful.[53]

As the U.S. economy moved in the 1990s toward a more information-based service economy, and away from "smoke-stack" industries, the ability of the Indian economy to respond to the challenge was called into question. Although more Indians than ever were graduating from high school, the relative number going beyond this level was still very small in comparison with Euro-Americans. Since higher education is a critical factor in the new economic order, the ability of Native populations throughout North America to share in the growth of such an economy seemed problematic.

ARTISTIC RENAISSANCE

It is in the "art" field that evidence of a "renaissance" among Native Americans is perhaps most clearly evident to outsiders. Contemporary North American Native art is a powerful expression of Indian thought and feeling in a form that communicates directly with non-Natives. The existence of this renaissance is known not only in America, but internationally. The most assiduous buyers of American Indian art, indeed, are Europeans, particularly Germans, as the book *Indianische Kunst im 20. Jahrhundert* edited by Gerhard Hoffmann suggests.

Contemporary Native American art emerges from a long tradition of skilled esthetic expression, rarely going under the name of "art," but infusing with beauty, nevertheless, the artifacts relating to Indian life and religion. The French anthropologist Claude Lévi-Strauss has described ancient Greek and Northwest Coast Indian art as comparable achievements of the human spirit. Ethnographic museums have assembled great collections of traditional Indian artifacts, whether of cloth, ceramic, metal, feathers, paint, or other material. These collections grace museums throughout the world, and are exemplified by catalogues such as that of Horst Hartmann, *Die Plains- und Prärieindianer Nordamerikas* (Berlin: Museum für Völkerkunde, 1979), which discusses some of the Plains Indian collections of the great Berlin ethnographic museum.

Traditional Indian arts have been assembled by public and private collectors since the earliest period of contact. The earliest explorers collected

---

[53] *Newsweek*, December 5, 1988.

such objects for "cabinets of curiosity" in the palaces of European noblemen and rulers. Later traders, and eventually tourists, collected "souvenirs," influencing, by their tastes, the character of Native American art. The influence of European buyers sometimes debased, sometimes elevated, sometimes left unaffected, the "quality" of indigenous "art." But it was only in the twentieth century, and particularly in the second half of the century, that Indian art came to represent not so much the traditions of the past, but the bold and imaginative expressive culture of contemporary Indian life.

The earliest expression of this "new" form of Indian art, in which the Indian creator saw himself as an "artist" in the context of the Western conception of "art," emerged in the 1930s, 1940s, and 1950s in the form of a cautious, carefully controlled representational art form that sought to utilize new materials and new techniques to recall a traditional Indian past. In the United States the work of Acee Blue Eagle (Creek-Pawnee), Fred Beaver (Creek-Seminole), Woody Crumbo (Creek-Potawatomi), Blackbear Bosin (Kiowa-Comanche), and Fred Kabotie (Hopi) was in this tradition. Some later Native American detractors of this style have designated it "Bambi art" to express their dislike for the delicate and finely drawn, but excessively idyllic and nonconfrontational, subjects of prancing deer and exotic Western landscapes that sometimes characterize the work of this school.

Such art was clearly related to the early development of traditional art as a "product" designed for a "market" of sympathetic tourists. The production of such art was understood to lead to economic gains for the tribe as well as for the artist-members of the tribe. An important landmark in the establishment of this tradition was the creation of the Indian Arts and Crafts Board of the Department of the Interior, which was established by an act of August 27, 1935 (49 Stat. 891). The importance of the encouragement provided by such a board, and by other activities designed to aid and assist the production and sale of what are seen by the outside world as art objects, cannot be denied. Nor is the fact that tourists provide the economic basis for this art a cause for denigrating its importance. The Inuit (Eskimos) of the Arctic Rim were encouraged by early visitors to experiment with painting, drawing, and carving in forms attractive to the outside visitor. The Natives suffered no loss of creative skill in producing such products for strangers. Indeed, the fact that Canada and (to a lesser extent) the United States are liable to identify their nations abroad by displaying images of Inuit, Northwest Coast, Pueblo, and Plains Indian art indicates the extent to which the creative product of the Native populations of Canada and the United States dominates the imagination of non-Natives. Artists have always worked with the needs and desires of clients or patrons in mind, whether in Renaissance Italy or contemporary America. That Indians and Inuit do the same should come as no surprise. Indeed, the largest portion of the twentieth-century Inuit economy has been the creation of objects for the art trade. As traditional methods of subsistence became less practical or profitable, art became a logical alternative.

Native American art in the United States has emerged in the second half of the twentieth century with the aid of another governmental organization, the Institute of American Indian Arts. Created by the Secretary of the Interior in 1962, the institute was established in Santa Fe, New Mexico, as a "progressive arts school which has encouraged its students to draw upon their cultural heritages while experimenting in nontraditional media as well as using traditional forms." The founders and early administrators of the school had high hopes for developing "extensions" through traveling exhibits, a permanent museum, and ultimately a National Native American Center. Many graduates of the institute carried its message of artistic liberation throughout the country. As James McGrath, who served as the Assistant Director of Arts and teacher of Indian Aesthetics, Basic Design, Exhibition Arts (Museum Training), Painting and Publication Arts, put it, proof of the "extensions" of Native American culture into everyday life in America was demonstrated by

the Native American theater group that started with I.A.I.A. students at La Mama Theater in New York City; former students of I.A.I.A who developed and managed their own tribal museums such as Harry Walters at the Navaho Community College; writers such as Ramona Cardin Wilson, Emerson Blackhorse Mitchell, Janet Campbell Hale, Anna Lee Walters, Larry Littlebird; painters such as Earl Eder, Linda Lomahaftewa, Kevin Red Star, Dan Namingha; sculptors such as Doug Hyde; filmmakers such as George Burdeau: ever so many who worked out of their Native traditions, beginning at I.A.I.A. . . . retaining their traditions for themselves, for others, functioning successfully in the American/world art milieu.[54]

In the 1970s and 1980s the institute suffered from poor management and divisive criticism. At a point when it was functioning at far less than its

[54] Testimony of Darrell Knuffke, Deputy Under Secretary, Department of the Interior in U. S. Senate, Select Committee on Indian Affairs, *Hearing on Development of Native American Culture and Art, July 29, 1980*, part 2 (Washington, D.C., 1980), 25–26; see also letter of James McGrath, April 4, 1980, to chairman John Melcher, printed in *Hearings* of same committee April 14, 1980, in Santa Fe, N.M. (Washington, D.C., 1980), 84–6.

capacity, the Secretary of the Interior decided to move high school students from the Albuquerque Indian School to the institute's Santa Fe buildings. Efforts were made in the 1980s to revive and expand the functions of the institute.

Whether or not the federal government weighs in with support for the training of artists and the extension of their influence, Indian art is in no danger of dying. Artists like the Crow Kevin Red Star (one of the graduates of the Institute of American Indian Arts), Randy Lee White (Lower Brulé Sioux), Virginia Stroud (Cree-Cherokee), Richard West, Sr. (Cheyenne), Fritz Scholder (Luiseno), T. C. Cannon (Caddo-Kiowa), R. C. Gorman (Navajo), George Longfish (Seneca-Tuscarora), Mike Kabotie (son of Fred Kabotie), and many others have produced paintings showing boldness in their use of color and design, as well as irony, sarcasm, and humor (especially in the work of Randy Lee White) in their handling of subject matter and in their evocation of the past (never in a slavish or cloying manner). Native Americans have produced unique visions – both personal and ethnic – from their own traditions.

Of special interest to the admirer of "Indian" art is the "hyphenated," multitribal cultural identity of many of the Indian artists. Far from being an impediment, this mixed character (which often includes non-Native American ingredients), may have served as a liberating element to free the individual vision of the Indian artist from the claims of any single Indian or non-Indian tradition. The tribally mixed character of the Indian artist will be seen again in the discussion of Native American writers, some of whom possess a similar strength and uniqueness deriving perhaps from the "hybrid vigor" of their origins.

The more traditional Native American art forms, such as pottery and weaving, tend to reflect a more controlled, formal, and older tribal character, as in the work of the Pueblo potter Maria Martinez of San Ildefonso. While Pueblo potters have experimented with new forms, there is a fundamental continuity between the pottery of earlier centuries and more recent work from the same villages, as in the work of Lucy M. Lewis of Acoma Pueblo.

Similarly, while silversmithing retains its vigor and is one of the traditional arts of the Southwest (even though, along with weaving, its "tradition" derives from the Spanish intruders), individual artists such as the Hopi Charles Loloma have reaped fame and profit while deviating from traditional designs. Being an artist of international reputation and attempting to continue to live as a Hopi was a severe strain for Loloma, who chose to live near, but not in, his Native village in a house built on the profits of his work, to the irritation of some, at least, of his fellow Hopis.

The artistic renaissance of Native Americans in the United States has been duplicated by a similar renaissance in Canada. The three dominant contemporary Native art traditions are those of the Inuit, of the Northwest Coast, and of the Eastern Woodlands. Each derives strength from its Native traditions but each has shown an ability to appeal to and enter the international art market. The leader of the Woodland school of Indian artists, Norval Morrisseau, an Ojibwa, has, since the 1970s, achieved a more powerful and controlled expression of emotion than most other Indian painters north or south of the border. Morrisseau's mind is on the Indian past, but his expression of that past bursts all bounds of conventional representation. Like other artists in the school, who are sometimes called "Legend Painters," Morrisseau fills his work with images of mythological figures drawn from Indian traditional tales.

Daphne Odjig, born on the Wikwemikong Indian Reserve, Manitoulin Island, Ontario, and a founding member of the Professional Canadian Native Indian Artists Association, is another Canadian Indian painter whose expressive technique matches that of Morrisseau in its incisiveness and power. Perhaps the most famous of the Canadian Indian artists is Bill Reid, a Haida whose work, following in the tradition of his Northwest Coast ancestors, now graces many museums in North America and Europe as well as occupying a prominent position in the Canadian Embassy complex in Washington, D.C.

The evolution of contemporary Canadian Inuit art can be documented to a particular individual and a particular time. Beginning in 1948 James A. Houston, a young artist from Toronto, spent fourteen years in the Arctic working as a civil administrator and encouraging Inuit to use their natural talents to create art objects that could be sold as a way of alleviating the severe Inuit economic problems. With the help of the federal government, cooperatives were established in the 1950s in northern Quebec, at Cape Dorset, and elsewhere to facilitate the production and marketing of Inuit art. In the meantime, Houston, who in 1958 studied with the Japanese print artist Un'ichi Hiratsuka, introduced Japanese papers and techniques at Cape Dorset and elsewhere. Inuit prints, which often take animals, birds, and marine life as well as Inuit legends and myths as their subjects, are designed by the artists in their homes and the finished drawings transferred to the print medium by other skilled craftsmen. The work of artists such as Kenojuak Ashevak and Lucy Qinnuayuak represents an artistic tradition that did not exist among the Inuit prior to Houston's 1948 trip, yet demonstrates the powerful artistic potential of the Native peoples of North America. Other art forms, such as sculpture, whose origins preceded the arrival of the Europeans, are represented by equally powerful artists, such as Johnny Inukpuk.

Native American art in both Canada and the United States has established itself as a force to be reckoned with in the contemporary art world. No longer is Indian art seen in terms of "arts and crafts" or as a way of rescuing an impoverished and "primitive" people from an economic and psychological slough of despond. It now functions on a plane of equality with Euro-American art. While still placed in an ethnic framework by most critics and observers, its assessment in the world art market of the future will determine its ultimate artistic as well as economic valuation. It is perhaps suggestive that in the new Canadian Museum of Civilization in Ottawa, designed by the Métis architect Douglas Cardinal (who was also chosen as the architect for the Smithsonian's planned National Museum of the American Indian), the Native tradition is fully represented as an integral rather than peripheral expression of Canada's past, both in its historical and artistic aspects.[55]

LITERARY RENAISSANCE

An efflorescence of Native American creativity perhaps even more spectacular than in the art field can be seen in the work of Indian writers, especially writers of fiction. For purposes of emphasis the year 1969 can mark the formal recognition of this phenomenon in the United States. In that year Scott Momaday, an Indian and professor of English at Stanford University, received the Pulitzer Prize for his novel *House Made of Dawn*. The book (the title taken from a Navajo healing ceremony) is about a young Jemez Indian named Abel from the Pueblo where Momaday grew up. Momaday was raised as "an outsider to Jemez Pueblo," as the critic Kenneth Lincoln has noted. He spoke English and some Navajo; he did not converse in his father's Kiowa. His mother was one-eighth Cherokee. Both his parents were artists and writers. Both in *House Made of Dawn* and *The Way to Rainy Mountain*, published in 1970, Momaday utilized Kiowa folklore to construct his tale. But, as Lincoln noted, "Momaday's intention is syncretic – to tend and nourish a life passed through his own family" and "in this sense he becomes a keeper of tribal culture and adds to the composing mosaic of Kiowa history."[56]

James Welch (Blackfeet/Gros Ventre) also emerged on the literary scene late in the 1960s and in the 1970s with novels such as *Riding the Earthboy* (1971), *Winter in the Blood* (1974), and *The Death of Jim Loney* (1979). Although dealing with his Indian past less directly than Momaday, Welch powerfully evokes the Indianness of his contemporary fictional characters. Simon Ortiz (Acoma) is another Native American whose poetry and use of words reminds us that Indian authors have contributed mightily to American literature.

"Native Americans are writing prolifically," Kenneth Lincoln has written, "particularly the women."[57] Leslie Silko (Laguna) has expressed herself most effectively in poetry, as has Wendy Rose (Hopi/Miwok). Paula Gunn Allen (Laguna), Roberta Hill Whiteman (Oneida), Joy Harjo (Creek), and Linda Hogan (Chickasaw) have all distinguished themselves with their writings.

Most recently Louise Erdrich, a mixed-blood Chippewa from North Dakota, has passed like a meteor through the literary atmosphere. Winning the American Academy of Arts and Letters prize in 1984 for the best first publication of fiction (*Love Medicine*), Erdrich, the wife of Michael Dorris (Modoc), another Indian writer and scholar, has published *Jacklight, The Beet Queen,* and other works showing a refined and exquisite sensibility in dealing with the contemporary Indian and non-Indian world of reservation and off-reservation life.

Native American writers, of course, do not reflect a single point of view. Gerald Vizenor, a Chippewa, writes with a humor and irony that, while deeply rooted in his Native origins, plays with and elicits – sometimes even mocks – elements of that past. In books such as *Darkness in Saint Louis Bearheart* (1978), *Earthdivers: Tribal Narratives on Mixed Descent* (1981), and other literary creations, Vizenor displays a striking originality of thought and phrase.

After being persistently portrayed as a totally foreign "other" in Canada's literary canon, Canada's Indians, Inuit, and Métis are beginning to assert their rightful place within that canon. While some of their work, such as Harold Cardinal's *The Rebirth of Canada's Indians* (1977) and Duke Redbird's *We Are Metis* (1980), is overtly political, in keeping with the

---

[56] Kenneth Lincoln, *Native American Renaissance* (Berkeley, Calif., 1983), 102, 103, 118.
[57] Ibid., xi.

political ferment of the recent past, other works, such as Norval Morrisseau's Ojibwa *Legends of My People* (1965) and Chief Dan George's *My Heart Soars* (1974), evoke the tradition of earlier Indian poetry, legend, and drama. Other Native authors include Maria Campbell (Métis), *Halfbreed* (1973); Lee Maracle (Métis), *Ravensong: A Novel* (1993), and *Sundogs: A Novel* (1992); and Tomson Highway (Cree), *The Rez Sisters: A Play in Two Acts* (1988). Inuit literary products, in the written Inuktitut language (devised by Christian missionaries in the mid-eighteenth century) as well as in English, are recorded in Robin Gedalof's *An Annotated Bibliography of Canadian Inuit Literature* (1979).[58] The tiny population of the Wendat (Huron) reserve near Quebec City has published an extraordinary number of works of history, philosophy, folklore, autobiography, poetry, and drama, all in the French language, but some of it has been translated into English.

How is it that so many Native Americans have seized the language of their colonizers and made it the vehicle of their unique feelings? Is this not a contradiction or a betrayal? Not at all. First of all many Native American writers share the heritage of two or more Native groups, to say nothing of occasional non-Native ancestors. While individual Native languages have persisted, they are at the local extreme from what clearly has become the world language: English. Any Native writer wishing a large North American audience – and most writers and artists are extremely desirous of having an audience – would do well to write in English. There may, indeed, be an advantage to being Irish or Welsh or Hopi or Ojibwa and absorbing the English language from the periphery. Writers not located in the centers of power can often see more clearly the character and effects of the culture that impinges on their own through the language of that culture. While the renewal of Indian life in the twentieth century has led many Indian leaders to encourage the study of Indian languages, and while these languages are enjoying a revival in Indian community colleges and in some cases in radio and journalistic media, English remains the preferred vehicle for Indian literary figures, whose sense of political awareness and cultural uniqueness is not eroded thereby.

Even if one accepts the appropriateness of a powerful English-language literature among Native Americans, how can one explain the sophistication, the subtlety, and the power evident in the specific language of the leading Native American writers? It is important to remember that expres-

---

[58] *Canadian Encyclopedia*, 725–6; Penny Petrone, ed., *First People, First Voices* (Toronto, 1983).

sive culture for Indians was traditionally oral in form. Language was not merely utilitarian in character. It was the "life-breath — the body's soul in Lakota belief — by which the world's powers could be called, prayed, sung, or chanted to, reasoned with, or admonished." The voice, or word, invoked and evoked power. Indian literature of the present is an extension of the stories and songs that formerly sought to tap the power in the universe that affected all human beings. Indeed, in *House Made of Dawn,* the novel ends with Abel singing the ancient chant "House made of pollen, house made of dawn. *Otsedaba."* Words make things happen. Hence the importance of ritual songs, sacred stories, prayers, and the like, in Indian fiction. Momaday calls tribal poets "men made of words," or keepers of the sacred word bundle.[59]

Native American literature has assumed its rightful role as an important part of both American literature and literature in English. Whether seen as the expression of one important element in North American society (such as Southern writers or Jewish writers), or as the expression of a culture alien to the Euro-American culture from which it derives its literary form, it is an important literature and one that has been reborn from the ashes of the historical process that engulfed Native Americans.

SCHOLARLY RENAISSANCE

Along with a dramatic increase in the number of Native American college graduates has come an increase in the number of Native American scholars. That increase has been helped by the willingness and, indeed, eagerness, of American universities to add Native American scholars to their faculties, often in conjunction with Native American Studies programs that proliferated in the 1960s and 1970s, and which have held their own in the succeeding years.

The scholarly fields into which Indian scholars have gravitated reflect both the culture and interests of Native Americans themselves, and the character and interests of the disciplines and institutions to which they have been drawn. The law has provided a particularly attractive subject matter for aspiring Native Americans both because of its practical utility in an era in which legal conflicts between Indians and Euro-Americans continue unabated but also because of the continuing support of organizations such as the Native American Rights Fund. NARF sought to create a national program to support the many federally funded local legal services programs that emerged in the 1960s to provide legal representation to poor and disadvantaged people. Originally under Euro-American leadership, NARF soon was filled with young Indian lawyers who have, in recent years, carried on a number of successful legal actions to protect Indian rights and resources. The priorities for NARF's work are: (1) the preservation of tribal existence, (2) the protection of tribal natural resources, (3) the promotion of human rights, (4) the accountability of governments to Native Americans, and (5) the development of Indian law. The opportunities for Indian lawyers in NARF's program and in related programs have provided a major incentive to Indians to specialize in the law.[60]

Even before the establishment of NARF, the subject of Indian law had become established on American university campuses. The American Indian Law Center at the University of New Mexico, established in 1967, is perhaps the most famous. The center, beginning at a time when there were only twelve Indian attorneys in the country, was soon turning out dozens of Indian attorneys annually.

Education has provided opportunities for Native Americans, as have other practically oriented subjects such as public health and medicine. The Arizona State University was the first university to offer courses on Indian education, with the establishment of the Arizona State Indian Education Center on the campus in 1954. The development of Indian-controlled lower schools, such as the Rough Rock Demonstration School on the Navajo Reservation in the 1950s and 1960s, led to the establishment of community colleges such as the Navajo Community College, founded in 1968. The first president of the college was Robert A. Roessel, Jr., a Euro-American who had married a Navajo woman, and who had been the force behind the creation of the Rough Rock Demonstration School. Roessel, an advocate of self-determination for the Indians, soon felt the effects of the doctrine turned against himself when the college decided that "non-Indian faculty members should have no voice in the decision-making process of this school." Roessel had urged the Board of Regents to try to tear walls down rather than to build them up. The college survived and grew, moving to a new facility at Tsaile Lake in 1972. Support for the college, and for other community colleges, came from the federal govern-

[60] Native American Rights Fund, *Annual Report for 1987* [Boulder, Colo.], 6.

ment through a sometimes skeptical Bureau of Indian Affairs. Roessel remained strongly supportive of Navajo initiatives in the educational field. Institutions, such as the National Museum of the American Indian within the Smithsonian Institution, have from the beginning been totally controlled by Native Americans.[61]

The emergence of scholarly advocacy among Native Americans was closely related to the efforts of Euro-American supporters of Indian causes in the nation's universities to support Native aspirations for a stronger political role. The American Indian Chicago Conference organized in 1960 by University of Chicago anthropologist Sol Tax (with the assistance of anthropologist Nancy Lurie) sought to elicit a unified Indian voice with which to confront the newly elected administration of John F. Kennedy. While not ignoring elected tribal leaders, Tax cast a wide net, attempting to get representative points of view from all elements of the Indian population, whether urban or reservation, young or old, elected or traditional. Contact with scholars at the University of Chicago, and the recognition of the role the Euro-American intellectual community could play in furthering Indian projects, turned some Indians toward an understanding of the way intellectuals as well as journalists and media specialists could influence public opinion. While a "Declaration of Indian Purpose" (which stated Indian goals and aspirations) was agreed upon by the conference, a splinter group of participants formed, in the same year, the National Indian Youth Council (NIYC) to distinguish their interests both from the views of their Euro-American supporters and of the established Indian tribal leadership. The NIYC spoke of "Red Power" and encouraged Indian activism. One of its members, Vine Deloria, Jr., in 1964 became executive director of the National Congress of American Indians. In 1969 he published *Custer Died for Your Sins,* subtitled "An Indian Manifesto," a book that defined the new activist Indian posture. By presenting Indian issues for Euro-Americans through an admiring and cooperating media, the Indian radicals seized the initiative from regularly constituted tribal leaders, as well as from the Bureau of Indian Affairs and, indeed, from the president himself. The activities of the radicals focused on immediate political issues, but helped lay the groundwork for a more scholarly consideration of Indian affairs.[62]

---

[61] Margaret Connell Szasz, *Education and the American Indian: The Road to Self-Determination since 1928,* 2nd ed. (Albuquerque, N.M., 1977), 166–79.
[62] Robert F. Berkhofer, Jr., "Native Americans," in *Ethnic Leadership in America* ed. John Higham, (Baltimore, 1978), 139.

The First Convocation of American Indian Scholars was held at Princeton University in March 1970 and was conceived, organized, and directed entirely by Native Americans. Participants were selected by a steering committee named by the American Indian Historical Society, an organization founded in San Francisco by Rupert Costo (Cahuilla) and his wife Jeanette. The papers at the conference and a transcript of the discussions were published under the title *Indian Voices: The First Convocation of American Indian Scholars*. Rupert Costo, in his keynote address, saw the convocation as "a moment of truth for the American Indian – a moment when we stand on the threshold of great change." Costo foresaw the possibility that it was "in our power . . . to perform a miracle of change in favor of a better life for our people." The consciousness of Native power and the belief that that power could make change possible in American society was perhaps the main message of the convocation. The close embrace of Euro-American scholars was shunned but non-Indians were not excluded. The need to utilize the intellectual structure of non-Native institutions, such as the university in which the convocation was held, was recognized. Ethnic pride was not absent, but the major participants – Alfonso Ortiz, then professor of anthropology at Princeton, Vine Deloria, W. Roger Buffalohead, Fritz Scholder, Bea Medicine, and others – shared a basic commitment to standards and values that transcended individual tribal interests. In the 1980s Jeanette and Rupert Costo established a chair in Indian history at the University of California, Riverside, one of the universities most sympathetic to Indian history.[63]

The growth of Indian-controlled community colleges also reflected the suddenly raised consciousness of Indians that they could shape their future. Twenty-four such colleges exist in the United States, almost all emerging during the 1960s and 1970s as an expression of the policy that looked to Indian initiative for Indian development. At the same time Indian Studies programs became fashionable at many American universities. Canada, with its higher proportion of Indians, Métis, and Inuit in the total population, has experienced a similar development of Indian community colleges, Native Studies departments, periodicals for Native readers, Indian clubs, centers, and other ethnic associations.[64] Among the more influential Indian centers of higher education is the Saskatchewan Indian Federated College at the University of Regina.

---

[63] *Indian Voices: The First Convocation of American Indian Scholars* (San Francisco, 1970), 3.
[64] John A. Price, *Native Studies: American and Canadian Indians* (Toronto, 1978).

The movement of Indians into the intellectual life of the United States and Canada is, along with the renaissance in literature and art, perhaps the most significant development in recent Indian–Euro-American relations. Vine Deloria, Jr., with his usual prescience, had noted in *Custer Died for Your Sins* that "it is vitally important that the Indian people pick the intellectual arena as the one in which to wage war." Cynical about Euro-American motives and actions, Deloria asserted that Indian people have "always been fooled about the intentions of the white man." "Never have we taken the time to examine the premises upon which he operates so that we could manipulate him as he has us."

Deloria, by putting his thoughts in a form that Euro-Americans could deal with on an intellectual level, risked his own credibility with his own people. He noted that "when one writes a book, or at least tries to write a book, a great deal of one's soul is surrendered and placed in print for all to see." As his "old friend Clyde Warrior" noted accusingly, Deloria reported, " 'I've sold out.' " Deloria experienced the same skeptical reaction among his Native American colleagues to his work as executive director of the National Congress of American Indians. As he sadly noted, "The useful national life of an Indian leader today is about two and half years." "After that," Deloria concluded, "he is physically and emotionally spent." The "absolute dependence on their leaders" makes Indians at once excessively demanding of, and periodically disillusioned with, their leaders.[65]

Deloria, although retiring from direct involvement in pan-Indian organizations, has moved to the equivalent of a mountaintop where he continues to exert an intellectual influence over the course of Indian affairs through his writings, interviews, and conversations. While many disagree with his characterization of Euro-American opposition to Indian demands, all concede that he has elevated the terms of discourse to an intellectual level rarely seen in the continuing debate on Indian–Euro-American relations.

RELIGIOUS RENAISSANCE

The religious expression of Native Americans is at once complex and simple. Complex because in addition to numerous "traditional" religious beliefs and practices, Native Americans have absorbed and incorporated into their own religious life practices from outside, most notably from

[65] Vine Deloria, Jr., *Custer Died for Your Sins* (1st ed. 1969; Norman, Okla., 1988), 216, 245, 257, 268.

Christianity. Christianity among Native Americans, has, in turn, reflected the influence of Native religious thought.

Religion traditionally is more at the center of the daily life of Native Americans than it has been among non-Native Americans. Indeed, as the Swedish scholar Åke Hultkrantz put it in his *The Religions of the American Indians*, "religious attitudes and values permeate cultural life [of American Indians] in its entirety and are not isolated from other cultural manifestations."[66] As a result American Indians normally lacked a word to denote what non-Natives called religion. Whether or not "God Is Red," as Vine Deloria asserts in the title to his book on Indian religious life, virtually every Indian people has traditionally put, and in many cases continues to put, religious rites and observances at the center of its life. This religious sense is often strongly focused on the natural environment, which plays a more prominent role in Native American religious thought than it does among other Americans. Whether among the Hopis of the Southwest, the Sioux of the Great Plains, or any of hundreds of other Native American groups, religious exercises and ceremonies – often in a setting in which nature provides both context and content – play a central role in the life of the Native community. No attempt will be made here to describe or categorize all the various forms of religious expression among American Indians, but important components of that life, such as the Sun Dance religion, will be discussed.

Just as Native Americans see power in the words and expressions of poets and writers, so they see power present in the spiritual world. Indeed, one of the reasons that Christianity was as successful as it was among Native Americans was that it was often characterized as having "power" – greater power – than the Indian "gods" that it challenged. Power – spiritual power – had practical consequences in Native American life: not only the power of shamans to cure the ill or predict the future, but the power that one achieved over one's own life, which was seen as both a gift of, and an extension of, the power of external forces, both malevolent and benevolent.

Joseph Jorgensen, in his study of *The Sun Dance Religion: Power for the Powerless*, in describing the Sun Dance ritual among the Utes and Shoshones, noted that a "generalized account . . . cannot, unfortunately, convey much of the beauty, vitality, and deep redemptive, religious signifi-

---

[66] Åke Hultkrantz, *The Religions of the American Indians*, trans. by Monica Setterwall (originally published 1967; Berkeley, Calif., 1979), 9.

cance of the ritual." Jorgensen nevertheless summarizes the ritual by observing that "the dancers forego food and water, experiencing considerable pain and privation, as they pursue power for their own good health, for the commonweal, for helping the bereaved whose close friends or kinsmen have recently deceased, and to make themselves shamans."[67]

The power, whose acquisition and control was the central concern of traditional Indian religions, dealt with spirits, ghosts, and other aspects of the supernatural that existed as real forces in human affairs. The supernatural was not a mere abstraction to Native Americans but "a living reality experienced by the Indians themselves." "The continuous, expected process of everyday reality is disrupted by the supernatural reality with its discontinuous, unexpected, and, above all, incomprehensible course of events."[68] When Native shamans proved unable to control the impact of European intruders, crises were faced by people after people. Struggles between shamans, or between culture heroes, to see who had the greater power, "are a widespread theme in North American Indian folklore," as William Simmons has pointed out in his *Spirit of the New England Tribes: Indian History and Folklore, 1620–1984*. In the case of New England the local groups, in the seventeenth century, were confronted by catastrophes such as military conquest, epidemics, and political domination that, as Simmons pointed out, "challenged their confidence and understanding and undercut the infrastructure of their societies." Christian missionaries, even seemingly obnoxious individuals such as Cotton Mather, were accorded the respect and fear due individuals whose control over the spiritual destiny of European settlers and Indians was clearly superior to that of Native shamans.

Thus began a process by which the Christian God was absorbed into the Indian spiritual existence. Yet at the same time traditional Indian practices were retained in the new amalgam. The Christian convert and preacher Samson Occom, for example, continued to recognize the power of Indian shamans to deal with the supernatural just as Christian ministers claimed a similar power to deal with the supernatural through the agency of Christianity. Converted Christians early began to refer to God in terms such as the Great Spirit or *manitou*. Even today, Simmons notes, "the modern role of 'medicine man,' a vestige of ancient shamanism, is a respected leadership role in contemporary tribal organizations." Dreams

---

[67] Joseph Jorgensen, *The Sun Dance Religion: Power for the Powerless* (Chicago, 1972), 177.
[68] Hultkrantz, *Religions of the American Indians*, 10.

also continue to be important in Indian life. Simmons cites the case of Eric Thomas, a Narragansett who helped prepare the Narragansett petition for federal recognition, which was finally achieved in 1983. Thomas attributed his political activism "to a dream in which he saw the spirits of the dead and the newborn leaving and returning to earth and in which he learned that the earth would end if the eastern Indians lost their land."[69]

A powerful modern example of the syncretism that anthropologists have noted in charting the interaction of Native beliefs and Christianity is afforded by the Lakota or Sioux people. Father Paul B. Steinmetz, S.J., from 1961 through the 1980s, lived and served among the Oglala Lakotas as a Catholic priest on the Pine Ridge Reservation in South Dakota. Steinmetz reported that he was accepted "not only as a Catholic priest but also as a 'holy man' in their own religious tradition." He was invited by Lakota medicine men to participate in the most sacred of their ceremonies, the Sun Dance, which he did. In addition, Steinmetz introduced into his own Catholic services, beginning in 1965, prayers with the Sacred Pipe. Steinmetz notes that "The night before the funeral [of Rex Long Visitor at Slim Butte] I had an inspiration that seized me emotionally, an intuition of the relationship between the Pipe and Christ." Steinmetz was thrown into the middle of a bitter debate between some of the older medicine men and the young American Indian Movement (AIM) radicals, who sought to prevent him, as a Euro-American, from participating in Indian rituals. Steinmetz persisted and was able to continue his work. In his church, Holy Rosary Mission, is a mural "expressing the Christian Trinity in Lakota religious symbols."

The work of redemption is expressed by an Indian-featured Christ on the Cross. The work of santification [*sic*] is shown by an eagle with twelve tongues of fire representing the Holy Spirit descending on the apostles on Pentecost day. Beneath the crucifix the Pipe represents man's offering of himself to the Trinity. As a dedication the patronage of the parish was changed from St. Elizabeth to Our Lady of the Sioux. This was a symbolic expression of the rationale of my relationship as a priest to the traditional Lakota Religion.

Similarities between Indian and Christian beliefs can hardly escape the notice of a careful observer. Even the self-torture of the Sun Dance ceremony, in which the Sioux torture the flesh, evokes equivalent Christian traditions of scourging and mortifying the flesh, and for similar spiritual

[69] William Simmons, *Spirit of the New England Tribes: Indian History and Folklore, 1620–1984* (Hanover, N.H., 1986), 73, 90, 92, 161, 261.

reasons. Similarly, the belief in a life after death, as Father Steinmetz has noted, parallels Christian doctrine. "I have never encountered any Lakota concept of the final destiny of the soul in the next life," Father Steinmetz writes, "distinct from the Christian one." To demonstrate the growing unity of Lakota and Christian belief, Steinmetz notes that "People famous in Indian Religion such as Black Elk about whom Neihardt and Brown wrote as well as the majority of medicine men all receive their Christian sacraments and burials."[70]

Steinmetz's rosy and optimistic view of a convergence of Sioux and Christian beliefs is not accepted by many scholars. William K. Powers, for example, asserts that "It takes not analytical ability but raw faith to see the Sacred Pipe as a foreshadowing of Christ." Powers notes that the two concepts have in common the "notion of mediation between common people and the supernatural," but asserts that while "from the perspective of raw faith there is always the possibility that Christ was a foreshadowing of the Sacred Pipe,. . . it is unlikely that any Lakota would *believe* that."

Powers further notes that the convergence of the two religions is complicated by the problem of language and translation. How, for example, was the formula "Lamb of God who taketh away the sins of the world have mercy on us" translated into Lakota by the early missionaries? Powers takes the translation of an early missionary and retranslates it: "Wakantanka's little mountain sheep suddenly puts badness in another place, pity us." "Not only is this translation ungrammatical in Lakota, despite the intrusive commas inserted to give the appearance of grammaticality," Powers notes, "but it lacks any reference to a meaningful cultural experience." Powers points out the additional confusion caused by the fact that most Lakota young people of today, who want to understand more about the religion of their grandfathers, do not speak Lakota. "Most were not instructed by medicine men," Powers notes, "and if they received any advice, it was in English and by analogy. Their great-grandfathers learned that 'God is like Wakantanka,' while they learn that 'Wakantanka is like God.' "[71]

Steinmetz discusses the Native American Church, famous for its use of peyote in the sacraments, and the Body of Christ Independent Church to

[70] Paul Steinmetz, S.J., *Pipe, Bible and Peyote among the Oglala Lakota* (Stockholm, 1980), 7, 36, 37, 49, 147.
[71] William K. Powers, *Sacred Language: The Nature of Supernatural Discourse in Lakota* (Norman, Okla., 1986), 105–6, 119.

demonstrate the extent to which the religious elements of traditional Lakota religion and Christian doctrine have been absorbed and assimilated by the Lakotas. To attempt to draw significant distinctions between the original and the introduced religious practices, he believes, misses the point.

Father Peter J. Powell, an Anglo-Catholic priest, has also concluded that Plains Indian religious practices "can be viewed as prefiguring the Church's life and faith." Powell, who worked among the Cheyennes and is the author of *Sweet Medicine: The Continuing Role of the Sacred Arrows, the Sun Dance, and the Sacred Buffalo Hat in Northern Cheyenne History,* could say of and to the Cheyennes that "I believed their sacred ways to have come from God himself" and that "I continue to believe, with the Cheyennes, in the supernatural power that flows from their sacred bundles and sacred ceremonies."[72]

How valid is the coming together of Christian and Native religious traditions from the Native American point of view? Joe S. Sando, in his *Nee Hemish: A History of Jemez Pueblo* (1982), recounts the amalgamation of Christian and Native feast days and celebrations within the context of his own pueblo. Sando notes that during the Christmas season "the Jemez people used to roast corn in the fireplace, and while that was going on, other members of the family would draw pictures of wild game animals and birds, as well as farm crops, on the wall next to the fireplace." "All this," Sando goes on to say, "was in hopes that the birth of Christ would also result in the birth of the animals and plants being drawn on the wall." Sando acknowledges that "skeptics may snicker that this is all superstition and ancient outmoded beliefs," but "the world is full of strange coincidences that are hard to explain sometimes."[73] Some mainline Christian churches, noting the similarities of Indian pantheism to New Age Theology, stress the incompatibility of pantheism and Christian theism. Yet even this attitude accords Indian beliefs more respect than the old fashioned idea of "godless pagans."

As important as the convergence of Native American and European religious traditions in recent times is the renewed emphasis upon traditional religious practices that fell into disuse or were banned in earlier periods. Thus the traditional Iroquois religion has been renewed among the Mohawks at Kahnawake (near Montreal) and Akwesasne (on both sides of the U.S.-Canadian border), although their ancestors professedly moved

[72] Peter J. Powell, *Sweet Medicine: The Continuing Role of the Sacred Arrows, the Sun Dance, and the Sacred Buffalo Hat in Northern Cheyenne History,* 2 vols. (Norman, Okla., 1969), xxiii–xxvi.

[73] Joe Sando, *Nee Hemish: A History of Jemez Pueblo* (Albuquerque, N.M., 1982) 217–22.

to Quebec in the seventeenth century in order to live as Christian trading partners of the French. The growing emphasis on "paganism" among the Mohawks in the course of the twentieth century seems to correlate with a resurgence of ethnic pride and political autonomy. The movement back to traditional religious practices can also be seen in the revival of the potlatch tradition on the Northwest Coast, and of the Sun Dance in Western Canada and the United States, religious traditions that were outlawed by the United States and Canada in an earlier period. These traditions survived "underground" and their emergence coincides with the resurgence of ethnic pride and demand for increased political rights characteristic of the 1980s and 1990s. At the same time Protestant evangelical Christianity is sweeping many Inuit communities as a means of coping with social problems such as alcoholism and abuse and is making inroads both on Roman Catholic and Anglican congregations and on traditional Inuit beliefs.

The survival and strengthening of Indian religious values has involved not only the Natives' innate strength and capacity to adapt and absorb, but also the increasingly supportive policy of the U.S. federal government. In 1934, Commissioner of Indian Affairs John Collier issued his Circular on Indian Religious Freedom and Indian Culture, which reversed the course of previous federal policy, a policy of prohibition and discouragement of traditional Indian religious practices, such as those associated with the Sun Dance. More recently, in the American Indian Religious Freedom Act of 1978, and in amendments in 1991 and 1993, the Congress broadened the protections extended to Indian religious practices. What such practices *are* is not always clear, and debate continues in the courts and in the tribal and legislative halls as to the proper definition. In 1988 the United States Supreme Court, in *Lyng v. Northwest Indian Cemetery Protective Association* (485 U.S. 439), upset many supporters of Indian religious freedom by denying the attempt of Yurok, Karok, and Tolowa Indians in California to prevent the construction of a paved road through the Six Rivers National Forest, on grounds that it would cause irreparable damage to sacred sites in an area of concern to some members of those tribes. Justice Sandra Day O'Connor, in her majority opinion (in which she was joined by four justices), concluded that "Whatever may be the exact line between unconstitutional prohibitions on the free exercise of religion and the legitimate conduct by government of its own affairs, the location of the line cannot depend on measuring the effects of a governmental action on a religious objector's spiritual development." Justice Brennan, in dissent, noted that "Native

American faith is inextricably bound to the use of land" and asserted that "The site-specific nature of Indian religious practice derives from Native American perception that land is itself a sacred, living being."

The leading Native American spokesman in the field of religion is Vine Deloria, Jr., whose *God Is Red* (1973) has been mentioned above. In his *The Metaphysics of Modern Existence* (1979), Deloria noted that "the most common feature of primitive awareness of the world [is] the feeling or belief that the universe is energized by a pervading power." Whether called *mana* as among the Polynesians or, as among Native North American peoples, *wakan, orenda,* or *manitou,* "there is general agreement that a substantial number of primitive peoples recognize the existence of a power in the universe that affects and influences them." Deloria observed that "It is sufficient to note that the observations and experiences of primitive peoples were so acute that they were able to recognize a basic phenomenon of the natural world religiously rather than scientifically." They refused to make a distinction between the spiritual and material as two distinct aspects of reality. Deloria commented that the Western attempt to shape the natural world into laws and regularities is "wholly artificial and may be understood by primitive peoples as the original sin." "Certainly," he asserted, "the acquisition of knowledge is understood in Genesis as the original sin, and it is ironic that in attempting to refine religious experiences into a more precise understanding that the great world religions commit the sin that alienates our species from the rest of the natural world."[74]

Thus Deloria asserts the superiority of Native American religions over the "world religions" and the sophistication they claim to possess. Deloria's views are generally shared by Indian peoples who believe that their perception of the universe, and of the natural and the supernatural, is more in touch with reality than is that of the questing, questioning, and never satisfied Euro-Americans. This attitude explains both the ease with which Indians are willing to absorb the rituals of outsiders, if they can be incorporated into their own scheme of belief, and why in other cases they feign ignorance of their own traditions or are uncooperative toward those seeking to "study" their religion. That the growing pride Native Americans have in reasserting their religious heritage is not merely an expression of ethnic vanity is shown by the attraction that such religious beliefs, and the related ethic of concern for the preservation of the environment, have

---

[74] Vine Deloria, Jr., *The Metaphysics of Modern Existence* (San Francisco, 1979), 152–4.

for many Euro-Americans.[75] While much Euro-American admiration of
Indian religion coincides with the growing strength of the environmental
movement among Euro-Americans and is related to the Natives' reputation as "natural ecologists," the reality of Indian ecological concern is a
debatable one, as Deloria, noting the casually scattered trash on Indian
reservations, has pointed out.

NATIVE HEALTH IN THE UNITED STATES AND CANADA

Not only have the figures for the Native populations of both the United
States and Canada shot up since the 1960s, but the health statistics of
both have shown a remarkable turnabout from the catastrophic record of
the past, only to confront new and sometimes puzzling challenges. Thus it
can be asserted that while earlier scourges have been largely eliminated in
both the United States and Canada, other serious health problems, such as
alcoholism, have come to the fore. These clearly reflect and contribute to
major social and political issues that have not been resolved.

Alcoholism, formerly defined as a behavioral problem, is now seen as a
health problem, and one of enormous consequences. Among Indians it is
currently the most important health problem. Deaths due to alcohol
dependence syndrome, alcoholic psychoses, and chronic liver disease and
cirrhosis, specified as alcoholic, in the 1980s were four to five times higher
among Indians in the United States than for the population generally. Yet
even this appalling figure is an improvement over the incidence of alcoholism deaths in the 1970s, which was six to seven times the United States
average. Some of the indirect consequences of alcoholism include child and
wife abuse, significant problems in both the United States and Canada.[76]

The two leading causes of death for American Indians and Alaskan
Natives aged twenty-five to forty-four in the period 1987–9 were accidents and chronic liver disease and cirrhosis, followed by suicide, homicide, and heart diseases. The pattern is similar for younger Indians fifteen
to twenty-four years of age, but in this age group chronic liver disease and
cirrhosis follow malignant neoplasms and heart diseases. While acute and
chronic infections have been eliminated as main causes of death, death by

[75] Niels Winther Braroe, *Indian and White: Self Image and Interaction in a Canadian Plains Community*
(Stanford, Calif., 1975), 131–4. See also William McLoughlin, *Revivals, Awakenings, and Reform*
(Chicago, 1978), 201–2.
[76] Indian Health Service, *Chart Series Book* (Washington, D.C., 1987), Table 4.23 (46); Snipp,
American Indians, Appendix 3, Tables A3.1 to A3.9 (349–59).

violence, suicide, and accidents, mostly alcohol-related, have increased proportionately. The extent to which alcohol played a role in the various causes of death is not precisely known in the United States, but is clearly significant. Many observers see alcoholism destroying traditional Indian communities. While the incidence of accidents and cirrhosis of the liver among Indians is five to twelve times greater than among the United States population fifteen to forty-four years of age, the incidence of homicide has steadily declined from a ratio of five times the rate in the United States population of all ages in 1955 to 1.6 in 1988. The ratio of suicides, while slightly above 1 (1.3) in 1988, has remained basically stable (between 1.1 and 1.8) since 1955.[77]

While it is true that alcoholism is playing a devastating role in destroying Indian individuals and communities, it is also true that in many ways Indians are coming to grips with the problem. Indian playwrights, such as Hanay Geigomah (Kiowa-Delaware), have dealt with the theme in an extraordinarily frank fashion, as in his play *Body Indian.* Individual Indians have recognized and overcome their addiction and gone on to successful careers.

The ravages of alcohol have affected the Native people of Canada as well as those of the United States. They have been especially deleterious in isolated northern Native communities and have stimulated some of them to respond by forbidding alcohol in their settlements. In an Ojibwa community in Ontario, a parent observed that alcohol was "a poison" and "a stronger power than love of children." This "poison" was directly responsible for the high incidence of infant death (about 22 percent of all deaths in the community compared with about 4 percent in the Euro-Canadian population of a neighboring town). Children were abandoned, neglected, and maltreated, usually when the mother was in a drunken state. Other social ills, such as gang rape and family breakups, were often directly attributable to alcohol.[78]

Research on the causes of alcoholism continues to fail to come up with satisfactory causal explanations. There is a prevailing skepticism about genetically or physiologically based explanations, and a preference for cultural ones centering on despair and depression brought on by deculturation. Until there is a scholarly understanding of the true causes of alcoholism, and

[77] *Canadian Encyclopedia,* 1453; Indian Health Service, *Trends in Indian Health – 1993* (continuation of *Chart Series Book*) (Washington, D.C., 1993), Charts 4.2, 4.3, 4.7, 4.9; *Statistical Record,* Tables 413, 418; Health and Welfare Canada, *Aboriginal Health in Canada* (Ottawa, 1992).
[78] Shkilnyk, *Poison Stronger than Love,* 48; A. J. Siggner, in Ponting, ed., *Arduous Journey,* 57–83.

an acceptance of the findings, a solution to the problem of Indian alcoholism will continue to elude searchers.

In 1985 age-adjusted mortality rates for American Indians affected by alcoholism were 321 percent greater than for the United States generally; for tuberculosis (still a scourge although enormously reduced from earlier periods) 220 percent; for diabetes mellitus 139 percent; for accidents 124 percent; for homicide 72 percent; and for pneumonia and influenza 34 percent.[79]

Life expectancy at birth for American Indians and Alaska Natives has increased from fifty-one years in 1940 to 61.7 in 1960 to 71.1 in 1980, four years short of the figure for the United States Euro-American population. Life expectancy for Canadian Indians doubled between 1950 and 1969 but remains about nine years shorter than the 76.5 year figure for all Canadians. The birth rate for Indians in the United States in the period 1983–7 was 28.4 per 1,000 population, 83 percent greater than the birthrate of 15.5 for the United States All Races population. The age profile of American Indians for 1987 revealed 32 percent younger than fifteen years, and 5 percent older than sixty-four years, in comparison with 23 and 11 percent for the comparable ages of the United States All Races population. In Canada, where the Native birth rate is likewise almost double the national average, 59 percent of status Indians are less than twenty-five years old, compared to 37 percent of all Canadians. The infant mortality rate for American Indians and Alaska Natives residing in Reservation States (the states in which the Indian Health Service has responsibilities for those – on and off the reservations – eligible for its services) dropped from 62.7 (rate per 1,000 live births) in 1954–6 to 9.8 in 1983–5, and 9.7 in 1986–8, a decrease of 84 percent. The rate is lower than the United States All Races rate for 1984, which is 10.8. In Canada the infant mortality rates in the mid-1980s were eighteen per thousand for Indians and thirty-four for Inuit compared to ten for other Canadians. With the transfer of responsibility for the delivery of health services in the Northwest Territories to the territorial government beginning in 1982, and the transfer of community health services to Indian communities if requested by band leaders, indices of Native health improved. By the end of the decade, infant mortality among registered Indians served by the Medical Services Branch declined from eighteen to ten per 1,000 live births (still

---

[79] For 1988 figures see *Statistical Record*, Tables 413, 421. Snipp, *American Indians*, Appendix 3, "Characteristics of American Indian Mortality," 349–59.

above the 1990 Canadian average of 6.8). Injury and poisoning are the leading cause of death (more than 30 percent) among status Indians and Inuit, while the fourth leading cause of death for the Canadian population generally. Yet the age-standardized Indian death rate from these causes has declined from 4.6 times the Canadian rate in 1978 to only 1.7 times greater in 1990. Suicide among Native peoples is twice the rate among Canadians as a whole: 22 per 100,000 compared to 11 per 100,000.[80]

The situation in Greenland parallels that in the United States and Canada. A thinly populated country – in 1992 the population was 55,000, up from 21,000 in 1921 – the number of live births per 1,000 population has declined in the 1980s to less than half of what it had been in the 1960s (twenty in 1984 compared with forty-nine in 1960). In the same period the infant mortality rate was more than cut in half. Since 1950 tuberculosis and other epidemic diseases such as measles, which had been prevalent, have been eliminated, while other diseases, particularly those associated with an increased life span, have become more common.[81]

Despite the steady improvement in the health and welfare of Native North Americans, they remain among the most socially and economically deprived ethnic groups in North American society. The disparity between the Native and non-Native populations continues to trouble both sides. Assured equality of results – in health, education, and employment – is sought by leaders in both Canada and the United States for all elements of their multiethnic populations, but the goal continues to elude those who seek to bring it about despite generous and prolonged government programs. Increasingly, equality of opportunity is being proposed as a more appropriate goal than equality of results around which to build programs of support. This shift in the approach to what was formerly called "the Indian problem" has raised doubts about many government programs devised in the supposed interest of Native Americans but which have in fact created dependency rather than independence and hobbled rather than liberated their supposed beneficiaries. Accompanying this shift in emphasis has been a growing conviction that the individual, rather than society, must bear a major share of the responsibility for his or her failure to adjust to societal norms. No one celebrates

[80] *Canadian Encyclopedia*, 1453; *Statistical Record*, Tables 398, 400, 448; Health and Welfare Canada, *Aboriginal Health in Canada* (Ottawa, 1992).
[81] Royal Danish Ministry of Foreign Affairs, *A Town in Greenland* [n.d.], 27; Royal Danish Ministry of Foreign Affairs, Press and Cultural Relations Department, "Facts about Denmark: Greenland" [n.d.], 14; Royal Danish Ministry of Foreign Affairs, "Greenland" (1992), 2.

the current economic and social situation of the Native American. But no one is certain of how helpful change is brought about. Yet change continues to occur, both formally and informally. Perhaps the continuing, but slowly diminishing, inequality of results between Native and non-Native is a reflection of the slow and uncertain processes by which Native people are regaining control of their lives.

Good will continues to exist on both sides of the divide. In Canada, a Royal Commission on Aboriginal Peoples, established by an Order in Council of August 26, 1991, was charged with investigating relations among aboriginal peoples, the Canadian government, and Canadian society as a whole. In its investigation of self-government it was charged with the task of "break[ing] the pattern of paternalism which has characterized the relationship between aboriginal peoples and the Canadian government." The commission held hearings and issued preliminary reports; its final report should help to facilitate changes that bridge the gap that continues to exist between Natives and non-Natives in Canada.[82]

CONCLUSION: A NATIVE RENAISSANCE THAT EXTINGUISHES THE NATIVE?

One would be wrong to conclude that the forces of assimilation and acculturation in U.S. and Canadian societies are pushing Native Americans into the culture of the majority society and overwhelming the political, legal, and cultural distinctiveness that has characterized what has been called in this chapter the Native American Renaissance. The meaning of assimiliation and acculturation – even as defined by the "majority" culture – no longer encompasses the loss of the minority's culture and the adoption of that of the newcomer. The United States and Canada have evolved as multiethnic societies that are able to accommodate virtually all the peoples of the world and allow them freedom of expression in a peaceful, prosperous environment. This achievement has been accomplished in part because the concept of culture accepted by all North Americans has allowed for, and indeed expected, change and evolution of cultures. Hence "Indianness" or "Nativeness" is no longer defined as earlier European settlers defined those terms any more than modern Euro-Americans are expected exactly to resemble their seventeenth-century fore-

---

[82] Privy Council, Canada, *The Mandate: Royal Commission on Aboriginal Peoples. Background Document* (August 1991), "Terms of Reference," 1.

bears. The new definition allows for Indian culture to meet the test of Indianness, even when that culture bears only a partial resemblance to that of the people on first contact with Europeans. An Indian writer with a Japanese computer (e.g., Vine Deloria, Jr.) is no more deracinated than his nineteenth-century Sioux ancestors mounted on descendants of Spanish horses and carrying American rifles or American bibles. And just as the Indian population of the United States is composed of two million Indians who live with what is called an "Indian" identity, while more than four times as many claim Indian ancestry without living as Indians, so Indian culture can be identified either as a central or peripheral element in a population identifying in one way or another as "Indian." While Indians continue to be marginalized to some degree by residual racist prejudice and by being stereotyped by some as primitive or drunken, such attitudes are no longer held by Euro-American opinion leaders, educators, politicians, religious figures, or business people.

But can an Indian Renaissance encompass peoples that have been, and sometimes continue to be, bitter enemies? Can one apply a pan-Indian gloss to cultures in opposition to each other, such as the Hopis and Navajos, Hupas and Yuroks, and other feuding peoples? Again the answer is yes. All Indian nations have, by the force of the majority culture's definition, as Robert K. Berkhofer has so effectively pointed out in *The White Man's Indian,* taken on a unified reality that might have remained fractionated but for the arrival of the Europeans. Even while proclaiming their differences, different Native peoples have become the sharers of a single culture in the eyes of the government, in the eyes of the people who have most profoundly influenced their fate, and, ultimately, in their own eyes. This tendency has been accentuated by the migration of nearly half the Indian population away from their traditional homelands to non-Indian centers of population, in both the United States and Canada, and by the growth of pan-Indian organizations and activities. Even those groups locked in seemingly endless conflict, such as the Hopis and Navajos, are bound together in the context of overarching rules imposed by the larger society of which they are a part. During the late 1980s the tribal chairmen of both the Navajo and Hopi tribes hoped that their common background as fellow students in the same BIA school would help them settle the bitter dispute between their peoples. This was not to be, but if the Hopi-Navajo relocation dispute is eventually settled it will be in terms defined by the United States of America as a whole as well as by the Hopi and Navajo peoples.

Does an Indian Renaissance make sense when the differences between
Native Americans of Alaska and those of the "lower forty-eight" states are
so marked? Whether or not the Alaska Native Claims Settlement Act of
1971 will be modified (beyond the amendments already made to it) to
reestablish tribal governments as they exist in the lower forty-eight, the
act has already brought Alaskan Natives into the larger U.S. economy as
corporate economic entities. Meanwhile, in the lower forty-eight, tribal
life is protected from external coercive change and tribal governments
possess a government-to-government relationship with the federal government. Just as the extraordinary flexibility of the U.S. system of government has allowed extraordinary changes in the relationship of each part of
the polity to the whole and to its other parts, so the differences in the
organization of Native societies in Alaska and in the lower forty-eight can
be encompassed in the American political system without violence or
distortion of the larger polity.

Are the Native peoples of Canada and Greenland also experiencing a
renaissance? Although at a slower pace, and in a more cautious and restrictive form, the Native societies of Canada and Greenland have wrested a
vastly enlarged political authority from those who formerly controlled
their destinies. In economics and health they have shown significant
improvements. Culturally, signs of a vigorous growth in the arts and
literature have emerged.

Prospects for the future of Native Americans throughout North America are favorable. Many alternative "futures" can be envisioned, but compared to the harrowing past through which the ancestors of the present-
day Native Americans passed, such futures can be looked upon with
confidence. Some will decry the optimism of this account. Too many
North American intellectuals will persist in seeing despair where there
should be hope, in judging the United States, Canada, and Greenland (but
not the rest of the world) by ideal standards that no one else tries to meet.
But judged by the standards of other nations, or by the record of the Euro-
American historical past, the future for the Native Americans of North
America can be assessed with optimism and confidence.

BIBLIOGRAPHIC ESSAY

The products of the massive 1990 U.S. Census are available from the Bureau
of the Census of the U.S. Department of Commerce in simple popular
pamphlets such as *We the First Americans* (Washington, D.C., 1993) or, for

the specialist, on Special Computer Tape Files showing data on the American Indian, Eskimo, and Aleut Population to meet unique data needs. Massive printed reports are available by subject title series, as follows: 1990 Census of Population and Housing, 1990 Census of Population, and 1990 Census of Housing. Under each of these categories are to be found data on Native Americans. For example, in the Census of Population and Housing are to be found reports on the social and economic characteristics of the American Indian, Eskimo, and Aleut populations. Many of these data have been incorporated in compilations such as the *Statistical Record of Native North Americans*, ed. Marlita A. Reddy (Detroit, 1993), and in the *Statistical Abstract of the United States, 1994*, 114th ed. (Washington, D.C., 1994). Material drawn from the 1980 census and data compiled between censuses are available in C. Matthew Snipp, *American Indians: The First of This Land: A Census Monograph Series* prepared for the National Committee for Research on the 1980 Census (New York, 1989), and in Paul Stuart, *Nations Within a Nation: Historical Statistics of American Indians* (New York, 1987). Canadian statistics are based on censuses taken every five years, the last in 1991, on the basis of which an Aboriginal Peoples Survey was conducted utilizing a sample of persons who reported Aboriginal origins. Included in the compilations prepared by Statistics Canada are such publications as *Profile of Canada's Aboriginal Population* (Ottawa, 1995) and *Ethnic Origin* (Ottawa, 1993), as well as more general publications such as *Canada Year Book 1994* (Ottawa, 1993). The *Canadian Encyclopedia*, 2nd ed. (Edmonton, 1988), also provides valuable data.

Voluminous records are kept by the Indian Health Service of the Department of Health and Human Services of the United States. Formerly published in what was called *Chart Book Series*, then as *Chart Series Book*, they are now continued, on a yearly basis, under the title *Trends in Indian Health – 1993*. The health statistics are selectively included in the statistical compilations noted above.

Graphic depictions of health conditions often appear in studies of individual Indian communities, and, particularly in its pathological aspects, in various literary forms, including poetry and plays. Anastasia M. Shkilnyk, *A Poison Stronger than Love: The Destruction of an Ojibwa Community* (New Haven, Conn., 1985) provides an appalling picture of the social and health effects of dislocation and alcoholism in a Canadian Indian community. Michael Dorris, in *The Broken Cord* (New York, 1989), provides an equally graphic personal account of the problem of fetal alcohol syndrome among Indian children.

The hearings carried on by the U.S. Senate Select Subcommittee on Indian Affairs provide rich detail about tribal government and activities, as the House Interior and Insular Affairs Committee did until recent years. Specific studies of individual tribes are almost numberless. Many carry the story to the present day, particularly as tribes are no longer seen in the "ethnographic present" of an earlier period, but as living, evolving societies. Examples are Helen C. Rountree, *Pocahontas's People: The Powhatan Indians of Virginia through Four Centuries* (Norman, Okla., 1990); and Loretta Fowler, *Arapahoe Politics, 1851–1978: Symbols in Crises of Authority* (Lincoln, Nebr., 1982). Increasingly Native Americans, such as Veronica Tiller, author of *The Jicarilla Apache Tribe: A History, 1846–1970* (Lincoln, Nebr., 1983), are adding to the tribal literature compiled by anthropologists and historians.

A general overview of the American Indian in recent years is D'Arcy McNickle, *Native American Tribalism: Indian Survivals and Renewals* (New York, 1973), in which McNickle, himself an Indian, sees 1961 as a "watershed" year. McNickle's own life story is told in Dorothy R. Parker, *Singing an Indian Song: A Biography of D'Arcy McNickle* (Lincoln, Nebr., 1992). Essays by two Native Americans, Alfonso Ortiz and W. Richard West, Jr., provide an insight into contemporary Indian attitudes, in *Indians in American History: An Introduction,* ed. Frederick E. Hoxie (Arlington Heights, Ill., 1988).

Accounts of the activities of radical Indian organizations are documented in Stan Steiner, *The New Indians* (New York, 1967); Alvin M. Josephy, *Red Power: The American Indians' Fight for Freedom* (New York, 1971); Peter Matthiessen's one-sided *In the Spirit of Crazy Horse* (New York, 1991); and *Where White Men Fear to Tread: The Autobiography of Russell Means,* with Marvin J. Wolf (New York, 1995).

A fascinating, skeptical, almost satirical series of observations of the interaction of contemporary Indians with the anthropologists, lawyers, and others whose work relates to them is James A. Clifton, ed., *The Invented Indian: Cultural Fictions and Government Policies* (New Brunswick, 1990). The collection covers such themes as "The United States Constitution and the Iroquois League" by Elizabeth Tooker, and "Pride and Prejudice: The Pocahontas Myth and the Pamunkey" by Christian F. Feest, as well as brilliant contributions by Clifton himself. It is enlivened by an appendix containing sixty-four Indian responses expressing irritation at comments about them made by anthropologists, historians, and other scholars.

For Canada the literature about recent Indian political activities is almost equally voluminous. Among the best general accounts of recent events are Sally M. Weaver, *Making Canadian Indian Policy: The Hidden Agenda, 1968–1970* (Toronto, 1981); Pauline Comeau and Aldo Santin, *The First Canadians: A Profile of Canada's Native People Today* (Toronto, 1990); some of the chapters dealing with the recent past in Bruce Alden Cox, ed., *Native People, Native Lands: Canadian Indians, Inuit and Metis* (Ottawa, 1991); and Olive P. Dickason, *Canada's First Nations: A History of Founding Peoples from Earliest Times* (Toronto, 1992).

The legal background of Indian–Euro-American relations and its influence on the contemporary status of Native Americans is discussed in Robert A. Williams, Jr., *The American Indian in Western Legal Thought* (New York, 1990), and in Wilcomb E. Washburn, *Red Man's Land/White Man's Law* (New York, 1971, rev. ed., Norman, Okla., 1995). Vine Deloria, Jr., has been an active contributor to the field. Deloria, with Clifford Lytle, published *American Indians, American Justice* (Austin, Tex., 1983), and *The Nations Within: The Past and Future of American Indian Sovereignty* (New York, 1984). Deloria has also edited *American Indian Policy in the Twentieth Century* (Norman, Okla., 1985). Charles F. Wilkinson, *American Indians, Time, and the Law: Native Societies in a Modern Constitutional Democracy* (New Haven, Conn., 1987) is another useful study. A more quixotic study is John R. Wunder, *"Retained by the People": History of American Indians and the Bill of Rights* (New York, 1994).

Other legal scholars who have contributed significantly to the literature include Monroe E. Price, *Law and the American Indian: Readings, Notes and Cases* (Indianapolis, Ind., 1973); Alvin J. Ziontz, "After *Martinez:* Civil Rights under Tribal Government," *UCD {University of California Davis} Law Review* 12(1) (March 1979), pp. 1–35; and Nell Jessup Newton, "Indian Claims in the Courts of the Conqueror," *American University Law Review* 41 (spring 1992), 753–854.

An interesting behind-the-scenes look at the "Indian bar" is Edward Lazarus, *Black Hills, White Justice: The Sioux Nation versus the United States, 1775 to the Present* (New York, 1991). There are many particular studies of specialized aspects of Indian law, such as water rights. An example is Charles T. DuMars, Marilyn O'Leary, and Albert E. Utton, *Pueblo Indian Water Rights: Struggle for a Precious Resource* (Tucson, Ariz., 1984).

Government publications contain the greatest amount of data concerning Indian economies, but theoretical approaches are not lacking. They range from analyses from a Marxist perspective, such as John H. Moore, ed., *The Political Economy of North American Indians* (Norman, Okla.,

1993), to analyses from a conservative perspective, such as Terry L. Anderson, ed., *Property Rights and Indian Economies* (Lanham, Md., 1992), and *Sovereign Nations or Reservations?: An Economic History of American Indians* (San Francisco, 1995).

Numerous studies of Indian art have been published. Among the most valuable are Christian F. Feest, *Native Arts of America,* updated edition (New York, 1992); and Gerhard Hoffmann, ed., *Indianische Kunst im 20. Jahrhundert* (Munich, 1985). The newly formed National Museum of the American Indian, Smithsonian Institution, has featured "art" from the enormous Heye Foundation collection, absorbed by the museum, in two volumes, *All Roads Are Good: Native Voices on Life and Culture,* ed. Terence Winch (Washington, D.C., 1994) and *Creation's Journey: Native American Identity and Belief,* ed. Tom Hill and Richard W. Hill, Sr. (Washington, D.C., 1994). The museum has also published, as a special issue of *Akwe:kon Journal* 11 (3,4) (fall/winter 1994), *Native American Expressive Culture,* which contains several essays on Indian art.

In addition to the works of individual Indian writers, there are several collections of critical studies of Indian literature. Laura Coltelli, ed., *Native American Literatures* (Pisa, 1989), brings together studies by both American and European literary critics, while Coltelli's *Winged Words: American Indian Writers Speak* (Lincoln, Nebr., 1990) focuses on the Indian writers themselves. Peter Nabokov, ed., *Native American Testimony: An Anthology of Indian and White Relations, First Encounter to Dispossession* (New York, 1978); Geary Hobson, ed., *The Remembered Earth: An Anthology of Contemporary Native American Literature* (Albuquerque, N.M., 1981); and Jerome Rothenberg, *Shaking the Pumpkin: Traditional Poetry of the Indian North Americas* (New York, 1972) are among the many anthologies of Indian literature. Perhaps the best study is Brian Swann and Arnold Krupat, *Recovering the Word: Essays on Native American Literature* (Berkeley, Calif., 1987). Swann has published another anthology, *Smoothing the Ground: Essays on Native American Oral Literature* (Berkeley, Calif., 1983), and *Coming to Light: Contemporary Translations of the Native Literatures of North America* (New York, 1995), while Krupat has edited *New Voices in Native American Literary Criticism* (Washington, D.C., 1993).

Essays on Indian literature with a more overt political point of view are collected in Bo Scholer, ed., *Coyote Was Here: Essays on Contemporary Native American Literary and Political Mobilization* (Aarhus, Denmark: *The Dolphin,* No. 9, April 1984). Charles R. Larson, *American Indian Fiction* (Albuquerque, N.M., 1978) represents the work of a more traditional literary critic.

W. H. New, ed., *Native Writers and Canadian Writing* (Vancouver, 1990), brings together studies of Canadian Native writing by Canadian critics. Penny Petrone, *First People, First Voices* (Toronto, 1983), is an important collection of the writings and speeches of Canadian Indians from the 1630s to the 1980s.

Specific studies of Indian religion, such as Richard B. Brandt's *Hopi Ethics: A Theoretical Analysis* (Chicago, 1954), are legion. Perhaps the best expressions of contemporary Indian religious thought are Vine Deloria, Jr., *God Is Red* (New York, 1973) and *The Metaphysics of Modern Existence* (San Francisco, 1979).

Other studies include Ed McGaa, Eagle Man, *Mother Earth Spirituality: Native American Paths to Healing Ourselves and Our World* (San Francisco, 1990). An Indian who has been able to speak persuasively about Indian spirituality and to use that spirituality to enhance Indian political goals is Oren Lyons, an Onondaga whose "Spirituality, Equality, and Natural Law," in *Pathways to Self-Determination: Canadian Indians and the Canadian State*, ed. Leroy Little Bear, Menno Boldt, and J. Anthony Long (Toronto, 1984), pp. 5–13, is an example of this ability. For other studies of Indian religious thought see the text of the essay.

There is a long tradition (that continues to this day) of Europeans and Euro-Americans passing themselves off as Indians, particularly in Europe, and particularly as Indians with special spiritual powers. Often it is impossible to determine the authenticity of the claim. A scholarly study of one such individual is Donald B. Smith, *From the Land of Shadows: The Making of Grey Owl* (Saskatoon, 1990). The ethnic background of Jamake Highwater, author of *The Primal Mind: Vision and Reality in Indian America* (New York, 1981), has been the subject of vigorous debate.

INDEX